RICHARD SHANNON

GLADSTONE

I
1809–1865

METHUEN

First published in Great Britain in 1982 by
Hamish Hamilton Ltd
Garden House, 57–59 Long Acre, London WC2E 9JZ

First published as a University Paperback in 1984 by
Methuen & Co. Ltd
11 New Fetter Lane, London EC4P 4EE

© 1982 Richard Shannon

Printed in Great Britain by Billing & Sons Ltd, Worcester

British Library Cataloguing in Publication Data
Shannon, Richard
  Gladstone.
  Vol. 1: 1809–1865
  1. Gladstone, W. E. (William Ewart)
  2. Prime ministers—Great Britain—Biography
  I. Title
  941.081'092'4   DA563.4
ISBN 0-416-36870-0 (University paperback 851)

To my mother
and the memory of my father

Contents

Illustrations

Preface

This book is offered on the assumption that a comprehensive new reading of Gladstone is necessary and possible. The quantity of fresh materials made generally accessible since 1968 at St. Deiniol's Library, Hawarden, at the British Library, and in *The Gladstone Diaries* constitutes something of an invitation in the imperative mood. Such, at least, was my sense when Messrs Hamish Hamilton invited me in 1974 to undertake a biography of Gladstone.

There has never been any stint of materials in Gladstone's case. Anyone who has had the temerity to contemplate tackling them in bulk will echo the awestruck comment of the first man so to do, John Morley: 'The first sight of the huge mountain of material at Hawarden might well make the stoutest literary heart quail.'[1] Subject only to the completion of the publication programme by the Clarendon Press at Oxford of the remainder of *The Gladstone Diaries* for the 1868–1896 period, one is now back in the situation in which quailing Morley stood when in 1898 he secured the commission from the Gladstone family to prepare the biography published by Macmillan's in 1903. We now have all the materials in our view. That view is no less daunting. As with a closer prospect of the Alps, 'Alps on Alps arise'.

The first great cache to be made publicly accessible was the political papers arranged by A. Tilney Bassett and deposited by the family in the British Museum in 1930. Though but a part of the whole, these 750 volumes remain still the largest archive of any of our statesmen, and the only one to be accorded the distinction of a separate catalogue by the Library.[2] Moreover, Gladstone published almost as voluminously as he corresponded or memorandised. *A Bibliography of Gladstone Publications at*

1 Quoted by M.R.D. Foot, 'Morley's Gladstone: A Reappraisal', *Bulletin of the John Rylands Library*, li (1969), 370. This and Foot's introduction to the first two volumes of *The Gladstone Diaries* (1968) provide the indispensable detailed information on the fortune both of Morley as biographer and of his materials. See also R. J. Olney, Gladstone Papers 1822–1977, PMP, iv appendix 3.

2 *Catalogue of Additions to the Manuscripts: The Gladstone Papers, Add. Mss. 44086-44835*, British Museum (1953).

Saint Deiniol's Library compiled by Patricia M. Long (Hawarden, 1977) lists 348 titles of books, articles, pamphlets and speeches: comprising 37 classical items, 41 on history and literature, 76 on domestic politics, 60 on foreign policy, 32 on Irish policy, 70 on religion and philosophy, and 32 miscellaneous. And Gladstone spoke copiously. He is estimated to have filled 15,000 columns of *Hansard* and to have featured in 366 volumes of that publication in over sixty years as a Member of Parliament (1832–1846, 1847–1895). Nor was he much less copious 'out of doors'. St. Deiniol's Library contains thirty-eight volumes of *Speeches and Pamphlets* and eleven volumes of *Speeches and Writings*, mostly press clippings.

These published materials had always been available at St. Deiniol's, Gladstone's own foundation (as, in many cases, elsewhere); but it was the removal in 1968 of the mass of private and family papers from Hawarden Castle to St. Deiniol's which marked the second great step in giving access to Gladstone. Scholars and historians such as J. L. Hammond and Sir Philip Magnus had been permitted, subject to certain restrictions (which in a greater measure had applied to Morley himself), to avail themselves of knowledge of the personal and intimate dimension of Gladstone's life. And indeed it was Magnus's *Gladstone* of 1954, the first study to treat this dimension in some depth, which prompted the notion of a full publication of Gladstone's Journal, since 1928 in the keeping of the Archbishops of Canterbury in Lambeth Palace Library. The first steps to this end were taken in the later 1950s on the advice of M. R. D. Foot, then Professor of Modern History at the University of Manchester. It was the appearance in 1968 of the first two volumes of *The Gladstone Diaries*, edited by Foot, which in turn prompted as a logical complement the transfer of the personal and family papers to St. Deiniol's. A further important step in this logical process was taken in 1970 when Messrs Macmillan deposited in the British Library ten volumes of political papers reserved by Morley as being too sensitive for general availability.[1]

Publication of the complete text of *The Gladstone Diaries* (now under the editorship of Dr. H. C. G. Matthew at Oxford) constitutes the fourth and last great step. Six volumes covering the years 1825–1868 have so far appeared. Gladstone himself referred in April 1895 to 'a succinct and very arid Journal which I kept for about 70 years'.[2] Succinct and arid the forty-one volumes of this Journal largely are; they are in form an account rendered of expenditure of the divine allowance of precious time. But they are also more substantially the record of intimate revelations of the utmost importance for any approach to an understanding of Gladstone's interior life. They need accordingly to be used with care and discretion.

1 These became Add. Mss. 56444-56453.
2 Add.Mss. 44776, 146.

They bear the character of Gladstone's witnessing against himself; the 'self-criticisms of morbid stringency' form a 'series of notes for the prosecution'.[1]

The question of what to do about the Journal had exercised the Gladstone family ever since Gladstone's death in 1898. It was clearly immensely important but also immensely dangerous. It contained matter of intense religiosity which could be subject to hostile misrepresentation. More to the point, it contained matter about Gladstone's relationships with prostitutes, and, in particular, relationships with certain especially attractive courtesans which went beyond the strict necessities of a mission of rescue and redemption. Gladstone's life had been subjected to a susurrus of rumour and scandal; it was not likely that he would be spared posthumously. When Morley undertook his commission it was made clear that he should eschew any attempt to deal with Gladstone's interior religious life, which included Gladstone's mission to rescue and redeem prostitutes. This restriction accorded well enough with Morley's own predispositions. He wanted to produce a grand public and Liberal monument. It was of no high moment to his purposes that, of all great public men, Gladstone's interior and exterior lives were the most integrally inseparable. Morley's use of the most intimate materials of his subject was thus fleeting, embarrassed, often tendentious, and in general gingerly insipid. Herbert (Viscount) Gladstone, the stateman's youngest son, remarked in 1928 that 'luminous and interesting' as were Morley's pages, they did not 'present, for those who did not know Mr. Gladstone, a true and complete view of his personality'; for 'the tendency of the modern writers' was 'to seek the truth about great men from the habits and affairs of their private life'.[2] The thought of what Lytton Strachey might have made of Gladstone's Journal indeed gave pause. What gave even longer pause was the thought of what a Strachey might have made of an edited version of the Journal. Such a version was in fact prepared in typescript by Herbert Gladstone in 1917, and made available to the eyes if not the pens of discreet scholars in due course, along with correspondence of a similar intimacy: 'to be seen but not published'. This was a perfectly sensible arrangement. It was a question of awaiting the right time. Meanwhile, the Journal was stored at Lambeth and a preparatory typescript made by H. W. Lawton. And, just as the 1917 version was made discreetly available at Hawarden without reference to Lambeth, so the Lambeth version was slipped to Tilney Bassett by the Rev. Claude Jenkins while Librarian there without reference to Hawarden. This was helpful to Bassett in his edition of Gladstone's letters to Catherine Gladstone, *Gladstone to his Wife* (1936). This, together

1 Foot in *Diaries*, i, xxxiii; and to the present author, February 20, 1982.
2 *After Thirty Years* (1928), xiii.

with D. C. Lathbury's *Correspondence on Church and Religion of W. E. Gladstone* (2 v., 1910), did something to fill the gaps left by Morley. Eventually the signal to go ahead with a complete publication of the Journal was, as has been indicated, given by the success of what, in effect, was the *ballon d'essai* of Magnus in 1954.

The present work attempts to take all this into account. It attempts also to take into account important recent scholarship on Gladstone: especially the suggestive introductions by H. C. G. Matthew to the two series of the *Diaries* published respectively in 1974 and 1978, and his seminal articles on Gladstone's religion (*Studies in Church History*, xv, ed. D. Baker, 1978) and budgetary policy (*Historical Journal*, 1979). The crucial aspect of Gladstone's sense of the relationship of religion and politics has been much illuminated by Derek Schreuder (*The Conscience of the State*, ed. P. Marsh, 1979) and by the former assistant-editor of the *Diaries*, Perry Butler, in *Gladstone: Church, State and Tractarianism* (1982).

To the extent that this book succeeds in such ambitiously comprehensive attempts it is indebted to the expertise, kindness and patience of many people. Sir William Gladstone provided generous hospitality at Hawarden in 1979, and his permission to make use of material in the Gladstone collections is most gratefully acknowledged. My debt to M. R. D. Foot is threefold: as first editor of the *Diaries*, as pathfinder for Gladstonian scholarship in his 1968 critique of Morley, above all as close and alert and unsparing reader of my draft, immensely to its benefit. Professor Derek Beales of Cambridge has likewise put his copious Gladstonian learning liberally at my disposal in his attentive reading of the text. Professor John Vincent of Bristol and Mr. Neville Masterman at Swansea (whose father abridged Morley in 1927) have been invariably helpful friends of this book. Mr. Christopher Sinclair-Stevenson of Hamish Hamilton has been an editor of rare patience and fortitude. Mr. C. J. Williams of the Clwyd Record Office and the Rev. Peter Jagger of St. Deiniol's Library and their staffs have been of great assistance. To the Right Hon. the Earl of Clarendon and to Mr. E. G. W. Bill of Lambeth Palace Library and to the Oxford University Press and to the trustees of the Mountbatten Settlements I offer due acknowledgment of their permission to quote copyright material in their care. My former colleague at the University of East Anglia, Dr. Michael Sanderson, has been a mine of information about Gladstone and the Theatre. My colleague at Swansea, Dr. Muriel Chamberlain, has generously allowed me to read the text of her forthcoming biography of Lord Aberdeen. The University of East Anglia and the University College of Swansea have been generous with funds to assist my researches. Mrs. Pat Rees and Mrs. Nancy

Williams typed intrepidly as well as accurately. Nor must I neglect to mention that my Gladstone special subject class at Swansea has been a constant and fruitful stimulus.

Richard Shannon
University College, Swansea
April 1982

Abbreviations used in Footnotes

Argyll   Eighth Duke of Argyll, *Autobiography and Memoirs*, 2 v. (1906)

Bassett   A. Tilney Bassett (ed.), *Gladstone to his Wife* (1936)

Butler   P. Butler, *Gladstone: Church, State and Tractarianism. A study of his religious ideas and attitudes, 1809–1859* (1982)

Checkland   S. G. Checkland, *The Gladstones. A Family Biography, 1764–1851* (1971)

CG   Catherine Gladstone

Conacher   J. B. Conacher, *The Aberdeen Coalition, 1852–1855* (1968)

D   M. R. D. Foot and H. C. G. Matthew (eds.) *The Gladstone Diaries, 1825–1868* 6 v. (1968, 1974, 1978)

DDCP   J. Vincent (ed.), *Disraeli, Derby and the Conservative Party. Journals and Memoirs of Edward Henry, Lord Stanley, 1849–1869* (1978)

EHR   *The English Historical Review*

G   Gladstone

GGP   Glynne-Gladstone Papers, St. Deiniol's Library, Hawarden

Gleanings   W. E. Gladstone, *Gleanings of Past Years*, 7 v. (1879)

G & P   P. Guedalla (ed.), *Gladstone and Palmerston* (1928)

GP   Gladstone Papers, British Library

Greville   Lytton Strachey and R. Fulford (eds.), *The Greville Memoirs, 1814–1860* 8 v. (1938)

H   *Hansard's Parliamentary Debates* (Third Series)

HJ   *The Historical Journal*

Kilbracken   *Reminiscences of Lord Kilbracken* (1931)

Lathbury   D. C. Lathbury, *Correspondence on Church and Religion of W. E. Gladstone* 2 v. (1910)

LQV   A. C. Benson, Viscount Esher, G. E. Buckle (eds.), *The Letters of Queen Victoria*, 9 v., 3s (1907–32)

Magnus   P. Magnus, *Gladstone* (1954)

M & B	W. F. Monypenny and G. E. Buckle, *Life of Benjamin Disraeli* 2 v. (1929)
Morley	J. Morley, *Life of William Ewart Gladstone* 3 v. (1903)
MRDF	*auctoritate* M. R. D. Foot
PMP	J. Brooke and M. Sorensen (eds.), *The Prime Ministers' Papers: W. E. Gladstone* 4 v. (1971–81)
Purcell	E. S. Purcell, *Life of Cardinal Manning* 2 v. (1896)
Q & G	P. Guedalla (ed.), *The Queen and Mr. Gladstone* 2 v. (1933)
QR	*The Quarterly Review*
Reid	T. Wemyss Reid (ed.), *Life of William Ewart Gladstone* (1899)
Rendel	F. E. Hamer (ed.), *The Personal Papers of Lord Rendel* (1931)
Tollemache	L. A.Tollemache, *Talks with Mr. Gladstone* (1898)
Vincent	J. Vincent, *The Formation of the Liberal Party, 1857–1868* (1966)
Wilberforce	A. R. Ashwell and R. G. Wilberforce, *Life of Samuel Wilberforce* 3 v. (1881)

NOTE

To avoid a needless profusion of references, I have not usually footnoted quotations from *The Gladstone Diaries* where the date in question or an indication of tolerable proximity is provided in the text. And it should be noted that all quotations from GP Add. Mss. 44527–44535 are from a secretarial hand, not from that of Gladstone himself; which accounts for the often odd orthography.

R.T.S.

CHAPTER I

THE FORMATIVE VALUES, 1809–1832: 'I HOPE TO LEAD A SEVERE LIFE'

[1]

In November 1832, shortly before being elected to the House of Commons, Gladstone confided to his diary that his 'State' was 'at present one of danger'. His cup overflowed with 'personal blessings'. He had loved Eton; he had loved Oxford no less, and graduated in an aura of conspicuous brilliance. He had completed a grand tour of the Netherlands, France, Switzerland, Italy and southern Germany of the utmost interest, profit and enjoyment. Now, shortly before his twenty-third birthday, he was the candidate of the Duke of Newcastle for the Duke's borough of Newark. Reserving with Evangelical scruple, as always, his deficiencies in godliness and mastery over his sins, Gladstone indeed confessed that he knew 'not what to desire'. But set against these blessings was danger of a 'singular kind': the circumstances of his family were far different from his own. He was acutely aware of a disturbing tension. He, the youngest of four brothers, was the one item of undoubted and satisfying success in a family dedicated to very comprehensive notions of success.

As Gladstone put it with rather opaque allusiveness, God Almighty had seen fit to overrule 'many plans and prospects which had been entertained'. By this it can be inferred that he had in mind primarily his father's thwarted ambition to crown a prosperous mercantile career with the parliamentary representation of Liverpool, his adopted city. By 1832, also, it was clear that Gladstone's eldest brother, Thomas, was not going to fulfil his father's hopes of carrying the Gladstone name into the first rank of politics. The two middle brothers, Robertson and John Neilson, had settled for careers of public inconspicuousness, the one in his father's Liverpool business, the other in the Navy. Almighty God, moreover, had often clothed his 'visitations' upon the Gladstone family in the form of sickness. Anne, the eldest child, the admiration and pride of the family for charm of personality, intellectual talent and saintly piety, had died after a lingering decline early in 1829, in her twenty-sixth year. Gladstone's mother had lived most of her life as an invalid; and indeed had less than three years to live. The youngest child, Helen, then aged eighteen, was bidding fair to emulate her mother as a professional invalid, as well as displaying incipient signs of the hysterical eccentricity which was to make her publicly conspicuous in a manner highly embarrassing to the family.

On top of all this, Gladstone's analysis of the way in which his family had been 'singularly dealt with' focused, with a sense of what almost could be called grievance, on the circumstance that it was, for practical purposes, homeless. John Gladstone, the father, had set himself up handsomely in Liverpool and in a substantial country house at Seaforth outside Liverpool. The first reflected his station as a merchant prince of the greatest English port apart from London; the second reflected his ultimate ambition to represent that great corporation by the side of Canning or Huskisson at Westminster. But the obstinate refusal of Liverpool to fall in with John Gladstone's plans, relegating him to the unsatisfactory recourse of representing, with varying degrees of exorbitant expense, vexation and brevity, the dim boroughs of Lancaster, Woodstock and Berwick, soured his relationship with the city. His wife's invalidism fitted in conveniently with John Gladstone's gradual withdrawal from Liverpool life. He was quite content to manage his multifarious business concerns by post from spas and resorts in the south: Malvern, Gloucester, Bath, Torquay, Leamington. William Gladstone was acutely aware of this rather odd pattern of family life. His vacations from Eton or Oxford would as likely be spent in a spa hotel as at home in Liverpool or at Seaforth House: 'snatched', as he put it, 'from a position when we were what is called entering society, & sent to comparative seclusion, as regards family establishment'.

John Gladstone's frustration led him in 1829 to signalise his spurning of Liverpool by purchasing the estate of Fasque, with a large new castle-like house, in Kincardineshire. But it would not be until 1833 that he moved in and the Gladstones could think of it as the family estate. Meanwhile the Liverpool establishments were let out. This, together with John Gladstone's abandonment of parliamentary ambitions,[1] represented a distinct defeat: 'prevented,' as William summed it up, 'from assuming the situation which seems the natural termination of a career like my Father's'.[2] That career, after all, had been no less than the stabilising and rationalising of grain provision for the Lancashire of the early industrial revolution: a system crowned by the mechanism of the Liverpool Corn Exchange. Looking back in his old age, William concluded that even for all his father's success as a merchant, 'considering his long life and means of accumulation the result represents a success secondary in comparison

1 His last effort was actually a humiliating failure at Dundee in 1837.
2 D, i, 584–85.

with that of others whom in native talent and energy he much surpassed.'[1]

It was all, indeed, rather a sad disillusionment of so many expectations, constituting in fact, in William's view, a 'noble trial' for himself personally, to 'exercise a kindly & unselfish feeling', if 'amid the excitements & allurements' now near him he was enabled 'duly to realise the bond of consanguinity, and *suffer with* those whom Providence has ordained to suffer'. John Gladstone, nearly seventy in 1832, had almost another twenty years to live on his Scottish estate, lively, busy, always formidable, a widower from 1835, but consoled by the vicarious pleasure of witnessing his youngest son's rise to political fame. He had early recognised in William the outstanding family talent – 'you shall be my biographer, William,' he had remarked to his fifteen-year-old son[2] – and had the satisfaction not only of having his own eminence and philanthropy marked by the honour of a baronetcy in 1846 but of living to see William a privy councillor and a secretary of state already widely mentioned as a future prime minister. He also had the satisfaction in 1851 of dying at the head of a commercial, agricultural and investment concern valued at something like three-quarters of a million[3].

[2]

In retreating to Fasque, John Gladstone had consciously returned to his Scottish roots. The Gladstones were of purely Scottish descent on either side. John's father, Thomas Gladstanes or Gladstones, had migrated from Biggar to establish himself at Leith as a modestly successful merchant. He married, advantageously, Nelly Neilson, the daughter of a merchant in Springfield, near Edinburgh. His was a family without pretensions. William later made the best of an unpromising genealogy by insisting that while admittedly there was no trace of their gentility among the Gladstones since 1660, he had 'never heard of them in Scotland until after the Restoration otherwise than as persons of family'.[4] John, born in 1764, the oldest of what was to prove a total of seventeen siblings, was the most talented and forward of their sons. He was tall, strong, craggy-visaged, of driving energy and obsessive determination to succeed in the kind of mercantile line of life open to one of his obscure origins and limited education. He emulated and surpassed his father's migratory policy in 1787 by selecting Liverpool as a mercantile centre appropriate to his capacities. Once settled in Liverpool he dropped the 's' from his

1 GP, 44790, 17.   2 D, i, 66.
3 Checkland, 414–15.   4 GP, 44790, 13.

surname, as being commercially ambiguous (though this in fact was not legally regularised until 1835[1]). He married in 1792 Jane Hall, daughter of a Liverpool merchant. It was not a brilliant match, but there were promising connections with the Church and Eton. To receive his wife and the family he hoped to have by her he had a fine house built in Rodney Street (then no. 1, now no. 62) in an area on the south-east of the town being developed and in which John made large and judicious purchases. Jane, however, was sickly and left him in 1798 a childless widower. By this time he was worth something like forty thousand pounds.

In 1800, on April 29, in St. Peter's Church, Liverpool, John took as his second wife Anne Robertson, daughter of Andrew Robertson, the Provost of Dingwall in Ross-shire. The Robertsons were a family in genteel circumstances, mixing landowning, local politics, and the law in laird-like degrees, and, though worth nothing like as much as John Gladstone in realisable cash, possessed qualities he recognised as not merely desirable but essential to a way of life far transcending anything old Thomas could have dreamed of in Leith. The Robertsons were Episcopalian; indeed William Gladstone would later characterise them, on the strength principally of the pedigree of Andrew's wife, *née* Mackenzie, as 'stoutly Episcopalian and Jacobite'.[2] Mrs. Robertson's clan chief (at least in her own estimation) was the Earl of Seaforth; and, when John Gladstone came in 1815 to build an imposing country house on an estate to the north-west of Liverpool between Bootle and Crosby overlooking the Mersey estuary, he named it Seaforth House in deference to his wife's putatively impressive connections. John accordingly relinquished his family links with the Kirk, and its Unitarian manifestations in Liverpool, and adopted his wife's denominational colouring, which was not merely Episcopalian, but – of immense consequence to the later development of the family and especially William – of pronouncedly Evangelical tinge. Evangelicalism of the kind relished by Mrs. Gladstone was not in fact available in Liverpool, whose Anglicanism was of an unregenerate and unenthusiastic character. John Gladstone attested his commitment to his new ecclesiastical loyalty by building his own churches and installing his own incumbents both in Liverpool and at Seaforth. To the latter he added a school, where his children could be given their preparatory education under strict and immediate parental supervision.

This he could well afford to do. By 1820 he was worth over £333,000. Nearly a third of this fortune was derived from investments in estates in Demerara in the West Indies worked by slave labour. This was perfectly in accordance with the traditions and habits of Liverpool, a port grown rich on the slave trade. But it caused problems for the Gladstones, for

1 Checkland, 16, 283.   2 GP, 44790, 13.

Evangelicalism was the prime ingredient of the anti-slavery campaign. This was a tension which remained long unresolved, far beyond indeed the legislative success of the abolitionist agitation in 1833. And it caused William acute embarrassment in his election at Newark in 1832.

But those were circumstances remote from John Gladstone's calculations in 1800. His second wife, frail and delicate like his first, but more beautiful, proved also more fertile. She bore six children: Anne Mackenzie in 1802, Thomas in 1804, Robertson in 1805, John Neilson in 1807, William Ewart (named after John's principal friend and business collaborator) in 1809,[1] and Helen Jane in 1814. By the time of the birth of his last child John Gladstone was fifty, with patriarchal habits and manners, not least in a confirmed disposition to need to dominate any environment he found himself in. In this respect his home life was no problem, since Mrs. Gladstone was wholly self-effacing, asking only to set the religious tone of the household at a somewhat fanatical level of intellectually undemanding piety, and to guide her husband and immerse herself in a suitable variety of philanthropies and charities. She found the duties in an alien land of running two large houses distasteful and the obligations of being the hostess of a rising business and political luminary quite terrifying. For her, ill-health became a way of coping with pressures she could not otherwise deal with.

Nor did John Gladstone have serious problems in imposing his dominance in business. He had a talent for quarrelling and an effective technique for choking off rivals in his partnerships. Thus he got rid of his brother Robert in 1821. All his other six brothers were clustered about him in Liverpool in positions of dependence. Nor did it appear that unchallenged dominance of Liverpool politics would be beyond his long reach. Originally a Whig, he shifted his ground towards support of Pitt's war policy, and in 1812 was foremost among the citizens of Liverpool who invited the illustrious George Canning to become one of the members for the city. John Gladstone became Canning's agent and prided himself on his mentorship of the brilliant younger man, a relationship characterised by a certain clumsy deference on his part and a patient politeness, occasionally wearing thin, on Canning's.

For John Gladstone, Canning was an image of what he would have liked to have been, but could not be. Canning was a feasible model also for what John Gladstone's sons might become. An upstart of dubious origins in an intensely aristocratic social and political world, Canning exemplified what innate talent combined with the processing offered by Eton and Christ Church, Oxford, could achieve. The Gladstone children were bred up in an atmosphere heavy with devotion for this image and this model. The resonances of the great metropolitan world of affairs and

1 December 29, at Rodney Street.

the ideal of the pagan polish of a classical education permeated the Gladstone household, mingling uneasily with the native forces of provincialism and sanctimony. The tensions thus set up afflicted the family in a manner which William, the only one who surmounted the problem successfully, half sensed but could not, in the nature of such things, accurately explain. They set John Gladstone off on his painful and ultimately futile quest for national political eminence. They reduced Mrs. Gladstone to feeble nullity. Anne had the wit to cope, but not the strength. As soon as she was of years of discretion, she effectively replaced her mother as the domestic linch-pin. As William's godmother she played a crucial role in his early intellectual and religious formation. Thomas was hit hard. He was too old to be sustained by his sister. On his shoulders, as the eldest son, rested the burden of living up to his formidable father's requirements. After a cosy childhood education at the family school at Seaforth, he was abruptly thrust into the rude and boisterous world of Eton. Neither of his parents could offer him any help, nor indeed had any notions of what help he needed. All they could do was veto Tom's pathetic pleas to be allowed to leave Eton.

Robertson, a decidedly more robust character, avoided direct confrontation with the family problem by being willing to fall in with his father's desire that one of his sons should follow him in the business. For this purpose Robertson was removed after a brief passage at Eton and sent to the Glasgow Academy for a sound, practical preparation for a commercial career. Robertson alone stayed on in Liverpool, prospering, and asserting his independence by marrying a Unitarian and later professing that creed,[1] and by moving in a distinctly radical political direction. John Neilson also avoided the problem by the simple expedient of removing himself from the family circle by insisting, much against his father's desire, on a career in the Navy. This, in the end, came to a commandership in 1842[2]; and John Neilson eventually followed his eldest brother Tom in ineffectual and rather resentful mediocrity as a backbench member of parliament. Helen was the only one of the children who could be said to have reacted strongly against her family. Much of her later rather bizarre career, from her conversion to Roman Catholicism to her financial scandals and bouts of alcoholism and drug addiction, has about it something of an unconscious mode of revenge. Fifteen years of age when her elder sister died, Helen became her mother's companion in her career of ill health, cures, spas, doctors and medicines, taking on, whether by sympathy or self-protection, much of her mother's habits of invalidism. When Mrs. Gladstone died in 1835 Helen became in turn her

---

1 Although G was shocked by this, the family had regularly attended Unitarian services in Liverpool until John Gladstone provided himself with his own church and amenable Anglican preachers. (MRDF).   2 Captaincy on retirement in 1860.

aged father's domestic prop. Released from this burden sixteen years later, she gravitated immediately out of the family orbit, spinning erratically, much to the dismay and scandal of her very proper brothers.

This leaves Willy, who unquestionably succeeded his elder sister Anne as the darling and favourite of the family. Everything, indeed, rather conspired in his favour. He was the youngest son of fairly elderly parents: his father was forty-five when he was born, nearly sixty when he started at Eton, nearly seventy when he graduated at Oxford. His elder brothers stood, in effect, as buffers between him and the full impact of John Gladstone's alarming personality. Unlike Tom, William did not have to be the first of his family and generation to brave the outside world: indeed, when William went to Eton in 1821, Tom was still there to ease his youngest brother's passage, which he did with fraternal unselfishness. William had Robertson and John Neilson to stand between himself and their father's wish for a son to go into the family firm. There was nothing very obvious or immediately important that William had to live up to. Moreover, William had the benefit, denied to his older brothers, of the ripening maturity of mind and character of their sister Anne, much the acutest brain, apart from himself, in the family. Anne took her duties as William's godmother seriously, and was the first influence upon him of a distinctly fine intellectual kind. 'In her later years,' as William wrote quite truly, 'she lived in close relations with me & I must have been much worse but for her.'[1] It was Anne who first made William aware of the deeper and wider spiritual and intellectual values of their religion, a feat quite beyond the capacity of their mother and quite outside the interests of their father. Anne began, in fact, on the issue of baptismal regeneration, in 1828, that movement in William's mind that led him shortly after to repudiate the stifling narrowness and mental meanness of the religious discipline of his boyhood.

Certainly there was little else, other than Anne, which might have given William that first, vital impulse to transcend the values of the family. Gladstone later recorded, probably quite accurately, that he was not by nature a 'devotional child', and had no recollection of 'early love for the House of God and for Divine Service'.[2] He accepted the religious attitudes current 'in the domestic atmosphere without question and without interest'.[3] He had 'no recollection of being under any moral or personal influence whatever' from Rawson, the Evangelical clergyman selected by his father (on the advice of the great Simeon at Cambridge) to run the church and school at Seaforth.[4]

It was not, however, such incipient capacities for criticism which endeared Willy to his parents and siblings. He was a child of much natural

1 GP, 44790, 11.   2 *Ib.*, 19.
3 GP, 44791, 1.   4 GP, 44790, 23.

charm and winningness, with unexceptionably precocious ways. He would a little later be described as 'the prettiest little boy that ever went to Eton',[1] with especially fine dark eyes like his mother's. Moreover, he gratified his father with early evidences of determination to succeed. William himself remarked on his early tendencies to 'priggish love of argument'.[2] John Gladstone was always a great arguer, and a bad loser at the art. This paternal characteristic of disputatiousness in William, which was to remain with him all his long career, gave him a distinct advantage in his father's estimation. More important, perhaps, were the evidences William displayed of simply being more efficient than his brothers at being a successful schoolboy. William had a way of getting on and not causing his parents anxiety or making difficulties. It is not without significance that Gladstone's earliest abiding memory of his infancy was of 'struggling or fighting' his way up a staircase, encouraged by his nurse.[3] The infant struggler or fighter up the ladder of success was very much the father of the man as well as being the son most like his father.

Otherwise, Willy's childhood memories reflect faithfully the life of Liverpool and Seaforth: being put on the dining table in front of Canning in 1812, in a red frock, and directed to say 'Ladies and Gentlemen' to divert the company; travelling with his parents in Scotland and to Cambridge, where Simeon was consulted about the incumbent for Seaforth (Gladstone remembered Simeon as 'a venerable man, and although only a Fellow of a College was more ecclesiastically got up than many a Dean or even here and there perhaps a Bishop'); attending with his father a thanksgiving service in St. Paul's in 1815 and sitting in a gallery just above the Prince Regent and looking down on him from behind; visiting with his mother the redoubtable first lady of Evangelicalism, Hannah More, and being presented with a copy of her *Sacred Dramas*.

[3]

Clearly, when the time came for decisions about William's more serious formal education, there was no question but that only the best would be good enough. What Tom had started out on, with rather dismal results, as the eldest son of the house, William would follow as its rising hope. In September 1821 he filled the place at Eton vacated when Robertson was transferred to Glasgow. Tom was his fagmaster until he left, without attaining to the distinction of the Sixth Form, in July 1822. Eton to William

1 By R. I. Murchison: C. E. Mallet, *A History of the University of Oxford*, iii (1927), 217.
2 GP, 44790, 23.   3 *Ib.*, 6.

was nothing like the traumatic shock it had been to Tom. At that time two-thirds to three-quarters of the boys lodged in Dame's Houses, at quite cheap rates. In William's experience, the 'system answered', and he never ceased in later years to deplore its ending. He did not care for his first Dame; and he was taken aback by the entire absence of the devotional atmosphere so assiduously cultivated at Seaforth. Sermons mumbled by 'toothless old Fellows' were a 'mockery'. Later he recalled only two sermons that left any impression on him at Eton. One was a diatribe against Roman Catholic emancipation by Vice-Provost 'Pug' Roberts; the other was at his confirmation, when the Bishop of Lincoln extolled a 'sober religion, neither declining on the one hand into lukewarmness, nor transgressing on the other into enthusiasm'.[1] But he adapted himself readily enough, conforming to the conventions of his new environment as unquestioningly as he had accepted those of the domestic atmosphere. He does not seem to have drawn unwelcome or hostile attention to himself. His *parvenu* background was not unusual in the Eton of those days. He enjoyed the advantages of being at once personally prepossessing and inconspicuous. One of his fags later described him as 'a good-looking, rather delicate youth, with a pale face and brown, curly hair, always tidy and well dressed'.[2] Evidences are not lacking of commonplace schoolboy instincts about fighting (though as a spectator only), cricket and football – though, acknowledging lack of skill or prowess in these sports, Gladstone resorted to sculling on the river as his preferred exercise. He never rated himself as being good at any bodily activity except walking, at which he put himself in the 'rapid and enduring' class, having both 'speed and "bottom"'.[3] He later recalled proudly that at Eton he slept invariably with his window open, winter and summer, for all that it looked on to the most crowded churchyard in England; and he 'scoffed at the idea of unhealthiness'.[4] He was boyishly enthusiastic about coaches and coaching, knowledgeable about routes, 'Bang up', 'Mercury', 'Irishman', and others, not least because of the vagaries of his family's places of residence. Gladstone later remarked of his Eton life that the 'plank' between himself and 'all the sins' was 'so very thin'. 'I did not love or habitually practise falsehood, meanness or indecency: but I could be drawn into them by occasion and temptation.'[5] A definition, it might be said, as to morals, of a not uncommon type of schoolboy.

In another very important respect, however, William was a decidedly uncommon type of schoolboy: he had the capacity to excel at the scholastic exercises most esteemed at his school. Command of Greek and

1 *Rendel*, 139–40; A. West, *Recollections* (1899), 56.
2 Morley, i, 34.   3 *Rendel*, 122.
4 *Ib.*, 114. The point here was hostility to cremation.   5 GP, 44790, 18.

Latin came easily to him. He drew attention to himself quite early as a promising classic, with a knack for versifying. Indeed, his sophistication in this respect was such by 1826 that he could criticise the Eton classical curriculum as being 'a great deal too exclusively attended to', involving a needless amount of drudgery.[1] Beyond his classical competence, Gladstone gave abundant evidence in these early years of that taxonomic passion for systematising, classifying, ordering, arranging and allocating that was one of the abiding characteristics of both the private and public spheres of his life. Possibly the efficiently commercial atmosphere in the family left its mark: certainly Gladstone learned early the art of docketing memoranda. A curious instance of this bent in his Eton days took an architectural form. 'Drew a plan of an Inn – an old propensity of Mine' (inspired doubtless by many a bad experience in his coaching journeys). Again: 'Drew plan of a house.'[2] (Significant also in this respect was his memory of having as a child 'a great affinity with the trades of joiners and of bricklayers'.[3])

The first important figure to notice Gladstone at Eton was Edward Hawtrey, then an assistant master to Keate, the head, and later himself a reforming headmaster and provost. Gladstone was not in fact his pupil, being up to him only for one term in 1822, when in the Upper Reserve of the Fourth Form. His regular tutor, the Rev. H. H. Knapp, took little notice of him, confining himself to the advice that Gladstone should model his poetical taste on the botanical epics of Dr. Erasmus Darwin. Hawtrey was much impressed by Gladstone's exercises, sent for him and went through his verses 'very carefully'. 'The novelty of the situation,' Gladstone recalled, 'was to me extreme, for he all the way through maintained the kindest manner, and appeared to feel an interest in me which I, as a boy of twelve, thought singular and unaccountable, but at the same time enjoyed with much flattering and a thrill of new hope and satisfaction.' Hawtrey 'sent Gladstone up for good', in the Etonian formula, to the diminutive but awesome Keate. 'It was an event in my life', and Hawtrey and it together then 'for the first time inspired me with a desire to learn and to do'.[4] Gladstone in fact never lost the momentum thus gained. He was 'sent up' to Keate in all three times, establishing a firm reputation in Eton for exceptional scholarship.

Eton and Gladstone, in general, approved of one another. In neither

---

1 Checkland, 211. In the case of arithmetic, however, the future Chancellor of the Exchequer, together with the future Dean Stanley, were reputed in their schooldays as being 'dolts in the matter of *arithmetic*!!' 'Uncle W. said himself he never took to it till he had worked hard at mathematics, to which he had a dislike at first, but which his father urged him into.' J. Bailey (ed.), *The Diary of Lady Frederick Cavendish* (1927), ii, 29.
2 D, i, 64, 65.   • 3 GP, 44790, 24.
4 GP, 44790, 1.

case was the approval uncritical. Gladstone might question the desirability of the classical monopoly of studies. And he was even quite iconoclastic about one of Eton's most hallowed institutions, the custom of Montem, whereby Eton boys arrayed in fancy dress importuned for money and spent a spring day in procession and archaic frolic. Gladstone's first experience of this event, in May 1826, proved a miserable disappointment, despite the presence there of his brothers Tom and John. 'The whole thing a wretched waste of time and money; a most ingenious contrivance to exhibit us as baboons; to most or all Eton fellows a day of fatigue, smothering, idleness – & – a bore in the full sense of the word. Hope twill soon be abolished.'[1] So incensed was he by his disillusioning experience that Gladstone composed a 'tremendous' series of verses 'abusing it vehemently; as I think properly'. His tutor was much pleased, but said it would not do to send up, as Gladstone had taken the 'unpopular side of the question'.[2] (Gladstone heartily supported Hawtrey when he finally abolished the custom in 1847.) There were, also, the rare occasions when Gladstone actually ran foul of the system. He was beaten once, for honouring the schoolboy code by not reporting some other boys who should have been beaten.[3] Quite late in his career he was summoned before Keate for dereliction in producing work, earning an imposition – 'a job & a jaw too. I am certainly not in his good books.'[4]

But mutual approbation was the rule. Gladstone was made captain of the Fifth Form in October 1826, and Keate promoted him to the élite Sixth Form in February 1827. In turn Gladstone responded to Keate's special attentions to the Sixth. 'Keate treats one with much more civility,' he observed with great satisfaction.[5] Gladstone carried away from Eton an affectionate awe of the tough little doctor. 'To him nature had accorded a stature of only about five feet, or say five feet one: but by costume, mien, manner (including a little swagger) and character he made himself in every way the capital figure on the Eton stage.' Keate's departure from Eton in 1834 marked for Gladstone the end of the 'old race of English public school masters' of which Busby at Westminster in the seventeenth century was the prototype.[6] Gladstone responded also to the opportunities offered by Eton's latitude in allowing for activities outside the formal courses of studies. Canning's example in making Eton a training ground both for oratory and for literature was a compelling precedent. Canning's fame and glory as Foreign Secretary from 1822 and Prime Minister in 1827 coincided with Gladstone's Eton years; and, though the statesman had exchanged his Liverpool seat for the less exacting representation of Harwich, his career was still the staple of family political

1 D, i, 48.   2 *Ib.*, 49.
3 Checkland, 203.   4 D, i, 98.
5 PMP, i, 189.   6 GP, 44791, 64.

discussion and the focus especially of Gladstone's ardent hero-worship. He gained election to the debating society at Eton in October 1825, and thereafter the society's affairs became one of his most absorbing concerns. Again, the weekly paper of entertainment and amusement produced by Canning and his circle at Eton, the *Microcosm*, was the model aspired to by Gladstone and his circle in producing, forty years later, *The Eton Miscellany*.

These activities, in which Gladstone emerged as a leading figure, mark important stages in the development of his self-awareness, both by providing him with a forum for expression in speech and print and by linking him in friendship with fellow-Etonians at a critical point of his adolescent emotional life. Among these was George Selwyn, later Bishop of New Zealand and then of Lichfield, inspiration of a Cambridge college, who was joint editor with Gladstone of the *Miscellany*. Gladstone recorded frequently the names of Milnes Gaskell (who described Gladstone in 1826 as 'one of the most sensible and clever people I have ever met'), Francis Doyle, William Farr, Edward Pickering, Gerald Wellesley (later Dean of Windsor, and Gladstone's principal adviser on ecclesiastical patronage), Charles Canning (son of the statesman), and above all Arthur Hallam, son of the Whig historian. These were the core of the society. Their debates were historical (Was the fall of the Roman Empire a blessing rather than a misfortune? Was Cranmer admirable? Was chivalry beneficial?), literary (Was Virgil as great a poet as Shakespeare?) and political to the extent that historical allusion could be ingeniously employed to circumvent Keate's ban on issues nearer than fifty years. There was, however, a unanimous decision to subscribe to the relief of distressed weavers in manufacturing districts on May 13, 1826, in which Gladstone seconded Selwyn's 'most excellent motion'. His specific political professions were of a distinctly Canningite liberal stripe. 'I am far from liking the Corn Laws as they at present stand,' he announced on October 31, 1826; and, as to tithes: 'I do not like the present system.'[1] Gladstone took his responsibilities as secretary and president with characteristic seriousness. 'Got Pickering mai fined for taking a paper out of the room without leave, & Doyle for not filing the papers nor entering the question in time.' 'Got Wellesley fined.' He opposed the introduction of a chess board and of *John Bull*, a scurrilous (if Canningite) paper; and eventually contrived to have at least the paper thrown out. The degree of their commitment to the society is indicated by a letter written by Hallam to Gladstone during the Christmas vacation in 1826, in which Hallam describes himself as indulging in 'many reveries about the Society, & its Right Hon. Chairman, & Treasurer. We must have a glorious session next half: your Administration must not pass over our heads

1 PMP, i, 182.

undistinguished, or unheeded. I assure you, we expect miracles from that arithmetical head of yours in the way of reduction of public burdens, & progressive amelioration of our system'.[1]

There were many occasions rather more irresponsibly carefree. Gladstone records in November 1826 a 'scrambling & leaping expedition' with Hallam, Doyle, and Gaskell. He wrote a song about Gaskell, 'abusing him: to be sent to him'. Wine parties were a regular feature of social life (Gladstone's father sent him parcels of wine and insisted that he drink it; according to the testimony of Charles Canning, Gladstone was known among his Eton cronies as 'Mr. Tipple').[2] Sculling Hallam on the Thames was a favourite recreation. Indeed it was one such expedition which caused Gladstone to miss meeting his political hero Canning, who called unavailingly to see him in June 1826. The very intense friendship which developed between Gladstone and Hallam became for Gladstone the great landmark of his Eton period, much as for Tennyson shortly afterwards Hallam's friendship transfigured his time at Cambridge. *In Memoriam* testified to Tennyson's sense of loss and desolation at Hallam's tragically untimely death in 1833, and of the spiritual solace attainable by poetic retrieval of the ideal moral quality of their relationship. In Gladstone's case the intensity of the relationship became a powerful element in his effort in the Eton years to construct the beginnings of a moral system adequate to control the pressures and urges bearing on his temperament as he emerged into adulthood.

[4]

Already, in July 1825, Gladstone had taken a decisive step towards forming a set of values for his future development by deciding to keep a daily account of his expenditure of time. This was a discipline to which he was to remain faithful in forty-one closely written volumes, until December 1896. That vast human span is a measure of the significance of the exercise for Gladstone as a test of spiritual seriousness. Such journals or diaries were a not uncommon feature of the Evangelical tradition of soul-searching, of setting down in cold script the essential items of action and thought so as to form a measure by which moral and spiritual self-criticism could accurately be gauged. That such a record would inevitably and necessarily be the basis of self-indictment was an integral feature of the discipline. Gladstone's case did not differ materially from the general pattern of such exercises, except in the sheer grandeur of its patiently majestic unfolding through seven of the most crowded and

1 Hallam to G [Christmas, 1826]. GP, 44352, 11.   2 Reid, 89.

consequential decades that any man ever lived. In such pilgrimages, it might be said, it is the first step which counts. That Gladstone took such a step in his sixteenth year indicated a seriousness of purpose which owed much, no doubt, to family training and influence, but which expressed also his awareness of a wider world of experience and challenges opening before him. As a good Calvinist, the young Gladstone was doctrinally very well aware of his hopelessly sinful nature and his unregenerate helplessness in the absence of divine grace. A reading of Southey's *Tale of Paraguay*, for example, provoked him to commenting in March 1826 on the dangerous doctrine of human innocence in the state of nature.

All Gladstone's deepest prepossessions precluded his assuming that he could live a life at Eton 'presenting those features of innocence and beauty' which he had 'often seen elsewhere' – for example, in that 'perfect saint', his sister Anne, so manifestly touched by grace. Many years later, Gladstone offered an apology, in guarded terms, for his moral obliquity at Eton: 'The best I can say for it is that I do not think it was actually a vicious childhood. I do not think . . . that I had a strong nurtured propensity then developed to what are termed the mortal sins.' What he did have was an inner life that was 'extraordinarily dubious, vacillating, and (above all) complex'.[1] Which is to say no more, perhaps, than that Gladstone underwent the normal adolescent emotional turmoils; and that the task he set himself of having honestly to record his daily life *sub specie aeternitatis* was probably the best devisable means of keeping that daily life within the bounds of the conventional decencies, subject, possibly, to certain areas of exception which might be considered as a kind of compensating release of tension, and which could yet be honestly presented as involving in all essentials the initial moral and spiritual premises of the exercise. It was not until Gladstone went to Oxford that he started experimenting with such an area of exception in the form of conversing with prostitutes and reading associated literature which he described, strictly accurately, as pornography. Meanwhile, at Eton, he immersed himself assiduously in his 'business', that is, his schoolwork, in the debates of the society, in plans for literary publication, and in the friendships engendered by them. Above all, perhaps, he found in his sister Anne a spiritual mentor upon whom he could rely for moral advice, intellectual stimulus, and emotional soothing at a time when he was most in need of such comforts.

Gladstone carried over into Eton the routine religious exercises drilled into him at Seaforth. Nightly prayers and bible readings were routine. He was a connoisseur of Eton sermons, dryly unenthusiastic though they might be. He read voraciously among anti-Roman pamphlets and novels, with approval and enjoyment. He kept up the early charitable and

1 GP, 44790, 18.

philanthropic causes among the poor at Seaforth in which he had been initiated by his parents. He read Gibbon, giving particular attention to the 'obnoxious chapters', judged his style beautiful, but deplored his 'sneering at Christian religion, partially disguised'.[1] He decided to take to early rising as a practical test in self-discipline. His journals in these years are punctuated with lamentations about his shortcomings in this respect. There was a constant tension between the absolute values represented by his mother's loving doctrinal severity and the very relative values engendered by his father's ambitions formed for him as represented by Eton. William was clearly aware of a weight of paternal expectation. But it is perhaps the most telling evidence of the unproblematical ease of his passage through Eton that this weight never seems to have constituted anything of pressure or burden. The Canning model radiated a benign and painless inspiration. 'From the faint idea which I am able to form of my future profession,' wrote the fourteen-year-old Gladstone to his father in November 1824, 'I should suppose (am I right?) that it was of consequence to me to begin the study of the law as early as possible.' Already he was calculating the matter of his entering Christ Church. There would be three years and three months intervening, he informed his father, allowing for getting into the sixth form at Eton two years hence. And as to that: 'A year in the sixth form would almost certainly make me Captain of the Oppidans; which I think I have heard you say you wished me to be.'[2] But tension was far from being the keynote of Eton life. William enjoyed cards, billiards, above all the theatre, that *bête noire* of Evangelicalism. Perhaps he learned this taste from his tutor, Knapp, a fanatical theatre-goer (who, having ruined himself by his addiction, eventually absconded to France). Theatre would eventually become something of a passion for Gladstone. But at this stage of development and lack of confidence there were anxieties. The moral code being instilled into him by Anne permitted cards and alcohol, but frowned upon the stage: 'the end of these things is Remorse,' she warned William in 1827, 'even if it please God to give us that Repentance which is unto Life.'[3] Attendance at his first ball in Gloucester on January 13, 1826 warranted three exclamation marks. From 1826 he began to use his birthday as an occasion of formal self-examination, arriving invariably at dismal conclusions as to his unregenerate wickedness. The physical manifestations of adolescence undoubtedly played a part in these self-denunciations: he records purchasing a manual on sexual hygiene while book-buying at Liverpool in August 1826.

Confirmation early in 1827 came for Gladstone as a peculiarly plenary *rite de passage*. He endeavoured to prepare himself for the 'sacred and awful rite' by an ejaculatory orison as to his helpless need for divine

1 D, i, 21.   2 Bassett, 8–9.   3 Butler, 13–14.

assistance. On February 1, 'most unworthy of so great a privilege', Gladstone was confirmed with upwards of two hundred other Etonians 'according to the apostolical rite preserved in the Church of England'. In fact, as he later recalled, it was administered as the merest matter of form by a bishop, Pelham of Lincoln, notorious even among Hanoverian prelates for his 'greed of lucrative office'. It was unfortunate but somehow contributing an extra note of solemnity that the dispenser of the sacrament should have died immediately afterwards. It was indeed a rather vicious winter, having already killed the Duke of York. It was at his chilly January funeral at Windsor, in fact, that both the Bishop and George Canning caught fatal colds. Canning managed to survive into the summer.

Gladstone, meanwhile, was entering into the particular spiritual intimacy which distinguished the last two years of his sister Anne's life. He recorded on February 11, 1827 having received a 'long & most excellent & pious letter from my Beloved Sister – unworthy am I of such an one'. In January 1828 he had a 'very long conversation with A.M.G. on many interesting subjects. The more one sees, the more one *must* admire.' A serious acceleration of Anne's wasting disease in July 1826 had come as a crisis in the family and a shock to Gladstone, who coached post haste to Seaforth, missing the 'great day' of the Eton break up. Anne became increasingly important to William as a kind of surrogate parent, by the end taking on for him the character of sanctity. After reading over her letters a few years later he exclaimed: 'O is it possible that such a saint could have held communion with such a devil?'[1]

All this happened within the encompassing glow of Arthur Hallam's friendship. He and Gladstone first met in 1824, and their friendship began, according to Gladstone, 'more at his seeking than mine'.[2] Though lodged at different ends of Eton, they arranged to mess together at breakfast in one another's rooms on alternate weeks. Hallam was more than a year junior in age to Gladstone, evidently a youth of exceptionally winning charm and sweetness of character. He made up for the disparity in their ages by having been bred in a household redolent of his father's easy latitudinarianism and graceful Whiggish culture. Doubtless part of the attraction of Hallam for Gladstone was that he embodied something quite different from most things that Seaforth House stood for. There was nothing about Hallam of struggling and fighting up the ladder of achievement and success. His attractiveness had to do rather with a certain softness and passivity. Gladstone eventually summed him up as 'one of those to whom it was more given . . . to *be* rather than to *do*'.[3] Their relationship slackened for a while, when Hallam transferred his affections elsewhere; and then recommenced in 1825 at Gladstone's impor-

1 D, i, 353.   2 *Ib.*, 258.   3 GP, 44790, 84.

tunity. By September 1826 Gladstone, after walking with Hallam, could analyse thus: 'I esteem as well as admire him. Perhaps I am declaring too explicitly & too positively for the period of our *intimacy* – which has not yet lasted a year – but such is my present feeling.'[1]

Their intimacy had about it much that is characteristic of schoolboy romances. Hallam wrote to Gladstone in the summer vacation of 1825 pleading for a letter: 'I had begun to fear you had reasons for not doing so of some unpleasant nature.'[2] They disputed vigorously about politics. 'You are severe,' wrote Hallam, 'on my Whiggism . . . An opponent of Reform, Sir, I was for a few days, misled by a few specious arguments of Mr. Canning: but I have long since been contrite for my error.' They could agree on Canning's 'Liberal Tory' politics of Catholic Emancipation, commercial freedom and challenge to the Holy Alliance of reaction on the continent, and especially his espousal of the cause of the Greek emancipation for which Byron had in 1824 offered his martyrdom. But otherwise the one could merely wonder at the other's obtuseness. Hallam:

> Look around you, Gladstone, look at the country groaning in the eleventh year after peace under a load of unparalleled miseries, look at Ruin by your own account staring our Trade in the face – & then sit down calmly, IF YOU CAN, & write me word that you approve of the late war, of Pitt's infatuated administration, of all those measures, big with horror & desolation, which have brought England to the verge of a precipice I shudder to gaze at.[3]

They disputed also about history. Hallam was reduced to placatory apologies for having grievously offended Gladstone by his levity about Charles I.[4] It is curious to find Hallam enquiring of Gladstone in April 1827 whether he had read the 'new Vivian Grey', the sequel to the original anonymous and notorious 'society' novel by the young Benjamin Disraeli.[5] There were no arguments about religion, perhaps because of Hallam's wholesome fear of being hauled to account for himself before what he described to Gladstone as the 'bar of your severe morality'.[6] It has been judged 'a distinctive feature' of Gladstone's Eton days, and most curious and unusual for an Evangelical, that he apparently made no effort to impress the strength of his religious convictions upon his fellows.[7] This inhibition was certainly not due to any general recessiveness of character. Was it that as a slightly uneasy provincial he feared public

1 D, i, 75.
2 Hallam to G [August 1826]. GP, 44352, 3.   3 *Ib.*, 5.
4 Hallam to Gladstone [August 13, 1827], *Ib.*, 31.
5 Hallam to Gladstone [April 1827] *ib.*, 23. Gladstone did not read it until fifty years later, when he correctly judged it 'trash'. R. Blake, *Disraeli*, (1966), 53.
6 *Ib.*   7 Butler, 18.

mockery? In any case Gladstone had no reservations about Hallam's moral fitness. He pronounced his Eton life an 'ideal life', without 'deviation from the ideal, in temper, word, or act'.[1]

That there was a repressed or unconscious homosexual aspect to this friendship 'rather exceptionally close'[2] is very probable, given the combination of a propensity to emotional attraction to their own sex common among adolescents together with the monastic absence of young females at Eton. The relationship was certainly quite proper, indeed as to external conventions quite formal: they were always 'my dear Hallam' and 'my dear Gladstone' in their letters and, it may be presumed, in their intimate conversation. There is no need to assume that either youth was immune from what it was perhaps that Gladstone a little later described as 'rankling passions' which disturbed him profoundly; 'passions which I dare not name – shame forbids it & duty does not seem to require it'.[3] But in any case it was the ideal that prevailed over any rankling passions there may have been below the surface of a relationship, which, as in the case of Tennyson, was 'so lofty, so fraternal'.[4]

It was in such a mood of exalted emotion that Gladstone took his leave of Eton in December 1827. He carved his name both on the door near Keate's desk (uncharacteristically miscalculating the space he would need to complete his beautiful Roman characters) and on the stone wall near his House. He did not achieve his father's ambition for him of becoming Captain of the Oppidans (the majority who were not scholars on the foundation). Hallam had already left, on his way to Trinity, Cambridge. John Gladstone exerted himself to mobilise his connections to secure William a place at the equivalent regal and magnificent foundation at Oxford, Christ Church, though this could not be arranged until the October of the following year. Hallam departed in July with heartfelt pledges of future friendship and an exchange of books: Burke for Hallam and Hallam's father for Gladstone. Gladstone had a year to fill in, partly back at Eton, partly in preparation for Oxford. In such circumstances Eton was poignantly void. Worse: Canning died in August 1827 after a mere three months as Prime Minister, and Gladstone had an extra occasion for lamentation and an aggravated sense of loss. He paid a visit of homage to Canning's grave in the Abbey on his way back from Seaforth to Eton in September, composed elegiac verses, purchased a portrait and a bust. On December 2, 1827 he sat down to write 'with a heavy heart' an account of his last Eton day and his feeling 'that the happiest period of my life is now past'. He prayed that God might make his feelings 'produce the salutary effect of teaching me to aim at joys of a more permanent as well as a more exquisite nature'. 'But oh! if any mortal thing is sweet, my Eton years,

1 GP, 44790, 84.   2 *Ib.*
3 D, i, 334.   4 GP, *ib.*

excepting anxieties at home, have been so! I am perhaps very foolishly full of melancholy.' He took formal leave of Keate and his tutor on the following day, visited the room of the society as an honorary member, and left Eton, 'my long known and long loved abode', for London, where he saw Kemble as Falstaff at Covent Garden, and Madame Vestris in *Don Giovanni*, which he did not like.

[5]

To none have the towers and spires and domes of Oxford beckoned more enticingly than to Gladstone in 1828. He had arrived at Eton in a condition of boyish insensibility; he left it having seen enough and read enough to place himself in a perspective in which a developed self-awareness could be related to wider awareness of his times and circumstances. Eton had been a high point for him, but there was never any likelihood that Oxford would be anything less than a higher point. Partly this was the struggle and the fight up the staircase of achievement. In this sense the purpose of a high point was to reach points yet higher. Eton had revealed to him that he had the power to excel in a manner well regarded in the wider world. Oxford would put those powers to the test. This in itself added an extra dimension to Gladstone's new, semi-adult self-awareness. He knew that the kind of religious belief which Liverpool and Seaforth had inculcated in him and which marked him decisively in his dealings with the outer world was an effort to renew the spiritual life and values of the Anglican Church, lately sunk in the stagnant latitudinarianism and materialistic Erastianism of the previous century. He was coming to question the content of some of those values; but never their life-renewing programme. Oxford, in the full panoply of its majestically unreformed devotion to the Church of England, stood for so much more in that kind of outlook than did Eton. Possibly, had Oxford remained without any more signs of revival than were evident in, say, Canning's time, John Gladstone might have thought Cambridge more suitable to William's requirements. The traditions of 'High and Dry' Churchmanship were never as strong in that cradle of the English Reformation.

But Oxford undoubtedly was stirring with new life. To some extent this can be measured in mechanical reforms. The New Examination Statute of 1800 began the process by which the honours schools in *Literae Humaniores* and Mathematics and Physics were established, and gained quickly in prestige. Robert Peel's double first-class in 1808 was a great public event. A new statute in 1825 became necessary to cope with the press of candidates eager to establish reputations in this new and rather dramatic manner. Peel was by no means a political hero to Gladstone in 1828. He had refused to serve with Canning in 1827 and was the leader of die-hard Protestant resistance to Catholic Emancipation. Even after Peel's capitulation on this issue in 1829, Gladstone was inclined to have reservations. He was distinctly unenthusiastic when in 1830 his father suggested that Peel might be the best man to replace Huskisson, accidentally killed by the new invention of the railroad locomotive, as M.P. for Liverpool. Gladstone's father's instinct here was surer than his son's. Peel was the purest and most prominent representative of a rising bourgeois social force engaging in a process of symbiosis with the traditional aristocracy precisely by means of the socializing institutions (in Peel's case Harrow rather than Eton) through which Gladstone himself was passing. The brilliance of his performance in the schools came to be seen in itself as a kind of portent of the coming of higher moral values in public life. Peel's example stood before Gladstone in 1828 with an irresistible cogency.

Even more cogent were the evidences that Oxford itself was beginning to respond to the instinct for renewal stirring in the Church. Copleston, Whately, Keble, Hawkins, Arnold, Newman, Pusey, Wilberforce, were the new names coming to the fore. Gladstone could reconcile his urge for achievement and success with religious and moral values by dedicating them to the service of reviving and purifying the Church; and the reviving and purifying of Oxford integrally involved with such a larger spiritual renewal in turn augmented and enhanced those tests of excellence provided by Oxford to encourage zeal for success and achievement.

In fact Gladstone could hardly wait to get to Oxford. He wanted to go up in the Trinity Term before the long vacation in 1828. Obliged instead to wait until October, he nevertheless made a point of visiting the university in January to matriculate, subscribe to the Thirty-Nine Articles of religion, and call upon his future dean and the vice-chancellor. He then went on to Wilmslow, south of Manchester, where he had arranged to be coached for the university by the rector. He discovered that his classics were in a 'bad way'. From the rector he got several introductions to the leading Evangelicals in Oxford. Then he went off to spend an Easter vacation with the family in Edinburgh. This was an occasion of considerable importance. One of his introductions was to a former Oxford Evangelical, the Rev. Edward Craig, now minister of St. James's Chapel in Edinburgh. At Craig's hands Gladstone underwent a severe course of extreme Calvinism: in effect a kind of doctrinal ordeal. Craig exposed to him unwittingly the tensions inherent in Evangelical theology.[1] At the same time Gladstone entered into the last and most intense phase of his relationship

1 Butler, 20–21.

with his sister Anne. 'Her mental gifts were considerable, her character most devout and fervent: her religious rearing had been in the Evangelical tenets but her mind was too pure for prejudice. She must have infused into me some little warmth, and I think she started me on some not very devious bypaths of opinion.'[1] The principal bypath was the doctrinal question of baptismal regeneration (which Craig most vociferously repudiated). The extent to which this matter became the germ of profound changes in Gladstone's churchmanship is indicated by the irony of the circumstance that the great controversy upon the question of baptismal regeneration which rocked the Church in 1850 and ended for good Gladstone's ideal of a new Church and a new State, was provoked by a clergyman whose opinion was identical with Gladstone's in 1828. The doctrine, with its 'High' stress on the efficacy of sacrament, had 'of course', as Gladstone recalled, 'been registered as a heresy in my mind'. Under his sister's influence he studied an article on the question in the *Quarterly Review* which adduced all manner of patristic testimonies in its favour. 'But what struck me most was that Saint Augustine was included among the witnesses: for I had always heard of him as a truly Evangelical Christian . . . ' Gladstone revealed to Helen on 24 August 1828 his new conviction ('Fool that I was' to have refused assent 'to a doctrine I cannot deny and a reason I cannot refute').[3] Thus 'lifted up to the level of Baptismal Regeneration', Gladstone was led on to reading Hooker's works which he found in his father's library. There was no dramatic mental explosion: Gladstone's mind fermented quietly. He left again for Oxford, praying that God might render useful to him the fruits of his communion with Anne. Surviving a coach upset near Walsall, Gladstone arrived back at Oxford early in August to consult his future tutor.

On his first night in Oxford he records meeting 'a woman' and having a 'long conversation' with her. The following night he 'met the poor creature again, who is determined to go home'.[4] This is probably the first instance of his propensity to what he came to call 'rescue work', meeting prostitutes and trying to persuade them to give up their abandoned way of life. Gladstone's knowledge of females, apart from his immediate relatives and servants, was practically nil. He idealised his mother and sisters as creatures hardly on a merely human plane. For him the problem of polite feminine society presented itself in these years as bristling with difficulty, anxiety, and embarrassment. He was shy, ill at ease, and painfully aware of his social clumsiness and lack of poise and emollient small talk. He was unhappily aware that his manner 'tends to turn every conversation into a debate'.[5] He knew that his opinions were those of 'a

1 GP, 44791, 1.   2 D, i, 187 (June 30, 1828).
3 Butler, 23.   4 D, i, 193.   5 *Ib.*, 428.

censorious and fastidious man'.[1] He knew also that his letters had not seldom the 'air of memoranda intended to clear his own mind'.[2] This worked well enough in the company of his family and of rather solemn and somewhat priggish male adolescents well aware that they represented the coming generation of great men in Church and State. But with, for example, the Misses Pocklington, daughters of a Leamington colonel, Gladstone was uneasily out of his depth. He confessed that he liked 'both daughters much especially Miss Jane, with whom I got upon delicate ground about the Vicar's preaching'. But he covered his embarrassment by raising characteristic objections about self-indulgence: 'All this time I ought to be asking myself, do I mix in society (wretchedly incapacitated for it as I am) for the gratification of self?' He was willing to arrive at a judiciously cautious response to his own question: 'My opinion of it has in some measure been changed: or rather I have had little opportunity previously of forming one. But it seems to me that female society, whatever the disadvantages may be, has just & manifold uses attendant upon it in turning the mind away from some of its most dangerous and degrading temptations.'[3] Probably the Misses Pocklington would not have been flattered by this analysis of their moral utility. It is probable, moreover, that for Gladstone prostitutes could play a curiously similar role.

Clearly the young Gladstone was most out of his depth with what could be termed the 'middle range' of females, between the status of family and the status of servants. With the former his spiritual relationship was that of a miserably unworthy sinner conversing to his infinite benefit with saints and angels. With the latter he was, though indeed himself a miserably unworthy sinner, in a position to assume some kind of superior, directive spiritual office. Indeed, it was his plain duty so to do, and all his life Gladstone took pains to arrange and minutely supervise the religious life of his servants. With prostitutes, those dropouts from the servant class, his position was even stronger, clearer, and to that extent easier and unembarrassed. The Evangelical missionary impulse to 'save' unregenerate souls from sin could have no more imperative justification than with poor creatures whose sinfulness was the very badge of their degraded profession. Gladstone could feel uninhibited in accosting a woman of the streets at a time when he would be nervously awkward at having to chat to a charming and accomplished young lady of his own social rank. There is no doubt, moreover, that for Gladstone the unction of his mission was in some large measure proportionate to the beauty of its object. This, again, had its prophylactic side. If the company of beautiful young ladies could help to turn his mind away from dangerous and degrading temptations (perhaps of the kind

1 GP, 44981, 2.   2 Lathbury, i, x.   3 D, i, 338.

too shameful even to name), the company of beautiful prostitutes could be a sensual pleasure sublimated by the exercise of a spiritual office.

This became and remained an important aspect of Gladstone's private life, a vocation later to be codified and institutionalised; but at this stage he was taking only tentative steps. Undoubtedly one of the contributing impulses at this time setting him along this sublimatory direction was his battle with the temptations of masturbation. Self-adjurations in this matter were a fairly regular feature of his journals in the Oxford years ('beast, fool, blackguard, puppy, reptile', was an entry for November 17, 1829). He was still pleading for 'God's help for Christ's sake in this besetting sin', which returned upon him 'again and again like a flood' in April 1831.[1] But with the climax of his academic career coming upon him a few months later he appears to have overcome the 'blackness' of his 'natural (& vigorous) tendencies'.[2]

From his initiative with the 'poor creatures' at Oxford Gladstone moved on to Cuddesdon, where his Christ Church tutor was vicar, for a second bout of preparation. Clearly he understood that he would enter Oxford as an undergraduate marked by his Eton reputation as being of rare promise; and he was determined that Oxford should not be disappointed. After having written up a list of books read, 'wh. is humiliating', he dined with the Bishop of Oxford (whose palace was nearby), who seemed 'a remarkably kind man'. Shortly afterwards, on August 23, 'Mr. Newman, of Oriel', came to dine. Gladstone's only comment was 'Draughts at night'. Whatever grounds Gladstone may have had for so nonchalant a response on a first encounter, it reflects with a curious faithfulness the generally rather cool attitude he was to take to Newman in the later years when both men were making their indelible mark on the life of their times. A certain prescience is again, perhaps, indicated by Gladstone's comment a few weeks later: 'An *excellent* sermon from Mr. Pusey.'[3]

On October 10, 1829 Gladstone moved in to temporary rooms at Christ Church, removing to rooms in the then Chaplain's Quadrangle (where the Meadow Buildings now are) on the 15th. He thought his lodgings 'very dirty indeed', but knew he was lucky to get them considering the pressure on space in the college, which a succession of recent deans had made a point of cramming to the hilt. He had the pleasure of unpacking a large box of wine on the 25th; and settled down happily in his first term. His academic duties did not tax him. He read steadily and voraciously. Biscoe's teaching of Aristotle was an important reinforcing influence on the already well developed systematizing turn of his intellect. He saw much of Pusey, and lamented, as at Eton, the stagnant condition of religion in Oxford, making the contrast between the reality of Oxford and

1 *Ib.*, 351; see also 250, 276, 285.   2 *Ib.*, 400.   3 *Ib.*, 202.

Oxford's claims and potentiality a 'most painful spectacle'.[1] Services at Christ Church itself were 'scarcely performed with common decency',[2] and Gladstone was obliged to look about Oxford for some more satisfying source of religious sustenance. His introductions to the Evangelical element at Oxford, clustered mainly in St. Edmund Hall and at St. Ebbe's Church, under its curate, Bulteel, were not entirely satisfactory. Bulteel, an extreme Calvinist, eventually left the Church and became one of the Plymouth Brethren. Gladstone, who occasionally found a way to hear his sermons even when he was under the Church's ban, found him partly attractive and partly repellent.

But there was little about Oxford religion or Oxford teaching of religion to jolt Gladstone into any direction radically at odds with his inherited loyalties. Hooker's doctrines on the Church remained as yet a 'mere abstraction'.[3] Even Bishop Butler, the great ornament of eighteenth-century Anglican theology, recently come into vogue in Oxford divinity, and later to become Gladstone's greatest theological admiration and preoccupation, shocked him by his lax doctrine of human nature. Nor, by his last year in Oxford, had the great names of the future 'Oxford Movement' made any decisive impression on his mind. Of Newman: 'much singular not to say objectionable matter if one may speak of so good a man.'[4] Of Keble: 'Are all of his opinions those of Scripture & of the Church?'[5] Although he 'knew and respected' both Pusey and Bishop Lloyd, 'neither of them attempted to exercise the smallest influence' over his religious principles. At Pusey's rooms in Christ Church he met Newman again, and was inclined later to think him 'very able indeed';[6] but no spark was struck. Whately on the other, 'liberal', side of Oxford theology, offended him by antisabbatical doctrine, 'as mischievous as it is unsound'.[7] Maurice, a migrant from Cambridge, he knew well at Oxford, but got 'little solid meat from him', finding him 'difficult to catch and more difficult to hold'. Henry Wilberforce, 'already a High Churchman & very sarcastic as well as acute', scandalised Gladstone by treating with contempt a sermon which Gladstone had thought 'very Christian'; and Gladstone was also scandalised when Vaughan Thomas spoke in the university pulpit of '*Calvin* and Socinus, and other like aliens from Gospel truth'.[8] Thus the integrity of Gladstone's Evangelicalism survived the Oxford years essentially intact. This was certainly just as well, for a crisis in his religious life coinciding with his almost manic excitement over the Reform issue in politics in 1831 would probably have disrupted his academic progress beyond retrieval.

In the meantime, he had quite enough other things to disturb him.

1 Lathbury, i, 2.   2 D, i, 370–71.
3 Lathbury, i, 6–7.   4 D, i, 347.   5 *Ib.*, 366.
6 *Ib.*, 405.   7 *Ib.*, 382–83.   8 GP, 44791, 1.

Towards the end of his first term, Anne's increasing debility became critical. The Seaforth Christmas was overshadowed by a sense of anxiety, for all that good cheer remained the official rule (on her birthday on December 24 Gladstone recorded himself as 'romping at night'). Back at Oxford in the new year, Gladstone received a series of melancholy bulletins from his father, culminating on February 21 with the news that Anne had died suddenly on the 19th. Gladstone immediately left for Seaforth in a state of 'abstracted' shock, 'at first much dismayed: but afterwards unable to *persuade* myself of the truth of the news'. This for Gladstone was the first serious breaking of a family link. He attempted to forge a replacement by making a solemn pact with his younger sister Helen that they should henceforth collaborate and monitor one another's religious and spiritual development in memory of their sister. This proved more troublesome than edifying. Helen, now a rather 'difficult' fifteen-year-old, was in no mood to submit to William's rather officious direction. Helen's distress in turn upset her parents, who depended increasingly on her domestic presence. By October 1831 the situation reached the point where Tom had to be called in to write to William asking him politely to desist from 'religious speculations' with Helen.

Nor were Gladstone's relations with Hallam at this time any more satisfactory. He was possessed by a morbid fear that Hallam was neglecting him, or that Hallam did not admire his literary productions. Hallam was obliged to write reassuring letters to appease Gladstone, who was clearly in a state of emotional tension.[1] Gladstone's account of Anne's death produced from Hallam a pious declamation of a distinctly uncharacteristic style.[2] But by September 1829 Gladstone could note that there was 'almost an uncertainty, very painful', whether he might call Hallam his friend or not.[3] Gladstone was elected to the Oxford Union the following month, and there was a happy encounter in November when Hallam came across from Cambridge as one of the members of the Cambridge Union to debate the merits of Shelley *versus* Byron at Oxford. Hallam assured him that the future great poetic genius of the era was one Alfred Tennyson, at Trinity, and promised to send his poems. But by 1830 they were back to a state of rather petty recrimination, with Hallam reduced to a stiff, defensive formality.[4]

Gladstone by no means restricted his efforts at spiritual oversight to his family. He still kept his local philanthropy in repair. It was a typical occasion when, in the company of a cousin, he visited a 'poor blind invalid'. 'She seemed in a most happy state. We each read her a sermon.' His Oxford friends were no less the objects of a vigilant solicitude. In this

1 E.g., Hallam to G, August 12 [1828]. GP, 44352, 72.
2 Hallam to G, [March 17, 1829]. *Ib.*   3 D, i, 259.
4 Hallam to G, June 23, 1830. *Ib.*, 158.

respect, Gladstone decidedly overcame the inhibition so marked at Eton. Anstice's spiritual health he diagnosed in January 1830 as 'very good'; Gaskell's case was 'not more painful than usual'. But that of Doyle was 'exceedingly distressing'. It was at this time that Gladstone, high in the favour of the Christ Church authorities for piety and zeal, became a prickbill, monitoring undergratuate attendance at chapel. It was his perhaps rather priggish zeal in this office which contributed to the unpopularity which led to his being beaten by 'a party of men' in his own rooms, some time between midnight and one in the morning of March 24, 1830. (He had reported 'a most disgraceful disturbance in Chapel' on the 22nd.) He soon, as he related, 'ceased to resist', and consoled himself with thanks to God for the salutary mortification of his pride and for the chance to exercise the faculty of forgiveness. He took it for granted that 'I shall be despised by some for it. I hardly know what to think of my own conduct myself'.[1] He later characterised himself as being 'not by nature brave.'[2] This 'hostile and unkind conduct', however, did not prevent Gladstone from speaking on the following day to Doyle, 'I trust plainly on religion – but the weapon is weak in such hands as mine'. On the day after that he was gratified by a 'long & satisfactory conversation' with Gaskell, which to some extent compensated for Doyle's apparent incorrigibility ('Called on Doyle. A week of debasement, but alas not of abasement'). At Oxford, as at Eton, Gladstone found time for a wide range of enjoyable social occasions – wine parties, teas, walks, dinners, outings such as the 'exceedingly pleasant' visit to Henley in June 1829 to watch the first Oxford and Cambridge boat race. Although never noted as a dandy, he was as 'tidy and well-dressed' as ever; and always an admirer of high sartorial tone. In his last period of residence at Oxford, in the 1890s, he still spoke with respectful awe of those exquisite young men of his time whose trousers were cut so tight as to prohibit their sitting. But there were also times when he was liable to be oppressed by the difficulty of reconciling the rather grand secularity of life at Christ Church with the insistent demands of his religious preoccupations.

Such occasions of anxiety and difficulty were exceptions to a rule of academic distinction and growing university eminence. Gladstone signalled his competitive intentions by attempting two of the university's most coveted awards, the Ireland scholarship in March 1829 and the Craven in May. He failed both attempts, but his tutor reported gratifyingly on his Craven effort. He succeeded, however, in being declared first among the candidates for the Fell exhibition at Christ Church in November 1829. Christ Church began looking at him seriously. His tutor enquired whether he intended to go into the Church, and whether there would be a chance of his staying on at Christ Church and taking pupils.

1 *Ib.*, 290–91.   • 2 Bassett, 164. But see Foot, D, i, xxxix.

Then in December he was made a junior student (or senior scholar) of the college, a mark of considerable academic advance. As he wrote to his brother John Neilson: 'A Student's gown is full and flowing and very different from that scanty and odious concern that hangs on Commoners' shoulders.'[1] In the new year he celebrated this dignity by moving to a set of rooms in the Canterbury quadrangle, on the first floor in the staircase in the north-eastern corner. These 'good & comfortable' chambers were in what was held to be the most fashionable and desirable quarter of the college. Meanwhile, following election to the Union (despite a distressing black ball, as at Eton, a not surprising indication that he lacked universal popularity), Gladstone decided also to repeat his Eton success by forming an essay society, with a nucleus of his Etonian contemporaries. A letter from Hallam at Cambridge spurred Gladstone to this venture. 'It is nearly on the model of one at Cambridge,' he reported to his father, 'which has existed long, and had many distinguished members: that goes by the somewhat inappropriate and extraordinary name of "the Apostles".'[2] This, called after his initials, the Weg, met first in New College in November 1829, when Gladstone was chosen secretary. He made his maiden speech in the Union in February 1830, and was elected to the committee. By May he was secretary and by November president. Back in Oxford in January 1831, Gladstone looked forward to ten or twelve hours a day of work. This would be the year of the supreme intellectual test. He failed narrowly in a second attempt on the Ireland scholarship in March, pulled down by too much 'superfluous matter' and an essay 'desultory beyond belief'.[3] He was rather dashed to discover that the winner was a schoolboy at Shrewsbury; and his tutor was scathing on Gladstone's disingenuousness, as for example trying to get away with answering the question, 'Who wrote "God Save the King"?' by 'Thompson wrote "Rule Britannia".' Still, he took this 'ludicrous defeat', as he described it to Charles Wordsworth, in good heart.[4] It is the opinion of a Regius Professor of Greek that 'Gladstone would not have made a good classical scholar'.[5] Nevertheless Gladstone was winding himself up into a state of formidable academic effectiveness.

[6]

There was also, throughout all this, the nagging question in the background as to what he should do after taking his honours schools at

1 Bassett, 18.   2 *Ib.*, 15–16.   3 D, i, 348–49.
4 J. Brinley-Richards, 'Mr. Gladstone's Early Politics', *Temple Bar* (c.1883), 212.
5 Hugh Lloyd-Jones, 'Gladstone on Homer', *Times Literary Supplement*, January 3, 1975, 15–17.

the end of 1831. At Eton his assumption was that Oxford would be followed by an Inn of Court as the standard preliminary to public life. At Oxford he began to sense a call from religion. This worried his father. At the end of 1828 his brother Tom had acted as an intermediary, stressing to William their father's opinion against any hasty decision, adding his own doubts as to William's capability as yet to take any course of action depending upon mature judgment.[1] By the end of 1829 Gladstone noted that his mind was continuing 'strongly inclined to the Church'.[2] Almost certainly this was part of his response to the psychic shock of Anne's death. His elder sister had been much the most important influence on Gladstone of an intellectually fine kind in his early formative years. If his father's influence represented secularity and public honours, Anne's pointed Gladstone to the higher life of sanctity and religious devotion. What could be a more fitting tribute to her memory than to dedicate himself to the profession of Holy Orders?

The summer vacation of 1830 found Gladstone in a state of intense distraction and perplexity as to his future course, and especially as to whether he was capable of discerning the 'right path' for himself. He felt a compulsive urge to press directly for ordination. Walking alone in early August in the garden at Cuddesdon, where he was on a vacation reading course, Gladstone felt a 'fearful weight' on his mind, asking himself why he was 'slumbering & trifling over matters which have at best but an indirect connection with religion, while souls throughout the world are sinking daily into death'. 'Strange thoughts' of his future life passed through his mind, 'giving up home, friends, University'. He was intimate at this time with another pious undergraduate, Joseph Anstice, with whom he conversed especially on the fraught topic of purity of motive.[3] On August 4 he wrote a feverish and 'very long letter' (in truth, of nearly 4,000 words) to his father declaring his desire for the 'ministerial office'.[4] But by the 8th, wavering, he had come independently to the conclusion that on such an 'awful subject' he was as yet too immature to decide: 'For I must not I think consider myself as a man exercising the unfettered judgment of a man: but as a being not yet competent for self-direction nor fitted to act upon his own uncorrected impressions, but under the guidance of others for his present course.'[5]

John Gladstone manoeuvred his son gently away from this latest infatuation and back to his earlier commitment to politics by allowing William to argue himself to a standstill. He replied soothingly to William on August 10 (from Leamington) that 'whenever your mind shall be finally made up', and 'whatever that determination may be', he could

1 Butler, 28.   2 D, i, 276.   3 Butler, 29.
4 Morley, i, 635–40; together with his father's reply of August 10, 640–41.
5 D, i, 316–17.

only trust that it would be 'eventually for your good'. 'Let nothing be done rashly; be consistent with yourself, and avail yourself of all the advantages placed within your reach.' In the absence of paternal prohibition, William could be relied upon to produce its equivalent for himself. Given his devotional cast of mind, his insistence on his being the 'chief of sinners', his constant self-adjurations to 'practical self condemnation' leading to a 'true self abhorrence', it was impossible for him to admit that, in a free choice of careers, he deliberately chose secularity and political ambition. It was later to be a great feature of Gladstone's own mythology about himself that it was the 'desire of my youth' to 'be a clergyman'. 'My mental life (ill represented in the moral being) was concentrated in the Church'; and that the 'change in the professional direction of my life' 'took place in deference to my father's wish'.[1] It was much more likely to have been a case, rather, of his own peculiar and complexly pious kind of collusion or complicity with what he knew his father's wish to be. Perhaps this was at the bottom of his ritual but ferocious self-condemnation on December 24, 1830, 'dearest Anne's day of birth in the human state': 'I, the hypocrite, and the essence of sin, am indeed deceitful above all things and desperately wicked, desperately wicked.' In the competition for his allegiance between his sister's and his father's influences, the latter had two decisive advantages. Gladstone took after his sister in fineness of intellect; but he took after his father in fortitude of mind. Unlike his three elder brothers, but very much like his father, William was a fighter and a competer who loved success and was well capable of attaining it on the world's terms. Moreover, Gladstone had already climbed the staircase of endeavour at Eton with conspicuous success and applause. He enjoyed that experience enormously. Apart from the one intense phase of yearning for ordination in the summer of 1830, evidence as to what course of professional life Gladstone desired in youth tends decidedly in the secular direction. Possibly the most telling early evidence of this predisposition is the back of a letter from his old Etonian friend Pickering in August 1829, covered by Gladstone with exquisitely penned doodles: lists of ministers, many facsimiles of Palmerston's signature (as well as the grand formula, 'Lord Viscount Palmerston, M.P.'),[2] many facsimiles also of the Marquess of Clanricarde (Charles Canning's brother-in-law); and two lists of his friends bearing the honorific dignity of privy councillors: the Right Honourable Members of Parliament included M. Gaskell, A. H. Hallam (twice), Sir P. A. Pickering (twice), F. H. Doyle, G. A. Selwyn, C. J. Canning (twice), A. C. Wood, W. W. Farr, and, modestly but decisively there, the Rt. Hon. W. E. Gladstone.[3]

1 PMP, i, 145, 148.
2 At this time the most promising of the Canningites.   3 GP, 44352, 130.

By the end of 1830 Gladstone noted: 'Politics are fascinating to me. Perhaps too fascinating.' After the fever of the yearning for ordination the elections and the Reform crisis came as a therapeutically absorbing distraction. It was a kind of stabilising reversion to type. It had been, as he put it, 'my Debating Society year'.[1] He had carried the debate on November 11, 1830 (the occasion he was elected president) on a motion that the Duke of Wellington's government was undeserving of the confidence of the country: so strong were his Canningite loyalties still. As at Eton, every aspect of the Oxford debating society engrossed Gladstone. It provided an arena giving fullest scope to the extroverted side of his personality, his verbally combative temper and his disputatious talents. And, unlike Eton, the Oxford Union debated current and immediate political issues. Moreover, there was always Liverpool to keep Gladstone gingered. And in Liverpool political passions were running high in the by-election to replace Huskisson. Gladstone's father, having failed (puzzled to the end) in his last bid for Liverpool's approval, was in the thick of managing a particularly corrupt and unpleasant campaign against the son of his old friend William Ewart. At Oxford Gladstone, who fully shared his father's bitterness at Liverpool's ingratitude, identified himself with the fortunes of the paternal faction and lamented its defeat and the distressing outcome of the end of friendly relations between the Gladstones and the Ewarts.

Canning's death in 1827 had robbed Gladstone of some of his zest for national politics. The break up of Canning's posthumous ministry at the beginning of 1828 left him unmoved. He was not sorry, as he told an Etonian friend, that the Whigs were out, for he thought that they, 'poor things', were born 'destined to the opposition benches'.[2] But Wellington and Peel, those deserters of Canning, pleased him even less, even though they conceded Catholic emancipation in 1829. With the Whig-dominated coalition of Grey in office in 1830, committed to a parliamentary reform bill, however, Gladstone began to have regrets about the Tories. He remembered Canning's arguments against the folly of attempting to replace the organic creation of centuries of history and experience with the paltry contrivances of presumptuous radicalism. He read Mr. Canning's Reform speeches at Liverpool and made extracts; he read Mr. Canning's great 1822 speech against Reform; he went back to the source of wisdom and devoured Burke. There was little doubt now as to career. In January 1831 Tom (himself preparing for the Bar) wrote: 'I cannot tell you how I rejoice at your having determined upon the Law.'[3] In March 1831 he trusted in God that the Reform Bill would not be carried. It scraped through the Commons by one vote on March 22. The Lords

1 D, i, 336.
2 G to Handley, January 23 [1828]. GP, 44352, 43.   3 Butler, 31.

rejected it by a majority of eight a month later. On April 22 he found that the 'excitement of politics' was too much for his reading. With a dissolution of the Commons imminent he read 'all the papers with harrowing interest'. He attempted unsuccessfully to get the Union to proscribe Cobbett's *Register*. By the end of April he was busy raising subscriptions for an 'Antireform fund', and netted £41. He went to the vice-chancellor about his 'struggle', received a 'gracious address', and went off to write placards.[1] Gladstone, in fact, was working himself up into a panic about Reform, a matter he was often later to recall with shame and apologies, pleading that he was deluded and misled into the pit of Tory reaction by his very loyalty to Canning on the one issue in which, unhappily, Canning was on the side of darkness instead of light. His father, pragmatically disposed to accept the inevitability of some measure of reform, failed to persuade Gladstone that the High Tory sentiments of uncompromising resistance which went down well in Oxford had relatively little influence in the country at large.

These later liberal apologetics were unimaginable to the Gladstone who threw himself furiously into the Oxford elections in May 1831. He found himself being 'hustled below the town hall', making 'an immense row'. He procured a horse to take part in the Tory cavalcade. He recorded on May 5 being 'quite hoarse and my throat sore from hollowing yesterday, with much cold and frequent nose bleeding'. There was much ado about the hustings again on the 10th, with Gladstone walking at night in procession to the Angel, shouting 'valorously'. He got himself pelted while out riding, and for a time it looked likely there would be a town and gown riot. He had a 'variety of adventures' while 'argufying', and 'twice narrowly escaped hustling'. It was on May 17 that he made a speech in the Union in which, for nearly an hour, he poured forth with passionate urgency his certain conviction that reform threatened 'not only to change the form of our government, but ultimately to break up the very foundations of social order'. He made a startling and profound impression on his audience, one of whom happened to be the Earl of Lincoln, a Christ Church friend and son and heir of the Duke of Newcastle. There was uproar afterwards and adjournment; and two days later Gladstone carried the division by 94 to 38: the 'result was delightful'.[2] Less delightful, however, from his point of view, was the decisively pro-reform majority produced for the government in the election, including Oxford city and Oxfordshire. The university and the Duke of Marlborough's borough at Woodstock stood unavailingly against the tide.

Thus stimulated, Gladstone set about getting up a petition of resident bachelors and undergraduates of the university against the second Reform Bill introduced in the Commons by the government in June. He

1 D, i, 356.   2 *Ib.*, 359–60.

records working hard in Brasenose College for signatures, 'with good success'. He noted that it had happened to him 'of late' since his union speech that he received 'more compliments than usual'; and it seemed worthwhile to write it up, fortified in his labour by more copious draughts of Burke. His anti-reform zeal was such as to lead to his 'skipping chapel' thrice in five days, 'of which I am really ashamed', and for which he atoned by writing an imposition. By June 11 he had finished collecting signatures – he secured 770 – and was accorded the cordial approbation of his college in the form of an invitation to dine with the dean. He noted on July 7 an 'excellent speech of Peel's'. For Gladstone Peel was beginning, as the leader of resistance to Reform, to take on an enhanced stature. The second bill passed the new House of Commons on September 21.

The new term began in October 1831 with the great debate in the Lords. Gladstone, through the good offices of Lord Clanricarde at the instance of Charles Canning and other friends and useful contacts at Christ Church, gained the *entrée* and was present, in a fever of excitement, at the five nights' debate from October 3–8. The pressure was tremendous. For four nights he sat precariously on a 'transverse rail' in full view of the peeresses for nine or ten hours, sleeping at the Albany chambers of his brother Tom. It was a week of intoxication and enchantment, in which his appreciation of rhetoric momentarily took precedence over his partisanship. He thought Brougham 'most wonderful'; Grey's speech 'most beautiful'; Goderich and Lansdowne 'extremely good'. Exhaustion in the end compelled him to abandon what he later vividly recalled as his 'partial and *cutting* repose' on the rail,[1] oppressed with grave thoughts of the consequences of the Lords' voting against the bill by 199 to 158: 'God avert them – but it was an honourable & manly decision, & so may God avert them!'[2]

Back in Oxford, Gladstone was obliged to forego the excitement of politics and concentrate his mind on the imminent final honours schools. Fearing a breakdown, he decided that the strain of attempting the examination in mathematics and physics as well as classics would be too great. It was entirely characteristic of him that, having got his father's permission to abandon mathematics, he could not bring himself to act upon it. As in the matter of his future profession in August 1830, the absence of a paternal obstacle forced William to create his own. Gladstone consoled himself by taking wine with his Christ Church friend Martin Tupper, the later poetaster and author of *Proverbial Philosophy*. The schools for *Literae Humaniores* commenced on November 9. 'In the schools Wed. Thur. Fri. each day about 6¼ hours at work – or under. First – Strafford's Speech into Latin – with Logical & Rhetorical questions – the latter somewhat abstract – & wearying.' On

1 PMP, i, 39.   2 D, i, 387.

Thursday: 'a piece of Johnson's Preface in morng – in evg. critical questions, which I did very badly, but I afterwards heard better than *the* *rest*: which I could not & cannot understand.' On the Friday there were historical questions in the morning – 'wrote a vast quantity of matter, ill enow digested' – with Greek to translate and illustrate in the evening. He heard 'cheering accounts' of his performance indirectly. The Saturday Gladstone accounted 'in great measure an idle day': he had a good ride with Gaskell and read only about six hours. On Sunday, to mark the gravity of the occasion, he attended chapel thrice, and was edified by a sermon on Bethesda, 'which could not have been more appropriate if written on purpose for those who are going into the schools'. He was on Monday to be tested by the public *viva voce* examinations, for which, as one 'cold, timid, and worldly, and not in a healthy state of mind', he felt himself 'utterly – miserably unequal'. 'God grant that He who gave himself even for me may support me through it, if it be his will: but if I am covered with humiliation, O may I kiss the rod.'[1]

Once the oral examination started the following morning he was 'little troubled by fear'. His answers on divinity were not as he could have wished; but he had a 'beautiful examination' with every circumstance in his favour from R. D. Hampden, Fellow of Oriel, who made some gratifying remarks on his construing. Then followed a 'very clever examination' in history and an 'agreeable and short' one on poetry. 'Everything was in my favour: the examiners kind beyond anything: a good many persons there, and all friendly.' On the Wednesday there was another written paper: a 'moral essay on a very fine but very difficult subject'. Gladstone 'wrought hard' for five hours without any notion as to how effectual he was being. Six hours of papers in the schools on his classical books on the Thursday completed the ordeal.

A week later, on November 23, the class lists were to be announced. Gladstone tried to work at his mathematics, but was 'much disturbed & excited'. The list came out at 4.30 p.m. To his infinite pleasure and relief Gladstone found himself one of the two candidates in the first division. He rode to Cuddesdon the following day to sequester himself for a fortnight while preparing for the mathematical schools, reading about ten hours daily. Pickering at Cambridge wrote on his own and Hallam's behalf congratulating Gladstone, and trusting that the same result would follow for the mathematical side. He invited Gladstone to come to Cambridge to hear Hallam recite his Prize Declamation in Trinity chapel on December 16.[2] Gladstone was delighted at the idea. The mathematical examinations took place on December 9–14. Saline draughts were prescribed to quieten Gladstone, his 'pulse being high and some excitement existing which hinders sleep'. The very fact that he found

1 *Ib.*, 391–2.　　2 Pickering to G, December 4, 1831. GP, 44352, 213.

neither pleasure nor interest in mathematics made success in a way even more important as a test of self-discipline. He heard Newman preach an 'able discourse' on the Sunday, and on Wednesday found himself listed once more in the first class, and 'felt the joy of release'. It was for Gladstone 'an hour of thrilling happiness, between the past & the future, for the future was I hope not excluded'.[1] The bustle of packing and preparing to leave for Cambridge made a last round of visits pleasantly hectic; and after a night in London Gladstone found himself at Cambridge before five on the 15th, 'excellently lodged and most kindly received by the Master of Trinity', the father of his Oxford friend Charles Wordsworth. That night he endeavoured to find Hallam but failed. He heard Hallam's declamation on the 16th and dined with him in Trinity hall, then to tea and supper, renewing his acquaintance 'with the *old* Hallam'. He enjoyed the sights of Cambridge, but was disappointed at Simeon's preaching (the text was on there being 'much filthiness of the spirit'). To Gladstone's 'great joy' Hallam invited a renewal of their lapsed correspondence – 'to my *very* great joy'.[2] By December 21 he was in Liverpool, where he received a hero's welcome from his father and Robertson and John Neilson. Back at Seaforth with more 'great joy' he completed the round of salutations. The Oxford test had been triumphantly surmounted.

[7]

The next great step would be a Grand Tour to finish the process of creating an English gentleman started at Eton and brought to such a satisfactory state of refinement at Oxford. (A further essential refinement was added in January 1832 when Sir Robert Inglis, the Tory who had replaced Robert Peel as M.P. for Oxford University, put Gladstone's name up as a candidate for the United Universities Club). Gladstone was to travel with his brother John (now a lieutenant, R.N.), and a valet-factotum, Luigi Lamonica. But there still remained the crucial problem of what Gladstone was eventually to do as a finished product. There was never any question but that his father wanted a political career for his most gifted son. Gladstone took the extreme *dévot* view that a parental wish was equivalent to a divine command. But John Gladstone was far too shrewd to attempt to take advantage of his son's posture of submissive filial piety. His technique (as in the case of August 1830) was to allow William to talk himself to a psychological standstill on the question of ordination, and then, by not forbidding it, thereby to oblige

1 D, i, 397.   2 *Ib.*, 398–99.

William himself to withdraw his own request and thereby, as William put it, 'meet all my wishes'. At Seaforth on January 7, 1832 Gladstone sat up late composing an elaborate memorandum for his father on his future profession. He worked on it on the 8th, reconsidered it on the 15th, 'reperused and began to rewrite' on the 16th and eventually on the 17th finished it and gave it to his father. Gladstone manoeuvred himself into a political career by arguing that the present crisis of humanity put all established attitudes and ideas in doubt. Parliamentary reform would lead to an attack on the Church establishment. It was his duty to prepare himself to assist in responding to the coming formidable vicissitudes of public life rather than to withdraw into a cloistered vocation as he had argued in August 1830 in 'the belief I formerly entertained, that duty might be more extensively and effectually performed in the clerical profession'. Gladstone now felt himself 'free and happy to own, that my own desires as to my future destination are exactly coincident with yours insofar as I am acquainted with them – believing them to be a profession of the law with a view substantially to studying the constitutional branch of it, and on experiment as time and circumstance might offer on what is called public life.' And if the will of Providence should deny 'what is called success' to such a venture, then so much the better for a lesson thus taught 'to a craving ambition'.[1] Gladstone had the gratification, high indeed, of hearing from his father that it met his wishes and 'my dear Mother's. God be praised.'[2]

There were to be further bouts of mental and emotional restlessness about this decision. Had he 'veiled' to himself under 'specious names' a 'desertion of the most High God'? He had come to a decision not only in utter ignorance of the goodness of the decision but also, and worse, 'of the purity of the motive'.[3] Had he not confessed, in effect, to a 'craving ambition'? A 'harrowing fear' would come to him that he had betrayed the cause of God to his worldly ambition, 'and sold even the cross of Christ for the love of earth and the things of earth'.[4] His sister Helen clearly thought so; and in Gladstone's eyes Helen still stood as something of a surrogate for the values of the late, sainted Anne.

Fortunately, in view of his creative capacities for devotional self-accusation, Gladstone was allowed little time for introspective rumination. The family was in the last stages of its abandonment of Seaforth. There was much bustle and packing. Gladstone took a melancholy leave of the house of his boyhood on January 20. He had to return to Oxford to pack up the belongings he left there on his ecstatic jaunt to Cambridge. (The first leg of this journey, from Liverpool to Manchester, was his first and much enjoyed experience of the railway.)[5] He took his bachelor's

1 PMP, i, 220–29. As in August 1830, some 4,000 words.   2 D, i, 403–04.
3 *Ib.*, 404–05.   4 *Ib.*, 414.   5 Checkland, 253–4.

degree on the 26th, lunched with Tupper, settled his accounts, and set off for London and the continent.

The six months' continental tour, launched on February 1 with a rough Channel passage and the first of many bouts of sea sickness, took the brothers through Belgium, Paris (with excursions to St. Cloud, Versailles and Fontainebleau) and through France to Turin, where they arrived on March 2. Calvinistic loyalties led to an excursion of homage to the Protestants of the Vaudois before proceeding to Genoa. They were in Florence from March 16–27 and in Rome for most of April. Most of May was devoted to Naples and environs; then back to Rome until setting out on June 5 for Venice, the Tyrol, thence back down to Milan; finally, early in July, the return through France and Belgium, and London once more on July 29. After a service at St. James's, Piccadilly, Gladstone observed that it was 'no small matter to have regained the stated ordinances of our beloved Church'.

Naturally, Gladstone was fascinated by what he observed of religion in the Catholic lands of Europe. He took great pains to see, hear, explore, investigate all the aspects of the Roman system that offered themselves to his assiduity and keen attention. His experiences had a profoundly important effect on his own religious development. He arrived at Ostend with his Seaforth Evangelicalism still essentially intact. And indeed most of his specific experiences on the continent, and his explicit comments on them, tended to reinforce his anti-Roman prejudices. He was shocked by the shameless mariolatry everywhere apparent. He was constantly scandalised by what he considered the indecent slovenliness of many Catholic services and offices. He was offended at direct confrontation with the provocative arrogance of Roman doctrinal claims and jurisdictional assertions. The physical pomp and spiritual pride of Rome itself stirred his most Protestant emotions to their depths. Half the time he was appalled at the fearful threat to religious truth and liberty posed by a Roman church in the flush of its triumph over the principles of the Revolution and in the confidence of its ultramontane reinvigoration of the worst and most reactionary tridentine traditions; the other half he was appalled at what he interpreted as the manifest evidences of Rome's hopeless decadence and imminent collapse. Nevertheless, Gladstone, confronted with the imposing magnificence of Rome, felt himself stirred by new and less negative emotions.

Partly this derived from his sense of history and his sense of theatre. Attending the Easter benediction at St. Peter's, Gladstone was over-whelmed by a vision of what such an occasion, 'sublime' as it was, must have been in the 'palmy days' of the papacy. 'Nothing could be finer than this scene to the eye – even now it has too many claims on the mind – but admit the assumptions of Rome, and its grandeur transcends everything.'[1] That Gladstone could speak already of 'claims on the mind' indeed signified that something subconsciously portentous was occurring. His first visit to St. Peter's on March 31 had excited mixed feelings. On the one hand, Gladstone was assailed by a sense of 'the pain and shame of the schism' which separated the Anglican Church from Rome. Yet he was clear that the guilt inseparable from schism surely rested not upon the 'Venerable Fathers of the English Reformed Church' but upon Rome itself.[2] Unconnected experiences and their mental impressions accumulated in Gladstone's mind; they would soon constitute a critical mass of sufficient energy eventually to be released in a convulsive intellectual spasm. One of these isolated but accumulating experiences had been the pilgrimage of Calvinistic piety to the Protestant Vaudois of Piedmont. Having framed a 'lofty conception' of these victims of popish oppression as 'ideal Christians', Gladstone underwent a 'chill of disappointment' at finding the heroes of Milton's sonnet very much like other men.[3]

Pressing hard behind this primary religious concern, however, were both politics and art. A great part of Gladstone's objections to Roman Catholicism, indeed, was that its corruptions tended to give conservatism a bad name. The bad name of liberalism he took as an axiom. He had an early opportunity, in Antwerp, where a Dutch garrison was still holding out against the forces of the newly proclaimed Belgian state, of regretting the deleterious principles and policy of Lord Palmerston, now Lord Grey's Foreign Secretary. Gladstone's sympathies were wholly Dutch. Later, in northern Italy, he was to be equally sympathetic to Austria. He was meticulous in noting both at Bologna and Ferrara how generally popular and respected were the Austrian soldiery. At Innsbruck he had the gratification of witnessing a civic reception for the Emperor Francis and his Empress (though candour obliged him to record that the appearance of the last of the Holy Roman Emperors was 'ordinary enough', and that of the Empress 'ordinary more than enough').[4] But the magnificent new Austrian roads across the Alps and the cleanliness and good order of Milan more than compensated for these personal imperial deficiencies. On a visit to the mint at Paris Gladstone remarked of himself and his brother that 'we neither of us like liberalism' – the occasion was a feeble pun on the demand of the guide for a liberal gratuity, but the sentiment was nonetheless serious. In the Panthéon the inscription to Voltaire as a teacher of freedom to the human spirit provoked the sharp retort that 'another kind of freedom was taught before him, and will live after him'.[5] His observations of continental society confirmed Gladstone in his already very high opinion of the character and qualities of the

1 D, i, 480.   2 *Ib.*, 462.
3 GP, 44791, 1.   4 D, i, 537.   5 *Ib.*, 427–28.

English aristocracy: 'These nations conceive a *milord Inglese* quite a different being from one of their own half & half nobility – and they are right.'[1]

On the cultural monuments of antiquity and the Renaissance, and on the features of the scenery through which he passed, Gladstone was as assiduous and exhaustive in his attentions as only one could be who, for example, devoted nearly 500 words, including a quotation from Virgil, to jot down his response to the Venus de Médicis. Gladstone's opinions on art were copious but as yet indiscriminate. He admired what was conventionally admired. He was well aware of this as a weakness. Of contemporary practitioners his particular admiration in Rome was for the Danish neo-classical sculptor Bertel Thorwaldsen. There were far too many distractions. There was the vast question of religion. There were questions of morals and manners: the laxity of the Parisians with respect to the sabbath; the rascality of the Neapolitans with respect to everything. There were problems, earnestly debated with John, about the propriety of attending theatres and balls. Most insistently, in the background, was horrifying news of English politics. At Rome, at the end of May, Gladstone read 'with many a thrill of horror' the debates in the Lords on the new Reform Bill. So uniformly disastrous were the reports that by his last day in Rome, on June 4, he could declare that 'even terrible news is now becoming dull & commonplace'. It was in Venice on June 16 that, in the midst of admiring the Austrian naval arsenal, he read the 'disastrous but expected news' that the Reform Bill had passed the Lords.

Two particular events made his continental tour ever memorable for Gladstone. The first was the eventual release of the energy generated in the accumulated critical mass of new religious impressions. The convulsive intellectual spasm occurred not in 'that most gorgeous temple', St. Peter's, in 'that city crowned with a thousand rays of glory, each bright enough to ennoble a nation's history',[2] but in the much less appropriate setting of Naples, where Gladstone moreover had cause to have grave suspicions about the genuineness of the liquefaction of the blood of St. Januarius, which miracle he had shortly before attended. On Sunday, May 13, 'something I know not what set me on examining the Occasional Offices of the Church in the Prayer Book'. Gladstone was struck particularly by the significance of the Order of Baptism. This linked back with his earlier introduction by Anne to the theological problems connected with baptismal regeneration. Now, on 'coming into Catholic countries, and to some few books', Gladstone felt he owed 'glimpses' of the 'nature of the Church, and of our duties as members of it, which involve an idea very much higher & more important' of it than he had previously conceived.[3] This sudden revelation of the Church as a

1 *Ib.*, 500.   2 *Ib.*, 480.   3 *Ib.*, 495.

teacher, through its doctors and traditions and sacraments, of divine truth made on Gladstone that day a mark never to be effaced. It presented to him Christianity under an aspect in which he had not yet known it: 'its ministry of symbols, its channels of grace, its unending line of teachers joining from the Head: a sublime construction, based throughout upon historic fact, uplifting the idea of the community . . . and of the access which it enjoys . . . to the presence of the most High.'[1]

While absorbing this inward revelation, Gladstone, nearly two months later, in Milan, was recalled to awareness of the demands of the secular world by a letter 'of extraordinary import' from his Oxford friend Lord Lincoln offering him the influence of his father the Duke of Newcastle at Newark in the impending general election. Lincoln had recommended Gladstone to his father on the strength largely of Gladstone's Union speech against Reform. What Gladstone had prospectively defined to his father as his readiness to undertake the profession of the law, 'with a view substantially to studying the constitutional branch of it, and a subsequent experiment, as time and circumstances might offer, on what is termed public life', now took on a dramatic and urgent immediacy. This 'stunning and over-powering proposal', 'an event in the life of any person at my years', left Gladstone for the whole of the rest of the evening of July 6 'in a flutter of confusion'. As often in such flutters, Gladstone pulled himself together by an exercise in excessively high-minded sanctimoniousness. 'Had it devolved on me at once to send a reply to this proposal, how great & how insuperable my difficulties would have been. Happily, God, who established the order of nature, & who seals parental wisdom & experience by parental authority, did by this order relieve me. To learn His will, the first human means is to refer to my parents – and this was done.'[2] There were inhibiting considerations: did the Duke, a bitter critic of Canning, realise the devotion of the Gladstones to that statesman? And what were the implications of the Duke's offer of financial subsidy? The highly expectable response of parental approval having been received, the two brothers resolved to set off immediately for England, which they reached on July 28.

[8]

The Duke of Newcastle's interest and influence in the borough of Newark meant a high probability of success, but not certainty, especially in view of the unforeseeable consequences of the Reform Act. Newark, no longer merely a pocket borough, was now a constituency of 1,600 voters,

1 GP, 44791, 1.   2 D, i, 543–46.

keeping its two members, instead of the pre-1832 constituency of a little over 500 scot and lot voters; and there was unquestionably a new and unpredictable popular spirit abroad in the political atmosphere. Gladstone would have to work for his prize. But this was a situation by now very familiar to him, and his capturing of Newark was an experience in its boisterous way not entirely unlike his winning of Eton and Oxford. He had his Address ready for the electors by August 4, 'induced by the most flattering assurances of powerful support', to venture to offer himself to their suffrages as a professor of 'warm and conscientious attachment to our Government as a limited monarchy', to the union of Church and State, and an unswerving determination to 'admit facts, and abstract principles only in subservience to facts', as the 'true foundations of commercial, agricultural, and financial legislation'. He cited 'the defence in particular of our Irish establishment', the 'amelioration of the condition of the labouring classes', 'measures for the moral advancement and further legal protection of our fellow-subjects in slavery' and the 'observance of a dignified and impartial foreign policy' as objects of his solicitude.[1] To an Old Etonian friend who lived near Newark Gladstone defined his politics at this time as of a cast 'rather melancholy and severe, than violent or ultra in the ordinary sense of these words'.[2] After recuperating at the family's new temporary base (this time Torquay), Gladstone prepared to throw himself into combat with zest. Rudely startled out of his assumption that he was going to enjoy a tranquil and pious Torquay Sunday on September 23, Gladstone found his father bursting into his room at 7.45 a.m. with the news that the canvass had begun and his presence on the spot was imperative. Gladstone break-fasted hurriedly and, with 'infinite disgust', spent the day travelling (though at Exeter he availed himself of the chance to slip into the cathedral and hear some prayers, and handed out tracts in the coach). At Newark he found Robertson and John Neilson and 'affairs in prosperous condition'.

At Torquay he had not in any case been idle: he wrote to solicit the interest and influence of Lord Middleton, a South Nottinghamshire magnate, only to get from Wollaton House a dusty answer ('I beg leave to say, it is not at present my intention to use any influence I may be supposed to have in Newark, in favour of any one & as an entire stranger to me, I must be allow'd to express my surprise that you should thus early have applied to me').[3] From Lord Winchilsea, however, Gladstone got regrets that Winchilsea's tenants in Newark had not offered that 'warm & unanimous support' their landlord had expected; and also assurances that his agent would see to it that any 'erroneous notions' entertained among the tenants and dependants would be duly 'corrected' and that

1 GP, 44722, 4.   2 G to Handley, August 9, 1832. GP, 44352, 243.
3 Middleton to G, September 15, 1832. GP, 44352, 267.

everything would be done to help secure his election.[1] The Duke of Newcastle's agent performed the same crucial office. Rather innocent in such matters (despite his father's and brother's experiences in being unseated for bribery), Gladstone was later taken aback to find out how much money had been disbursed on his behalf. Gladstone himself paid his respects to the Duke, in some trepidation, in a visit to Clumber Park on October 9, where he was received 'most kindly' and dined *en famille*, with something of a sense of drowning in a sea of Clinton children, four young lords and four young ladies being present. On the 10th and 11th he had long conversations with the Duke mainly concerning expectation of events 'so awful that the tongue fears to utter them' in preparation for the 'grand struggle between good and evil', a principal feature of which would be the downfall of the papacy. Patron and protégé were well pleased with one another, the protégé especially being reassured as to the 'virtues of an ancient aristocracy, than which the world never saw one more powerful or more pure'.[2] The patron was content with the bargain to pay half the expenses of the election contracted with John Gladstone.

The only sour note in the campaign was the slavery issue, which the supporters of the Whig candidate Serjeant Wilde (later Lord Chancellor Truro) naturally exploited. Gladstone countered with accounts of his father's enlightened estate policy and of how essential it was to prepare the way for eventual emancipation by gradual stages, as well as the equally conventional line about factory children in Britain. Slavery, he informed the electors of Newark, was a 'momentous question' upon which he would not allow 'irresponsible' parties to interpose between himself and them. As regards 'abstract lawfulness', this was recognised in Scripture, and hence was not 'absolutely and necessarily *sinful*'. The 'moral bondage' was the thing to concentrate on first, instead of risking exchanging 'weightier evils' for immediate emancipation. 'Let *fitness* be made the condition of emancipation.'[3] To himself he confided: 'In my soul and conscience, as I shall answer on the day of judgment, I do not feel that I have any bias in that question; nor is this at all laying claim to superior impartiality: for I think I could account for it intelligibly enough to any moderate person.'[4] Gladstone added to his advocacy of '*adequate remuneration*' to labour and 'correction' of the poor laws a proposal for 'allotment of cottage gardens' which startled the Duke and had curious echoes fifty years later.

Parliament was formally dissolved on December 3. Nominations at Newark were made on the 11th. Gladstone spent between six and seven hours on the hustings, revelling in the charged atmosphere much as he had done in the Oxford elections in the previous year, revelling also in the opportunities to exert his powers of platform rhetoric which Oxford had

1 Winchilsea to G, October 8, 1832. *Ib.*, 281–2.   2 Magnus, 15–16.
3 GP, 44722, 63.   4 D, i, 565.

first revealed. 'A stormy scene. The yells rung around my head – but wrought little effect . . . I was most powerfully escorted to the Clinton Arms.' The Duke's machine was working effectively; and, though the Newcastle influence was 'somewhat diminished' by the Reform Act, the Duke was able in the next decades 'usually' to return one member.[1] From a window of the Town Hall Gladstone harangued a 'hustling' mob in the market place. He reported to his father that one 'Blue' flung a stone 'which came within twelve inches of my head'.[2] The poll was declared on the 14th. Gladstone led with 887, his Tory colleague Handley became the second member with 798, and the Whig Wilde was defeated with 726. 'Near Fifty Reds dined together. The utmost enthusiasm was displayed . . . Too much wine was drunk by some of the party.' Gladstone, M.P. for Newark a few days short of his twenty-third birthday, noted that neither he nor Handley was received with much cordiality by the mass of (mainly non-voting) Newark citizenry. Newark was a triumph for the anti-Reform cause; but it soon became clear that the results were 'generally melancholy enough' for what was shortly to become known as the 'Conservative' party: Gladstone would enter the House when the session opened in January as one of a party of 172 opposing 486 supporters of Lord Grey's ministry.

Resiliently, Gladstone pressed on with defiant articles for the *Liverpool Standard*. He indulged also in doom-laden pathos. Christmas day evoked reflections that 'before many years, we may not be permitted to celebrate this festival as now'. Doom stalked also on the continent ('Antwerp gone! God help the poor oppressed Hollanders'). But there was still time for literature ('Paradise Regained, two books. Very objectionable on religious grounds?'). He had the pleasure of franking his first letter as an M.P. on December 19. But on his twenty-third birthday he thought fit to warn himself of the dangers now confronting him. 'I have now familiarised myself with maxims sanctioning and encouraging a degree of intercourse with society perhaps attended with much risk, nay perhaps only rendered acceptable to my understanding by cowardice and a carnal heart.' Yet still did Gladstone think that 'mirth may be encouraged, provided it have a purpose higher than itself'; and nor did he think himself 'warranted in withdrawing from the practices of my fellow men except when they really *involve* the encouragement of sin': in which class Gladstone certainly did rank 'races and theatres'. He hoped 'to lead a severe life'. On New Year's Eve Gladstone noted the end of an 'eventful year' for the poor country at large as well as for his own prospects; and prayed for the mercy of God to provide in His wisdom against national sins and failings; especially that the 'stormy elements of agitation which are now aroused' might be 'overruled by Him to the glory of His name'.[3]

1 C. R. Dod, *Electoral Facts from 1832 to 1853 Impartially Stated* (1972 ed.), 222.
2 Bassett, 27.   3 D, i, 595–96.

CHAPTER II

FIRST VOCATION, 1833–1841:
'I HAVE BEEN LONG AGO
PLEDGED TO THE SERVICE OF THE CHURCH'

[1]

The family kept its Christmas at Leamington, and Gladstone moved to London on January 24 to take his seat in the Commons. He entered Lincoln's Inn and ate his first dinner there on the 25th. He looked for rooms, eventually moving into Albany, chamber L2, the lease of which his father had already purchased. John Gladstone set up his son in his new career by transferring to his account £10,000 of capital stock in Messrs. Gladstone and Co. of Liverpool (to which he added £300 for furnishing the Albany apartment).[1] He took his seat in the Commons on the 29th, 'provided', as he recalled, 'unquestionably with a large stock of schoolboy bashfulness' in the presence of the Keate-like Speaker, Manners-Sutton. He observed that the 'corporeal conveniences' of the House were 'marvellously small'.[2] Hayter's portrait of the first reformed House of Commons depicted the darkly handsome young Gladstone crowded next to his brother Tom on the opposition back benches. (He would, in fact, suffer the inconveniences of the former chapel of St. Stephen only for two sessions: fire destroyed it on the night of October 16, 1834. Gladstone, away at Fasque, missed the furious spectacle.[3]) On March 6, 1833 he was elected to the Carlton Club, recently established as the Tory response to the Reform Club.

As a Member of Parliament, Gladstone early distinguished himself for exhibiting what a leading article in the *Globe* in December 1834 described as 'the most zealous adherence to the most antiquated and obnoxious principles of his party'.[4] A few years later Macaulay would dub him indelibly with the famous delineation as 'the rising hope' of those 'stern and unbending Tories' who chafed mutinously under Peel's moderate leadership. The occasion of Macaulay's phrase was his brilliantly hostile review of Gladstone's book *The State in its Relations with the Church*,

1 GGP, Secret Account Book, 93/13, 1.   2 Morley, i, 100–101.
3 Until the opening of Barry's and Pugin's new Commons in 1852 the Commons used the old Lords' chamber, the peers moving into the royal robing room until their new chamber was ready in 1847.
4 D, ii, 144, n.7.

published in 1838. In that book Gladstone endeavoured to lay firm
foundations of principle for establishing the manner and extent to which
the State should be obliged by its Christian conscience to enter into
alliance with the Church. Thereby, also, he hoped to set out a programme
of political action for himself, combining the vocation of service to the
Church he persuaded himself he had originally yearned for with the
vocation of service to the State into which his father allegedly had
diverted him. He would 'witness for the principles of the Church in the
Councils of the State'.[1]

In formulating the ideals and principles of this dual vocation Gladstone
depended heavily on the help and influence of two friendships which
ripened from 1835 onwards. Henry Manning, Rector of Woolavington in
Sussex and in 1840 Archdeacon of Chichester, was at this time moving
from an Evangelical to a Catholic stance much like Gladstone himself.
James Hope (later Hope-Scott on inheriting Sir Walter Scott's Abbotsford
estate) was much the most important single influence on the Catholic
development of Gladstone's religious sensibility in the later 1830s. A
barrister and fellow of Merton College, Oxford, Hope dedicated his life
and career to a lay apostolate, considering himself to have taken the 'first
tonsure'.[2] He and Gladstone were acquaintances rather than friends at
Eton and Oxford. Their renewed acquaintance and growing intimacy
developed from 1836. Gladstone would always remember Hope as 'the
most winning person of his day'.[3]

'Politics,' Gladstone told Manning in 1835, 'would become an utter
blank to me, were I to make the discovery that we were mistaken in
maintaining their association with religion.' And this, he insisted, despite
the 'present miserably relaxed condition' of the Church. But why should
this dismal situation be permitted to continue to prevail? To Gladstone it
had long been apparent that 'the Church of England must have her
legislative constitution revived'. He hoped, trusted and prayed 'that *then*
without having forfeited any of the incalculable advantage of an
Establishment, we may have got rid of the burden and shame of its
present state, oppression on the side of the government attended with
constant reviling on the score of the debility which that same oppression
has produced, and practical shortcoming in the performance of its
functions, and in the attainment of its high and noble ends'.[4] 'Restrict the
sphere of politics to earth,' he had observed in 1832, 'and it becomes a
secondary science.'[5]

In those days Gladstone was quite sanguine about the prospects of
success in this endeavour. In later years, wondering at the powers of self

1 G to Manning, March 15, 1838. GP, 44247, 41.   2 GP, 44819, 48.
3 R. Ornsby, *Memoirs of James Robert Hope-Scott* (1884), ii, 275.
4 G to Manning, April 5, 1835. GP, 44247, 3.   5 Butler, 42.

delusion, he tended to foreshorten and contract this period of faith. But in the 1830s, despite the grim face of things, with reforming majorities in the House of Commons, Erastian Whiggery and infidel Utilitarianism in the ascendant, a distemper of grievance and impatience with established institutions abroad generally in the land, Gladstone could still count on some formidable countervailing and consoling considerations. First, there was his faith in the ultimately benevolent purposes of divine providence, and of his own humble appointed role within that providential order. 'Unless I altogether delude myself,' he confided to his journal on his twenty-fourth birthday, 'I still continue to read in the habitual occurrences of my life the sure marks of Providential care and love: I see all things great and small fitted into a discipline.'[1] Secondly, Gladstone's confidence in the validity and efficacy of his political opinions was unshaken by his party's crushing defeat in the elections. This is not uncommonly the case with young, vigorous candidates whose electoral success runs against the general political tide. His position in the House was much more conspicuous as part of an attenuated and embattled minority than it would have been obscured in the mass of a triumphant majority. He had an early opportunity of demonstrating his powers in the 1833 session. Already he had made a very brief intervention concerning a petition against the election at Liverpool, which allowed Gladstone the pleasure of informing the House that 'the Reform Bill had not produced at Liverpool the effect which had been anticipated from it'.[2] The great issue of Negro slavery, which had been such a sore point for him on the Newark hustings, was now before the House. Gladstone ruminated on the 'solemn and awful question', of which it was 'the lightest part' that it involved the 'properties of many thousand Englishmen: for it also involves the heavy responsibilities of an entire nation and the temporal and eternal interests of an extensive and an oppressed population'.[3] Stanley's speech opening the debate on May 14 dwelt on cruel punishments inflicted in Demerara. Howick made specific charges against John Gladstone's management of the Vreeden's Hoop estate, alleging especially a correlation between increased productivity and higher mortality. Tom (misidentified by the confused *Hansard* reporters as 'Mr. William C. Gladstone') refuted the allegations on May 17.

On June 3 Gladstone found at last, after an agony of frustration, an opportunity to intervene in his father's defence and to defend the West India interest generally from what he felt to be excessive and uninformed criticism. His maiden speech of some fifty minutes was received 'very kindly' by a House full of men who regarded family loyalty as being on the level of a cardinal virtue. 'It was a charge,' as Gladstone said in rebuking Howick, 'affecting moral character.' The speech was in his best

1 D, ii, 78.   2 H, xv, 1030.   3 D, ii, 10–11.

Oxford Union vein, indignantly argumentative, rounding off with a peroration pathetically invoking sympathy for the maligned West Indian planters and concluding with a rhetorical flourish of an unction later to become characteristic: 'England rested not her power upon physical force, but upon her principles, her intellect, and virtue.'[1] Macaulay, writing to his sister Hannah at 11.30 that night in the Commons library, was interrupted by his friend Vernon Smith with the report that 'Gladstone had just made a very good speech and Howick is answering him'.[2] Stanley was still sufficiently nettled four days later to tack on to his compliments to Gladstone for 'calmness, a clearness, and a precision, which might operate as an example to older Members', the sardonic observation that he had 'never seen greater ability and ingenuity' than that with which his honourable friend 'insinuated' that millions of money should be given to the colonists.[3] Gladstone relaxed after the ordeal with tea at the Carlton; and two days later he had the gratification of hearing himself, at Harrow, praised 'most kindly' by that eminent Harrovian Peel.[4] An invitation from Peel to dine came before the end of the month, when the Conservative leader did his young follower the favour of asking him to take wine. Gladstone consolidated these early good impressions by delivering on July 8 a short but vigorously bigoted defence of the Church of Ireland against Whig propositions that it had far more wealth and far more bishoprics than it needed.

This kind of thing was good for morale. And, much as Gladstone felt himself under the obligation of viewing the prospects of his temporal existence with the somewhat despairing hope which his theology imposed upon his assessment of his chances of eternal salvation, he nonetheless found occasion for a modest degree of reassurance. It was a comfort, for example, to reflect upon the grounds for defending hereditary aristocracy, and to refute the assertion that it had an 'unavoidable necessity of producing more evil than good'. For was it not evident as a premise that inequality was '*essential* to a good state of society'? And was it not clear that inheritance of title and power had a 'mitigating effect on the inheritance of property', for 'property with birth goes to form a more elevated and disinterested character, than property alone'? Warming to his theme, Gladstone reflected that 'loftiness of sentiment and honour, which is certainly the *besetting virtue* of an aristocracy *per se*, though not amounting to the excellence or usefulness of Christian principle, yet ranks very high among human motives, and is well worthy of being admitted into that compound, to which, (taking the best material which the nature of the case affords) we are to commit to the work of legislation'.

1 H, xviii, 330–37. Reid, 171–2.
2 T. Pinney (ed.), *The Letters of Thomas Babington Macaulay* (1974), ii, 25.
3 H, xviii, 505.   4 D, ii, 33.

Gladstone went on to considerations with a distinct bearing on his own social situation: the 'moderate aristocracy of England' was 'not too closely approximate to the money-making classes – for it would deteriorate in its high bearing'. But neither was there 'any impassable barrier between them'. The transition was 'gradual and gentle'. Wealth was 'an introduction to an advance in society', and in return that society 'fosters the growth of liberal and elevated habits of thought in the possessors of wealth, until they become qualified to wear the permanent insignia of honour without affixing a blot on them or earning exposure and derision for themselves'. Thus for Gladstone an unmitigated bourgeois deference was yet the ground ultimately, perhaps, of honourable aspiration to transition to that exalted sphere of social and political life whose past record enabled him in April 1833 to appeal with confidence to the history of England 'and to the present state of the peerage generally, or at least more so up to the end of 1830', invoking Magna Carta, the resistance of the barons to papal encroachments, the Glorious Revolution, the Act of Succession, and to that aristocratically pragmatic English political tradition which related means to ends in a 'moderate and reasonable form'.[1]

Still, for all his theoretical defences of the aristocratic dispensation in society, Gladstone continued to wrestle with his conscience on the regulation of social intercourse with his fellow men 'by one whose mind is awakened to a strong sense of religion'. Was it possible without 'violating the primary social duties' to withdraw oneself from the society of those who disagree or who 'at best give no distinct evidence of agreeing' on the 'most important of all questions'? Or should one on the other hand aim at unity with them and participate even in their amusements, so far as might be 'without infringing that law of perfect obedience to God and regard for his Glory in all things', which clearly was the only rule of life adequate to the requisitions of Christianity? Gladstone pondered anxiously the examples offered in the life of our Saviour, which seemed to bear in favour of the latter of these principles. Had He not attended a marriage feast, sat with publicans and sinners, and feasted with rich Pharisees? No doubt there were other passages of Holy Writ suggestive of an 'awful caution' on this subject; the approaches of pleasure were insidiously 'covert and oblique'. Gladstone's initial instinct was to withdraw from the allurements of the great world now opening glitteringly upon his sight. But yet: were there not inescapable duties to and in society? He concluded that his principle of action must be to follow the example of his Saviour while continuing a vigilant resistance against all seductive allurements and 'the lust of the eye and the pride of life'.[2]

But, undoubtedly, the mere fact of constant proximity to the great had

1 GP, 44722, 194.   2 *Ib.*, 315.

its insensibly insidious effect. Gladstone did his best to bridle any temptations to pride. After a reception at Peel's in April 1834 he records having done 'a very absurd thing in speaking to him: as usual'.[1] Yet vigilance was very likely to have been relaxed when after a House dinner at the Carlton in July Sir Robert was 'in good spirits and very agreeable'.[2] In that same month Gladstone was introduced to the insidiously charming Lord Melbourne, on the verge of becoming Prime Minister. 'He said most of his family had broken with him on account of his political principles: his brother Henry (I think) had not spoken to him for two years.'[3] Encountering Daniel O'Connell (in an open carriage driving to Coggeshall) was no doubt a rather different kind of occasion, but not thereby lacking interest. The Irish Tribune discoursed vividly on Protestantism, absenteeism among the landlords, and denied allegations that the descendants of ejected Roman Catholics would get their lands back after a repeal of the union.[4] Rather more formidable was the task of coping with H.R.H. the Duke of Cumberland, to whom Gladstone was presented at a reception at Lord Salisbury's. The manner of the Duke's conversation was disconcerting to the young parliamentarian – '"My dear Sir", and thumps on the shoulder after two minutes' acquaintance'; and the matter was equally startling. 'He is fond of conversation, and the common reputation which he bears of including in his conversation many oaths, appears to be but too true.' The Duke, according to his loyal interlocutor, 'made many acute remarks, and was I should say most remarkably unaffected and kind – these are fine social qualities for a prince, though of course not the most important'. The Duke certainly spoke 'broadly and freely' and delivered himself 'much on the disappearance of the Bishops' wigs, which he said had done more harm to the Church than anything else!' Gladstone, however, could forgive much in a man who confided that he had made a point of sending his son to be edified by witnessing George IV's funeral, 'thinking it an excellent advantage for a boy to receive the impressions which such a scene was calculated to convey. And (it appears) he burst into an uncontrollable fit of weeping, as the coffin was placed in the vault and disappeared from his eyes.'[5]

These were years in which Gladstone had time to clear his mind and form his notions of things. He addressed grave discourses to himself on such things as the 'cardinal ideas of human nature', especially the delusion of 'happiness' ('For such is our state. The fabric of God's workmanship is in ruins: but the traces of its beauty and its glory though

1 D, ii, 101.   2 GP, 44819, 5.
3 *Ib.*, 3.   4 *Ib.*
5 GP, 44819, 27. Prince George of Cumberland (1819–78), King of Hanover as George V, 1851–66. Already going blind, the child had few further events of any kind to benefit from as a witness.

dim are still discernible ... they survive amidst the desolation of humanity, like garlands suspended on the gravestones of a cemetery, the pale emblems of life amidst the forcible realities of death.')[1] Of political science as a feasible study he had grave doubts ('For let us remember how subtle and profound a subject is the agency of an individual man: the counterpoise of his principles and passions: the passive, and active, capacities, and the final sovereignty of his will').[2] With *aides mémoires* on Predestination and Baptismal Regeneration he marked his passage out of Evangelicalism into Catholic High Churchmanship. A small treatise on Church Establishment sketched the general lines of his book later in the decade. He thought much on education and the Irish Church. In literature there was much verse, a sharp critique of *Candide*, and some thoughts 'On the sincerity of authors, especially poets'. He kept his French, Italian, and German in tolerable working order. In the summer of 1835 his first affair of the heart provoked a burst of love poetry. More abiding was the beginning in 1834 of his great literary love affair with Dante. 'The intense contemplations of Dante's Paradiso,' he would be writing by 1840, 'are to my mind without exception the loftiest work of human art, or rather of divine truth & feeling under the handling of human art ...'[3] Gladstone's introduction to Dante came in an essay in Arthur Hallam's *Remains* privately published by Hallam's father. His first reading of the *Paradiso* early in 1836 opened crucially to his mind the profound theme of the 'quenching of false or unfulfillable desires by divine charity', which 'makes us long for what is our true vocation to love'.[4] For Gladstone, Dante became the most important 'symbol of a high Catholic faith'; and he particularly stressed that he associated his first meeting with Hope 'with the preparation of mind created by the study of Dante'.[5]

By 1835 Gladstone had developed distinctly in social and political poise. Finishing Tom Paine's *Rights of Man* he could offer a rather blasé comment: 'They do not startle me now.'[6] Peel, on the look-out for promising talent among the new Conservative members, could hardly fail to mark Gladstone. When William IV dismissed his astonished Whig ministers in November 1834 and called Peel back from his vacation in Rome, Gladstone was among those summoned to attend the new Prime Minister-designate. Gladstone received Peel's 'serious call' on December 17 in Edinburgh. After getting his father's advice to 'take anything with work and responsibility',[7] Gladstone saw Peel about eleven on the 20th. He was received 'very kindly', though Gladstone was scrupulous to reflect that it was 'to be expected that under the circumstances his

1 *Ib.*, 44722, 30–32.   2 *Ib.*, 44726, 321.   3 D, iii, 28.
4 O. Chadwick, 'Young Gladstone and Italy', *Journal of Ecclesiastical History*, xxx (1979), 250.
5 *Ib.*, 252.   6 D, ii, 154.   7 *Ib.*, 142.

expressions should be warmer than would otherwise have been the case'. Peel assured him that his letter was one of the first he wrote, and that he did so 'without communication with anyone and simply from his own opinions and feelings towards me'. He offered Gladstone the choice of a junior lordship of the Admiralty or Treasury Boards, though recommending the latter as being in more confidential communication with himself, and as thus likely to afford much general insight into the concerns of government. Gladstone was later gratified by being told by Lord Granville Somerset that Peel intended Gladstone to do some of his work for him. He had in fact been unofficially alerted to the effect that he would get an appointment at the Admiralty: a post which had little intrinsic attraction to so profoundly civilian a temperament as Gladstone's. Possibly Peel did not know his man well enough at this time to be aware of such a circumstance; but in any case he had the graciousness to add that Lord Lincoln would be a colleague at the Treasury, 'for I know he is a friend of yours'. This immediately obliged Gladstone to admonish himself that while people indeed called Lord Lincoln his friend, and while he acted as such, it was well for him to remind himself of the 'difference of rank between us'.[1]

[2]

In the new elections called by Peel in January 1835 asking the country in effect to endorse William IV's call for a halt to further organic reform, Gladstone had the pleasure of being returned for Newark unopposed. He was now a man of note and consideration, far different from the callow tyro two years since. And, though Peel failed to achieve a majority, he reduced decisively the margin of Whig preponderance from something well over 350 to little more than 100. Gladstone prepared for the session fortified both by the éclat of office and the comfort of massively augmented Conservative benches. The new government manifestly had before it a short prospect of life. The elections had shown conclusively that the Court could no longer make a parliamentary majority for its chosen minister. William IV would soon be obliged to reappoint Melbourne. But meanwhile Peel and his administration had a golden chance to enhance their new political credit.

Hardly had Gladstone settled in at the Treasury when on the afternoon of January 25, 1835 Peel summoned him and offered the War and Colonial under-secretaryship. The original appointee had failed to retain his seat in the election; and Lord Sandon declined Peel's consequent appeal. Thus

1 GP, 44819, 7.

two strokes of luck placed Gladstone in a position rarely occupied by a young man just turned twenty-five. Peel put the matter (allowing the case of the Younger Pitt in 1782 as being quite outside conventional categories) with succinct accuracy: 'You know there perhaps never was such an opening for a young man.' Gladstone would be responsible for a great department in the Commons (the Secretary of State was Lord Aberdeen); and a privy councillorship with all its parliamentary privileges and prestige would be regarded as an appropriate embellishment within a measurable time. (Only the brevity of Peel's tenure, it may be assumed, put this distinction off until 1841.) 'His manner,' Gladstone recorded, 'was not only friendly: it was, as from an older man to a young one – unless his cheerful spirits and any self-love deceived me, what may be termed affectionate; and above all when I came away he said what I take it is not the usual salutation of a statesman to his follower – "Well, *God* bless you, wherever you are". *That* word was emphatically sounded, that word of high sacred and sustaining import.'[1] Perhaps Peel was getting to know Gladstone better.

Or perhaps the pious Scot Lord Aberdeen had marked Gladstone out as one of his own; for Peel told Gladstone that, in spite of Aberdeen's never having spoken to Gladstone, it was Aberdeen's 'particular wish' that Gladstone should have the appointment. Gladstone went off immediately to meet his new chief, who had indeed largely figured in Gladstone's mind as the object of Byronic invective and Canningite prejudice. Now he was to commence a special relationship, eventually deeper even than that with Peel, with a man he would soon describe as pre-eminent for his 'statesmanlike mind, calmness of temper, warmth of benevolence, high principle, and capacity for business'.[2]

Such circumstances of conspicuous political success would tend naturally to sustain buoyancy of spirits; which was perhaps why, when meeting in 1835 the gloomy John Wilson Croker for the first time, Gladstone was able to demur somewhat at the Conservative sage's 'darkest prognostications' of future radical and revolutionary triumph. 'I confess my mind recognises a preponderating probability in most of them, and the most material, but while the struggle is making, I feel it my duty to resist that decisive depressing preponderance, which hinders us from girding up the loins.'[3] It is true that, a little later, when Peel's government tottered on its way to defeat in April 1835, Gladstone's anguish at losing office led him to the rather hyperbolical interpretation of Peel as 'not indeed the last hope, for God still reigns', but the 'last, ordinary, available, natural resource against the onset of revolution'.[4] This mood of near-despair was evanescent. Gladstone's intellectual

1 *Ib.*, 9.   2 *Ib.*, 22.
3 *Ib.*, 13.   4 Magnus, 22.

resources were too powerful to permit so grandly facile an assessment of complex times and events to persist.

Gladstone in fact had formulated for himself, from the viewpoint of a strong high Anglican and anti-Liberal, a sophisticated assessment of the situation of the 1830s. He was acutely – perhaps excessively – aware of the underlying intellectual trends inimical to his own beliefs. Probably his most influential contemporary guide in this respect was Coleridge. 'The genius of the present day,' he noted, 'is remarkably averse to the pursuit of moral philosophy.' In part this was to be ascribed to the account of the ethical writers themselves, who dealt 'in a niggardly and unworthy manner with the principles of revealed religion, while composing their own systems, and to a consequent jealousy on the part of pious and excellent men, of a branch of study which had heretofore been and which may again be made to clash with the authority of the Bible, and to vitiate and hamper men's perceptions of religious truth'. But there was also, in Gladstone's analysis, 'another cause of more efficacious and universal operation, to which the neglect, not to say contempt, of ethical studies may be ascribed: it is this: intellect is now moving along a line having a very different direction: it is employed, with unexampled activity and success, in the means of multiplying physical comforts'. At least, Gladstone argued, this would be found to be the final object of its endeavours; and it was for that reason that the science of political economy had been called into existence, with its 'restless activity exercised in discussing the laws of labour, of wages, of capital, of currency'. The science of politics, meanwhile, had 'fallen into almost total desuetude, so far as regards its higher forms . . . as affecting the spiritual and mental characters of individuals'. Hence likewise the 'multiplication of inventions intended to facilitate physical processes: inventions which it would be unreasonable not to admire and accept': but which came attended with many dangers when they came *'alone'*. For they had, Gladstone was convinced, a 'tendency to attract an undue share of our regard'.

All these tendencies led to a general disposition to 'see God the creator of all things diminished'. Likewise was the disposition diminished to live in Christian dependence upon Him and in union with Him; and also, thereby, the faculty of attracting 'that admiration and consequently that assiduous culture, which a man . . . owes rather to the higher faculties of his nature . . . as a creature endowed with the powers of lofty heaven-borne Thought, with the perception of Truth and Beauty, and with the transcendent privileges of a member of the Church, that is, the body, of Jesus Christ'. There, it seemed to Gladstone, were the 'tendencies, the besetting sins of the "mechanical philosophy", as it has been aptly termed, now prevalent'. There had been a 'rapid and disproportionate advance in that lower faculty which has been termed by some the understanding'. The great need was for more systematic study of ethics founded on apprehensions of the purity and simplicity of religion; for a much better balance of the varied and 'reciprocally proportionate' faculties of 'pure reason' and 'imagination', 'now little exercised'.[1]

The Coleridgean flavour of this analysis reflects accurately Gladstone's debt to the most considerable critic of the 'mechanical philosophy' before the years of Carlyle's celebrity. Equally evident is this influence in Gladstone's analysis at this time (about 1835) of the principles of concession and resistance to be offered to the contemporary radical or revolutionary demands.

Partly Gladstone formed his principles from the historical evidence furnished by the cases of Charles I and Louis XVI. But his central concern was to demonstrate that 'the principles of morals, limitable by circumstances, have an application to politics, and have within the bounds of that applicability an authority as true and cogent as that more definite command which they exercise over the actions of an individual'. He argued that 'if the conscience be convinced of the suitableness of monarchical and ecclesiastical institutions to the national character and circumstances permanently considered and thereby to the national happiness, then in such a case, under no pressure whatever of immediate exigency ought the vital and organic principles of the Constitution to be surrendered by the individuals in whose charge they are placed'. Gladstone's thesis, quite tough-mindedly resistant in general tone, was that those who 'preach concession' were 'generally wrong in this: that they do not draw in their own minds a due distinction between matters not of principle which may be conceded, and matters of principle, which may not'. Conscience here as in private life must be the 'guide through slippery places'.[2] Gladstone, moreover, was at pains to clear his mind on the question of the 'true position of will in government', with particular implication for democratic assumptions about the plenary claims of popular opinion. It was, he insisted, 'our duty . . . firmly to grasp by the understanding the truth that human will as will, though it has power has not authority, in the fundamental matters of government'.[3]

When Manning in 1838 remarked to Gladstone that civil government was becoming the 'expression of popular will', Gladstone agreed: 'I see daily that it is too much so, and threatens to become entirely so.' But, 'God be praised that there is much truth in the mockery of some foreigners, who approaching England with her strange medley of institutions, compounded partly of modern and partly of Gothic elements, bear a most trustworthy witness to the fact, that we are as yet very far from the idea and the practice of a merely popular government:

1 GP, 44723, 407.   2 GP, 44725, 184.   3 *Ib.*, 207

however true it be on the other hand that we are on the road to both the practice and the theory'.[1] It was encouraging in this respect to note the steady number of defections from the government's camp. As each major item of legislation passed on into law – the Reform Act itself, the Abolition of Slavery, the Factory Act, the New Poor Law, the Municipal Corporations Act – so another group of ministerial supporters, gaining a particular end, lost a general motive for keeping longer in power a government seemingly at a loss to cope with economic distress and popular unrest, increasingly prone, with Palmerston at the Foreign Office, to be meddlesome and quarrelsome in Europe, and, above all, disclosing disturbing tendencies to appease its Irish Catholic supporters with measures inimical to the Established Church of Ireland. Both Stanley and Graham resigned from the cabinet in 1834 in protest against proposals to appropriate Irish Church revenues for secular purposes. After a brief interval as an independent group (dubbed by O'Connell the 'Derby Dilly') they came across to the Conservative opposition in 1835.

A further part of Gladstone's general analysis of his times in the 1830s was his formulation of his view of the 'principles actuating the two political parties'. Whigs and Liberals were guided by a 'principle of self-government'; the Tories or Conservatives by a 'principle of obedience'. It was for Gladstone a deep and difficult question how a conclusion was to be reached in assigning a just role to both elements, and 'one in which we must perhaps rely mainly upon perceptions and persuasions incapable of analysis and ranking among the ultimate facts of our nature'. The 'details of Revealed truth' seemed to Gladstone to 'bear out the choice' which his mind had made. They indicated that 'we are as children and pupils seeing in a glass darkly, appointed to self-government for the purposes of growth and strength, but not intended to regard it as an end valuable in itself'. And, moreover, while on the other hand self-government was 'necessary', it was '*less* necessary, than the counterpoising principle of obedience'; while the two together formed the 'active and the passive principle from the harmony of our nature'.[2]

In these years Gladstone presents a distinct degree of contrast between what may be termed the 'public image' of reactionary resistance as received by the editorial writer of the *Globe* or by Macaulay, and the composer of private memoranda anxiously arguing with himself about the fundamentals of the relationship between truth and public policy. There were certainly abundant evidences of the former role: Gladstone the defender of the scriptural propriety of slavery; Gladstone the presenter of petitions against admitting Dissenters to Oxford; Gladstone the defender of the intolerance of the Church of England on the grounds that

1 G to Manning, February 18, 1838. GP, 44247, 38.   2 GP, 44726, 21.

its fruits were superior to the intolerance of either the Independents or the Roman Catholics[1]; Gladstone the parliamentarian receiving the congratulatory approbation of the great bogey of the radicals, the Duke of Cumberland; Gladstone the railer against the appointment of his genial erstwhile examiner Hampden to the Regius Chair of Divinity at Oxford as 'nefarious' and an 'act of infatuation'.[2] And even as late as 1840 Gladstone could be acutely perceptive about Peel (in a conversation with the notoriously authoritarian High Church Bishop of Exeter, Henry Phillpotts) on grounds which were implicitly critical of the Conservative leader's propensity to the two heresies defined by Gladstone as excessive respect for the validity of popular will and excessive confidence in the principle of popular self-government. Phillpotts condemned Peel as feeble and Wellington as obstinate; both thereby leading the country into decline. Gladstone responded shrewdly: 'There is a manifest and peculiar adaptation in Peel's mind to the age in which he lives and to its exigencies and to the position he holds as a public man. What the ultimate and general effect of his policy may be is a question too subtle and remote for one strongly to presume upon.'[3]

That Gladstone would himself soon be following Peel's lead along those heretical paths was in this particular case a matter for irony but not, in a more general sense, something absolutely lacking any grounds of preparation or foreshadowing. The cast of mind of a man who depended ultimately on the 'details of Revealed truth' as the foundation of his political principles was not likely to be a conventional or narrowly consistent party-political man. There was, possibly, a certain element rather of unpredictability about the course of a politician whose crucial concern was the moral conscience of the State as a body owing allegiance to its divinely-ordained spiritual counterpart, and who, in the 1830s, had convinced himself that what he called 'Church principle' (that is, the Catholicity in which he was now educating himself) would in time 'pervade the Establishment', and that if the Church fell, it would 'fall with the State and not from it'.[4] This rather apocalyptic 'all or nothing' attitude would increasingly become vulnerable to the accumulating pressure of the exigencies of the age in which Gladstone, as much as Peel, lived. It was indeed Gladstone's fixation on witnessing for the Church in the councils of the State which gave him the detachment requisite for so shrewd an assessment of Peel; but, once deprived by circumstances of any grounds of prospective success in the realisation of his witness for Church principle in public life, would Gladstone have any better defence than Peel against the 'spirit of the age'? He would very likely have to confront the logical alternatives of leaving public life for good or of

1 *Ib.*, 23.   2 *Ib.*, 44247, 7.   3 *Ib.*, 44819, 50.
4 G to Manning, February 18, 1838. GP, 44247, 38.

turning to some different, or at least crucially readjusted, basis of action.

But the culminating crises of that problem were as yet many years distant. Meanwhile, Gladstone offered sufficient testimonies not to a disposition to waver in any serious degree from his carefully formed and considered opinions in politics, but certainly to a capacity for absorbing without fear or favour elements of experience which, in certain contingent circumstances, could have a potential for shifts and adjustments within and even beyond those opinions. Against the influences on him of Coleridge's notions of a spiritually intuited higher reason as the foundation of politics could be set the much more pragmatic (and 'concessionary') conservatism of Alexis de Tocqueville's *La Démocratie en Amérique*, which Gladstone judged in 1835 'a most able book'.[1] Also in 1835 he was occupying his mind with notes about the relationship between free trade and Toryism[2]; to the effect that the Navigation Act of 1652 manifestly owed nothing to Toryism; that the Act of 1667 against the importation of Irish cattle was passed in spite of the Court; and that things such as the Commercial Treaty of 1713, and Mr. Pitt's Commercial Treaty and his Irish Propositions by no means gave any grounds for assuming that, say, Canning's 'liberalism' in this respect was in any degree a deviation from Tory tradition. And it was to his widow, Lady Canning, that Gladstone recorded in 1836 his obligation for new insights into English history: 'from her almost alone have I heard that comprehensive statement of the abuses of the half-century of Tory governments, and indeed of the whole period since 1688.' This insight (veiled from historians for long after Gladstone's time) was that those abuses were 'intimately connected with the greatest political benefits'. The Revolution 'wrought in this country a substitution of Patronage for Prerogative as the chief *mechanical* stay of regal government'. Thus the abuses with which the country had since been vexed 'flowed out of that substitution'. 'Were they therefore to be retained? Certainly not: and accordingly they were in course of diminution since the first accession of Mr. Pitt [to] office: a course of increasing efficacy, for the three years preceding the Reform Bill.' Here was indeed the germ of a general view of politics incorporating an intrinsic principle of reform together with an implied emphasis on overall continuity of action not to be interrupted by the Reform Act. Gladstone's historical formulation harmonised with the more pragmatical doctrine of Peel's 'Tamworth Manifesto' of 1834 accepting the Reform Act as 'final and irrevocable' and pledging a review of grievances without compromising the essential elements of the great institutions of the country. 'But he alone,' Gladstone concluded, 'will truly estimate those abuses, and wisely regulate the *manner* and *time* of their removal, who sedulously bears in mind, that even these were on the whole a

1 D, ii, 204.   2 GP, 44724.

comparative advantage: otherwise, forgetting that they replaced something worse, how likely are we to replace them again with something worse.'[1]

[3]

The first spell of office lasted only until April 1835, but it gave Gladstone time and opportunity to reassure Peel and Aberdeen that they had not miscalculated on him as an investment. He did, it is true, give Aberdeen some evidence, on the question of education policy in the West Indies, of that punctilious stickiness on points of principle which was later to exasperate his chiefs.[2] For his own part, Gladstone had nothing but praise. Peel's reported intention of stopping Sunday dinners and cutting back on Sunday cabinets and refreshing his mind instead with the best divines was 'very delightful'.[3] And he regretted especially dissolving his official connection with the 'equity and gentleness' of the serious and earnestly benevolent Aberdeen.[4] His parliamentary duties, during the few weeks of the session which the government survived, were not heavy. Apart from steering the technicalities of a Passengers Bill, Gladstone's only major contribution to debate was a trenchant defence of the Church of Ireland from the impiously Erastian threats of the Whigs and Radicals and the menacing jealousy of the Irish Catholics. 'The Government, as a government,' Gladstone affirmed, 'was bound to maintain that form of belief which it conceived to contain the largest portion of truth with the smallest admixture of error.'[5] (This was the speech which earned the Duke of Cumberland's rather too hearty approbation.) The fate of the Irish establishment of the Anglican communion was taking on for Gladstone a crucial importance. He had already, in the 1833 session, made himself conspicuous as one of its champions. Ireland, where the Church was exposed in circumstances of manifest peril, struggling to fulfil its mission in a land overwhelmingly given over to Roman error and idolatry, was for Gladstone a grand testing ground. On the parallel question of Irish education policy he was prepared to make tactical concessions, but only to reinforce the grand strategic mission of emancipating the Irish from Rome. His argument was that the government was bound to promote a school system in Ireland not opposed to the principles of the Protestant establishment of the country, even if it did not specifically promote those principles. The 'National' schools he advocated would be Christian and non-Roman Catholic: thus

1 GP, 44819, 21.   2 D, ii, 156–57.
3 GP, 44819, 17, 20.   4 *Ib.*, 44777, 31.   5 H, xxvii, 512.

Gladstone could use the words 'impartial' and 'neutral' about the propagation of 'Scripture or Extracts' under a 'mixed Board' of management.[1] The principles he stood for in witnessing for the cause of true religion in politics were subjected in Ireland to pressures and stresses which tested them to the very extremes of their capacity to resist and survive. 'How few people,' he would later remark, 'care for a *naked* principle.'[2] There was no principle more naked than that of propping up the beleaguered Anglican establishment in Ireland.

It was in the same spirit of unmitigated pursuit of the logic of naked principle that Gladstone in these years made himself conspicuous in asserting the necessity of maintaining the Anglican monopoly of the universities of Oxford and Cambridge. In answer to a move by the Radical Joseph Hume to restore those ancient foundations to the nation at large, Gladstone insisted that the universities were 'national institutions, but only so far as they were connected with the National Church', and that they had an 'important place in the moral constitution of the State' which merely secular universities such as those in Germany did not pretend to occupy.[3] Likewise in the same spirit Gladstone appeared prominently at the head of the Oxford Church pack hunting down the newly appointed Regius Professor of Divinity, Hampden, for his relaxed and liberal doctrines ('his delineations of truth are such as to ordinary minds must prove shadowy and impalpable').[4] Equally trenchant was his rebuttal of Dissenters' grievances about compulsory payment of church rates. After some rather offensive remarks making light of the allegedly tender consciences of the Dissenters, Gladstone confessed:

> The principle of an Established Church, he grieved to say, had not hitherto been acted on; we had not had a due or adequate sense of our obligations; but because that had been the case up to the present period, did it therefore follow that men were to perpetuate that injustice – that we were to commit a crime of so deep a dye as to renounce these obligations, and to refuse to observe the duties to which they bound us. Was there no difference between temporary forgetfulness and entire neglect of them?[5]

This plea both for intellectual acceptance of the inexpressible importance of the sway of religion over State and policy and for sympathetic forebearance to a Church establishment desperately seeking means to renew itself and fulfil its ideal purpose defined for Gladstone the essential terms of the bid he was about to make to open the way towards a glorious new era of Church-State relations.

1 'Irish National Education', GP, 44727, 12.
2 D, ii, 386.   3 H, xxv, 636.
4 GP, 44726, 306.   5 H, xxxvii, 495.

Meanwhile, Gladstone lodged comfortably at Albany, which combined, as Macaulay put it, the advantages of the metropolis with the convenience of an Oxford or Cambridge college set. He cultivated his oratorical powers by declaiming sermons, both to himself and to his servants, whom in any case he led in prayers daily. He had his clubs. The Carlton (then in Pall Mall) was an essential amenity for a Tory M.P. But Gladstone always remained fonder of the United Universities Club in Suffolk Street, to the committee of which he was elected on March 9, 1837. In 1840 he was elected to Grillions, the select parliamentary dining club, which met generally once a week during the session. This 'embarrassing honour', which Gladstone felt quite alien to his temperament,[1] certainly testified to his growing stature as a House of Commons man. For a while he kept his dining terms at Lincoln's Inn, although, like that other notable Lincoln's Inn man, Disraeli, he never proceeded as far as to qualify to practise at the bar.[2]

The family, also, was now more comfortably situated. At last, in 1833, John Gladstone, now a patriarchal seventy, was able to abandon his nomadic existence and install himself and Mrs. Gladstone and Helen at his austerely imposing new country seat at Fasque, made available by the happy chance that Sir Alexander Ramsay bankrupted himself in building it to the designs of (probably) John Paterson of Edinburgh, the most distinguished of the school of Robert Adam. Gladstone paid his first visit there in August after the end of the parliamentary session. The place delighted him, though it never quite displaced the memory of Seaforth in his affections. The abandoned Merseyside house Gladstone could not visit without a twinge. There he felt, as he remarked in August 1834, 'what is the power of a child's imagination: how the local associations of boyhood can neither be eradicated, nor replaced'.[3] Gladstone never found the conventional country pursuits appropriate to the much larger estate at Fasque congenial. He was too mediocre a shot to enjoy the sport. Nor was he scrupulous to observe the minor sporting conventions. He recorded shamelessly having killed two rabbits 'sitting'; later that same season (1834) he was abandoned enough to fire at and wound 'a *fox*'.[4] Gladstone relished the Kincardineshire country itself. Although he missed the furious spectacle of the burning Houses of Parliament, a sublimely violent storm which caused sad devastation among the trees inspired thirteen stanzas of 'A Congratulation to the beeches of Garrol Hill, on their escape from the storm of October 23 and 24, 1834'. John

1 D, iii, 6.
2 *The Records of the Honorable Society of Lincoln's Inn*, iv (1902), 200, record that at a Council on April 15, 1839 'Upon a petition of W. E. Gladstone a Fellow of this Society, praying that his name may be taken off the Books, he having given up his intention of being called to the Bar – Bond cancelled on payment of all arrears.'
3 D, ii, 122.   4 *Ib.*, 128, 132.

Gladstone had also again invested in a London house, 6 Carlton Gardens, which helped to underpin the family's new domiciliary stability. Gladstone was never one to dedicate himself to an ideal of bachelor independence, and it cost him no pangs in February 1837 to abandon Albany and move in to share Carlton Gardens. It would be time enough to set himself up in an independent establishment when he married. The search for a suitable wife was, indeed, one of Gladstone's intensest preoccupations at this time.

Whether at Albany or Carlton Gardens, the House and society could fill as much of his time as Gladstone cared to allot. In the spirit of his resolution in 1833 to fulfil decently his obligations to the 'primary social duties', Gladstone entertained and was entertained on principles of rational enjoyment. He was a reluctant diner-out on lenten Fridays, but otherwise readily favoured friends with the 'cultivated beauty of his baritone'. Possibly his rather curt refusal to subscribe to the cause of aged and infirm actors and actresses as proposed by the Covent Garden committee[1] indicated that the old Evangelical suspicion of the theatre had taken a new lease of life in his mind. It was a joy and a privilege, in any case, to breakfast with old Wilberforce in July 1833 – a few days only, as it happened, before the Saint's death – and hear him leading his family at prayer. Equally a joy and a privilege was it to receive Wordsworth at Albany, being particularly touched when the venerable poet, arriving early and finding Gladstone directing his servants at prayer, insisted on participating. Gladstone, a fervent believer in the moral and Christian message of Wordsworth's poetry, joined issue warmly with others of his guests, including the reverend wit Sydney Smith and the brilliant Irish politician Sheil, who dared to find fault with the future Laureate. 'Glory is gathering round his later years on earth,' thought Gladstone, 'and his later works especially indicate the spiritual replenishment of his noble soul.'[2] Smith he met at Henry Hallam's house in 1835, when the Whig cleric assured him in his droll manner of the great improvement in the standard of the clergy, offering himself as an example of the bad, superseded type. One particular social occasion in 1835 assumed a curious retrospective significance: dining at Lord Chancellor Lyndhurst's on January 17, the young Junior Lord of the Treasury was impressed with the company of the 'flower of the bench'. The only record Gladstone left of his reaction to the rather disreputable Lyndhurst's rather disreputable protégé, the society dandy and novelist about whose recent novel Hallam had earlier enquired, was of the 'singularity' of Disraeli's dress.[3] Disraeli, five years Gladstone's senior (and sharer of Lady Sykes's favours with the Lord Chancellor), still unsuccessful in his efforts to win a seat in the

1 GP, 44722, 167.   2 GP, 44819, 214.
3 A. F. Robbins, *Early Public Life of Gladstone* (1894), 217.

Commons, certainly noted 'young Gladstone', possibly from motives of envy more than anything else. He thought his fellow guests 'rather dull' in any case, judging the swan on the table as the best company there.[1]

Such were Gladstone's routine social engagements. He was to be seen in fashionable salons, such as that of the ancient and eccentric Lady Cork. Peel received him at Drayton in January 1836, where he mingled with a grand house party, had much interesting talk with old Lord Harrowby, observed the Duke of Wellington closely, heard Peel speak edifyingly on religion and the Church, and left after a week with 'regret'. But his mood in these years tended more in the direction of melancholy than of sociability. He was oppressed by cruel evidences of mortality. His first season at Fasque was rendered hauntingly memorable by the news, received on October 6, 1833, of Arthur Hallam's sudden death at Vienna on September 15. Gladstone had rejoiced to renew in London his old Etonian friendship; now, all that Hallam represented to Gladstone in charm, attractiveness, and promise was abruptly cut down. Gladstone remembered Eton, and recalled, as probably a 'forecast of the mournful future'[1], how whenever he entered Hallam's room after Hallam had been closely engaged in work, Gladstone used to find him 'flushed up to the very eyes, in a way quite beyond his usual colour, which was always high'.[2] Alfred Tennyson, Hallam's great friend at Cambridge, called at Carlton Gardens in 1835. Gladstone's rather cool comment on this 'unexpected honour' being due to no other tie than his 'having been in earlier life the friend of his friend' perhaps testified to an 'odd undercurrent of jealousy' between the two young men who both preened themselves as having been Hallam's best friend.[3] They met again, a little later, in 1839, at a breakfast at Samuel Rogers'; but anything in the way of even ostensibly amicable and regular acquaintance was more than two decades away.

A second poignant loss was that of his ailing mother, who died at Fasque on 23 September, 1835. Gladstone consoled himself by composing a long memorandum in the edifying Evangelical manner of her last hours, as she departed 'in seraphic peace, like the gentleness of her own disposition'.[4] His mother had never been for Gladstone much more than a dimly benign figure in the background. Probably he was quite unconscious of the irony of his pious reflection that, 'tender, affectionate, unwearied in love and devotion as she was, she is perhaps nearer us than ever'. Then, in March 1836, came news of the death of another of his closest Oxford friends, Anstice, Professor of Classical Literature at King's, London, which provoked elegiac verses. Thus, as his public reputation burgeoned, Gladstone's private circumstances grew increas-

1 Blake, *Disraeli*, 123.   2 GP, 44790, 84.
3 R. B. Martin, *Tennyson* (1980), 232.   4 GP, 44724, 164–75.

ingly problematical. He was vulnerable to moods of turmoil and distress. He was capable of responding to external stimuli with a kind of morbid intensity indicative of suppressed emotions, and, without doubt, frustrated sexuality. On reading Scott's account of Napoleon's last days and death – Gladstone early became and remained a great connoisseur of death beds – he 'literally felt an internal weakness and my stomach turned, with such a feeling as is excited upon hearing of some sudden and terrible catastrophe – with such a feeling as I should behold the sun removed out of the face of the heaven'.[1] He wrestled with his conscience about the question of suppression: were we not strictly justified, he asked himself in a long and intricate memorandum, 'in saying that the man who feels himself inclined to obey the will of God, and yet unable to find a compensating satisfaction amid the pains and sacrifices of obedience, is of all others the man who ought to examine himself whether the cause be not that he is afraid [of] opening his whole case to the great Physician'?[2] He had recourse to the prophylactic office of accosting prostitutes. He recorded conversing on February 25, 1837 with two women who blamed their 'miserable calling' on the deaths of their husbands. There was another instance in the following July.[3]

It is significant that these two encounters occurred in the interval of two failed quests by Gladstone for a wife. Matthew's judgment that he was surely virgin before his marriage in 1839 seems unquestionable.[4] The first object of his intentions was Caroline Farquhar, sister of one of his Eton friends, whom he met in 1835. As with all Gladstone's matrimonial suits, including his last and successful bid, his instinct, or policy, was hypergamic. The Farquhars, though of professional (medical) origins, had risen through banking to baronetical status; and, had his suit been successful, Gladstone would have had the daughter of a duke as a sister-in-law. Caroline was a beauty, and Gladstone persuaded himself that she conformed to his exacting requirements in the matter of religion. On the former score Gladstone was always quite decisive. He would later characterise himself as one of the most 'convinced and uncompromising assertors of the substantive character of beauty', in opposition to those who taught that it was conventional or that it took rank 'below the dignity of an independent and changeless principle'. Gladstone inclined to the view that 'Beauty is in Metaphysic what Pleasure is in Ethic'.[5] Caroline Farquhar also, presumably, conformed to the prescriptions regarding female excellence which Gladstone in 1834 had laid down in a conversation with Doyle: that, if their goodness was greater than men's, their intellect was less.[6] The combined intellects of Miss Farquhar and her parents were certainly in any event capable of grasping that this rather

1 D, ii, 4.   2 GP, 44726, 30.   3 D, ii, 305.
4 D, iii, xliv.   5 GP, 44791, 68.   6 D, ii, 127.

alarmingly earnest suitor would be hopelessly unsuitable. A tradition in the Farquhar family has it that Miss Farquhar saw Gladstone walking across the park at Polesden Lacey (there having been a hitch in transport arrangements) and remarked decisively: 'Mama, I cannot marry a man who carries his bag like that.'[1] They managed to fend Gladstone off, though he was agonisingly slow to take the hint. The Farquhar quest dragged its unintentionally comical way through the summer of 1835 into the autumn and through the winter, with Gladstone obstinately reluctant to accept failure. It left him bruised and sulky. His brother Tom's engagement to the daughter of a Norfolk gentleman in that summer of 1835, as his own suit foundered humiliatingly, tempted William to express reservations which almost provoked a fraternal confrontation. And poor Robertson specially suffered some by-blows of Gladstone's sense of grievance when he announced his engagement in November 1835 to a Unitarian lady, a Miss Mary Ellen Jones, of Larkhill, Liverpool. William and Helen whipped themselves up into a rictus of sanctimonious objectionableness and had to be robustly called to order by their exasperated father. Gladstone perforce attended the wedding in January 1836, under protest, but departed as soon as decently possible to restore his ruffled composure at Hawarden Castle, the home of an Eton and Oxford friend, Stephen Glynne, near Chester. It is probable that this emotional distemper accounted for the extraordinary feebleness of Gladstone's participation in the debates of the 1836 session, in which he made but two interventions, neither of much moment. Perhaps it was the irritating spectacle of Robertson's matrimonial bliss which provoked William to compose a sonnet on the theme:

I know not whether any other boon
Except the holy treasure of a wife
Could make me love this anxious load of life.[2]

That was in September 1837. By October Gladstone was reassuring himself of the 'peculiar dignity' of marriage in its 'sacred and sacramental character', by which it was distinguished from the 'sacraments peculiarly so called, and from Ordination', in that it was 'not founded upon our fallen state, having been instituted in Paradise and without reference to anything of human corruption or impurity'.[3] His thwarted yearning for matrimony led in January 1838 to a state of emotional tension marked by what Gladstone convinced himself was an angelically borne scriptural visitation. Staying at Tom's parents-in-laws' place at Shotesham Park, Norfolk, Gladstone attended a service in Norwich Cathedral after having received an 'extinguishing letter' from the Farquhars. The music of the organ seemed to Gladstone's bemused state to raise Psalm 128 ('Thy wife

1 MRDF.   2 GP, 44727, 175.   3 *Ib.*, 206.

shall be as a vine') to an unearthly pitch as if borne on angels' wings.[1] He would afterwards cite this as the first of a series of such angelic visitations at moments of 'sharp pressure or trial'.[2]

In a mood of renewed fervour, Gladstone set off on his second matrimonial quest. The objective now was Lady Frances Douglas, eldest daughter of the Earl of Morton, a Scottish grandee. The pattern of the second suit was much like that of the first. A rather precipitate and alarming proposal to startled parents, flustered parental fending off what, from their exalted social station, would be a dubiously advantageous alliance, followed ultimately by a formal request to desist. To their infinite relief, the Mortons contrived to marry Lady Frances off to the heir of Earl Fitzwilliam. Gladstone indulged in introspective reflections about his failures in love and the 'icy coldness' of his heart.[3] At the funeral of a relative in June 1838 Gladstone's self-pity led him to find the cemetery 'beautiful and soothing', tempting him to a 'desire to follow'. He knew he ought to be happy in the world of affairs 'having the means to be useful: yet I live almost perpetually restless and depressed'. More than ever Gladstone was aware of a need for 'active duty', which brought peace; 'what I have then to pray for is to be kept always at it'.[4]

The House of Commons naturally provided much active duty. William IV's death in June 1837 and the accession of his niece, the eighteen-year-old Victoria, meant the dissolution of the House of Commons and new elections. Gladstone was once more unopposed at Newark, where his address to the electors dwelt on the hopes for the Queen of 'tender years and gentle sex', and confidence that with her 'noble nature' she would resolutely maintain 'under God, that settlement of the Monarchy in Church and State, which had hitherto been found, after every allowance for human imperfections, their efficient guarantee'.[5] It was distressing that his father should have been humiliatingly defeated at Dundee (this was to be his last, sad bid); and also that Tom was at the bottom of the poll at Leicester. But the national results in August were gratifying to Peel and his party. They gained nearly fifty seats, leaving Melbourne with but a tenuous and crumbling majority. Gladstone, against his will, had also been nominated for the recently enfranchised borough of Manchester, where he came at the bottom of the poll behind the two successful Liberals. This was irritating, but it was also in its way flattering. There was talk of reserving him a seat in South Lancashire if needed in the next elections. Gladstone attended the great dinner at the Merchant Taylors' in May 1838 when Peel, Stanley and Graham harangued 300 Conservative Members of Parliament, confident that their party was once more on the brink of office, but unaware of how awkward an obstacle the

1 D, ii, 334.   2 D, iv, 617.
3 D, ii, 367.   4 *Ib.*, 375.   5 GP, 44727, 60–68.

young Queen would prove herself. There were, moreover, already premonitory indications of the difficulties Peel was going to have in keeping together a party ranging in spectrum between deep-dyed and resentful Ultras to palely-converted ex-Whigs. Gladstone indeed noted that Sir Robert was not at his best at these after-dinner occasions. Still, he much enjoyed the Queen's coronation at Westminster Abbey in the following month. The service was noble, the sight magnificent, though the chanting was 'greatly wanting'. He went to the Carlton to see the procession, watched fireworks in the evening at Bath House, and ended the memorable day at a reception at the Duke of Wellington's.

As a former Colonial under-secretary, Gladstone conscientiously made it his business to keep abreast of the affairs and problems for which that department was responsible. He was vigilant in defence of the West India planters' interest, especially in connection with the new system of apprenticing former slaves. He was vigilant also (in the opposite direction) to defend the Church Missionary Society's activities in New Zealand, aimed at protecting the interests of the Maori aborigines from the incursions of British settlers. The Cape was a particular cause of concern, with the Afrikaner *Voortrekkers* pushing out beyond the limits of British rule across the Vaal and challenging the Zulus in Natal. It was this question which occasioned in November 1837 Gladstone's first official contact with the Duke of Wellington's 'plain but kind' manner.[1] It was the crisis in the two Canadas, however, which claimed most of Gladstone's parliamentary attention. Popular resentment and rebellion in Upper Canada (Ontario) against the oligarchic 'Family Compact' and similar hostility in Lower Canada (Quebec) to the 'Château clique' embarrassed the Whig government, which tempered the severity of the repression of the disorders by sending out Lord Durham to report on the most effectual basis for future policy. In a major speech on March 8, 1837, Gladstone delivered himself, after some acid comments on Hume's prolixity ('an economist with everything but the public's time'), of impeccable and unyielding Tory sentiments on the theme that all colonies 'were to be regarded as the children of the parent country', that the government's coercive measures deserved support, and that French-speaking Lower Canada should not be allowed to secede from the Empire.[2] To the unhappy affairs of Canada he reverted in the two following sessions, in the same high and resistant temper.

There were possibilities of active duty of a more private kind. M.R.D. Foot remarks on the juxtaposition of projects for religious good works with the crises of Gladstone's failed matrimonial quests. He wrote about wanting to 'have *one* work of private charity' on his hands on the day he admitted defeat in the Farquhar suit; he drew up plans for a new religious

1 GP, 44819, 32. GP, 44355, 266.   2 H, xxxvii, 95–96.

fraternity shortly after his rejection by Lady Frances Douglas.[1] But it was his long-considered and steadily maturing plans for a signal witnessing for the Church in the councils of the State which towards the end of the 1830s provided Gladstone with a vocation that kept steady the keel both of his emotions and his career.

Here the friendships with Manning and Hope were decisive. Gladstone needed like minds to rub against his own. He needed critical but sympathetic guidance. He needed the stimulation of powerful and pious intellects in full cry after 'naked principle', who could yet offer alternative perspectives and suggest different ranges of emphasis to set against his own conclusions. It was Hope who recommended William Palmer's *Treatise on the Church of Christ* (1838), a conservative and 'full-scale attempt at an Anglican systematic theology', which probably influenced Gladstone more profoundly than any other contemporary work of theology.[2] 'I have not had a conversation with you for years,' he wrote to Manning on February 20, 1837; 'do remember my claim if you come to town.'[3] It did Gladstone good in the following months to be forced by the ecclesiastical and spiritual severity of Manning's mind to defend both the policy of the Conservative party and the generally well-intentioned, if imperfect, behaviour of Parliament.

A preliminary question between them was the kind of role a person in Gladstone's situation and circumstances was to sustain. 'Now I fully believe with you,' Gladstone told Manning on March 29, 1837, 'that there is in the public councils of this realm, and especially in the House of Commons where after all the brunt of the social battle is to be borne, a "most blessed calling" open to us, a work which does indeed cry aloud for men to work it, and that is the application of the searching test of Christian Catholic principles to those numerous measures of the time which are in form or substance or both calculated to bear powerfully on religion.' But where to find men 'the joint state of whose minds and hearts' would permit them to discharge that function? And Gladstone feared that, apart from their inevitable fewness, their 'mental composition' was for the most part 'of too fine a texture readily to undergo the rude handling of a popular election, and the subsequent contact with party combinations and with every form of worldly motive'. Such rare beings would require a 'large gift of grace' to have the strength to carry 'through the crowd so precious and so delicate a burden'. Gladstone defended the Conservative party leaders for failing to develop in their speeches what the 'study and cloister' had only within the past few years revealed to the country. For he believed that the form of Christian feeling which was now wanted 'as applicable to statesmanship, involving a mixed and justly proportioned regard for the body and spirit of

1 D, i, xxx.   2 Butler, 57–58.   3 GP, 44247, 11.

institutions', was one 'different from personal piety even where combined with intellect, still more different from any combination of secular motives', and indeed 'only realised by a few persons under the most favourable circumstances, requiring time to spread over and tinge the general sentiments of the nation'. And Gladstone was clear that such an ambition was less likely to prevail as its practitioners were in contact with the excitements and the pressures of detail unavoidably accompanying the political life. There were also problems such as having to address the Commons in terms intelligible within its conventions. Gladstone confessed to Manning his own consciousness of failure in carrying himself 'upwards during a speech to that region of pure principle and at the same time retaining the sympathy of the hearers'.[1]

Might Gladstone, despite this frailty, and given the chance of favourable circumstances, be such a rare being, fortified by a sufficient gift of grace? He assured Manning that there was no danger of his being 'seduced by ambition' into a conventional political career. Indeed, so far as he knew himself, he felt that his 'personal danger' lay 'another way';[2] which Manning probably interpreted correctly as signifying out of politics into some more directly comprehensive mode of substituting for the abandoned vocation to orders. Certainly he hoped that 'other and more competent persons' might appear to fulfil the mission of spreading over and tinging the general sentiments of the nation with the proposition that the State had a conscience capable of distinguishing between truth and error in religion, and that as it realised by means of its conscience that religion was the indispensable foundation of the ethical welfare of society, the State was bound to promote true religion and to discountenance its false, or perverted, manifestations. Hope, for example, so copiously gifted with grace, was eminently the type of too fine a texture to endure the hurly-burly of political life. For his part, Gladstone was always rather guiltily aware of his own relish for the rude transactions of the hustings and the platform. He saw himself as a comparatively coarse-grained public practitioner dependent upon Manning's priestly asceticism and upon Hope's delicately-fibred legal intellect much in the manner in which he used to upbraid himself at Eton for failing to be worthy of Hallam's ideal character.

But where were the other and more competent candidates? The publication in 1837 of the first part of the *Remains* of the late Hurrell Froude, that lamented young luminary of the new High Church 'Tractarian' group in Oxford, filled Gladstone with dismay. If this was a specimen of the best and brightest that the school of Oxford Catholicity guided by Keble, Newman and Pusey could produce, with his radical contempt for every aspect of the Reformation and his rather ludicrously

1 GP, 44247, 13.   2 G to Manning, March 15, 1838. GP, 44247, 41.

épatant attempts to be more popish than the Pope, Gladstone could only express 'repeated regrets' at the 'very singular' materials.[1] Never particularly close to Oxford Tractarianism, Gladstone found little reason to feel more attracted and much to disturb. A little later (15 April 1838) he began reading Newman's *Lectures on Justification* with grim foreboding: 'I tremble.'[2]

On the other hand was Lord Ashley (later 7th Earl of Shaftesbury), a friend Gladstone could admire intensely, and devoted no less than Gladstone to the ideal of 'our national homage to God, which is the meaning of a Church Establishment'. Yet Ashley remained fixed in the narrow Evangelicalism from which Gladstone had emancipated himself; and their respect and affection for one another could never bear the intellectual fruits of Gladstone's intercourse with his ex-Evangelical friends Hope and Manning.[3] Gladstone's efforts in his speech on church rates in 1837 to widen and strengthen the grounds of his convictions as to the efficacy of a polity based on a state religion by appealing to the precedent of ancient Rome shocked Ashley by its comparative or relativistic implications at the expense of the unique revelation of the Christian gospel. Gladstone was here, in fact, beginning to grope his way towards those notions of pagan presaging of Christian revelation which would later, especially in his Homeric studies, constitute a large part of his intellectual concerns.[4] For the present, he stood his ground by insisting that only the 'assignment of a gigantic cause' was adequate to account for the 'principle of vigour and permanence' in the phenomena presented by Roman institutions. Such doctrinal collisions as these gave Gladstone further impulse and motive to clear his mind and set out in public a fully developed vindication of his ideal.

Gladstone had for long contemplated a major literary production to project his ideas on State and Church. In April and May 1838 he attended a series of lectures by Dr. Thomas Chalmers, Professor of Divinity in the University of Edinburgh, on the establishment of religion. Gladstone was disconcerted to hear a future breaker of the Scottish establishment and founder of the Free Church flog the apostolical succession grievously, 'seven Bishops sitting below him', and 'the Duke of Cambridge incessantly bobbing assent'.[5] Chalmer's handling of the theme, with his thesis that it was no part of the duties of the State to be concerned with questions of theological doctrine and that one Protestant establishment would do as well as any other, so dissatisfied Gladstone that he was provoked into action. By May 14 he was setting out his plan to Manning:

1 D, ii, 355–57.   2 *Ib.*, 363.
3 Butler, 53: 'It is curious how unaware Gladstone was of the strength of moderate evangelical opinion in the 1830s.'
4 PMP, ii, 76–79.   5 Lathbury, i, 12.

This is a matter which lies I think equally within the province of ecclesiastics and politicians: and my plan is this: to state the several theories upon the subject of Warburton: of Paley: of Coleridge: of your friend Leslie: of my friend Chalmers: and perhaps some others: then to give a theory of the subject from a politician's point of view: then to consider the history of the connection since the Reformation, and the influence of Protestantism upon it: its present state: and probable destiny with the results.[1]

'Your thoughts,' Gladstone told Manning after reading Manning's response, 'are all intrinsic to the Church, mine are extrinsic to her.' Manning tended to look at the terms and relations between Church and State; Gladstone 'simply at the law of conscience written upon the heart of the state which obliges it to enter into such relations, and at the gradual and growing relaxations of that law'. Chalmers had done Gladstone the 'benefit of goading and reanimating intentions which had flagged and on which I now seriously hope to act'. The principles to be established and defended were 'loaded under our circumstances with every possible disadvantages [sic], and the question is shall we strive for the one along with the dross. I speak,' added Gladstone, ever anxious to avoid misinterpretation, 'not of our Church, but of our Church and State alliance'.[2]

By July Gladstone was writing hard, complaining ruefully: 'My materials very unruly.'[3] He reported to Manning: 'I have been labouring of late to throw into shape my old and tumbled thoughts on *my* department of the subject of Church and State: i.e., not the terms of the relation, and the manner which the State should act through the Church, but its obligation to act through the Church alone.'[4] To Hope he explained how much he wished that something should be published by someone on the subject, 'and that speedily, to begin to draw attention to a subject on which men's minds are so sadly undisciplined. When set in motion the ball will roll, as I anticipate.' Could Hope kindly suggest improvements for the bad arrangement of the materials? 'As regards myself, if I go on, and publish, I shall be quite prepared to find some persons surprised, but this if it should prove so cannot be helped: I have not knowingly exaggerated anything: and when a man expects to be washed overboard he must tie himself firmly with a rope to the mast.'[5]

The devoted Hope agreed to read and criticise the manuscript; the greater part of which Gladstone was able to send off to him on July 20. The intense intellectual effort cost Gladstone dear in troubled eyesight (he had been advised by an oculist as early as November 1837 not to read or

1 GP, 44247, 49.   2 G to Manning, May 17, 1838. *Ib.*, 51.
3 D, ii, 382.   4 G to Manning, July 11, 1838. GP, 44247, 53.
5 G to Hope, July 18, 1838. *Ib.*, 15.

write more than a quarter of an hour without rest). He got the remainder of the draft off on the 23rd; and perhaps the sense of rather exhausted grievance common to authors in such a situation, resentful at not having done themselves full justice, led Gladstone in a conversation that day with Philip Pusey to confess 'for himself only – I thought my own Church and State principles within one stage of becoming hopeless as regards success in this generation'.[1] By the 26th he was thanking Hope for invaluable and painstaking suggestions which amounted to a virtual rewriting of the rather tortured text; and reporting that Lord Mahon had suggested 'Church and State considered in their connection' as a title. But the defect of this, Gladstone yet again insisted, was that he 'did not *much* consider the Church in its connection with the State'; but it gave him the idea of a modification: 'The State viewed in its connection with the Church.'[2] Further clarifications: 'It is not my business to prove the reasonableness of the Anglican doctrine: but only to show that it was not such as works out into influences hostile to the connection between Church and State.'[3] He was consulting John Murray, the publisher, by the beginning of August. After a final conference with Hope, Pusey and T. D. Acland[4] about publication on August 2, Gladstone began forwarding the manuscript to Murray's. He had set the ball rolling. *The State in its Relations with the Church* (for that was the title pitched on in the end at Hope's suggestion) would appear before the end of the year. It would be dedicated to the University of Oxford.

No doubt, as the point of no return approached, Gladstone was oppressed even more by his awareness of the menacing disadvantages under which his cause laboured. He had already, in 1837, emphasised to Manning his sense of 'that hard and formidable question which must not be evaded, how the principle of Catholic Christianity is to be applied in these evil and presumptuous days to the conduct of public affairs'; and among the formidable obstacles menacing the principle of Catholic Christianity particularly instanced by Gladstone at this point was the crucial issue raised by the annual government subvention to the Roman Catholic seminary of St. Patrick's, Maynooth, outside Dublin.[5] Normally this was a routine item in the Committee of Supply, a mere matter of eighteenth-century expediency; but now it was both appropriate and ominous that, almost at the moment of his completion of his manuscript, Gladstone, on July 30, 1838, delivered in the Commons a brief and aggressive statement of his objection to the proposal to renew the grant 'because it contravened and stultified the main principle on which the

1 D, ii, 386. P. Pusey, M.P. for Berkshire, was the elder brother of E. B. Pusey.
2 G to Hope, 26 July 1838. GP, 44247, 31.
3 G to Hope, 31 July 1838. *Ib.*, 31.
4 Christ Church contemporary; M.P. for West Somerset; later 11th baronet.
5 G to Manning, 2 April 1837. GP 44247, 18.

Established Church of England and Ireland was founded'.[1] Earlier in the month he had caused great offence to O'Connell and the Catholic party by his objections to the provision of Catholic chaplains in prisons. Now more deliberately than ever he was giving notice of intention to prosecute his politics strictly in accordance with his intellectual convictions. Here was the nub of a point which would press ever more painfully upon Gladstone until it called eventually into question not only the possibility of his continuing a political career but also the very unity of the Conservative party.

[4]

Everything suggested at this juncture a change of scene. The parliamentary session was nearing its end; Gladstone was *désoeuvré* and exhausted; Hope could be relied upon to attend to the irksome details of seeing *The State in its Relations with the Church* through the press; his inflamed eyes badly needed rest; he was oppressed at remaining longer at the scene of his failed marital quests; and his sister Helen, in a state of physical and emotional distress, was insisting on quitting her closeted domestic role at Fasque and escaping abroad. The spa resort of Bad Ems, in the duchy of Nassau near Koblenz, was fixed upon as the refuge for her and her companion. Gladstone saw them off from London on August 5 and prepared to follow on the 11th to rendezvous at Ems and then continue down to Italy for a recuperative vacation. It was arranged that at Rome he would join forces with the Glynnes, the Flintshire family with whom he was on friendly terms. Sir Stephen Glynne, 9th and (as it happened) last baronet, of Hawarden Castle, near Chester, had been a contemporary of Gladstone's at Eton and Christ Church. A gentle, amiable and unworldly antiquarian, whose life's work consisted in surveying 5,530 English churches, he was now a silent M.P. for Flintshire. The family party consisted of his dowager mother (still rather ailing from a stroke in 1834), his brother Henry (Rector of Hawarden)[2] and his two sisters, Catherine and Mary. Gladstone had already stayed at Hawarden: it was in fact there that he had paused to recruit his spirits and smooth his ruffled feathers in January 1836 after the distressing affair of Robertson's *mésalliance* in Liverpool. It is not clear that Gladstone met Catherine on that occasion. Gladstone recorded a breakfast party on July 23, 1838 at the house of the poetical banker Samuel Rogers, at which he noted the

1 H, xliv, 817.
2 The rectory of Hawarden, the advowson of which was in the gift of the Glynne family, was worth near £3,000, an income greater than that of some bishoprics and of all deaneries. It was one of the great plums of Church preferment.

presence of the 'Miss Glynnes'. Possibly this was the occasion Catherine Glynne remembered later as her first sighting of a young MP who that day finished writing a rather abstruse treatise, 'and having him pointed out to her as a future Prime Minister'.[1]

On August 16 Gladstone arrived at Ems, whither John Neilson had also gone to assist, to find Helen settled contentedly. The Glynne family, on their way to Italy, paused briefly at Ems, giving the elder daughter Catherine an opportunity to observe the tender delicacy of William's attentions to his 'invalid' sister. The Rhine rather disappointed Gladstone: the hills were not high enough in relation to the river's width; and the vineyards were a 'sad delusion'. 'They *sound* everything that is beautiful, and are the most insipid of all possible ingredients in a landscape.' He was, however, charmed with the situation of Koblenz on the confluence of the Rhine and Moselle. And the picturesque setting of great castles frowning feudally over their lesser fellows bore witness, for Gladstone, 'however rude and imperfect, for great truths of humanity'.[2] He was curious to observe the young Czarevitch, Alexander Nicholaevitch,[3] also at Ems that season, on a matrimonial reconnaissance. He corrected the proofs of *State and Church* and returned them to Hope, and by mid-September was able to resume touring. Passing through the Tyrol, accompanied now by Arthur Kinnaird, Liberal M.P. for Perth, Gladstone reached Milan on September 21, after stopping at Monza to see the Iron Crown with which the Emperor Ferdinand of Austria had just been crowned as King of Lombardy-Venetia. In Milan he sought out the celebrated writer Manzoni, eventually tracking him down in his villa outside the city, and discoursed on religion. Concerned as ever to say a good word for the Austrian régime, Gladstone heard how the Milanese had gone to law with the government about some public works, and won the case. 'This shows like more freedom than we give credit for.'[4] By the end of September he was in Florence, delighting in a new sense of power and confidence in his artistic appreciation, and deploring the 'unnecessary profusion of nudity' in Bronzino's 'Descent of the Lord'.

Both in Milan and Florence Gladstone debated with himself as to the propriety of taking so leisurely and self-indulgent a tour, with his lonely father bereft of Helen, and his tender eyes in any case suffering from too much picture-gazing and the strong sunlight of Italy. He resolved that, if it came to the necessity of green spectacles, he would turn homeward. (Green spectacles became in due course necessary; but there was no turning homeward.) His conscience was sore also on the point that he had left Helen 'under the escort of persons not of her own family'.[5] 'A word or

1 *Rendel*, 134.   2 D, ii, 392, 396.
3 Czar Alexander II, 1855. Assassinated 1881.
4 D, ii, 412.   5 *Ib.*, 431.

syllable' would have turned him back. But no letter came, and Gladstone proceeded to Rome, and his rendezvous with the Glynnes.

The party travelled south to Naples on October 11; and Gladstone and Kinnaird set off on the 13th for a tour of Sicily. By now he was captivated by Catherine. This did not make him any less indefatigable as a traveller and sightseer. He liked Palermo: were it furnished with an English church it would make a delightful place of residence. At Sciacca they happened upon the King and Queen of the Two Sicilies making a tour of their domains. 'The throng was dense: but an Englishman always has an advantage in a foreign crowd: particularly if he have been educated at Eton.'[1] This spirit of gusto carried Gladstone serenely through every Sicilian hazard. He bade farewell to his mule on November 1, reflecting on the sadness of parting after a service of nearly 400 miles without being able to like the beast. Taking passage for Naples from Messina, Gladstone was delighted to identify Scylla, 'still conspicuous as when Virgil wrote', and exercised himself enjoyably in speculating about the site of Charybdis. The voyage turned out a nightmare of storms and sea-sickness. Their ship turned back for Messina, and it was not until November 7 that the travellers crossed the straits and journeyed to Naples by road through Calabria. The thousand-mile tour taxed even Gladstone's superb powers of endurance. Back at Naples – 'which, after Sicily and Calabria, seems like my house in London' – he confessed that 'the luxury of a reasonably good bed was for once indescribable'.[2]

No doubt it was refreshing also to be back with the Glynne ladies, who lodged at the same hotel. Gladstone does not record whether they were present at a distressing occasion at the San Carlo theatre, when he saw 'part of the Ballet'. He left abruptly, hoping 'never to see another and can have no doubt about any ballet Establishments. Indeed it has always been that as reputed, which has to my mind, formed the definite reason for avoiding the Opera in London.'[3] Leaving the Glynnes in Naples, Gladstone was back in Rome by early December, looking forward to a good month's stay in that city of solemn delights. But a nasty jolt awaited him at the post office: news that Helen at Ems had become engaged to marry a young Pole, Count Leon Sollohub. The Count's parents disapproved, and were insisting that Miss Gladstone must be converted to Greek Orthodoxy and live in Russia. No wonder Gladstone reeled rather than walked away from the office.

It was consoling that Manning arrived in Rome shortly after. Lord and Lady Lincoln were also there, with many other familiar ornaments of English society. The Glynnes soon appeared too. The arrival of a parcel of copies of his recently published book was an agreeable distraction. He proudly distributed them, including one for Catherine. A letter from

1 *Ib.*, 448.   2 *Ib.*, 502.   3 *Ib.*, 505.

Helen herself about her intended was reassuring. In St. Peter's on Christmas Eve, as the Pope attended Vespers, Gladstone was accosted by his fellow M.P. Macaulay, who conversed entertainingly, as yet unaware that he would be reviewing Gladstone for the *Edinburgh*. 'He received my advances with great empressement indeed,' Macaulay recorded in his Journal. 'We had a good deal of pleasant talk.'[1] Gladstone's appetite for religion and art continued strenuous. On the side of art he frequented the studio of the painter Joseph Severn, to whom Gladstone introduced himself as an admirer of Severn's old friend, Keats. Severn particularly noted Gladstone's hostility to the papal government. He recalled Gladstone on one occasion, riding in the Campagna, flinging his cap into the air on leaving Roman territory and shouting 'Long Live Liberty!'[2] Much of Gladstone's Italophilism was stimulated by anti-popery. On the side of religion an intended conversation of Catholicism of half an hour with the noted Theatine monk Padre Ventura extended itself to two and a half hours, with copious memoranda; and that after a previous conversation of an hour and a half. He introduced Manning to Dr. Wiseman, head of the English Catholic community: an occasion with ironic overtones for the future. The state of his eyes made attendance at as many sermons as possible a duty as well as a pleasure. Wiseman gave him a lesson on the Roman Missal; there were precious evenings with Manning on 'Church matters and that large circle which lies around them'. In thanking Hope for his devotedly self-sacrificing help with his book, Gladstone emphasised the subordination of his political life to the 'polestar' of his existence: 'I have been long ago pledged to the service of the Church.' He was aware that such clearness and symmetry of views as *The State in its Relations with the Church* possessed owed more to Hope than to himself. But he was content that his perplexities should honestly reflect the perplexities of the time. Above all, Gladstone did not for a moment regret having made an attempt to stir and raise so momentous a question, even though he was aware that his belief in the 'visibility of the Church', and the 'doctrine of Catholic consent upon the intepretation of disputed Scripture' would inhibit the book's progress.[3] A long and complimentary article on the book in the *The Times* of December 19 arrived in time to close the year gratifyingly.

But it was the Glynnes who were the focus of Gladstone's more intimate concern: dining with the Glynnes; with the Glynnes at Santa Maria sopra Minerva; discussing plans for the return journey with the Glynnes; dining again with the Glynnes; to the Sistine chapel with the

1 Pinney, *Macaulay*, iii, 276.
2 S. Birkenhead, *Illustrious Friends. The Story of Joseph Severn and of his son Arthur* (1965), 108–09.
3 G to Hope, January 11, 1839. GP, 44214, 60.

Glynnes; to St. John Lateran with the Glynnes; tea with the Glynnes; tea again with the Glynnes; with the Glynnes to the baths of Caracalla; to Severn's studio with the Glynnes. The attraction of '*Gia*' – their nickname for Gladstone – to Catherine was obvious enough, though there was tacit agreement to pretend that nothing was afoot. Catherine was beautiful, vivacious, pious, much the most spirited member of her otherwise rather effete if well-connected family. It was, eventually, on a visit to the Colosseum by moonlight on the night of January 3, 1839 that Gladstone managed, amid a setting unequalled for romantic suggestiveness, to say something to Catherine Glynne. Miss Glynne did not, despite the prompting of eighteen storied centuries, respond positively. Possibly it was not clear to her what Gladstone was getting at; probably she was in two minds as to whether she wanted to know. When Gladstone, having found no subsequent chance for a private word, wrote to her on January 17, two days before his departure, putting his heart and his hand at her disposal, she replied with bland disingenuousness that he had taken her quite by surprise. His tone was formal and all that could be asked in terms of respectful humility, but the syntax, convoluted even by Gladstone's high standards of verbal reticulation and mastery of the art of subordinate clauses, betrayed a profound agitation. It was only with tenacity indeed that Gladstone's meaning as to heart and hand was to be extracted. Catherine told Gladstone that if he required an immediate answer it would have to be in the negative. Her feelings would have to grow warmer before she would accept his proposal. A 'conversation and a walk' about noon on the 18th confirmed Gladstone in his fear that, incorrigibly, once again, he had been precipitate. Yet he sensed also that his declaration had not been so entirely surprising as Catherine had alleged. He was left rueing the worthlessness of his affections but still nursing a hope that all was not lost. After a last tea with the Glynnes he packed and prepared his departure on the morrow, more reluctant than ever to leave the 'mysterious city', 'whither he should repair who wishes to renew for a time the *dream* of life'.[1]

Gladstone travelled back with Henry Glynne, admiring once more the monuments of Paris but shocked more than ever by the sabbatarian laxity of the Parisians. He arrived at London Bridge on the early afternoon of January 30, and hastened to Carlton Gardens, where he found his father 'delightfully well'. He settled down to catching up with the interrupted business of life.

1 D, ii, 570–77.

His immediate concern was the fate of his book. He anticipated, as he told Hope, that *The State in its Relations with the Church* would set in motion a ball which would then roll on of its own impetus in the furthering of the grand design, providentially blessed, by which the men of Oxford Catholicity would complete the work of building the *Ecclesia Anglicana* commenced by the men of Cambridge Protestantism. The root, as he assured Manning, was striking deep and far and wide. Doubtless he would provoke opposition, hostility, even incredulity, because he was challenging the prevailing values and prejudices of the time. The first great need of the Church had been to emancipate itself from the jurisdiction of a debased and corrupted Romanism; for that purpose it needed to place itself under the protection of the State. But the consequences of what was in the sixteenth century an unavoidable circumstance had by the nineteenth century revealed themselves in many respects (though in much lesser degree) to be debasements and corruptions.

The great need now, Gladstone argued as his fundamental premise, was to correct the false situation in which the State stood in relation to the Church by persuading it to reverse the Erastian trend which made the establishment of religion a contrivance for stifling and fettering the spiritual energies of Anglicanism. He asserted that the State had a 'true and a moral personality', and should therefore profess and practise a religion. Having a conscience, the State was both competent and obliged to choose between truth and falsehood in religion. The State's sphere of duty included 'particular obligations to adapt the laws to the principles of the State religion on all points of definite contact between them'. It was likewise under an obligation to provide for the 'maintenance and the perpetuation from age to age, of the chosen system of belief and worship'. It had obligations to 'instruct the young as they grow into consciousness and responsibility'; to supply 'sacred ordinances to the poor, who are so engrossed by physical necessities that they have not the means of providing and supporting them on their own account'; and to supply 'a pervading machinery for soliciting the unwilling and the spiritually dead through the agency of suasion'.[1]

Gladstone argued eloquently for the principle of national established religion as being most evidently in accordance with divine purposes, revealed and unrevealed. The English people had achieved a moral primacy among the civilised nations of the world because it had connected itself with (for all its shortcomings) the best and purest form of Christianity, Catholic and Reformed, tracing its credentials and pre-

1 *The State in its Relations with the Church* (4th ed. 1841), i, 190.

rogatives through the episcopate and the apostolical succession back to the very foundation by Christ of His Church Universal. The Scots, less historically fortunate, had secured for themselves the benefit of establishment of reformed religion but, wickedly and needlessly provoked by the restored Stuart monarchy, had been tragically goaded into casting aside the unspeakable blessing of episcopacy. Gladstone was not without hopes that the unfortunate legacy of 1690 might be gradually superseded by a revival of apostolical principles in the Kirk, thus removing the unfortunate and embarrassing anomaly of two incommunicate establishments under the same Crown. As for the Irish case, Gladstone was as firm as ever that the western branch of the United Church of England and Ireland must be sustained in the full strength of its established privileges to renew the work of rescuing the unregenerate mass of the Irish from the corrupt and debased form of Catholicism ruled by the Pope. The great Irish tragedy was that the penal laws, instead of being exploited consistently and intelligently as an opportunity for mass conversion, had been allowed to become merely a system of defensive protection. The unfortunate fact that the Church of religious truth in Ireland comprised but a small minority of the Irish made it more, not less, imperative for the State to look to its conscientious obligations to uphold its appointed ecclesiastical partner.

In his efforts to provide a convincing theory of national established religion conformable to the circumstances of the nineteenth century, Gladstone was concerned to refute what he held to be the deleterious influence of two of his most prominent and applauded predecessors in the field, Bishop Warburton and Paley. The great Elizabethan Doctor of the Church, Hooker, was of little use in this respect, for he could assume a complete identity of religion and nationality which events in the seventeenth century entirely vitiated. Gladstone had to cope not only with the stubborn persistence of Irish Catholicism and English Dissent but also with the malign consequences of the 'emancipation of philosophy' which 'gave us Lockes and Paleys, instead of Dantes and Lord Bacons'. The eighteenth-century latitudinarianism of Paley and Warburton founded the idea of religious establishment on expediency and numbers: what was biggest was best. Warburton would have advocated the establishment of Roman Catholicism in Ireland if he had dared. 'Here is the fulfilment of the declaration of Burke, that the age of economists, sophisters, and calculators has arrived.' Here was the 'twin sister of that degraded system of ethics or individual morality, the injurious legacy of Locke, which received its full popular development from Paley, and was reduced to forms of greater accuracy by Bentham'. Of contemporaries, Chalmers was so unsatisfactory as to have provoked Gladstone's own effort; and Coleridge alone, 'the man of our own day who has stood pre-eminent for the powers of speculative thought, far above all others of his generation in this country', had 'laboured with might and main to re-establish the natural relation between theology and all other science', and to provide a true notion of the reciprocal ends of Church and State.[1]

Granting his theological assumptions, Gladstone's book (especially its revised and enlarged edition) was effective, even formidable, by no means the naively unworldly anachronism it has usually been depicted. It has faults of style and presentation not uncommon to writers in their twenties, but its great merit was its logic and coherence. It was precisely these qualities which caused offence. Gladstone's logic inescapably raised questions of intolerance, persecution and disqualification. If the State was bound to promote true religion, what must its attitudes to false religions consequently be? Gladstone considered the possible, desirable or expedient forms of action with becoming gravity. His motive, again, was to trim the balance of public attitudes away from what he considered the excessive and injurious prevalence of facile and irresponsible indifference and libertarianism. Gladstone in fact rejected persecution. But he did not reject disqualification. He offered what he hoped could be a working theory of negative intolerance: the State was bound not to offer any forms of encouragement, benefit, or inducement to dissenting forms of religion. 'Inasmuch, therefore, as dissidence, taken in the whole, however the rule may be qualified or even reversed in particular cases, implies a failure in one of the conditions of full national life, it also implies a defect, be it more or be it less, of competency for public office, whose holders act on behalf of the nation. The State, therefore, in certain circumstances, may disqualify.'[2] Gladstone's was a theory of the means by which pressures against religious dissent applied as a matter of deliberate public policy might be restrained by considerations of prudence and warrantability within bounds classifiable as persuasive and dissuasive as distinct from coercive. In terms of such a doctrine, Gladstone's State would, for example, have to consider seriously whether it would be proper to continue the *Regium Donum* to Protestant Dissenting ministers in Ireland; or the annual grant to maintain the Roman Catholic seminary of St. Patrick's, Maynooth.

Gladstone aimed his book against the 'proud, ungodly spirit, which brands the forehead of the age'. He eagerly scanned the public scene for evidences that the modest ball he had set rolling promised to gather weight and momentum. He noted in his diary on February 6: 'I have been anxiously receiving and even seeking testimonies respecting my book.' He needed assurance that he was not talking in a public void. 'I wish,' he told Lord Lyttelton, 'you knew the state of total impotence to which I

1 *Ib.*, 115, 149, 167.   2 *Ib.*, 337.

should be reduced if there were no echo to the accents of my own voice.'[1] There was no lack of confirmation on that point. Bishops and clergy were pleasantly surprised to find their Church taken very seriously indeed in a becomingly solemn manner. Even Dr. Arnold at Rugby, no friend to Oxford Catholicity, welcomed Gladstone's attack on Warburton's 'wretched doctrine' that the State had only to look after 'body and goods'.[2] From his point of view, even if the argument was half erroneous, no doctrine owing so much to Arnold's master Coleridge could fail to do some good.

In reporting to Manning at the beginning of February that the book had just gone to the press for a third printing, Gladstone could set against 'some infamous avowals of non-concurrence' and 'some darkened and half averted brows' and a 'baddish article' in *The Times* of January 21 reversing its previously favourable notices, and a possibly ominous silence from 'our political people', the following items: the Bishop of London's letter was everything he could wish; there were several testimonies in his favour from Prussian sources (where a reformed State Protestant establishment was a great feature of the times); and his 'dear Father', who might well have been 'offended or startled, if any', was really 'just as I could wish'. The author moreover, was unapologetic to those readers who found the book 'stiff work': 'so did I.' On balance Gladstone felt as yet unrepentant and convinced that even a year's delay in publication 'would have been wrong'.[3] *The Times* explained that its earlier praise for Gladstone's boldness, dexterity, completeness, trenchancy and profundity had been accorded in an insufficient awareness of the underlying harmony of Gladstone's argument with 'divers dogmas of the Pusey school'. Viewed in that revealing and sinister light, *The State in its Relations with the Church* stood exposed as replete with 'popish biases' and as 'contaminated' with the 'new-fangled Oxford bigotries' being currently propagated by 'certain stupid and perfidious pamphlets entitled "Tracts for the Times"'. Newman indeed grieved for 'poor Gladstone'. He had not read the book, but its consequences in *The Times* spoke eloquently enough for it. 'Poor fellow!' as he wrote to Frederic Rogers. 'It is so noble a thing.'[4]

Keble, however, did read the book; and his review, in *The British Critic* (edited by Newman), had repercussions on Gladstone's thinking which started him off, by insensible degrees, on a track increasingly removed from the principles of 1838. Ever since his fulmination against the Irish policy of the Whig government in 1833 which had come to be generally marked as inaugurating the Oxford or Tractarian movement for Church renewal, Keble had been outspokenly sceptical about the benefits of

1 Lathbury, i, 50.   2 Reid, 231.
3 G to Manning, February 2, 1839. GP, 44247, 53.   4 Reid, 231.

religious establishment. He found Gladstone's fervent hostility to 'Voluntaryism' disturbing.[1] In his solicitude to define the proper role of the State, Gladstone was in danger of neglecting those autonomous and divinely ordained essences within the Church upon which alone its highest spiritual fulfilment depended.

Keble's review is credited by Lathbury as bringing home to Gladstone the truth that while he began his book as an Evangelical, he ended it, in great measure, as a High Churchman. 'But the moment he read Keble's words he recognised the truth that he was in search of. The process of emancipation had begun . . . ' Keble exposed the spiritual implications of the English Church, which to Gladstone at that time was more significant than Macaulay's exposure of the secular implications of the Irish Church. Gladstone wrote to Hope in November 1839 that Keble had the gift of prophecy, 'so accurately does he interpret many hidden meanings that are in my mind rather than my book'.[2]

This, for Gladstone, was matter for intense concern, but not dismay. His confidence was still undented. Macaulay, his recent acquaintance in Rome, was, he had heard, to review it for the *Edinburgh*. Macaulay indeed reported to his friend Ellis on February 9 that he had bought Gladstone's book. 'Verily the Lord hath delivered him into our hands.' But, recalling their pleasant encounter in Rome, Macaulay would 'put him on the hook tenderly, and as if I had a love for him'. Gladstone himself, Macaulay wrote on the 18th, 'is an excellent fellow: good-natured, honest, industrious, and well-read. For the sake of his high personal character and of some civilities which passed between us at St. Peters . . . I shall be very courteous to him personally'. 'He is both a clever and an amiable man with all his fanaticism.'[3] Gladstone could certainly anticipate from that Whig and Erastian quarter an appropriately unsympathetic response; but since the ratting of *The Times* from the cause he had tasted hostility and was able to assert to Manning that for such he did not give 'a *mezzo bajoccho*'. There was still no reaction from his political leaders. But the Prussian Minister in London, Bunsen, reported that the Crown Prince of Prussia[4] had read it and was talking of a letter. And altogether there were grounds for thinking that the cause was far from hopeless. Manning was too prone to exaggerate fears about the threat of Rome.

> Compare the Church of England with what it should be, and one would despair: compare it with what it has been, and hope would swell into presumption: but the compound of these opposite forces is I do believe in a well-ordered mind, a temper of cheerful though grave

1 G. I. T. Machin, *Politics and the Churches in Great Britain, 1832–1868* (1977), 84–86. Butler, 87–89.
2 Lathbury, i, 17–18, 46.   3 Pinney, *Macaulay*, iii, 275–78.
4 Reigned as Frederick William IV, 1840–1861.

anticipation of those changes which even in embryo are rocking the foundations of society.[1]

Gladstone's grave cheerfulness was grounded partly on his belief that religion was 'gradually occupying the hearts and wills of a greater and still greater number of individuals'. And the point of his publication was that such growth would be 'no sufficient consolation, if it be also true that it is losing its influence upon the national life and public institutions. For it is losing ground which is more permanent, and gaining ground which is less permanent'.[2] And a cause of grave cheerfulness in Gladstone but a source of grave weakness in his book was that he was 'totally, and inexcusably', unaware of the growing strength of Dissent. Even as late as 1851 he was astonished at the evidence of Dissenting expansion as revealed in the Religious Census of that year.[3]

Lay opinion, moreover, was hardening against doctrines which presumed to reverse four centuries of intermittent but ultimately decisive Erastian subordination of the Church. Wordsworth, listening to Henry Crabb Robinson reading the book, agreed with *The Times*'s strictures on Gladstone's 'Anglo-Papistical pretensions'.[4] Sir James Graham professed himself unable to understand what Gladstone was getting at. Much more serious was the reaction at Drayton Manor. Richard Monckton Milnes, a guest at the time Gladstone's somewhat nervously proffered offering appeared, recorded with malicious delight that 'Peel turned over the pages of the book with somewhat scornful curiosity, and, after a hasty survey of its contents, threw the volume on the floor, exclaiming as he did so: "That young man will ruin his fine political career if he persists in writing trash like this".'[5] Gladstone noted despondently that when dining at Peel's on February 9 there was 'not a word' from Peel, Stanley, or Graham 'yet even to acknowledge receipt of my poor book: but no change in manner, certainly none in P's or G's'. But it was bad enough that Peel betrayed a 'peculiar, embarrassed shyness' on next meeting Gladstone; and in June 1839 his leader's evident constraint on passing in the street so unnerved Gladstone that he ran back after Peel to ask what was wrong, whereupon he was told that the publication was regrettable.

Doubtless, Peel's sense of regret had been made all the keener by the appearance in April of Macaulay's review in the *Edinburgh*. For that – in Macaulay's own inimitably philistine formulation – 'spirited, popular, and at the same time gentleman-like, critique'[6] did more than anything else to arrest such momentum as Gladstone's ball had received from the propulsion of his admirers. The issue was, as Macaulay well realised,

1 G to Manning, February 23, 1839. GP, 44728, 61.
2 GP, *ib.*, 39.   3 Butler, 84.   4 Reid, 231.
5 T. W. Reid, *Life of Lord Houghton* (1890), i, 316.
6 Pinney, *Macaulay*, iii, 275–76.

adapted perfectly to his manner. When he read the book he exulted: 'a capital shrove-tide cock to throw at. Almost too good a mark.' The nature of the case allowed Macaulay to indulge to the hilt his *persona* as candid, honest, practical man-of-the-world at grips with mysticism, reaction and priestcraft. He hit both his mark and Peel squarely with his celebrated opening sentence, saluting Gladstone as a 'young man of unblemished character, and of distinguished parliamentary talents, the rising hope of those stern and unbending Tories, who follow, reluctantly and mutin-ously, a leader, whose experience and eloquence are indispensable to them, but whose cautious temper and moderate opinions they abhor'. That these rather gratuitous words would stick to the point of becoming one of the most frequently exchanged coinages of journalistic currency of the times was probably better apprehended by Peel than by Gladstone.

Macaulay's celebrated review bore the character, then and since, of so completely crushing a refutation of Gladstone's argument that the book has survived only by virtue of the *Edinburgh* notice. This is to overestimate the merits of Macaulay and to underestimate those of Gladstone. It was easy for Macaulay to triumph on the stronger side. But, as he confessed to his editor, Napier, 'I wish that I could see my way to a good counter-theory; but I catch only glimpses here and there of what I take to be the truth'.[1] Gladstone had put himself in the exceedingly vulnerable position of offering a comprehensive notion of truth. And Macaulay's essay in demolition was not made the harder by his technique of pushing a principle tentatively proposed by Gladstone to its logical and absurd extreme. Gladstone was quite justified in protesting: 'What political or relative doctrine is there, which does not become an absurdity when pushed to its extremes?'[2] A sense of the validity and relevance of Gladstone's attempt to delineate the grounds of a moral conscience for the State derived from its relationship with religion would revive with the reaction in the twentieth century against the mechanistic secularism of the values too complacently celebrated by Macaulay.[3] *The State in its Relations with the Church* was a work of rather noble pathos, notably lacking in characteristics definable as those of 'worldly wisdom'. Macaulay, an unrivalled purveyor of that commodity, revelled in the opportunities to set against Gladstone's rather stilted, somewhat prig-gish solemnities and earnestly edifying adjurations a brilliantly deployed mass of crassly down-to-earth cases and ostentatiously homely instances.

Macaulay revelled also in his opportunity, as one who himself had passed through the fire of the Evangelical discipline, to catch Gladstone

1 *Ib.*, 277.   2 *State in its Relations with the Church*, i, vii.
3 This is the argument urged by A. R. Vidler, *The Orb and the Cross. A Normative Study in the Relations of Church and State with Reference to Gladstone's Early Writings* (1945).

out on a biblical quotation, and threaten him with a wigging from that 'zealous primate', Laud. Above all, Macaulay revelled in the opportunity to deploy his immensely capacious resources of learning, experience, wit and irony in defence of the principles of Warburton: 'We consider the primary end of government as a purely temporal end, the protection of the persons and property of men.' Gladstone's book he judged 'not a good book', but showing more talent than many good books. It was, indeed, in one respect, 'a very gratifying performance'. It was 'a measure of what a man can do to be left behind in the world'. It was 'the strenuous effort of a very vigorous mind to keep as far in the rear of general progress as possible'.

The real sting of Macaulay's critique, however, came in its tail: he contrived, in pursuing Gladstone's principles with respect to the Churches of England and Scotland, to open the way for a peroration which contrasted all the more effectively the vulnerability of Gladstone's position on the Church of Ireland. His method was to demonstrate that on grounds of utilitarian expediency the religious settlements of England and Scotland conduced to the welfare of their peoples. This happy result was achieved not because of but in spite of those principles most heavily insisted on by Gladstone to sustain the pretensions to singular purity of Anglicanism, the apostolical succession and unity of doctrine. Further-more, the separated Churches of England and Scotland conduced to the unity of the State: 'The nations are one because the Churches are two.' On these principles Macaulay conceived that a statesman, 'who might be far indeed from regarding the Church of England with the reverence which Mr. Gladstone feels for her', might yet firmly oppose all attempts at disestablishment. And with at least equal ease Macaulay's statesman would find reasons for supporting the Church of Scotland. But if there were, in any part of the world, 'a national church regarded as heretical by four fifths of the nation entrusted to its care', a church 'established and maintained by the sword', a church 'producing twice as many riots as conversions, a church which, though possessing great wealth and power, and though long backed by persecuting laws, had, in the course of many generations, been found unable to propagate its doctrines, and barely able to maintain its ground', a church 'so odious that fraud and violence, when used against its clear rights of property, were generally regarded as fair play', a church 'whose ministers were preaching to desolate walls, and with difficulty obtaining their lawful subsistence by the help of bayonets, such a church, on Macaulay's principles, could not be defended. 'We should say that the state which allied itself with such a church postponed the primary end of government to the secondary; and that the consequences had been such as any sagacious observer would have predicted.' Moreover: the 'sounder the doctrines of such a church, the most absurd and noxious the superstition by which those doctrines are opposed', the stronger were the arguments against the policy which had 'deprived a good cause of its natural advantages'.

The effect on Gladstone of more than twenty thousand words of this pungent censure was bracing. On April 10 he ruefully addressed to Macaulay – the article was anonymous, but, like most of Gladstone's own later productions, 'signed in every line' – his sense of honour and appreciation at having been the target of so illustrious an armoury of literary weaponry. Gratified, Macaulay confessed he was 'half afraid when I read myself over in print, that the button, as is too common in controversial fencing, even between friends, had once or twice come off the foil'.[1]

The weight of Macaulay's attack knocked the wind out of Gladstone for the moment but did not convince him that Macaulay had right as well as might on his side. Macaulay represented the forces of the praisers of accomplished facts; he was in the enviable position of being able to assure a public generally eager for such assurance that British society and politics were progressing on the right lines; and he employed Gladstone as a measure by which that public might reckon the extent of its advance and its grounds for self-congratulation and self-confidence. Gladstone's estimation of Macaulay's credentials as a spokesman for what later became known as the 'Whig interpretation of history' can be accurately enough gauged in the drubbing he was to administer to the M.P. for Edinburgh in the Commons in 1840 for Macaulay's support for the arrogant and aggressive policy being pursued by Palmerston in China. And in any case criticism quite different from Macaulay's was likely to have a much more profound impact on Gladstone. Macaulay's attack would make Gladstone all the more conscious of the reality of his remark to Philip Pusey of the near hopelessness of expecting decisive success for his principles with the existing generation. Macaulay confirmed Gladstone's fears that he would have to be more patient as well as more persuasive. Keble's criticism was for Gladstone infinitely more fruitful in terms both of the ends to be aimed at and the means of their attainment.

If one logical alternative presented by Macaulay was unthinkable and unthought of – recantation and joining the ranks of the winning side – the other alternative presented itself all the more insistently. That was to leave politics and continue to work for the Church, perhaps in the manner of Hope, 'in the intermediate region' between clergy and laity. He discussed this possibility in a long conversation with Hope on March 17,

1 Pinney, iii, 283–84. Trevelyan's assertion that Macaulay marked his sense of the worthiness of his antagonist by leaving Gladstone's letter uniquely unburned was inaccurate: Macaulay kept many letters. (G. O. Trevelyan, *Life and Letters of Lord Macaulay* (1909 ed.), 376.)

1840. Was there 'a point, actual though very difficult to be exactly discerned', at which the 'service of the State became lifeless or polluted: at which a man who sought employment for the service of the Church, must institute his search in some other quarter'? From which position would a 'refluent Christianity', in the course of 'expulsion from our institutions and public life' best be served? Hope's advice to Gladstone was 'let every man abide in the calling' he was in. Gladstone, who perhaps wanted to hear something different, thought Hope urged this principle 'even over strongly'.[1]

In the larger view, Gladstone could remain confident in the superior validity of his credentials. He found no reason to doubt Hope's assertion that 'the spirit of Christian Chivalry seems to be awakened whether it will or not'.[2] He was sustained partly by the sheer dynamism of his Church activities. He remarked in February 1839 that he had '*ten* committees on hand', mostly religious, other than his already pressing concerns of family, parliament, and study. This last alone provided Gladstone with occupation enough for the undivided energy of most men. An efficient economy in the expenditure of time was becoming for Gladstone a fine art. At a meeting in Willis's Rooms, St. James's, in May 1839 of the Friends of the National Society for Promoting the Education of the Poor in the Principles of the Established Church, Gladstone found himself together with the recently elected Conservative M.P. for Maidstone, Benjamin Disraeli.[3] To these undertakings he would soon add the absorbing scheme in which along with Hope he was a prime mover to found a college in Scotland both for the training of prospective candidates for the Episcopalian clergy and as an equivalent of an English public school for the sons of the Scottish gentry. More importantly, he was sustained by the intellectual sympathy and response attracted by his book. Bunsen was assiduous in his attentions. He recommended Rothe's *Anfänge der Christlichen Kirche*, which Gladstone reported to Hope as being 'full of research' and of an extraordinary exegetical ability. Rothe argued that 'at a future period of the development of human nature' the Church would be 'swallowed up, and State thoroughly sanctified will be everything'. 'This can give you no idea of him: but if you are in quest of any reading of that sort, he is worth your attention.'[4]

For Gladstone, this kind of ideal of a sanctified state, similar to the Coleridgean ideas which had strongly influenced his thinking, would now in fact begin to fade. The implications of Keble's kind of thinking would correspondingly begin to colour and form Gladstone's outlook. Within a few years he would be denouncing Bunsen as a bane. The ultimate outcome of this shift in intellectual emphasis would leave

1 GP, 44819, 48–49.   2 Hope to G, November 1, 1839. GP, 44214, 72.
3 GP, 44728, 99.   4 G. to Hope, November 6, 1839. GP, 44214, 74.

Gladstone, after tortuous stages of development which astonished both Macaulay and Keble, a pronounced High Churchman in the devoted service of a State formed by the principles and values represented by Macaulay and in amicable consultation with the leaders of moderate Dissent. He would be no less devoted to the service of the Church, but a Church essentially autonomous, linked to the State as a matter of convenience and mutual utility, fulfilling itself not by permeating the State but rather by resisting permeation by the State. Gladstone's version of Coleridge's idea of a 'clerisy', a ruling élite of guardians dedicated as much to the moral as to the political well-being of the nation, would find a secular rather than a 'national religious' expression. It permeated his zeal for reform of the Civil Service. It would be of the essence of his '*étatisme*' of later years. This, however, was an ultimate outcome undreamed of by Gladstone in 1839 and 1840. On the contrary, he was distressed at that time to find that he had caused more offence than had been apparent from Keble's review of his book to 'those friends of the Church who have recently become cool in their desires for the continuance of its connection with the State'. The Oxford Tractarian party, ever suspicious of the Erastian State, was additionally bruised by the universal execration or regret provoked by the indiscreet publication of Froude's *Remains* and by the general hostility with which their *Tracts for the Times* were being received. Gladstone disliked the notion of 'party' in the Church, which he thought incompatible with the 'first principles of Catholicity in religion'; but he asked Hope to reassure those 'eminent and admirable men at Oxford whom it pains us to hear reviled and to whom the Church has so much reason to be grateful' of his profound respect and admiration. He would rather be thought to be wholly with them than to be thought 'indifferent or even lukewarm respecting certain great principles which they have been so splendidly instrumental in bringing out into due prominence'. Still, for all the personal kindnesses 'indeed many and great' he had received from Dr. Pusey, these, he would contend, were not to be 'paid off in compromises of principle'.[1]

His thoughts were focused immediately on an intellectual counter-attack on his critics: to enlarge and revise his *State in its Relations with the Church*, and to publish another book, eventually to be titled *Church Principles considered in their Results*. On the other side, his active dynamism in no wise abated. He could list in September 1840 ten 'plans at present in view', including the two books, the 'Scotch college' and churches built by his father at Liverpool and Fasque. It was at Fasque that autumn that he worked on the remodelling of his book. It was a measure of increased confidence in one sense that he could write to Hope in December that he was 'astonished' at its 'crudeness'.[2] On the other hand, it was with a

1 G to Hope, February 13, 1840. *Ib.*, 84.   2 G to Hope, December 19, 1840. *Ib.*, 127.

somewhat chastened sense of the need to make himself more intellectually accessible and plausible that he planned a new publication. Gladstone was prepared to concede that his urging that the State ought not only to know Christian truth but also to act logically in consequence of that knowledge was, in the circumstances, asking too much. But he was not prepared to admit that truly Christian principles could find an equally satisfactory alternative. Gladstone never repudiated the *a priori* foundations of his 1838 programme. They remained his official credentials as a Churchman in politics. On what other foundation and by what other credentials could he remain in politics? His new publication would not offer an alternative ideal so much as an alternative mode of action. In a defiant preface to his revised 1841 edition of *The State in its Relations with the Church* Gladstone put powerfully the case that: 'In an age which inclines to secularise the State, and ultimately to curtail or overthrow civil liberty by the subtraction of its religious guarantees, to declaim against intolerance becomes a secondary duty, and it is infinitely more important, and . . . more rational, to plead earnestly for those great ethical laws under which we are socially constituted, and which economical speculations and material interests have threatened altogether to subvert.'

[6]

The other great unfinished business awaiting Gladstone back in England in 1839 was the question of Catherine Glynne. The siege had been long, and frustrating. Like William, Catherine had been wounded by earlier disappointments. In 1837 Francis Harcourt had jilted her in favour of Lady Charlotte Jenkinson. Unlike William, she was consequently cautious. From the point of view of the Glynnes and their vast ramifying aristocratic cousinhood a Harcourt match would be proper and desirable. A Gladstone match would be neither. William Gladstone was personable, promising, and available. But his background was raw; and it would be a 'high' match for him at a time when 'New men did not then easily make such matches'.[1] (The Gladstones were not armigerous until the baronetcy in 1846.) The capitulation came eventually on June 8 at Lady Shelley's house near Fulham. 'We walked apart, and with an effort she said that all doubt on my part might end.' Gladstone 'intreated her to try and know me well'. He also confessed to Catherine what was his 'original destination and desire in life', and 'in what sense and manner' he 'remained in connection with politics'. He was relieved to observe that 'all this produced no revulsion in her pure and lofty spirit'. Catherine 'asked

1 *Rendel*, 134.

for the earliest communion, that we might go together to the altar of Christ. Blessed creature!' That rite was celebrated the following day. Gladstone showed Catherine the letter he had written in 1835 to Lady Farquhar unfolding his ardent hopes as to her daughter. Gladstone had made 'an inward compact' with himself to leave Catherine free until she had understood and accepted his earlier passion. This she did; and Gladstone could 'freely and absolutely call her mine'; and kissed her cheek in token of an engagement now publicly proclaimable. Then to St. Paul's. On the Monday the couple were summoned to be blessed by the Archbishop of Canterbury, which Gladstone managed to slot in between conferring at Sir Robert Peel's on education and delivering a speech in the House on Jamaica; on the Tuesday Gladstone presented his father and Helen at the Glynnes' Berkeley Square house; that afternoon he drove out and called on 'a tribe of Catherine's relations'. He must have struck them as a rather odd, stiff young man, with a tendency to bourgeois mannerisms such as addressing his seniors formally as 'sir'. No doubt the Robertsons of Dingwall had so looked upon the gauchely impressive young John Gladstone in somewhat similar if less grand circumstances forty years before. There would be no more vexatious delay. The wedding was fixed for July 25 at Hawarden.

The happy news was conveyed to Manning (a widower since 1837): 'this you know is an excuse for the general *bouleversement* of designs, breach of promises, and contempt for obligations.' Gladstone could assure Manning that his more intimate relations with Catherine day by day more and more convinced him of her 'rare excellence'. 'If Catherine Glynne does not aid me in the fulfilment of God's will concerning me, and does not bring me more in to him in the body of His Son, it will be not less my fault than my misfortune.' Gladstone was 'not equally sanguine' about the benefits to be derived by Catherine from the union; but as against that he was certain that Manning would pray for them both.[1]

Hawarden was *en fête* for the great occasion on July 25. It was to be a double event: Catherine's younger sister Mary was betrothed to George, the 4th Lord Lyttelton. Francis Hastings Doyle was Gladstone's best man; and old John Gladstone beamed about him in a haze of pride in this brilliant new connection for his clan. The rejoicing village was a mass of flowers. The procession was 'in about 12 carriages'. 'Uncle George', the Rev. G. Neville Grenville, Master of Magdalene College, Cambridge, officiated impressively. 'There were many many tears.' The wedding presents glittered with social as well as material refulgence. (The Archbishop of York gave a copy of Milton.) There was one awkward exception to the general gush of delight: Lady Glynne remained alone in 'uneasy depression' at the Castle. The Lytteltons set off for Hagley, the

1 G to Manning, June 14, 1839. GP, 44247, 63.

Gladstones for Norton Priory, Cheshire, the seat of Catherine's cousin Sir Richard Brooke. The wedding night was preceded by readings of two Second Lessons and Scott's *Marmion*. The following day was inaugurated by Bible reading together: 'this daily practice will I trust last as long as our joint lives.' After nearly a fortnight at Norton revelling in 'this glory & poetry of life' Gladstone conducted Catherine and the Lytteltons on an extended tour of the Scottish Highlands, centring on Fasque.

In truth Gladstone's earlier frustrations turned out most fortunately for him. Catherine proved herself indeed a match of 'rare excellence'. She understood sufficient of the serious side of Gladstone's character (that is to say, most of it) to merge with it sympathetically and without strain. In a household at Hawarden consisting of a vaporous mother, a devoted younger sister and two rather dimly recessive brothers she was unaffectedly pious, the confident leader and manager. Catherine was symmetrically adjustable to Gladstone's formidable devotional requirements. In almost every other respect her personality was asymmetrical to Gladstone's in a manner most advantageous to him: she was easy, natural, relaxed, always full of quips, jokes and whimsy. Communication at Hawarden tended to be conducted in 'Glynnese', a code vocabulary combining comical, witty and slangy elements.[1] Catherine delighted in informal company and family society though she shared William's distaste for merely frivolous amusement. Even the rather fraught atmosphere at Fasque, with Helen flouncing in her queen of tragedy role, did not daunt her. Gladstone remarked thankfully on her 'perfect sweetness and naturalness of manner' among his rather dour relatives there.[2]

In one important respect the asymmetry of Catherine and William might have been the occasion of serious difficulty instead (as proved to be the case) of relatively minor irritation. Whereas Gladstone had an obsession for method, order, and punctuality, Catherine was constitutionally vague, grossly untidy and shiftless, incorrigibly unpunctual. She carried about with her an air of inimitably breezy disorder, where no details were ever quite right but somehow the ensemble succeeded splendidly. 'Clothes tumbling about her' was a typical comment on 'Atie Puss' by her niece Lucy Lyttelton.[3] This rule applied to her household management as much as to her dress. She twinkled her way through all problems. Hussey Vivian later diagnosed her as 'really a sensible woman with a silly manner, but all there.'[4] A problem for Gladstone with

1 See *Contributions towards a Glossary of the Glynnese Language* by a Student (George William, Lord Lyttelton), printed privately 1851; reprinted 1904.
2 D, iii, 71.   3 *Diary of Lady Frederick Cavendish*, i, 265.
4 Averil Stuart, *Family Tapestry* (1961), 182. Vivian (1821–94) was Liberal M.P. for Truro, Glamorgan and Swansea; Lord Swansea 1893.

Catherine was that she disliked formal entertaining. This was one reason why his breakfast parties on Thursdays after Easter at ten became such an important feature of his social life. Much of this problem arose out of Catherine's intensely protective commitment and loyalty to her family, especially her sister Mary. This family fixation in turn was reinforced by the circumstance that Lady Glynne's dependence led to the arrangement whereby Catherine continued to keep up a presence at Hawarden, which thus in a manner became Gladstone's country seat. Both Catherine and William could enjoy a kind of complementary status: Catherine remained in effect châtelaine of her stately family house in which her husband remained technically a guest of his brother-in-law; and in view of the marked ineffectualness and presumed unprogenitiveness of the two remaining male Glynnes, Sir Stephen and the Reverend Henry, Gladstone emerged unofficially but decisively as the dominant male inhabitant of Hawarden Castle and the extensive Glynne estates. This suited both of them. It gave Catherine a sense of independence which was an important aid to her in coping with the problem of being married to a formidable man. In turn, it gave Gladstone a delightful country retreat (much more convenient as well as more agreeable than Fasque); and, more important, it gave him the hypergamic assurance he seems to have been seeking. Lady Glynne did not, in any case, remain long, electing to withdraw to her younger daughter's care at Hagley, leaving a vacuum at Hawarden which Catherine and Gladstone inevitably filled.

[7]

What manner of man had Catherine Glynne married? Within nearly five months of his thirtieth birthday, Gladstone preserved (as he long would) the prepossessing form of youth. Testimony agrees as to the general outlines: slightness of the figure; paleness of the complexion; brilliance of the eye. Testimony differs as to the impression of his stature. In Italy in 1838 he was observed as being 'tall, with a pale resolute face, an upright carriage and an expression somewhat severe'.[1] Possibly it was the uprightness of the carriage which gave an effect of height. George Holyoake saw Gladstone speaking in the Commons in 1842: 'seemingly a young-looking man, tall, pallid-faced, with dark hair.'[2] To others he seemed 'a slight man of moderate height';[3] or even 'short of stature and

1 Birkenhead, *Illustrious Friends*, 108–09.
2 G. J. Holyoake, *Bygones Worth Remembering* (1905), i, 289.
3 D. Hudson, *Munby* (1972), 226.

slight'[1] (though this was a description of his old age). In fact Gladstone in his prime stood 5 feet 10¾ inches in slippers (December 26, 1859), or 5 feet 11 inches in shoes and weighed 11 stone 10½ pounds (September 16, 1861). By contemporary standards this put him well above average height for adult males (the Metropolitan Police Act of 1829 stipulated a minimum of 5 feet 7 inches without shoes for recruits).

'Without being strictly handsome'[2] – Gladstone possessed rather too much of his father's nose – there was no doubt as to the general winningness of the effect. Of Gladstone at about this time a journalist wrote: 'His complexion is pale, with a slight tinge of olive, and his dark hair sets off both that and the brilliance of his intellectual eye. He wears his hair close to his head, and ... has no whiskers'.[3] A physician who examined Gladstone at the age of seventy-two declared that he was built in the most perfect proportion he had ever seen of all the parts of the body to each other, 'all without a flaw, like some ancient Greek statue of the ideal man'.[4] Moreover, Gladstone habitually took a valetudinarian's pains to keep himself out of harm and in trim. His preferred exercise was serious walking. He would walk as a matter of course from Chester to Hawarden or from Birmingham to Hagley. It was not until the early 1850s that he took to tree-felling. He rode a good deal in London in the 1850s and 1860s; but walking remained his natural physic, whether in the country or in London (where of course it was usually part of another serious purpose, his 'rescue' work). Certainly Gladstone's physical regimen answered: his energy and his capacity to apply it were alike phenomenal. The essential fact about him, thought his secretary Godley, was the 'extraordinary intensity and vehemence of all his impulses'.[5] Goldwin Smith, who knew him well in connection with Oxford reform, judged his 'physical and mental force' as 'enormous'.[6] This force Gladstone regulated by his capacities as a 'first-rate sleeper' and by his knack of throwing off official responsibilities whenever he needed relief from pressure. This knack could give an effect of carelessness. 'What I fear in Gladstone,' Archbishop Tait once declared, 'is his levity.'[7]

As far as appearance went the eyes provoked most emphatic comment. 'His eye was intensely bright,' recalled Goldwin Smith, 'though in the rest of the face there was nothing specially indicative of genius.'[8] It was possible for a stranger coming upon the 'pale-faced, slim figure' of

1 C. R. L. F[letcher], *Mr. Gladstone at Oxford, 1890* (1908), 36. In Algernon West's *Recollections* (ii, 193), there is a reference to G as being 'remarkably short' as a boy (indeed this was G's own testimony). *Notes and Queries*, 9 series (1900), v, gives various estimates of G as 5 feet 8 inches or 5 feet 10 inches (129, 189–90). G himself related in 1894 that he was then 5 feet 9 inches, but had been 5 feet 11 inches in his prime.
2 Morley, i, 194.   3 Checkland, 344.
4 Magnus, 293.   5 *Kilbracken*, 123.
6 Goldwin Smith, *My Memory of Gladstone* (1904), 2–3.
7 *Ib.*, 18.   8 *Ib.*, 2.

Gladstone 'to think rather poorly of his appearance until he met a glance from his eye, which caused him to pass on "with a sense of having been in that instant examined, commented upon, summed up, and dismissed".'[1] The 'rapt, intense gaze' of 'his brilliant flashing eyes'[2] could indeed be formidable. Holyoake was struck particularly by Gladstone's 'gleaming eyes'; and the doorman of the Treasury door at the Commons assured him: 'Yes, there have been no eyes enter this House like Mr. Gladstone's since the days of Canning.'[3] By old age their colour, described in boyhood as dark, seems to have faded to 'blue-grey'; but while 'in ordinary conversation' they were 'essentially mild', they could still 'light up so much as to be describable as "fierce"'.[4] Unquestionably it was his eyes which contributed most to the 'carbonarist countenance' of a photograph of Gladstone in 1847, from which flashed a 'sense of fires smouldering beneath the iron control of the sitter's will'.[5] Men of the theatre, with whom Gladstone mingled freely in later years, were especially conscious of his 'eagle eye'. Johnston Forbes-Robertson recalled him as 'a lonely figure on the O.P. corner of the stage, pale of face with gleaming eyes'.[6]

As to manners, Gladstone suffered from much the same kind of critical comment made about Peel: there was a *parvenu* quality which grated upon a certain highly bred sensitivity. Caroline Farquhar's reputed opinion of Gladstone's deportment was a case in point. Lady Augusta Bruce, a bedchamber lady to the Queen, would note that he was pleasant enough, but perhaps a shade too 'systematic'; it was Lady Augusta's opinion also that 'Mr Gladstone has no possible understanding of a joke', and that he knew 'nothing of human nature'.[7] This, again, was a partial and prejudiced viewpoint. Certainly Gladstone's severe approach to life prohibited anything in the way of frivolity. Marriage and family life would, however, greatly enlarge his sense of the scope of 'rational amusement'. Among the children of Hawarden and Hagley he would prove himself capable of being 'quite unaffectedly joyous and engaging'. Gladstone's problem lay rather in his dealings with sophisticated ladies and gentlemen 'of the world', in whose company he was often in need of preliminary signals.[8] Emily Eden remarked to Lord Clarendon that there

---

1 *Kilbracken*, 109–10.   2 Hudson, *ib.*, 200.
3 Holyoake, *ib.*, 294.   4 Fletcher, *ib.*, 36.
5 M. R. D. Foot, 'Gladstone and Panizzi', *British Library Journal*, v (1979), 50.
6 J. Forbes-Robertson, *A Player under Three Reigns* (1925), 153.
7 Dean of Windsor and H. Bolitho, *Later Letters of Lady Augusta Stanley, 1864–1876* (1929), 59–60.
8 'Like Bright, he could reduce the Commons to tears; unlike Bright, he could also reduce it to rollicking fits of laughter, and no humourless man could do that. He was enormous *fun* in private company; but felt it wrong as a rule to smile in public. Unlike Victoria, he detested smut; that doesn't mean he was humourless.' (MRDF) Perhaps Margot Asquith best summed up the problem: 'Gladstone, not exactly lacking a sense of humour, but not often in the mood to be amused.' C. J. A. Gere and John Sparrow (eds), *Geoffrey Madan's Notebooks* (1981), 44.

was 'something in the tone of his voice and his way of coming into a room that is not aristocratic'.[1] It was much in the same spirit that an 'old Whig' commented on Gladstone's presentation of the 1860 budget: 'Ah, Oxford on the surface, *but* Liverpool below.'[2] Certainly the accent was of a distinctly Lancashire provenance. Gladstone pronounced 'prefer' as 'prefurr'; 'conform' became almost 'confurrm' – 'but not, you understand, the Scottish "r";' 'gyarden' for 'garden' – '(almost)'; 'propourr-tion'. Occasionally he elided an h: 'erb, 'armony.[3] Gladstone habitually spelt 'controul'. 'Constitootion' was another characteristic pronunciation. Disraeli declared of his accent that 'Gladstone was provincial, but a very fine voice.'[4] Johnston Forbes-Robertson declared it 'the deepest-toned voice I ever heard'. It was the copiousness of the flow of Gladstone's words rather than the accent by which they were pronounced which caused most comment. Russell remarked that Gladstone had 'a wonderful vocabulary'.[5] Readiness with words, or redundancy of words, established itself in Gladstone's boyhood as a commanding characteristic. It was often thought odd in this respect that Gladstone never did more than acclimatise himself tolerantly to the 'Glynnese' vocabulary in which his new domestic life at Hawarden and Hagley expressed itself. One of his secretaries, Godley, considering the merits of Glynnese for humour and forcibility of expression, thought 'his abstention was curious'.[6] 'Sitting tight!' as he wrote to Catherine on January 19, 1844: 'I suppose a Glynnese expression. It is most provoking, for five years I have been trying with all my might to master that language & I have not yet succeeded.' It was generally held that Gladstone's only contribution to its vocabulary was his use of 'addled' to mean 'perplexed', a remnant of his Etonian slang usages. Otherwise Gladstone's role in the Glynnese glossary consisted in having fun poked at his idiosyncracies, such as immense distress at everything spilt on the tablecloth, making a list of his coats when setting out on a journey, his 'pleasingly childish greed' for sugar and sweets, and the marked manner with which he shovelled up dirt brought inside by others and threw it on the fire 'in the very eye of the offender'.[7] Glynnese was not to be 'mastered'. It required

1 Maxwell, *Clarendon*, ii, 224.
2 W. Bagehot (ed. R. H. Hutton), *Biographical Studies* (1881), 86.   3 Fletcher, *ib.*, 39, 61.
4 H.M. and M. Swartz, *Disraeli's Reminiscences* (1975), 93. Sir Herbert Maxwell (M.P. for Wigtonshire, 1880–1906) denied G's provincialism: 'If by the aid of the phonograph it is proposed to store up a sample of standard English pronunciation of the latter half of the nineteenth century a better specimen could not be obtained than from Mr Gladstone.' And three Lancashire ladies were 'decidedly' of the opinion that G did not have a Lancashire accent. However, Professor Walter Skeat heard Gladstone in Cambridge in 1859 and detected 'slight . . . traces' of a northern accent: G said *'strenth'* for *'strength'*; and Skeat, a famous philologist, said to himself 'North.' Finally, a Mr J. A. Picton, a Lancashire and Liverpool man: G's 'tones and mode of utterance are decidedly of Liverpool origin'. *Notes and Queries*, 7 series (1888), vi, 'Does Mr Gladstone speak with a Provincial Accent?', 124-5, 153, 178, 210.
5 *Ib.*, 99.   6 *Kilbracken*, 143.   7 G. Battiscombe, *Mrs Gladstone* (1956) 93.

innate empathy. Gladstone had very little of that. The expository power for which Gladstone came to be celebrated derived at bottom from anxiety. His obsession with method was both consequence and cause of anxiety. Equally in self-incriminating devotional outpourings and in triumphant financial statements Gladstone's concern was a logical completeness, without gaps or leaks. He could lose a night's sleep on recollecting omission in debate of a material point (as on December 17, 1852). With him diffuseness was a means to imperviousness. An attentive critic described one of his speeches as that 'of an able & accustomed speaker, not of a great orator. The oratorical effects of false emphasis & constant repetition of ideas was glaring'.[1] He had a good memory though, as he explained later to Disraeli, 'not for passages. He never could command them.'[2] Gladstone never lost the habit acquired at Eton and Oxford of debating in order to win. His oratory was for that reason particularly recommended as exhibiting the pragmatic utility of great eloquence and selection of words and rhetoric 'with a style not a bit above debate'.[3]

Others found this relentless will to win not so recommendable. Arthur Balfour found Gladstone's speeches and writings alike 'hopelessly *dull*'. The only things Gladstone could do to perfection, Balfour alleged, were to speak about the procedure of the House, 'and to make a speech at a wedding breakfast'.[4] Perhaps such an opinion needs to be a little discounted as coming from an intolerant younger generation which knew not Gladstone in his great days of the 1850s and 1860s. Still, Balfour's explanation that 'Gladstone was naturally deficient in personal emotion' has to be taken into account. Nearly sixty years of successful marriage and happy family life might be considered a sufficient answer to that charge were it not for the two considerations that Gladstone made it clear to Catherine that his first love would always be religion and the Church and that he was to find his most intense human emotional release outside his marriage. As he put it to Manning, Gladstone saw Catherine essentially as an 'aid' in the 'fulfilment of God's will' concerning him. Possibly Catherine saw this as a role she was willing to play. There were important advantages from her point of view. Marriage altered her way of life much less than was normally the case. She remained châtelaine of her own home, Hawarden; her close relationship with her sister remained unbroken, even intensified by a new Hawarden-Hagley family axis.

On the superficial level of 'style' there is no lack of evidences of the kind of deficiency to which Balfour alluded. Gladstone's relationship with his wife was a curious amalgam of confidences and reservations. Having debated with himself whether on the political side Catherine should be

1 Grosskurth, *John Addington Symonds* (1964), 57.   2 Swartz, 6.
3 Morley, i, 193.   4 D. Newsome, *On the Edge of Paradise* (1980), 276.

told everything or nothing, he came to the conclusion that it would be best to tell her everything. As they lived apart quite often – probably more so than most couples even in public life – his correspondence is unusually revealing. His letters to Catherine, gradually becoming more hasty and fragmentary in shape, mix hair-raising political indiscretion with stereotyped formulas of endearment. It became a joke in the family that Gladstone's standard subscription to 'My own Catherine' was 'Ever yours affty W. E. Gladstone'.[1] He rang the changes with 'My beloved Cathie', 'My beloved C', 'My dearest Cathie', 'Dearest Cathie', 'My own dearest', 'My own Cathie', 'My own beloved'; but the furthest he would go in a rare relaxing of the severity of his subscription was 'From your old WEG'. 'Affty' was very much Gladstone's marital keyword. He and Catherine were always a devoted couple. Their relationship worked. A mutual friend observed that marriage had 'improved' Gladstone 'very materially'. His 'manner is not so ascetic as it was; he really seems to enjoy life independent of the consideration that it is a sphere for the exercise of duties'. He was an instance 'of superior men selecting superior women'.[2] Gladstone was ready to acclimatise himself to a much warmer domestic atmosphere than had ever been known among his own family. Catherine in return relished the 'grub' of confidences which Gladstone offered. Apart from occasional slips (indulgently treated) and a tendency to leave vital letters drifting about the house, Catherine proved herself adequately discreet. But two special aspects of Gladstone's devotional life were reserved from Catherine. One was the spiritual-emotional recourse he would come to in 1849 of ritual self-flagellation; the other was his later relationship with Laura Thistlethwayte.[3]

It also seems to be the case that in personal relationships Gladstone could exude something of an aura of not being entirely master of his own time: there was always a higher purpose which had first call. Gladstone soon found himself in 'deadly conflict' with Catherine over chess: 'It is too great an expenditure perhaps of thought & interest.'[4] One of his secretaries, Edward Hamilton, in almost every other respect a fervent admirer, said of Gladstone that it was 'a fact that he is not a considerate man. Consideration for the convenience of others has never been numbered among his best qualities.'[5] By that time, it is true, Gladstone was 'an old man in a hurry'; but a secretary of an earlier vintage made the same point rather guardedly: Gladstone, said Algernon West, was an 'appreciative rather than a considerate master'.[6] Something of the same character was remarked of Gladstone's conversational manner. Arthur

1 'This formula was, though, absolutely normal among the nineteenth-century bourgeoisie.' (MRDF)
2 Battiscombe, 43.　　3 See Matthew's comments, D, v, lxiv-lxv; and below, 534.
4 D, ii, 623.　　5 D.W.R. Bahlman, *The Diary of Sir Edward Hamilton*, (1972), li.
6 West, *Recollections*, i, 346.

Severn, son of the painter Gladstone met in Rome, commented that he was 'always a good listener if he thought people could tell him anything he did not know'.[1] Goldwin Smith testified that 'there was certainly no lack in him of social affability or charm'; but there was always something of a blankness: 'he never was very open to argument.'[2] Later, Stuart Rendel said of his conversation that, however delightful, Gladstone 'did not talk to people; he talked before people. He did not talk for his hearer's sake; he talked for his own.' Gladstone 'could and occasionally did converse. He could give and take, whenever there was something to take', but 'he was always happy with an intelligent listener'. With another man, Rendel concluded, 'I should have said that that single conversation bound us in some measure to some lasting recognition of each other's personality. With Mr. Gladstone I was never under such illusion.'[3] Even the devoted Catherine would in moments of exasperation burst out with some such sharp comment as 'if you weren't such a great man you would be a terrible bore'.[4]

The exasperations between Catherine and William more usually arose out of the temperamental contrasts between the shiftlessness of the one and the obsessive precision of the other. Throughout his life Gladstone lamented: 'Horrid confusion of papers: what a science it requires to keep them in manageable order!'[5] He set about laying the foundations of that science in an elaborate memorandum in 1837, 'Of keeping books and papers', with nine classifications of 'mechanical rules', and the warning motto *'Haud ignara mali'*.[6] In March 1847 he was still complaining that the 'machinery even of my private life is very heavy & cumbrous'.[7] This, after all, was hardly surprising when, for example, Gladstone insisted on checking whether applicants for posts of service in his household were communicant Anglicans; because, if not, Gladstone then imposed upon himself the duty of instructing them; which, as he complained to Catherine, was very time-consuming.[8] In his bachelor days this office had not been too burdensome ('endeavoured to explain the sacrament to my serv. at night'; 'started Best with his French Grammar; tried to explain how such things should stand, there is *one* more important'). After marriage Gladstone found it expedient to make an inventory and arrange a 'little library for the servants: about 60 vols'.[9]

For all its cumbrousness, Gladstone's private life was a triumph of machinery over confusion. In no other manner but the strict application of 'mechanical rules' could so complex and multifarious a range of activities and preoccupations and mass of materials have been kept in

1 Birkenhead, *Illustrious Friends*, 170.
2 Smith, *My Memory of Gladstone*, 47, 80.   3 *Rendel*, 23.
4 Battiscombe, 82.   5 D, ii, 220.
6 GP, 44727, 256–58.   7 D, iii, 608.
8 G to CG, January 20, 1844. GGP, 28/2.   9 D, ii, 136, 143; iii, 31.

manageable order. There were ludicrous aspects of this: as when Gladstone enjoined upon his children the improving habit of thinking while eating of four bars of common time written in quavers as an aid to chewing each mouthful thirty-two times (though he admitted this to be a 'counsel of perfection').[1] The middle and later 1830s were a period of rich development of Gladstone's apparatus of theological, philosophical and literary studies and educational schemes and philanthropic projects. Apart from a few months in 1834–35 he was not in official employment. After the crisis of Anne's death and the question of his vocation in 1829–32 there would be no recurrence of critical spiritual turmoil until 1843, following Helen's perversion to Rome in 1842 and Newman's ominous slide at Oxford in the same direction.

This freedom led not only to major publications, *The State in its Relations with the Church* and *Church Principles*; it enabled Gladstone to establish a pattern in the allocation of the chief interests of his life which he was determined that neither marriage nor office in the future should be allowed decisively to disrupt. After marriage in 1839 and office in 1841 and in more than thirty of the years which followed, Gladstone defended his ground of private studies and activities with a systematic tenacity. 'Study method,' he enjoined as one who by 1858 could fairly claim mastery of the art, 'in the disposal particularly of time & money; it is the secret of independence of ease and of great results from small means.' As for the disposal of time, Gladstone's doctrine was that 'relaxation & refreshment are properly to be found in the alteration of different employments: of these some may be serious & others light but all should have an end: vacuity and dawdling have no end and should at all times & under all circumstances be avoided'.[2]

Gladstone's vast reading was the most conspicuous case of successful application of his doctrine. He was omnivorous in areas congenial to him. Theology and ecclesiastical history and affairs easily predominated. He conscientiously kept abreast of the major periodical reviews. In literature generally, ancient and modern, he was well found, by no means disdaining current fiction. In 1839 he was reading Hazlitt, Carlyle, and Landor. Always loyal to his Oxford friend Martin Tupper, Gladstone read his poem *Geraldine*. He perused Lady Blessington's memoirs. Of novels in that year he read Waddington's *Janet*, Haliburton's *Clockmaker*, Dickens's *Oliver Twist* and *Nicholas Nickleby*, and Sophie Cottin's *Mathilde*. As Stuart Rendel was later to observe severely, Gladstone was 'easy and accommodating with books to a fault.[3] There were, however, large gaps. Some found puzzling Gladstone's 'extraordinary want of, and apparently even interest in, all knowledge of the Sciences of Nature'; and there were 'strange gaps even in that knowledge, e.g., of ecclesi-

1 Tollemache, 61.   2 D, v, 320.   3 *Rendel*, 80, 97–98.

astical and constitutional matters, which did not interest him'.[1] Goldwin Smith noted a deficiency in Gladstone's 'multifarious reading' in the areas of history and political philosophy. He noted also that Gladstone 'left among his writings nothing of importance in the way of political science', nor did he seem 'even to have formed any clear conception of the polity which he was seeking to produce'.[2] (The short answer to these strictures was that Gladstone always had more faith in providence than in science.) It was true also that Gladstone was not immune from the intellectual fashions of his day. He seems to have had a weakness for phrenology: witness his recording a 'phrenological conversation' in 1837 with Thomas Wakley, the Whig MP for Finsbury. Gladstone 'turned the conversation to Sir R. Peel's head' and got the benefit of Wakley's opinion that it was 'out of sight the best head in the House', though its 'prodigious' powers of intellect were 'rather restricted in their development' by Peel's 'organs of caution and secretiveness which are immense'. No doubt it was reassuring to be informed that O'Connell's head was in general 'very inferior.'[3]

Temperamentally a slow and deliberate reader, he absorbed the enormous volume of his reading by dint of exploiting 'unconsidered intervals'. A 'five minutes reader', Gladstone read by 'morsels', instantly deep into a book and just as instantly clean out. This facility was a deliberate discipline of the mind, perfected by training. His reading became a kind of mortar which bound his time into shape. As a matter of principle Gladstone never stood about or passed time. When in office his secretaries commented upon his fidgety uneasiness whenever by chance he was in want of immediate employment.[4] For himself, Gladstone could truly say 'I have never known what tedium was, and have always found time full of calls & duties, life charged with every kind of interest.'[5]

As for disposal of money, Gladstone's doctrine was equally uncompromising. 'It is wrong to say we ought not to care about money,' he insisted in 1836. 'We ought to care about money. We might as well say we did not care about time; or did not care about health & bodily strength; or did not care about our mental faculties: for all these are referable to one and the same class, namely the class of means and instruments which God has put into our hands . . .'[6] Gladstone was destined shortly to have his hands full. In that year his income was a modest £1,551, and his expenditure £655. Of the balance he disbursed £200 on 'charity and religion'. To the £10,000 of Messrs. Gladstone and Co. of Liverpool capital stock held by Gladstone since 1833 John Gladstone added in 1837 £1,000 of East India stock, worth £2,510; which was topped up in 1840 by a £2,000 allowance on marriage for furnishing his new establishment. In the

1 *Kilbracken*, 127–28.   2 Smith, *My Memory of Gladstone*, 37.   3 PMP, ii, 85–86.
4 *Kilbracken*, 87.   5 D, v, 183.   6 GP, 44726, 147.

background, John Gladstone further decided in August 1839 to sell up his Demerara properties, worth something above £50,000, and set up a trust for his children, Robertson in Liverpool having the management. William felt 'this increased wealth so much beyond my needs with its attendant responsibility is very burdensome, however on his part the act be beautiful'.[1] The marriage settlement itself brought Gladstone an additional £8,666 mainly as Catherine's portion under her father's settlement. This sum Gladstone lent out to his father on mortgage on lands and houses at Seaforth at 4 per cent (re-lent by his father at the same interest so there was no account between them). Further, through Catherine, Gladstone received from the Glynne agent Boydell £950 in cash and a twentieth share in Oak Farm Iron Co. stock of £500. He estimated the value of Catherine's wedding presents, including Lady Glynne's diamonds, at £600.[2]

With the mortgage arrangement with his father raised on Catherine's marriage settlement Gladstone purchased Lady Cholmondeley's house and furniture at 13 Carlton House Terrace for £7,800 in February, 1840. He estimated the probable total value of his property and goods on March 1, 1840 at £34,270; his annual income at £4,260 and his expenditure at £2,168. (By 1846 they would be £6,987 and £4,007 respectively.)[3] Between 1831 and 1843 he expended £4,250 on charity and religion.[4] Taking pride of place among his goods were books (on which he spent lavishly) and objects of art. Gladstone purchased art as a duty as well as a pleasure. He estimated the value of his collection in December 1842 as follows: marble busts of Catherine and Lady Brabazon £100; three casts (one of his father) £10; 'St. Anthony by Salvator' £50; 'An Architect by Giovan Bellino' £50; a copy of the Raphael 'Madonna della Seggiola' (with frame) £21; all of which represented a gratifying increase over cost of £53.[5] The following year Gladstone would add £189 worth of paintings: two Italian landscapes by Joseph Severn, Bradley's portrait of his father, and a painting by the earliest of the 'pre-Raphaelite' school, William Dyce, whose expression in art of High Church principles made him an object of Gladstone's keen attention.

Gladstone rather preened himself as a connoisseur of the arts, with high notions of the duties of patronage as befitted a son of the Liverpool of William Roscoe, celebrated scholar of the Medicis and the Italian renaissance.[6] He certainly addressed himself very seriously to both literature and the visual arts; but to no telling effect. He relaxed decidedly his self-adjuration of 1832 against the theatre to the extent in later years of

1 D, ii, 623–24. Checkland, 313, 414–15.
2 GGP, Secret Account Book, 93/13, 1, 7
3 *Ib.*, Rough Book 'A', 94/11, 1, 35, 47.
4 *Ib.*, Secret Account Book, 167.   5 *Ib.*, Rough Book 'A', 171.
6 M. Pointon, 'W. E. Gladstone as an Art Patron and Collector,' *Victorian Studies*, xix (1975).

becoming something of an anecdotal prop for theatrical memoirs (one of which records him sleeping through a reading of Ibsen's *An Enemy of the People* at the Haymarket).[1] He composed large quantities of stilted verse on the ground of his theory that 'the office of poetry is to represent things, actual or imagined, with reference to beauty'.[2] Whatever might be objected to a judgment about Gladstone's deficiency in personal emotion, there seems to be no convincing appeal against Stuart Rendel's verdict that he was 'in no sense remarkable as a man of taste, though he aspires to be a man of taste, and is ignorant that on the side of art he is comparatively weak'. Gladstone had a very unsure critical grasp of contemporary literature, with a weakness for liking 'every book almost that is fairly good of its kind'.[3] Religion always remained Gladstone's ultimate aesthetic criterion. He paid relatively little attention to classical sculpture. In 1842 he was involved in a scheme to establish a 'British Institute of Christian Art', whose scope would be architecture, music, painting and sculpture, and whose programme would be to apply religion to art and art to religion.[4] It was perhaps just as well that Gladstone eventually decided to concentrate his aesthetic powers together with his financial investment on porcelain. 'And yet', as Rosebery later commented, 'Mr G. was reputed to be an enthusiastic ignoramus about china. His collection realised very little.'[5]

Nor was Gladstone any less 'easy and accommodating' at the table, his primary gastronomic concern being to avoid any waste of food as being in the same deplorable category as waste of time or waste of money. He had a tendency positively to tease Catherine by proclaiming a taste for the mundane dish of mutton chops. One of his rare positive dislikes was for oysters: a dislike he made clear to the Mumbles oysterwomen when on his visit to Swansea in 1887. With alcohol, however, especially wine, Gladstone, as befitted the 'Mr. Tipple' of Eton days, took a rather higher tone. He remarked of himself later that whereas he had no taste for cards (September 8, 1839 at Fasque: 'did duty at the whist table') and a definite disinclination to any form of gambling (August 6, 1846 at Hawarden: 'spectator of Vingt Un') he 'remembered well the pleasure and stimulus to the brain given by sipping wine and could well imagine in himself a turn for drink'.[6] He was tolerant of occasional drunkenness;[7] and was perfectly capable as a solitary diner (which he much disliked) of disposing of a bottle of champagne. Gladstone thought bitter beer 'a divine drink' (θεῖον πότου).[8] And he could thank a thoughtful Liberal M.P. for the gift of a bottle of Danish cherry brandy: 'I know its quality from happy experience.'[9]

1 E. Robins, *Both Sides of the Curtain* (1940), 265.   2 GP, 44726, 324.
3 *Rendel*, 97–98.   4 GP, 44729, 198.
5 MS note in copy, once his, now MRDF's, of Tollemache, 30.   6 *Ib.*, 79.
7 Magnus, 379–80.   8 Tollemache, 62.
9 G to Moffat, September 14, 1863. GP, 44533, 166.

Such were the leading characteristics and idiosyncracies observable by the world. How would Gladstone himself have defined the inner substance of his being and purpose in the world? He spent a good deal of time and trouble attempting precisely to answer that question both for his own and posterity's benefit. His diaries and papers are replete with introspective self-analysis and conjecture as to the fulfilment of God's will concerning him. Certainly no figure of comparable historical stature has attempted more copiously and deliberately to leave evidence bearing on the question and the answer. He felt himself very much aware at this time of the need of a means of reading the meaning of events. 'Why have I not come by this time habitually to recognise *my* proper & peculiar exercise?', he demanded of himself on March 21 1841. 'So far from this I hardly begin to perceive the truth: I faint & murmur continually: & have not yet got that higher natural theology, which reads & applies to practice *design* in all the forms of incident that beset & accompany our daily course.'[1] It was his pertinacity in this quest together with his immense natural energy and talents which made Gladstone so formidable. In his search to penetrate meaning and elucidate design Gladstone in effect constructed a career in politics of a singularly consistent and well-marked configuration. By the end of his life Gladstone was convinced that he had trained himself sufficiently in the 'higher natural theology' to read and perceive the great truth about the relationship between design and himself:

There is a Providence that shapes our ends
    Rough-hew them how we may.
I think that no one can be more deeply penetrated with
these words, than I am or ought to be.
The whole of my public and exoteric life has been
shaped as to its ends for me, scarcely rough hewn by me.[2]

Together with this teaching of the higher natural theology Gladstone also offered a view of himself as a creature subject to the discipline of the supernatural theology of revealed religion: 'I don't believe in any new systems. I cling to the old. The great traditions are what attract me. I believe in a degeneracy of man, in the Fall, – in *Sin* – in the intensity and virulence of sin, & sin is the great fact in the world to me.'[3] The tension engendered by being a public man in such a world fascinated Gladstone. 'The experience of my life', he was able to conclude in the 1850s, 'has impressed me with the belief that of all the classes of human characters (and they are many) politicians present to us those which are most complex.'[4]

1 D, iii, 92.   2 GP, 44791, 19.
3 W. S. Peterson, 'Gladstone's Review of *Robert Elsmere*', *Review of English Studies*, new. ser. xxi (1970), 451.
4 GP, 44746, 66.

[8]

The Gladstones moved into 13 Carlton House Terrace on February 11, 1840. Catherine gave birth to their first child, a son, on June 3. He was christened William Henry, and declared to be extremely like his father, with his mother's mouth. Hope and Manning were his sponsors. Soon Gladstone was drawing up the first of a series of genealogical sketches he would make in the coming years showing Willy's maternal descent from Sir William Temple and his links with the Dukes of Buckingham, and thereby with Grenvilles, Wyndhams, and Pitts.[1] By September Gladstone felt obliged to discuss the question of the child with Catherine: clearly people were generally assuming that William Henry would be the heir of Catherine's family. 'We agreed that we should not merely be silent, but never even think, about any such thing: not only because of the uncertainty, but also because of the harmless change of feeling that would arise if one of her two brothers did marry; which I doubt either has ever wanted to.'[2] Thus, as early as 1840, the prospect of a Gladstone inheriting Hawarden had obtruded itself rather awkwardly on William and Catherine; yet not entirely, it may be fairly assumed, as an unwelcome contingency. By August 1840 Gladstone was already inspecting the Glynne estates. He found especially interesting the new concern of Sir Stephen's, Oak Farm, a coal, ironstone and brickworks property near Stourbridge, a small share in which he (and Lyttelton) had received as part of the marriage settlement. This was a venture designed to rescue the somewhat embarrassed Glynne finances. Sir Stephen sold £55,000 worth of land in 1840 to maximise his investment. Gladstone looked over it with the Glynne agent, Boydell, who, in partnership with his brother-in-law, C. B. Trevor-Roper of Plas Teg, Mold, was enthusiastically promoting it as a winning investment. Gladstone went over the whole affair 'which is very large and seems a good concern even at the present low prices of 4.5 for pig and 7.20 for bar'. He 'had no time to see the books'.[3] This was perhaps extremely unfortunate. For Oak Farm, far from being a winning investment, soon proved to be a heavy liability, which dragged the entire Glynne estate down to the brink of bankruptcy and which in the coming years was to cost Gladstone much tedious labour and weariness of spirit in devoted and time-consuming nursing of his wife's family's estate back to financial health.

If the outlook on the Glynne family front promised well, the atmosphere among the Gladstones was strained. Perhaps it was Gladstone's new sense of married maturity and independence which made him chafe at his father's imperturbably patriarchal requirement that his youngest son continue as ever to perform endless tasks of secretarial drudgery. He

1 GP, 44729, 107.   2 D, iii, 58 n.4.   3 *Ib.*, 55, 125 n.2.

edified himself with an agitated and conscience-stricken memorandum on the divinely ordained duty of filial submission. But in fact his father's ascendancy in the family was fading in the face of the brilliance of William's achievements. Rejection by the electors of Dundee sharply underlined the equivocal nature of John Gladstone's 'success' in life. William's eldest brother Thomas, out of Parliament since 1837 and painfully conscious of William's impressive public eminence, displayed symptoms of grievance and hurt pride. He nursed his public failure and hit back at William's new High Churchmanship by stoking his zeal for the family's traditional Evangelicalism.

Much more disturbing was the case of Helen. Her engagement to the Polish count had been terminated by his parents. Sequestered once more as her father's companion, Helen lapsed into depression and hysteria. The doctors prescribed laudanum and alcohol as tranquillisers. Soon addicted, Helen sought her own tranquilliser in the form of Romanism.

From the summer of 1840 onwards Gladstone noted a series of 'sad' letters from his father and 'painful' conversations about Helen's reported attendances at Roman Catholic places of worship. This was disturbing to him as a convinced and indeed militant anti-Roman; it was embarrassing for him as one whose public career was increasingly stigmatised as part of the Puseyite conspiracy to undermine the Protestantism of the Church, a conspiracy which dropped its mask in February 1841 with the publication of Newman's notorious *Tract XC* demonstrating that the Thirty-Nine Articles of the Church could reasonably bear a thoroughly Catholic interpretation. Gladstone's comment on 12 March was: 'ominous.' He had already diagnosed his sister's case as betokening the 'deepest delusion'. But it was an awkward fact that William himself had led Helen along with him in joint explorations of Catholicity. He was not in the least disposed to sympathy for Helen's predicament, trapped as she was at Fasque without her own life or any hope of a career. He subjected both her and their father to a good deal of overweening and even hectoring advice. Probably he was only too aware of how near he himself could come to the kind of breakdown which overwhelmed Helen. All his life he had been aware of powerful and intense passions being restrained only by a rigidly systematic self-control.

Meanwhile, Gladstone was busy enough at his regular avocations. He delighted in visits to Eton – 'this sweet place' – to examine for the Newcastle scholarship and to attend the quatercentary dinner. He conversed in London in March 1839 with Charles de Montalembert, the former disciple of Lamennais and the chief of the Catholic party in the French Chamber: 'a very interesting person', and indeed as a liberal Catholic very *à propos* of Gladstone's current preoccupation. His second book came out in August 1840. *Church Principles considered in their Results,* 'completed beneath the shades of Hagley', revealed Gladstone realigning his argument on a historical and ecumenical ground. If his 1838 ideal of a National Church was improbable, then the great 'signs' of Anglicanism, its visibility, its apostolicity, its authority in matters of faith and of the things signified in the sacraments, could be made to bear not only upon the relations of Anglicans one with another, but also 'with the members of other religious communions, under the peculiar circumstances of the present day'. The alternative mode of action was now a reunited apostolic Christendom.[1] For Gladstone the historical dimension now superseded the *a priori* foundations of *The State in its Relations with the Church. Church Principles* made, not surprisingly, no great public impact. Its implications were remote and, indeed, in a sense, 'foreign'.[2] But it was these principles which prepared Gladstone to receive in a few years' time the uneffaceable impact of Döllinger.

Spiritual philanthropy continued unabated. In 1840 he joined (together with Hope) a small brotherhood founded by the elder Thomas Dyke Acland devoted to works of mercy and charity. This was the germ of a rather more ambitious scheme developed a few years later by Acland's two sons. He was much immersed in the affairs of the Millbank penitentiary, the show place of penal reform. His earlier tentative explorations in the area of female prostitution had faded away in the intense pressures of public life and marriage; it was not until the mid-1840s that other kinds of pressures, emotional and psychic, led him to resume 'rescue work' on something like a systematic scale. He was determined to provide the workmen at Oak Farm with the blessing of a church. The plan for an episcopalian seminary and school in Scotland was eventually realised in 1841 in the form of Trinity College, Glenalmond.

His speeches in the Commons in these years largely rehearsed well-defined themes: defence of the West India interest (including yet another warm passage of arms on behalf of his father's reputation); insistence that British authority must be upheld in Canada with a firm hand; above all, advocacy of the claims of the Church. He objected to the government's plans to aid popular education on the grounds of insufficient provision for religious instruction. He had the satisfaction of helping in February 1839 to strike a blow against theatrical amusements at Drury Lane during Lent. He denounced the policy of allowing the alienation of clergy land reserves in Canada. He declared his grave doubts about the propriety of permitting Jews to sit in Parliament; and on March 31, 1841,

---

1 *Church Principles*, 28–29. On this theme generally see Butler, 59–66 and H. C. G. Matthew, 'Gladstone, Vaticanism, and the Question of the East', in *Studies in Church History*, xv (1978), ed. D. Baker.

2 Macaulay thought it best to let it alone: 'I have no disposition to split hairs about the spiritual reception of the body and blood of Christ in the Eucharist or about Baptismal regeneration.' Pinney, iii, 344.

after a clash with Macaulay, was defeated in an attempt to prohibit the election of Jews to municipal office.

[9]

Politics were in a state of flux and impending crisis. Melbourne's reduced majority of 1837 was crumbling away. Only the fatherless young Queen Victoria's vehemently affectionate attachment to her widowed and childless and fatherly Whig Prime Minister and her spirited resistance to Peel over the question of new Tory ladies of the bedchamber had prevented Peel's forming a government in 1839. Dearest Lord M. as father-figure began to be eclipsed in 1840 when Victoria married her adored cousin, Prince Albert of Saxe-Coburg. Albert had no motive for encouraging Melbourne's further presence; and he and Peel were temperamentally likely to find one another congenial. Gladstone observed Lord Home expressing pleasure at the Queen's beginning to 'tinge her dinner-parties a little less faintly with Conservatives'. Yet he feared it was true that 'Lord Melbourne had urged her to invite Sir Robert Peel & that she had been reluctant'.[1] Melbourne managed to hang on into 1841. This delay was probably a good thing for Gladstone. Peel needed time to get over his disgust with Gladstone's book. Gladstone needed time to make himself more adaptable to the exigencies of politics. He dined at Peel's at the beginning of February 1840, when there was 'much rumination on the probable course of politics and party'. Gladstone was unhappily aware that he was being pointed at as one of the '*respectable* bigots' whom Peel was responsible for allowing to share the councils and headquarters of his party. Perhaps Gladstone's election to Grillion's Club at the end of January was especially fortunate for him from his point of view. He found the honour 'embarrassing' and conviviality with his parliamentary colleagues alien to his temperament, especially after marriage. But the 'rules of society' obliged him to 'submit'. He duly attended the fish dinner for the Speaker at Greenwich in June, and seemed to enjoy the 'great merriment'; but privately he avowed himself 'ashamed of paying £2.10.0 for a dinner'.

That the probable course of politics and party showed fair for Conservatism in 1840 was manifest. Much of the evidences of burgeoning Conservative strength in the constituencies came from the response of those elements of the political nation whom Peel had assiduously solicited ever since the publication of his Tamworth Manifesto in 1834: that 'great and intelligent class of society' which was 'much less interested in the

1 GP, 44777, 62.

contentions of party than in the maintenance of order and the cause of good government'. But it was equally clear that a powerful agency of Conservative revival derived from the resurgence of confidence in the Church and the public sentiments which fed that resurgence and which fed from it. Such sentiments might not generally regard favourably Gladstone's alleged Puseyism; but they certainly regarded with suspicion the kind of cautious moderation in religious opinion characteristic of Peel. A 'careful review of institutions, civil and ecclesiastical, undertaken in a friendly temper', 'not actuated by any illiberal or intolerant spirit towards the Dissenting body', was a formula possibly appropriate to the circumstances of the early 1830s, with the old State and the old Church reeling under the impact of Reform; but by 1840 such circumspect attitudes seemed to many advocates of unapologetic Toryism entirely out of place. It was perhaps just as well from this point of view that Peel's spell of office in 1834–35 had been so short. His accommodating temper in areas increasingly regarded as sacred by many of his party's most zealous adherents, such as church rates, tithe commutation, marriage, and Irish Church revenues, indicated the likelihood of many points of friction in the future. It would be a deep question for Gladstone as to how he would adjust his position in such circumstances. How could the author of *The State in its Relations with the Church*, committed to an ideal of political service to the Church, reconcile himself to continued service of an administration which failed to mount a determined and principled counter-attack against the proud, ungodly spirit which branded the forehead of the age, the spirit of indifferentism, Erastianism, liberalism, 'pluralism'? Ashley, from the Evangelical angle, was already convinced of the dangers threatened by Peel's love of expediency, his perpetual egoistry, his dread of an immovable principle, his delight in the praise of men, which would 'attract him more than "Hast thou considered thy servant Job?"'[1] Gladstone himself was fully aware of what he had earlier described to the Bishop of Exeter as the 'peculiar adaptation in Peel's mind to the age in which he lives'. 'If I have differences from my leader', he noted on 9 May 1841, 'they are as I am convinced not political but religious.'[2]

But for the time being, as the Whig majority disintegrated, such speculations and apprehensions could be subordinated to the immediate requirements of the party. Gladstone certainly signalled a major new initiative in his political development in April 1840 when he launched a vigorous assault in the Commons on Palmerston's 'Opium War' against the Chinese Empire (no doubt Helen's addiction added an edge to his indignation). Possibly Macaulay's defence of Palmerston's policy was an additional incentive for Gladstone; but his note of May 14 that he was 'in

1 Machin, *Politics and the Churches*, 149.   2 PMP, ii, 137.

dread of the judgments of God upon England for our national iniquity towards China' testified to an overriding conscientious conviction of the hypocrisy of the government's allegations and Macaulay's defence of them. Palmerston and Macaulay admitted the formal right of the Chinese government to ban the importation of opium, though Macaulay expressed his doubts as to the wisdom of attempting to exclude 'a drug which, if judiciously administered, was powerful in assuaging pain, and in promoting health, because it was occasionally used to excess by intemperate men'. But, as Gladstone charged, every practical action of the British government and its agents exhibited them as supporters of the British merchants engaged in the contraband trade and as obstructers of the Chinese efforts to suppress it. Palmerston, instead of obstructing, should have collaborated with the Chinese; and, although the Chinese were 'undoubtedly guilty' of much absurd phraseology, of no little ostentatious pride, and of some excess, justice, in Gladstone's opinion, was with them; and 'whilst they, the Pagans, and semi civilised barbarians, have it, we, the enlightened and civilised Christians, are pursuing objects at variance both with justice, and with religion'.[1]

This was Gladstone's first incursion into the field of foreign affairs. In it he set a tone and a direction which would become increasingly evident and characteristic in the coming years. His attitude, as yet but dimly formulated, had to do essentially with a notion of Britain's moral obligations to an ideal of a community of the nations. His teacher, to the extent that so definite a concept of educational development is appropriate, was Aberdeen, himself the disciple of Castlereagh. Much more distinct and palpable was the object of Gladstone's growing dislike and hostility: the jaunty, arrogant, morally libertine Palmerston, with his doctrines of British prerogatives in the world and British rights to intervene in the affairs of other peoples who were imitating the 'proud example of this country, by obtaining the inestimable privilege of a representative Government'. Palmerston compounded the mischievousness of his interference in Spain and Portugal by his reckless challenge to the French government over the Near East. It was annoying enough that Palmerston should presume to claim the inheritance of Canning; it was doubly annoying that Palmerston should have been formally crowned with Canning's laurels in July 1840 by the *Edinburgh Review*. It was comforting to reflect along with the *Quarterly Review* in 1841, however, that Palmerston's reign of misrule at the Foreign Office would soon be terminated. 'The Conservatives may well congratulate themselves on their great, their growing, and speedily triumphant force, increasing honourably and rapidly, in despite of the influence of the most corrupt of governments, and without the predilections of a misinformed

1 H, liii, 808–819.

and misguided court.'[1] Gladstone helped the good work along by aiding his brother John Neilson to capture Walsall in a by-election in February 1841. In the course of doing so he had a brush with the anti-Corn Law agitator Cobden, who was offended by Gladstone's curt refusal to accept his challenge to public debate.

Melbourne's government duly collapsed in June 1841 after fatiguing itself fatally in its efforts to push through the provisions of its rather desperate and controversial budget. It attacked three great and powerful interests, sugar, coffee and timber, in an effort to overcome the chronic deficit which had plagued the Whigs. Peel manoeuvred skilfully, and timed his attack well on June 5, beating ministers by 312 to 311. Parliament was dissolved and elections for a new House of Commons started at the end of June. By mid-July it was clear that the Conservatives would have a good majority. Gladstone was teamed at Newark with another Conservative candidate, Lord John Manners; and, as there was a Liberal in the field, a poll was held, in which Gladstone came top with 633 votes, Manners second with 630 and the defeated Liberal Hobhouse a poor third with 394. Gladstone's admiration for feudality had not flagged. He remarked on the 'enthusiastic and beautiful' scene at Newark where 'the Duke's tenantry thronged round him, and he did his part with the grace and dignity of a prince'.[2] Gladstone hurried over to Flint to help his brother-in-law Sir Stephen (most outrageously accused of homosexual perversion)[3] in his campaign. Glynne was defeated (though he regained the seat in the following year on a petition). Gladstone, admiring in Sir Stephen the 'meek unshaken courage of a Christian', consoled himself for failure by observing the touching loyalty of Hawarden: 'here is one of the best forms of feudalism, still thank God! extremely common among us.'[4] Meekness was far from being Gladstone's own mode of electioneering. He was accused by Lord Westminster's agent of 'tampering' with the Grosvenor tenantry, who were to be delivered to the victorious Mostyn.[5] It was a pity also that John Neilson lost his so recently gained seat at Walsall; and poor Tom ended up at the bottom of yet another poll – this time for Peterborough. However, Gladstone returned to Westminster for the new session beginning in August as one of Peel's majority of near eighty. The government was defeated on an amendment to the address on August 27 by 360 to 269, and the Queen reluctantly bade farewell to Melbourne and summoned Sir Robert to Windsor. 'What a change since I came into Parliament!' reflected Gladstone. 'We were barely 140 out of 658. So expires the ninth life of the Government.'[6]

That Gladstone would be a member of the new administration was

1 QR, lxvii (1840–41), 302.   2 D, iii, 122.
3 Joyce Marlow, *Mr and Mrs Gladstone. An Intimate Biography* (1977), 33.
4 D, iii, 124.   5 PMP, ii, 148–51.   6 D, iii, 134.

beyond any reasonable doubt. He was one of the small group constantly being called together by Peel to consult about policy and tactics. He records such meetings on May 20 and June 7; again on August 21, and on Sunday the 22nd (Peel's house being 'beset with spies') at Aberdeen's ('I attended this meeting with some pain: but I did not think it *right* to refuse'). The personnel of these conclaves could quite reasonably be deduced as in effect a shadow administration. Gladstone certainly had grounds for assuming that Peel would include him in the new cabinet. He had served his apprenticeship as an under-secretary. He recorded on August 2 that 'since the address meetings the idea of the Irish secre-taryship had nestled in my mind'.[1] That had been Peel's own *entrée* to high office at the age of twenty-four. And indeed in Bonham's draft list of appointments Gladstone is twice noted as a possible Irish secretary (though not necessarily in the cabinet).[2] Gladstone had already pon-dered the problem of the contingency of being offered office. All his reflections brought him 'more and more to the conclusion that if the principle of National Religion (a principle, which is my bond to parliamentary life) is to be upheld, or saved from utter overthrow, it must be by the united action of the Conservative party'. This did not necessarily mean 'every member of it, nor only of its members, but yet of the party as a whole and moving under its leaders'. The constituencies could not be expected to make the nice points of politics the study of their lives; they must elect on 'grounds few, simple, comprehensive'. Hence the nature of the system required the 'principle of party', representing and expressing a faith 'upon some general and leading terms'. He thought both the cast of Peel's sentiments and his abilities were such as to be 'a great Providential gift to this country, wonderfully suited to her need'. His duty to support Peel, despite Peel's lack of response to the ideal of the 'Catholic Church historical and visible', remained para-mount.[3] There were 'many fast friends of the Union of Church & State' who said 'Stand aloof from office or Party, proclaim the truth from an independent position & so you will maintain or revive the true principle of the constitution'. Against this Gladstone reminded himself that he had 'ever thought & held that when the Church is divorced from the State, they cannot be reunited by any agency of Catholic principles in Parliament'. It might be difficult 'to determine the point of declension at which institutions in themselves wholesome must be surrendered': but he was sure that, in retrospect, 'the practical issue' would 'in most cases approximately at least decide it'.[4] In any case, that time was not yet.

Having thus primed himself as to the general propriety of accepting office, and having been so constantly among the intimate inner circle

1 Morley, i, 244. 2 Peel Papers, BL Add. Mss. 40489, 393–94.
3 D, iii, 105–08. 4 GP, 44729, 108.

of the party, it came to Gladstone as a distinct let-down when Peel summoned him on the morning of 31 August and offered him the office of Vice-President of the Board of Trade as spokesman in the Commons for the President, who was to be Lord Ripon. This was the alternative disposition proposed in Bonham's lists: 'Gladstone (if not Ireland) V̲ P of the Board of Trade.'[1] Bonham's emphatic underlining of the 'V' expressed possibly a determination that Gladstone should get no more than his deserts; or, conversely, indicated an awareness that the junior status had about it an element of anomalousness. Peel covered the offer with many flattering remarks about 'the great struggle in which we have been and are to be engaged', and the chief importance to be attached to questions of finance, and the highest importance of the office in question. Gladstone's immediate, rather crestfallen, response was that he was really not fit for it, having no general knowledge of trade matters and no special competency for them. Upon Peel's then remarking that Gladstone would be impossible for Ireland, but that something in the Admiralty might be available, Gladstone 'rather interposed' to make it clear that he was even less fitted for 'anything connected with the military and naval forces of the country' – a fact which Peel no doubt appreciated quite keenly. He thus adroitly manoeuvred the deflated Gladstone into a sulky acceptance: 'I will not decline it: I will endeavour to put myself into harness; and to prepare myself for the place in the best manner I can; but it really is an apprenticeship.' Doubtless Peel took the point of Gladstone's allusion to having already served his apprenticeship at the Colonial Office. Gladstone covered his retreat by raising possible difficulties about China policy, which Peel gently deflected. Gladstone came away after a bad quarter of an hour convinced of the distastefulness of his designated employment. 'I must forthwith go to work, in sum, as a reluctant schoolboy meaning well.'[2] The additional appointment annexed to his responsibilities of Mastership of the Mint if anything underlined the point of his complaint that, wanting to govern men, he was instead put to governing packages.

Ruminating later on his disappointed expectations, Gladstone felt himself entitled to conclude that, considering the 'degree of confidence which Sir Robert Peel had for years, habitually I may say, reposed in me, and especially considering its climax, in my being summoned to the meetings immediately preceding the Debate of the Address in August', and allowing for the 'delusions of Selflove', there was 'not a perfect correspondence between the tenor of the past on the one hand, and my present appointment and the relations in which it places me to the administration on the other'. Was it possible that Peel had not intended on August 21 to make him the offer he made on the 31st? Was Gladstone

1 Peel Papers, *ib.*   2 PMP, ii, 158–61.

altogether deluded to imagine that Ireland with the cabinet was originally in Peel's mind? Gladstone was 'sorry now to think' that he might have been guilty 'of an altogether absurd presumption, in dreaming of the Cabinet'. But he insisted to himself that it was 'wholly suggested' by the tone of Peel's summons. And Gladstone persisted in thinking that 'there must have been some consultation and decision' relating to him 'in the interval between the meetings and the formation of the new ministry, which produced some alteration'. Gladstone was 'distinct' in his recollection that there was 'a shyness in Peel's manner and a downward eye when he opened the conversation and made the offer', not usual with him in speaking to Gladstone.[1] Perhaps Gladstone should have recalled the incident in the street after the publication of *State and Church*. The Board of Trade was Peel's way of bringing Gladstone down to earth. There may well have been a touch of satire in the decision. And Gladstone's own account of the interview indicates that in Peel's quite sensible view Ireland was far from being the most suitable post for so aggressive an exponent of the highest claims of the Irish Church as Gladstone. But in any event Gladstone decided it was 'easy to recognise the mercy and wisdom of God in the arrangement as it stands'. And to sweeten the pill there was, at last, the privy councillorship. Gladstone became right honourable and magnificently gold-braided on September 3, 1841, along with Lord Ernest Bruce, the Duke of Buckingham and Chandos, Lord Eliot, the Earl of Lincoln, and the Earl of Liverpool. It was some consolation; but it was one thing to be an under-secretary at the age of twenty-five and quite another to have the same effective rank, even as a privy councillor, at the age of thirty-one.

1 *Ib.*, 162–63.

CHAPTER III

'A FURTHER DECLENSION IN THE RELIGIOUS CHARACTER OF THE STATE OF THESE REALMS': 1841–1845

[1]

'I can digest the crippled religious action of the State,' Gladstone had conceded in August 1841, contemplating the imminent approach of office. In a Lenten rumination in March 1842 he interpreted his notion of a crippled action thus: 'the adjustment of a certain relations of the Church to the State.' Not that he thought that the action of the Church could be 'harmonised' with the laws of the State: 'We have passed the point at which that was possible'; and he did not expect to see it recovered. 'The materials waste away daily.' The 'whole doctrine of Reserves for the Church,' he pointed out, had been 'much damaged not only by democratic sentiment in politics & religion, but by crude & defective arrangements'.[1] But it would be 'much' if the State would 'honestly aim at enabling the Church to develop her own intrinsic means'. And Gladstone had a second 'prospective object' for which he hoped his public employment might 'if not qualify yet extrinsically enable' him. That second object was 'unfolding the Catholic system' within the Church in some 'establishment or machinery', 'looking both towards the higher life, and towards the external warfare against ignorance and depravity'.[2]

. In his birthday retrospect in December 1843, after more than six months in Peel's cabinet, Gladstone avowed: 'Of public life I must certainly say every year shows me more and more that the idea of Christian politics cannot be realised in the State according to its present conditions of existence.' For purposes Gladstone believed 'sufficient', though 'partial & finite', he was 'more than content' to stay where he was. But it seemed to him that 'the perfect freedom of the new covenant' could only be 'breathed in other air'; and the day might yet come when God would grant him 'the application of this conviction'.[3] His conscience remained sore on China. 'My heart I am pained to say,' he assured Francis Palgrave, 're-echoes your denunciation of the Chinese proceedings, & sympathises in yr anticipation of judgements on acct of them.' He had never, he

1 G to Palgrave, November 11, 1841. GP, 44527, 49.
2 D, iii, 190.   3 Ib., 336.

insisted, 'knowingly done anything to favor them: & I am at all times ready to contribute, were it in my power, to stop them'. But the 'deadness of Parlt in general' made him 'sorrowfully conclude last year, that until some new conjuncture, humanity forbade to stimulate those poor sheep destined for slaughter to prolong an unavailing resistance. Alas for England. I know not where, except only in the Slave Trade, to find a parallel to this shame in our annals.'[1]

The programme of 1838 had thus far been drastically curtailed. The State could not be the active and positive organ of Christian politics. It would henceforth be enough if the State did not hinder the Church in its work. Was Gladstone deluding himself with his notions of a 'perfect freedom' which could only be 'breathed in other air'? It is easy to fall into a habit of coining portentous utterances of vague import which have the effect of stilling an uneasy conscience. How 'partial and finite' were the purposes 'sufficient' to keep him contentedly in his political role – a role increasingly marked by the worldly insignia of fame and success? 'Dim and distant' indeed were the 'purposes' which must take their form as God wills 'from the course of events under His Providential guidance'.[2] Meanwhile: perplexity. 'The longer our sins remain in us the more do they benumb our spiritual instincts and the faculty of discerning the will of God in order to follow it.' There was, too, the point that 'even a small amount of sin but within a range often & often exerted' might generate a 'determined bias extensively impairing the powers of moral judgement, hard indeed to be redressed'.[3]

'Other air' might, however, be breathed in the second prospective object he had in view of an 'establishment or machinery' within which the 'Catholic' system might be unfolded as a way of helping the Church to develop her own intrinsic means of realising her purposes. The ideal of a group of pious laymen bound together in a fraternity dedicated both to contemplative devotion and practical good works took an increasing hold on Gladstone's imagination in these years. As the religious aspect of the State wasted away into an ever more palsied debility the attractions of a compensatory 'intrinsic' renewal of spiritual life and strength suggested themselves with corresponding cogency. There had always been a side of Gladstone's inner emotional life which leaned in the direction of the 'cloister'. In his early hopes of leading a 'severe life' Gladstone feared the seductions of the great world to which his talents exposed him. He always saw himself much in need not only of self-adjuration but of external support. That was perhaps the single most important function of his friendships with Manning and Hope. Gladstone needed them as censors, props, almost as external standards of reference by which to judge

1 G to Palgrave, November 11, 1841. GP, *ib.*
2 D, iii, 190.   3 *Ib.*, 337.

himself. Hope's 'tonsured' status in a kind of lay apostolate, a version of a tertiary member of one of the great medieval religious orders, especially appealed to him. But he hankered as well for some kind of institutional corset. He was a member of a like-minded group of Catholic High Anglicans who congregated at the Chapel of All Saints, Margaret Street, whose leading spirits were the Aclands and whose spiritual mentor was Keble.[1] A feature of the spiritual life of this group especially appealing to Gladstone was a version of the confessional, not as a sacrament administered by a priest, but as a mutually supportive private aid or boon. 'Certainly an atmosphere of devotion, a reality of earnest concurrence in the work of holy worship pervades the place, which I know not where else to look for.'[2] In Gladstone's papers of about 1842 or 1843 is an outline of a 'Rule' evidently for a group engaged in an Easter Retreat in a 'Clergyman's Country House'. The regimen for the 'Inmates' Gladstone sketched as follows: bell rings for rising at 5.30; prayers at 6; morning service at 9; visiting sick or instructing poor until 2 (a service at 12 for those not so engaged or who have been at private devotions); a general service at 3; private devotions at 6; family prayer at 9. Fasting on Wednesdays and Fridays. There were also details of 'Vigils' and 'Festivals'.[3] There are no evidences of Gladstone's actually going into such a retreat; but the ideal obviously had for him a powerful attraction.

Sharing in the life of some such spiritual 'cell' in the Church promised for Gladstone rich private edification and blessed consolations in the way of philanthropic activity. But what of the Church itself? In his perplexity Gladstone oscillated between despondency and confidence. News from Oxford gave occasion for both. He was sure that 'were Newman & his friends in intention hostile to the peace of the Church (& they are far otherwise)' it would be 'not even within their power to interrupt and sever the profound comprehensive movements towards the true basis of unity in the Church of England'. It would be difficult, after all, too, 'for their disservice to come near to outweighing their service.'[4] A few days later Gladstone anxiously expounded to Manning his 'private apprehensions of Oxford opinions'. Newman on the doctrine of justification he could wish 'forgotten altogether'; and on the horrors thus conveyed by Romish notions of human desert were superimposed the horrors threatened by the Protestant scheme of the Jerusalem bishopric to be shared with the Prussians. He informed the Bishop of London of his inability to become a member of the Bishopric of Jerusalem Trust. He

1 All Saints was a proprietary chapel within the parish of St Marylebone. When the new church of All Saints designed by Butterfield was consecrated by Tait, the Bishop of London, in 1859, the parish of All Saints was established. The incumbent from 1839 to 1845 was Frederick Oakeley, noted as the translator of the Latin hymn 'Adeste fideles' ('O come, all ye faithful').

2 D, iii, 192.   3 GP, 44731, 142–43.   4 D, iii, 94 (March 30, 1841).

was fearful that his negative response would lead to interpretations of 'Tractarianism', 'wh I do not really entertain'; and despite the work and good will of 'my excellent friend' Bunsen, the project 'yet raised a scruple in my mind' about the 'seemingly simple appellation of "Protestant"' and the status of the Confession of Augsburg.[1] And what of the power of the new bishop to ordain priests without subscription to the Thirty-Nine Articles? To Bunsen himself Gladstone insisted that it was 'a cause of grief & nothing less to me, thus at the moment of the apparent consummation of yr benevolent & pious labors, to interpose doubts & questions, wh beset my own individual conscience.'[2] While staying at Nuneham Courtenay in April 1841 Gladstone took an opportunity to inspect Newman's church at Littlemore. Catherine's verdict was 'Nothing there to make one jump.'[3] To both Manning and Hope Gladstone wrote a word of excited despondency in November 1841 on the Jerusalem bishopric, that 'saddest & most anxious' subject, 'full of confusion, instability, darkness, conflicting interpretations, precipitancy – to say nothing of the prejudices & passions, which it necessarily arouses'.[4] 'God help this labouring church, and send us no more of such disastrous years.' Oxford at 'deadly strife with herself' over *Tract XC* and the poetry professorship made even Cambridge seem to Gladstone's incredulous eyes to have 'pretentions' to a 'juster equilibrium'.[5]

The painful irony behind all this was Gladstone's rising reputation as what the violently Whig and Protestant *Morning Advertiser* defined as 'lay leader of the Puseyites, or Oxford Tract Party'. It was bad enough that Gladstone should find himself accused of fomenting 'monstrous notions' to restore the medieval authority of the Church and to extinguish both Dissent and the liberties of England by 'fire and sword'. Much worse was the attack on Peel as deliberate harbourer of the chief conspirer of this malign conspiracy of swarming Puseyites: 'And to crown all, Sir Robert Peel receives, with open arms, into his new government, the most noted among them. The effect of this in increasing their numbers must be fearfully great.'[6]

[2]

As ever, Gladstone's best answer to perplexity was 'active work'. His capacity in this respect soon became a matter of widespread comment. Graham, the new Home Secretary, noted admiringly that 'Gladstone

1 G to Bp of London, October 28, 1841. Gp, 44527, 46.
2 G to Bunsen, November 3, 1841. *Ib.*, 47–49.   3 Battiscombe, *Mrs Gladstone*, 44.
4 G. to Manning, April 22 and November 30, 1841. GP, 44247, 91, 103.
5 G. to Hope, November 25, 1841. GP, 44214, 196.
6 *Morning Advertiser*, September 16, 1841.

could do in four hours what it took any other man sixteen to do, and he worked sixteen hours a day'.[1] One of his secretaries in later years calculated that if an ordinary man were measured for 'internal force' in 'units of horse power' as 100, and 'an exceptionally energetic man to be 200', then 'Mr. Gladstone's horse power was at least 1,000'. And 'this tremendous force' could be turned 'in any direction and for any purposes great or small'; like a steam hammer, it could 'break a bar of steel or crack a nut'.[2] In this aptitude for intense application Gladstone emulated Peel's own laborious habits. In these years government was groping its way towards a new expertise in political economy to enable it to cope with unprecedented transformations in society. In later years Gladstone looked back in wonder not only at his own ignorance but at the ignorance of ministers in general. Peel imagined that Ripon was a 'master of the craft'; and Gladstone frankly avowed his own first major operation, the tariff of 1842, 'a bungling business'.[3] His duties in his first two years at the Board of Trade and the Mint required him to master the business of customs duties, railways, corn importation, copyright of designs, tariffs, colonial preferences, half-farthings and silver coinage, commercial treaties, Stade duties with the Elbian lands of Germany, sugar duties, the Fisheries Convention, Brazilian sugar and slavery, problems of coopers and coal whippers, problems of the watchmaking trade beset by new technology. Should the birth of the Prince of Wales be marked by striking a commemorative medal? Gladstone anxiously consulted Lord Wharncliffe and failed to find a precedent in the case of George IV. Gladstone was not hobbled at the Board by the presence of a formidable president. Ripon, the former Goderich and 'Prosperity Robinson' as Lord Liverpool's Chancellor of the Exchequer in the 1820s, was now ambitious merely to redeem his failure as prime minister with a successful elder-statesmanship. As the minister who had actually introduced the Corn Law of 1815, Ripon felt a certain proprietary interest in the corn issue; but he had neither the energy nor the ability to play a decisive role in forming cabinet policy. Gladstone later recorded that he came 'in a very short time' to 'form a low estimate of the knowledge and information of Lord Ripon'.[4] It was as well that the President was content to let his voracious subaltern have all the work he wanted. But the new Vice-President never really reconciled himself to the indignity of 'governing packages', though he admitted it to be a wholesome discipline and education for wider spheres of public life. He was still apologising to the House in 1843 for the 'wearisomeness' of the subject of export duties on coals.

Did it cost Gladstone any pangs in October 1841 when, after much

1 Lathbury, i, 259.   2 *Kilbracken*, 123.
3 *Rendel*, 119; PMP, i, 46.   4 PMP, i, 74.

fruitless negotiation with reluctant grandees about the Indian governor-generalship, Ellenborough himself left the Board of Control and went off to Calcutta, Peel filling the awkward gap with Vesey Fitzgerald, hitherto unplaced in the ministerial arrangements? In any case, the later fate of Fitzgerald would as it happened bear very directly on Gladstone's fortunes. Probably, at that juncture, Gladstone was too preoccupied with fulfilling Peel's first major call on his services. He warned Catherine in December 1841 that the devotion of his time to 'public purposes' would 'render it imperative on me to be more than heretofore a recluse in my own house – I do not mean as to you and the boy, and as to Lady Glynne'; he was anxious that Catherine especially should not suffer loneliness because of his absorption: 'but absorbed I must be, and I cannot be otherwise without taking my mind, I believe, beyond its powers of healthy operation.'[1]

The department which Gladstone came to have effective responsibility for was dominated by officials schooled in the traditions of Huskisson and the practices of Poulett Thomson, who managed the Board for the Whig government first as vice-president (in a similar relationship to Lord Auckland as Gladstone was to Lord Ripon) and then as president up to 1839. The Canningite evocations of Huskisson's reputation would certainly attract Gladstone; but there was little else to make him warm to the Board and its servants in 1841. The tone and temper of its officials was rancorously anti-landowner and anti-aristocratic; it conducted a propaganda campaign for the dismantling of the existing mercantilist apparatus of customs and excise strong on *a priori* free trade and utilitarian ideology but weak on reliable information and statistics. Peel rightly disliked and distrusted the Board for these reasons, and looked to Ripon to call it to order and suppress its Whiggish excesses. Gladstone was left to educate himself in the business of his office. He was much in communication with various uncles and cousins in Liverpool for first-hand information. 'I learned the cause of the different trades,' as he later recalled, 'out of the mouths of the deputations which were sent up to remit our proposals.' (February 21, 1842: 'Saw six deputations, a hard day, & discussion with different members on different matters nearly all the evening.' One such member was a young man in Quaker dress whose interventions were 'rather fierce, but very strong and very earnest': John Bright.) In the process he soon felt the 'stones' of which his protectionism was built up 'get uncomfortably loose'; and by the end of the 1842 session his faith in protection 'except as a matter of transition' was crumbling 'rapidly away'.[1] Along with Peel, Gladstone moved towards free trade along a path of investigation essentially independent of its vociferous official propagandists.

1 Bassett, 40.   2 PMP, i, 74.

Gladstone described himself as setting to work at the Board of Trade 'with all my might as a learner', putting in as a rule fourteen hours a day. Ripon attended to the administrative side; and, given thus the 'advantage of being abľe to apply myself with undivided attention', Gladstone's apprenticeship in the 'government of casks and packages' was short. By the end of two months Gladstone was a tolerably complete master of the department's business. The officers of the Board, for all their political objectionableness, were more technically and administratively competent than in most government departments of the time. In R.W.Rawson and (in 1842) Stafford Northcote, Gladstone had very able private secretaries. By November 1841 he was preparing memoranda advising Peel on the conclusions he had drawn from his initial labours. His schoolman's mind was offended by the untidy clutter into which the tariff system had got, replete with anomalies, confusions, and endless occasions of lobbying, wire-pulling, petitioning and litigation by commercial interests manoeuvring for advantage in the interface where mercantilist government and governmentalised commerce grated against one another. John Gladstone had proved himself a ruthlessly successful practitioner of the arts of survival in this world. His son was to prove himself ruthless in another direction. Gladstone's method was precisely that which he had applied to the equally anomalous and unsatisfactory relations between State and Church. His rigorous logic in that earlier case had caused offence as being at odds with the spirit of the time; his no less rigorous logic in this present case would gain approval on the same grounds. But it was the logic in either case which Gladstone attended to, not the grounds. He dealt with 750 delinquently inefficient tariffs in the same mood of Oxonian Aristotelianism in which he castigated the slipshod morality of the State and the Erastian frailty of the Church.

Peel was determined to break out of the financial impasse into which the Whigs had got themselves and to cure the commercial depression lowering over the country by a bold and decisive stroke of budgetary policy in the coming session of 1842. He did not come into office with a preconceived plan of implementing a 'free trade' policy as understood by the Board of Trade or the Anti-Corn Law League. His starting point was a much more empirical position of curing the budget deficits which had plagued the Whigs since 1837. This led him towards shaping governmental response to social distress and unrest. The doctrines prevalent in the Board implied distinctly a subsistence theory of wages; and the greatest problem the League had was to counter the charge that it advocated cheap bread as an excuse for manufacturers to reduce wages. Peel was also pragmatically aware that the Whigs, at a loss for a large and popular policy, were hovering on the brink of a general commitment to free trade as the new bandwagon upon which they could climb to restore their political fortunes. Peel wanted to put his government and his party in a position to pre-empt such a bid, if necessary. His leading idea for 1842 was to shift the greatest burden of revenue-raising away from duties on imported staple foodstuffs and raw materials for industry. To compensate for the temporary (as he anticipated) loss of revenue thus incurred, Peel needed a sure and flexible source of direct taxation. The precedent of Pitt's tax on income naturally occurred. Peel started canvassing his senior colleagues as soon as he knew the likely result of the elections. Probably he had already made up his mind; and his motive was educational. Pitt's tax had been a wartime measure and carried with it that character of something to be resorted to only in dire circumstances. Peel had to accustom his colleagues' minds to the notion that so desperate a recourse was appropriate in the economic and social conditions of the early 1840s. Ripon and Wellington, two old 'friends of the late Mr. Pitt', were quite amenable. By October Peel got around to sounding out the Vice-President of the Board of Trade.

'The reply he received,' as Peel's biographer put it, 'was a formidable demonstration of his young colleague's intellectual powers, even though what it exhibited was more the clarity and force which Gladstone could bring to practical matters than any depth of economic experience and judgement.'[1] Gladstone, impressed by his father's inveterate hostility to the income tax as an inquisition and a provocation to fraud, argued for the alternative of resuscitating the old house tax, repealed in 1834. Goulburn (the new Chancellor of the Exchequer), Graham, Stanley, Herries, and the other party seniors had no difficulty in convincing themselves, despite Gladstone's insistence that most objections might be 'mitigated by a careful graduation',[2] that even the income tax was decidedly preferable. Gladstone thus, unwittingly, proved Peel's point for him.

But Gladstone had a much larger point yet to prove to Peel. If his advice about income tax did not find approval his advice about tariff reforms certainly fitted neatly into Peel's developing outlook. The depth of Peel's economic experience and judgment was leading to the conclusion that the enormous new importance of Britain's industrial and manufacturing sector, and the social instability threatened by a 'regression in manufactures', made expedient a critical revision of the existing apparatus of restrictive, discriminative and prohibitive tariffs which arguably had the effect of inhibiting industrial growth by making imported raw materials and semi-finished products dearer. Further, tariff barriers being erected by foreign governments against British industry could be reasonably counteracted only by removal or lowering of British tariffs on foreign produce. That this would tend to lower the price of foodstuffs could be seen as an additional 'social' bonus. The best argument against the Corn

1 N. Gash, *Sir Robert Peel* (1972), 302.   2 G to Peel, November 16, 1841. GP, 44527, 50.

Law was that it was bitterly resented by foreign wheat-producing countries which were markets for British industrial exports.

The peculiarly crucial role the Board of Trade would play in such a policy consisted in the simple fact that, of a total tax revenue (in 1840) of £47 million, £35 million came from customs and excise duties, with sugar, tea, tobacco, spirits, wine, timber, and coffee the principal items. Even allowing for the relatively restricted proportion of national wealth tapped by a mid-nineteenth-century government, a fiscal shift of such dimensions as Peel envisaged could be reasonably calculated to make ultimately a more than marginal contribution to alleviating what was becoming known as the 'Condition of England question'. Peel thought in terms of threefold approach to the question: first, a budget early in 1842 to set up the income tax (at 7d in the £) and start off the process of general tariff reductions; second, a new corn law later in the 1842 session to reduce substantially the existing scale against importation of corn; third, as soon as practicable later, a special provision to solve the vexed question of the sugar duties – vexed because they were entangled in problems of the vested interests of the West India producers, moral problems of slave-grown and cheaper foreign sugar, above all the problem that sugar was the largest single revenue-producer among the customs duties.

His auxiliary but indispensable part in these great transactions during 1842 gave Gladstone a considerable depth of economic experience and judgment. By the beginning of 1843 he could publish (anonymously) in the new *Foreign and Colonial Quarterly Review* (which he favoured because it replaced the defunct Tractarian *British Critic* as the organ of High Church principles) a masterly exposition, copious and authoritative, of the government's 'Course of Commercial Policy at Home and Abroad', in the form of a review of a series of new works on tariffs.[1] By then Peel had inaugurated his income tax and tariff policy in such a way as to enhance his reputation and prestige. The Corn Bill had caused much more trouble and aroused murmurs of resentment in his party at the sacrifices land was being asked to make by a government held by most of its supporters to be peculiarly the defender of the landed interest. Gladstone thus wrote at the optimum moment for the government's general economic strategy. Things would never look quite as promising again. The government fended off Whig efforts to exploit the corn issue in the 1843 session, and by the opening of the 1844 session, to all appearances, had the situation well in hand. But Peel's bid in that session to resolve the sugar problem, compounded by an earlier quarrel with a large body of his party over the Factory Bill and further exacerbated by the subterranean mood of persistent resentment about corn, ended in disaster. Finally, Peel forced his will on his party but the bonds of esteem and loyalty which in 1841 had

1 January 1843, pp. 222–273.

given him an unprecedented political ascendancy were irretrievably broken. Maynooth in 1845 virtually completed the process of divorce between Peel and the mass of the Conservative party. When corn was pushed forward again by the Irish famine in 1845, Peel almost eagerly took the opportunity to ram down the throat of his choking party the logical completion of his 1842 compromise. Thus in the end Peel got rather more of his policy of 1841 through than he could have anticipated; but his great instrument, the Conservative party, had broken apart in his hands.

In all this Gladstone remained unwaveringly loyal to his chief, even to the point of voting ultimately in favour of Peel's Maynooth policy. For Gladstone there was never a question of doubting the merits of Peel's case against that of his restless or mutinous party, even though he would on occasions advocate a less provocative means to the desired end. Gladstone was by nature prone to be psychologically vulnerable to the kind of benignly authoritative herculean high-mindedness so completely incarnated by Peel. He was prone also, as was Peel himself, to be by nature a 'man of government'. Though he confessed the religious action of the State to be 'crippled', he disavowed nothing of the high and authoritative character he urged for the State in his 1838 book. The sheer administrative grandeur of Peel's vision of the transmuting of economics into morals captivated Gladstone. It was from Peel, as of from a mighty alchemist of state, that Gladstone first learned the sublime art of turning the base metals of politics into gold. For this he would in the end resist the inner voice telling him of a 'perfect freedom' to be 'breathed in other air.' This new and exciting awareness imbued the exalted temper of the 'Course of Commercial Policy' article.

The great policy of Peel as expounded by Gladstone was to endeavour for the first time to 'apply general rules and reasons' to Britain's system of import duties. And these rules were now available for future inclusions not yet dealt with (Gladstone no doubt had butter, cheese and sugar primarily in mind) for which the 'simple and essential interests of the revenue' demanded temporary exemption. Prohibitory duties had been generally abolished. The great mass of raw materials and accessories of manufacture had been liberated from 'sensible charge'. There was now a new system of low duties on ores and metals. Timber, one of the items which had brought the Whigs to grief in 1841, was dealt with resolutely in the same spirit, despite the protests of Canadian and shipping interests. Foodstuffs were likewise relieved from charges tending to enhance their price. The necessities of life were raw materials to the extent that they entered into the costs of labour. The revised Corn Law of 1842 had reduced the duties on foreign corn by a half. Prohibitions on the importation of cattle and other food animals were removed. All fresh meats were now admissible. The duty on salt provisions for home consumption was reduced by a third to a half, and to such provisions was opened the victualling of the British merchant marine. Duties on vegetables and seeds were lowered to a half, or even a twelfth in the case of 'that important esculent, the potatoe'. On the other side of the economic equation, all *'great* articles of manufacture', excepting so far silk, were now admissible at much lower duties; and only in some minor articles of manufacture where there were problems with raw materials were rates kept as high as 30 per cent, but even so were considerably reduced. Prohibitions on the export of machinery, except in so far as regarded linen manufacture and the spinning of linen yarns, had been withdrawn. The export trade was generally relieved of small but mischievous burdens. There would be many new facilities for the employment of shipping in the colonial trade.

These 'late commercial changes', Gladstone pointed out, had been 'of such extent in themselves, and moreover so decidedly of a nature to indicate a determined and comprehensive purpose,' as to constitute a 'shock' to received notions of tariff policy. Gladstone was sufficiently Burkean to salute healthy prejudice – it would be 'an evil day for this country when its people have no prepossessions in favour of its laws' – but his argument was that new circumstances dictated new policies. The overwhelming testimonies to 'sharp and widely extended sufferings of the people in the manufacturing districts, with the stagnation and decrease of trade', and the grim evidence of 'their moral, their social, their spiritual condition', exposed the lack of imagination and insight of the 'high doctrinarians' from their theoretical models. Behind the government's 'determined and comprehensive purpose' was a philosophy of the beneficial 'growth of the processes of reciprocal dependence between nations', of the 'increasing measure of the interest felt by each in the commercial and material concerns of its neighbours', 'whereby benefits – benefits only of this world it is true, but yet in their proper place and nature real, if inferior benefits – are exchanged between the several families of the human race'.

The melancholy picture of the sufferings of labouring people, the afflictions of penury and want despite their 'dauntless spirit, their skilful fingers, their indefatigable arms', was the consequence of a loss of demand. How was this to be accounted for? Britain began the year 1843 with the home market – *'so far as that market depends upon the high scale of remuneration to the growers of agricultural produce and to the owners of the soil'* – in a flourishing condition. It was the 'paralysis of our foreign trade' which had been the cause of much of this distress. What had signally flourished in the home market was the high price of food; redress must come in the stimulation of 'beneficial exchange' in foreign trade on the principle of consenting 'to buy from other nations that which Providence has enabled them to give you upon better terms than you can give it yourselves'. The notion of an opposition between foreign and domestic trade was 'fictitious and delusive'. Because of Britain's great success and wealth as a manufacturing country she was more dependent than ever on reciprocity and interdependence. This remained true despite the retrogressive and deplorable tendencies towards protectionism in France, America, Russia, Spain, and despite the 'anti-commercial ideas' of Dr List in Germany. Britain herself, of course, had not been innocent in the past: 'We shall not here inquire whether the acts of our commercial policy have been defensible: we shall not examine, for example, whether the Corn Law of 1815 was or was not in error.'

But in reality the implication of Gladstone's arguments bore heavily on the merits of the Corn Law. He was well aware of the simmering resentment among the Conservative county members at the new cheap food policy. His article, indeed, aimed precisely at allaying and rebutting the notions beneath it. He recognised the problem of the welfare of agricultural labour. There was the 'old and vexed question of burdens on the land'. He knew that there were 'those who think that it has been the height of folly in Sir Robert Peel to make these changes, and to select such a period for their introduction'. (One such, indeed, was Gladstone's own father, for whom Huskisson represented the furthest limit of commercial liberalism.) On the other hand, Gladstone was scathing on the 'fanatics' who supposed that repeal of the Corn Laws would inaugurate a 'commercial millennium'. But the thrust of his argument was resolutely unapologetic. Where were the evidences of doom and disaster, ruin and collapse, so confidently prophesied during the 1842 session? 'Our great manufacturers have thriven under the . . . generally wholesome, stimulus of competition. We think it can hardly be said that of late years this principle has been brought sufficiently to bear upon the growers of agricultural produce.' Agriculture had large resources yet untapped in improvement and efficiency. The same principles were essentially applicable to both manufactures and agriculture. The growth of commerce and population would help agriculture.

Gladstone denied that he subscribed to any 'doctrinal optimism'. It was rather a matter of 'most plain and proximate utility', or really of 'iron necessity', that Britain should enter into general competition with the markets of the world. Peel, the colleague of Huskisson in 1825, had divined that severe distress among many sections of the working population had 'arisen from causes closely connected with our economical condition, and lying much nearer its foundations than any of our statutes'. No amount of 'wisdom or of courage in the work of legislation' could prevent the 'recurrence at intervals of distress analogous in its character'; but yet 'wisdom and courage were not precluded from doing something, from offering some contribution, towards the alleviation of that distress', and they 'dictated and required those changes in our tariff which Sir Robert Peel had carried into effect'. Clearly, for Gladstone, it was the moral dimension of Peel's policy which carried greatest weight. There was the setting of a great international example by not excluding from the benefits of the new arrangements even those countries whose simultaneous enactments of a hostile character caused Britain to suffer. Britain's capacity thus to offer international moral leadership crucially depended on the fact that the high place which Britain occupied as the first among the commercial nations of the world had been assigned to her in the order of providence, not by a 'fortuitous concurrence of events nor by any artificial or temporary combination of them', but as the 'natural and proper consequence of her possessing, in a superior degree, the elements of industrial greatness'; and not merely its physical elements, but its 'moral elements, resolution, energy, skill, perseverance, and good faith'. As if to leave no doubt in the public mind as to his authorship of the piece, Gladstone stressed that at the foundations of the great series of tariff changes lay the conviction that 'religion and Christian virtue, like the faculty of taste and the perception of beauty, have their place, aye and that the first place, in political economy, as the means of creating and preserving wealth'.

The 'Course of Commercial Policy' article was Gladstone's second major exercise in public propaganda. Formal anonymity allowed him greater scope for more forthright expression than would have been expedient in parliament. As such it marked a distinct point in the development of his mind. Certainly, protectionist hackles were roused: as he reported to Catherine, 'Morning Post don't like it at all'.[1] Gladstone was soon dismayed that 'so much misapprehension & suspicion' should be excited by it; and that it was 'impossible not to foresee' that he 'should be challenged upon its authorship'. For that reason he later refused even to read a manuscript on commercial policy sent to him by the *Foreign and Colonial* editor, the Rev. Dr. Worthington: free trade zealots like Charles Villiers were being 'inquisitive'.[2] For that reason Gladstone declined Worthington's proposal of another article for the July 1843 number. 'The very great & general depression in the prices of agricultural produce', he explained, 'has produced a degree of sensitiveness in the minds of those generally who are connected with the land at which I cannot feel surprise, but which disposes them very easily to take alarm at any expressions falling from a person in office which are in any degree capable of a construction that implies so much as the possibility of future relaxation in

1 G to CG, January 26, 1843. GGP, 28/2
2 G to Worthington, February 15, 1844. GP, 44527, 170.

our commercial code.' His January article had, Gladstone believed, tended from this cause to 'increase a prevailing sentiment of uncertainty growing out of fears on the one side and arts on the other, but very mischievious to the public interest'. Thus he was unwilling at this time to indulge 'in anything like freedom of discussion'. Gladstone was also unwilling to cover himself under the 'usual secrecy of writers'. He had deliberately in the January article 'wholly avoided' any attempt to 'foil' detection; but to use words which one *'knows'* will be misunderstood 'amounts to wilful mischief'.[1]

Exponents of free trade doctrine later cited the article as a revelation of a decisive degree of movement: a 'startling realization of the progress made by Mr. Gladstone during his year of office';[2] exhibiting 'more clearly than any of his speeches in Parliament the extraordinary progress of his mind . . . It is not too much to say that after a year's work at the Board of Trade Gladstone could not harbour another Protectionist thought.'[3] Putting aside the question-begging connotations of 'progress' as well as the fact that the tariff of 1842 still remained protectionist in principle and purpose, it still remains important to draw attention to the point that the movement of Gladstone's mind at this juncture was as much lateral as linear. He was certainly teaching himself to follow the line that would lead him to free trade; but equally he was learning the great lesson of reconciling his preoccupation with the religious conscience of the State with a growing awareness of the moral dimension of political economy. Gladstone made no comment on his reading in the summer of 1843 of Carlyle's *Past and Present*; nor is there any reason to suppose that he would have been vulnerable to its bullying rhetoric; but he could not have avoided recognising it as a 'sign of the times'. 'This is a time,' he told Catherine in August 1842, 'when we may reflect on the thorough rottenness socially speaking of the system which gathers together huge masses of population having no other tie to the classes above them than that of employment, of high money payment constituting a great moral temptation in times of prosperity, and the reductions in adversity which *seem* like robberies, and which the poor people have no discipline of training to endure.'[4]

[3]

Behind this triumphant affirmation of purposive government lay the

1 G to Worthington, April 21, 1843. *Ib.*, 125–26.
2 F. E. Hyde, *Mr Gladstone at the Board of Trade* (1934), 85.
3 F. W. Hirst, *Gladstone as Financier and Economist* (1931), 57.
4 Lathbury ii, 25.

problematic relationship of Conservative leadership and Conservative party. Peel, bred in the school of Pitt with its Chathamite and Shelburnian traditions of 'carrying on the king's government', looked on the Reform Act as having registered the end of the old system whereby the executive 'made' a House of Commons. What then, in the future, was to 'make' a Commons? Peel could not envisage, let alone desire, any notion about 'opinion' in the 'country' as embodied in 'party' being the ultimately legitimate maker of a Commons. Peel saw the role of party not as providing a programme but as embodying and representing the ability of the executive to make a Commons. As such, party was merely a consequence, not formatively the çause, of government. Peel accordingly wanted his party to be strong, aggressive, and resourceful in the country, but docile, self-effacing and obedient in the Commons. While out of office Peel had relatively few problems, one of them being, indeed, his dislike of the notion of being in 'opposition'. But once in office incompatibilities tended to reveal themselves. Peel's bidding was thus grossly contradictory; and his party not surprisingly displayed early symptoms of neurosis.

Peel's rationale was that only a strong executive could cope with financial deficit, economic depression, and social dislocation and the challenges to public order and parliamentary sovereignty being made 'out of doors' by the burgeoning Chartist and Anti-Corn Law movements. He insisted that the executive was in an incomparably better position to form a judgment on issues of public policy than any body of backbench parliamentarians. He refused to contemplate abdicating any degree of responsibility founded on that decisive advantage. His consistent pattern of response to party refractoriness was to exploit his immense personal ascendancy and face down disaffection by sheer weight of reputation. Peel was too shy and too proud to stoop to ingratiation or treat for popularity with his backbenchers. He never wavered in his confidence that the Conservative party needed him more than he needed the Conservative party. Any notion of sharing authority with his party Peel regarded as a betrayal of his trust with the Crown and as such unconstitutional. This kind of relationship would have been problematic enough for a government with modest and negative objectives. But Peel's turn in the direction of more ambitious notions of applying wisdom and courage in the work of legislation towards the alleviation of social distress added an enormous complication to an already sufficiently fraught relationship.

Gladstone had long been a shrewd observer of Peel's 'manifest and peculiar adaptation' to 'the age in which he lives, and its exigencies'. It was ironic that, by the end of 1841, Gladstone was, if anything, rather ahead of his chief in the matter of adaptation to the age. Gladstone's immense labours at the Board in the autumn of 1841 left him in no doubt about the dangerously retrogressive effect a maladjusted tariff system could have on manufacturing industry. On the vital and delicate subject of corn importation the Vice-President's view, on careful consideration of the evidence at first hand, was for a cautious and tentative but distinct abatement of the protective duty. He placed in Peel's hands in November 1841 a 'long paper' on the subject in which he advised a move in this sense. Gladstone was not as well aware of the fragility of the government's position in its particular relationship with its protectionist Conservative following as he might have been. He learned his lessons in trade and political economy at the Board immersed in a somewhat innocent detachment. But, if he was no longer quite the 'rising hope' of 1839, the Tories were no less stern and unbending and following reluctantly and mutinously. On the other hand Gladstone was much more sensitive to the larger problem of social order. The progress of the 'democratic principle, supervening upon a state of division and disorganisation in respect of Church Communion', as he told Christopher Wordsworth, worried him more than the 'dark and dubious' prospects of the connection between Church and State.[1] To Manning he wrote in 1843: 'You ask me, when will our Bishops govern the Church? My answer is by another query – when will anybody govern anything?'[2]

Early in 1842 Gladstone found occasion to reveal the degree to which his new convictions in the matter of corn had become less cautious and tentative. On January 10 he conferred with Peel 'on Tariff 4-6¼' ('Read "Plenary & Verbal Inspiration" by way of relaxation'). Peel on January 21 propounded to his colleagues his scheme for a revision of the tariff scale. Gladstone was 'so forward as to think it quite inadequate'.[3] 'The present law I am sorry to say appears to me to have been a very stringent & severe one.' He was impressed by Ripon's confession that the ministry had forced the 'celebrated amendment' to the law in 1827 despite having had the worst of the argument. He convinced himself that Peel 'would not be averse to abatement – but wishes to feel the pulse of the agricultural folks'.[4] In conversations with Ripon, Peel and Graham on February 2 Gladstone could see that all were 'aware the protection is greater than necessary'.[5] Gladstone rather let his new enthusiasm run away with him at a meeting with Peel, Ripon, Graham, Stanley and Granville Somerset on February 5. 'I hinted at retirement as being perfectly ready to adopt it if that could be done without perplexing the Government.' Peel was not surprisingly vexed with this jejune temperamentalism: 'so entirely taken

1 Lathbury, i, 60.
2 G. to Manning, August 14, 1843. GP, 44247, 166.
3 PMP, i, 74.   4 GP, 44819, 74–76.   5 *Ib.*, 76.

by surprise that he hardly knew what to say – he was thunderstruck.' He considered Gladstone to have consented to the scale he proposed on January 21; and anyway the extent of difference on which Gladstone was sticking 'seemed a small one – that it was impossible for everyone to have precisely that which he thought best'. Gladstone had a painful memory for the rest of his life of Peel's 'sulky displeasure' on this occasion.[1] He feared, with good reason, the Peel was 'much annoyed & displeased for he would not give me a word of help or of favourable suggestion as to my own motives & belief'. Gladstone wished he 'could have seen that he was at all soothed: he used nothing like an angry or unkind word, but the negative character of the conversation had a chilling effect on my feeble mind'. Gladstone went home 'well intimidated, and in very low dumps indeed',[2] '& told all to Catherine, my lips being to everyone else, as I said to Sir R. Peel, absolutely sealed'.[3] He was intensely relieved to note on February 7 that 'all was smooth & cordial today after the ruffle of Saturday at P's'.

In the debate early in the new session on the ministerial proposal for a revised Corn Law Gladstone rather redeemed himself on February 14 with a long and cogent statement of his departmental brief. He stressed the point that the existing law 'pressed with very considerable severity on the consumer'; and recommended the government's compromise scheme of a relaxed sliding scale as the least of the choice of evils available. The note of apology was perhaps too evident for good tactics. Certainly there was evidence of a lack of total conviction among ministers. Gladstone recorded Graham as saying to him: 'This measure [corn] is the Euthanasia of the Corn Law: if we can maintain it ten years I shall be satisfied: and then I trust that our agriculture will not want it.'[4] Possibly Gladstone's speech two days later rather overdid the delicate and dangerous theme of the 'noble sacrifice' being made by the agricultural classes in accepting the new graduated scale; especially as he underlined the point that the sacrifices were not more than 'the commercial and the general interests of the country' had a right to demand. Nor would the Conservative country members rejoice at Gladstone's eulogy of them as deserving consideration for exhibiting the same skill and energy 'as in our commercial and manufacturing greatness'. Nor would they be enchanted by Gladstone's argument that free trade would displace a vast mass of agricultural labour, and that the issue was not so much a landlord's question but more of a labourer's question. Nor was his rebuttal of the charge that the new law was 'but the precursor of ulterior change' very convincing.[5] Still, as an honest but

1 PMP, i, 74.   2 *Ib.*, 45–6.   3 GP, 44819, 77–79.
4 GP, 44819, 81 (March 7, 1842).
5 H, lxi, 374–79 (March 9, 1842).

not counter-productively candid argument of the government's case Peel would have every reason to be satisfied with Gladstone's effort. And, for his part, Gladstone was greatly impressed by Peel's tenacity in holding steadily to his compromise ground. On purely 'abstract considerations' Peel would have proposed a 'lower protection'; but the 'extraordinary sagacity of his parliamentary instinct' led him to the right point of equilibrium.[1]

The Conservative leader's ascendancy was as yet directly unchallengeable; but there was little chance in any case that the worst suspicions of the agricultural interest would fail to be excited in the circumstances of 1842. And Gladstone personally could not fail to become the focus of much of the disaffection so aroused. His role in the first great tariff revision and in the epochal budget of 1842 was so conspicuous. His handling of the intricacies of the tariff reductions was a parliamentary *tour de force*; and his success in persuading the Commons to sacrifice nearly one and a half millions of Customs revenue by reducing or abolishing duties on more than half the 1,200 articles on the tariff was the crucially essential prerequisite for the success of Peel's budgetary proposal to revive the income tax for three years at nearly three per cent, to cover both the tariff loss and the inherited deficit. Gladstone early exhibited the calloused temper of confident executive power ('Copper, Tin, Zinc, Salmon, Timber, Oil, Saltmeat, all are to be ruined, & all in arms').[2] He disposed unceremoniously of Monckton Milnes's Pontefract licorice manufacturing constituents ('the demands of your people as to amount of duty are very excessive').[3] John Gladstone had the pleasure of receiving from Peel in June 1842 a tribute to his son: 'At no time in the annals of Parliament has there been exhibited a more admirable combination of ability, extensive knowledge, temper and discretion.'[4] Perhaps it was Gladstone's conspicuous assiduity at Peel's right hand, passing up papers as the great man expounded his daring strokes of fiscal mastery, that led to Cobden's judgment at almost the same moment: 'Peel is a Free-trader, and so are Ripon and Gladstone. The last was put in by the Puseyites, who thought they had insinuated the wedge, but they now complain that he has been quite absorbed by Peel, which is the fact. Gladstone makes a very clever aide-de-camp to Peel, but is nothing without him.'[5] Perhaps Cobden had a sour memory of Gladstone's haughty refusal to debate with him at Walsall in 1840. Gladstone certainly would soon have a clearer perception of how 'worrying' Cobden was to become; and Cobden soon came into possession of a more accurate appreciation of Gladstone's capacity to be his own man.

1 GP 44819, 79.   2 D, iii, 187.
3 G to Milnes, May 24, 1842. GP, 44527, 79.
4 Hirst, 42–3.   5 J. Morley, *Life of Richard Cobden* (1879) 242.

The session of 1842 was decisive in establishing Gladstone's political reputation as an effective manager of a great department of state. This was purchased at spiritual cost. He lamented the deficiencies of his Lent 'in outward means'. 'I persuaded myself that I had not strength to spare.' It had its brilliant social side as well. The Gladstones were commanded to dine at Buckingham Palace in April – 'the whole machinery beautiful & the Queen gracious'. Gladstone dreaded the presentation, with memories crowding in of his trepidation with Keate at Eton and the Duke of Newcastle at Clumber.[1] Strict sabbatarian principle necessitated, however, a refusal to dine with the Archduke Frederick at the Austrian Embassy.[2] But in the end, despite the *éclat* of the government's success, the abidingly important fact of 1842 was that the disaffection of the bulk of its supporters remained persistently and ominously unappeased. In December, shortly after having commenced his celebratory and evangelistic 'Course of Commercial Policy' article, Gladstone fell in with Philip Pusey at the Carlton Club. Pusey told him 'that the county members had gone with Sir R. Peel to the very utmost point they could go with respect to corn: and that to speak plainly, if Sir R. Peel should become convinced that a further change was requisite, they considered that he ought to leave it to the Whigs to carry it, & resign accordingly'. The farmers, Pusey reported, were much disappointed with both the tariff and the corn bills, fearing large importations and falls in prices. They were also 'much alarmed from a notion that Peel is going to make some further change – from his having spoken of the present measure as an experiment'. Gladstone sturdily resisted these pressures, avowing himself 'very glad' at Peel's statement that 'laws of this kind were not Magna Charta, they were in their nature mutable', due regard being had 'to the increasing pressure of the population upon the production of food'. Gladstone's position was that the law could survive with good harvests; but a bad or late harvest with prices driven up would be fatal to it: 'the people had been sadly ground down by the high prices of provisions for the last four years & I was convinced they would not bear it again.' He lamented agricultural distress, and said 'it seemed to me the fall in prices proceeded & mainly from the poverty of the people, not from the Tariff'. As to Sir Robert, Gladstone quite stiffly rejoined that the Prime Minister would of course 'be governed by his convictions of what might be requisite for the safety & well-being of the country in judging hereafter of the question whether the law ought to be maintained or not and so it was clear he ought to be, independently of the further question what course he ought personally to take as to remaining in office'.[3]

1 D, iii, 192.
2 *Ib.*, 242.
3 *Ib.*, 244.

[4]

The vast issues of the reformation of public life involved in the budget, the income tax, the new tariff, the revised Corn Law, insensibly drew Gladstone into a new frame of view as to what he defined in his Lenten rumination of March 1842 as the 'prospective objects' of his continuation in public employment. The faintness of his hopes about adjusting the relations between Church and State faded even further in the new light being radiated by the moral and religious power immanent in political economy properly understood. Still, the residue of the old commitment remained stubbornly intact. There was, specifically, the question of Maynooth. Gladstone had occasion in October 1841 to recall his earlier 'disapprobation of the original principle of the grant' and his vote against it in the Commons. However, problems of reconciling disapproval in principle with the 'strength of that equitable claim wh seems to me to have grown up since 1795', transmitted through the hand of many ministries '& of some peculiarly conscientious ministers', had led to his inability on the last occasion to bring himself to 'resist the grant when it was proposed by a Govt wh I did not support'; and he could not 'with consistency have accepted the office under the present administration which to my knowledge or full persuasion intended to renew the proposal, if I had meant on a future occasion to alter my course in this respect'.[1] Thus Gladstone voted for the renewal of the grant to the Irish seminary at Maynooth in July 1842, 'reluctant but convinced'.[2]

Such a vote at least had the merit of public courage; for it was indeed in early July 1842 that his sister Helen's Romanism burst forth in public scandal. Gladstone spoke with his father on May 26 about Oak Farm 'and Helen's proceedings as to Romish worship.' The 'stunning & awful announcement' of the 'lamentable visitation' of Helen's perversion was received by Gladstone on May 30. The catastrophe provoked from him a letter 'keen & piercing' ('This delusion is not your first. . . You are living a life of utter self-deception. Not in religion alone, but in all bodily and mental habits').[3] 'I write, as one would drag a woman by the hair, to save her from drowning.' There was a very painful interview between brother and sister on June 11, following Gladstone's reading a letter to their father from Dr. Wiseman. Gladstone adopted the attitude he would in substance maintain for the rest of Helen's life: that her behaviour was not spiritually honest. 'The source of your malady is not religious', he informed her. 'It is private will.'[4] Did Gladstone take up this ungenerous stance from a guilty sense of responsibility for having led Helen along a path of danger and temptation? His meticulously

1 G to Lord, October 8, 1841. GP, 44527, 37.   2 D, iii, 213–4.
3 Magnus, 59.   4 Checkland, 330.

precise memorandum of their conversation on 11 June was in effect an exercise in self-exculpation. This was the theme also of his correspondence with Wiseman. Certainly in the family there was a strong sense – expressed pointedly by Tom – that William was blameable. He wanted their father to cast his errant daughter out of his house. But old John had not his youngest son's fanaticism. He depended on Helen and felt a kind of compassion for her. William noted with quite uncompassionate regret that his father's 'flinching' had sacrificed peace for himself and 'humanly speaking' all hope for Helen. John resented William's hectoring; and William felt 'the vital principle being expelled from all our relations'. John made no secret of his feeling that William's attitude to Helen was one of 'over-refinement, scrupulosity, or uncharitableness'; the latter no doubt partly because of William's resolution to 'limit poor Helen's intercourse with our children'. At a new height of public triumph Gladstone tasted the bitterness of family discord. And as a consequence of his father's weakly adopting this 'fatal course' of indulgence Helen appeared at the dinner table at No. 6 Carlton Gardens and startled poor Sir Stephen Glynne by 'asking if there were not 4,000 Puseyite Clergymen in the Church of England!'[1]

Helen's rebarbative talent for calculated indiscretions was the least of William's troubles. There were others asking the same awkward question – but from Protestant motives. Gladstone's public reputation was severely compromised by his sister's lapse. There were many who saw Helen as a victim of her brother's crypto-Romanism. There were others who scented danger of a different kind. Manning wrote on July 10: 'I can have no rest till I write to you to be assured, one way or the other, respecting a paragraph I have this moment seen in the Oxford Herald. To be abrupt – it states that Miss Gladstone has been received by Dr. Wiseman in the Roman Church, at Birmingham. I forebear all expressions – which may be needless – and only ask, as a privilege of our friendship, a few words from you.'[2] Gladstone replied immediately that the report was only too true; that the 'visitation' to the family was 'greater, even than you would suppose'; that he could not write for lack of time and that he would 'shrink from it' even if he could.[3] Gladstone was 'still groaning under Helen's case' at the end of 1842. 'I do not accuse myself: except for not having set her a better example.'[4]

Groanings under Helen's case were no doubt exacerbated by grim news of Oxford opinions. A report on the 'general view of the ulterior section of the Oxford writers and their friends' in July 1842 he found 'startling'. They looked 'not merely to the renewal and development of the Catholic idea within the pale of the Church of England: but seem to

1 D, iii, 208, 277.   2 GP, 44247, 142.
3 *Ib.*, 145.   4 D, iii, 248.

consider the main condition of that development and of all health (some tending even to say of all life) to be reunion with the Church of Rome as the See of Peter'. All this was indeed 'matter for very serious consideration'.[1] On top of this Gladstone reeled under two further personal blows in 1842. In September, shooting partridge near Hawarden, his unorthodox method of reloading one barrel while the other was at full cock led to the shattering of the forefinger of his left hand. A five-minute operation at Hawarden removed the remains. 'I have hardly ever in my life had to endure serious bodily pain: this was short.'[2] There was of course occasion for self-rebuke and mortification, particularly as Catherine was pregnant and within three weeks of confinement. She displayed a 'fortitude equal to her tenderness'. Gladstone displayed a formidable recuperative fortitude. After sleeping well he spent the following day reading 'Church Intelligence', including the Bishop of Chester's recent Charge, Dryden's *Maiden Queen*, and Southey's *Sir Thomas More*. He concluded that Samuel Warren's novel *Ten Thousand a Year* with 'humour & interest' had 'more heart & *positive* good (thus distinguished from Dickens who is but negative) than any book of the kind I know'. He read also that season Macaulay's *Lays of Ancient Rome*: 'liked them very much.' The second blow fell in November. His old patron, the Duke of Newcastle, bankrupted by injudiciously ambitious purchases of land on borrowed money, was obliged to put his affairs in the hands of trustees. Lincoln spoke to Gladstone of his difficult children, '& of his father's ruin – which he meets with a truly English heart'.[3] It would not be long before Lincoln's marital problems also became acutely critical. The one great compensation for Gladstone in all this scene of woe and anxiety was the birth on October 18 of a daughter, christened Agnes, 'large, with dark hair, deep blue eyes, & lungs strong enough for two months old'. In his retrospect of his thirty-third year he could not find much comfort in the 'enigma' of his soul: 'Is it single and true in its self exposure & self renunciation before God? Or is its inward life toward Him a tissue of self-deceit?' Yet he found his 'public acts' a 'comfort in that I believe that they are honest before God however poor'.[4]

[5]

The new session opened in 1843 under the shadow of the murder of Peel's private secretary, Drummond, shot by a Scottish lunatic in mistake

1 *Ib.*, 216.
2 Thereafter G habitually wore a black finger-stall over the stump: 'the family noticed that this minor, but very visible, disability was never used against him by cartoonists' (MRDF).
3 D, iii, 240.   4 *Ib.*, 248–49.

for Peel himself. Ministers had no ambitious plans for the session. The general disposition was to let things consolidate after the exertions of 1842. Corn was best left alone. As Graham had remarked to Peel in December, 'the next change must be the last'; and 1843 was too soon for a decisive alteration to 'open trade'. It would be sufficient meanwhile to fend off Whig pressure for a low fixed rate. Tariff relaxation could be continued, with consideration of delicate matters of colonial preference. There were embarrassing problems about an unforeseen gap between the tariff reductions of the last session and the first instalment of the new income tax. Gladstone would be busy enough. 'I rather comfort myself,' he told Catherine, 'that in writing daily I have spoken to you longer than I should have done if you had been here.'[1] There were worries about India, with Ellenborough committing the government to ambitious and aggressive policies. The condition of the labouring population continued to exercise Peel; and Graham had ready a Factory Bill to improve conditions and provide educational facilities for children. Ireland promised to be troublesome, with O'Connell's Repeal movement beginning to look formidable. Graham and Stanley, like the former Whigs they were, were keen on a policy of educational concessions to Roman Catholics. 'As to Maynooth,' as Graham put it to Stanley, 'if it were not for Protestant feeling, the last thing I would refuse to the Catholics should be money.' It was a measure of Gladstone's enhanced political reputation that his 'scruples' and hesitations on this matter should have been thought a major obstacle.[2] Peel in any case inclined towards proving that O'Connell could be firmly outfaced before offering concessions.

It was gratifying to Gladstone that Peel should now have raised with him for the first time the question of Church affairs – giving him a mass of 'difficult and interesting papers to read on these questions of Church property, of which my head is now full', as he reported to Catherine – even if in the form of Peel's dissatisfaction with the Church's management of its estates, and consequent impairment of its pastoral efficiency among a spiritually deprived populace. Gladstone, nervous of Peel's impatience with clerical ways, pleaded for the Church to be allowed to work from her own means rather than from the 'secularising & demoralising system' of a public grant. He assured Peel that it would be in his power not only to make the present system tolerable 'but to call forth a great amount of sympathy from the best friends of Church', among whom Gladstone cited Hope and Manning as valuable specimens whence much aid could be got in such a cause. Peel, characteristically, was not convinced, thinking religion far too serious a matter to be left to *dévots*. He tried to get included in the Speech opening the new session a

1 G to CG, January 26, 1843. GGP, 28/2.
2 C. S. Parker, *Life of Sir James Graham* (1907), i, 358.

statement that it was desirable to 'notice the question of increased pastoral care', with particular reference to improved management of Church estates. It took the Archbishop of Canterbury's distinct unresponsiveness, with Stanley 'somewhat keenly' in support, to scupper Peel's initiative. Gladstone was hoping to turn the occasion to advantage by getting money for new bishoprics in under-episcopalised northern industrial areas. He was the more agitated about this issue in that the current scheme for doing this involved the amalgamation of the two ancient bishoprics of North Wales, Bangor and St. Asaph, which raised distressing memories of callous Whig policy in Ireland in the 1830s. Gladstone did not fail to make known to Peel and to Graham his *'desire'* that one of these historic sees should not be sacrificed.[1] The challenges of the time to episcopal authority were alarming: 'we live in a state of things when the masses are so possessed not only with prejudice but with self-opinion that they will not allow their appointed teachers to instruct them in the truth;' and it was distressing to calculate the extent to which the 'whole power of the episcopate would be but in peril if our spiritual fathers were to speak with the unrestrained and apostolic freedom of our relaxed state as to doctrine discipline and life which is needed in order to restore their tone'.[2]

Property and bishoprics were among 'many Church matters' Gladstone discussed with Manning at this time. But more painfully immediate was the 'whole subject of the practicality of any measure to arrest the inclination to Romanise, or at least to disclaim all disposition either to encourage it or to treat it as a light evil'. Gladstone had a notion of a 'solemn assurance' to the Archbishop of Canterbury; but Manning thought this 'excessive': it would encourage the evil by making it seem too important.[3] Otherwise sessional affairs kept Gladstone sufficiently busy: this was why, as he explained to Catherine who remained up at Hawarden, 'I am *hard* about absence'. He worried moreover that Catherine was not keeping herself warm enough. 'Sleeping alone at No.13 *I* do not find two doubled blankets & a counterpane too much.' Had Catherine ever thought of replacing her silk sheets with cotton? 'There is no chill in getting into them.' As for communication: 'You know I never have any political gossip.' Catherine might well find his letters 'shabby'; but, as he assured her on Thursday, January 19, 'I have not yet been able to find time to read some that came for me on Tuesday'.[4] There was much ado with the problems at the School of Design and its director, William Dyce (Gladstone consulted Mr. Etty); coinage designs were

1 GP, 44819, 85–6, 91.
2 G to Worthington, May 19, 1844. *Ib.*, 44527, 177.
3 G to CG, January 17 and 18, 1843. GGP, 28/2.
4 G to CG, January 19, 1843. *Ib.*

always a great problem; and an even greater problem was Signor Pistrucci's project for a Waterloo medal. On the social side he was busy enough as well: 'I dine at 22 Bedford Square tomorrow – have sent them a brace of pheasants. Monday the Duchess of Beaufort. Wedy the Gold-smiths' Company. Wednesday week Peel, stuck up party.' Catherine could thus feel reassured that William was getting enough to eat. 'My Aunt,' he reported, 'has made me a delightful little stall' for his finger stump, 'or as my Father calls it (with *great* anxiety that it should be the right shape etc.) stool!' Domestic difficulties had to be coped with at both ends. At the London end John Gladstone was conducting an epic quarrel with the painter Bradley about his portrait; and there was the great scandal of his under-butler stealing and selling forty-four pounds of used candles. John flinched from prosecution (he had just paid the man fourteen guineas for half a years' wages); but William and Helen urged him on. There was also the awkward difficulty of giving the ass which supplied the milk for the children enough exercise in London; and getting the creature back to Hawarden was equally fraught. Gladstone much missed the 'ass-wisdom of Bill Williams', the Hawarden servant.[1]

The parliamentary briefs which kept Gladstone so occupied were to defend an income tax of which he disapproved and a Corn Law which he deemed quite excessive. This he did with appropriate aggression, tempered only by reflections on the 'melancholy feature' of the social state of the country: increased distress and privation on one hand and accumulation of wealth and luxuriousness on the other. It was possibly these reflections which led him on February 13 to stumble over the 'main question' upon which all attention was really 'concentrated': the Corn Law. In the course of refuting the Whig case for a fixed duty instead of a scale of duties varying according to the rise and fall of prices, Gladstone observed rather carelessly, as Peel unavailingly tried to gesture him into discretion, that there was one particular answer to that observation, which appeared to be of itself conclusive, 'although I admit it is conclusive only as a temporary measure'. At this point Gladstone was interrupted by ironic cheers.[2] He confusedly pressed on to explain his point, only to stumble further into indiscretion. For the next few days Gladstone's 'temporary' was hunted joyfully like a hare or a fox by the baying opposition.[3] Peel had much ado to smooth things over and soothe the country Tories.

Gladstone had even more ado to soothe himself. It was alleged that he had been supposed to 'play with the question' and 'prepare the way for a departure from the Corn Law of last year': and he was sensible that he so far lost his head 'as not to put well together the various, & if taken

1 G to CG, January 20, 23, 27, 1843. *Ib.*
2 H, lxvi, 496.   3 *Ib.*, 610, 741, 771.

separately conflicting considerations, which affect the question'. Though the new law had 'more of the slide in it (practically)' than Gladstone at the time thought necessary, he was not prepared to part from it 'as in the nature of a settlement for a period at least'. But it so happened that besides this he spoke 'under the influence of a new & most sincere conviction, having reference to the circumstances of recent legislation abroad – to the effect, that it would not be wise to displace British labour for the sake of cheap corn, without the counteracting & sustaining provisions which beneficial exchange ... not distorted by tariffs all but prohibitory, would supply'. This was, it was clear to Gladstone, 'a slippery position for a man who does not think firmly in the midst of ambiguous & diverse cheering – and I did my work most imperfectly, but I do not think dishonestly. Sir R. Peel's manner, by negative signs, showed that he thought either my ground insecure or my expressions dangerous.'[1]

It was a relief to go away to Nuneham for Easter after a week in which it had been impossible to get to church. Lent once more had not been satisfactorily severe. Gladstone broke off his 'semifast' 'on account of my strength, admonished by signs. The night work of Parlt requires much physical support; a true but slippery doctrine.' Easter Monday was notable for meeting Newman '& conv. *on the road*'. But back in London a persistent mood of misunderstood rectitude and injured innocence no doubt contributed to Gladstone's snappish snub to J.L. Ricardo on April 25 when, nettled by an interruption from the free trade nephew of the late economic sage, Gladstone retorted in accents of impeccable Toryism that the people of this country were not favourable to abstraction in political science or in commercial regulations. He took the opportunity with zest on May 9 to redeem himself with a forthright assault on the Cobdenite Villiers' annual motion against the Corn Law. Why should corn not get protection? It was not enough for Cobden to allege that our great manufacturing interests did not want it. Even the linen industry asked for protection. The revised tariff was still a generally protective tariff, with corn likewise dealt with. And there were gross exaggerations of hardship. The wants of the people were not to be compared with an abstract state of perfection, but with what it was at former times, when wheaten bread was unknown, and not only in Ireland and Scotland. The present law deserved a 'fair trial on its merits'.[2] Gladstone noted gratefully that both Peel and the Secretary of the Treasury were 'pleased with my long dull speech on Corn'.[3]

Peel indeed was very pleased with so competently deployed a departmental brief. He had, also, a problem of cabinet reconstruction on

1 D, iii, 264–65.
2 H, lxix, 58–75 (May 9, 1843).   3 GP, 44819, 91.

his hands. Vesey Fitzgerald, the President of the India Board, was dying. Ripon wanted to succeed Fitzgerald, or to have the reversion of any cabinet place vacated by Fitzgerald's successor. With Gladstone in virtual command of the Board of Trade, Ripon was anxious to dispense with a rather fictitious reponsibility. Fitzgerald died on May 11. Gladstone made no reference to this sad event in his diary, perhaps because he was preoccupied with the distressing case of his former underhousemaid who was being committed for trial at the Old Bailey for theft. ('God forgive me if by any neglect she may have been led into this misery.') His plea for mercy got her off with a light sentence. The social round was also at this moment rather intense. There was dinner with John Gladstone and then an evening party and music at home on the 11th; on Friday the 12th there was dinner at the Archbishop of York's and then to Lady Wicklow's in Cavendish Square. Meanwhile Peel's dispositions slotted in smoothly. He consulted the Queen immediately and offered Ripon the vacant India Board. On 13 May Gladstone received Peel's letter offering him the Presidency of the Board of Trade with a place in cabinet.

Characteristically, Gladstone's first move was to compse a memorandum for use in discussion with Peel later that day, listing the obstacles to his accepting the offer. When Peel received Gladstone there were preliminary compliments. Gladstone thanked Peel for the 'indulgent manner in which he had excused my errors and more than appreciated any services I might have rendered'. Protesting that he had gone to the Board of Trade 'without knowledge or relish', Gladstone declared that he was happy to stay in his present position where he had come to enjoy his work and had all the responsibility he desired. Peel spoke 'most warmly of service received', discounted any 'personal considerations', and insisted that his proposal was 'obviously the right arrangement'. Then Gladstone announced that it was his duty to examine his mind about some questions 'coming closer home than others as involving matter of principle & of character'. As to opium, Peel pointed out that immediate power and responsibility lay with the East India Company; but that in any case it was a 'minor subject' compared with other imperial issues constantly demanding attention. As to Gladstone's reservations about educational matters Peel was doubtful if they could be carried through the House anyway. Peel spoke of the 'compromises and adjustments of opinion necessary to ensure the co-operation of a Cabinet composed of any fourteen men', citing the example of the Duke of Wellington's having 'surrendered his opinion' on the American boundary question, '& added that his own individual sentiments were not favourable to the present Corn Laws'.

When Gladstone in his 'simplicity or silliness' brought up the point he imagined would be of least difficulty, the North Wales bishoprics, Peel responded that that was a 'more serious matter', as involving a 'practical course'. Gladstone explained that his main anxiety was not a sentimental attachment to the sees because they were ancient, but from the 'connection of the question with that of the increase of episcopal supervision in general', and that since 'the health of the nation depended in great part on the operation of the Church upon the lower class' it was to his mind a matter of 'very great magnitude'. 'Much was said', as we may well believe, on this topic. Gladstone asked for time to consider his position. Hope and Manning were both out of town, and consultation was essential. 'I have to consider with God's help by Monday whether to enter the Cabinet, or to retire altogether: at least such is probably the second alternative.'[1]

On Sunday, May 14 Gladstone divided his devotions between Holy Communion at St. Martin-in-the-Fields in the morning and St. James's, Piccadilly, in the afternoon. In between he wrote to Hope and came to a view of his problem which gave him 'satisfaction'. In the occurrence of the 73rd Psalm among the services of that day Gladstone saw 'another of those minute but striking Providential adjustments' which he had often had occasion to remark. The case of the prophet, wounded by diffidence, but prevailing in a temptation because knowledge of God's purpose gave him the means of victory, was indeed appositely construable. That evening Gladstone addressed his servants on the case of the poor underhousemaid.

On the Monday morning Gladstone conferred with Hope and Manning 'which led to some variation of my view of yesterday, but sent me still with a settled mind & judgement to Peel – where I explained & accepted'. Then off to relay the great decision to Catherine and father. Gladstone attended his first cabinet that day, at which it was decided that since Repeal meetings in Ireland involved no breach of the peace there was no case for interference. To Manning that day Gladstone wrote: 'I am in. I made the statements I believe exactly according to what passed between us, & no difficulty presented itself. Remember that my perils are increased. . .'[2] Gladstone impressed upon Peel the strong feelings held within the Church; and that he would never go against those feelings. He envisaged the possibility of 'the evil of hostility between the Govt. & the Church'. 'I told him in evidence of the strength of my feeling upon that subject, that I had in my own mind contemplated the resignation of my seat as well as my office, in case the misfortune should happen to me of separating from him on a question of that sort.' For, if the present administration came to a breach with the Church, Gladstone was sure, 'her battle is hardly to be fought against them in Parliament. Her warfare

1 GP, 44819, 92–3.
2 G to Manning, May 15, 1843. GP, 44247, 160.

must be withdrawn, it seems to me, from the places of this world, to more appropriate scenes where the Heavenly Door can never cease to overhang her banners and where her victory is assured.' Peel soothed Gladstone with more compliments about not recollecting 'any former instance of a single vacancy in a Cabinet, on which there was an entire concurrence', and assured him that on the bishoprics question 'in practice no obstacle or uneasiness would arise'.[1]

Cabinets were full of Irish and Indian affairs. There were problems about Graham's Factory Bill, the Dissenters objecting strongly to its educational clauses giving the Church the privilege of teaching the factory children. Peel decided to drop the bill for the present session. Gladstone stuck to his old Board of Trade last. Before long he was back to the dreary task of trying to convince the rightly distrustful Tory rank and file that the government was to be trusted on the Corn Law. Answering Lord John Russell, Gladstone animadverted indignantly on that 'fertile theme' which was being exploited as a 'weapon of attack on the Government', namely, 'the supposed intention of the Government to abandon the present law, and be guilty of double-dealing with the farmers'.[2] That, together with a defence of the differential duty to benefit 'free' sugar and the introduction of a Coal Whippers Bill to emancipate the colliers in the Port of London from the system of being employed casually in gangs recruited by publicans, was about the sum of Gladstone's direct parliamentary responsibilities for the remainder of the session.

As the session dragged its weary way along, Gladstone grew weary with it. The second act of the Fall of the House of Pelham-Clinton added a further burden of distress. At the end of May Lincoln disclosed to Gladstone his 'domestic situation': his wife (a daughter of the Duke of Hamilton but, perhaps more relevantly, a grand-daughter of Beckford of Fonthill) was starting on the wayward career that would lead to her pregnancy by Lord Walpole in 1849, her divorce in 1850, and her marriage to Monsieur Opdebeck, of Brussels, in 1860. 'In a long conversation I was almost stunned by the view he gave me.'[3] Lincoln named Gladstone one of the guardians of his children. At a cabinet on July 25 the vexed issue of religious instruction in schools drove from Gladstone's usually highly alert mind the fact that it was his wedding anniversary.

There were, also, certain delicate domestic issues at Hawarden. Gladstone's role as father of the putative heir-presumptive gave rise to awkwardness. Misapprehension that he was the lord of the manor was already widely received. He joked uneasily to Catherine: 'The Morning Post of today actually made Stephen visit himself at Hawarden Castle!'[4] And already Henry Glynne at the Rectory was taking steps on behalf of

1 GP, 44819, 96.   2 H, lxix, 1476–79 (June 13, 1843).
3 D, iii, 284.   4 G to CG, January 13, 1844. GGP, 28/2.

his sense of family. In August 1843 Gladstone was taken aback by indications of Henry's matrimonial intentions. 'Certainly any one that could conquer Henry could conquer Gibraltar.' Gladstone professed himself not surprised should Stephen arrive in London announcing the 'catastrophe'.[1] The intended was George Lyttelton's sister Lavinia. Gladstone lightened the atmosphere with badinage for Catherine: 'I use the carriage almost every day more or less – dine on mutton chops – & have the shower bath three mornings in the week.' 'On Thursday when I came home for my mutton chops. . .' He yearned for release. 'I could almost jump out of my skin, as the saying is, at the thought of freedom! A boy's vacation is nothing to it.'[2] On Saturday, August 12, Gladstone felt 'quite tired & good for nothing' and in the evening went off to Astley's theatre and circus. He was amused by wonderful feats of strength and agility but not by the 'wretched farce' that followed. Peel's outlining of the formidable agenda for 1844 must have been in itself rather exhausting. Peel 'spoke out very freely about commercial matters', declaring that were he not 'hampered by party considerations' he would propose a new Corn Law uniting the fixed with the sliding principle at a much lower rate. The revenue showed such little elasticity that, unless there was a great improvement during the coming autumn, 'some further great operation' would be necessary next session. Income tax must be extended for five years; and he hinted it would be well if it were raised to five per cent. 'Cotton, Wool and Sugar duties must at all events be dealt with next year – and also Silk.' Some further efforts to relieve trade might also be necessary; and 'that if an increase in the income tax were found requisite it must be combined with relief to the consumer'.[3]

Hopes of an early release were sadly disappointed by this press of business; 'but the consolation is that it is one's duty.'[4] At last by late August the Gladstones arrived thankfully at Fasque, where William spent seven weeks relaxing with Catherine and the children, riding, walking, playing whist, music, and shooting once more. John Gladstone, though troubled with decaying sight and hearing, continued alert and formidable, engaged in heavy polemics against the Free Church seceders from the Church of Scotland and heavy investment in railway stocks. Somewhat to William's embarrassment, his father was also at this time deep in controversy against the 'corn repeal mania'. His assets in 1843 totalled over £600,000. The children were generously provided for. William, along with the other younger brothers, had an annual allowance of £2,000; and in 1843 an additional provision of £15,000 was added to the trust managed by Robertson. Gladstone's brooding over Church affairs

1 G to CG, August 2, 1843. *Ib.*
2 G to CG, August 11, 12, 17, 1843. *Ib.*
3 D, iii, 308–9.   4 G to CG, August 18, 1843. GGC, 28/2.

during September led to another article, published in the *Foreign and Colonial Quarterly Review* in October: 'Present Aspect of the Church'. In this Gladstone distinguished between the 'spurious and morbid' and the 'legitimate powers & tendencies' of the Oxford Tractarians. The scandal of Helen clouded its pages. Ironically, that very month of October would see the crucial point of the beginning of the end of Newman as an Anglican.

The Fasque interlude ended in mid-October with Henry Glynne's marriage to Lavinia Lyttelton in St. George's, Hanover Square. 'May every blessing rain down upon them.' Did the thought of a Glynne heir to Hawarden pass through William's and Catherine's minds?

In any case there were soon to be more compelling and burdensome distractions. Gladstone had been painfully startled in 1842 by new insights into the 'ulterior section' of the Tractarian party. Since then Pusey had been suspended from preaching at Oxford. Now came the news, via Manning, that Newman had resigned his cure at St. Mary's, Oxford, because of the 'general repudiation' of *Tract XC* by the Church. Gladstone registered 'pain and dismay'. 'May God restrain and confirm his steps: they seem to waver. He has considerably weakened his powers for good: they remain great for mischief: but we may yet trust he will not be abandoned.'[2] To Manning Gladstone wrote that he read Newman's letter with 'a heavy heart'. How could one wonder at Newman's difficulties in restraining some of his followers from lapsing into Romanism when his own foundations were so apparently 'undermined'? Gladstone was persuaded that this 'powerful man' had suffered much in the healthful tone of his judgment from 'exclusiveness of mutual habit, and from affections partly wounded through cruelty, partly overwrought into morbid action from gloating as it were continually & immediately upon the most absorbing and exciting subjects'. 'The Newman of 1843 is not the Newman of 1842, nor is he of 1842 the same with him of 1841'; and 'how different, how far drifted down', were any of these from the Newmanism of the early Tracts, which indeed it always appeared to Gladstone were 'even too jealous of the suspicion of Romanism, too free in the epithets of protest and censure'. Gladstone found it 'frightful' to reflect upon the fact that such a man as Newman was – for was it not so? – wavering in his allegiance 'upon any ground so impalpable as what he terms the general repudiation of the view contained in tract 90': for it was the manner and the language, not the substance, of that tract which gave offence.[3]

But worse was to come four days later. Another letter from Newman to Manning, forwarded to Gladstone, announced Newman's conviction,

1 D, iii, 319.   2 *Ib.*, 321.
3 G to Manning, October 24, 1843. GP, 44247, 171.

held since the summer of 1839, that the Church of Rome was the Catholic Church, and the Church of England not a branch of the Catholic Church because not in communion with Rome. Newman's 'alarms' had been revived recently by the Jerusalem bishopric project. He was now 'relieved of a heavy secret'. Gladstone's first thought, as he wrote to Manning, was 'I stagger to & fro like a drunken man, & am at my wit's end'. But even out of the 'enormity of the mischief' Gladstone could still detect a 'gleam of consolation'. Newman had been waiting under this fatal conviction for four or five years; 'he has waited probably in the hope of its being changed – perhaps he may still wait – & God's inexhaustible mercy may overflow upon him & us'. What Newman termed a conviction was, perhaps, 'not a conclusion finally reached in his mind, but one which he sees advancing upon him without the means of resistance or escape'.

All this was 'sad enough, and more than enough'. But Newman must be helped with means of resistance or escape, if only, Gladstone was convinced, to make his conduct *'honest'*. Newman's descriptions of himself in his transactions with the Church authorities since 1839 was *'as it stands thus* frightful: forgive me if I say it, more like the expressions of some Faust gambling for his soul, than the records of the inner life of a great Christian teacher'. Gladstone could not therefore 'take this letter as it stands to be his'. All the more important was it then for Manning to redouble his efforts to prevent the catastrophe.[1]

The threat of Newman's defection Gladstone counted as the 'greatest crisis & the sharpest that the Church has known since the Reformation'. It would be the apostasy of 'a man whose intellectual status is among the very first of his age, and who has indisputably headed the best movement & the nearest to the seat of life that the Church has known for at least two centuries'.[2] 'Northcote has an alarming rumour,' Gladstone reported to Catherine, 'that a meeting of the Romanizing party has been held at Oxford & that about seventeen were going over. I do not think this carries the semblance of being very likely: & may God grant it may prove wholly baseless.'[3] On November 7 Gladstone received Hope, Manning and Frederic Rogers to what must have been a rather fraught dinner. Manning had shown Newman's letters to a 'grieved & shocked' Pusey.[4] Hope, shattered, was inclined to 'withdraw from active interposition: not in itself a cheering sign: but he has in view a scheme for an institution for charity & selfdenial', a 'refuge for the Houseless', a 'design full of spiritual benefits'.[5] Another letter from Newman to Manning which Gladstone sent to Catherine ('remember it is strictly secret & send it back to me by

1 G to Manning, October 28, 1843. *Ib.*, 175.
2 G to Manning, October 30, 1843. *Ib.*, 179.
3 G to CG, November 9, 1844. GGP, 28/2.
4 D, iii, 325.   5 *Ib.*, 324, 330.

return post') removed 'immediate alarm' but confirmed 'that which is ulterior'. 'But it is melancholy to see so great a mind pressed in such a manner: it is however the letter of a great man.'[1] Gladstone made his own plea to Newman. Hope's doubts about the efficacy of 'active interposition' with Newman were well-founded: Newman's message was that Gladstone's arguments convinced him of the ' "Hope*less*ness"' of meeting the views of a class of persons whom he much respected'.[2] Gladstone was pleasantly surprised that Newman took his letter so kindly ('so like the operation of a clumsy bungling surgeon, upon a sensitive part')[3].

[7]

These were appropriately wintry thoughts. (Gladstone informed Catherine that he had 'mounted a new great coat which is expected to meet your approbation'.) Preparation for the 1844 session plunged Gladstone back into public affairs amid such a scene of gloom and impending disaster on the Church side. Domestic life at Carlton Gardens offered busy distractions. There were new bookcases to be arranged ('a critical matter'). George Richmond's portrait of Catherine was now completed (the account was for £36.15s). After a laborious day at the Board of Trade he unbent and 'wrote divers verses, our nursery maid wanting an epitaph for her Aunt'. There were rumours that one of the members for Oxford·University, Estcourt, would not stand at the next elections; rumours also that Gladstone was interested in the possible vacancy. Oxford certainly would have been attractive to Gladstone, and doubly attractive as a citadel of the Church. But he reassured his agent that he had no intention of 'deserting' Newark.[4] There were obligations of friendship: it was a delicate task to persuade the dilettante Monckton Milnes that his political career was not so insignificant as to justify his applying for the secretaryship of the Paris legation.[5] He wrestled with intricate problems of a new commercial treaty with Brazil and disputes with Hanover and other north German states over Stade duties in a mood of profound disenchantment with the prospects of his guiding 'idea of Christian politics'. The 'perfect freedom of the new covenant' could only be breathed 'in other air', as he told himself at Hawarden on his

1 G to CG, November 21, 1844. GGP, 28/2.   2 D, iii, 331.
3 G to CG, November 22, 1844. GGP, 28/2. Newman on G: 'He talks of divinity as a
   clergyman talks of geology.' (Gere and Sparrow, *Geoffrey Madan's Notebooks*, 38).
4 G to Caparn, November 24, 1843. GP, 44527, 155.
5 G to Milnes, October 23, 1843. *Ib.*, 145.

thirty-fourth birthday at the end of 1843. But how to judge the respective utility to religion and the Church of remaining where he was ('more than content' to be so for 'sufficient' purposes) as against abandoning his brilliant political prospects for 'other air' which might be perfect freedom but also extremely thin? When his brother Tom carped (with Helen's case very much in mind) to their father about William's 'meddling' with matters outside his competence in his 'Present Aspect of the Church' article, William told his father that 'Tom would scarcely urge his objections if he knew the relative position which secular and church affairs occupy in my mind. I contemplate the former chiefly as a means of being useful to the latter.'[1]

There was much indeed to be done in 1844 to further the great work of tariff liberalisation and thus the moral dimension of political economy. Gladstone also had in view a bill to establish parliamentary oversight over the tremendously expanding new railway system. In a larger view, there appeared to be no serious obstacles in the way of Peel's programme for the session. True, Wharncliffe, the Lord President, wanted a specific statement about the need for continued protection for corn; but to this, as Gladstone noted, Peel 'avoided a direct answer'. 'Silence rather than stoutness' was his line.[2] Indeed, Peel, in December, in conversation with Aberdeen and Gladstone, had 'expressed obiter a strong opinion that the next change in the Corn Laws would be total repeal'.[3] So discretion at this point was certainly the better part of valour. How long the party rank and file would continue patiently to suffer silence rather than stoutness was another matter. It so happened that Graham's reintroduced Factory Bill, shorn of its controversial educational clauses, was the occasion, in February, of the first great explosion of Tory party impatience.

Ostensibly, it was a matter of conflict between the Tory group led by Gladstone's Evangelical friend Lord Ashley, who wanted the maximum hours per day workable by women in textile factories to be set at ten, and Graham and Peel, who, while reducing the hours worked by children, thought best to leave hours workable by women at twelve, the level set in 1833. In substance, it was a chance for the seething resentment building up in the party at the style of Peel's leadership and the tone of his policies to vent itself. Ninety malcontent Conservatives voted with Ashley and, with Whig support, defeated the government. Gladstone's part in this was to express conciliatory and concessionary opinions, and propose a compromise eleven hours. He was amazed at the passion into which his leaders worked themselves. Gladstone had noted in 1842, in his own brush with Peel over the sliding scale for corn, how Peel overreacted and mishandled him: 'He might ... have gained me more easily by a more open and supple method of expostulation.' Certainly Peel was 'not

1 Checkland, 347–8.   2 Gash, *Peel*, ii, 429–30.   3 GP, 44777, 108.

skilful' in the 'management of personal or sectional dilemmas'.[1] Instead of trying to cajole his refractory following with some tactful awareness of their fears and insecurities, Peel brutally harangued them with threats and set about booting the bill through. He and Graham were convinced that if they saddled the industrialists with shorter hours the government would not be able to avoid making the compensatory concession of Corn Law repeal. Peel whipped his sulking party into reversing its vote in favour of Ashley's ten hours; but he and Graham had to wait until June before they got their original bill through. It was an episode which left Conservative morale shaken and Gladstone ruminating on the strange ways of experienced and senior statesmen in their selection of issues of principle to stick at. He ruminated also as to the point of his continuing in politics: 'It is becoming a very serious question', he told T.D. Acland, 'whether there is anything left worth contending for here.'[2]

Gladstone himself enjoyed his work in the session, industriously pressing on with a second great batch of tariff abatements and piloting his pet project, his Railways Bill. Railways had become, in a short period of immense expansion, a great new social and economic presence; and, given their unavoidably monopolistic character, it was expedient for government to ensure that railway companies did not abuse their monopoly privileges at the public's expense. There was the sore issue of the cavalier treatment of the third-class passengers. Gladstone had no doubt that this was a perfectly proper area of parliamentary and governmental intervention, while yet holding to the general principle of abstention. His insistence on the 'competency and right of Parliament to interfere in this matter' led to the introduction of cheap and regular 'parliamentary' trains, providing improved accommodation to persons of the humbler classes at one penny per mile; and to the right of the State (never actually exercised under the Railways Act of 1844) to purchase railways twenty-one years after they had been built.[3] A move to oblige railway companies to run cheap trains on Sundays, however, perturbed him extremely: 'I do not know how to reconcile it to myself', he told Peel, 'to be responsible either for the enactment or the execution of a law containing a provision so dangerous in its immediate and ultimate results to public morality.'[4] In any case railways were an important aspect in Gladstone's education in '*étatisme*'. But already, even as Gladstone contemplated with satisfaction this modest but in its implications portentous exercise in sharpening the State's conscience, he was about to be confronted with an issue of principle at which, to the consternation of those sticklers for the twelve-hour Factory Bill, Peel, Graham and Stanley, he stuck fast.

1 PMP, i, 45.   2 Butler, 125.
3 H, lxxii, 236–37; D, iii, 387.   4 G to Peel, July 26, 1844. GP, 44527, 185.

Peel's calculation was that, having stood firm against the worst that O'Connell's Repeal campaign could do in 1843, the government was in a favourable position to offer Ireland a programme of reforms in 1844, conceded from strength rather than extorted, as in the normal manner, by panic. Gladstone could remark that 'everything has gone in Ireland as favourably to the Govt and public order as was possible'; but 'any combination of events which in that country places the State and O'Connell as adverse parties before a jury is of necessity formidable'.[1] He was in touch with his brother Robertson as Mayor of Liverpool about matters of intelligence on collections among the Irish of Repeal and 'Proclamation' money; and trusted that, 'looking at the state of Ireland', Robertson's successor as mayor might also be 'a man of vigour'.[2] There would be concessions in the municipal and parliamentary franchise; in educational matters; and there would be an enquiry on Roman Catholic endowments, including especially St. Patrick's College, Maynooth. Gladstone read the 'devastating dialectic'[3] of Peel's circular paper on Maynooth on February 11. The essence of Peel's argument was that the British State and the Irish Roman Catholic priesthood needed to come into a new relationship of co-operation and mutual good-will; and that a preliminary foundation of such a relationship would be adequate financial provision on the part of the State. After an 'anxious morning of reflection' Gladstone informed the Cabinet that the views he had expressed in his book in 1838 were unchanged. From Goulburn alone did Gladstone get any sympathy. He had no hopes that any good would come of the proposed enquiry and was sure that the measure implied in the proposal of a substantial increase in the grant to the college would precipitate a demand for State payment of Roman Catholic clergy. At a second cabinet on the 13th Gladstone, although reluctant to put difficulties in the way of the government, insisted that 'considerations of character were not on any account to be set aside – that only a great and decisive change of sentiments' could justify his participating in such a proposal; and 'no such change had taken place'.[4] In an enormous memorandum, comprising fifteen headings and six sub-headings, Gladstone set out his objections with agitated meticulousness, asserting that such a new departure in the State's relationship with Roman Catholicism would be 'a great shock to the religious feeling of the country', and would 'weaken confidence'. He was sure that his colleagues 'deluded themselves' with 'visionary hopes of improvement, of control, of conciliation', all of which by the means proposed were 'entirely beyond reasonable expectation'. It was merely 'purchasing peace by the hour'.[5]

1 G to Milnes, October 27, 1843. *Ib.*, 147.
2 G to Robertson G, October 31, 1843. *Ib.*, 149.
3 Gash, ii, 421.   4 D, iii, 347–8.   5 GP, 44777, 119–123.

A riposte came from Peel at the end of the month, provoking Gladstone to anxious reflection on the 'very serious question not whether I shall assume or avoid responsibility but whether I shall choose on the one hand the responsibility of participating in that endeavour, or on the other hand by retiring of giving a signal for disunion suspicion & even conflict in that political party by which alone as I firmly believe the religious institutions & laws of this country are under God maintained'.[1] Gladstone could see in Peel's measure 'no rational hope' of conciliating the Roman Catholic body or of altering the Roman Catholic priesthood for the better; he could foresee plainly a 'further declension in the religious character of the State of these realms'; he saw with dismay in Peel's proposals an 'acknowledgement of the priests as instructors of the Irish people', and an acceleration of demands that the wealth of the minority Church of Ireland should be largely transferred to those instructors. After what he had published, *even* if he had changed his mind, it seemed clear to Gladstone, resignation would have the merit of paying 'just tribute to public character and consistency'. The 'path of duty' was clear.[2]

On the evening of March 1, seeing Peel setting off homewards, Gladstone 'plucked up courage, & asked to walk with him'. He pleaded for Peel to make a 'private enquiry' before going ahead. Peel would not be deflected. There was no time to spare; 'we could not remain as we were.'[3] Growing desperation inspired Gladstone to hit upon a new delaying tactic. Peel had been considering the expediency of establishing diplomatic links with the Vatican; Gladstone tried to convert this into an essential preliminary to any movement on Maynooth. He insisted: 'intercourse with the Papal Court ought to be renewed for the sake of the good conduct even of existing relations', but even more so for the sake of giving 'a hope of success to the contemplated measures'. Everything about the history of Maynooth, it became clearer to Gladstone, underlined the necessity of 'including the Court of Rome as a party'.[4] Thus on Saturday, March 2 – an 'awful day' – Gladstone produced for Peel and the Cabinet another monstrous memorandum, stressing the need for a direct link with Rome and mentioning the contingency of his resignation. In a pre-cabinet interview with Peel, full of the 'utmost frankness & kindness', Gladstone was rather put out by the robust secularity of his chief's comment that, after all, 'no one could remember' any words Gladstone might feel pledged him. Ruffled, Gladstone chose to excuse this crassness as 'inadvertence'. In cabinet there were several flattering testimonies from his colleagues. The Chancellor held that Gladstone's departure would create an extreme party and leave the government without friends in Ireland. Wharncliffe thought that an 'extreme high church Protestant party' would be formed. Graham spoke of popular clamour and

1 D, iii, 350–51.   2 PMP, ii, 237.   3 GP, 44777, 165.   4 *Ib.*, 182–83.

combination. Peel referred to his own repressed inclination in 1829 to quit office and support the Duke from an independent position. Buccleuch proclaimed his strong Protestant feelings but after careful consideration had no scruple in adopting Peel's proposal. Gladstone felt himself under heavy pressure but not under the temptation to take refuge in any of the many available interstices of compromise.[1]

On the following Monday heavy pressure was renewed in the formidable person of Lord Stanley, who for two hours at the House of Commons stressed to Gladstone the 'extreme seriousness' of the situation. He tried to curdle Gladstone's blood by painting a lurid picture of the Maynooth policy as the last chance of saving the Church of Ireland from ultimate despoliation; for such a policy of disestablishment and disendowment might well have to come, urged Stanley, unless something decisive to head it off by reconciling the mass of the Irish people to the established church and the union were not done in good time. And, he added for good measure, 'he might so act' in such circumstances. The irony of this threat by the ex-Whig and later champion of the Church of Ireland to the later ex-Tory and its disestablisher and disendower no doubt often recurred to both men in the fullness of time. For the present, Gladstone could only protest that a great patrician like Stanley who had already proved his fidelity to the Church of Ireland, 'like an old General who can well afford not to fight a duel', was in a very different position from one like himself, 'whose courage has never been tried', who had 'no position, no rank or stake of property in the country'. The public might with reason regard him as a 'mere adventurer' if he should be thought to part company with character.[2]

The more Gladstone felt himself pushed into a corner, the more obsessed he became with the notion of a direct link with the Vatican as a brake upon the remorseless movement of events. On April 19 he read to Catherine, corrected and copied out a memorandum on 'Relations with the Court of Rome', which he then presented to Peel. A few days later he tried anxiously to read the significance of Peel's reception of it; and the absence of an immediately negative response led Gladstone too easily to assume that Peel saw 'daylight' in it.[3] In fact Peel saw nothing but obfuscation and nonsense in it, and was not prepared to humour Gladstone, as he had done in the case of the income tax question, by entering into a painstaking refutation. He allowed it to lapse quietly into limbo.

While this incipient drama gathered pace behind the scenes, the humdrum business of the session had to be attended to. Gladstone found himself on March 12 answering an attack by Cobden on the Corn Law, 'five-sixths of which', as he remarked to Hope after the end of the session,

1 PMP, ii, 238–41.   2 *Ib.*, 244–7.   3 D, iii, 369.

'I should have been glad to have spoken'.[1] Possibly it was a sense of Gladstone's prevaricative difficulty with the question which led the House to greet his motion that there be not a committee of enquiry on the effects of the law on account of its 'complicated and unsuitable nature' with a shout of laughter.[2] On top of this there were endless troubles over Ellenborough in India, with poor Ripon trying to fend off the demand of the directors of the East India Company for his recall.

Amid the turmoil Catherine gave birth on April 4 to a boy, baptised Stephen after his maternal uncle, with the Bishop of Salisbury standing sponsor. Gladstone thought him very like old John Gladstone: that is to say, with a larger mouth and bigger nose than the other children. There were anxieties about a recrudescence of a troublesome abscess in one of Catherine's breasts, but all went well. There was the constant pressure also of obligations to society. He dined at the Palace again on April 20; there was a dinner at the Comte de Saint-Aulaire's on May 1 to celebrate King Louis Philippe's birthday. (Gladstone had dined at Whitehall Place on April 30 '& missed div. on Scottish Tests. Now I ought to feel this as a sin & confess it as such.') He was captured by a remarkable romance entitled *Ellen Middleton*, written by Lady Georgiana Fullerton (daughter of Lord Granville), whose pious Catholicity made her fiction irresistible to Gladstone; who proposed to turn his 'Whitsun holydays to account' by writing something for the *Foreign and Colonial*.[3] For Whitsun he retreated to Brighton, where Catherine remained after May 30 to continue her recuperation. He did not neglect his own health and strength ('I charged Aunt J. to tell you particularly of the execution I did upon the beef at N.6 luncheon').[4] It was, however, a sign of recrudescent political troubles that Gladstone, dining with his father on May 2, should have had 'much conv. on Sugar Duties'.[5] And there was always Stanley to press upon him heavily unsubtle reminders calculated to give him pause about resigning. Shortly before he left for Brighton Gladstone had another strong dose of Stanley's medicine, this time on the theme of the 'dearth of young men of decided political promise on our side of the House, & on the other, always excepting Cardwell'. This was a prelude to Stanley's telling Gladstone that 'you are as certain to be prime minister as any man can be, if you live – the way is clear before you'. Gladstone replied primly that he 'dared not speculate on the future'. Trying another tack, Stanley dilated on the difficult position of poor over-worked Peel, harassed and plagued by all the insubordinate young men. Gladstone could indeed agree that Peel did the work of three or four men already; and was innocently puzzled

1 G to Hope, August 20, 1844. GP, 44214, 256.
2 H, lxxiii, 906.
3 G to Worthington, May 19, 1844. GP, 44527, 177. The piece eventually came out in *The English Review*, July 1844.
4 G to GC, May 30, 1844. GGP, 28/2.   5 D, iii, 372.

that Stanley could 'hardly have recollected our former conversation' of March 4.[1] There is every reason to suppose, on the contrary, that Stanley had that former conversation very much in mind.

Stanley's remarks on insubordination were much to the point. By mid-June the Conservative party was embroiled, by way of the Sugar Duties, in an even more painful and damaging quarrel than the one it had suffered over the Factory Bill in February. Sugar had the effect of combining several elements, harmless in themselves, into a dangerously combustible compound. One was the fact that the West India interest had enjoyed a virtual monopoly of supply, being protected by a 25s. duty per hundredweight as against 63s. for foreign sugars. The problem here however was that the West India interest could not keep pace with the growing demand for sugar on the British market. On its side, the government was generally disposed to the idea of freer importation of sugar, subject however to pressures hostile to 'slave grown' sugars such as Brazil and Cuba produced. On this point, however, the commercial treaty with Brazil restricting importations of other foreign sugars lapsed in 1844, giving Britain the opportunity of opening her markets to non-slave produced sugars, such as the Dutch East Indies might supply. Meanwhile, prominently in Peel's calculations, was the fact that since sugar was much the most lucrative single item of customs revenue, accounting for one third of the dutiable returns, it offered itself as the obvious means of leeway in reduction of duties on basic consumables to balance his probable need to extend the income tax. Hence, from the government's point of view, the importance of sugar as a manipulable fiscal resource, combined with the opportunities for a freer trade opened by the lapse of the Brazil treaty, added to the general pressure for free trade reconcilable with the principle of favouring 'free' sugar as against 'slave' sugar, all pointed irresistibly towards Goulburn's proposal to admit 'free' foreign sugar at 34s. per hundredweight.

Against this could be combined, on an artful motion, two otherwise irreconcilable interests: the West India interest, which opposed any reduction in the imperial preference; and the free traders, who opposed any restrictions whatever. The protectionist reflex of the Conservative rank and file put them instinctively on the side of the West India interest. The link between Peel's fiscal requirements and freer trade gave to rank-and-file loyalty to the West Indies the extra inducement of grievance against Peel's style and tone of leadership. By June 11, despite two speeches from Gladstone defending the government's policy of encouraging free-grown sugar and maintaining a reasonable margin of advantage for the West Indies, Peel sensed apprehensively a repetition of the Factory Bill fracas. Determined not to be taken again by surprise, he

1 GP, 44777, 186 (dated June 1, 1844, but referring probably to May 20).

summoned a meeting of the party at his house on June 13: 'the most unsatisfactory meeting he had ever known.'[1] Far from nipping mutiny in the bud, Peel provoked resentment and resistance. As Gladstone was later to remark, 'upon the question of the Sugar Duties, it was not always easy to tell which was the ministerial side of the House'.[2] By June 15, after the government had been defeated by a combination of Whigs and Conservative dissidents, Gladstone was referring to 'the Crisis'.[3]

At a cabinet on Saturday, June 15 Peel spoke of resignation, while Gladstone, much in the manner of the Factory Bill case, tried to be a soothing and conciliatory influence. There was a meeting of ministers again on Sunday at Aberdeen's house. Gladstone went there in a state of high agitation 'almost direct from the altar'.[4] Peel was determined either to force his party back into obedience or confront them with the consequences of a ministerial crisis. Gladstone thought it was 'evident that Peel's mind and the others leaning the same way' – Stanley and Graham – had been influenced 'not principally by the difficulties of the individual question, but by disgust with the immense uncheered labour of their position and with the fact that their party never seems to show energy except when it differs from the leaders'. Gladstone confessed, however, that 'in choosing to attempt the re-establishment of our own plan' the ministers were too hard on their malcontents and that 'some small & secondary concession' ought to have been offered to ease the way towards reconciliation. But Gladstone nevertheless felt that 'Peel's final inclination must and ought to guide the Government'.[5]

Through all this hectic party turbulence, as the government wrestled desperately to subdue its supporters, stalked the majestic and serenely unaware figure of the self-invited Emperor Nicholas of Russia, with the little King of Saxony in tow, augustly negotiating the future of Europe with a somewhat distracted Aberdeen. At a reception at the Palace on June 7 Gladstone was moved to note that the Emperor was a 'grand sight, in form & in bearing'; the King of Saxony, on closer acquaintance a week later, had the merit of being 'very unaffected'.[6] The sedate passage of these exalted guests formed an almost farcically antithetical backdrop to the Conservative turmoil. At a further cabinet, Peel reluctantly allowed himself to be persuaded into a token concession – 'some change not of an essential character might wisely be made in order to enable persons who were desirous to change their course to do so at least without indecency'. Gladstone himself leant towards renewing the old duties for nine months in order to allow things time to simmer down. Peel's speech later in the

1 Gash, *Peel*, ii, 447.   2 H, lxxviii, 1271 (February 26, 1845).
3 D, iii, 381.   4 *Ib.*, 382.
5 *Ib.*, 383.   6 *Ib.*, 380–81.

House almost wrecked the compromise plan. Gladstone listened to it with 'great pain'.

> The tone was hard, reserved, introspective: & when he came to the part when he said it was his duty to consider what encouragement would be afforded by a concession from him to the renewal of similar conduct in future, & the formation of fresh combinations between friends & opponents against his policy, I had what in *Glynnese* is called a creep – I felt that injustice was done though unintentionally to honourable men and cordial friends, and also that the venerable dignity of a British Parliament was offended.

At the end of the speech Peel's colleagues felt they were out. 'The House seemed resolved into its primordial elements.' Gladstone was later convinced that a 'deep wound had been inflicted upon the spirit & harmony of the party: that a great man had made a great error'.[1] The tense situation created by Peel's captiousness was saved by a brilliantly 'rattling' speech by Stanley, who, as Monckton Milnes put it, employed a temperate tone 'with the sort of advantage that an ill-tempered man has when he chooses to be good-humoured; the House was flattered that Stanley thought it worthwhile to be conciliating'.[2] By November, after the lull of the vacation, Gladstone could report to Catherine that 'questions relating to the admission of sugar which were the ugliest I had in view on coming up [from Fasque] are likely I think to be disposed of without very serious difficulty'.[3]

In such an unconvincing and unresolved manner the Conservative party and government cobbled themselves together again. The corn problem remained as tender and sore as ever. Gladstone was vulnerable at the Board of Trade. Even his intervention on the Dissenters' Chapels Bill, in which, counselled by Hope, he defended the rights of Unitarians lapsed from Presbytery to keep their chapels, laid him open to the mischievous wit of Sheil, who professed himself delighted 'to hear from such high authority' that this bill was 'perfectly reconcilable with the strictest and sternest principles of State conscience'. Sheil could not doubt that Gladstone, 'the champion of free trade', would ere long become 'the advocate of the most unrestricted liberty of thought'.[4] Gladstone in fact found a deputation of aggrieved Unitarians 'somewhat horrid'; but was clear that justice was more with than against them.[5] And certainly, along with his rather sympathetic view of the disrupters of the Church of Scotland and the formation of the Free Church in May 1843,

1 *Ib.*, 383.
2 R. Stewart, 'The Ten Hours and Sugar Crises of 1844: Government and the House of Commons in the Age of Reform', HJ, xii (1969), 46.
3 G to CG, , November 7, 1844. GGP, 28/2.
4 H, lxxv, 377.   5 G to CG, June 1, 1844. GGP, 28/2.

this case was a straw in the wind of Gladstone's withdrawal from strict and particular establishmentarianism. More disturbing was Gladstone's growing inability to make the House keep a straight face on the corn issue. When Villiers launched a motion on June 25 to abolish the Corn Law he knew it was a forlorn hope as far as winning the division was concerned; but it was a highly effective tactic to draw Gladstone out to repeat all his old defences of the 1842 measure and thereby expose his flanks to stings and arrows. Gladstone claimed 'something like stability for the decisions of Parliament [*Laughter*]. The noble Lord and hon. Gentlemen opposite laughed at what he has said. Possible it was that they might perceive a meaning in his words of which he himself was totally unconscious [*renewed laughter*]. . .'[1]

As he later explained to Hope, Gladstone was still convinced that 'our course in these matters has been generally right', but it involved 'progression'; and it was a high probability that 'one bad harvest or at all events two would break up the Corn Law and with it the party.' Hitherto it had worked better than could have been hoped; but it was undeniably 'a law mainly dependent on the weather'. Moreover, Gladstone was 'strongly and painfully impressed with recent disclosures concerning the physical state of the peasantry: for whose sake mainly, as my notion has been, we have maintained the Corn Laws'. On the immediate and personal level, Gladstone had grounds other than of modesty for insisting that 'as connected with trade', he was 'certainly a cause of weakness and not of strength to Sir Robert Peel in the *two* houses of Parliament'.[2] He told Augustus Stafford O'Brien, the Conservative and later Protectionist member for Northamptonshire, that it 'neither offends nor surprises me that I should be regarded with mistrust by the friends of protection in general', though insisting that the government had acted with 'strict and severe good faith towards the agricultural body'. Gladstone declared himself not so worried by differences in the Conservative party about measures of trade 'provided we were all agreed in placing them upon the ground of secondary matters, and that we could broadly distinguish between these and the larger and deeper principles which form the groundwork of our party connection'. Gladstone professed 'a strong impression that the disposition to confound these things together is likely to work out at some future period into very evil results'.[3]

The 1844 session ended with a further turn of the Maynooth screw. Peel summoned Gladstone on July 8, and after smoothing the way with matters connected with Gladstone's current concern, the Railways Bill,

1 H, *ib.*, 1412–19.
2 G to Hope, August 20, 1844. GP, 44214, 256.
3 G to O'Brien, August 2, 1844. *Ib.*, 44527, 187.

went to the nub: the government would respond positively to a motion on Roman Catholic education. Gladstone stood by his objections raised in the spring. He could not be the *'author'* of such a measure; but on the other hand thought it would not be his duty to oppose it when proceeding from a government which he knew 'adopted it as being on the whole the best means of defence for the Church of Ireland'. He was well aware of the 'evils of *any* secession' on such a question, 'and anxious to gain time at all events if practicable without dishonour, to go out in the recess rather than now'. He suggested to Peel that Easter would be a good time as affairs at the Board of Trade would leave him 'tolerably free to retire without causing any inconvenience'.[1] Gladstone talked with Hope on each of the following three days. He also spoke with Catherine 'on special matters'; perhaps the beginning of a new phase of 'rescue' work with prostitutes?[2] Or possibly he raised some preliminaries concerning his part in the fraternity of the Margaret Street Chapel which would be unfolded in November.

On July 12 Gladstone wrote to Peel on Maynooth, raising again the issue of reopening official diplomatic relations with Rome, going so far this time as to offer himself as plenipotentiary; wisely adding that he did not consider himself entitled to a reply. Reply there was none, and Gladstone dined the following day at Peel's in a rather guilty awareness of his chief's 'astonishment on receiving such a letter'. Later, in listing this episode among his 'Recorded Errors', Gladstone owned that he tried Peel hard by a 'most indiscreet proceeding'.[3] After making such a point of keeping Gladstone out of any office in which he could have continued to dip his fingers into religious controversy, Peel must have blenched at the vision of so notorious a Puseyite and so ingenuous a diplomatist earnestly pursuing along the mazy corridors of the Vatican 'opportunities that might be afforded' for 'bringing about in Latin quarters a more just estimate of the English Church'. Peel's announcement of the government's decision drew from Gladstone sombre reflections on the necessity for 'forms and principles of government' to 'bear an analogy' to the 'inward tone and life' of the people. 'And to judge by our tone and life the higher theory however true in itself is no longer true to us – that is, it is an untrue representative of the result issuing from the concourse of wills and forces that make up our national system.' The only people who 'really view the State as having a conscience which shall disapprove and exclude, fasten that conscience not upon the positive idea of the Church but upon the negation and repudiation of Popery'. It seemed to Gladstone then that the time was 'drawing near for a change of scenes and parts' – and that this was indeed the commencement 'of a great transition'.

1 D, iii, 388.
2 So Foot and Matthew suggest: *ib.*   3 PMP, ii, 127–28.

The most revealing clue to the movement of Gladstone's mind at this crucial moment, however, is provided in his deduction from the lamentable but now undeniable fact that the 'higher theory' of the 'forms and principles of government' bore no meaningful relationship to the 'inward tone and life' of the 'wills and forces' constituting society: 'That Government has a mind or is the presiding mind of the community is a doctrine which when the idea of mind and spirit become thoroughly dissociated one should perhaps wish extinct.'[1] The peculiar agony of the Maynooth issue for Gladstone derived not so much from his steadfastness to true principles of 'disapproval and exclusion' as from an amalgam of despairing convictions that he was publicly committed to steadfastness on grounds which he could now admit to himself that he wished no longer existed.

[8]

After a 'very interesting' and in 'the last stage astonishing' excursion by rail to Folkestone and Dover with Catherine and Willy, with speeds of nearly 60 m.p.h. between Tonbridge and Ashford, and then his first ministerial whitebait dinner at Greenwich, Gladstone arrived for his customary retreat at Fasque early in August.

From Fasque on August 20 Gladstone wrote to Hope that the purpose of parliamentary life resolved itself with him 'simply and wholly into one question': would it ever 'afford the means under God of rectifying the relations between the Church and the State', and give Gladstone 'the opportunity of setting forward such a work'? The 'general objects of political life' were not Gladstone's objects. On the whole he did not expect, from the 'good sense of the English people, the force of the principle of property, and the conservative influence of the Church', 'less than the maintenance of our present Monarchical and parliamentary constitution under all ordinary circumstances'. And Gladstone did not flatter himself by imagining this would be better done by his remaining to take part in it. The 'real renovation' of the country did not depend upon 'law and government'.[2] Were Gladstone's reasons for pursuing the purpose of parliamentary life thus 'sufficiently' formulated? How 'sufficient' was Gladstone's distinction between 'rectifying the relations between the Church and the State' as a purpose for which in 1844 he could still presumably justify continuing in political life, and his earlier dictum that the point had been passed when the action of the Church could be 'harmonised' with the law of the State? And what weight did the

1 PMP, ii, 268 (July 19/20, 1844).   2 GP, 44214, 256.

second 'prospective object' of some 'establishment or machinery' to unfold the Catholic system within the Church add to his ultimate decision to continue in politics? To Newman he put the question: how were those 'whose destiny is cast in public life' to (in Newman's own words in his earlier sermon on 'The Church and the World') 'kindle their fire from the altar of God'? How were they to 'regulate that large portion of their agency in which they are partly (though from year to year in lessening degrees) the directors of a civilised power, made up of almost innumerable and thoroughly heterogeneous wills?'[1]

In truth Gladstone was in these years deploying a schoolman's casuistry to avoid the logic of his own deepest avowals. He had already admitted to himself, if not to Hope, that 'one might perhaps wish extinct' the doctrine which he proclaimed still to be the purpose of his parliamentary life. His agility in this ritual intellectual dance verged in its later stages somewhat between frenzy and farce. By 1846, after the shock of Maynooth and resignation, after Newman's despairing abandonment of Anglicanism for Rome, when both Manning and Hope were being pushed by events inexorably towards that same resolution, Gladstone had come to the pass of expressing to Manning a wish that he could get a 'synodical decision' in favour of his 'retirement from public life'. For he professed to remain there, as he reminded the possibly slightly (by this time) unimpressed Archdeacon of Chichester, 'for the service of the Church'; and his views of the mode of serving her were getting 'so fearfully wide of those generally current that even *if* they be sound they may become wholly unavailable'.[2]

To which Manning might have responded (uncharitably) something to the effect that how 'unavailable' do views have to become before appropriate logical consequences are deduced? How threadbare does a garment of principles have to get before intellectual decency demands its replacement? For Gladstone to speak (even if half-jokingly) of needing so bizarrely unattainable an item of 'establishment or machinery' as a 'synodical decision' to do for him what he was evidently unwilling to do for himself was tantamount to a decision to set unfulfillable terms for his so oft-repeated and declared undertakings as to his life's priorities. Gladstone, in short, was being guided by a 'determined bias' which quite possibly extensively impaired his powers of moral judgment; quite possibly his sins were so.persistent as to benumb his spiritual instincts and his faculty for discerning the will of God. At all events, he was never to intuit any providential guidance telling him that his political game was up.

Why? That he was possessed by a healthy degree of political ambition is

1 Butler, 126.
2 G to Manning, March 8, 1846. GP, 44247, 289.

sufficiently attested by his disappointment in 1841 at not getting a cabinet office. The child struggling up the stairs at Rodney Street was still very much the father of the man. Gladstone found his 'public acts' a 'comfort' in a rather uncomfortable world. His 'technical fascination' with 'working the institutions of the country' grew apace.[1] Did Catherine's influence at this time help to hold him to politics? More than any one else she would have been aware of his need for business and occupation to keep him steady. Yet Gladstone's protestations that the 'general objects of political life' were not his objects held good. If service to religion and the Church was the mainspring of political action then the power, influence and reputation bestowed by cabinet status were not to be impiously despised. Still, when Gladstone did finally resign his cabinet office at the beginning of the 1845 session he most decidedly did not do so as the first step to a general political disengagement.

[9]

Fasque in the late summer and early autumn of 1844 produced copious sheafs of notes on sixteenth- and seventeenth-century theology and church history: Stephen on the Church of Scotland, Burnet, Paul on the Council of Trent. It was also notably distressing for domestic tensions. Helen, with her addiction to 'abominable opium and other stimulants' and her 'deep delusion with regard to most questions of conduct', kept the household in a state of barely repressed hysteria. One resident aunt, Johanna Robertson, suffered, not surprisingly, from severe depressions; and there were exasperating problems about the housekeeping. Tom also was becoming a problem. He had failed in politics (after gaining a seat for Ipswich in June 1842 he was unseated on a petition in August). He had failed to produce a son (Louisa presented him relentlessly with a succession of daughters). Would John Gladstone deprive his eldest son of the inheritance of a sufficiency of his fortune needed for the upkeep of Fasque? William dropped a bombshell on Tom when he told him on October 4 1844 that their father 'happened to mention what was new to me . . . that by his Will, as it stands, you would have Fasque as *constituting* your extra share, and except for that, would have the same as the other sons'.[2] William took the view that Tom had 'little pleasure or interest' in Fasque, and his wife Louisa even less. Hawarden seemed foreclosed by Henry and Lavinia Glynne; so, if Tom wished it and John Gladstone consented, 'one of us' – by which William meant himself – might take Fasque over. William was in love with the idea of a country estate. Tom

1 Matthew, D, iii, xxx.   2 Magnus, 62.

resented both being asked to give up his inheritance and being deprived of the means to live up to it. He left William 'painfully impressed with the needlessly gloomy character of his views, I cannot help thinking in a great measure the result of want of steady occupation'. Tom's distress Gladstone conveyed to Catherine ('it only goes to you as with the inner chamber of my mind. It makes one rather sad').[1] He pointed out to Tom that George Lyttelton with very little money somehow managed to keep Hagley going. Having thus consoled Tom, William consoled himself by writing on 'The Theses of Erastus and the Scottish Church Establishment', published later in the *Foreign and Colonial Quarterly Review*, a tribute to the newly-founded Free Church of Scotland for its resistance to deleterious Erastianism. (Nor did he neglect the opportunity to slip in a boost for the recently-established Trinity College at Glenalmond.) As an extra bonus he launched into Oxford religious controversy with a polemical critique of W. G. Ward's anti-Anglican *Ideal of a Christian Church*. He administered in the *English Review* a sharp rebuke to Lord John Russell for presuming, as a mere latitudinarian Whig, to dabble with the sublime Dante. In much the same terms as he was later to recommend Tennyson, Gladstone declared his assurance that if his countrymen were to 'advance in their moral health and intellectual vigour', Dante 'must advance in their estimation'.[2] He also recommenced in August the practice of reading daily a chapter from the Bible with Catherine. Another consoling feature of the vacation was that, after much prodding and exploitation of Catherine's lighter touch, Gladstone persuaded his father that it would be an excellent thing to build a chapel at Fasque. Gladstone had on occasion found himself inconvenienced when, the nearest Episcopalian church at Laurencekirk not being available, he had perforce subjected himself to the Calvinist grimness of the local kirk at Fettercairn. Prospective avoidance of that hazard was an additional cause of joy as the Gladstones eagerly immersed themselves in the details of this new project.

By the end of October Gladstone was back from Scotland, pained at having missed his religious observances at Liverpool because of the boat's lateness, and upset that attendance at the opening of the new Royal Exchange in the City should have caused him to neglect his sacred duties yet again. He made up for these lapses with his Catholic devotions, though even he occasionally found the pace a little hot. 'Have just been to Margaret Chapel,' he recounted to Catherine, who remained at Hagley. 'We had a short discourse tomorrow being All Saints – he made the Blessed Virgin the Queen of Angels as well as Saints, which seemed to me a little strong.'[3] The Margaret Street Chapel fraternity was indeed about

1 G to CG, October 31 and November 2, 1844. GGP, 28/2.
2 Chadwick, 'Young Gladstone and Italy', *J. Ecc. Hist.* (1979), 256.
3 G to CG, October 31, 1844. GGP, 28/2.

to undergo an important transmutation in the shape of a more formally constituted 'Engagement', with provision for 'disciplines' evidently both of a mortifying and confessional character. Gladstone sent this account to 'My beloved C.':

> The inclosed paper was given me by Acland . . . last night – and the matter is one so important and full of interest, especially when one considers that anything good of the kind ought never to part from one on this side of the grave, that I do not stir further in it without sending for your perusal the paper itself and the letter I propose to send back.
>
> The paper seems to me on the whole drawn with an admirable judgment: it is done by Keble, the 'sweet singer of Israel'.
>
> For years I have been talking about discipline and some opportunity and hope of help in it appears to have come into view. My conscience is weak and wants aid – not to say that it is crooked, more than you know or can know, and wants a straight rule for its correction.
>
> The laxity of habits, which my occupations entail, forms another good reason for taking some means to ascertain that it does not degenerate into a mere pretext for selfish indulgence.
>
> I am quite at ease also in this matter as the movement is one not only within but almost required by the injunctions & spirit of the Church.
>
> It often occurs to me what a blessing it will be to our children if they can be brought up in the habit of constantly disclosing the interior of their minds: then that is met by the thought that while thus governing them we should or at least I should also have made already some provision still nearer home.
>
> This seems to me so healthy & so simple, that I confidently anticipate its appearing so likewise to you – and I say nothing therefore with the view of obviating apprehension or suspicion. If the eye be steadily fixed on the salvation of the soul, how precious does every real help appear! How do we love the holy songs of the Church, which are such helps! Let us then love other true helps also, though not of such unmixed exterior sweetness.
>
> G[eorge Lyttelton] & M[ary] may I think see the paper: but they will understand the subject to be confidential. Show my letter too if you wish it but only then.
>
> Yours most affty
WEG[1]

Catherine's only objection seems to have been to Gladstone's insistence on the crookedness of his conscience, more than she knew or could know. 'If I do not dispute your relative unworthiness,' he told her, 'it is not because I believe it. Let us on that subject hold our contrary opinions.

1 G to CG, November 24, 1844. *Ib.*

I am blessed in you to the whole extent of my heart's desire – & increasingly as time goes on. What can I say more?' Gladstone would not further enter 'into professions of the great need I have for help & even for inward relief, because such things become worthless by repetition, & while we go into detail upon them the evil thought creeps in "what a good boy am I"'.[1]

Thus sustained spiritually by this new version of his old ideal of a 'severe life', Gladstone confronted the severities of politics and bachelor London living ('No fear, love, about my feeding. Among other things I have put my teeth into the old Cheshire Cheese; which I declare to be *very good*')[2]. He needed all the physical sustenance he could get. During November and December Peel brought the Maynooth question formally before a series of cabinets. Gladstone had 'to *do the deed* over again'.[3] His convoluted explanation to his colleagues confused Stanley into supposing that he was hostile to the new policy. After receiving a letter from him at the beginning of January 1845, Peel commented to Graham: 'I really have great difficulty sometimes in exactly comprehending what Gladstone means. . . I take it for granted, however, that the letter means to announce his continued intention to retire, and I deeply regret it.'[4] Gladstone described his 'uncomfortable' situation to Catherine on January 13: 'I may remain a couple of months, or only a week – may go at any time on 24 hours notice.'[5] It was provoking that an invitation to Windsor should have come at so delicate a moment. 'It is like an event in one's life to go there,' he told Catherine; but perhaps this was not the time. By January 20 Peel gave up his last lingering hopes that Gladstone could be persuaded to stay in, and started the difficult business of reconstructing the administration. Gladstone's birthday adjurations to himself at the end of December had about them a special poignancy of regret at finally committing the deed he had been setting up for years as a promise to himself: 'Now commences as it were the downhill of my life. The last years have woven strong cords upon me that I had not before: but my vocation does not seem as yet to struggle against them.'[6]

While Gladstone underwent the anguish of the loosing and the breaking of these strong cords, he was distracted by the Oak Farm problem. He had fitted in a cursory visit there in mid-November, and found the industrial spectacle 'a wonderful sight'. But a more than cursory study of the books presented a far less wonderful sight. Neither Stephen Glynne nor George Lyttelton had any capacity for business. Gladstone had no experience; and in any case little time to spare. They let

1 G to CG, November 27, 1844. *Ib*.
2 G to CG, November 1, 1844. *Ib*.
3 PMP, ii, 270.   4 Gash, *Peel*, ii, 457.
5 G to CG, January 13, 1844. GGP, 28/2.   6 D, iii, 422.

the agent Boydell have his head. John Gladstone, who had stepped in with both advice and money, grew increasingly uneasy at the dangerously exposed position William would be in if the concern were to collapse under the pressure of Boydell's over-sanguine and extravagant management. He warned his son in November 1844: 'Events the most disastrous are *possible*.'[1] 'Lightly & imperceptibly', as William noted of himself and Lyttelton, 'we have been drawn there into immense liabilities.'[2] John Gladstone, increasingly precipitate, talked of joining William at Liverpool to confer with Boydell. Gladstone was anxious at the 'cruel' pressure on his father ('at the present moment his rapidity, tho' I am not myself exactly dilatory, makes me afraid'). There was also an annoying aspect to it: 'It is very singular but my Father writes to me just as if I had nothing whatever to do here – however he does not know the real pinch of it.'[3] The Gladstones insisted on a 'plan for our release', which was consummated the following year, the brothers-in-law securing themselves by retiring . from the company and taking out instead mortgages on its assets.[4]

As yet Oak Farm was no more than a cloud on the horizon, a nagging anxiety in the background of life. Pressingly immediate was the facing of the new session. Gladstone had to make explanations of his conduct which would satisfy the House, the government, and not least himself. On January 30 he apprised the Duke of Newcastle of his intention, stressing that there was no blame to Peel in 'the character of the times and of the religious and political sentiments which prevail'.[5] He recorded himself as ruminating on the 'dangers' of his explanation 'right and left'; and it made him 'unusually nervous'.[6] The matter was very delicate. The Tory party was deeply and instinctively Protestant. Memories of the great betrayal of 1829 were undimmed in the minds of many of its members, as Peel well knew. In his last efforts to hold Gladstone, Peel had used this as a weapon: 'I wish to speak without any reserve, and I ought to tell you I think it will very probably be fatal to the Government.'[7] Gladstone had already been slightly offended at Peel's tendency in public to 'say more' than he had indicated to Gladstone privately.[8] Peel also pressed rather heavily for control over the details and language of Gladstone's statement, insisting that Gladstone should stress 'perfect concurrence' between them on matters of trade and keep within the compass of an agreed formulation. Gladstone pledged that he would not join in any 'no Popery' cry. Peel also insisted that an audience with the Queen was indispensable. Indeed, there was something punitive about it: though

1 Magnus, 61.   2 D, iii, 416.
3 G to CG, November 23 and 25, 1844. GGP, 28/2.   4 Checkland, 353.
5 G to Newcastle, January 30, 1845. GP, 44528, 7–8.   6 D, iii, 431.
7 PMP, ii, 272.   8 *Ib.*, 268.

long since parted from the easy latitudinarian influences of dear Lord M.,
Victoria was no less likely to receive unsympathetically the kind of
apologies Gladstone would offer, reeking of casuistry, Puseyism, and
distinctly unhealthy morbidity of conscience. Politely mystified regrets,
tempered by desultory conversation on the 'reduced condition' of
Chartism, were all Gladstone got in the private sitting room at the Palace.[1]

Perhaps, after this, the House of Commons was easier to confront on
February 4. Gladstone struck the balance pretty near the right point. Peel
had no cause for complaint, apart perhaps from Gladstone's representing
the new policy as implying eventual payment of the Roman Catholic
priesthood; the House, rather like the rest of Gladstone's colleagues and
the Queen herself, were probably too puzzled by the intricacies of
Gladstone's position to realise that a cause for complaint was there to be
had. Even Hope wanted 'more explanation'. Parties did not understand,
he told Gladstone, whether he repented of his book; or why, meaning to
support the bill, he 'disturbed the public mind by quitting office'.[2] John
Cam Hobhouse's puzzlement was widely shared: 'why or wherefore no
one seems exactly to know.'[3] Gladstone had, as he told the House,
published deliberately and in detail views on 'the relation of a Christian
State to religion and to the Christian Church'. He had a 'strong
conviction' that 'those who have thus borne the most solemn testimony to
a particular view of a great constitutional question' ought not to be
'parties responsible for proposals which involve a material departure
from them'. He was not inflexible or immutable in his views; but he
believed his opinions as published still to be 'the best and most salutary
scheme for the regulation of the relations between a Christian State and
the Christian Religion'. If, however, the time had come when, owing to a
great advance of religious divisions and very great modification of
political sentiments, 'what remains of that system must be further
infringed', then he could 'not undertake to draw any line of distinction'
unfavourable to his Roman Catholic fellow subjects, in Ireland in
particular.[4] Hobhouse felt of Gladstone's explanation that 'although it
was not quite what Mr. Plumptre afterwards called it, unintelligible', it
was 'not well done. It was too long, and he dwelt too much on his own
book.' Again: 'Why the deuce did he quit the Cabinet? Everyone asks
this.'[5]

Lincoln, Dalhousie and Aberdeen all spoke to Gladstone of a short
separation, commensurate with the rather esoteric nature of Gladstone's
impediment of conscience. To which Gladstone could only feebly
respond 'sufficient for the day', and that no man was master of events in

1 *Ib.*, 274.   2 *Ib.*, 276
3 Lord Broughton, *Recollections of a Long Life*, vi (1911), 135.
4 H, lxxvii, 77–81.   5 Broughton, *ib.*, 136, 140.

public life, nor could answer even for himself.[1] *A propos* of which it might fairly be remarked that the scrupulous intensity of his conscience about his cabinet responsibility for the Maynooth policy was rather inversely proportioned to a somewhat acquiescent disposition to allow himself to be mastered by events and to renounce the opportunity to 'answer for himself' at a juncture when active and positive testimony might have been thought overwhelmingly appropriate. In short, Gladstone determined that he would not jump off; he would have to be pushed. As he told Stanley on March 4, 1844: 'the lower ends of a State ought to be fulfilled even when the higher ones become impractical.'[2] Like the general of a defeated army, he deliberately exposed himself to the victorious enemy's fire on the field of battle, allowing providence the opportunity of fulfilling the logic of defeat. He survived unscathed to lead other armies in other battles.

1 PMP, ii, 273.   2 D, iii, xxxii.

CHAPTER IV

'MY WORK IS GONE': THE END OF THE IDEAL OF STATE AND CHURCH, 1845–1851

[1]

Resignation of office over Maynooth enabled things on the surface to remain the same. Having made his gesture, Gladstone was free to continue to debate with himself and his friends as if his options remained open and equally available. Seemingly resolute and self-sacrificing, in fact resignation for Gladstone was an exercise in irresolution and the art of survival. When in May 1843 he envisaged the 'evil of hostility' between the government and the Church, he told Peel that in the event of separating from him 'on a question of that sort', he contemplated resigning his seat as well as his office. Now, abandoning office noisily was a way of quietly not abandoning politics. There was an element in it simply of procrastination: the old argument against 'precipitancy'. Gladstone was to do his best in 1850, when the Gorham case confronted the Church with an even more crucially significant issue of principle, to manoeuvre both Hope and Manning into adopting the same irresolute tactic. His failure then to hold them for the Church became, in effect, the signal for his own emancipation from the fetters of mission and commitment to serve the Church in the State with which he had loaded himself ever since he had first persuaded himself that his vocation had really been for the Church and that he had gone into the State only at his father's command.

But was there in resignation at the beginning of 1845 something deeper than mere procrastination, of hoping against hope that the future would somehow rescue him from his self-imposed dilemma? To what extent was Gladstone aware that although things on the surface could, for the time being at any rate, remain the same, subterranean shifts and pressures were already imposing themselves ineluctably upon him: that in effect he was contracting almost unawares new missions and commitments? Naturally, both his public and private rhetoric proclaimed the superficial primacy of the 'sacred' mission. But by 1847 (on the issue of Jewish disabilities) he was publicly using rhetoric of an almost crassly profane and Macaulayesque 'march of mind' character; which, moreover, he was prepared to subsume within a curiously adapted concept of the 'providential government of the world'. And his partisanly Liberal biographer Morley could rejoice that by 1850 Gladstone (on the issue of reform of Oxford) had recorded 'the last manifestation, on a high theme and on a broad scale, of that toryism from which this wonderful pilgrim had started on his shining progress'.[1]

The notion of Gladstone the reluctant but ineluctably compelled 'march-of-minder' is attractive because of its intense charge of dramatic irony. Clinging hopelessly to the last enchantments of the *ancien régime*, Gladstone registers decisively and conclusively the righteousness and inevitability of his ultimate commitment to the values of Liberalism by the very fact that he came upon them unawares. His quest was for a moral mode of political action. It turned out, somewhat to his chagrin, that it was Liberalism he was seeking. Nor is the plausibility of this 'pilgrim' interpretation to be denied. Gladstone was quite vulnerable to the temptation to accredit the march of mind by equating it with eternal moral verities. But the process was far from being a simple one of transference, a conventionally transitional replacement of old values by new, conveniently legitimised by the plausibly alleged validation of divine providence. In these years Liberalism as a concept was unformed and as an entity unplaced. There was no fixed frame of reference by which Gladstone's 'progress' could be measured. There is a good case to be made for Peel as the 'progenitor of Gladstonian Liberalism';[2] there is certainly a convincing case to be made for Peel as progenitor of Gladstone's Liberalism. In either case the complexity of the process is sufficiently underlined. Gladstone's eventual discomfiture at finding himself 'a member of a Liberal government' 'in association with the Liberal party' was to have consequences highly discomfiting for Liberalism. The pressures of the 'profane' new subterranean values broke through to the surface and gradually replaced the old 'sacred' values. But these latter, being driven underground, were by no means obliterated. Rather, under the new pressures now imposed upon them by the force of their displacement, they underwent a change of constituence. The sacred values lost in this metamorphosis their old formal and increasingly impotent primacy; but they gained a new potency, all the more effective because unacknowledged and occult. Thus the power exerted within Gladstone's political and public existence by commitment to a concept of spiritual mission, of moral redemption of the world, of a great service to mankind by means of his devotion to Christ crucified and immanent within His Church Catholic, underwent no essential diminution. For the very reason of ceasing to be in itself the doctrinally proclaimed programme of his motives, actions, and purposes, the 'sacred' dimension of

1 Morley, i, 498.   2 B. Hilton, 'Peel: a Reappraisal', HJ (1979), 614.

Gladstone's energy became freer to seek its public purposes outside conventional bounds; or to transfer concepts of 'mission' and 'redemption' from a private and a personal or individual sphere into the sphere of secular policy.

For Gladstone the immediate assessment of his political situation was that, if his old high notion of the state had failed, perforce he had to accept a new low notion. This was simply to confuse the failure of his ideal of State and Church with the failure of either the State or the Church. He did not for long remain imprisoned in this confusion; but for the time being it was at the centre of his explanatory letter to his Newark colleague, Lord John Manners.

> You I have no doubt are disappointed as to the working of a conservative Government. And so should I be if I were to estimate its results by comparison with the anticipations which from a distance and in the abstract I had once entertained of political life. But now my expectations not only from this but from any government are very small. If they do a little good, if they prevent others from doing a good deal of evil, if they maintain an unblemished character, it is my fixed conviction that under the circumstances of the times I can as an independent member of Parliament, for I am now virtually such, ask no more... The principles and moral powers of government are sinking day by day, and it is not by laws and Parliaments that they can be renovated.

From this superior – or perhaps sulky – position of disillusionment Gladstone could adopt a loftily dismissive view of the 'mournful delusions' entertained by the Carlylean and 'Young England' critics of the new dispensation with whom Manners was associated.

> It is most easy to complain as you do of *'laissez-faire'* and *'laissez-aller'*: nor do I in word or in heart presume to blame you: but I should sorely blame myself if with my experience and convictions of *the growing impotence of government for its highest functions*, I were either to recommend attempts beyond its powers, which would react unfavourably upon its remaining capabilities, or to be a party to proposed substitutes for its true moral and paternal work which appear to me mere counterfeits.

Moreover, the 'constant declension' of the moral powers and principles of government was 'not only augmenting the burdens and diminishing the satisfactions of public men, but limiting within narrower and narrower bounds their real liberty of choice'; and already they were 'perhaps the least free portion of society'. As for his own position Gladstone declared that he understood and felt 'that it was a grave practical question' whether 'persons entertaining the dark view' which he entertained of the 'conditions and prospects of government' should 'meddle with public affairs'; but: 'that question I have settled for myself upon very definite grounds which I will not now explain because it would be opening a fresh chapter of egotism'. He concluded by assuring Manners of his conviction that if work were to be carried on by the 'Conservative body' it could only be done by the 'greatest forebearance on all sides', by 'giving credit for good motives', by readiness 'to adopt favourable constructions and allow for difficulties unseen and therefore not accurately measured', by 'trusting much to those in whose general ability and integrity we believe', and in fine 'by a faithful observance of all that is essentially necessary to keeping what is now the organ of Government, a parliamentary majority together with the party it places in power, in such a state of mutual respect and confidence' as was necessary for the performance of that work.[1]

This was Gladstone's own version of what was to become an interpretation of him first proposed publicly by Walter Bagehot in a famous essay in 1860. In contrast to the 'pilgrim' thesis of positive quest and 'shining progress' adopted by Morley, Bagehot proposed a thesis of Gladstone's 'adaptive mind': 'Mr. Gladstone is essentially a man who cannot impose his creed *on* his time, but must learn his creed *of* his time.'[2] Others have stressed, following this line, the 'secondary, and almost accidental, character of Gladstone's liberalism'.[3] It was certainly a commonly enough expressed criticism of him among the rabbis of the 'movement' that 'as a Liberal he had no clearly thought-out political philosophy'.[4] All Goldwin Smith could detect was that Gladstone 'perhaps' derived 'something from Russell, whose leading principle was that people needed only responsibility to make them act wisely and rightly'. As far as Smith could see, Gladstone had, 'apparently, no notion of any system of government other than party, which he seemed to treat as though it had been immemorial and universal'. Even 'as to the workings of the British Constitution', his opinions were 'not very clear'. All that Gladstone could supply to fill the gap noted by Smith in political science or the absence of any clear conception of the polity he was seeking to produce was a 'guiding idea, when once he had broken loose from his early Toryism', of 'liberty, which he appeared to think would of itself be the parent of all good'.[5] Smith's ultimate diagnosis of the essential Gladstone boiled down to the fact that he was 'ambitious, happily for the

1 G to Manners, January 30, 1845. GP, 44528, 8–9. Morley, i, 304–05.
2 W.Bagehot (ed. R.H.Hutton), *Biographical Studies* (1860), 94, 112.
3 Vidler, *The Orb and the Cross*, 147.
4 Smith, *My Memory of Gladstone*, 37.   5 *Ib.*, 37–39.

country; he wanted to recover the means of doing great things. His admirers need not shrink from that avowal.'[1]

Undoubtedly there is a larger element of validity in this general interpretation of Gladstone's adaptiveness to his times and the consequent elements of fortuitousness and even emptiness of his Liberalism than is to be found in the Liberal pieties of Morley. Public testimony by Gladstone himself, writing on the role of the orator in his *Studies on Homer*, was appealed to by Bagehot:

> His work, from its very inception, is inextricably mixed up with practice. It is cast in the mould offered to him by the mind of his hearers. It is an influence principally received from his audience (so to speak) in vapour, which he pours back upon them in a flood. The sympathy and concurrence of his time, is, with his own mind, joint parent of his work. He cannot follow nor frame ideals; his choice is, to be what his age will have him, what it requires in order to be moved by him, or else not to be at all.[2]

Yet, allowing for this, there would always be at the same time with Gladstone the implications of what he referred to as 'joint parentage'. The whole point of Gladstone's career after 1845 was a tension between the consequences of his disillusionment with the 'principles and moral powers of government' for 'its highest functions' and his indefatigable determination to find 'substitutes for its true moral and paternal work' which were decidedly not 'counterfeit'. He was unable to forge his true alloy until the 1850s and 1860s; the two great elements of his compound would be a vision of a new potency of government and a new public opinion responsive to that potency. He would achieve a 'joint parentage' precisely at the epoch when the values of political economy denounced by Manners and grudgingly acknowledged by himself in 1845 would be at the highest peak of their reputation and authority. This was the 'mould' in which 'practice' was cast for Gladstone; and the 'flood' which he would 'pour back' upon it was indeed 'inextricably mixed up' with that practice. After 1845 he offered few challenges to his times. But what he did eventually offer by way of interpreting how his age would best have him and how its requirements would best be catered for at his hands was a mode of political operation characterised above all by wilful manipulation and executive arrogance. This contradiction was at the heart of the tension in Gladstone's politics. Bagehot himself unwittingly exposed the contradiction when he remarked that Gladstone 'has the same sort of control over the minds of those he is addressing that a good driver has over the animals he guides: he feels the minds of his hearers as the driver the mouths of his horses'.[3]

1 *Ib.*, 28.   2 *Studies on Homer and the Homeric Age* (1858), iii, 107.   3 Bagehot, *ib.*, 95.

This was profoundly true. And given that Gladstone, upon 'very definite grounds', had elected to continue to 'meddle with public affairs', his meddling would consist essentially in reconciling the contradiction between the old sacred values and the new secular values in such a way as to put him in a position derived from the former as a driver and a guide driving and guiding in a manner conformable with his interpretation of the requirements of the latter. Just as Gladstone rarely thought after 1845 to challenge his age (the divorce issue being one of the few decided instances in point), so he never thought that the authority and prerogatives necessary for resolving the tension of the contradictions of his posture in relation to that age could come from his own unaided resources. His first duty would be to explore new possibilities of a higher, revealed accreditation.

[2]

It was probably as well for Gladstone that events crowded so thickly upon him early in 1845 that he had no time to brood on his predicament. No sooner had he explained himself to the bemused House of Commons than his attention was diverted by the 'astounding announcement' from Oxford that the Heads of Houses had decided to submit to Convocation formal censure of Newman's *Tract XC*. This was supplementary to the proposal to degrade W. G. Ward to the status of an undergraduate to punish him for his insolently Romanist *Ideal of a Christian Church*. Perturbed letters were at once despatched to Professor Pusey and the Dean of Christ Church. To the Provost of Oriel Gladstone expostulated on the 'incredible' and indecent haste of the proceedings, citing in mitigation the ferocity of Newman's former writings against the Roman Church.[1] Gladstone's agitation broke through the scholarly air of a breakfast party at Macaulay's when, after innocuous conversation on Aristotle's *Politics*, talk on Oxford proceedings led to Gladstone's growing 'hot'.[2] Conferences with Hope and Manning led to agreement on a Declaration of Thanks to the Proctors (who had announced their intention to veto the censure on Newman). Gladstone hastened to snow-girt Oxford for the dramatic séance in the Sheldonian Theatre on February 13, where he saw the Protestant majority ('very fair for a mob', as he described them[3]) thwarted by the resolute proctors (one of whom, R. W. Church, was to become one of Gladstone's most influential ecclesiastical confidants). There was no need to waste sympathy on the duly degraded but ebulliently irrepressible Ward. It was more distressing

1 G to Provost of Oriel, February 8, 1845. GP, 44528, 10–11.
2 D, iii, 432.   3 Mallet, *Oxford*, iii, 274.

that Frederick Oakeley, the minister of the Chapel of All Saints in Margaret Street, should have declared his solidarity with Ward. Gladstone pleaded with Bishop Blomfield on Oakeley's behalf on the strength of his sense of personal debt to 'a restorer of the inward life and spirit of Divine Worship among us.'[1] Oakeley was received into the Church of Rome in September 1845. Most distressing of all was the awareness that the proctorial veto could only delay Newman's departure for Rome. Gladstone had indeed every cause to share Pusey's being 'sadly apprehensive about Newman'. He envisaged with dread the view thus opening up of 'important and continuous secessions to Rome' constituting the 'one frightful circumstance in the prospect of Catholicity within the English church'. And indeed the 'catastrophe' at Littlemore of Newman's decision to resign his fellowship occurred on June 1.[2]

Smarting from this blow by his beloved but incorrigibly Protestant Oxford against Anglican Catholicity, Gladstone consoled himself with the 'inward relief' provided by the discipline of the Engagement, the group of lay Anglo-Catholics formed in 1844 by the brothers Thomas D. and A. H. D. Acland under the patronage of St Barnabas, whose Rule, framed by Keble, he had in October shown to Catherine. This characteristic expression of the 'Tractarian' impulse of the times consisted of a dozen or more members, including Frederic Rogers (later Lord Blachford) the eminent civil servant, J. D. Coleridge the equally eminent judge, Roundell Palmer (later Earl of Selborne) a future Lord Chancellor, and William Butterfield the architect (who rebuilt their spiritual centre, the Chapel of All Saints, Margaret Street, as a model for Anglo-Catholic liturgical design).

Members of the Engagement bound themselves to twelve rules: some regular work of charity; attendance daily at religious service; observance of the fasts of the Church; observance of certain daily hours of prayer; special prayer observances; observance of rules for hours of sleep and recreation; observances of meditation and self-examination; a portion of income to be spent on works of mercy and piety; to consider a direction of confession and absolution; failing a spiritual director, to follow the judgment of one or more of the Engagement in the case of a breach of the rules; payment of extra funds if unable to perform a regular work of charity; and to meet regularly, compare results and consider amendments to the rules.[3] Gladstone had no great difficulty in conforming to most of these rules. Some of them were already more or less a part of his routine. In 1844 he subscribed a total of £920.15.9d to charitable and religious purposes; his 1848 total of £772.10s.4d. (hit by Oak Farm) was distributed among 61 items. He started to note the number of hours spent each day in sleep, meals and recreation (his total in the first week was 67½);

1 Butler, 191.   2 D, iii, 444, 458.   3 *Ib.*, 435–6.

and, though he gave up the habit of computing them on departing for Germany at the beginning of September 1845, his regular way of life in normal circumstances adequately guarded against self-indulgence. He certainly considered the question of a confessor. It was a not unusual practice among Anglo-Catholics at the time. Edward Pusey had given a lead in this direction at Oxford. But Gladstone evidently felt no compelling need for it as a formal spiritual office. His Journal provided in some ways for this purpose; and Manning he could look to in some degree for spiritual direction. His major initiative within the framework of the Engagement was to convert his early fascination with prostitutes and their 'rescue' from moral abandonment into a major feature of his work of charity. He made his first, tentative moves in talking to prostitutes and endeavouring to persuade them to escape from their lives of sin in the following summer, noting five such occasions between July 9 and August 24 1845. Catherine knew of and approved these rescue activities at a later stage (from 1850), but it is not clear whether she was aware of the inception of the practice. In any case, Gladstone did not undertake any such direct rescue work in the streets between August 1845 and July 1849, when it could be said to have started in earnest.

Instead, Gladstone channelled the charitable vocation required by the terms of the Engagement in these years within doors; into the institutionalised work of redemption which took its cue from James Hope's project in 1843 of a 'Refuge for the Houseless'. In 1846, under the supervision of the Bishop of London, a former workhouse, No. 9 Rose Street, Soho,[1] was purchased and converted for the temporary relief of the homeless and destitute 'with such offices of personal kindness, advice and instruction as each individual case may require', and with a view to a 'Christian effect on the poor population'. The St. Barnabas House of Charity opened in January 1847. It catered for both sexes (though distressed females predominated); a second refuge, managed by an Anglican sisterhood, the House of Mercy at Clewer, near Windsor, was more specifically geared to the reformatory work in which Gladstone mainly engaged himself. It would be a question for Gladstone whether his work in the St. Barnabas House and at Clewer would offer a sufficient remedy for his problem. His great need was to sublimate sexual tension by a vicarious diversion of emotional energy. It was possible that no such mode would substitute satisfactorily for the kind of release he seemed to get by direct accosting in the streets.

On the public side, Gladstone adjusted as best he could to being out of office for the first time since September 1841. He spoke from the front

---

1 Now No. 14 Manette Street. (The street name, evoking Dickens's character in *A Tale of Two Cities*, was changed in 1895.) The House of St. Barnabas-in-Soho still continues its work around the corner in No. 1 Greek Street. See below, 461.

bench halfway between the Treasury Bench and the bar of the House with all the authority of a privy councillor on such subjects as railways and sugar. Cobden's persistent and tasteless charges of bad faith on the part of the landlord class irritated him; and he had some sharp words for that 'very peremptory' association, the Anti-Corn Law League.[1] But unavoidably it was Maynooth that overshadowed all else. Gladstone consulted Hope and Manning prior to the debate, in which he took an early opportunity of intervening on April 11. He declared his conviction that the minority in the House who opposed Peel's policy of appeasing Irish Catholic sentiment represented the 'general and prevailing sentiment of the great majority of the people of England and Scotland'. He was nevertheless prepared, he assured the even more bemused House, 'in opposition to his most deeply cherished predilections', to give a 'deliberate and even anxious support' to Peel's measure, in opposition to his own constituents. He could find no 'great principle of the Constitution, sufficiently grounded in the actual convictions of the people', upon which resistance could be founded. The old principle of 'exclusive support of the national religion' had for 'so many years, and in so many ways', been 'grievously impaired', that it was no longer possible to urge it as forming in itself a conclusive reason for the rejection of a measure that applied public money to the purposes of some other communion. Peel's measure was one with 'an equitable and comprehensive regard to the actual circumstances of the period and of the country', especially in view of the 'practice of the State of Ireland, as it is, and as it is likely to remain'.[2]

A novel feature of the 1845 session was the emergence of Benjamin Disraeli as a leader of Tory dissidence. There was in his attitude a strong element of personal vendetta against Peel. That Gladstone, so conspicuously bred in Peel's school, should suffer some by-blows from this malevolence was to be expected. Disraeli was no longer merely the flamboyant dandy and scandalous society novelist of his earliest political days. The break-up of the Conservative party, with most of the ministers cleaving to their leader and the mass of backbenchers falling away, gave Disraeli an unparalleled opportunity to reveal his formidable talent for invective and his genius for projecting himself as the heroic spokesman for the cruelly betrayed Tory majority. He possessed, unfortunately for Gladstone, one unusual qualification for a member of parliament: he had taken the trouble, spurred no doubt by mischief rather than piety, to read Gladstone's book. This put him in a good position to tease Gladstone with sardonic expressions of mock disappointment that Gladstone had not supplied, 'subtle a casuist as he may be', the new principle of government upon which the country must now stand. Disraeli professed

1 H, lxxvii, 1284.   2 *Ib.*, lxxix, 522–53.

himself astonished that Gladstone should, on the issue of Maynooth, 'so completely have given up principles'. He had looked up to Gladstone 'as the last paladin of principle, the very chivalry of abstraction'. These were telling as well as mocking phrases. And he was able, by pouncing on a rather footling precedent of the time of Spencer Perceval pedantically appealed to by Gladstone, to conclude witheringly that he never supposed that it would be Gladstone of all people 'who would come and give the House the small change of circumstances to settle this great account'.[1]

To be thus exposed to mockery by a political adventurer was galling. All the more so since Disraeli had put his finger accurately on Gladstone's weakest point. What indeed *was* the new principle of government upon which the country must now stand? Gladstone's resignation offered no relevant guidance, no lesson of substance from which national politics could benefit. Moreover, what were the implications in Gladstone's rather despairing appeal to the special circumstances of Ireland for the Church of Ireland? No wonder Gladstone on April 16 'lay long thinking on the Irish Church question'.[2] He braced himself on April 18 to vote with the majority on the Maynooth division. The Conservative party was shattered, never to recover its unity or morale for a generation. It split nearly evenly, driven to the point of destruction by Peel's 'reckless determination'.[3] Peel thus got his bill by grace of the Whigs; but, since Gladstone had always been 'anxious to avoid any sanguine anticipations as to its results', he could not share the confidence of Peel, Stanley, or Graham that it would help the Church of Ireland. As he later explained to Manning, 'as to my book I believe people could show from it if they chose that I am bound after Maynooth, so far as consistency binds, to strip the Irish Church'.[4] Doubtless Disraeli would have so chosen. 'The Irish Church question', Gladstone moaned, 'is on me like a nightmare.'[5] It would, he warned Lincoln, 'lead us very far'. How could it be separated from the 'general question in Ireland'? If the Irish Church could not be defended on grounds of truth and duty could it be defended on grounds of the poverty and numbers of the Irish Roman Catholics?[6] He could not overcome his 'dread' of the issue: 'It is a Trojan horse, full of armed men.'[7]

There was also, of course, the awkward question of Newark and the Duke. His Grace was not amused at this recurrence of the disgraceful betrayal of 1829. His voters were very much of a mind with him. Gladstone was put to shifts to mollify an anti-Maynooth deputation from Newark on April 30. He put it to Lincoln, by way of discreetly communicating back to Clumber, that he could not think of retiring from

1 *Ib.*, 556–8.   2 D, iii, 448.   3 Gash, *Peel*, ii, 477.
4 G to Manning, March 8, 1846. GP, 44247, 289.
5 D, iii, 450.   6 *Ib.*, 452.   7 *Ib.*, 455–6.

his seat 'unless in the event that it should be distinctly alleged by the Duke or by my constituents that they had been *misled* by me'.[1] Gladstone was confident that a bold front would keep Newark in hand.

More perplexing was the problem of keeping Hope in hand. He lacked Gladstone's casuistic resilience. Maynooth hit him hard. It was worrying that Hope declined Gladstone's invitation to join the 'guild or confraternity' of the Engagement within which 'some humble and humbling offices' would be discharged.[2] Rather in a panic that Hope was slipping out of reach along with Newman, Gladstone addressed a passionate plea that 'we have in the Church of England, even among her mutilated institutions, large and free access to our Lord and a communion with Him sufficient to form in ourselves . . . all the lineaments of His Divine Image'. Gladstone believed firmly that the 'rulers of the Church of England' would 'put down' the 'heresy and latitudinarianism that range within her if they could'. But was not authority 'resolutely set on the side of those equally awful evils' which had a 'freer scope within the Roman Church'? It was also a plea, in effect, for Hope to accept Gladstone's decision to hold to politics. 'In the midst of the most painful oppression of heart, under a deep conviction that the civil power is moving itself farther and farther from God, and in a word beneath a pressure of anxieties not personal so heavy as to reduce to perfect insignificance the anxieties connected with the personal question whether I or any who may think similarly shall make utter shipwreck even of what is commonly termed public character in the effort', Gladstone avowed himself 'fastened down to the conviction that it is the duty of us who are in public affairs to remain where we are, and not effectually to separate ourselves from a general course which we believe to be one tending to evil, for the sake of the Church of God, and of the great opportunities, the gigantic opportunities of good and evil for the Church, which the course of events seems (humanly speaking) certain to open up'. And who could conceive a nobler vocation 'than that of one of the sentinels of the Church of England on the side looking towards the Church of Rome', defending, but defending 'in love'? The Church of Rome was both the 'very best and the very worst of all the Churches of Christ' – a sentiment 'clearly and strongly pronounced as to substance in Dante, that prodigy of humankind'.[3]

On precisely what terms to 'remain where we are'? Gladstone could afford to be more depressingly explicit on this theme in private than would be suitable in pathetic special pleadings to shore up Hope's morale. In a long memorandum on the sad prospects for halting the secularisation of State and Society Gladstone despairingly asked: 'Are

1 PMP, ii, 277.   2 Ornsby, *Hope-Scott*, ii, 63,71.
3 G to Hope, May 15, 1845. GP, 44214, 267, 276; Ornsby, *Hope-Scott*, ii, 60–61.

there now living the men whom God has appointed as his instruments for that work?' The State would adhere longer to religion 'in a vague than in a defined form'; but Gladstone could not be a party to 'tearing up the seamless garment of the Christian Faith in order to patch the ragged cloak of the State'. Therefore: 'Keep religion entire, and you secure at least to the individual man his refuge. Ask therefore on every occasion not what best maintains the religious repute of the State but what is least menacing to the integrity of Catholic belief and the Catholic Church.'[1] Which was pretty much the sceptical and even suspicious view of the State establishment of religion enjoined by Keble in his review of *The State in its Relations with the Church* in 1839. Gladstone had reached the point of turning his original programme inside out.

It was no doubt a relief amid all the 'pressure of anxieties' to make one last flourish in the parliamentary session: Gladstone distinguished himself on July 15 in a carefully prepared and satisfyingly virulent assault on Palmerston. He enjoyed his performance as a service he could render Peel, who needed his expertise on the matter in question (Spanish colonial sugar). But he enjoyed drubbing Palmerston all the more as a way of paying him back on Aberdeen's behalf for the 'tenacious animosity' with which the former foreign secretary had attempted to undermine Aberdeen's patiently unassertive policy of rebuilding good relations both with the conservative governments of Europe and with the United States. It was a significant stage in Gladstone's forming a pattern of critiques of Palmerston, linking his China speech of 1840 with the speeches he would make in 1850 on the case of Greece. It was also a particular pleasure because he earned from Peel, 'the most conscientious man I ever knew in spareness of eulogium', the tribute, 'that was a wonderful speech, Gladstone'. In 1896 Gladstone proudly allowed himself the pleasure of recording so signally rare an event.[2] Certainly Peel was in need of all the help he could get in the aftermath of Maynooth. Naturally he hoped to regain his disciple for his government. Gladstone was touched when at the end of the session Peel, in the role of weary Atlas sustaining the world of politics, complained of the 'pressures of a sense of fatigue upon the brain, I mean a physical sensation', caused by the immense multiplication of the details of public business, and the enormous tax imposed upon available time.[3]

From that point of view being out of office certainly had its attractions. In parliament Gladstone was free to pick and choose his occasions. He could take the opportunity to air his old hobbyhorse about the need for diplomatic relations with the Court of Rome.[4] Otherwise he was free to take Willy around Eton 'by way of initiation', to make arrangements for

1 GP, 44735, 38 (May 1845); *ib.*, 34 (June 19, 1845).
2 PMP, i, 128.   3 GP, 44777, 229.   4 H, lxxx, 1260–61.

Helen to go off to Baden-Baden and Munich for treatment (he saw her off, with well-founded foreboding, on July 20), to rejoice at the birth on July 27 of another daughter (Catherine Jessy), to admire the lovely Raphael at Lady Sykes's (one of Disraeli's former mistresses), to view the cartoon and fresco exhibition for the new Houses of Parliament, to arrange his books and make a catalogue (a never-ending source of enjoyable fussing), to worry about Hope (a report on August 10 gave him 'no comfort'), to urge 'Reasons for augmenting the incomes of the Scottish Bishops', to discuss with the Indian philanthropist Dwarkananth Tagore the admission of Indians to parliament, to devour theology and Church history. There had been a course of Dante in April; by July he was deep in Bishop Butler, the great eighteenth-century Doctor of Anglicanism, whom he had first tasted at Oxford, but whose magisterial disposing of deists seemed now even more crucially *à propos*. Perhaps it was this rather more relaxed atmosphere which led Gladstone in July and August to take tentative steps in accosting prostitutes. He had a 'touching conversation, not free of shame to me', with a woman who came from the vicinity of Hawarden.[1] There was talk with Philip Pusey and Hope of an autumn 'walking tour' of Ireland, which would have given Gladstone a view of that land on the brink of famine and demographic catastrophe. 'Ireland is likely to find this country and Parliament so much employment for years to come', Gladstone told Hope, 'that I feel rather oppressively an obligation to try and see it with my own eyes instead of using those of other people, according to the limited measure of my means.'[2] But the opportunity, ungrasped, slipped away. And in any case it became clear that, if Gladstone were to make an autumn tour, it would be to Germany to rescue Helen.

[3]

In the meantime, however, Bishop Butler was the pressing concern. For Gladstone now in the aftermath of Maynooth an urgent task was to find new intellectual brick and mortar with which the crumbling grounds and 'prospective objects' of his continuance in public life could be bolstered and secured. He needed a higher, revealed accreditation which had the power to resolve the contradiction between accepting defeat and not accepting defeat. He needed to be able to infuse convincingly such residue of the 1838 programme as survived within the 'crippled religious action of the State' into the moral and religious power immanent in political economy properly understood. He could not continue to wander

1 D, iii, 467.   2 Ornsby, *Hope-Scott*, ii, 62.

around the battlefield of defeat in a daze. He must make shift to set up new lines, if only at first of retreat in good order. Abandoning the fortress of his Maynooth position meant that he was now in open country, looking for cover. The sad news of Oxford opinions aggravated his sense of the need for fresh moral reinforcement, of redrawn mappings of spiritual terrain, of new resources both of attack and defence for a workable Christian idea of politics. Where to find it? In relating State to Church Gladstone had found Coleridge his most suggestive teacher. He was looking now for a doctrine which more comprehensively applied Christianity to the world. Formerly he had seen himself as a Churchman seeking political accreditation. Now he was a politician seeking religious accreditation. His duty was to turn to Anglican authority; his instinct was to seek something resonant and revered yet readily adaptable for his practical purposes. Bishop Butler answered these requirements in a manner Gladstone took to be, in itself, providential. The great modern (he was not yet a century dead) Anglican doctor of the moral government of the world, of God as 'Almighty Maker, Governor, and Judge',[1] Butler was to be for Gladstone a lifelong obsession. His intellectual valediction in 1896 was an edition designed to recommend Butler for the edification of the contemporary world. One of his great griefs was the 'blot' on Oxford for not restoring Butler to its curriculum.[2] 'The supreme value of Butler will probably be found in the future, as it has been in the past, to lie in this; that the works of the Bishop are singularly adapted to produce that mental attitude required for treating the questions which concern the dealings of God with man.'[3]

    In an elaborate 'Exercisus Butleriani' of 1845,[4] Gladstone began his great wrestle with the Bishop. He did not need Butler for what hitherto he had most been famed, as a prop of faith against the seductions of deism or infidelity, as the Christian advocate recommended by Pitt to the doubting Wilberforce, as the proponent of a doctrine of probabilism and sufficient evidence who almost saved even James Mill for the faith. Butler's peculiar utility for Gladstone consisted both in his 'mental qualities' and his method as well as in his teaching on the bearings of divine purpose in the world for those Christians setting out to apprehend it as best they might. It was Butler's 'strength of tissue' which so recommended him to Gladstone, 'always dealing with the heart, never with the surface of the question', with 'no outside, no mere skin, to his writings', with a unique 'closeness of contact between the author and his argument'; above all, where every single sentence was like a 'well-

1 *Studies Subsidiary to the Works of Bishop Butler* (1896), 84.
2 Tollemache, 42.   3 *Studies Subsidiary*, 16.
4 GP, 44731, 66–120 (undated, and catalogued as of 1842; but almost certainly the fruit of Gladstone's delving into Butler in the summer of 1845).

considered move in chess'.[1] *The Analogy of Religion, Natural and Revealed, to the Constitution and Course of Nature*, by arguing that the difficulties of Revelation were no greater than the difficulties of the natural order of Creation, offered a means of deducing moral politics within a Christian providential scheme: 'an argument for religion at large, drawn from the course of natural government at large.' In the opening up of this argument, which in Gladstone's judgment stood out 'among the master-pieces of the human mind', Butler 'unfolded to us the entire method of God's dealings with his creatures; and in this way the argument which he offers is as wide as those dealings themselves'.[2]

This grand comprehensiveness did not of itself dispel human ignorance (Gladstone was sure that no part of Butler's teaching was 'more urgently required' in the nineteenth century than his 'strong but carefully bounded view of human ignorance'[3]); but by offering a method of interpreting 'the dealings of God with men in the kingdoms of Nature, Providence, and Grace',[4] even men who could know but 'a most insignificant portion of the whole order of things'[5] could reliably deduce that the 'intelligent Author of nature is also moral, for He takes sides in that conflict between virtue and vice, which incessantly prevails in the world'.[6] Thus 'Butler's pursuit, and the labours of those who study him, are incessantly conversant with the relation between the lower and higher world, between all the shapes of human character and experience on the one side, and a great governing agency on the other'. The evidences of this providential scheme of moral government were a system of 'moral desert and punishment for sin' and 'marks of distributive justice in the world'.[7]

Gladstone interrogated Butler more specifically for his purposes as a Christian politician. 'By his argument he has set forth to us with remarkable closeness and precision . . . the method of the government of God, and . . . the provision supplied to us for the discharge of our several offices under that government; taking the two together, he has here supplied us with the main substance of a philosophy of life.' The evidential links between the governing agencies of the higher and lower worlds were grounded on the fact that Butler 'chose for his whole argument the sure and immovable basis of human experience, from his earliest tracings of natural government, up to his final development of the scheme of revealed religion'.[8] For 'while the *Analogy* purports to exhibit God's method in one department only, that which deals with religion, it is equally applicable to the whole of our moral experience; first, in every study, in philosophy, history and the rest; and secondly, in conduct, in

1 *Studies Subsidiary*, 86–87. 2 *Ib.*, 8–9.
3 *Ib.*, 104.   4 *Ib.*, 76.   5 *Ib.*, 46.
6 *Ib.*, 15.   7 *Ib.*, 51.   8 *Ib.*, 2.

the entire weaving of that web, whereof our whole life is made up'. A theory of probability and presumptive evidence is indeed well calculated for the purposes of men of affairs (Gladstone could even cite Voltaire's testimony in support).[1] 'To know what kinds and degrees of evidence to expect or to ask in matters of belief and conduct, and to be in possession of an habitual presence of mind built upon that knowledge, is, in my view, the master gift which the works of Butler are calculated to impart.' Especially is this gift valuable if this 'mental habit' is developed 'in that field of thought which above all others is occupied by the science of the indeterminate': which is to say (following Bacon) politics. With the method of such a theologian as Butler, the politician, the lawyer, and the scientist also, was twice armed. It might be noted particularly that for Gladstone it would seem to have been a potent recommendation of Butler's doctrine that the Butlerian politician's weaponry was so amply provided in his function as an agent of virtue against vice, as an exponent of moral desert and punisher of sin and as an awarder of marks of distributive justice.

'Undoubtedly,' Gladstone concluded, 'if my counsel were asked, I should advise the intending politician, if of masculine and serious mind, to give to Butler's works, and especially to the *Analogy*, a high place among the apparatus of his mental training.'[2] Gladstone began in 1845 to equip himself with this apparatus and to put himself in possession thereby of the appropriate habitual presence of mind. His 'four "doctors"', as he was soon telling Manning, Aristotle, Augustine, Dante, and Butler, 'are doctors to the speculative men; would they were such to the practical too!'[3]

[4]

A family crisis called Gladstone away from Butler. 'Sad letters from Fasque' about Helen's state of mind and body in Munich reached him in mid-September. He consulted Dr Wiseman. He had notions in any case of resuming his acquaintance with the solemn delights of Rome. Perhaps Helen might somehow be established there? But Wiseman did not think there were any 'persons or establishments in Rome that would take charge of Helen in the way I hoped'. ('I told Dr. W. in justice to Helen that personally I knew she had every kind feeling towards me.') Gladstone now considered his going to Rome '*almost* put out of the question: I cannot at present think it would be my duty to go there for the purpose of showing it to her'.[4] It was, equally, his duty to go to Munich for the

1 *Ib.*, 335.   2 *Ib.*, 6.   3 Morley, i, 247.
4 G to CG, September 23, 1848. GGP, 28/2.

purpose of restoring her to her family, armed with a letter from Wiseman telling her to obey her father. Gladstone lost no time in setting off on a fraternal rescue mission. A missed boat at Brighton led to a sharp letter of complaint to the Steam Navigation Company; complaint also about missed devotions or of 'prayers in a corner' was the keynote of his swift passage through Calais and Paris. He stopped by at Passy on the fringe of Paris to call on Guizot, former ambassador in London and now the strong man of Soult's ministry, with a message from Aberdeen about international copyright. Guizot (a Protestant) congratulated Gladstone on Peel's Maynooth policy and assured him that England would have the 'sympathies of Europe in the work of giving Ireland justice'. Gladstone 'saved and pondered' this remark, as he later reminded Guizot, as opening for him an insight into a European view of the Irish question.[1] Then on he pressed through Toul, Strasbourg, Kehl, Stuttgart, and Ulm. But at the opera at Augsburg he was soothed by 'Mozart's soft luxurious music, exquisite of its kind' in *Don Giovanni*.[2] He reached Munich on September 30 to find that Helen had skipped out of the way, back to Baden-Baden. For want of immediate occupation (he even contemplated attending a race-meeting, to 'see & inquire') he found himself in the company of Bavarian scholars and divines, among whom was one Hope had urged him to seek out, Dr. Ignaz Döllinger, professor of ecclesiastical history at the university and one of the more prominent of the Roman Catholic theologians of the liberal stripe. Gladstone, rejoicing no doubt that his laborious practice of German had left him sufficiently well found in that tongue, took to Döllinger instantly. They spent five hours together on Gladstone's first evening in Munich, with which Gladstone found himself 'greatly delighted'. The following evening he saw Döllinger again (the other guests left at nine '& I sat with Dr. D. till 1'). By October 3 it was a matter of note for Gladstone that he saw Döllinger for but one hour only ('but a good one'). He decided to postpone his pursuit of his sister for a few days.

Döllinger marked an epoch in Gladstone's intellectual and religious life. At a time when Catholicity in the Church of England seemed to tremble on the brink of discredit and ruin, when the kind of Italianate-Irish Romanism represented by Wiseman was raising its head in anticipation of an era of advances and triumphs, it was reassuring to find an entirely different face of Roman Catholicism. Eminently learned, Döllinger was theologically sympathetic and intellectually congenial, leaning liberally towards the Reformation as Gladstone leaned conservatively towards Rome. Döllinger's historical approach to theology and the Church Gladstone found particularly sympathetic. He relished especially Döllinger's scepticism on the doctrine of purgatory. 'I often

1 Morley, i, 874.   2 D, iii, 485.

think of Dr. Döllinger's assurance to us,' Gladstone recalled in 1850, '– expressing I am sure his own conviction – that the Church had no judicial function, no authority beyond the grave. I wish this were the real Roman doctrine.'[1] Döllinger's influence solidified and ratified the development in Gladstone's mind of distinguishing an 'historical' course of religious thought, accepting the 'visibility' of the Church, from the 'ultramontane' course which accepted the papal monarchy (and from the 'protestant evangelical', 'deistic' and 'negative' courses).[2] Gladstone manifested his delight in this meeting of minds in copious and careful memoranda of their conversations. They were indeed 'of great comfort to one who views the unity of Christians as I must do'. When they bade farewell Döllinger said, 'Well, we are in one Church by water – upon that I shall rest.' Gladstone responded that it was his happiness 'to be allowed to go farther'.[3]

This serendipity of missing Helen and finding Döllinger could not long be allowed to deflect Gladstone from duty. He tracked down the hapless Helen at Baden on October 8, finding her full of laudanum and hysteria. She proved highly refractory, refusing to go back to her family and having to be held down by force to be leeched. 'Use deadens us to frightful things,' he wrote on October 12 to Catherine; 'and I feel it ought to seem to me more piercingly frightful than it does seem.' But in fact the distracted, intense, and almost feverish tone of this long letter makes it evident that frightfulness took a severe toll. Gladstone was having 'odd dreams': 'one that *John* had turned R.C. & would not listen to me trying to dissuade him: the other that (last night) Lady M. Farquhar was being confirmed in a house of mine, & Sir W. brought her a *huge* mass of roast meat just at the beginning: this event turned me out of my bed below stairs & I thought I would go up to you as a surprise! What a creation is the brain of man.' Away from his wife and children Gladstone felt himself especially exposed to temptations to impurity. 'This absence from you & them is so unnatural, and makes one feel so lawless.'

His talks with Döllinger brought home to Gladstone, as he told Catherine, 'what a crisis for *religion* at large is this period of the world's history – how the power of religion and its permanence are bound up with the Church – how inestimably precious would be the Church's unity, inestimably precious on the one hand and on the other to human eyes immeasurably remote – lastly how loud and how solemn is the call upon all those who hear and who *can* obey it to labour more and more in the spirit of these principles, to give themselves if it may be clearly and

1 D, iii, 275. Matthew, 'Gladstone, Vaticanism and the Question of the East', *Studs. in Church Hist.*, xv, 423.
2 'The Courses of Religious Thought' (1876); *Gleanings*, iii, 101.
3 PMP, iii, 6.

wholly to that work'. It seemed that amid the painful pressure and turmoil and loneliness Gladstone sensed the beginnings of an outline of an alternative mode of giving himself. 'It is dangerous my Cathie to put indefinite thoughts, instincts, longings, into language which is necessarily determinate. I cannot trace the line of my own future life, but I hope and pray it may not be always where it is: not that it may now cease to be so, nor while a reasonable hope remains of serving God there to more purpose than elsewhere: but that that hope may come to an issue if it be His will.' The implications of the Maynooth case for the Church of Ireland, exacerbated perhaps by Guizot's words, pressed themselves upon Gladstone with the eerie clarity of yet another bad dream.

> I see too plainly the process which is separating the work of the State from the work of the Christian faith. Even now as a consenting party, in a certain sense, and relatively to certain purposes, to that process of separation, I am upon the very outside verge, though with full consciousness, and an undoubting support from within, of the domain which conscience marks to me as an open one. I have a growing belief, that I shall never be enabled to do much good for the Church in Parliament (if at all) except after having seemed first a traitor to it and being reviled as such. I mean that it is now for the highest interest of the Church to give gold for freedom . . . Ireland, Ireland! that cloud in the west, that coming storm, the minister of God's retribution upon cruel and inveterate and but half-atoned injustice! Ireland forces upon us these great social and great religious questions – God grant that we may have courage – to look them in the face and to work through them.

Were these questions worked through, 'were the path of the Church clear before her as a body able to take her trial before God and the world upon the performance of her work as His organ for the recovery of our country' – how joyfully would Gladstone 'retire from the barren exhausting strife of merely political contention'. Nor did he suppose that Catherine would be 'very sorrowful' for such an issue.

> As to ambition in its ordinary sense, we are spared the chief part of its temptations. If it has a valuable reward upon earth over and above good name, it is when a man is enabled to bequeath to his children a high place in the social system of his county. That cannot be our case. The days are gone by when such a thing might have been possible. To leave to Willy a title with its burdens and restraints and dis-qualifications, but without the material substratum of wealth, and the duties & means of good as well as the general power of attending it, would not I think be acting for him in a wise and loving spirit. . . But oh!

my beloved have I not seen promise, apparently as fair, utterly, awfully blighted – how narrow a bridge are a few short years to connect childhood almost angelic with the wreck so to speak of heart & body at the very commencement of maturity!¹

'Great as is one's joy in *them*', the children, Helen's collapse served as a grim warning. Henry Glynne's marriage (he already had daughters) seemed to close an avenue of legitimate expectation.

The personal frightfulness of Helen's case mingled for Gladstone with the political frightfulness of his own. Yet, as ever, he stipulated very high conditions for his retirement from politics. His 'growing belief' that he would never be able to serve the Church 'except after having seemed first a traitor to it and being reviled as such' suggests both a parallel with Peel's travails and something of a notion of an analagously grand Peelite political mission. The most significant and revealing insight exposed in his letter to Catherine of October 12 was his 'full consciousness' and 'undoubting support from within', that there was a 'domain' before him which his conscience marked to him as 'open'. His vocation, following his sense of the turn of the 'process' which separated the 'work of the State from the work of the Christian faith', would reflect the extent to which its original form had become turned inside out. Just as Peel set out to defend protection and was now reviled as a traitor to it, Gladstone could discern the outlines of a great work open to him of fulfilling the logic forced ineluctably upon him to labour for the principles of '*religion* at large in this period of the world's history'. His 'treachery' to the national Church programme of 1838 would take the form of an ecumenical commitment to Catholic unity. This was the vision congruent with the contrast between the historicity of *Church Principles Considered in their Results* and the *a prioristic The State in its Relations with the Church*. Such a commitment would be wide and 'open' not only ecumenically: history, as Gladstone pointed out, forced upon him great social questions as well as great religious questions.

In the intervals of coping with Helen and her numerous attendants and medical specialists, Gladstone diverted himself with excursions. (At Strasbourg he much disliked the *Louis Quinze* monument in the cathedral to Marshal Maurice de Saxe, so much of a 'spruce or as we used to say at Eton dapper figure' about to step into his tomb in full regimentals.²) There was cheering news of Samuel Wilberforce's appointment to the bishopric of Oxford: 'on the whole it would be a very good one & honourable to Peel.'³ The lamentable news of Newman's final submission to Rome reached Gladstone amid the incongruous promenades of the grand-

---

1 G to CG, October 12, 1845. GGP, 28/2; Bassett, 63–65.
2 D, iii, 491.   3 G to CG, October 25, 1845. GGP, 28/2.

ducal watering-place. He wrote to Manning, much in the mood of his earlier appeal to Hope, on the theme of the plenitude of the efficacy of Anglicanism and (with Newman in mind) on the duty of stepping into the place of a comrade fallen from the Church 'as a rear rank man when his front rank man falls in battle'.[1] Having thus distributed a meed of stoic cheer, Gladstone exercised his mind by grappling for two and a half hours in conversation with a young Jesuit priest. As he explained to Catherine, 'I am rather deep in German divinity that is as far as my very narrow knowledge will allow me to go'.[2] Enforced leisure also gave him the opportunity for an elaborate exercise in self-examination as enjoined in the rules of the Engagement. On October 26 he set out a 'sketch of my besetting sin', that is, irrepressible curiosity over 'impure' books and prints. He resolved, in a series of 'remedies', 'not to look over books in bookshops, except known ones', and the same 'as to looking in printshop windows'.[3] It was in a mood thus chastened that Gladstone wrote to Catherine:

> I am well assured that if we stood together before God's tribunal our relative positions would be the reverse of what you suppose. Let us however only ask ourselves, my beloved, how we can help one another, how raise one another upwards, how enable one another through Him to enter into the performance of that great work which is waiting to be done for Him among us. O may we be found really pressing forward, striving towards the mark, for the prize.[4]

The prize of rescuing Helen, however, eluded him. His mission undoubtedly resulted in doing Helen good; but he failed to entice her to accompany him home. He got her as far as Cologne, but further she would not budge in his company. Foiled, but consoled by a midnight view of the cathedral, Gladstone had no choice but to leave Helen to her own devices and to return alone. By January 1846 Helen was declining to communicate with either Tom or William.

[5]

Back in England by November 17, after a harrowing passage and sitting in the Dover Customhouse for the night, Gladstone found Catherine and the children happy and well at Hagley. Once more in London he was soon caught up by the quickening pace of political developments. Russell

1 G to Manning, October 20, 1845. GP, 44247, 273.
2 G to CG, October 28, 1845. GGP, 28/2.
3 D, iii, 491–2.   4 G to CG, October 28, 1845. GGP, *ib.*

on November 22 announced that, with famine impending in Ireland, he was a convert to total repeal of the Corn Law, and advocated public agitation to encourage the government to take the plunge. Lincoln was Gladstone's contact with the great world and his link especially both with Peel and the Duke of Newcastle. They had much talk on December 6 on Church matters. On the question of the hour, the Corn Law, Gladstone told Lincoln that in his view the old law had been a 'delusion', as virtually equalling prohibition. The new modification of 1842 would be all right if it realised the purpose of the scale then introduced. Although the 1815 Law was a 'gross error' Gladstone did not feel himself at liberty upon the terms of his election in 1841 to unsettle the new one. On the other hand, if it were found to have the same deficiencies as the old one, he held himself at liberty to vote against it, 'and could justify the vote to my constituents and contend it was the same which they in my place must as fair and honest men have given'. Gladstone, it is clear, had no notion of the depth of the crisis confronting Peel and the government; nor, indeed, of the depth of the crisis which would shortly be confronting him at Newark. Lincoln, much better informed but not at liberty to divulge cabinet confidentialities, remarked that the new law was not working well, and that Peel and Graham 'apprehended a great deficiency'. (Peel had circulated on December 2 his crucial memorandum about the need to find fresh sources of food for about three million people in the United Kingdom, and in view of that whether to maintain, modify, or suspend the Corn Law.) Lincoln was clear that the government was in a 'false position': it was 'especially desirable to disengage the Corn Law if possible from the general interests of the aristocracy which were now more seriously compromised by it'. All this was a jolt for Gladstone: 'It is manifest that something is in the wind – and something serious.'[1]

On December 16 Gladstone, immersed congenially in refuting Newman's *Essay on the Development of Doctrine* and reading St. Cyprian, Dryden, and Ovid, was called away by politics: 'Devoured the newspapers: I do not yet understand why the crisis came now & not later.'[2] Peel, with both party and now cabinet hopelessly divided, resigned, and Russell undertook on December 18 to form a ministry. However, though bold enough to urge Peel to take the plunge, Russell seemed not to relish the notion of matching his brave words with deeds. After a feeble parody of negotiations he hastened to return the 'poisoned chalice' to the Queen, who perforce passed it on back to Peel. Exasperated by Russell's trifling, Peel determined on one last great stroke of decisive ruthlessness. Gladstone was full of foreboding and apprehension. Repeal could not be done 'in conformity with the due relation between the constituent and the representative body and without con-

1 PMP, iii, 11–13.   2. D, iii, 503.

victing us either of folly or fraud either now or in 1841' – 'unless upon the special facts of the Irish case which I did not yet know'. And afterwards: 'Upon what were we to rally as a party? Were we to be a party, separate from the Whigs?' Gladstone dreaded 'beyond all things' that 'these processes should run into series'; that the same pattern of rallying the country to defence of a great interest or institution should be followed after a certain period by successive abandonments; that this 'factious baseness' might apply, for example, to the Irish Church. 'This must not be,' Gladstone concluded; 'but plainly our having this in the background made the present subject far more difficult to manage.' It seemed certain that Stanley and Buccleuch would resign; equally certain that Peel would send for Gladstone to stand by him at his supreme hour of need. Gladstone prayed that God would 'exclude the pest ambition' from his soul.[1] 'I have been & am still in a great whirl,' he wrote to Catherine. 'Both private & public affairs are such as to defy repose & even *my* nervous system has lost a little of its steadiness. . .'[2]

On Sunday, December 21, after Holy Communion at the Margaret Street Chapel, Gladstone met Peel at Lincoln's house. Stanley had indeed resigned and Peel asked Gladstone to fill his place at the Colonial Office. Never did Gladstone feel a 'poorer creature'. But he needed to be convinced that the Irish situation was so critical as to 'entirely alter the case'. On the 22nd he read the Scarcity and Crisis papers previously circulated to the Cabinet on the situation in Ireland. He saw Peel again at three and accepted office, 'in opposition', he had the consolation of feeling, to his 'leanings & desires: & with the most precarious prospects'. So much for that 'pest', ambition. Peel was 'most kind, nay fatherly – we *held* hands instinctively & I could not but reciprocate with emphasis his "God bless you".'[3] Defending his decision later to his protectionist father, Gladstone pointed out that he had invariably up to that time spoken of protection 'tenderly and cautiously'; but 'It *then* appeared to me that the case was materially altered' by events in Ireland; 'it was no longer open to me to pursue that cautious course.' A 'great struggle was imminent, in which it was plain that two parties only could find real place, on the one side for repeal, on the other side for *permanent* maintenance of a corn law and a protective system generally and on principles.'[4] It was a more difficult matter defending his resumption of office to those who had looked to him as (in William Palmer's words) 'a faithful son of that Church which you have in past years strengthened and edified by your admired writings, and which . . . looked up to you as her greatest earthly Hope.'[5] Gladstone accepted office in August 1841 to serve the Church; he accepted office in December 1845 to serve the State. He excused himself

1 PMP, iii 14–19.   2 G to CG, December 20, 1845. GGP, 28/2.
3 D, iii, 506–7.   4 *Ib.*, xxxviii-ix.   5 Butler, 117.

awkwardly to Hope: 'I have sought for the best alternative, honestly, so far as that term is applicable to any of the operations of my mind. I am sure you pray for me.'[1] A few days before his thirty-sixth birthday Gladstone was a secretary of state. But would he remain Member for Newark? Appointment to office meant submitting himself for re-election, and putting the 'fairness and honesty' of his constituents to the test.

The interstices of these political transactions Gladstone filled with his campaign to hold Manning to the Church – a matter he regarded as of at least equal importance. His ploy on this occasion was to lure Manning by propping up Newman as a tempting punch-bag. Newman's new book, Gladstone informed Manning on December 23, 'interests me deeply, shakes me not at all'. He placed Christianity 'on the edge of a precipice; from whence a bold & strong hand would throw it over'. Gladstone was 'more sanguine' than Manning about the 'ultimate issue'. He was persuaded 'that Bishop Butler if he were alive would in his quiet way tear the whole argument into shreds wonderful as is the book, so that we should wonder where it had been'. Why should Manning not be the Bishop Butler of their time? Why not tear Newman's argument into shreds and strike a famous blow for Anglicanism?[2] Perhaps Gladstone should have reflected that Butler, who started his career as a Dissenter, was suspected of having ended it a Roman Catholic. For Manning was lured into measuring himself against Newman, but found the task disturbing and unsettling to his Anglican faith.[3]

Gladstone's fears about Manning's susceptibilities in the light of Newman's fall and Hope's weakness were all the livelier since Manning was the nearest thing Gladstone had to a spiritual director. Another of Gladstone's pious ploys at this time was to press upon Manning a variety of issues relevant to this quasi-office. Did he hope thus to bind Manning with one more thread? From Manning Gladstone received guidance that three hours of religious devotion per day – prayers, fasting, festival, private devotion and scripture – was a reasonable expectation. Gladstone still thought the three hours a 'scanty allowance', but designed charitably for ordinary persons. Gladstone submitted his own regimen for Manning's inspection: when '*in London and in office*', family prayers twice a day; Sundays were reserved for devotional offices 'with rare exceptions', and it was Gladstone's practice to receive communion. On weekdays, of daily services 'except a little before and after Easter', Gladstone could not claim one a fortnight; perhaps one a month. Such were the consequences of the 'sad irregularity of public life'. The practice of guarding his Sundays in fact, Gladstone was convinced, had kept him alive and well. He

1 *Ib.*, 131–32.
2 G to Manning, December 23, 1845. GP, 44247, 277–79.
3 Purcell, i, 318.

pleaded that his constitutional need for sleep was great; though he admitted that he *could* economise on his reading. On average, over the last year, he could claim not over ten hours per day for sleep, food and recreation – though of course 1845 had been a 'holiday year' as to pressure upon mind and body.[1] 1846 clearly was going to be different.

[6]

Between settling in at the Colonial Office and seeing the New Year in as the guest of the Queen and Prince at Windsor Gladstone barely had time for a rather scrambled Christmas at Hawarden. There was a pleasant family atmosphere at Windsor, though Gladstone was bound to confess that it was 'difficult to look at the little Prince of Wales without a sigh'.[2] From Windsor he sent off his re-election address to Newark. 'The town is much disposed to kick against the Duke,' he deludedly assured Catherine. 'The Duke has not got a man & they say will have much difficulty. If *he* is determined to keep me out, very likely a League[r] may come forward!'[3] Matters at Newark, he reported on January 7, 'continue in a curious state – my old supporters have fought a good battle & I think they will very likely beat the Duke'.[4] Beat the Duke they did not. Gladstone protested vainly to his agent: 'If there were a candidate ready to offer himself with the Duke's recommendation, I should retire, but not otherwise;' '*simply* retire I cannot: recede I will, if the Duke of Newcastle has another candidate.'[5] Gladstone seems to have calculated that he could bluff the Duke by stipulating that the Duke would have to take the distasteful initiative of producing an alternative candidate. But if so he miscalculated; for the Duke did not need to. Gladstone's erstwhile 'principal & best supporters among the Electors' did the job for him by providing John Stuart, Q.C.,[6] in the protectionist interest, with the Duke's fervent blessing. Gladstone was outraged, and considered himself dishonestly supplanted. He renounced his candidature in the highest dudgeon. 'Stuart had behaved ill,' he told Catherine, 'and I have had to write to him at great length . . . there is great discontent and indignation in the town.'[7] He was not used to defeat, and took it badly. His supplanter in the borough's affections, moreover, had the effrontery

1 Lathbury, ii, 266–9.
2 G to Manning, April 19, 1846. GP, 44247, 306.
3 G to CG, January 3, 1846. GGP, 28/2
4 G to CG, January 7, 1846. *Ib.*
5 G to Caparn, January 10, 1846; to J. Stuart, January 13, 1846. GP, 56444.
6 Later Sir John Stuart (1793–1876), Vice-Chancellor (1852), Bencher of Lincoln's Inn.
7 G to CG, January 9, 1846. GGP, 28/2.

to add insult to injury by suggesting he might apply to the alternative borough of Dudley. Gladstone was hurt and bitter: 'The Duke of Newcastle has committed an error: he has made Newark a watchword, ready for a conspicuous place in some future Reform agitation – but I am not his judge.'[1]

It was humiliating thus to have forfeited the Duke's countenance; and it was embarrassing to be claimed eagerly for one of their own by the Liberals and Leaguers of Newark. 'Avowed' members of the League expressed 'consternation' at Gladstone's enforced retirement, and assured him of the support of 'nearly all your former opponents'. 'Time has been, when the Party with which I am concerned,' a Mr. Jackson assured him, 'did not think well of your political views, circumstances have changed, and we agree.'[2] And from a certain W. Andrews, an 'extreme Radical': 'the Electors of this Borough are very generally disposed to support you ... in Opposition to any Person who may present himself as the Advocate of unrestricted Monopoly and as the Candidate of the no Popery party.'[3] There was even a requisition forwarded by the local secretary of the Anti-Corn Law League that Gladstone stand avowedly in the free trade interest. Appalled at this box of horrors he had unwittingly opened, Gladstone hastened to reassure his agent that he had made no declarations of any compromising kind to such persons. Instead, he began to make shift to find himself a new seat: 'Somewhere or other I must woo again as soon as possible.'[4] Ripon, Wigan, Liverpool, Dorchester and Chester, were wooed early; Oxford City, Scarborough, Aberdeen and the Montrose Burghs wooed later; all wooed in vain. There was talk again of South Lancashire. There was no reason, as Gladstone grumpily pointed out to Robertson, why they 'should not have had me if they liked it'. Evidently, as he had to conclude sourly, they did not like it.[5] Even at the Whips' office Bonham's unrivalled expertise was baffled by the task of placing so odd a political specimen as the new Colonial Secretary.[6] Gladstone, unseated as it happened until August 1847, was obliged during his six-month tenure of the Colonial Office, and through the high drama of the fall of Peel's government, to remain a frustrated spectator in the Commons' gallery.

Quite apart from this exasperating lack of a constituency, Gladstone found his tenure of his new office an exasperating task. He was later to complain eloquently about the difficulties peculiar to the Colonial

1 G to Caparn, January 12, 1846. GP, 56444.
2 James Jackson to Gladstone, January 7, 1846. *Ib.*
3 W. Andrews to Gladstone, January 8, 1846. *Ib.*
4 G to Caparn, January 15, 1846. *Ib.*
5 G to Robertson G, July 3, 1846. GP, 44528, 72.
6 G to Bonham, January 16, 1846: 'I am not exactly aware of the steps that a man in office and out of Parliament should take in order to remove the anomaly by supplying himself with a seat.' J. B. Conacher, 'Mr Gladstone Seeks a Seat', *Canadian Historical Association Annual Report* (1962), 57.

department: problems of distance and delay, problems of partial information, interventions invariably too late, an immense mass of business of which nine out of ten issues bored the Commons and the tenth was decided on an unintelligently partisan basis.[1] But in any case Gladstone was in a great muddle about colonies. He indulged himself with the delusion that it was possible to draw 'the broadest and most marked distinction between questions of a local and imperial character'; and that upon the foundation thus securely laid could be erected a 'general doctrine of the necessary supremacy of the mother country over a colonial dependency'.[2] In the dispute between Lord Elgin and the Canadians in 1849, for instance, Gladstone's partisanship for Elgin earned a rebuke from Russell for needlessly embittering the question.[3] But the most revealing instance of Gladstone's unsureness of touch was his harsh dismissal of Sir Eardley Wilmot from the governorship of Van Diemen's Land. Wilmot had been sent out to reform the corrupt transportation system so as to allow its continuation and expansion, an object much desired by the British government and by Gladstone. It was a hopeless undertaking. Gladstone, impatient with Wilmot's failure to achieve the impossible (and shocked by reports of rampant homosexuality among the convicts), credulously received misinformation from Church sources in the colony (who were in conflict with the Governor) about Wilmot's personal morals. Humiliated, Wilmot became a colonial hero; and Gladstone was lucky that Wilmot's death in the colony prevented his return to drum up a campaign to clear his reputation. Gladstone behaved throughout with perfect good faith but woeful insensitivity.[4]

One dimension of Gladstone's muddle was impeccably 'liberal'. He was clear that colonial policy ever since the American War of Independence had been unsuccessful and expensive. He was clear that what ought to be kept in view was not separation or connection as such or expenditure as such but the great 'work and function' assigned by divine providence to Britain of 'laying the foundation of mighty States in different quarters of the world'. What ought to be kept in view was the cherishing and fostering of those infant communities on 'principles that are sound and pure – on the principle of self-government'.[5] Thus, on the question of franchises in Australia, Gladstone fully concurred in 'the policy of giving free institutions' to the colonies, and indeed warned against setting the franchise so high as to produce a dangerously oligarchical form of government, 'which possessed the character of freedom in relation to this country, but in relation to the great mass of the population a very different character'.[6] But the other dimension of

1 H, cvi, 983–4 (June 26, 1849). 2 *Ib.*, 193–4, 225. 3 *Ib.*, 225.
4 See K. Fitzpatrick, 'Mr Gladstone and the Governor,' *Hist. Studs., Australia and New Zealand* (1940), 31–45.
5 H, civ, 354–5. 6 H, cv, 1129.

Gladstone's muddle, deriving from his schoolman notions of necessary metropolitan supremacy and colonial dependency and consequent categories of imperial and local jurisdiction, led him to suppose, in that same case of Australia, that the policy of transporting criminals could not only be maintained, but extended. And he was quite clear that this should be done despite the 'ill odour' into which the transportation system had fallen with the Australian colonists.[1] It rankled with Gladstone also that the colonists had a tendency to look to the British taxpayer. Part of his penchant for self-government was the idea that the colonists must be given free institutions upon which to found their own responsibility for their acts, and the taxation by which to pay for them.[2] In other words, if they wished to wage war against Kaffirs or Maoris, they must bear the financial burden involved.

These opinions, expressed primarily because Gladstone continued for a few years to be the Peelite spokesman on colonial issues, hardly mattered as far as his transient and embarrassed tenure of the Colonial Office in 1846 was concerned. It was eloquently expressive of his sense of futility that he referred to the 'thirteen noblemen and gentlemen who have in such unhappily rapid succession flitted through this Office to which, in the penury of the times, I have been brought'.[3] His immediate cares in any case tended to be such problems as the enlargement of the Order of the Bath and, above all, appointments to jobs and coping with the mass of applications and recommendations for jobs. Indeed, one of his first acts was to appoint Catherine's brother-in-law George Lyttelton to be his under-secretary. Lyttelton, as chairman of the Canterbury Association, a body dedicated to planting colonies of an Anglican tincture, in fact represented the one aspect of colonial affairs (apart of course from tariffs and trade) in which Gladstone had hitherto taken any interest, beyond his old devotion to the West Indies. It cannot be said that such concern as Gladstone took in colonial affairs in 1846 either did much good for the colonies or for the general enlargement of Gladstone's political sensibility. He left the Colonial Office in June with notions, conventional enough, now that the West Indies interest had decided into insignificance, which equipped him with a sufficient mistrust of colonists, dislike of expanse and expansion, and a shrewdly pessimistic overall sense that the empire was a hindrance rather than a help, to provide himself with ready rules-of-thumb by which to measure colonial affairs for the rest of his career. These rules-of-thumb he wrapped in generous doctrine which served for all purposes: the connection between the colonies and the mother country would subsist upon the basis of local

1 H, ciii, 422–3. It is fair to add that G substantially modified his views as to maintaining the 'connection between British colonies and British crime'. He hoped to relieve (temporarily) the burden on Australia by spreading transportation to Nova Scotia, New Brunswick, Gibraltar, Bermuda, the Ionian Islands, and the Cape. See GP, 44735, 191–94, 264–79.
2 H, cxvi, 268.   3 G to Stephen, April 8, 1846. GP, 44528, 35.

self-government and imperial supremacy for as long as it was good for either that it should subsist; and, when it ceased, he hoped that instead of bloodshed it might 'arise from the natural and acknowledged growth of these communities into States perfectly fitted for self-government and independence', and would 'still subsist in similarity of laws and institutions, and in a close unity of affection'.[1]

At the end of March 1846 Gladstone tried, with confessed lack of conviction, to convert his involuntary absence from the House of Commons into something to be grateful for: 'A most gracious purpose of God has spared me the most wearing part of the labours that my resumption of office should have brought: the bitter feuds of Parliament: but my heart does not answer as it should in lively thankfulness.'[2] Certainly the feuds were bitter. Gladstone noted after Disraeli's great philippic against Peel on January 22: 'Read last night's debate. The skies are dark enough.'[3] It was vexing not to be able to be at Peel's side when he most needed help. When Peel proposed his Corn Law measures to the House on January 27 Gladstone was loyally in attendance in the gallery (Prince Albert was present for the occasion also, in much the same mood and for much the same purpose). After a cabinet dinner at Peel's on February 11 the Gladstones held a reception 'attended by all Young England'. The era of such social amenities between the Conservative factions was almost at an end. He was not present to witness the division on February 28, when a devastating two-thirds of Peel's party voted against their leader. He was indisposed with influenza on May 15, the occasion of Disraeli's most virulently brilliant onslaught. Gladstone had given his first cabinet dinner on May 6, noting despondently: 'We were thirteen.' The gloomy days were enlivened by occasional trips to Brighton, whither Catherine had removed herself and the children (Gladstone treated himself to a salt shower bath).

Perhaps it was this climate of despondency on top of the aftermath of Maynooth and Gladstone's new jitters about the Irish Church which influenced once more his bruised conscience on the matter of his duty to retire from public life. It was on March 8 that he startled Manning with his bizarre yearning for a synodical decision to tell him to retire. Manning could only respond as he had always done: there was work to be done for the Church in parliament; and that anyway there were no 'new and distinct signs' to warrant so anomalous an act.[4] And indeed the effect of Gladstone's tortured argument was to convince himself of the unavoidable necessity of staying where he was. But a psychological imperative required him to verify this regrettable conclusion from time to time, probably by now as much for Manning's benefit as for his own. The 'process in which I am actively engaged in carrying on', Gladstone

1 H, civ, 354–5.   2 D, iii, 528.   3 *Ib.*, 515.
4 G to Manning, April 5, 1846. GP, 44247, 298.

reminded Manning, 'is a process of lowering the religious tone of the State, letting it down, de-moralizing it, i.e., stripping it of its ethical character, and assisting its transition into one which is mechanical'.[1] And had he not pledged himself to fight this process in his book? And did not the burden of proof therefore rest on the side of the argument for his remaining in public life? And had not Manning 'unconsciously given me what I ask for'? Precisely what Gladstone was asking for might well have puzzled Manning at this time. Gladstone's consistent tendency was to deprecate anything in the way of a decisive action. He agreed, for instance, with Pusey that the Jerusalem bishopric 'bodes no little good and more evil'; but he urged that any attempt to be rid of it would 'rivet it, if not in the affections, in the prejudices and antipathies of many'.[2] What Manning did offer, by way of remarking that Peel's policy neither helped the Church nor let the Church help herself, was a text wherefrom Gladstone could wring the moral that he must stay where he was for the time being, because the time being included the possibility that Peel's policy of obstruction might be succeeded by one allowing the Church to help herself; and for as long as that possibility existed, and in the event of the 'work of emancipation' actually being implemented, Gladstone felt bound to the place where he stood. But 'so soon as that is over, the force of original & never abandoned Election, whatever that may be, draws me away from it'.[3] 'Whatever that may be'! Did Manning shrug? In any case the practical point was that the decision was thus in effect postponed until the Greek Kalends. A fortnight later Gladstone reduced his opaque verbiage to prosaic bathos: 'In all probability the Church will hold her nationality, in substance' beyond his and Manning's day. It would hold it 'as long as the monarchy subsists, & that will last when we are gone'; and '*so* long, undoubtedly, the Church will want political and parliamentary defence'.[4]

The rite of validating his public credentials thus becomingly observed, Gladstone was free to turn his attention to affairs. In the Church itself there were painful tensions. Newman's secession provoked something of an Evangelical witch-hunt led by Ashley, who had, Gladstone believed, 'every good point about him except a tendency to violence and intolerance. But Ashley has been of late the leader of a party in the Church; he is hand in glove with Bunsen who in my opinion has done the Church of England more mischief than any man alive. . .'[5] (On Bunsen's *Church of the Future* Gladstone's verdict was: 'It is *dismal*: and I must write to him to say so as kindly as I can.')[6] Royal occasions included losing 8d at cards at

1 G to Manning, April 19, 1846. *Ib.*, 306.
2 G to Pusey, April 12, 1846. *Ib.*, 44528, 36.
3 G to Manning, April 5, 1846. *Ib.*, 298.
4 G to Manning, April 19, 1846. *Ib.*, 306.
5 G to CG, May 1, 1846. GGP, 28/2.   6 G to CG, October 12, 1845. *Ib.*

the Palace and explaining to the Queen why the Tory dissidents were being so cruel to poor Sir Robert ('the English character is apt to mistake that to which it is closely wedded for matter of principle').[1] There were discussions with Acland about the Soho House of Charity and plans for a new church in Leicester Square which would cater conveniently to the constituency of fallen sisters. After a Council at the Palace for the birth of Princess Helena, he travelled down to Winchester to persuade Charles Wordsworth to take on the wardenship of the new college at Glenalmond. There was much ado exercising his talent for economy in selling to a tavern landlord a live turtle which had been presented to him. Economies at Oak Farm were more difficult to achieve. 'Boydell has been up in town', Gladstone told Catherine on April 29; '– again in difficulties. Every fresh occasion deepens my impression of his untrustworthiness: which would not be much greater if he were distinctly dishonest. I wish it were possible duly to impress upon Stephen and George that they *may* still have heavy losses to sustain by the O.F.'[2]

Meanwhile, Peel's government staggered towards its end. As Graham mordantly put it, the country gentlemen could not be more ready to deal the death-blow than ministers were to receive it. 'The political sky is quite impenetrable', Gladstone informed his Oxford contemporary Governor Harris of Trinidad on June 15. 'Tomorrow night probably the Corn Bill will come out of Committee. The opponents I understand reckon on a majority of three. . . The supporters are sanguine too and talk of a large majority their way. . .' What clearly attracted Gladstone was the assessment that upon the whole 'the chances, so to speak, are that the relation between us will be dissolved by my disappearance from the desk at which I write. . .'[3] The Whigs duly gave Peel a majority for his Corn Bill; but having given, they prepared to take away. Gladstone was gratified by a by-product of imminent defeat: Peel commissioned him on June 20 to convey the Queen's offer of a baronetcy to John Gladstone; 'who was pleased but much less moved that he wd. have been by a small matter affecting one of his children.'[4] Old John in any case was too much a critic of free trade to rejoice in an honour at the hands of a man who had broken both protection and the Conservative party. There was to be a division about special coercive legislation for Ireland. Defeat was almost inevitable. Should the government resign or recommend a dissolution and new elections? Wellington, rightly in Gladstone's view, was strong for fighting on and dissolving. On June 26 Peel held the shortest cabinet Gladstone had ever known: merely announcing that, as a consequence of defeat on the second reading of the Protection of Life (Ireland) Bill, he intended to resign forthwith. So evidently weary and eager for release

1 PMP, iii, 17–18.   2 G to CG, April 29, 1846. GGP, 28/2.
3 G to Harris, June 15, 1846. GP, 44528, 61.   4 D, iii, 545.

was the Prime Minister that his colleagues did not have the heart to resist.

Although Gladstone never wavered in his conviction that Peel was wrong and Wellington was right on the merits of appealing to the electorate, he was not sorry to divest himself of the anomalous role of holding office without a parliamentary seat. What most ruffled him about the government's demise was Peel's valedictory eulogy on June 29 on Cobden. Gladstone held that Cobden's tone had always been 'most harsh', and his 'imputation of bad & vile motives to honourable men incessant', even though his power of discussion might be great and the end he sought good. 'I do not think the thing was done in a manner altogether worthy of Peel's mind.' Like smaller men, Peel was 'very sensible of the sweetness of the cheers of opponents'.[1] Aberdeen went so far as to interpret Peel's regrettable tone as designed deliberately to make it 'impossible that he should ever again be placed in connection with the Conservative party as a party'; that Peel had made up his mind never again to lead it, never again to take office; that he was 'fixed to the idea to maintain his independent and separate position – taking part in public questions as his view of public interests might from time to time seem to require'. Gladstone was convinced that such an attempt on Peel's part to abdicate his leadership while remaining in the Commons was impossible: as convinced, in fact, as only a man can be who thirty years later would insist on doing precisely the same thing, with precisely the same awkward consequences pointed to by Gladstone as likely to be the case with Peel in 1846. With his 'greatness' Peel could not remain there 'overshadowing and eclipsing all governments and yet have to do with no government'; that 'acts for such a man' could not be isolated, but must be in series and in relation to one body of men rather than another.[2] As for himself, Gladstone quitted the Colonial Office with almost school-boyish glee at the prospect of release. On July 6 he went to the Palace to hand in his seals, as he told Governor Harris: 'And now goodbye Council, goodbye representative institutions, goodbye Emigration & Immigration except the Emigration out of office and out of Parliament [of] men from town in this frying season, and their immigration into the country.'[3]

[7]

So worried, however, was Gladstone by Aberdeen's revelations as to Peel's intentions that before departing in mid-July for his usual long retreat at Hawarden and Fasque he made an excuse to see Peel (a matter

1 *Ib.*, 547.   2 PMP, iii, 19.
3 G to Harris, July 7, 1846. GP, 44528, 73.

relating to New Zealand affairs) and pressed the point on him that he could not hold himself aloof from the 'great movements of political forces' in the Commons. Peel, appropriately laid up after an accident, attempted to deflect Gladstone by discoursing fervently on the unimaginable labours and anxieties of managing a government. But, with the ruthlessness of a vigorous thirty-six year old, Gladstone insisted that Peel had but two choices: either retirement from the Commons, or leadership in the Commons. To which Peel could only mutter that he might well give up parliament altogether.[1] Perhaps Gladstone might have put his case more tactfully. Possibly it might have been better to have allowed Peel more time to recuperate and unwind. But the sense of something like panic in Gladstone's reaction to the prospect of losing Peel's leadership suggests that he was quite as much worried for himself as for country or party. His emphasis on Peel's being the 'strong man of this Parliament – of this political generation', on Peel's having been a masterful prime minister in a sense which none other had been since the time of Pitt, on Peel's having 'performed an extraordinary task', on Peel whose 'labours have been incredible', hints in Gladstone at something of a peculiarly personal dependence on Peel's leadership, or upon an ideal of Peel as leader. Gladstone had often given indications of a deliberate cult of filial or juvenile submission to a person or principle of authority in every aspect of his life and career. By now he had moved distinctly beyond the range at which his father's authority was anything more than a matter of form or pious fiction; perhaps Peel had come for Gladstone somewhat to fill the role of paternal authority thus vacated. Certainly Gladstone tended to be rather obsessive over the next few years on the theme of Peel's failure to do his duty and fulfil his ordained function as the strong man of politics.

No doubt benefiting from a sense of relief at having thus acquitted himself with Peel, Gladstone set off for Hawarden (leaving London by the 11 a.m. train and reaching the Castle by 9 p.m. – 'How easily do we now perform these journies: & how ungratefully') and settled into the congenial routine of his vacation occupations. He loved Hawarden and had made himself very much at home there. He records soon after arrival a walk with Catherine 'to enjoy the place: & arranged my nest'.[2] It was during these ample retreats that Gladstone had time to engage himself deeply and comprehensively in search of nutritious and sustaining literature. Dante and Bishop Butler were now great figures in his literary pantheon; Homer would join this select category in the winter months of 1846–47 at Fasque. Gladstone quarried an enormous mass of Homeric notation in 1846 primarily to combat Karl Lachmann's theory that the Homeric epics had been cobbled together out of many isolated fragments. A convinced 'unitarian', Gladstone argued also that Homer lived near to

1 PMP, *ib.*, 28–30.   2 D, iii, 560.

the time of the events he described. This case for one man describing a
real world came out in the *Quarterly* for September 1847. Gladstone's
literary enthusiasms always had a very practical, if often very idiosyncratic, bearing. Dante's anti-papalism was not the least of his attractions. The
Christian uses, or abuses, to which Gladstone would later put Homer
became a scandal of classical scholarship. And Butler fulfilled many
rather odd purposes. Thus when Lord John Manners, Gladstone's former
colleague at Newark, visited Hawarden in August 1846, Gladstone found
him, though 'by no means heady and precipitate', yet distressingly prone
to find his ruling impulse in antipathy to Peel. 'I think,' was Gladstone's
considered judgment, 'had he studied Butler it would have been a
powerful corrective to him.'[1]

So much did Gladstone relish these opportunities for reading that he
felt constrained to guard himself against the dangers lurking in a kind of
indulgence. 'It has now become a very important part of my duty,' he
warned himself at Fasque in November 1846, 'to take care that the
absorbtion of my time in study, which is a great delight to me, does not
also become a snare & an occasion for the unsuspected, & even therefore
vigorous, action of selfishness.'[2] There were also the insidious temptations of impurity. Aretino's *Ragionamenti*: 'horrible, but also incredible, as
I think.' (Perhaps it was the problem of credibility that led him to re-read it
in 1854: 'an evil book, an extraordinary picture.')[3] He found himself
reading Petronius 'chiefly by way of glance: but this is a clear offence agt.
my rules of Oct. 26 1845 which were made with the conviction that
instruction derived from such a source is impure to me: I cannot afford or
bear it. . .'; 'Thus I record my sin.' Still, he insisted that Petronius had an
'attractive as well as a repellent influence'.[4] On the dangerous pages of
Boccaccio's *Decamerone*: 'a book that some should know: but they should
be better men than I.'[5] These hours of study were also the occasion of
self-communings of a desultory but highly relevant character on general
social and political issues. Thus, on the morality of capitalism: Was the
'system of modern industry' not merely liable to abuse but fundamentally
and essentially at variance with the principles of the gospels? Gladstone's
answer had to be 'deliberately . . . in the negative'. The accumulation of
stock or capital, the crucial element upon which hung all the rest, arose
out of the division of labour; which meant, practically, the economising
and multiplying of its productive power; and so, by preventing each
individual from supplying his own wants as was the case among mere
savages, it thus required him 'to purchase, & to live upon stock while he
prepared what he was to sell; and thus it became a beneficial and laudable
use of faculties given by God', '& one that honours the Giver'.[6]

1 PMP, iii, 31–2.   2 D, iii, 581.   3 *Ib.*, 335; iv, 635.
4 D, iii, 594.   5 *Ib.*, iv, 236.   6 GP, 44736, 12.

Fasque at this time still had for Gladstone a special dimension of family cares and concerns. Some of them were pleasurable enough. The building of the chapel offered Gladstone a wide range of congenial problems to fuss about. Trinity College, Glenalmond, was also a source of deeply rewarding concern. There was a grand occasion in September 1846 for the laying of the foundation stone. Sir John Gladstone spoke with 'great earnestness and energy', followed by the new warden, Charles Wordsworth; to whom the 'Presbyterian workmen & country folks listened devoutly'.[1] Then in October came the long-awaited moment of the opening of St. Andrew's Chapel at Fasque. Gladstone was in an ecstasy of excitement ('Once or twice but for my co-practitioners I should have broken down completely'). There were exasperating hitches: the new chaplain forgot to bring his gown, and Gladstone discovered indignantly that the local people considered bell-ringing beneath them. But Gladstone doted on this Gladstone foundation. Nothing made Fasque so dear to him as the opportunities provided by the chapel to indulge his tastes in ecclesiology and family piety. He soon busied himself collecting various family coffins from earlier graves for reinterment in the family vault. He brought in his mother and an uncle from Fettercairn kirk; and he noted later that dear Anne's remains removed from Seaforth were temporarily stored in the north bedroom.[2]

Fasque also had its peculiar difficulties. Helen, long since returned from her German escapade, remained unrivalled at the head of the family agenda of problems. When Manning proposed himself for a visit, Gladstone welcomed the idea but warned him: 'It is only fair to you to state that there is reason the other way, I mean the presence of my poor sister in the house, whose change of religious profession combined with some other points of character make it a delicate matter for clergymen in your position to manage a common intercourse with her.'[3] Apart from occasional 'fits' Helen was prone to delusions of 'little people' running around her room and constantly accused her family of plotting against her.[4] Manning might also have found himself in difficulties had he encountered Gladstone's huge brother Robertson, who displayed distressingly Unitarian tendencies and who was apt to express 'violent opinions in a very excited manner about the Church, Bishops, & religion'.[5] There was also the delicate matter of the ultimate disposal of the aged Sir John's immense estate. And conversations with his father at this time, apart from tedious harangues against free trade, raised in Gladstone's mind fresh anxieties about Oak Farm. Sir John had always warned him against placing too much trust in Boydell; now William

1 D, iii, 570.   2 *Ib.*, iv, 71.
3 G to Manning, August 31, 1846. GP, 44247, 314.
4 D, iii, 658.   5 *Ib.*, 569.

signalled a sense of his own guilty responsibility by professing to be disturbed at Sir John's unwarranted indulgence to the reckless agent and to be pleased that his father was now determined to call a halt: 'He is justly incensed with B. & and has at last announced that there can be no *more* aid without a systematic investigation.'[1]

Anxiety about Peel's negative attitude to his future political role was the one thing seriously troubling Gladstone in the early months of the Russell administration. He felt the Whigs had made a 'good start', apart from their addiction to doctrinaire free trade in the sugar question. 'Indeed,' he assured Manning in August 1846,[2] 'if their aspect should remain for another twelvemonth as Conservative as it now is, we shall see the radical party fall away from them and they must depend upon the support of former opponents.' Gladstone could not profess to have *confidence* in them, considering their former conduct in government and the *manner* in which they had recently obtained power; but the 'only subject of *immediate* moment' on which he felt apprehensive was their disposal of Church patronage. (And it was true that Russell was to lose no time in preferring the egregious Hampden to the see of Hereford in 1847.) Gladstone had no apprehension 'as yet' of anything but sobriety in the Foreign and Colonial Offices, in which more than in any other departments 'fears of a disposition to extravagate might have been entertained'. It was indeed a measure of Gladstone's Peelite disposition to hope for the best from the Whigs that the succession of Palmerston to the place of good Lord Aberdeen did not provoke dire prognostications; and in fact it was not long before 'Pam' was extravagating quite in his old manner.

The early months of 1847 were darkened by an awareness of the consequences of famine in Ireland: this 'greatest horror of modern times'; a 'calamity most legibly divine'.[3] But they were enlivened personally for Gladstone by the circumstance that, with a general election in view, a seat for Oxford University might be available. Gladstone 'desired it', as he was later 'not ashamed to own' publicly, 'with an almost passionate fondness'.[4] Representation of the University of Oxford meant in effect representation of the largest body of clergymen in the Church of England. It meant for Gladstone something of a substitute for his forsaken vocation. He relieved himself of his feelings about the Roman Church and its fraudulent inducements to Anglican defectors by a fulmination in the *Quarterly* for June 1847, asserting his faith that the English character, with its 'energetic love of freedom', made impossible any widespread acceptance of the 'rankness of the Papal system'.[5] Other personal matters

1 *Ib.*, 580, 585.
2 G to Manning, August 14, 1846. GP, 44247, 312.   3 Lathbury, ii, 274.
4 *A Chapter of Autobiography* (1868), 36.   5 Butler, 207.

were less satisfactory. Plans for a rigorous Lent somehow went awry and a further visit to Fasque at the end of March revealed Sir John suddenly as a 'visibly older man', losing his grip and engaging in degrading altercations about Helen and the housekeeper. Gladstone was shocked by a 'very *disgraceful* ebullition' from Aunt Johanna. He complained ruefully to Catherine: 'Though I thought I was coming to a quiet place, it has proved far otherwise.'[1] Clearly Sir John's need of his own London residence was now in question, and Gladstone and Catherine looked over 6 Carlton Gardens 'with a view to the *possible* flitting thither' from along the street in Carlton House Terrace.

Meanwhile, on May 12, a meeting of members of Oxford Convocation announced support for Gladstone as a candidate to replace the retiring Estcourt. Gladstone was far from being a universally popular candidate. A strong anti-Tractarian countermove got under way. Ashley thought of offering himself in the Evangelical interest. It was awkward that Edward Cardwell, cited by Stanley as the most promising of the younger Peelites along with Gladstone himself, should have allowed his name to go forward; and Gladstone's committee had a delicate task in easing him out of the way.[2] In the end Professor Charles Round was put up against the 'mystified, slippery, uncertain, politico-Churchman, a non-Romanist Jesuit', as Ashley described Gladstone.[3] Thus, for the first time since the Reform Act there would be a contest for a seat regarded as being sedately above the common broils of politics. One immediate embarrassment was that Tom indicated that his Evangelical and protectionist principles would be a barrier to giving fraternal support to William. Sir John frothed at this breach in family solidarity. The inevitable *canards* about William's perverting influence on Helen also made their appearance. Gladstone did his best, under Hope's guidance, to present an innocuous front and produced a short and 'tranquillizing' address to the university electors rather than a dangerously expansive one. The delicate issue was the Irish Church. In 1846, learning the lesson of Maynooth, Gladstone had refused to oppose the Russell government for not pledging itself against further appropriation of Church property in Ireland. His ingenious position now for the benefit of the Oxford voters was that he did not anticipate any proposal hostile to the Church of Ireland which would receive his support. Gladstone heard of his formal nomination when at Fasque at the end of July, listening to his father speaking of Tom with 'great pain & dissatisfaction'. The wretched Tom was duly brought to heel and his reluctant vote helped Gladstone safely to the second seat in the poll at the

1 G to CG, 9 April 1847. GGP, 28/3.
2 J.B. Conacher, 'Mr Gladstone Seeks a Seat', *Canadian Historical Association Annual Report* (1962), 66.
3 G. Finlayson, *Shaftesbury* (1981), 261.

end of August.[1] His intense anguish as to success made the election 'harrowing'; in 1853 he recalled: 'I never can forget my anxiety not to lose the battle in 1847.'[2] He was both immensely relieved and proud to hold a seat that Peel had been proud to hold. (John Neilson lost at Ipswich, and soon joined Tom in complaining of William's hurtful manner to him.) The Whigs scraped home with a bare majority and Russell would need Peelite support to sustain his ministry. Peel's followers, 119 at the time of the break in 1846, now numbered something between 108 and 113.

But as Gladstone rejoiced at being once more a member of parliament, and amidst the high festival of the formal consecration of St. Andrew's Chapel at Fasque, where 'another root of the tree of healing' was 'planted for all time' with impressive ceremonial showing Gladstone 'more & more what our liturgy *may do*' (unfortunately the Bishop of Aberdeen's sermon turned out to be cribbed), news came of the collapse of the Oak Farm concern. Gladstone was actually called away to hear of the catastrophe from the very services and offices of consecration which he had lovingly and minutely planned. As he explained to Manning, he now had on his hands a 'concern in bankruptcy, with £250,000 of liabilities' as the consequence of the 'hare-brained' schemes to turn iron into gold of a 'reckless agent unduly trusted'. The fact was that Gladstone was as responsible for undue trust as anyone else. The collapse inflicted serious financial damage on Gladstone – who calculated his loss as £12,834[3] – and crippling damage on Lyttelton; but the effect on Stephen Glynne's position was devastating. His entire estate and the 'social position of his family' were now in jeopardy. It was a question either of parting with the estate or of fighting a severe conflict to restore its viability.[4] Gladstone's habits of self-training in kissing the rod by which an inscrutable higher power chastised him for his own good now proved extremely useful: 'most providentially instructive,' he commented as the fruits of ecclesiastical delight at Fasque turned to ashes, 'and surely not ill but *well* timed, & this not in spite of but *because* of the way it presses on these moments. It makes one a little understand what is the night & what is the day.'[5]

It would be long before Gladstone saw daylight on Oak Farm. 'Tearing anxiety' continued throughout 1847 and into 1848. It brought Sir John down to London and reduced William to the misery of confessing that the defaults involved 'true dishonour. Here is their sting.'[6] On top of all this, the Gladstones suffered a shock on discovering that Catherine's maid 'whom after 6 or 7 years experience we thought modesty itself' had

1 Inglis, 1700; Gladstone, 997; Round, 824.   2 D, iv, 485, 617.
3 GGP, 94/13. Secret Account Book, 8.
4 G to Manning, March 12, 1848. GP, 44247, 343.
5 D, iii, 645.   6 *Ib.*, 670.

earlier lived in a state of 'unlawful intercourse' with another of the servants, now her husband. 'Alas alas for the children of Adam. There could scarcely be to us a greater downfall. I may say we loved them. But more, I was *vain* of them: and am well chastised.' Gladstone wrote 'a long & solemn address to our poor servants – which C. gave to her woman'.[1] And there was a fright in September 1847 when their daughter Agnes contracted erysipelas. Gladstone was so relieved at her recovery that he proposed a thanksgiving window in the new chapel (a project vetoed by Sir John in deference to Tom's susceptibilities). Catherine gave birth in November to a daughter, 'plump & pretty', baptised Mary. But Gladstone betrayed the disturbing impact of events upon him by succumbing that very day to 'pornographic' temptation. This was to become something of an epidemic in 1848. Boydell remained 'impudently unrepentant' about Oak Farm. 'The works generally are a deathly solitude,' Gladstone reported to Catherine, 'of a most unnatural aspect: huge hammers hang lifted in the air as if waiting to fall, & vast wheels to revolve, and as if some unseen decree arrested them: all the means & appliances of labour scattered about in confusion, but all spell-bound.'[2] He was relieved to find the principal Oak Farm creditor, Lord Ward, 'perfectly good humoured' at an archery meeting at Westwood in August 1848. There was talk of letting Hawarden out to 'any good tenant'. When Lavinia Glynne at last gave birth to a boy in January 1848 it seemed the ultimate irony of the Glynne fortunes. 'All Hawarden' did its best to respond joyfully to the birth of an heir whose inheritance seemed at best dubious. But in any case the child lived only a few hours. Hawarden was not in the end let out. Sir Stephen resumed residence in 1852. In January 1848 Gladstone had started work on a plan to commute his and his father's claims on the concern into land.

The burden of the rescue fell unavoidably upon Gladstone. The Glynne brothers were of no use: they took a much more relaxed, aristocratic attitude to financial failure than the commercial Gladstones. 'Good as he is,' Gladstone remarked to Manning of Stephen, 'accomplished as he is acute and sensible & prudent as in many ways he is he has not the smallest capacity for managing these affairs and the whole weight nearly of them comes on me in his stead, not because I am competent to bear it but because I am in one degree less disqualified.' Gladstone of course had an enormous appetite for work. Though he rather portrayed himself as a martyr to the Oak Farm disaster, it is difficult to conceive that anyone else, however competent, would have been allowed elbow room in the affair. The sting of what he felt as his own share of the responsibility goaded

1 *Ib.*, 646. G became godfather to the Hamptons' *second* child: 'a nice forgiving touch' (MRDF).
2 G to CG, February 5, 1848. GGP, 28/3.

Gladstone to repair the damage as an imperative moral obligation. A 'vast & complex business to be recast, very heavy and early demands to be provided for, large sums of money to be borrowed and realised, and a constant uphill fight to be carried on against difficulties which are to all appearance all but & only not insurmountable', certainly tested Gladstone's capacities very severely. 'How I get on with them I hardly know: they often make me faint & sick at heart.'[1] He complained that these distractions made it 'quite impossible for me to discharge my duties properly in Parliament'.[2] Under pressure he confessed to Catherine: 'I am much addled and have plenty to say if it would come out but it is all so jumbled.'[3] 'I have had Roper with me today,' he told Catherine on February 23, '– in great distress and like a child, without resource, having nothing practical to propose and working apart from Boydell whom he seems inclined to avoid, and no wonder.'[4] Gladstone's feat in rescuing the Hawarden estate proved in the end to be a work not merely for the sake of his wife and his wife's family but a decisive part of the process whereby Hawarden eventually passed into the possession of his own branch of the Gladstone family. But that outcome was not at all evident in 1848. Lavinia Glynne might well give birth to another son. Catherine and William would like their line to inherit Hawarden; but that was one of several possible contingencies, and in the new circumstances of 1848 such an inheritance promised to be more of a bane than a blessing.

In January 1848 Gladstone explained his land commutation scheme 'at great length' to Sir Stephen and the Reverend Henry. There was also much work to be done on Lady Glynne's annuity. Gladstone could barely repress a note of bitterness in his comment that after much labour over Glynne's 'dark, but not hopeless' affairs, 'Stephen went off: light-hearted enough'.[5] Perhaps Gladstone should have been thankful for light-heartedness. Sir Stephen certainly should have been thankful for such a brother-in-law. Gladstone's mother-in-law's response to the crisis provoked him by September 1848 to considering seriously whether the 'process of mesmerism should not be tried on Lady Glynne'.[6] His tenacity, however, allowed him to get on top of the Oak Farm problem during 1848. His relationship with Ward continued good. And there was one great compensation: ever after he would insist that training in such a hard financial school prepared him better than anything else for the Exchequer.

1 G to Manning, *ib.*
2 D, iv, 12.
3 G to CG, February 9, 1848. GGP, 28/3.
4 G to CG, February 23, 1848. *Ib.*
5 D, iv, 11.
6 *Ib.*, 66.

[8]

It was lucky for Gladstone that he was hit by Oak Farm while out of office and with his party so disorganised that he was spared heavy public responsibility. He still complained of Peel's unworthy holding aloof from party and office. He pressed keenly for measures to keep the parliamentary group of 'Peelites' intact and united. The group would need to be led by Peel or at least in constant and formal communication with him. The first session of the new parliament met in November 1847. To Gladstone the great danger was that without Peel's gravitational pull many of his followers would drift back into 'some other section' of parliament.[1] Any strengthening of the 'rump' Conservative party, now led by Stanley in the Lords and by a collective leadership including Bentinck and Disraeli in the Commons, was to be deplored; and especially if it threatened the stability of Russell's Whig ministry, which for the time being promised well in rounding off the free trade policy. To the general sense of antipathy which divided the two sides of the Conservative party was added in Gladstone's own case a furious quarrel with Bentinck over an accusation of corruption in a colonial judicial appointment. After consulting with Peel, Goulburn and Cardwell on the budget and income tax in February 1848 Gladstone thought Peel 'does not seem to allow himself to realise his position: but power is surely coming near him, & likely to be forced upon him'.[2]

One of the measures of the new Whig ministry which Gladstone felt it expedient to support was the removal of Jewish parliamentary disabilities, following the precedents of 1828 for Protestant Dissenters and 1829 for Roman Catholics. This was an awkward posture for a representative of the University of Oxford in 1847, especially as his senior colleague, Sir Robert Inglis, was a leading advocate of the argument for keeping parliament all the more Christian if it could not be kept exclusively in the hands of established religion; and the more so, no doubt, in view of Gladstone's own earlier attitude in March 1841, when he clashed with Macaulay on the issue of municipal disabilities. (He was not a member of Peel's government when it resolved that issue in 1845.) Inglis represented also the argument that if parliament could not be kept Christian, could Oxford be kept Anglican? Gladstone was ready in 1847 to plead for 'natural justice' for Jews in parliament; but he was to sing a very different tune in 1850 about the threat to dismantle Oxford's Anglican exclusivity. The extraordinary feature of Gladstone's response to Jewish disabilities in 1847 was the extent to which his argument in favour of relaxing them, for all that he pleaded 'pain' and 'deep regret' to Oxford, was an effusion of 'march-of-minding' which Macaulay himself might have been proud to

1 PMP, iii, 32–4.   2 *Ib.*, 34–5.

own. The arguments for a 'Church Parliament' which he himself had formerly urged, Gladstone told the House in tones of one who had been through it all before, and well knew the lesson of inevitable defeat, then arguments for a 'Protestant Parliament', and now arguments for a 'Christian Parliament', were all hopelessly vulnerable 'owing to profound and uniform tendencies, associated with the movement of the human mind – with the general course of events, perhaps I should say with the providential government of the world'. It hardly mattered after that if Gladstone added the reassurance that, after all, the link between religion and politics would not be entirely severed, and that the vast majority of members of parliament 'will long, will, as we trust and pray, always continue to be Christians'.[1]

These were forthright words indeed not only for Gladstone the Churchman but for Gladstone the representative of a body which still guarded its Anglican exclusivity with a jealous zeal. True, the likely practical consequences of the issue even were the bill passed (which it was not), compared with those of 1828 and 1829, were trivial; and Gladstone could thus not have chosen a safer occasion on which to unleash such evidence of a new political sensibility. Still, he was clearly registering the existence of such a sensibility, possibly – though not necessarily – with portentous implications. It was one form of logical expression in positive form of certain negative conclusions about the politics of State and Church which circumstances had been impressing upon him for many years. It was the beginning of his argument that the Church should give gold in return for freedom. The same would be true of his much more relaxed view evident from 1849 on the church rates question. The portentousness of the implications should not be accorded, for the 1840s and 1850s, an overwhelming significance. Gladstone had given evidence of a capacity to accommodate conflicting ideas without disabling strain. He had already admitted to himself the conceivability of being justified in wishing that one did not hold the opinions which one held. That same doctrine would be applied equally to new opinions. To assume that Gladstone was feeling his way towards a new political equivalent to his free trade sympathies would be to overestimate the degree of conscious endeavour in his thinking. It would also read too much of Gladstone's future into his present. As a Canningite, Gladstone was of a tradition and a generation which could see the party of Pitt as the party of freer trade; which could see the coming of the Whigs to power in 1830 as the saving of the Corn Law from the abolition which would

---

1 H, xcv, 1282–87. The Jewish Disabilities Bill, consequent on Lionel de Rotnschild's election for the City of London in 1847, was passed by the Commons but rejected by the Lords. Two further measures in 1849 and 1851 suffered a similar fate. The point was not gained until 1858.

certainly have resulted from a continuation of Tory rule; which saw Whig conversion to Corn Law repeal in 1845 as much in the same tradition of bandwagon mounting as Whig conversion to parliamentary reform in the late 1820s; which had no need of lessons from the Manchester School, and which looked upon Cobden with a considerable resentment and distrust.

That Gladstone did not have a state of mind so much as states of mind is indicated at this time by his response to the parallel question of extending Roman Catholic relief. He was willing to allow Roman Catholic Orders to return to England (with certain reservations about the Jesuits). But he stuck at the re-establishment of a Roman episcopal hierarchy with concomitant territorial jurisdiction. This would, Gladstone thought, be 'open to objection' as establishing 'somewhat of a false and unnatural relation between the Papal Court and ourselves – between the Pope as a temporal Power and the British Government'.[1]

Three other features of interest in relation to Gladstone in early sessions of the Whig parliament deserve notice. The first was a major speech on March 10, 1848 defending the Conservative budgetary and fiscal policy of 1842, marking Gladstone's emergence as a first-class force in the broad field of financial policy and as a natural claimant to succeed Goulburn as the Peelite Conservative candidate for the increasingly important Chancellorship of the Exchequer. This would be a crucial matter should Gladstone's sense of a new vocation take a distinctly financial turn. In this speech Gladstone also declared on behalf of Peel's friends that the government deserved their support 'without any regard to party feelings or considerations', especially at so critical a period, with Europe embroiled in revolution.[2] He reinforced this approving attitude with specific endorsement of the government's policy of further relaxing the Navigation Laws and in continuing the 'recent commercial legislation' of freeing trade.[3]

Secondly, Gladstone defined in relation to his general support for free trade policy his reservations as to what might be called Cobdenite ideology. In the course of defending the government's relaxing of the Navigation Laws and endorsing Prussian claims for equality of treatment in shipping policy – 'the day has gone by when we can look down upon other countries in this respect, and arrogate to ourselves privileges which we are not prepared to yield to them'[4] – he took some care to distance himself from Manchester School doctrine. His personal resentment at Cobden's mannerless rancour died hard. (He had already that session delivered a pained rebuke to Bright for hard language against the bishops.)[5] But the consistency with which he abided by this definition throughout his career points to the presence of strains and traces of

1 *Ib.*, 845; xcvi, 747–8.   2 *Ib.*, xcvii, 453.
3 *Ib.*, xcix, 253.   4 *Ib.*, 253.   5 *Ib.*, xcvii 1285–6.

opinion much more persistent than passing resentment. It was as the heir of Canning and Huskisson that Gladstone insisted in 1848 on the need to continue the system of allowing the Navy resort to the resources of the mercantile marine in the event of war or sudden national emergency. While agreeing with Cobden 'in entertaining a sanguine hope that the commercial legislation of this country, with its benign contagion, so to speak', would 'spread itself slowly among other nations, and become the rule of general legislation', and that it would 'prove a tie which will much strengthen the bonds of unity which unite different countries, and diminish the frequency of wars', Gladstone could not concur in Cobden's 'sanguine prophecy', and 'anticipate that universal peace will immediately follow the declaration of freedom of commerce'.[1] Apart from the traditions of Canning, Gladstone had a healthy respect for the efficacy of the doctrine of original sin and the natural depravity of mankind. It was in 1848 indeed that he drew up a memorandum on this subject: 'Those who have denied the doctrine of original sin have been hard pressed to account for all the evil and misery in the world.' They had, perforce and unconvincingly, to fasten the blame upon government; and it was true, Gladstone noted, 'that the class in question have in a very considerable degree been opponents of established government and given ... to favour innovation'.[2] And as if further to mark his unabashed attachment to old loyalties Gladstone, *à propos* of the sugar duties issue, distinguished himself in yet another heart-rending appeal on behalf of the West India interest ('Do not let it be said that the plan of emancipation, mighty and gigantic as it was, was based upon the ruin of private fortunes ...').[3]

The third feature was Gladstone's extolling the behaviour of the Thames coal whippers in offering their services as special constables against the Chartist agitation. (Gladstone himself had been sworn in as a special constable on March 11.) He spoke warmly of the 'encouragement given to all classes of labourers by the tribute of approbation which, on our part, such conduct will never fail to receive'. But his deeper purpose was to bring to the attention of the Commons an example of the positive response given by workers in gratitude for their being rescued six years earlier (at Gladstone's instigation at the Board of Trade) from a morally degrading thraldom.[4] For Gladstone the coal whippers' case was the germ of an idea which was to grow into an entire dimension of his public awareness: a sense of mission to rescue the morally deprived masses from the degrading consequences of their deprivation and thereby to engage their newly engendered moral energies in the cause of a higher and purer politics. This sense of mission owed something no doubt to the older Evangelical tradition represented by Wilberforce as well as to current

1 *Ib.*, xcix, 256.   2 D, iv, 82.
3 H, xcix, 1031.   4 *Ib.*, xcvii, 458–9.

notions of Tory paternalism. But the force that was to make it so crucially important an element of Gladstone's consciousness came essentially from a much more intimate and idiosyncratic source within himself, a conviction of personal election. It was integrally related in origin to his private vocation to rescue prostitutes; it could be said to be an extension into the public and political sphere of that same vocation. Being thus a very deeply and restrictedly personal phenomenon, Gladstone's 'social rescue' impulse had little relation to such contemporary manifestations of social conscience as Christian Socialism. Indeed, Gladstone was careful to clear himself from any imputations of 'socialism'. He took an early opportunity to do this in May 1848, on the master and journeymen bakers question. He insisted that the coal whippers' case did not set a precedent for legislative interference between employers and employees. He had rescued the coal whippers from a demoralizing dependence upon publicans: that was all. The issue in the bakers' case was that there should be a law restricting the hours of labour in the bakery trade. This Gladstone thought 'would be so entirely abhorrent to the genius of the constitution and people that it would not be endured'. The remedy lay in the two parties concerned being 'aided a little, and perhaps rebuked a little'.[1]

[9]

On the whole, especially with Oak Farm hanging over him ('Under nothing has my heart oftener sunk')[2], Gladstone felt himself in 1848 subjected to many pains and penalties and few mercies. Among the latter, in public affairs, he could count the country's deliverance from the revolutionary turmoils which overturned governments in France, Germany, Italy and Austria. He dined at Aberdeen's on March 22 with Guizot and Jarnac; and at Peel's on the 29th with Guizot again and Duchatel; and no doubt he heard much on the dangers threatening civilized society. On duty as a special constable on April 10 he was relieved profoundly at the collapse of the Chartist challenge: 'May our hearts feel profoundly the mercies of this very remarkable day.' An Address to the Queen by the Vicar, Churchwardens and inhabitants of the parish of St. Martin-in-the-Fields, moved by Gladstone, thanked God for the failure of the 'attempt of some misguided persons to overawe the established Authorities.'[1] And it was highly gratifying to receive an honorary doctorate of civil law from Oxford that summer. Attempts to block the nomination failed; there were a few non-placets at his

1 *Ib.*, xcix, 97–8.   2 D, iv, 88–9.
3 GP, 44737, 29 (April 22, 1848).

presentation at the Sheldonian Theatre but he was spared the indignity of a scrutiny. (He was saved from the solecism of presenting himself in black neck-cloth only by the resource of a horrified and alarmed Sir Robert Inglis.)

But pains and penalties unquestionably predominated. 'My father's illness, C's narrow escape from miscarriage, Helen at worst, Agnes's illness, Oxford, Tom's disaffection, feud about the chapel, Hampton and his wife': such was Gladstone's litany of woe. Gladstone still insisted, as he told Hope, that Helen had turned to the Roman Church 'not on grounds of a religious change but as a powerful means of excitement'.[1] Had Gladstone been aware at this time how much Hampden's appointment to Hereford had jolted both Manning and Hope in the direction of Rome his litany of woe would have been immeasurably aggravated. Helen surpassed herself in October 1848 with a prolonged cataleptic fit which she could only be induced to end by a 'miracle' wrought by Wiseman with the 'knuckle bone of some female saint'.[2] Gladstone was unhappy too with his political position and that of the Peelite group. Peel, as usual, had failed to give a lead when Goulburn, Graham, Lincoln and Gladstone were asked to talk with Ellenborough and Lyndhurst on the protectionist side about their respective positions. Before the end of the 1848 session Gladstone noted despondently that communications among the Peelites had 'dropped oddly'.[3] On the private side Gladstone found that the Soho House of Charity had become 'less suitable than it was for affording me ever so little scope for works of mercy'.[4] What the Soho establishment did not provide was the 'needed counterexcitement' of direct personal accosting of girls in the streets.[5] His obsessive anxiety in these years was indeed recurrence of his 'principal besetting sin', 'impurity' or prurient curiosity. 'I have fallen more seriously within the last month than for between 2 & 3 years', he commented in June 1848. 'Here is cause for much sadness, may it also be fruitful.'[6] Five weeks later he added an explanatory memorandum to his elaborate 'account' drawn up in Baden Baden in October 1845 on the practical means for correcting his 'dangerous curiosity & filthiness of spirit', an activity of the intellect on impure subjects,'covering itself with the plea of innocent and useful ends'.[7] Since August 1845 he had not canvassed prostitutes; now his resumption of that practice in May 1848 was part of his struggle to ward off by prophylactic questing the appalling temptations of 'allowing and entertaining of positive desire'.[8]

On the Church side he had worrying readings of David Strauss's *Life*

1 Butler, 206n.   2 Marlow, *Mr. and Mrs. Gladstone*, 48, 54.
3 PMP, iii, 35–6.   4 D, iv, 42.
5 Marlow, 53–54.   6 D, *ib*.
7 *Ib.*, 51–55.   8 Marlow, 51–52.

of Jesus (translated by the Misses Brabant and Mary Ann Evans: 'a painful book but wh has its uses as well as its dangers')[1]; and worrying conversations with Manning, lately returned from Rome (where he had been received in audience by Pius IX) not only about his own political course, but the course of Manning's thinking about religion. To Gladstone Manning described the 'searching trial' he had undergone to test his position in the Church of England.[2] Gladstone reassured himself that Manning's allegiance to Anglicanism remained unwavering; but in fact Manning was profoundly unsettled by his Roman experiences. In view of what happened later Gladstone held that Manning deliberately misled him on this and other occasions in these years.[3] The Church of England was at this time itself undergoing a 'searching trial', or rather a series of searching trials. Soon after talking to Manning Gladstone immersed himself glumly in the latest materials on the unpropitious Gorham case. This case concerned the Rev. G. C. Gorham, whom the Bishop of Exeter, Henry Phillpotts, had refused to institute to the living of Brampford Speke on the grounds that he held heretical views on the doctrine of baptismal regeneration, and that he was therefore unfit for a cure of souls. (Gorham in fact took a sceptically Calvinistic view of the doctrine, a view which Gladstone himself had held before Anne had commenced his emancipation from uncatholic error.) Gorham, a tenacious man, was in the process of appealing to the Court of Arches against the bishop's ruling; and gave every indication of taking his appeal if necessary to the ultimate stage, the Judicial Committee of the Privy Council. This was a body of laymen, but competent in the existing state of the law to pronounce on the legality of Church doctrines. The horrid prospect was thus opened that either way the Church would be exposed and suffer: if the Court of Arches found against Gorham his appeal to the Privy Council would in itself, even if the lower court's verdict were upheld, subject the Church to the profound indignity of having its doctrine pronounced upon by representatives of the State. And if the judgment of the Court of Arches were to be reversed in Gorham's favour, the much more appalling situation would have arisen that a body claiming apostolic and catholic status would be pathetically revealed as in harsh reality the mere creature of the State. It was precisely the possibility of this unacceptable situation, even though it might not actually arise, which was exercising Manning's imagination.

So Gorham could now be added to Oak Farm and Helen and 'impurity' as an element in the series of chronic anxieties in the texture of Gladstone's life. (Helen, if anything, improved on her performance as a problem: Gladstone was shocked to discover that she was in the habit of

1 *Ib.*, 76. Mary Ann Evans: 'George Eliot'.
2 *Ib.*, 49.   3 Butler, 203.

using books by Protestant divines as lavatory paper. 'The subject makes me wish I could find myself even a calumniator'; 'I tried to consider it much & not act beyond the occasion.')[1] Another personal grief struck with Lincoln's telling him on August 2, 1848 of Lady Lincoln's 'clandestine & very sudden journey': her abscondment abroad, in fact, with Lord Walpole.[2]

That Christmas and New Year at Fasque were much taken up with Sir John's will and entail. Oak Farm was inescapable. Gladstone complained to Catherine: 'A note from Stephen rather frightens me with the notion that now (as before with my Father about selling some land) he does not see that as to all matters of money either he must manage *or I* and that without the slightest exception.' New Year did have its lighter moments. Gladstone recounted to Catherine on January 10: 'Yesterday Aunt J[ohanna] accused me of taking part in a hoax upon her of which I was innocent so today in revenge I have been getting up a note to her from Lord Panmure, sent through Guthrie, announcing Lord P.'s desire to make her acquaintance and that he will call on her *next Sunday at eleven o'clock*. Last night talking of Lord P. my Aunt maintained that there was a great deal of good in him as he always made his servants go to Church.'[3] But such moments were rare; Gladstone desponded about his spiritual 'wounds' sustained in his 'secret conflict'.[4]

It was against this background of general malaise that Gladstone recorded on January 13, 1849 that 'having been much tempted during the week I made a slight application in a new form of the principle of discipline: with a good effect at the time, and how thankful ought I to be to God if I should find it so continue'.[5] By this Gladstone meant self-flagellation with a small whip or scourge. Possibly he found encouragement or precedent for this practice among members of the Engagement. In any case, though not so much used among the new Catholic High Church school as the confessional, mortifications of this physical kind were by no means unknown. Already in 1843 Gladstone had speculated as to 'how far satisfaction and even an action delighting in pain may be a true experimental phenomenon of the human mind'. Might not 'such a virtue often exist, as shall find when the lower faculty is punished or straightened, a joy in the justice and in the beneficial effects of that chastisement, which shall do more than compensate and counteract even at the moment the suffering of the punishment itself? In which case be it observed not only are the pleasure and the pain simultaneous & the first superior, but the latter is actually the occasion, the material,

1 D, iv, 80.   2 *Ib.*, 58.
3 G to CG, January 10, 1849. GGP, 28/3. The first Lord Panmure (d. 1852) was a brother of the Earl of Dalhousie and a Forfarshire figure.
4 D, iv, 88, 90.   5 *Ib.*, 92.

the substratum of the former.'[1] Gladstone's pressing motive for some signal new recourse to moral discipline was his shame and distress at his inability to overcome his temptations to 'impurity'. He noted four more flagellations in the first half of 1849; though by April he was remarking on its declining efficacy: he had been 'trusting unduly' to it, and the danger was that he could use it as a too convenient cover for unabated impurity. For two Sundays he abstained from receiving communion to mark his sense of sinful unworthiness. 'Man as God made him is wonderfully made: I as I have made myself am strangely constituted. An ideal above the ordinary married state is commonly before me & ever returns upon me: while the very perils from which it commonly delivers still beset me as snares and pitfalls among which I walk.'[2] He tentatively recommended direct 'rescue' work in May 1849; but a more consistent resumption did not occur until a year later.

The new session in 1849 offered no consolation as far as Peel's vexing neglect of his responsibilities was concerned. The disunity of the Peelites was exposed humiliatingly over the Navigation Law question in March. Gladstone felt strongly that by making support for the government at all costs his one and only rule, Peel had renounced the privilege of judging and voting freely. While bowling along in Aberdeen's pony trap in Scotland Gladstone denounced Peel's position as 'false and in the abstract almost immoral – as he, and still more Graham, sit on the opposition side of the House professing thereby to be independent members of Parliament but in every critical vote are governed by the intention to keep ministers in office and sacrifice everything to that intention'.[3] Gladstone was obliged to submit to jeers at his partyless plight from such as the bumptious and rather coarse Radical Roebuck.[4] This he resented more than Disraeli's 'good-humoured and brilliant' sarcasms.[5] Of Disraeli at this time Gladstone was inclined to severity: 'It is a very unsatisfactory state of things', he told his father in July 1849, 'to have to deal with a man whose objects appear to be those of personal ambition and who is not thought to have any strong convictions of any kind upon public matters.'[6] Disraeli certainly owed Gladstone gratitude for his pleas for 'natural justice' to Jews on the question of parliamentary oaths.[7] But Gladstone's most substantial intervention in the 1849 session was an attempt to block liberalisation of the marriage law. His passionate celebration of Leviticus and Deuteronomy was quite in his old style of the State's obligation to uphold in its institutions the teachings of the divine law. It must have done wonders to restore his credit in the more orthodox and unyielding quarters of Oxford, shaken by his attitude to the 'Jew

1 D, iii, 250–51.   2 D, iv, 117.
3 PMP, iii, 38–9, 46–47.   4 H, cvi, 281.
5 *Ib.*, ciii, 1254.   6 D, iii, xxxix.   7 *Ib.*, cii, 925.

Bill'. But Gladstone's passion derived not only from his defence of the strictest legal expression of the marital sacrament; he sensed also the shadow of the Gorham case hanging over the marriage issue. If the Marriages Bill were to pass into law 'the consequences which it must draw after it would be to bring the whole religious belief of the subject within the sole vote of Parliament'. Where was such legislation to stop? A stand must be taken on the 'positive injunction of the word of God and centuries of practice'.[1]

[10]

Immediately Gladstone had satisfied himself as to his obligations to his parliamentary duties, he turned to the domestic problem of the Lincolns. Lincoln told Manning in November 1848 that 'you will not be surprised that the people who are endeavouring to assist me in saving my unhappy Wife from utter destruction if it is yet possible are William Gladstone and his admirable Wife'.[2] 'New & very painful evidence' that Lady Lincoln might have committed 'the last act of infidelity' – that is, conceived a child adulterously – came upon Gladstone in June 1849. The practical problem was to establish whether or not this evidence was correct. If it were not correct, and Lady Lincoln could be persuaded to return, a scandalous divorce case (for which special legislation would be needed) could be avoided. If, on the other hand, the evidence was correct, it would be necessary for Lincoln's application to parliament for a divorce that this fact be substantiated by reliable testimony. Who was to go to Italy to establish the facts of the case, perhaps persuade Lady Lincoln to return, or be prepared to testify as to her adultery? Lincoln was very much in need of devoted friends who could find time to travel and who might be sufficiently in Lady Lincoln's confidence to effect a private rather than a public resolution of the problem. Clearly Gladstone was a prime candidate. He saw Lincoln and then Peel early in July to talk of a 'mission'. Lincoln mentioned Manning as well. Gladstone was keen on the idea of a joint mission. He startled Manning with a proposal to go to Naples (where the lady had last been heard of) '*now & with dispatch*'.[3] Speed indeed was of the essence, for if Lady Lincoln were pregnant she might unload the crucial evidence of it before her guilt was detected. It was not within Manning's power to assist. But at Peel's on the 11th it was decided that Gladstone would go in any event. The enterprise was not

1 *Ib.*, cvi, 619–30.
2 V. Surtees, *A Beckford Inheritance. The Lady Lincoln Scandal* (1977), 94.
3 G to Manning, July 7, 1849. GP, 44248, 8.

without its comical aspect (a point on which Sir John had lively feelings, much resenting William's compromising his family's dignity). Mary Lyttelton instructed her husband: 'Take in that *Thesiger* and *Peel* were the two who advised the journey abroad.'[1] Yet it had a very specifically practical motive. And no doubt above all, from Gladstone's point of view, it combined a certain novel romantic knight-errantry with his old attachment to the ideal of a mission to rescue fallen virtue.

Gladstone rather enjoyed his hectic trip of 3,000 miles in twenty-seven days. There were the usual complaints about Sundays spent in travel and the appalling stench of Marseilles; but against this were the rewards of meeting 'an intelligent & not irreligious Italian' who was 'keenly against the Pope'.[2] Italy in the year of the Counter-Revolution offered many sights of interest. Gladstone arrived in Rome only a few days after the end of the 'Roman Republic' and the beginning of the French occupation. There were also moments of sweet nostalgia. Gladstone was overwhelmed by the 'sights and the thoughts of this almost electric visit' while at the Crocelle Hotel in Naples. 'But this place, this house, & on this day,' he wrote to Catherine, 'is full of our own associations. I feel myself to be beneath the roof where near 12 years ago when Kinnaird & I could not get our bell answered at dinner we were told it was because *una grande famiglia Inglese* had just arrived & put the house in confusion – it was yours, & you had been guided hither to bless my life.'[3] Nor was tourism disdained: 'The plot thickens for I have been buying a lot of Roman bronzes with which I hope & think you will be pleased.'[4] With the same assiduity with which he had earlier tracked Helen in Germany, Gladstone dogged Lady Lincoln through the length of Italy. She eluded him in the south but he was soon on her traces and she could not shake him off. Gladstone had her eventually, as he reported to Manning, 'a few posts advanced, in full flight' from him at Lecco. She had resolutely shut her door against him at Cerno; and he decided not to overtake her by 'fear of consequences if I persevered and the almost impossibility of doing good under those circumstances by force'. Eventually he brought her to bay at Como where his administrative talents and generous bribery furnished him what he wanted. He enlisted the services of the governor of the province, the chief of police, the landlord of his hotel, Lady Lincoln's courier, the midwife, '& had the laquais de place incessantly at work'.[5] There was much standing on tip-toe and attempting to penetrate curtained carriage windows. He told Manning: 'You will be shocked and stunned to learn that I can entertain no moral doubt whatever of the fact

1 Surtees, 94. Frederick Thesiger, later Lord Chancellor Chelmsford, had been Peel's Attorney-General.
2 D, iv, 139.   3 G to CG, July 25, 1849. GGP, 28/3.
4 G to CG, July ?21, 1849. *Ib.*   5 D, iv, 142.

that the unhappy subject of our cares is within a few weeks, probably a
few days, of her delivery – this tells all.'[1] Gladstone could not doubt there
would be a suit for divorce; though for one who had denounced any
notions of legislation to make divorce more readily available it was a
perplexing problem. Could any Act of Parliament, he asked Manning,
'*touch* the mystical union'?[2] Manning shared Gladstone's perplexity.
Meanwhile Gladstone mused on 'poor miserable Lady L. – once the
dream of dreams, the image that to my young eye combined everything
that earth could offer of beauty and of joy. What is she now!'[3] He grieved
for the 'triumph of hellish wickedness over a woman of the rarest gifts,
and the utter devastation of heart & home & profanation of the holy
mystery of marriage. Lord have mercy upon us, Christ have mercy upon
us, Lord have mercy upon us.'[4]

[11]

As usual with Gladstone, travel had a tonic effect. His affairs on his return
soon seemed to have a rather less dismal aspect. He had taken the first
major step towards repairing the Oak Farm disaster by the purchase of
the lease and subsequently in April offering the property for sale at
Birmingham. Gladstone named £130,000 'in perfect *bona fides* but with
fear & trembling';[5] and also unavailingly. Even Lord Grey's purchase of
13 Carlton House Terrace was a weight off Gladstone's mind, 'tho' at
what would be called a wretched price'.[6] Still, it was a great saving for the
family to move to Carlton Gardens. At Fasque old Sir John was now
declining fast, no longer capable of business and driving William almost
to distraction with senilely obsessive 'assaults' on free trade. But as the
once formidable father declined, Helen seemed to respond by blooming
into life again. The days of Protestant lavatory paper were no more. Such
was the degree of reconciliation between brother and sister that William
christened his new daughter, born on August 28, 1849 ('very plump', and
the future Vice-Principal of Newnham), after Helen. Gladstone devoted
himself happily at Fasque to planning a series of breakfast parties for the
next London season. (Carlyle was not likely to be a guest: Gladstone had
dined at Lord Ashburton's where the Sage 'spoke very painfully about
religion, and I must add in a manner the most intolerant'.)[7] Fasque that
vacation was anjoyable also for visits to Lord Aberdeen, a source of useful
if depressing information on such things as the religious opinions of the

1 G to Manning, August 10, 1849. GP, *ib.*, 14.
2 Surtees, 115–16.   3 D, iv, 144.   4 Surtees, 109.
5 D, iv, 119.   6 *Ib.*, 136.   7 *Ib.*, 131.

Queen and Prince Albert (Aberdeen had dry anecdotes about the Queen's less than reverent attitude to archbishops and about her pleasure in throwing off her Anglicanism altogether when in Scotland; the royal couple were, it seemed, positively 'keen' in their favour of the deplorable Hampden).

Meanwhile, the slow fuse of the Gorham case burned steadily away. The Court of Arches duly upheld in August 1849 the Bishop of Exeter's decision. Gorham then, with a malignant obstinacy worthy of the lowest of Low Churchmen, proceeded to appeal to the Privy Council. That lay body had as learned assessors for the case the Archbishops of Canterbury and York and the Bishop of London. But it was not likely that even the first three prelates of the Anglican hierarchy would sway the judicial committee to refusing a clerk in holy orders institution in a benefice (to which he had been presented by its patron, the Lord Chancellor) on grounds of heresy. Who was to define what was heretical in the Church of England? The Queen, the head of the Church, was 'keen' in favour of Hampden, the new Bishop of Hereford; yet Hampden was as furiously denounced as a heretic by the Evangelical Gorham as by the High Church Phillpotts. Gladstone pondered the oddness of speculative political 'lucubrations' with Manning 'at a time like this when my political future at any rate is made so peculiarly uncertain on account of the uncertainties overhanging the Church. It is quite possible that the judgment about Mr. Gorham may impose duties upon me which will separate for ever between my path of life public or private and that of all political parties. The issue is one going to the very root of all teaching and all life in the Church of England. . .'[1] In a conversation with Phillpotts in February 1850 Gladstone was reassured to gather 'plainly' that the sturdy Bishop of Exeter would not 'succumb' to an 'anticatholic decision'.[2]

That decision was duly announced a month later: Gorham's appeal was upheld. As Gladstone put it to the Bishop of Oxford, by the Gorham Judgment 'a foundation is laid for emptying of all their force the articles of the Creed one by one, as public opinion by successive stages shall admit and encourage it', and also 'for habitual assumption by the State of the office of interpreting the Creed, as well as the other documents of the Church'.[3] The day was indeed not far distant (in fact, fourteen years) when a mock-epitaph would be devised for an English judge: he 'abolished . . . the Eternity of Punishment', 'dismissed Hell with costs, and took away from orthodox members of the Church of England their last hope of everlasting damnation'.[4]

The Erastian cat was truly at large in the Tractarian dovecote. The

1 G to CG, February 25, 1850. GGP, 28/3.   2 D, iv, 183.
3 GP, 44740, 1. Memo. January 22, 1852.
4 J. B. Atlay, *The Victorian Chancellors*, ii (1908), 264.

flapping and consternation was in measure to the enormity of the implications of the judgment. Manning's version has it that he went immediately to see Gladstone, ill in bed with influenza, to break the news. 'Starting up and throwing out his arms, Gladstone exclaimed, "The Church of England is gone unless it releases itself by some authoritative act".'[1] How and what? Gladstone, 'rocked as by an earthquake',[2] conferred for several days in agitated sessions with Pusey, Hope, Manning, Phillpotts, Robert Wilberforce and Henry Wilberforce. The Church had been stripped rudely of its pretensions to apostolic autonomy and exposed in humiliating nakedness. Already Newman was preparing his lectures *On the Difficulties of Anglicans*. Gladstone displayed symptoms of apocalyptic despondency; nor was he above posturing and dramatising himself a little: he recorded dining at the Palace on 7 March 'probably . . . for the last time'.[3] Was this not the revelation at last of that long-predicted 'point of declension at which institutions in themselves wholesome must be surrendered'? What was there left now of the union of Church and State? But, for all his apocalypticism and posturing, the salient feature of Gladstone's response to the Gorham Judgment was to urge Hope and Manning to follow his own predilection for judicious delay and not to fall into unwarrantable precipitancy. 'To be calm and rational,' Gladstone urged, 'is a high duty under these circumstances of pain and peril.'[4] It was not long before Hope was referring to Gladstone in his letters to Manning as a 'hindrance'.[5] When it came to a proposal for an address to the episcopate, to be signed by the very cream of Anglo-Catholicism, Gladstone receded; and, even though they were assembled on 18 March in Gladstone's own drawing room, he was 'not with them'.[6] His motives for this refusal are obscure. It was not, as Manning thought, because he was a privy councillor;[7] possibly it was because of his plan for an address to the Bishop of London, whom he had seen on March 13. This moment of bathos was the first distinct and serious breach with Manning. (Manning's biographer did not scruple to point out that there were thirteen present on that occasion, and if Manning clearly played the Christ-role, there was equally no doubt as to who played the Judas.[8])

Gladstone spent an enormous amount of time and trouble during the spring and summer of 1850 trying to repair this damage to relationships he prized so dearly. He put himself forward in a move for an address to the Bishop of London to be signed by laymen only, pleading that the bishop take counsel with his right reverend brethren to find a remedy against the 'general unfitness' of a court so composed as the Judicial

1 Purcell, i, 528.   2 GP, 44738, 147.
3 D, iv, 191.   4 GP, 44738, 222.   5 Purcell, i, 529.
6 D, iv, 194.   7 Butler, 212.   8 Purcell, i, 530.

Committee of the Privy Council to deal with matters of doctrine.[1] But for Manning and Hope by this time Gladstone's role must have seemed that of a grinder out of tired and mechanical and irrelevant old phrases. 'The main question is,' he told Manning on April 4, 'should we try to act for the Church *in* the state or *on* the State'? He had been asking that question since the early 1830s and seemed no nearer to an answer. Sidney Herbert's declining to sign the address to the Bishop of London appeared to Gladstone 'a sign to prepare for making that change soon: for the reluctance of other men in politics to commit themselves in any degree of course must tend to drive me forward, as the keeping in company with them would tend to hold me back'. But how soon was 'soon'? And were not Gladstone's 'states of mind' rather uncomfortably like the hosts of Lars Porsena as recently depicted by Macaulay: where those behind cried 'forward', and those before cried 'back'? 'It is for ever, and for all, that this battle is to be fought in the Church of England.' Yet Gladstone's trumpet-calls, so frequently sounded, had a tendency to die ever more fitfully away. 'I am unfeignedly desirous,' he assured Manning, 'of asking the very least that will rescue the Church from the present hideous system. For upon that minimum must be made a stand involving certain tremendous issues.'[2] Manning could no longer be impressed by 'very least' and 'minimum' as the keynotes of resistance.

The strategy of resistance proposed by Gladstone began by demonstrating the 'dishonesty' of holding that the Church 'must ask the State again and again for a change in the law until she shall obtain it', on the grounds that 'as long as she continues to ask she cannot be responsible for failing to obtain'. This was a path merely to 'infinite demoralisation'. Gladstone put his faith in 'the BISHOPS' as being the benign power within the Church which would deliver it from its travail. From the Carlton Club Gladstone wrote optimistically to Catherine about the bishops: 'Hear that the *great* majority of them are now disposed to try for a settlement which ought to satisfy at least until it breaks down on trial. They may not get it but it is something that they should try for it; & those who try in earnest, if they fail, will not stop there.'[3] It was 'with them and under them that we are now to labour for the truth' in the form of a great counter-attack from the House of Lords.[4] Manning probably had a less sanguine view of both the willingness and the ability of the Anglican episcopate to play this heroic part.

1 GP, 44738, 117, 121.
2 G to Manning, April 4, 1850. GP, 44248, 36.
3 G to CG, April 30, 1850. GGP, 28/3.
4 GP, 44738, 226.

[12]

For the past few days Gladstone had been 'dissipated and unmanned' by
the disturbing illness of his second daughter Jessy. On April 2 the dread
condition of cerebral meningitis was diagnosed. The four-year-old child
died after a horrific week of agonised convulsions which left the
Gladstones shattered. Gladstone was reported as being 'for some hours
in a state of such violent grief as to cause positive alarm to those around
him. Then, suddenly, his sense of duty got the upper hand; thencefor-
ward he was perfectly calm, and returned in all respects to the demeanour
and habits of his everyday life.'[1] With intense emotional impulses thus
under iron control the stricken father took the remains up to Fasque for
interment in the family vault. This was Gladstone's first loss within his
own household. The elaborate necrology he composed is some measure
of his emotional shock.[2] The chapel was crowded on April 13 for the
funeral, 'but few were able to sing'. He reported to Catherine, prostrate in
Brighton: 'We then placed the Coffin in its proper place: on the upper
stone slab, south side, with the head towards the south, and as nearly as
possible just below the altar step, where she received her first lessons of
earthly worship, close by you at the organ. I have kissed the coffin where
it lies: but the stones will not be laid down until tomorrow is over: and
therefore my last visit is not paid.' Gladstone 'got through pretty well':
'not so weak as when I have been by you, and as when therefore I ought to
have been strongest.'[3] While at Fasque he kept the key to the vault and
paid long visits there every day. Old John Gladstone did not help with his
senile complaints about the 'evil of short visits from his sons'.[4]
Gladstone considered that Catherine stood 'in real need of a Book at this
time with reference to the inward fruits of the exercise through which we
have been passing: and I send you accordingly the work of Thomas à
Kempis on the Imitation of Christ, itself not improperly to be called
inimitable, & for all times invaluable: God bless you & it to you. Yours
affty W. E. Gladstone.'[5]

[13]

It was not until the end of April, at Brighton, where he had gone to join
Catherine, that he forced his mind to turn again to the Gorham issue,
which now at least had the merit of providing an absorbing diversion. 'I

1 *Kilbracken*, 126.   2 GP, 44738, 122–141.
3 G to CG, April 13, 1850. GGP, 28/3.
4 G to CG, April 14, 1850. *Ib.*   5 G to CG, April 23, 1850. *Ib.*

have two characters to fulfil,' he told Manning, 'that of a lay member of the Church, and that of a member of a sort of a wreck of a political party. I must not break my understood compact with the last and foreswear my profession, unless and until the necessity has arisen. That necessity will plainly have arisen for me, when it shall have become evident that justice cannot, i.e., will not, be done by the State to the Church.'[1] The evidence for that necessity might, of course, take a very long time to determine. Apparently, the 'disastrous news' that Bishop Blomfield of London's bill to amend the law of appeal to the Privy Council on matters of religious doctrine was rejected by the Lords on June 3 did not constitute such evidence. Blomfield found support from only one of his brethren, Samuel Wilberforce of Oxford; and the crucial speech which killed the bill was delivered by Connop Thirlwall, Bishop of St. David's. No less than four bishops (Durham, Down, Worcester and Norwich) actually voted with the majority. Lord Redesdale, one of the signatories to the laymen's address to Blomfield, made some cutting remarks on the 'want of courage in the bench of Bishops'.[2] Archbishop Sumner did not attend: 'Canterbury was absent!!!' as Gladstone remarked to Robert Wilberforce. 'Why, Cranmer opposed the Act for the Six Articles. But Cranmer's weakest moments were heroism itself and ideal glory compared with the present shame and degradation which carries that honoured name.'[3] For Gladstone it was a cruel disillusionment. Never again would he look upon the Anglican episcopate with the reverence of old. 'I find it no part of my duty, my Lord,' as he wrote indignantly to the Bishop of London on June 4, 'to idolise the Bishops of England and Wales. . .'[4] In his desperation he turned to the Scottish episcopate, with notions of how their freedom from state influence and state power could make of them 'the great Providential instrument for effective resistance to anarchical designs' by way of an institutional system as developed in the colonies whereby a 'lay element' in 'regular organization' could be set up under a 'College of Bishops' to give 'increased vigour to legitimate authority, along with increased scope for reasonable freedom'.[5]

One consequence of the severely oppressive combination of private and ecclesiastical griefs seems to have been a marked recurrence of Gladstone's urge towards accosting prostitutes and trying to persuade them to avail themselves of the facilities of the Soho or Clewer charitable institutions. Altogether he noted sixteen such incidents in May, July and August of 1850. One of them was after the occasion of the Royal Academy

---

1 G to Manning, April 29, 1850. GP, 44248, 39.
2 H, cxi, 639.   3 Butler, 223–24.
4 *Remarks on the Royal Supremacy as it is defined by Reason, History, and the Constitution. A letter to the Lord Bishop of London* (4 June 1850), 86.
5 *A Letter to the Right Rev. William Skinner, D.D., Bishop of Aberdeen, and Primus, on the Functions of Laymen in the Church* (1852).

dinner, where Gladstone sat next to Disraeli, who was 'very easy & agreeable'.[1] Doubtless Disraeli would have been highly intrigued had he known of his prim neighbour's post-prandial plans. Gladstone also had recourse twice in June to self-flagellation as a moral relief. In these circumstances his attention to public affairs in the first half of 1850 was understandably distracted. Nor did his literary energies falter. Fasque that winter produced an enormous volume of notes on Italian poetry and eventually an article on Leopardi in the *Quarterly* for March; the preparation of which cemented his growing friendship with the ex-Carbonaro Panizzi of the British Museum. He dutifully attended the dinner at the Mansion House to launch the Great Exhibition project for 1851, admiring Prince Albert's speech as a '5th Gospel, a New Evangel'. Here he met Lord Granville, whom Gladstone liked greatly: the beginning of another life-long friendship.[2] He dutifully gave evidence in the Lords on Lincoln's divorce bill; though not without making something of a spectacle of himself by answering the question whether he was on 'friendly terms' with Lady Lincoln by 'Yes, allowing for the difference in station, we were well acquainted with her ladyship'.[3] His sensitivity at being a member of 'a sort of a wreck of a political party' was as keen as ever, but his efforts to encourage cohesion among the Peelites as a basis for effective negotiation with the majority faction had little effect. Disraeli's motion on agricultural distress in February was attractive to several Peelites, Goulburn and Herbert and Gladstone himself among them. And there were grounds for co-operation with the Protectionists in certain circumstances. Sir John Tyrell pressed upon Gladstone the advantages of acting with the Tory majority as a party, allowing for his taking his own course on protection and other issues and providing that his 'personal honour and character was secured'. After all, the 'Throne was vacant' in the Commons and there was nothing to prevent Gladstone's seating himself on it. Gladstone recoiled demurely from this 'startling' *démarche*. 'Questions of antipathy' would have to be more 'subdued', he told Tyrell, and 'questions of sympathy more pronounced, and worked upon', before such a contingency could be 'with honour or in fact'.[4]

By late June, however, Gladstone's spirits were sufficiently restored to allow him to play a major part in the famous 'Don Pacifico' debate, in which the Peelites joined with the Protectionists and the Manchester School faction of the Liberals in an attempt to bring Palmerston down. The Foreign Secretary had 'extravagated' to a quite extraordinary degree in a dispute with the Greek government over the misfortunes in Athens

1 D, iv, 207.
2 *Ib.*, 194. The Tractarian writer Lady Georgiana Fullerton was Granville's sister.
3 Reid, 349.   4 PMP, iii, 48–9.

Doodles by Gladstone at Oxford, 1829: *'Politics are fascinating to me. Perhaps too fascinating.'*

Gladstone, by Heinrich Müller, Rome, 1839: '. . . *this mysterious City: whither he should repair who wishes to renew for a time the* dream *of life.*'

Catherine Gladstone, née Glynne, 1840; after a portrait by F. R. Say at Hawarden: '*How much might I say of her as a hero-woman.*'

Gladstone as a young man, an engraving by F. C. Lewis from a drawing by
George Richmond. *'The lower ends of a State ought to be fulfilled even when the
higher ones become impractical.'*

James Hope (later Hope-Scott), by George Richmond, and Henry Manning, by F. Holl after Richmond: *'They were my two props. Their going may be to me a sign that my work is gone with them.'*

Sir Robert Peel, by J. Linnell, 1838: 'There is a manifest and peculiar adaptation in Peel's mind to the age in which he lives and to its exigencies and to the position he holds as a public man.'

George Hamilton-Gordon, 4th Earl of Aberdeen, by John Partridge, c.1847: 'He is the man in public life of all others whom I have loved.'

Hawarden Castle, near Chester (south front): '. . . *this sweet place*'

Cliveden House, Taplow, Buckinghamshire, from the *Illustrated London News*, 1866: '. . . *what courtesy, warmth, and grace*'

Harriet, Duchess of Sutherland, by
F. X. Winterhalter, c.1850: *'Friendships with
women have contributed no small portion of my
existence.'*

Maria Summerhayes, by William
Dyce, as 'The Lady with the
Coronet of Jasmine', 1859: *'My
thoughts of S require to be limited and
purged.'*

Gladstone. A photograph, c.1847: *'The sympathy and concurrence of his time, is, with his own mind, joint parent of his work . . . his choice is, to be what his age will have him, what it requires in order to be moved by him, or else not to be at all.'*

of an allegedly Gibraltar-born Jewish money-lender. Palmerston's brazen and shameless bullying of a small and helpless country astonished Europe. The Greeks were confronted with more battleships than Nelson had commanded at the Nile. (Palmerston's substantial motive was to frighten the Greeks off meddling with the restless Ionian Islands protectorate.) The Peelites, as peculiar custodians of the traditions of the Conservative concert ideal embodied in Aberdeen's policy, were especially incensed. Aberdeen himself, who had suffered so much abuse at Palmerston's hands, led the attack with relish, and success, in the Lords, together with Stanley. There were hopes that the government might be toppled. A Stanley cabinet was 'drawn out on paper' with Gladstone at the Colonial Office and Disraeli at the Board of Control.[1]

But in the Commons Palmerston saved his skin by a speech superlative as to manner and unabashedly chauvinistic as to matter. His appeal to the baser patriotic instincts with his *'Civus Romanus sum'* tag was irresistible. Gladstone did his best in two speeches to try to turn the tide. He paid graceful tribute to the 'masterly character' of Palmerston's speech, 'alike remarkable as a physical and as an intellectual effort', when 'from the dusk of one day until the dawn of the next, . . . through the live-long summer's night the British House of Commons . . . hung on his lips'. But he begged the House not to be deluded, and to recall that a Roman citizen was the member of a privileged class, a conquering race holding other nations down by the strong arm of power. He pointed to the shameful irony that it was Nesselrode, the minister of the Czar, who spoke for the freedom of small peoples. He denounced passionately Palmerston's 'spirit of interference', the 'insular temper' and 'self-glorifying tendency' he encouraged among his countrymen. He objected to Palmerston's setting the British up as being 'universal schoolmasters' to the rest of the world. 'I object,' Gladstone insisted, 'to the propagandism even of moderate reform' in the absolutist European powers: and cited as an instance particularly objectionable the mission of Lord Minto in 1847 to encourage reform in the Italian states, like to 'nothing but the fabulous influence of the dim eclipse, which shed over the nations through which he travelled, disastrous twilight', perplexing rulers and ruled alike. The great need was a policy 'to conciliate peace with dignity' in conformity with the 'general sentiment of the civilized world'. In his second fulmination, on the following day (June 28), Gladstone expanded the last point by a eulogy of Aberdeen.[2] Disraeli fulminated also against Palmerston; and Peel assisted with a rather lack-lustre performance (destined to be his last). But Palmerston eluded his pursuers. Gladstone thought the division 'disgusting' not only on account of Palmerston's majority in itself but for the number of Peelites who allowed them-

1 DDCP, 22.   2 H, cxii, 547–90, 649–52.

selves to be seduced.[1] He was still sore on this point in November in Naples, where he declaimed after breakfast 'rather vehemently' against the Peelite delinquents, only to recollect that one of them was present.[2]

In high dudgeon, Gladstone went off with Catherine for a cricket match at Eton and ecclesiastical talk at the deanery at Windsor. On the morning of July 1 at Windsor he heard that Peel had been seriously injured in a riding accident two days earlier. Back in London, at a concert at the Palace, the Queen spoke of Peel's condition with 'most simple earnestness'. Gladstone called at Peel's the next day, and heard later of the 'great calamity' of his chief's death. Thus to the shock of death in his intimate family circle was added the shock of the death of Gladstone's political father-figure. He never recollected, he assured Manning, an event which more impressed him 'with the belief that God had taken the matter into his own hands and had a special meaning in the occurrence, a meaning we must trust of mercy, though we know not how'.[3] Gladstone seems to have made of the occurrence a distinct abatement of rancour with Disraeli and the Protectionists. Disraeli himself described how 'a day or two after Peel's death, Gladstone was at the Carlton, & said, "Peel died at peace with all mankind; even with Disraeli. The last thing he did was to cheer Disraeli. It was not a very loud cheer, but it *was* a cheer; it was distinct. I sate next to him".'[4]

Peel's tragic removal from the scene meant certainly for Gladstone a kind of emancipation. He no longer had a political senior of heroic stature who had been the dominant and imposing figure in politics in Gladstone's formative and impressionable years. Lord Stanley was cut off by protectionism and by the still not entirely subdued 'antipathies' of recent events. Neither Graham nor Goulburn among the Peelite seniority could arouse in Gladstone the kind of admiration accorded to Peel. *Faute de mieux*, he selected Aberdeen as a kind of father-figure substitute. (Lincoln's pretensions to take Peel's place he decisively choked off: 'I made my views distinctly known . . . He took no offence.')[5] The difference was that he respected Aberdeen deeply precisely for those qualities he found most deficient in Peel: a profound and fervent Christian piety together with a conviction that it was the first duty of a Christian politician to Christianise politics. This constituted a powerful attraction to Gladstone; and he never thereafter wavered in his allegiance to Aberdeen or to Aberdeen's memory. But it was an allegiance essentially of personal devotion. 'He is the man in public life of all others whom I have *loved*,' he would later say. 'I say it emphatically *loved*. I have *loved* others but never

1 D, iv, 222.   2 *Ib.*, 276.
3 G to Manning, July 8, 1850. GP, 44248, 77.
4 Swartz, *Disraeli's Reminiscences*, 33.   5 PMP, i, 72.

like him.'[1] Gladstone could not pretend to regard Aberdeen as an adequate political replacement for Peel. Aberdeen simply did not have Peel's capacity for public mastery. Gladstone himself, moreover, was now forty and a seasoned office-holder. He had made his reputation in Peel's shadow; and the removal of Peel's giant figure from the political scene correspondingly enhanced Gladstone's stature.

It would take something rather electric to jolt Gladstone out of the benumbed state into which private and public tragedy had reduced him. Russell provided such an issue later in the session. With characteristic precipitancy and absence of consultation, he had earlier decided to take over on behalf of the government a routine Radical demand for the 'nationalization' of the ancient English universities. Now he proposed that there should be a Royal Commission to investigate Oxford and Cambridge with a view to advising parliament as to reforms calculated to bring those institutions into line with the requirements of the modern world. There were many questions involved: teaching, scholarship, organisation, finance. But above all was the great question of the integral relationship of Oxford and Cambridge to the established religion. By a logical progression a House of Commons no longer for its English members exclusively Anglican was demanding the abolition of Anglican exclusivity in the two most ancient, wealthy and prestigious English universities. Gladstone had conceded the abolition of a test of Christianity for membership of parliament precisely for the motive of removing irritating but inessential pin-pricks of religious privilege in public life, the better to defend those privileges which were important. The House of Commons would remain *de facto* overwhelmingly Anglican. Gladstone calculated that that would continue to be a sufficient guarantee that Oxford and Cambridge would be kept safe from their most jealous and predatory critics, the Dissenters and the infidels. Now Gladstone realised with dismay that he had reckoned without the susceptibilities of Whigs and Liberals and Conservatives who, though Anglican, could no longer countenance a system of higher education governed by Elizabethan statutes in the case of Cambridge and by Laudian statutes in the case of Oxford.

There was for Gladstone the aspect of proud and venerable corporations threatened with crass coercion from outside; corporations which, moreover, were quietly and independently reforming themselves from within. But overwhelmingly for Gladstone the universities question presented itself as yet another assault of implacable secularity against bastions of the faith. In the light of Maynooth, in the light of the

1 J. B. Conacher, 'A Visit to the Gladstones in 1894', *Victorian Studies*, ii (1958), 157. The occasion, at Pitlochry on July 3, 1894, was Gladstone's emphasising how little he loved Aberdeen's son Arthur Gordon, Lord Stanmore.

Gorham Judgment, with the Church's defences crumbling on every side, a stand had to be taken to stop the rot. This explains the rather absurdly combative character of Gladstone's opposition to the commission. His totally implausible panegyric on the Christian scholars and gentlemen of Oxford amounted practically to an unconscious satire. Nor did he scruple to stoop to dragging in the memory of Peel for pathetic effect as one who had loved his university 'to the very last with maiden ardour'.[1] Gladstone's stand was in fact logically as well as practically quite untenable. It was one thing to hope that the Church might regain control of her doctrine. But it was quite another to suppose that Oxford could be protected from institutional reform to which the Church itself in large measure had been subjected. How could he hope to preserve Oxford's immunity from 'profound and uniform tendencies, associated with the movement of the human mind', with 'the general course of events', perhaps even the 'providential government of the world', to which he had already conceded so much? Peel, for that matter, would almost certainly have accepted university reform as both unavoidable and desirable. Gladstone was attempting, in a hopelessly futile way, to use the universities question as a kind of compensation for his sense of helplessness over the Gorham case. Just as his attempt to block marriage reform owed much of its vehemence to forebodings about the impending appeal, so his attempt to block university reform needs to be interpreted in the fraught aftermath of the judgment.

The universities episode reveals the extent to which Gladstone was distraught and disturbed by the shocks of 1850. From this time for about six weeks until his departure for Hawarden in late August he immersed himself in a particularly intense campaign of rescue work. Probably his presence in the Adelphi Theatre to see an 'amusing farce with some social morality in it' is to be accounted for as part of this purpose. He began to haunt the notorious Argyll Rooms. After a success in inducing a woman to 'go to Mrs. Tennant', the keeper of the Clewer House, Gladstone told Catherine of his 'proceedings of last night – which she approved & with much interest'.[2] This appears to have been Catherine's first initiation into her husband's special work of charity. It marked the point also when rescue work, originally conceived as part of a wider 'humbling office' within the general framework of the Engagement, took precedence of that fraternity, which began to wither. Gladstone was restless, and yearned for repose. At Hawarden, unlet yet unlived in, he speculated with Catherine 'on the possibility of establishing a joint concern there next year'.[3] True, Lavinia Glynne was pregnant once again; but Sir Stephen, who in effect protected the Gladstones with his dedicated bachelordom, might well outlive them all. Sailing from Liverpool to Glasgow on his way

1 H, cxii, 1495–1518.   2 D, iv, 231.   3 *Ib.*, 234.

to Fasque Gladstone read Tennyson's newly-published elegy on Hallam, *In Memoriam*. His only comment was that the boat made a splendid passage. Possibly he was piqued at not having received either the trial printing or the first edition which Tennyson distributed carefully to selected friends. The 'buried rivalry' remained as intense as ever.[1] At Fasque he celebrated his reconciliation with Helen by climbing the Slogh with her to enjoy the grand view – 'over much so for my giddy head'.

The measure of relaxation provided by Fasque allowed Gladstone to devote time and thought to Hawarden. He told Catherine: 'I feel that nearly everything depends on the adoption of my plan about the Jointure.' If the trustees refused he would withdraw.[2] It allowed him also to devote time and thought to Manning. To save that rising hope of the stern and unbending High Church from teetering over the brink which had swallowed Newman was a task worthy of Gladstone's best devotion. The Bishop of Oxford was 'very apprehensive about Manning – and indeed I must be apprehensive about him & many more if the Church of England quietly sits down under the abominations that have been practised'.[3] His tone, after the Gorham fiasco, was still necessarily apologetic. Yet he contrived to combine, by way of apology, some exceptionally acute and penetrating observations about himself with an exceptionally obtuse misapprehension about Manning. 'My life has, I know and feel, had this tendency, to lay a heavy weight upon the movement of the understanding when solicited to depart from the main practical principles by which it has been anchored, and to make the movements of all such processes exceedingly slow.' Manning certainly had come to appreciate the truth of that statement. Then: 'Lagging behind you as . . . I always feel myself to do, on this occasion for the first time it occurred to me not because of the apparent interval between you & me, but between you and your former & recent self, can it be that, the shock of these awful times . . . his trenchant intellect has formed for him too sharp and too short a way through them?'[4] Did Gladstone's lapse at the end into the rather coyly distancing third person betray an awareness of a considerable degree of presumption? From Manning's point of view the irony of this plea was that, after all, it was Gladstone who, by the very fact of his laggard reluctance to move, was 'departing' from the 'main practical principle' by which his 'understanding' had, ostensibly, been applied to political life for nearly two decades. What right had Gladstone to speak of Manning's 'former self' by contrast with his 'recent self'? Manning stood consistently for a particularly high ideal of a Catholic and Apostolic Church. It was not his fault if Anglicanism either could not or

1 Martin, *Tennyson*, 330.   2 G to CG, September 10, 1850. GGP, 28/3.
3 G to CG, September 17, 1850. *Ib.*
4 G to Manning, September 22, 1850. GP, 44248, 102.

would not supply him with it. And if Manning was threatening to be 'sharp and short' over Gorham, was it perhaps because he felt that a decisive dose of intellectual honesty was long overdue? Not surprisingly, Gladstone's endeavours to persuade Manning to adopt his own mode of accepting the unacceptable were of no effect. What Manning described to Hope as 'two jarring and useless conversations' in October opened to Gladstone 'a still darkening prospect. Alas for what lies before us. . .'[1]

[14]

Lavinia Glynne died early in October 1850 after giving birth to yet another daughter. Would Henry remarry and try again to provide Hawarden with a Glynne heir? The question remained delicately poised for some time. (There were to be several determined females proposing themselves as candidates for the task.) Meanwhile, restless back in London, Gladstone decided to use the visit to Hawarden for the funeral as a springboard for escape. His ostensible motive for travel was that his daughter Mary's eyes were inflamed and that, somehow, wintering *en famille* in Italy would be the answer. Doubtless also he was acutely sensitive to any hint of illness after the tragedy of Jessy. Gladstone compounded his restlessness with a peevish humour. Crossing by the Boulogne boat on October 18 he was 'much incensed at the impudence of the captain in kissing and hugging Agnes: & was very hot'. Gladstone took the trouble to write to the offender, '*warning* him'. At St. Germain l'Espinasse he had 'a row with a stripling of that very unsatisfactory & greedy race the French postilions'. This led to a letter to the French Director of Posts, no doubt warning him also. There were endless disputes about Gladstone's obstinate resistance to seemingly reasonable charges for extra horses. Emotional shock worked its way out in aggression. However, Gladstone allowed himself to relax at the ballet in Paris. There was no question now of stalking out abruptly in a state of moral concussion; rather, there were appreciative comments of connoisseurship: Francesca Cerrito was a 'wonderful work of art, a statue made alive'.[2] After wandering at Versailles through the 'bewilderments of that wonderful palace', the Gladstones set off for Italy, where Gladstone specialised in collecting from liberal but not republican or irreligious Italians items of evidence tending to the discredit of the papacy. Before the middle of November they were settling in at Naples.

1 D, iv, 242. Butler, 220.
2 *Ib.*, 246.

The Italian excursion was intended as an escape from scenes of sorrow and circumstances of malaise and frustration. Gladstone badly needed to regain his equilibrium, and his instincts were all for the tonic soothings of tourism, art-purchasing, book-hunting, sermonology, theatre, light society. The last thing he anticipated was getting involved in Neapolitan politics. Had he not recently delivered a powerful critique of Palmerston's deplorable penchant for meddling in the affairs of other states? Had he not objected decidedly to the 'propagandism of even moderate reform'? Had he not mocked Lord Minto's mission of 1847? If anyone was to be dubbed as the embodiment of Lord Aberdeen's policy of non-interference and forbearance to foreign states grappling with difficult problems it would be Gladstone. When, at Lady Leven's for tea, Gladstone came across one Giacomo Lacaita, legal adviser to the British embassy – 'a very accomplished man', who had known one of Gladstone's current literary obsessions, Leopardi – he valued his company not for his dissident politics but above all for his indefatigable assistance as a cicerone for art-purchasing and sight-seeing expeditions.

The only politics to claim Gladstone's attention was news from home: Lord John Russell's brazen attempt to capitalise for Whig benefit on the outburst of anti-Roman Catholicism which followed the papal proclamation of the restoration of the Roman hierarchy in Britain. Russell took the opportunity for a side-swipe at the Anglo-Catholic 'enemies within the gate, indulging in their mummeries of superstition'. Gladstone groaned: 'All human influences, from all quarters, seem to combine against the poor Church of England.'[1] For here at last was the episcopate of England in full fig of truculent unity, boldly and bravely setting out to do battle against the Pope on an issue of somewhat marginal significance, having but a matter of months earlier, on an issue as Gladstone saw it of life or death for the true Catholicism and Apostolicism of the Church, exposed themselves as timorous lackeys of Erastianism. And was not the bishop very accurately selected by Russell as the most appropriate recipient of his notoriously aggressive protest against the Roman Aggression that very Bishop of Durham who had positively voted against Bishop Blomfield's bill? This affair powerfully reinforced Gladstone's sense of disillusionment with the Anglican bishops. Their undignified posture of compounding for their tame acceptance of penalties against themselves by energetically calling for penalties against others would lead Gladstone to reverse his earlier stand on the question of the restored Roman hierarchy. Meanwhile, he mused on the theme that the Church's hysterical behaviour on the question afforded 'a most powerful argument to Statesmen' against giving any relief of the kind sought after the Gorham Judgment. Were these things connected? They seemed most 'ominously

1 *Ib.*, 272.

conjoined'. 'New liberties for ourselves and new restraints upon others cannot stand together;' 'he who asks for the one practically renounces that is to say will never get the other.'[1]

Amid such rather morbidly paranoid broodings Gladstone was interrupted on January 3, 1851 when he heard with astonishment of the 'imprisonment of our friend Lacaita'. The following day he hastened to see Mr. George Fagan, first attaché at the embassy, friend of Lacaita – but 'how fruitlessly! One grows wild at being able to do nothing'.[2] Mr. Fagan was also the friend of another political dissident, accused of recent revolutionary activities by the government, Carlo Poerio; and that day Gladstone went to the Vicaria to hear Poerio defend himself. There was little Gladstone could do in any case, since he was due shortly to leave for Rome, where he looked forward to more solemn delights. But shortly before Christmas, Catherine, pregnant yet again, was shocked by a near-collision with a horse, and suffered a miscarriage on January 7. Rest was prescribed. This was awkward. By January 23 the Rome project had to be given up: Catherine could not be moved with perfect prudence. Regretfully Gladstone cancelled his arrangements for transport. Lacaita was by now out of prison and discussing a possible refuge in England with Gladstone. To Gladstone's broodings about the Church and his outrage about Lacaita could now be added frustration and irritation about Rome. What had been intended as a cure for his problems of emotional instability and repressed aggression began instead to aggravate his symptoms. The Neapolitan government gradually became the focus of a long-smouldering rage. By January 29 Gladstone's excitement had got to the point where at a social occasion he made ' a sort of clean breast about the Government to the Duchess of Sabriani: wh. was not very agreeable to either of us'.[3] A gesture of clemency by King Ferdinand at the beginning of February could no longer appease Gladstone's urge towards some kind of explosive emotional release. 'Loathsome!' He lay awake at night 'thinking what is my duty in this matter'. Lacaita was soon in fresh trouble; and Gladstone made notes in Poerio's case. On February 13, with feckless liberality, the authorities permitted Gladstone to visit the Bagno at Nisida, where most of the prisoners were held. He visited other prisons, interviewing and taking copious notes without hindrance, a distinguished and privileged guest of the Kingdom of the Two Sicilies. He arrived at the conclusion that this 'illegal government' was 'struggling to protect its utter illegality by a tyranny unparalleled at this moment, and almost without a rival amidst the annals of older atrocities'.[4]

Each element in this conclusion was a nonsense. The Neapolitan government, however illiberal, was as legal as any other established government in Europe. To talk of an 'unparalleled tyranny' (which

1 GP, 44740, 2.   2 D, iv, 297.   3 *Ib.*, 301.   4 PMP, iii, 66–70.

permitted visitors to examine its prisons and interview its prisoners) in view of what was happening and had happened elsewhere in the European counter-revolutionary clean-up was absurd. Gladstone had been reading for months past in such as the *Quarterly Review* or *Blackwood's Magazine* of the well-merited failure of the 1848 revolutions and of the stern and salutary measures being taken to restore legitimate authority. What was going on in Naples was a much milder and rather inefficient version of similar processes in, say, Hungary. Gladstone had been a stern enough defender of law and order against Canadian disaffection. There was no lack at the time of Irish efforts to solicit similar explosions of moral outrage and indignation. And to speak of the Neapolitan case in terms of unrivalled distinction in the annals of older atrocities was mere over-excited hyperbole.

It would be equally nonsensical to assert that the Neapolitan government was simply being made to pay for Gladstone's grievances: for what had happened to Jessy; for the loss of Peel and, in another sense, the impending loss of Manning and Hope; for the Gorham Judgment and the imbecility of the bishops; for Oak Farm; for the Marriages Bill and the Universities Commission; for the sad fact that the Engagement had lost much of its early vitality and coherence;[1] or, for that matter, 'impurity' and flagellations. Some such accumulation of emotional pressures certainly played a crucial part in generating the pent-up energy which was exploded by the trigger of the visit to the Nisida Bagno. What Gladstone witnessed there was no doubt distressing enough. As in any situation of counter-revolutionary (or revolutionary) repression there were serious problems of overcrowding. The Neapolitan police and criminal procedures had always been more or less tyrannical; but Gladstone had often been in Naples before without letting that worry him. And to that accumulation could be added three further aggravating elements. One, a general feature of Gladstone's outlook, was his animus against the Roman Church in Italy, not in the abstract or in theory but in its practical aspect as a prop of the reactionary system in Italy. There has always been a side of Gladstone, evident in his first days in Italy in the 1830s, which indicated awareness that a political implication of religious anti-Romanism led towards the sentiments he himself had expressed as he rode through the Campagna shouting, 'Long Live Liberty!' The implications of that germ of sentiment had developed further in his mind on every subsequent visit to Italy. His relish for the anti-Roman testimonies of a class of intelligent Italians, not willingly republicans or unbelievers, came, by the time of Naples in 1850, to a kind of logical climax. His friendship with Antonio Panizzi at the British Museum prepared the way for him. Lacaita and Poerio and their fellow victims in the Bagno were very much of that type. And this led to the second further

1 Butler,.162.

element. Gladstone witnessed the treatment as common criminals of persons he could identify with himself as gentlemen. 'The class persecuted as a whole in the class that lives and moves, the middle class, in its widest acceptation, but particularly in that upper part of the middle class which may be said embraces the professions, the most cultivated and progressive part of the nation.'[1] These were the first 'Liberals' with whom Gladstone came into close and sympathetic political connection. It was not long before he was deep in reading Farini, classic *Risorgimento* historian of *Stato Romano, 1815—1850* (1850), and composing memoranda designed to remove common English misapprehensions that Italian Liberalism was a conspiracy of republicans and atheists; and his central indictment of the radicals and Mazzinians was that they worked in effect for the King of Naples and were in fact 'entitled to rank with soldiers and policemen as forming together the triune support of the reactionary system in Italy'.[2]

The third further aggravating element was simply that Gladstone witnessed for the first time in his life at Naples what it was actually like to be on the receiving end of political repression. He was innocent of any experience of serious public manifestations of suffering or violence. The nearest he had come to it were occasional Eatanswill electioneering brawls and apprehensions of violence at the time of the Chartist attempt to overawe the authorities in 1848. No doubt he had quite approved of the resolute behaviour of the French provisional government in suppressing the challenge of the Paris proletariat in the 'June Days' of 1848. Had he gone to Ireland as he planned in 1845 he might have experienced something of the same shock of seeing a situation concretely which he knew only abstractly and distantly. In the abstract, before the shock of the revelations in Naples in 1850, Gladstone had had no quarrel with the Kingdom of the Two Sicilies.

His quarrel was, in any case, a matter of the merest chance. Had it not been that one of the accused ex-revolutionaries happened to become a part of his entourage and had not Catherine's state of health ruled out the Rome trip, Gladstone would not have surpassed Lord Minto as a dim eclipse, shedding disastrous twilight and exerting a fabulous influence in terrorising the reactionary régimes of Italy. In the event, he had just enough time to gather his materials before news about his father's health and the state of politics in Britain led him to depart from Naples on 18 February, leaving Catherine and the family to stay on for a further month.

Stephen had arrived to fill Gladstone's place as *paterfamilias*. Gladstone was in high form on the return journey. 'This Vesuvio makes her passages gallantly,' he reported from Leghorn, where he had time

1 D, iv, 307–8.   2 GP, 44738, 214–5. [Probably 1850].

enough to translate twenty pages of Farini, and could hope to 'dispose of 22 more which are all that remains of the *body* of the two volumes'.[1] He was much diverted when the passage to Marseilles was delayed by a sailor falling overboard and 'floating about in the sea very comfortably till a boat reached him' after perhaps half an hour.[2] At the Hotel Windsor in Paris the mood was more sober. 'I don't think any of Lord John's efforts at patching would comprehend me, nor is there any other combination seemingly in view'; but he should hasten in any case if only because 'friends of mine may be materially involved'. He thought Graham 'seemed to have spoken in the Disraeli debate in a manner *needlessly* keeping the breach open or rather widening it between himself & the Protectionists'.[3]

The Protectionists, meanwhile, were doing all they could to narrow the breach. On February 23 an evening was passed at Stanley's house in St. James's Square arranging a distribution of offices, 'on the two suppositions that Aberdeen and Gladstone do, and do not, join us'. Disraeli expressed his willingness to serve under Gladstone as Leader of the Commons; but Stanley was sure that 'Gladstone as leader would be equally obnoxious to Protestants and Protectionists'. In any case Stanley was on February 25 'despondent and depressed' at Aberdeen's refusal. He would not persevere 'unless strengthened by the accession of Gladstone'.[4] The object of these lucubrations arrived back in London on the morning of February 26, to be met by his old Oxford friend Phillimore with a copy of *The Times* when his train arrived at London Bridge station and to learn that Lord Stanley desired to consult him about the possibility of taking office in a new Conservative ministry. 'I had not any idea until that time that my coming would be so opportune.' He was more than half afraid that Stanley would make him an offer on terms he would find difficult to refuse. Lincoln (now Duke of Newcastle) had already intercepted him to warn against seduction, urging that if the Peelites 'held off now the crisis must end shortly in placing the *summa rerum* in our hands'. Stanley offered Gladstone '*any* office', subject to Canning's being given first refusal of the Foreign Office; and without any mention being made as to the Leadership of the Commons. But Stanley made it easy by insisting on a fixed duty on corn; and Gladstone's only problem was to speculate why Stanley should have thus wasted time.[5] Gladstone asked for the sake of form for a 'few hours for deliberation'; but his refusal was made known as early as four or five that afternoon, after he had seen Aberdeen. Gladstone was more interested, in fact, in a campaign to 'bruit abroad the fame of the Neapolitan government', which he inaugurated by

1 G to CG, February 20, 1851. GGP, 28/4.
2 G to CG, February 22, 1851. *Ib.*   3 G to CG, February 25, 1851. *Ib.*
4 DDCP, 45–48.   5 PMP, iii, 71–3.

buttonholing Lord Normanby at a levée. The dismayed protectionist Conservatives thus had their first taste of the perplexing problem of dealing with the Peelites; who seemed 'only to be had in the lot' and whom Edward Stanley suspected of aiming at forming a cabinet exclusively out of their own party.[1]

[15]

It was as well that the Neapolitan government provided Gladstone with an issue upon which he could release his hitherto repressed aggressive impulses without restraint. Lord Aberdeen had received as yet no hint of what was painfully in store for him on that score. Instead, Gladstone learned what was painfully in store for himself on the Church front. He heard from Phillpotts that the bishops were compounding their pusillanimity of the previous year by determining not to press for amending the law of appeal. Gladstone read a paper being prepared by the bench, 'very ruinous in my judgment'.[2] This threatened 'outrageous' episcopal manifesto was bad enough; but things with Manning and Hope were even worse. 'Will you believe,' he asked Catherine, 'I was three hours with M. and he never got to the subject, shrinking from it I suppose instinctively: which is no good sign.'[3] There was a 'sad conversation' with Hope on March 6, after Gladstone had spent an evening at Lady Granville's being prompted to discourse on 'Neapolitan horrors'. What Hope had to tell him 'came nearer home': '"Manning's mind I think is made up: I am not very far from the same." What piercing words. We argued for two hours, but what am I for such high work?' Something of Gladstone's distress and excitement was evident in his speech on March 25 attacking Russell's anti-Roman Catholic Ecclesiastical Titles Bill. It was observed that his 'peroration was one unbroken torrent of energetic declamation marred only in its effect by being too long'.[4] On March 30 Manning 'smote me to the ground by answering with suppressed emotion that he is now upon the brink: and Hope too'.[5] Gladstone recorded glumly being with Manning for two hours, 'Not at close quarters'.[6] He would always hold against Manning a lack of candour and confidence. A note from Manning on April 5 warned him that the 'blow' would fall on the following day. On the fatal 6th he had to go through a meeting at Aberdeen's on budgetary matters. 'A day of pain! Manning & Hope!' For Hope too had made his submission to Rome. 'They were my

1 DDCP, 50. Edward Henry Stanley (1826–93) succeeded his father as Lord Stanley in 1851 and as 15th Earl of Derby in 1869.
2 D, iv, 314.   3 G to CG, March 4, 1851. GGP, 28/4.
4 DDCP, 59–60.   5 D, iv, 313, 319.   6 *Ib.*, 317.

two props. Their going may be to me a sign that my work is gone with them . . . One blessing I have: total freedom from doubts. These dismal events have smitten but not shaken.'[1] He immediately executed a new codicil to his will striking out Hope as an executor and replacing him with his former secretary Stafford Northcote. He wrote to Hope much later expressing his sense of the occasion in 1851: 'What is in your view finding a sure anchorage is in mine one of the most deplorable errors ever committed by men in perfect good faith, from pure motives, and at heavy cost.'[2]

The stricken Gladstone wrote on Easter eve at Fasque 'a bitter thing' against himself: 'Whether owing (as I think) to the sad recent events [of the 6th] or not, I have been unmanned & unnerved & out of sheer cowardice have not used the measure which I have found so beneficial against temptations to impurity.'[3] Again, on May 11, after having 'crossed J. Hope on his stairs', Gladstone added: 'Having mentioned that name I must here record the saddest effect wrought on me by the disasters crowned by his & M's secession: the loss of all *resolution* to carry forward the little self-discipline I ever had.'[4] He wrote to Hope expressing an 'unaltered affection' and the wish that separation would not mean estrangement.[5] The threads of a social relationship with Hope were soon picked up again; but Gladstone and Manning remained strangers for a decade.

But the saddest effect wrought upon Gladstone by these disasters was rather the circumstances of his resumption of his measure of physical self-punishment in mid-July. Hitherto, use of the scourge had been related to the 'impurity' of temptations to what passed for Gladstone as 'pornography'. Now it became a feature of his rescue mission to fallen women. Such 'terrible blows' as the fall of Manning and Hope 'not only overset & oppress me but I fear also demoralise me'. Their shock jolted Gladstone to admit to himself that his rescue interests were 'Carnal, or the withdrawal of them would not leave such a void'. With one woman who came with him to his house twice ('a singular case indeed') he admitted that he was 'certainly wrong in some things & trod the path of danger'.[6] The crucial case which overbalanced him was one Elizabeth Collins, who 'much interested' him on their first meeting on June 11, 1851. During the following year he met her on twenty occasions and sought for her in vain five times. Early in July he advised her to make a day visit to Carlton Gardens and appeal to Catherine for advice.[7] On July 13 there was a 'strange & humbling scene' of two hours which led to

1 *Ib.*, 322. 2 G to Hope-Scott, November 1, 1868. GP, 44214, 396.
3 D, iv, 325. 4 *Ib.*, 329.
5 Ornsby, *Hope-Scott*, ii, 88–89.
6 D, iv, 319. 7 *Ib.*, 342.

Gladstone's flagellating himself.[1] Shortly afterwards he recorded 'another mixed scene somewhat like that of 48 hours before': again the scourge. Thus carnality had invaded charity. The sexuality which undoubtedly had always been a part, however firmly repressed, of Gladstone's philanthropic urge ever since his earliest essays in accosting on his first evening at Oxford, now broke through to the surface. His old doctrine of the 'substantive character of beauty', insisting that it was to metaphysics what pleasure was to ethics, was now given a curious new twist. Gladstone was both smitten and shaken by Elizabeth Collins's beauty. 'Half a most lovely statue,' he rhapsodised rather oddly (in Italian), 'lovely beyond measure.'[2] Her attractions led to Gladstone's being the first to leave a grand dinner given by Palmerston for the United States minister to spend two more hours with her, 'strange, questionable, or more'. Once more the scourge, together with confessions: 'Whether or not I have been deluded in the notion of doing good by such means, or whether I have sought it through what was unlawful I am not clear.'[3]

After their seventeenth meeting Gladstone told himself it was 'bad: & there must be a change'. But a few days later he groaned: 'I am surely self-bewildered.'[4] It was a real struggle for him to regain his emotional composure. His rescue mission could no longer bear its former even ostensibly unalloyed character as a charitable office of his membership of the Engagement. There are no grounds whatever for supposing that the Collins episode involved anything in the way of directly physical or explicitly sexual contact. But clearly Gladstone had crossed a crucial psychological threshold. In his smitten and unnerved state he allowed two very sensitive areas of his private life to break out of bounds and mix together. Once having mixed, 'impurity' and 'rescue' would be difficult to extricate. Moreover, Gladstone had been driven to admit to himself the possibility that his 'mission' was founded on 'unlawful' motives. And did not the horrid prospect arise that physical self-punishment which he already acknowledged as being paradoxically as much an encouragement to as a deterrent from impure temptation might play the same facilitating part in making the 'scenes' of his rescue missions even more 'mixed' or 'questionable'?

Manning's and Hope's going as a 'sign' that Gladstone's 'work' was 'gone with them' proved in fact the one positive consequence of the 'disasters'. Gladstone would now be free from the futile obligation of having to convince himself by convincing Manning and Hope that, despite everything, there were still good reasons why he should stay in public life for the sake of the programme of 1838. That they had been his two 'props' was very true: in one sense, their sympathy and even

1 *Ib.*, 344.   2 *Ib.*, 440.
3 *Ib.*, 346.   4 *Ib.*, 426, 429.

indulgence had been like intellectual crutches, permitting Gladstone for many years to get away with self-justifications of an almost ludicrous implausibility; in another sense, they had been barriers against Gladstone's being able to move freely enough to readjust his position in public life and reformulate his claims to political credentials. There is no doubt as to the genuineness of Gladstone's pain for himself as well as for the blow to the Church. He had grown too used to his crutches not to feel their loss acutely; and he had a very intelligently well-founded fear of his consequent freedom to move. He knew himself well enough to know how heavy a weight lay upon the movement of his understanding and how agonising would be the operation of detaching himself from the main practical principles by which his understanding was anchored. For this purpose anger was very helpful in its destabilising effect: anger at the Neapolitan authorities, anger at the bishops. ('I meet a squadron of Bishops now,' he noted after a dinner at the Bishop of London's Fulham Palace, 'with much altered feelings.')[1] This awareness of a fundamental displacement would be the keynote of the immediate future. The last 'two terrible years', he wrote in August 1851, had 'really displaced and uprooted' his 'heart' from the Anglican Church, 'seen as a personal and living Church in the *body* of its Priests and members'; and at the same time the two friends whom he 'might call the only supports' for his intellect had been wrenched away from him, leaving him 'lacerated' and 'barely conscious morally'. 'These misfortunes,' Gladstone added, probably with mixed or questionable 'scenes' in mind, might 'yet succeed in bringing about my ruin, body and soul'.[2]

1 *Ib.*, 338.   2 *Ib.*, 352–3.

CHAPTER V

'THIS WHIRL WHICH CARRIES ME OFF BALANCE': FOUNDATIONS OF A NEW VOCATION, 1851–1855

[1]

As if defiantly hitting back at fell circumstance, Gladstone dated his letter to Lord Aberdeen on the Neapolitan horrors April 7, the day following the catastrophe of Manning and Hope. In the void of displacement and instability compounded of his membership of a 'sort of a wreck of a political party' and the bankruptcy of his personal politico-religious programme, the letter represented the two solid and familiar and reassuring things Gladstone could cling to: his Peel-substitute leader and a cause embracing politics and morality in a dramatic and emotionally compelling degree.

Aberdeen was by no means anxious to fit into Gladstone's requirements and fulfil some kind of heroic Peel-role by intervening to restrain and correct the Neapolitan government. His permission to Gladstone to address the letter to him was a calculation reluctantly arrived at: possibly he might in some measure tone down Gladstone's obsessive excitement. The letter sent to Aberdeen on the 7th was, ostensibly, a private communication, and it was Aberdeen's hope to keep it that way. The supposition was that Aberdeen would aid Gladstone's purpose of diminishing a 'mass of human suffering' through his special and authoritative contacts with the conservative leaderships of Europe. As Gladstone put it in tones not far short of polite blackmail, he trusted that mitigation of these great offences to the eye of Heaven might be effected 'through your Lordship's aid, on the one hand without elusion or delay, on the other without the mischiefs and inconveniences which I am fully sensible might, nay in some degree must, attend the process, were I thrown back on my own unaided resources'.

Thus the hapless Aberdeen weighed with more than his habitual moroseness the likely chances of his swaying the policy of counter-revolutionary Europe against the likely consequences of Gladstone's running amuck with his own unaided resources. A public scandal would be meat and drink to Palmerston and the Radicals. Aberdeen's son, Arthur Gordon, later recorded his father's comments on Gladstone:

'eager and impulsive', 'be the consequences what they may', with no *'perspective* in his views. All objects, great and small, are on one plane with him; and consequently the tiniest sometimes assume the largest dimensions.'[1] Many years later Gladstone and Gordon disputed as to the precise terms of the understanding. 'My father thought you intended to appeal to Parliament or the public, but suspended the execution of that intention to allow him to intervene,' insisted Gordon. 'You meant to appeal to his intervention, but with the intention of publication should that intervention be refused, or fail.' Either way, however, it was Aberdeen's 'sore point' that it was for him and not for Gladstone to decide when intervention had failed.[2] He agreed to Gladstone's request 'provided he remained silent' in the meantime.[3] Gladstone promised Aberdeen that he would find the matter of the Neapolitan case 'painful, nay revolting, to the last degree'. Probably Aberdeen, who had witnessed the carnage of the 'Battle of the Nations' at Leipzig in 1813, was less pained and revolted than Gladstone innocently assumed. But he would not have been the less impressed by the dangerous power of Gladstone's insistent rhetoric on outrages 'upon religion, upon civilization, upon humanity, and upon decency'; on 'wholesale persecution of virtue when united with intelligence'; on 'total inversion of all moral and social ideas'; and especially by Gladstone's propagandist instinct for exploiting someone else's winged phrase: 'This is the negation of God erected into a system of Government.'

As against this excited rhetoric, together with copious (and occasionally inaccurate) circumstantial detail of the atrocities of gentlemen chained as if common felons, it availed little that Gladstone professed impeccably Conservative motives. Gladstone argued that the Neapolitan régime was doing the work of republicanism; and that 'as a member of the Conservative party in one of the great family of European nations', he was 'compelled to remember, that that party stands in virtual and real, though perhaps unconscious alliance with the established Governments of Europe as such'. In gentlemen of virtue and intelligence such as Poerio or Lacaita he could see himself. He did not sympathise with them as liberals; but as men unable to be conservative because their government forced upon them the choice only of tyranny or revolt. These distinctions, however, were too subtle to make much impression upon the public mind.

Gladstone's indictment of the Neapolitan régime was that it disgraced the cause of European conservatism. Aberdeen's problem was that,

1 Conacher, 532.
2 Gordon to G, February 19, 1893. GP, 44322, 140.
3 E. Jones Parry, *The Correspondence of Lord Aberdeen and Princess Lieven, 1832–1854*, ii, (1939), 590.

however much he 'would willingly have assisted, in the interests of Monarchy and good Government, to obtain some improvement',[1] he was dealing with a different kind of European conservatism from that with which he was familiar in the gentler times of Metternich and Guizot. The fulcrum for any leverage at Naples would have to be Vienna; and in place of the sympathetic Metternich was now Felix Schwarzenberg, rather ruthless and a little reckless, furious at the British government's support for Turkey in 1849 over the Hungarian refugees affair, offended at the insults more recently offered by the Southwark rabble to the *K.K. Feldzeugmeister* Haynau, and not inclined to cause himself trouble in Naples in order to accommodate an ex-foreign secretary to whom he was under no obligations of personal friendship. Moreover, Schwarzenberg tended to be impatient of British claims to criticise other governments for repression when British policy in Ireland, the Ionian Islands (and its by-product, the scandal of Greece and the Don Pacifico case) and Ceylon was far from being beyond reproach. If the *avvocato* Poerio was a victim of injustice, what of the Chartist barrister Ernest Jones? However, when Schwarzenberg received Aberdeen's carefully researched letter of May 2 he decided, out of consideration for Aberdeen's character and reputation, to respond to it with appropriate seriousness and good will. His own enquiries at Naples naturally took time; and he cautiously employed a personal messenger (Count Buol-Schauenstein, no less) rather than the postal service to despatch his reply to Aberdeen at the end of June. That response was indeed measured and, from Aberdeen's viewpoint, quite satisfactory and promising. But, before it reached Aberdeen, and to his intense consternation, Gladstone took it upon himself to publish his letter on July 11, despite Aberdeen's protestations that he was in decency 'bound to wait for the Prince's answer'.[2]

Given Gladstone's state of aggressive and unstable excitement, his impatience and precipitancy were understandable; but, quite apart from ruining the chance created by Aberdeen's studious diplomacy of practical ameliorations, Gladstone wilfully and inconsiderately put Aberdeen in an impossible position vis-à-vis Schwarzenberg; who received Aberdeen's embarrassed apologies and washed his hands of the affair. Gladstone felt that a lapse of over three months gave him the right to take the matter into his own hands. More importantly, it is clear that he would not be baulked of his prey.

The impact of the publication of *A Letter to the Earl of Aberdeen on the State Prosecutions of the Neapolitan Government* owed much to the incongruousness of the writer in relation to his theme. Not only was there the dramatically gross contradiction of his own Don Pacifico doctrine, seized upon eagerly by Palmerston as all the more apt for his purposes as coming

1 *Ib.*, 600–01.   2 *Ib.*, 591.

from the pen of a converted sinner; but also the startling revelation of a new Gladstone *persona*. Hitherto notorious for Puseyism and priggishness, a being somewhat remotely above the common level of *homo politicus*, Gladstone burst into the public arena apparently in something of the role of demagogue. His credit as an advocate of a popular cause was if anything enhanced by addressing his appeal to a disciple of Castlereagh. Aberdeen rightly felt himself hardly used to be thus exploited. 'Gladstone's ill-advised publication,' he reported to his old friend Princess Lieven, 'has produced the most extraordinary sensation here, amongst persons of all parties, and has given a great practical triumph to the Foreign Office.' The truth was, Aberdeen conceded, that 'too many' of Gladstone's accusations were 'well founded', though nothing could 'excuse his rash publication'. He groaned to learn that Gladstone was preparing a second letter in rebuttal of criticisms, and Aberdeen could only hope that, with 'all the advice I could give him', it would have 'a much better tone and spirit'. 'This Gladstone affair,' he lamented, 'has caused me a good deal of vexation; for I have been open to much misrepresentation; and although I would not, on any account, quarrel with a man whom I love and esteem as much as Gladstone, he knows perfectly well that I think I have great reason to complain of his proceeding.'[1] Gladstone, hard at work preparing his second letter, told Catherine: 'Ld Aberdeen does not much like the matter now but will not ask me to postpone any more and I think he sees tho reluctantly that I ought not.'[2] Aberdeen found it impossible to be resentful at Gladstone; but, as far as practical mitigations were concerned, he had much reason to deplore that Gladstone had 'done more mischief by his ill-advised proceedings than it is possible to estimate'.[3]

As with the response of the Liberals and Leaguers of Newark to his virtual dismissal by the Duke of Newcastle, Gladstone found himself in 1851 the object of some not entirely welcome applause. The *Edinburgh Review*, that notorious champion of the European Revolution, distinguished itself in offering congratulations and slyly confessing to envying his party 'a man, whose talents we have often admired, but whose generosity of feeling had not been sufficiently appreciated'.[4] Palmerston's exploitation of him Gladstone found almost as embarrassing as his exploitation of Aberdeen had been to Aberdeen; which was but poor consolation to Aberdeen. Palmerston made a great point of paying elaborate tribute to Gladstone in the Commons and ostentatiously arranged to have copies of the pamphlet distributed for the edification of the European Courts by British diplomatic representatives. Gladstone found himself now in company with one of the leading Radicals,

1 *Ib.*, 603.   2 G to CG July 14, 1851. GGP, 28/4.
3 Parry, 598.   4 *Edinburgh Review*, xciv, 1851 (Oct.), 491–3.

Molesworth, who was conducting his own campaign against the Neapolitan régime. But the immediate significance of the *Letter to the Earl of Aberdeen* was very much what Aberdeen himself diagnosed: impulsiveness and inconsequentiality. It owed much more to Gladstone's sense of having lost a past than to any strivings to find a future. The issue was far too remote and tangential to be of service in Gladstone's quest for a new political vocation. If anything, Gladstone's embarrassment at being hailed as a recruit for the 'march of mind' led him to a quite excessive stickiness and purism over the next few years in asserting the Conservative integrity of the Peelite group. As if to compensate for the Neapolitan escapade, Gladstone, like an embodied conscience of the Party of 1842, barred the door to Liberalism against the irritated Herbert, Newcastle, and even Aberdeen himself. Gladstone took himself seriously enough in this role virtually to drum the astonished Graham out of the Peelite fellowship. Far from hastening him on to Liberalism, the Neapolitan affair in fact retarded Gladstone's movement quite considerably.

At the same time, however, the Neapolitan affair registered the fact that there was movement. Displaced and unstable, Gladstone, bereft of his crutches and the old familiar bearings of his political ways, was indeed being powered, as he put it to the dismayed Aberdeen, by his 'own unaided resources'. Gladstone's determined lurch in 1851–53 towards what he took to be the bosom of the 'party of 1842' was just as much a symptom of instability as his Neapolitan lurch had been. The fact that the Neapolitan lurch of 1850–51 approximated better to his ultimate point of rest in 1859 than the 'party of 1842' lurch in 1851–53 tends to dignify the *Letter to the Earl of Aberdeen* with rather more resonance than it really merits. Given that at this time Gladstone was running rather out of control, he was bound to register at some point the direction in which he would eventually move. Thus the Neapolitan affair was random rather than purposeful, and certainly in no sense determinant. It was one lurch among several.

[2]

In the interval of addressing his letter to Aberdeen and the notoriety of its publication, Gladstone resumed his now rather bedraggled public career. On the Church front the rude jolt of displacement led him to formulate a much more severely Keblean view of the Establishment. 'If we can,' he noted rather ruthlessly at this time, 'we are bound to have Faith, Church, and Establishment together. If one must be parted with, however, it must be the Establishment of Religion. And if a second must be dispensed with, it must be the Church of England.'[1] Such was the sour fruit of much bitterness of soul. A good deal of this sourness had come out in the denunciation of Russell's Ecclesiastical Titles Assumption Bill in March 1851, disguised in the form of tolerant liberality ('the great principle of religious freedom') and a deliberately provocative tone of contempt for majority opinion ('fatal confusion of mind and ideas').[2] Gladstone's quite perfunctory apologies to Oxford were hardly an adequate explanation of his change of front on the issue of Roman Catholic dioceses and archdioceses. He seems in any case to have accepted the massive 'Protestant' majority for the bill as a kind of symbolic emancipation from his old State and Church programme. The paradoxical and ironic circumstance that the Commons, like the bishops, were on this point for the programme and he against it, only underlined Gladstone's sense of alienation. More distressing for him on this occasion was the end of the Peelites as a serious parliamentary party. The mass of Peelite backbenchers either drifted back to the Conservative party or faded away at the next elections. All that was left effectively was little more than the front bench rump, over which Gladstone appointed himself a kind of unofficial whip.

Of much more moment was Gladstone's response to Disraeli's criticisms of Whig financial proposals in April 1851. Protection or free trade had held the stage as the dominant political issue since 1844. Now finance was coming back to the fore, much in the manner of the early and great days of Peel's ministry, as the crux of the relationship between government and public. The rise of pressure groups such as the Financial Reform Association expressed this new awareness. This pressure for direct taxation, led in the Commons by Hume, helped to defeat Wood's budget proposal in 1851 to renew the unreconstructed and undifferentiated income tax. The failure of Wood's budget created an immediate and obvious ground of conflict as to by whom and on what terms the issues would be resolved. Though highly marginal in terms of gross national product, mid-nineteenth-century budgets were coming to create a state of 'psychological expectation', and to be thereby crucial in forming grounds of social balance, equity, and political stability.[3] As Peel's disciple, Gladstone was acutely sensitive to this dimension of politics. But far from seeing budgets in tandem with parliamentary franchise reform, Gladstone saw them as the sovereign remedy for creating social confidence and content and thus obviating the need for reform. He told his fellow-Peelites that the 'financial feebleness & the extravagance' of the

1 GP, 44738, 227.   2 H, cxviii, 263–6.
3 See on this theme H.C.G. Matthew, 'Disraeli, Gladstone, and the Politics of Mid-Victorian Budgets', HJ (1979), 615–31.

Whigs was the 'sure means of generating successive demands for reform'.[1] He also saw Disraeli as the obvious rival for filling Wood's place and commanding the possibilities of the central ground of political credit and reputation. He soon decided that Disraeli's financial plan contradicted the principles laid down by Peel of reducing taxes upon consumption of articles of industry.[2] Disraeli begins indeed at this point to take on something of the character of a target previously sustained by the Neapolitan régime. Much in the same mood of footloose aggressiveness was Gladstone's pursuit of Disraeli on the question of reintroducing the House Tax at the end of June.[3] Indeed, if Gladstone needed for the reassembling of his vocation some kind of demon or devil-figure, Disraeli would be admirably adaptable for such a purpose: Peel's unkindest critic, an adventurer of dubious origins and dubious morals, an ex-dandy and rake of rather Mephistophelean appearance, elevated to parliamentary eminence only by the tragic circumstances of 1846.

As Disraeli began to nestle in Gladstone's mind as possibly the focus of a kind of domestic version of the Neapolitan Horrors, so Gladstone at this time focussed also on an alternative source of moral regeneration. Again, it seems clear that he had an instinctive sense of the requirements of his new vocation. He needed a target of resentment, or moral evil. Was it not a duty positively enjoined upon him by the teachings of Bishop Butler? Disraeli might well (and indeed did) answer for this requirement. On the other hand, Gladstone needed also a new means of validating his public credentials. Peel was now but a memory: a potent memory to be sure, and one from which Gladstone would extract the maximum accreditation. Something more and something big and something in need of redemption and something with a bearing to the future was requisite. Eventually Gladstone would describe this as a 'public opinion' which he could 'form' and 'direct' towards ends divined by himself. For the present his initiatives in this direction were tentative and exploratory. His first exercise in exploring the phenomenon of what he would soon be describing excitedly as 'the *people*' took place at Shadwell on May 14, 1851, when he addressed a meeting of Thames coal whippers. This group of workers had become a hobby for Gladstone since his days at the Board of Trade, something of a proletarian version of his 'rescue' work. 'These men were delightful to see & hear,' he recorded, 'apart from the excess of their grateful feeling towards me – which made me feel much ashamed. I spoke at some length.'[4] What did the coal whippers make of a 'great burst' from Gladstone on 'Papal Aggression'? But it was nonetheless a conjuncture of some significance. That gratitude was in the coal whippers' minds when they invited Gladstone is clear; but what was in

1 *Ib.*, 625.   2 H, cxvi, 58–65.
3 H, cxvii, 1446.   4 D, iv, 330.

Gladstone's mind as he accepted and went off to so incongruous a locale as Shadwell?

There were occasions of less moment. Gladstone's attending the opening of the Great Exhibition put his father in a senile rage; which however was appeased; and indeed Sir John was soon insisting that he would go up to London himself for the Exhibition and stay in his old room at Carlton Gardens, with Helen lodged in the neighbourhood. Gladstone warned Catherine that this dread prospect was 'not wholly impossible'.[1] Gladstone found himself masquerading at a Court costume ball at Buckingham Palace in June as Sir Leoline Jenkins, a seventeenth-century M.P. for Oxford University ('some little work about my dress: resisted moustaches, & the imperial dropped off').[2] He thriftily wore the same costume again for Lady Ashburton's ball later that month. There were further visits to the Great Exhibition in July. There was one curious moment on July 9 when, on a chance rumour, Gladstone went to the Guildhall thinking the Emperor Nicholas of Russia would be there: 'as I reckon him a sight worth much'; so deep had been the impression of 1844. At Hagley the Gladstones heard George Lyttelton recite his 'Glynnese Glossary', the dictionary of the Glynne family's whimsical speech mannerisms, of which fifty copies were published that year by 'a little subscription among us.'[3] Gladstone would occasionally unbend for Catherine's benefit to a Glynnism ('Went last night to Saint Barnabas: Liddell praught . . .')[4]; but fluency still eluded him. In truth in these summer months of 1851 Gladstone was still reeling from the impact of Elizabeth Collins. He wrote to Catherine as their wedding anniversary approached:

> When you say I do not know half the evil of your life, you say that which I believe in almost every case is true between one human being and another; but it sets me thinking how little you know the evil of mine, of which at the last day I shall have a strange story to tell. That in which I join you unreservedly is looking back upon the day from which we have just measured twelve years with fondness and thankfulness, and a desire that I may be made less unworthy to realise its blessings. Self examination is a mournful task especially in one who feels himself made up, as I do, of strange and sharp contrasts. It is a fatal error to try to get over that pain otherwise than by the removal of the cause – and a serious fault to flatter others when they are in the mood of serious reflexion. I will not tell you my beloved that you have nothing to strive against: but how gladly would I change with you.[5]

1 G to CG, April 28, 1851. GGP, 28/4.
2 D, iv, 337.   3 Bassett, 40–41.
4 G to CG, November 8, 1852. GGP, 28/4.
5 G to CG, July 26, 1851. *Ib.*, 28/3.

Gladstone considered the question of a visit to Paris 'with the feeling that I am utterly over-excited'.[1]

At Fasque that autumn there was much ado with the Italian text of the Neapolitan defence against his indictment. But what had promised to be yet one more of a long series of Fasque vacations took a more serious turn. By December it was clear that Sir John was sinking. The family gathered to watch over the redoubtable laird's last fight. William diverted himself by reading Henry Mayhew's *London Life and London Poor*. Helen rallied to play her part admirably. Sir John died on the 7th. William was distressed that the old man refused the Holy Sacrament; and it was also rather unfortunate that his last words, *compos mentis*, were, 'Get me some porridge.' The kisses William placed on his dead father's cheek and forehead were the only ones he could remember.[2]

For Gladstone his father's death was an important emotional break, especially in its incidence within the death-ridden climate of the whole period since Jessy's atrocious death. But the human relationship between father and son had long since ceased to have anything more than a sentimental significance. What caused a more serious break was the new, and rather chilly, atmosphere which immediately obtained at Fasque. Sir Thomas, the new baronet, long overshadowed and resentful, lost no time in asserting his status as laird. William's presumptuous notions about inheriting Fasque were no more heard of. Such was the feeling between the brothers that William did not see Fasque again until he paid a visit of semi-reconciliation in 1858. The loss of so crucial a part of his routine of life added immeasurably to Gladstone's already depressed sense of displacement.

There was, also, the complex question of dividing up the immense estate. Sir John had commenced the division in earnest himself in 1849. William had Sir Stephen Glynne's bond for £30,000 transferred to him, together with £9,000 in cash, the house at No. 6 Carlton Gardens with furniture and stables (valued in total at £10,000), a second set of stables in St. Martin's Mews (£1,200), £4,000 of Edinburgh Gas shares, £6,000 of Monkland shares, £7,332 of Forth and Clyde shares, and 850 more assorted shares with a sale value of £4,272. This was topped up in 1850 with £2,000 of London and North-Western stock. The total capital Gladstone received from his father in the latter's life time amounted to £88,114 10s. In the final division in and after 1851 William was credited with £27,000 in the Residual Trust, together with smaller items (including some of the West Indian properties, part of which were left to Catherine).[3]

1 G to CG, July 31, 1851. *Ib.*
2 D, iv, 375. 'For the time and class, the behaviour was, I am afraid, normal; it may help to account for the impersonal intensity of G. among many other of his contemporaries.' MRDF.
3 GGP, 94/13. Secret Account Book, 3–5.

Helen received much less in 1849 and much less again in 1851 and the sources of her income remained largely out of her own control; and her resentment did considerable harm to her newly-found reconciliation with the family. (Her revenge was to leave as much as she could to the Roman Catholic Church.) Tom, the heir, got the largest share; but the younger sons each received in total something worth £151,000.[1] Part of William's share was Seaforth, which he purchased from the Trust at Robertson's sanguine valuation of £50,000; but on which in the end William lost something like £12,000. He was sentimentally pleased at inheriting this part of the patrimony, though the Liverpool estate was by now merely a matter of taking advantage of the city's north-westward development. He paid a visit of inspection in 1853, but did not find the place as enchanting as his early memories of it: his thoughts wandered around the sombre theme of his 'ungodly childhood' and the retrospect of 'selfishness and sin'.[2]

December 1851 ended for Gladstone his 'saddest year'. 'In truth the religious trials of the time have passed my capacity & grasp. I am bewildered & reel under them.' It had been a year of 'rending & sapping of the Church, the loss of its gems, the darkening of its prospects; as well as the ill fruit this has had on me individually'.[3]

[3]

Thus, though he had lost Fasque, Gladstone had gained wealth. This put him in a strong position in relation to Hawarden. What he had gained could be put to work to compensate for what he had lost. He realised £9,605 worth of shares in the autumn of 1850. The logic was obvious and cogent: Sir Stephen was, and would clearly remain, unmarried; his heir was his younger brother Henry, now a widower with daughters. There was a strong presumption that the Hawarden estate should be kept intact. It had nearly collapsed, but was now mending. In July 1851 Gladstone spoke pessimistically of Stephen's affairs being 'little better ten years hence than they are now, I mean his incumbrences [sic] little less'[3]; but by October 1852 he was planning to make 'a kind of wind up of the office I have held for the last five years, trying to convert myself into a mere referee, to be applied to when they think it necessary, instead of having the whole matter in my hands. The day when I can conscientiously do this,' he told Catherine, 'with a sense of its not being injurious to Stephen, will I can assure you not be the least happy of my

1 Checkland, 368, 375, 416.   2 D, iv, 568.
3 G to CG, July 24, 1851, GGP, 28/3.

life.'[1] By January 1853 Gladstone could remark on Stephen's affairs as 'materially improved'.[2] That material improvement had come about not only through Gladstone's exertions but also through infusions of Gladstone money. Gladstone now held Sir Stephen's bond for £30,000. The process of commuting Glynne debts to the Gladstone estate led by 1852 to Gladstone's being able to remark proudly that he walked from Chester to Hawarden 'thro' my land'.[3] There was not enough Glynne money to keep Hawarden in being. Had Henry, or any male line deriving from Henry, inherited, the estate in effect was doomed. Though perfectly capable of remarrying and supplying a Glynne heir, the new circumstances created by the Oak Farm crash and its consequences placed what amounted to a veto on any such proceeding on Henry's part. It was in many ways an awkward and delicate and somewhat embarrassing situation; and Gladstone was naturally sensitive to any obvious but quite misconceived sentiments or whispers on the theme of a Gladstone appropriation of the Glynne heritage.

The same logic that vetoed Henry Glynne invited the husband of Catherine Glynne. Now that Stephen could resume residence in the Castle (with his mother preferring to remain at Hagley with her younger daughter), the question of a joint residence with the Gladstones suggested itself as the natural solution to all their problems. Catherine and William discussed arrangements with Stephen in January 1852. Stephen formally registered the sense of the new dispensation by settling the estate on the eldest son of Catherine Gladstone. (Willy at that time was himself being settled – very unhappily – at Eton.) The legal arrangements drawn up in 1855 provided that Willy should inherit on the decease of the last male Glynne. This formally made proper provision for Henry, but with a tacit understanding that Henry should respond by not throwing all into the melting-pot once more by marrying. Confronted by these dry and unfeeling legal provisions, Gladstone recoiled. He was sensitive about misrepresentation; and tried to persuade the Glynne lawyer that the arrangements should be submitted to impartial outside parties for comment. He was anxious about the adequacy of the charges on the estate in favour of Henry's eldest daughter, and 'even on the main point that he is right in passing from Henry's male line to C's. I must consider carefully whether I can take any step to obtain a clearer view in this matter; for it touches both honour & justice very nearly.' The Glynne lawyer persuaded Gladstone that any outside opinions were best avoided: 'the dispositions might lead to remark.' The proposed arrangement was the 'most wise & equitable' solution to a difficult and complex case. Gladstone and Catherine talked it over '& agreed that it should be

1 G to CG, October 23, 1852. *Ib.*
2 D, iv, 486.   3 *Ib.*, 451.

kept deeply secret by *us*; Mary [Lyttelton] the only exception, if even Mary'.[1] All these dispositions were doubtless eased by Lady Glynne's death in May 1854. Gladstone marked the occasion by setting to work on her accounts, 'that I may close my stewardship in this department'.[2] In 1855 Gladstone finished arrangements for the £20,000 with which he took up Sir Stephen's Oak Farm mortgage.[3]

By October 1853 Gladstone was arranging his books and papers in the 'north room' at Hawarden. The ordering and arranging of new bookcases was a matter over which Gladstone took immense pains. By October 1855 he could report: 'Our room is growing characteristic; & I think of having in it our own furniture.' In November he busied himself enjoyably planning and laying out the Park walk up to Hawarden Church, which was to become over the years a, *Via Sacra*. Already in 1853 he had inscribed his initials over a gate on this route near the ruins of the old castle. In October 1852 he noted the felling of three beeches in the park: the beginnings of his most characteristic and famous exercise, prompted by the very practical motive of realising the assets of the Park.[4] Soon Gladstone was speaking on Stephen's behalf at the Hawarden Rent Dinner.[5] By December 1855 he was comfortably enough installed to exhibit proudly his new quarters to Derby's son Lord Stanley (whom he marked accurately for 'a high but perhaps agitated destiny').[6] Quarters indeed must have been rather cramped. Hawarden originally was a modest house, with some good eighteenth-century apartments. Sir Stephen's father enlarged it handsomely in the Regency gothick style. The irruption of the numerous Gladstone family would eventually necessitate, in the early 1860s, large additions on the north-west corner. Meanwhile, despite the rather makeshift character of these arrangements, Gladstone found in 'this sweet place' the solace he needed. He inaugurated his new domestic life 'with auspices somewhat less unhopeful for the family'.[7]

[4]

The early weeks of 1852 were dominated by the disintegration of Russell's ramshackle Whig government. Palmerston, obdurately opposed to Russell's project for a new Reform Bill and dismissed from the Foreign Office at the end of 1851 for recognising Louis Napoleon's *coup d'état*

1 D, v, 60, 62.   2 D, iv, 619.   3 D, v, 73.
4 G later told W.T. Stead that the advantage of tree-felling was that it *forced* one to relax one's mind by making it so dangerous to think of anything other than when the axe would next fall. D, i, xlvi, n.
5 D, iv, 485.   6 D, v, 79, 80, 81, 88, 91.   7 D, iv, 444.

without consulting either the Queen or the Prime Minister, had his 'tit for tat with Johnny Russell' over the Local Militia Bill on February 20. In his extremity in 1851 Russell thought of shoring up his crumbling position by bringing in some Peelites. He tried Newcastle for Ireland unavailingly; waved a *'large* offer' at Graham whose answer was merely 'coy'; and Hobhouse (now Lord Broughton) was willing to step down from the India Board to make way for Gladstone.[1] But Gladstone was no more enthusiastic for Reform than Palmerston. The Peelites themselves had dwindled and were no longer in a position to prop Russell up, even had they wanted to. Their problem indeed was that they did not know what to do: 'I fear,' Gladstone noted in January 17, 'we are not agreed on the practical course to be taken in regard to the Govt.'[2] Derby, summoned to form an administration, did not, as in the previous year, open negotiations with the Peelites; instead, he devoted all his energies to attracting the ex-Canningite Palmerston. He failed in this quest; but such was the confusion on the majority side of the House, with disaffected Palmerstonians, disillusioned Radicals, resentful Irish, dithering Peelites, and the sharp decline in Russell's credit and reputation, that Derby had very reasonable prospects of forming a minority Conservative ministry which might well coast along and gather support on the way. Since the Peelites still constituted much the greater part of Conservative front-bench strength, Derby was at shifts to construct a plausible cabinet. Perforce, most of its members had no previous ministerial experience. To the Exchequer went Disraeli, only partly encouraged by Derby's bluff assurance that he knew as much about finance as Mr. Canning did and that in any case 'they give you the figures'. Disraeli would also be leader of the House of Commons.

The Peelites looked upon this 'Who, who?' cabinet (so called because of the deaf old Duke of Wellington's incredulous questions as Derby read through the list of its members) with condescension and contempt. Gladstone was particularly withering about the Exchequer. 'Disraeli,' he wrote to Catherine, 'could not have been worse placed.'[3] Given the forming lines of his new vocation, the Exchequer presented itself to Gladstone as the *sine qua non*: to see Disraeli there constituted something of a special provocation and affront. But condescension and contempt did not resolve the Peelites' problem of how to respond to the new situation. Gladstone by this time was well into his lurch away from the Neapolitan excesses and towards a severe Tory notion of the duty of the friends of the late Sir Robert. A junction with the Liberals, he insisted, was 'our least natural position'.[4] He was dismayed to find Aberdeen leaning distinctly away from reunion with the majority Conservatives

1 Broughton, *Recollections*, vi, 292–93; J. Prest, *Lord John Russell* (1972), 338.
2 D, iv, 387–8.   3 Morley, i, 416–7.   4 PMP, iii, 103.

and towards association with Russell. Gladstone assumed that the Court was behind this. Graham was even worse: unashamedly anxious to reassume his former Whig colouring. Herbert and Newcastle were leaning dangerously in the same direction. Gladstone vigorously set about correcting these deplorable tendencies. The first step was to scotch any notions of a deal with Russell. We must, he urged on his colleagues, hold ourselves 'clear and free'; the Peelites must preserve 'our separate and independent position', to 'be free and ready to pursue whatever course in point of party connection the interests of the country might seem to require'.[1] Gladstone gave a dinner party to inspire and stiffen resolve: 'Ten to dinner: a Peelite party – *is* that name to die?'[2] He dealt vigorously with delinquents. Graham found himself called to task. 'It appeared to me that Sir J. Graham contemplated his own virtual reincorporation with the Liberal party and that our acting with him would have the analogous effect for us.'[3] Graham, much taken aback, had to admit this was true; though he might also have wondered by what authority Gladstone presumed thus to set himself up as the keeper of the Peelite conscience. Cardwell also needed to be kept in line. Gladstone had a rather 'warm' conversation with Newcastle on a sofa at the Carlton Club. Newcastle complained bitterly about the Conservative Protectionists; Gladstone defended them and argued that a position like Peel's on the liberal side of the Conservatives was preferable to being on the conservative side of Liberalism. He summoned to his aid in this dispute the great shades of liberal Conservatism: Pitt, Canning, Huskisson, and 'in some degree' Castlereagh and Liverpool.

Then there was the problem of where to sit in the Commons. Since 1846 the Peelites had been sitting on the opposition side of the House along with the Protectionist majority of the Conservatives. (The front bench had been tacitly shared, though there was always Peelite uneasiness at the prospect of finding oneself rubbing shoulders with such as Disraeli.) Now, with the Protectionists moving across to the ministerial benches, the Peelites were confronted with a decision of considerable, if symbolic, import. Cardwell, Newcastle and especially Graham were keen to stay on the opposition side of the House, with the Liberals. Herbert was more inclined to move across with the other Conservatives on the grounds that the issue which divided them was a dispute within a party and not between parties. Gladstone strongly urged this argument, convinced by 'instinct' that sitting by Lord John and not acting with him as a party was a thing not to be dreamt of. Gladstone's political doctrine at this time was that a Derby government must bring protection 'to a speedy issue'; it would inevitably be defeated, must resign, and the battle between free trade and protection thus having been finally resolved, the way would be

1 *Ib.*, 103–5.   2 D, iv, 398.   3 PMP, *ib*.

open for a return of the Peelites to a chastened Conservatism, and then the formation of a government 'mainly Conservative in its personal composition, connections, and traditions'.[1]

As it happened, the Peelite rump decided to remain on the opposition benches and sit with the Liberals: a foreshadowing of the coalition ministry which would be formed at the end of the year. The symbolic and psychological implications of this arrangement for Gladstone were simply that as yet free trade *versus* protection remained the formal dividing question in politics. He could still assure himself that as soon as that was settled things could get back to 'normal'. Beyond that vague aspiration he did not possess anything which could be described as a formed prospective view. Gladstone's 'instinct' against sitting with Russell owed much more to his own psychic disturbance and political instability than to any convincing analysis of the likely prospects of politics. An ideal of a reunited and regenerated Conservative party was for Gladstone another anchor to cling to in hope amid the turmoil of displacement, along with a Peel leader-figure and a great cause joining politics and morality. It remained an ideal only as long as Gladstone did not have to confront the practical implications of its reality. Once he had done so, he very briskly set about constructing obstacles in the way of attaining that reality. The major obstacle was Gladstone's discovery that, even if free trade triumphed, there was a new grand question of principle to keep the Conservative wings divided: financial policy.

Thus, characteristically, just as Gladstone had fought hardest to retain the trappings and colouring of Conservatism, so, once the decision had been made, in effect, to sit on the conservative side of Liberalism, Gladstone fought hardest to translate that symbolism into reality. It soon became clear anyway that Derby and Disraeli had no intention of committing suicide by directly challenging free trade. This afforded the Peelites even more grounds for condescension and contempt, but little in the way of a handle for a decisive confrontation. Russell, whose hunger for office was exceeded only by Disraeli's, wanted immediate joint action to bring Derby down; but the Peelites decided that, in all decency, the Conservative government should be allowed to survive on condition that it dissolved the House of Commons and called a new general election in the summer, and that immediately after meeting the new parliament in November it brought forward its fiscal and financial proposals. Disraeli accepted these stipulations readily enough (he would have conceded almost anything short of abject confession of sin and error); but in doing so he deprived himself of the time he would need to calculate his financial plans with care and finesse. As it was, he had to produce hugger-mugger an interim budget in April 1852, the materials for which

1 *Ib.*, 104–111.

he virtually took over wholesale from the preparations of the former Whig free-trade Chancellor, Wood. Disraeli, privately convinced that protectionism was 'not only dead, but damned', used the budget to shift the Conservative party away from Derby's disposition to maintain a modified but distinctly protectionist stance. And indeed Derby had to admit that he did not expect to get a sufficient majority in the Commons in the coming elections to restore a protective duty on imported grain. Conservative election addresses on this issue would be studiously equivocal.

Gladstone meanwhile found the first session of 1852 generally very restorative to his morale. The Peelite policy of circumspect co-operation with the government suited him temperamentally at this stage; and he was happy to contrast it with what he had always regarded as Peel's deplorably rigid commitment to the Whigs. Thus, though now sitting opposite the government, Gladstone could still plausibly indulge his ideals about eventual Conservative reunion. On the other hand the Neapolitan episode had proved salutary in its way. He had made a gratifying public stir (and there were still negotiations with Antonio Panizzi at the British Museum about revises of his pamphlet). His Church interests were now sufficiently recuperated to allow him to urge greater lay representation in the revival of the powers of Convocation and to promote legislation to put colonial bishoprics on the right footing (significantly, a non-established footing), and to defend the Rev. Mr. Bennett, a victim at Frome of Protestant bigotry. He relieved his feelings about the papacy ('a foul blot upon the face of creation, an offence to Christendom and to mankind') in a review of his own translation of Farini's *Stato Romano* in the April *Edinburgh* (his first publication in that organ). There were problems about the coal whippers which troubled him: the ballast heavers of the port of London were attempting to benefit from the coal whippers' precedent; and the coal whippers themselves were engaging in 'something in the nature of a strike' for higher wages. Gladstone was very nervous about the possible implications of his own earlier legislation, and advocated extreme caution to make sure that socialistic principles should not seep unawares into any new legislation on labour conditions.[1] Otherwise, there was plenty to keep him occupied: a third son, Henry Neville, was born on April 2. He dabbed mildly in the new craze for phrenology.[2] There was the Report of the Oxford University commissioners to be digested. There were proofs of his translation of Farini to be corrected. His London social life on occasion was so exalted that when he dined at Newcastle's he 'took the bottom of the table'.[3] And having money now in fairly free quantities opened up new avenues: Gladstone commissioned a sculpture of Paolo and Fran-

1 H, cxx (April 6, 1852). 2 D, iv, 415. 3 *Ib.*, 423.

cesca, inspired by his devotion to Dante.[1] By July 1852 he estimated the value of all his pictures and works of art and ornaments at £2,401; with Richard Wilson's 'Phaeton' (given as an heirloom by his father in 1847) holding pride of place at £1,200.[2]

But above and beyond all was the great question of his political future and the new 'work' which he would put at its head and front. That Gladstone was beginning to think himself into something of this kind is perhaps marked by a self-deprecatory quotation from Suetonius at the commencement of a new volume of his diary on March 1, 1852: 'he had a longing for immortality and perpetual fame – but an ill-considered longing.'[3] It is in these months that Gladstone began seriously to get Disraeli into focus as a target: as a symbol and symptom of something he could persuade himself was fundamentally and morally objectionable; a symbol and a symptom, moreover, with his hand on the levers of financial policy, the key to the politics of the future. Disraeli's efforts to ingratiate himself with free trade sentiment in his April budget evoked no gratitude from Gladstone. By continuing the trend to a direct tax policy following the recommendations of Hume's committee Disraeli's first 1852 budget 'marked the point at which the tories again began to act as a national party'.[4] Gladstone would have none of this. Disraeli, he decided, had failed to secure a proper balance between direct and indirect taxation by his neglect of tariff policy. By July he was remarking ominously that he found each successive financial speech by Disraeli 'more quackish in its flavour than its predecessor'.[5]

The elections were held that month. The ministerial Conservatives benefited from their cautious ambiguity about reimposing protection for corn and gained ground, but not sufficiently to form a majority in the Commons. It was gratifying to family pride that John Neilson should have been returned for Devizes. The Peelites, mainly from retirements and defections, were reduced to about 40; and the Whigs, Radicals, and Irish amounted to something rather more than the Conservatives, but not sufficient to challenge them effectively without Peelite co-operation. Thus the Peelites were still in a position to fend Russell off and hold to their policy of giving the Derby-Disraeli ministry an opportunity to bend its neck and pass between the caudine forks of Sir Robert Peel's fiscal and financial principles.

For his own part Gladstone displayed superb nonchalance over his Oxford seat. It was vexing that once again he was challenged by a 'Protestant' candidate; and he would have much to tell Stephen and Henry later about 'Oxford rascalities'; but, whereas in 1847 he almost had a nervous breakdown at the possibility of failure, he now chose to set off

1 *Ib.*, 394. 2 GGP, 94/11, Rough Book A (Accounts), 171.
3 D, iv, 406. 4 Matthew, HJ (1979), 621. 5 Blake, *Disraeli*, 328.

for a holiday in South Wales, basing himself at first at Tenby, with excursions to Pembrokeshire and Carmarthen, admiring the views of Towy vale; then to Builth – 'all beautiful' – Rhayader and Hereford. Oxford University meanwhile returned him on July 14 with a gratifyingly improved vote. He confessed to feeling a little 'odd' at being so insouciantly detached and insisted that he was not displaying pride. Convention, after all, debarred him from canvassing or publishing a personal address. He returned via Shrewsbury to Hawarden and London did not see him again until October. One of his principal occupations at Hawarden was venting his animus against the Roman Church by means of a bilious review for the December *Quarterly* of Montalembert's *Des Intérêts Catholiques au XIXe siècle*. He accused Montalembert of ingenuousness in supposing that he could evade the 'fundamental antipathy between ultramontanism and freedom'.

[5]

London included not only grand affairs of state but the beautiful and disturbingly attractive Elizabeth Collins. On October 13: 'remained some time mainly I hope to muse but ever with shame'. He busied himself distributing copies of *Uncle Tom's Cabin* to prostitutes ('it is a *great* book').[1] A few weeks later he had to adjure himself again to remember 'Hooker's Torch'; followed for good measure by a flagellation and then immersion in the bromidic Report of the Cambridge University commissioners. He indulged himself with a soothing visit to Oxford ('Dined in Ch Ch Hall & only left the Commonroom when Tom tolled'). Back in London on November 4 he 'saw a most beautiful unnamed girl of 18. I accompanied her to her house, where we lingered over a talk.'[2] Doubtless he learned with mixed feelings that Collins was planning to depart for Australia.

Derby's government returned to face the new parliament at the beginning of November. The recent death of the Duke of Wellington cast an august gloom over the occasion. Martin Tupper, Gladstone's old friend, produced a 'Dirge for Wellington'. His Muse, Gladstone avowed, reminded him of the 'magnificent composition of Manzoni on the death of Napoleon'. He assured Tupper he had shown it to Mrs. Sidney Herbert who was an 'enthusiastic lover' of *Proverbial Philosophy*.[3] Gladstone was deeply impressed by the splendidly solemn funeral ceremonies.

1 D, iv, 461.   2 *Ib.*, 465 (in Italian).
3 D. Hudson, *Martin Tupper* (1949), 164–5. Tupper was prepared to admit that 'Tennyson's ode is far better than mine, but he took (as he ought to have done) more time about it.'

Soon he was eager to assist at the obsequies of protection. He pressed Disraeli to declare whether the government had 'definitively, un-equivocally, and finally abandoned the idea of proposing a return to protective policy'.[1] Disraeli, desperately eager to stay in office and produce another budget, was willing to go to any lengths short of a definitive, unequivocal and final renunciation. Russell let slip his dogs of free trade, led by Cobden's henchman Villiers, and Disraeli had to be saved by Palmerston's good offices and by swallowing further doses of Peelite contempt. Herbert indeed allowed his contemptuous invective against Disraeli's personal integrity to spill over into anti-semitism, deliberately seeking revenge for what Peel had suffered. Gladstone expressed himself as 'especially warm and indignant' at the govern-ment's evasive shuffling. His 'opinion indeed of Mr. Disraeli's political character, indifferent before, had become worse since he made his speech on Mr. Villiers' motion'.[1] No doubt feeling that Herbert had said quite enough, he insisted he was *'glad* I had not to say out what was in me about Disraeli's speech'. Nervous excitement kept him awake for the first time in many years.[2]

This element of personal vindictiveness deeply disturbed Derby. He, rather innocently, assumed that now that the government had all but in name surrendered its ground on protection, the way would become clear for the great object of Conservative reunion. He took Gladstone aside at Lady Derby's evening party on November 27 and stressed the need to get rid of all 'personal questions' and to 'consider how all those men who were united in their general views of government might combine together to carry it into effect'. Rather pathetically he pleaded with Gladstone to assure him that Herbert had said 'more than he intended'. Gladstone insisted that there had been, on Disraeli's part, 'provocation'; and informed the disconcerted and no doubt irritated Prime Minister that the Peelites still demanded to be satisfied as to the government's financial plans.[3] Nervous excitement suggests clearly that Gladstone was building up, rather as before the Neapolitan explosion, to something big. And clearly 'personal considerations' had come to the fore with a curious force. Possibly on the next occasion Gladstone might well 'say out' what was in him about Disraeli.

Was it wholly Disraeli's fault? Certainly his political posture was undignified and not very creditable. He was sustaining a minority government by skilful prevarication and offering deals to anyone who would listen: Palmerston, the Irish, even John Bright, who was scandal-ized but amused by Disraeli's cynicism and his frank avowals that he was in politics to seek fame. Gladstone was willing to admit to himself but to nobody else that he was ambitious and sought fame. Such a man tends to

1 H, cxxiii, 97.   2 Conacher, 48.   3 PMP, iii, 129–30.

be excessively censorious of another who parades weaknesses which a proper shame transfigures by self-deprecation and decent concealment. Gladstone's excessive censoriousness had about it in origin much of this instinctive and aggressive externalising of blame and moral obloquy against an outside object who functioned as a means of transferring guilt; and who indeed in some degree deserved censure. But in Disraeli's case the desert was far below the blame. The extent to which during these years in the early 1850s Gladstone was building Disraeli as a demoniacally evil element into the structure of his general interpretation of the decline of politics is illustrated by his unpublished article of 1855, 'Party as it was and as it is. A sketch of the political history of twenty years.'[1] The plot of this curiosity febrile piece is the dramatic story of how a 'normal' and beneficent party system which had developed in the epoch of reform was destroyed by the powers of the 'great and massive' but tragically flawed figure of Peel, like some doomed hero of Aeschylus or Shakespeare. This, after all, in a much less dramatic form, had long been the central feature of Gladstone's regrets about the events of 1845–46. What was new was the now greatly enhanced role played by Disraeli not only as an exploitive but as a contributory principal in the grand tragedy. His 'attacks and invectives', actuated by a restless ambition, complemented with evil precision Peel's noble flaws. The 'subtle self-seeking which History will probably impute to Mr. Disraeli' fed like a devourer of carrion on the stricken field of political disaster. 'It is needless,' commented Gladstone with a quite undisarming disingenuousness, '. . . to enter into the moral of his singular career: and no one would gratuitously enter upon a task, which it would be so difficult to execute with fairness, at once to him, to the country, and to public virtue.'[2]

Disraeli's being thus constructed into a major and the morally most blamable component of Gladstone's theory of what had gone wrong with politics made him inevitably an equivalent component of any formulation of the role Gladstone would envisage himself playing in setting politics to rights. All the factors in the equation were beginning to assemble themselves with compelling cogency. Gladstone was in need of a great new work to replace the abandoned State and Church cause. Everything pointed to finance as the appropriate core of such a work. It followed naturally on Gladstone's lieutenancy in Peel's great fiscal and financial operations. Gladstone's celebration of the sublime art of transmuting economics into morals in his 'Course of Commercial Policy' article could be plausibly interpreted as a kind of anticipatory prevision or prophecy of his succession to Peel's role as the grand alchemist of state. Moreover, now that free trade had triumphed, financial policy was emerging more and more as the next great controversial issue of politics: the Peelites in

1 GP, 44745, 173–222.   2 *Ib.*, 181, 184, 190, 192, 195.

particular were obsessively stipulating that finance was now the sacred touchstone which would determine all. Disraeli was Chancellor of the Exchequer and would shortly produce his new budget. That Gladstone would explode against Disraeli and 'say out' what was in him on that occasion was so cogently in the nature of the case as to constitute, persuasively and indeed conclusively, the necessary fulfilment or resolution of the equation. That Gladstone would need, also, for the purpose of his new vocation, to establish convincingly his claims to succeed Disraeli at the Exchequer, was by no means the least important factor in that equation.

Disraeli produced his second budget on December 3. He was in a very awkward position. He had to offer something to the interests which felt themselves the victims of Peel's betrayal over the Corn Law. On the other hand he could not avow protectionism as his guiding principle. He was, moreover, severely hampered by the constrictions of the time limit imposed upon him by the Peelites. This meant hurry and improvisation. He did not have up-to-date returns of figures. In the circumstances Disraeli's performance was impressive. He argued that under free trade direct taxation must be largely increased. Hence retention of the income tax was unavoidable. Macaulay, by no means a sympathetic critic, conceded that it was 'well done, both as to manner and to language'. He characterised Disraeli's plan pungently as 'nothing but taking money out of the pockets of people in towns and putting it into the pockets of growers of malt'. He 'greatly doubted' whether Disraeli could carry it against the general prejudice of the majority in the House; but he was sure that Disraeli had 'raised his reputation for practical ability'.[1]

The budget of December 1852 became the focus of a quite disproportionate furore. It meant the term of the self-denying ordinance which the Peelites had imposed upon the majority of the House. The government had been granted leave to live until it brought forward its financial proposals. Now the option of pronouncing its death-sentence was available for use. This added fortuitously to the occasion a rather doom-laden atmosphere. Gladstone was excited. (There was another self-flagellation on December 9 after 'a conversation not as it should have been'.)[2] This atmosphere increasingly obscured the practical issues at dispute about house tax, income tax, malt tax, distinguishing between 'real' and 'precarious' incomes, surpluses and deficits. The veterans of Peelite and Whig finance, Goulburn, Graham, and Wood, were indeed captious and tedious deemsters. Disraeli, rightly, felt himself to be in a false position. He was being trussed up as a ritual retributive sacrifice on a free-trade altar set with pious hypocrisy before a monument to Peel. He responded, characteristically, with appropriate rebarbativeness. During

1 Trevelyan, *Macaulay*, 579.   2 D, iv, 475.

the invective of his concluding vindication on the night of December 16–17 an observer described the 'remarkable appearance' presented by the opposition benches: 'not speaking to each other, pale in the gaslight. It reminded one of the scenes of the National Convention of the French Revolution. To complete the effect, although in midwinter, a loud thunderstorm raged; the peals were heard and the flashes of lightning could be seen in the Chamber itself.'[1] Disraeli sat down at 1 a.m. on the morning of December 17 after what Gladstone described as a 'grand' and 'powerful' oration[2] adorned with his famous peroration about being confronted by a coalition whose triumph would be brief, for 'England does not love coalitions'.[3] John Bright thought it 'his greatest speech; he was in earnest; argument, satire, sarcasm, invective, all were abundant and of the first class'; 'never a man fought more desperately or with more skill and power.'[4] As both Chancellor and Leader of the House, Disraeli thus concluded the debate amid a storm of cheers and counter-cheers and the members began to shift themselves towards the division lobbies. Suddenly, in breach of all parliamentary convention, and amid a revived storm of astonished cheers and counter-cheers, Gladstone projected himself to the table and insisted that Disraeli's speech needed a reply, and 'that, too, on the moment'.[5]

It was an inspired decision. By instinct, or calculation, Gladstone seized precisely the moment of maximum dramatic impact. His intervention intensified the already highly charged atmosphere with an unprecedentedly direct and immediate element of personal, almost gladiatorial, challenge. At first he had to fight hard to gain a hearing against furious ministerial resentment at his presumption and at his embodying what they felt to be an ultimately unforgiving Peelite vindictiveness. Stanley saw Gladstone rise 'choked with passion, for which he could find no vent in words, and his first utterances were the signal for fresh explosions from each side of the House alternately'. 'Gladstone's look when he rose to reply will never be forgotten by me: his usually calm features were livid and distorted with passion, his voice shook, and those who watched him feared an outbreak incompatible with parliamentary rules. So strong a scene I have never witnessed.'[6] Ostensibly impromptu, provoked by what he considered the 'shameless personalities and otherwise' with which Disraeli disgraced his speech, Gladstone's attack in fact had been long 'fermenting' in him and he 'made notes for speaking' on the 16th.[7] He had already acquitted himself of his part in the debate by contributing two speeches hostile to Disraeli's proposals, on December 6 and 10. But his bold bid on the 17th to cap Disraeli was of an entirely different order of

1 M & B, i, 1262.   2 Morley, i, 438.   3 H, cxxiii, 1665–66.
4 P. Bright (ed.), *Diaries of John Bright* (1930), 130.
5 H, *ib.*, 1666.   6 DDCP, 89–90.   7 D, iv, 477. Morley, i, 438.

rhetoric. Gladstone was bidding beyond the budget; he was asserting himself as the bearer of credentials conferring legitimate authority to fulfil the purpose of his new vocation. He also released long pent-up aggressive energy. His excitement was that of a hunter closing in on his quarry: it was like 'a fox chase'.[1] 'To smash an antagonist across the House of Commons,' as he later remarked to Lady Mildred Hope, 'is sometimes not disagreeable . . . '[2]

In his onslaught Gladstone passed from strictures on Disraeli's bad manners to strictures on his bad policy. He made very heavy weather of the former; but since he claimed to speak ostensibly from a sense of irresistible obligation to administer the necessary rebuke, that could not be helped. Much of what he said on the latter is disfigured by the same kind of excited hyperbole as lay at the bottom of his Neapolitan indictment. Disraeli did not, in fact, threaten the national credit; nor was he 'guilty of high offence against the public' for providing no surplus in the canonical manner of Peel. Though the dazzling technical virtuosity ostentatiously displayed in the speech inaugurated the mythology of Gladstone as the great master of Victorian financial policy, it is rather more significant for its implicit revelations of Gladstone's view of Gladstone. The point of the speech really was in itself as a bravura performance, a kind of theatricalised politics, a morality play of finance, with Gladstone offering himself to the public as heroic rescuer of 'public virtue' from the clutches of the melodramatic villainy of Disraeli, presented here explicitly as the angel of the hosts of evil 'enchanters and magicians'. Not only was Gladstone's intervention on the moment an inspired opportunism; his mode of exploiting the opportunity he thus created was an achievement of high genius. At one decisive stroke he established himself on an entirely new and higher eminence of public reputation. Even more importantly, he signalled the onset of a crucial metamorphosis: as an exercise in both a new political style and a new rhetorical method the 1852 budget speech was an encouragingly success-ful experimental model providing an enormous potential for future development and enhancement.

Two features of this experimental model stand out prominently. The first was Gladstone's conspicuously draping the mantle of Sir Robert Peel about his own shoulders. The malt tax? 'That subject was explained by Sir Robert Peel in 1830.' Most of Gladstone's technical critique had to do with demonstrating that Disraeli had failed dismally to conform to the three grand principles of Sir Robert's financial system, of which he now asserted himself as spokesman and keeper. 'I may presume to have an opinion on the question of what were Sir Robert Peel's principles of

1 Morley, i, 438.
2 G to Lady M. Hope, October 18, 1859. GP, 44530, 96.

commercial reform.' Again: 'Long associated with a recollection that will ever be dear to me, and sharing in the first struggles that he made for that great object, I must necessarily have had many opportunities of observing the workings of his mind upon the subject.' He made a special point of appealing in Peel's name to the Conservatives opposite him to repudiate Disraeli's dishonesty and trickery and return to their former and proper obedience. 'Are you not the party of 1842? Are you not the party who, in times of difficulty, chose to cover a deficit and to provide a large surplus? . . . I appeal to you by what you then were.' The second feature was Gladstone's implied claim for the Exchequer in view of the almost certain fall of Derby's government. This was done mainly by underlining at every opportunity Disraeli's lack of experience as contrasted with his own rich maturity as a man of government and high office. The theme was that Disraeli did not 'know business'; he had learned a little, but he had much more still to learn. The tone was, perhaps, rather insufferably patronising; but Gladstone in effect took advantage of an opening Disraeli himself had in a mood of incautiously mocking self-deprecation offered: 'My own knowledge on the subject is, of course, recent. I was not born and bred a Chancellor of the Exchequer; I am one of the Parliamentary rabble.'[1] Gladstone certainly made every effort to establish that his knowledge was of long standing and that he was undoubtedly and in the traditions of the highest legitimacy born and bred a Chancellor of the Exchequer.

These two aspects of Gladstone's performance clearly were matters of deliberate calculation. To what extent was this true of his intervention as a whole? Gladstone himself asserted shortly afterwards to his Oxford colleague Heathcote: 'To tell you the truth all I have done . . . has in my view flowed so simply and distinctly from the absolute dictates of duty that in the main I have not felt that I had an option to exercise.'[2] This claim can be allowed substantially to stand, subject only to a stipulation that 'duty' requires to be more broadly defined than Gladstone's own explanation of his motives for his dramatically unexpected act. Unquestionably he felt himself propelled by pressures which could reasonably be defined as 'absolute dictates': in other words, the accumulated weight of the elements which now came together to form so persuasively coherent an argument for his new vocation. It is most unlikely that Gladstone consciously formulated this argument or consciously calculated the tactics or strategy required to launch his vocation with optimum advantage. It is much more likely that he was responding instinctively and impulsively to unconsciously apprehended urgings and promptings; but since those urgings and promptings themselves reflected an underlying coherence and logic, Gladstone's impulsiveness came to have the

1 M & B, i, 1259. On this aspect see Vincent, 14.
2 Conacher, 47–8.

appearance of calculation. He had to focus his ostensible motive of 'duty' consciously against Disraeli; it was a necessary and indispensable element in Gladstone's unconscious scheme of requirements that Disraeli should be so grotesquely enlarged in villainy as to comprehend a target adequate to the exalted moral purposes of the new vocation. The most revealing 'control model' in this respect is the Neapolitan episode: Gladstone's response to the pressures in that case seemed aberrant and untoward precisely because the pressures themselves did not add up to anything, politically speaking, coherent or logical. There was no way in the early 1850s in which Gladstone could gear a notion of political 'duty' to the energy released by his explosion over Naples. By contrast, the explosion sparked by the December 1852 budget could be immediately transformed into motive energy by a very potently efficient relationship of cogs and gears.

Gladstone's intervention postponed the division on the budget for a little more than two hours. Ministers were defeated by 305 and 286. It is very doubtful that Gladstone made any difference. He certainly failed to persuade the ministerial Conservatives to return to the 'party of 1842'. His speech had the effect of making the government's defeat seem more resounding that it would otherwise have been. He did not 'destroy the Administration' as the myth later had it,[1] but he gave a good impression of doing so. The House adjourned at 3.45 a.m. and Gladstone, the opposition hero of the hour, went off to the Carlton Club where, anticipating that he would soon be back in office, he wrote to Stafford Northcote, his former secretary at the Board of Trade, enquiring whether Northcote would be available for employment. Going to the Carlton was perhaps a foolhardy thing to do: Stanley went there also, noting that those who had voted with Gladstone 'prudently kept away: they would not have escaped insult'.[2] That night Gladstone slept only two hours. 'My nervous system was too powerfully acted upon by the scene of last night. A recollection of having mismanaged a material point (by omission) came into my head when I was half awake between 7 & 8 & utterly prevented my getting more rest.'[3] It was a moment, nevertheless, of supreme relief. 'Smashing an antagonist across the House of Commons' was indeed a sensation 'not disagreeable'. The cabinet decided to resign immediately and Derby went off to Osborne later on the 17th. The Queen sent summonses to Lansdowne and Aberdeen.

Most Conservatives, like Heathcote, were puzzled at the lengths to which Gladstone, hitherto noted as the most ministerially-leaning of the Peelites, went to make any future co-operation with Disraeli unlikely or even impossible. Naturally, having no inkling of the inward necessities imposed upon Gladstone by the exigencies of his new vocation, they

1 Hirst, *Gladstone as Financier*, 130.   2 DDCP, 90.   3 D, iv, 477.

supposed that his setting up of Disraeli as a monster of political depravity was of the same order of grotesque aberration as his Neapolitan performance. Gladstone, indeed, was hard put to explain his behaviour. He excused himself lamely to Heathcote with more rhetoric about Disraeli's 'dishonest & profligate scheme of finance' and by claiming, retrospectively, that he did not feel sure that, even had 'all obstacles been removed', he 'would have accepted the responsibility' of becoming Disraeli's colleague, 'while nothing would have induced me to lift a finger for the purpose of moving him from the leadership he has gained'. He tried, most implausibly, to put the blame on Disraeli for not being a Peelite: 'To *you* I must frankly state that in parts of the Budget . . . I read on his part . . . a determined intention that there should be no union with the Peelites; whose financial principles he knew very well.'[1] Derby was highly vexed, as well he might be having expended such efforts on peacemaking and reunion; and let his irritation show through clearly in his announcement in the Lords on Monday the 20th of his government's resignation. That night, after dining with Herbert and Newcastle, Gladstone found himself in the newspaper room at the Carlton in a 'lion's den' of tipsy and indignant Conservatives, who threatened to pitch him across Carlton Gardens into the Reform Club. Gladstone retreated, fearing 'actual ill-usage'. Stanley recorded that this 'unlucky incident is much noticed, and not to our advantage'.[2] *The Times* indeed gave the 'Disgraceful Scene in the Carlton Club' prominent notice.[3] For his own part, Gladstone ought perhaps to have had the tact and good sense to stay away on such an occasion.

[6]

Promptly, on December 18, Gladstone composed an elaborate memorandum which he read that afternoon to Aberdeen, who was poised to go to Osborne the following day. In this he had a two-fold purpose: his first, practical, motive was to impress upon Aberdeen's mind that a 'great and palpable exigency of State' existed in connection 'not only with respect to contingencies which may happen with our foreign affairs: but more visibly and immediately with regard to a subject on which the public mind is always accessible, ready, and receptive; with reference namely to finance'. Then, after much technical discourse: 'There is therefore a resistless call for a vigorous and united effort to settle and secure the finances of the country.' No doubt Aberdeen took the hint: Gladstone wanted the Exchequer. For despite the brilliant *éclat* of his

1 Conacher, 47–8.   2 DDCP, 92.   3 December 23, 1852, 5.

performance against Disraeli, his going to the Treasury was by no means
a foregone conclusion. Gladstone's second purpose was to define what
seemed to him the most desirable available form of government. He
urged a 'mixed government', by which he meant a coalition, as against a
'fusion of parties'. Neither the Liberal party simply nor the Conservative
party simply was adequate to the occasion. And since a coalition could be
'warrantable or auspicious' only when its members had a 'most thorough
confidence in the honour, integrity, and fidelity of each other' and when
they were 'agreed in principle upon all the great questions of public policy
immediately emergent', it followed that only a Liberal-Peelite arrangement satisfied the essential criteria. Having made Peelite co-operation
with the Derby-Disraeli Conservatives virtually impossible, Gladstone
now set out with equal resolution to make sure that co-operation with the
Liberals would in no way compromise the Conservative integrity of the
Peelites. He was indeed displaying an extraordinary and most impressive
capacity for wilful self-confidence.

As to the Exchequer, Gladstone knew there would be little difficulty
with Aberdeen. The problem would be with Russell. It was fortunate for
Gladstone that Russell's bargaining position was relatively weak and
Aberdeen's relatively strong, despite the vast disparity between the
respective numbers of their supporters in the Commons. Aberdeen was
the clear favourite of the Court. Russell had damaged his reputation with
his own party as well as the Court, to whom he was only marginally less
offensive than Palmerston. Moreover Palmerston, who carried weight in
the Commons, would not serve under Russell again. The possibility of a
Derby-Disraeli-Palmerston combination was not beyond conjecture. The
only Whig under whom Russell could serve without irreparable hurt to
his immense vanity was Lansdowne; but Lansdowne's health made him a
very uncertain contender. It required all the weight of Lansdowne's
seniority and prestige to convince Russell that there was no alternative
but to serve under Aberdeen – to become, as Disraeli later put it cruelly, 'a
subaltern of a former subaltern of Sir Robert Peel'. Mollified by an
informal understanding that Aberdeen in due course, once the Coalition
was solidly on its feet and in good working order, would make way for
him, Russell allowed himself to be persuaded; and thus a government
could be formed.

Aberdeen suggested Gladstone for the Exchequer or the Colonial
Office. Russell wanted Graham for the Exchequer, with Gladstone for the
Colonies. Graham was given his choice of the Home Office or the
Exchequer but consented 'to neither the one nor the other' – which
perhaps was fortunate for Gladstone. Delane of *The Times* tried to block
Gladstone from the Exchequer as unsafe on the income tax; and made
'unavailing remonstrances' for either Graham or Wood, the Whig (and

largely discredited) chancellor under Russell.[1] But the decisive tilt in the end came from the Court: Gladstone was the Queen's and Prince Albert's favourite for the Exchequer, and the rapport between the Court and Aberdeen was such that Russell could not resist.[2] After enormous difficulties, especially in suiting Russell himself, a coalition cabinet was constructed in which the Peelites secured six of thirteen places. Oddly, Peelites monopolised the armed services departments: Graham back at the Admiralty, Herbert as Secretary at War, and Newcastle as Secretary for War and the Colonies. Doubtless at the time Gladstone considered this most satisfactory: his particular friends would be in the great spending departments. Palmerston, barred from the Foreign Office, which went briefly to Russell and then to Clarendon, took the Home department; Wood took India, and Molesworth, the token Radical, the department of Works. Lansdowne, Argyll and Granville joined Aberdeen himself, Newcastle and Lord Chancellor Cranworth in handling government business in the Lords. Gladstone only just managed to scramble up through a hurricane to Hawarden in time for Christmas. He presented himself at Windsor on December 28 for his seals of office and 'got in a good evening of work' later.[3] The tension was marked by another scourging on December 30. There was an unpleasantly narrow squeak in his re-election for Oxford University. The Low Church and anti-'Jew Bill' forces put up a candidate, the son of the former prime minister, Perceval; and Gladstone only scraped in by 1,022 votes to 898. At one critical point he was reduced to resuscitating old, familiar and threadbare phrases: defeat 'may improve my hope of rendering any poor service in my power to the Church generally'.[4] To be obliged to fulfil his oft-promised undertaking to abandon the State and devote himself to the Church would have been in the circumstances of January 1853 the supreme irony of Gladstone's life and career.

Not only did Gladstone display at this time wilful self-confidence: he displayed formidable powers of work. He had remarked at the time of his term at the Colonial Office: 'What a mercy that my strength, in appearance not remarkable, so little fails me.'[5] The abiding impression his son Henry had of his father in the 1850s was 'a vivid sense of his great physical strength'.[6] Gladstone himself commented at the end of 1853 on the 'singular blessing' of '*health*'.[7] In his early forties, he embarked on the building of his new vocation certainly at the height of his physical maturity, and very nearly at the height of his intellectual powers. Gladstone, moreover, seized his moment at the Treasury in the spirit of zest and zeal of one who felt himself, politically speaking, regenerate. He

1 *Greville*, vi, 384–85.   2 LQV, ii, 421.
3 D, iv, 482.   4 *Ib.*, 485.
5 D, iii, 514.   6 Hirst, 301.   7 D, iv, 579.

regularly put in enormous hours: on February 20 he recorded as a marvel that he had managed to relax to the extent of taking a *'walk'*. There was, in addition, all the fuss of moving to Downing Street and letting out Carlton Gardens. And there was the vexing wrangle with Disraeli over official furniture and the Chancellor's robe. Disraeli wanted a certain sum of money from Gladstone as reimbursement for the customary sum he had earlier paid for furniture to his predecessor, Wood. Gladstone claimed, wrongly, that under the provisions of a recent alteration in the relevant regulations Disraeli should apply to the Office of Works. Gladstone, in turn, requested Disraeli to deliver the Chancellor's official robe. Disraeli, believing the robe to be that once worn by Pitt, had no intention of passing it on to Gladstone: and skilfully used Gladstone's rather guileless obstinacy on the matter of the furniture to confuse the issue. The robe in question remained in Disraeli's hands.[1] Their correspondence degenerated into an acrimonious third person, adding a ludicrous dimension of private quarrel to their public rivalry.

There were indeed quarrels enough afoot. Tom was being particularly tiresome, complaining of William's neglect ('Robertson writes to me in great wrath about Tom's note – and says Mary Ellen was extremely cut up about it').[2] Perhaps the birth in April 1852 at long last of a son[3] to Tom made him more sensitive to what he considered William's lack of consideration. Gladstone did not allow himself many other distractions. He planned to produce a budget to replace Disraeli's defeated version by April. Nor would it merely be a budget; it would, in effect, be his evangel, his new *State and Church*. He had to make sure not merely that it succeeded, but that it succeeded convincingly, indeed grandly, that it more than lived up to the lively expectations generated by the dramatic events of December. Still, the routine of life and politics claimed more of his time than he willingly allowed. One of Russell's conditions for accepting the coalition was that the Jewish question should once again be reintroduced; and this meant Gladstone's having to listen to Lord Adolphus Vane quoting from *The State in its Relations with the Church* and claiming to be 'a less exalted person but a more consistent politician', than its author.[4] There was much ado with the Canada Clergy Reserves Bill and the Colonial Church Bill, introduced by Gladstone in the 1852 session. He set about ensuring value for money in the Ordnance Survey mapping project. Gladstone had to deal with the delicate question of the cleaning of pictures in the National Gallery and was glad to reassure the Commons that 'nothing of an unwise or indiscreet character' had been done.[5] He regarded it as part of his duties to keep an eye on Christie's

1 The National Trust now displays it at Hughenden.
2 G to CG, January 10, 1853. GGP, 28/4.
3 John Robert: 3rd baronet, 1889–1926.   4 H, cxxv, 98.   5 *Ib.*, 1116–7.

sales for possible acquisitions for the National Gallery. He spoke to Aberdeen in March about a Tiberio d'Assisi and a 'passing of the Red Sea purporting to be by Raffaelle when a boy'.[1] One of the more congenial aspects of his work at the Treasury was in contemplating the matter of duties on wine. He indulged himself in a lyrical passage on the possibility of decreasing the duty on 'one of the great gifts of Providence to man', dilating on the 'many useful and wholesome ends it subserved in connection with his physical temperament'.[2] He was in touch with Robertson, a leading member in Liverpool of the Financial Reform Association, which pressed for direct taxation: should customs and excise reductions be preferred, where there was a choice, to stamps and excise? Gladstone warned his brother in any case that the surplus budgeted for by Disraeli was not likely to be realised; and that next year it would probably be absorbed by increased expenditure on education and defence. But he had hopes of making a 'real and permanent impression' on expenditure by reductions on military and ordnance establishments for the colonies.[3] There was the question also of a pension for Martin Tupper. Gladstone pointed out to Aberdeen that the author of *Proverbial Philosophy* had done much to promote 'kindly feeling between England & America' because the scale of his sales there, unremunerative because of the absence of a copyright convention, *'approaches* to that of Uncle Tom's Cabin in England'.[4] In April 1853 he took part in the inspection of the ground and the plan for the Reading Room extension of the British Museum. He grudged the time spent at the Lord Mayor's dinner: 'a lamentable hole in my evening 6½–12. Came home & worked until four on Budget Plans of Finance of all kinds – and on Customs' Reform Minute.'[5]

Another of his minutes of this time was to bear a signal reputation: the Treasury Minute of April 12, 1853 commissioning an enquiry into the Civil Service with a view to reducing its costs and improving its efficiency. When on the very morning of his triumph over Disraeli on December 17 Gladstone wrote to Stafford Northcote recalling him to service, Northcote responded by asking for the vacant place on the Treasury Committee inquiring into the organisation of the Board of Trade. A series of such committees under the aegis of the Assistant Permanent Secretary of the Treasury, Sir Charles Trevelyan, had been since 1849 investigating various departments to economise in numbers and expense and improve performance. Trevelyan was eager to break out of his restricted and fragmented frame of reference and to consider broad questions of principle and policy about the recruitment and training of the Civil

1 GP, 44528, 109. 2 H, *ib.*, 634–5. 3 G to Robertson G, February 21, 1853. GP, 44528, 101.
4 G to Aberdeen, February 20, 1853. *Ib.*, 99. 4 D, iv, 509.

Service. He was convinced that the time was ripe for replacing the prevailing system of recruitment by patronage by a system of selection by merit founded on some objective criterion such as a public examination. The ripeness of the time for Trevelyan, as an old India hand, had much to do with the legislation being prepared by Charles Wood, now at the India Board, to renew the Charter of the East India Company and incidentally to reform the system of recruitment and training for the Indian Civil Service. Northcote quickly established a good working relationship with Trevelyan, to whom he became the 'perfect foil'.[1] Northcote in turn soon interested Gladstone in the potential importance of Civil Service reform: the principle of the morality of merit would fit in perfectly with his notions of a new political evangel; and from his angle, also, Civil Service reform might fit very neatly and advantageously into current ideas about Oxford University reform; and, not least, there was the irresistible lure of applying ruthless schoolmen's logic to the untidy and expensive clutter of anomalies and deficiencies of the Civil Service.

There was a brief recuperative interlude at Herbert's family house, Wilton, at the end of March, with excursions to Stonehenge ('a noble & awful relic, telling much, & telling too that it conceals more') and Salisbury Cathedral ('a wonder of harmony & beauty').[2] There was some 'stiff work' in the early part of the session, with annoying defeats for the government instigated by Disraeli, 'who unlike all other leaders of opposition stimulates and spurs faction instead of endeavouring to keep it within bounds'.[3] By April 9 Gladstone was ready to discuss his budget proposals with Prince Albert, who reacted very approvingly and encouragingly. So far, apart from Disraeli's spoiling tactics, Gladstone had come across no obstacles. His technique in dealing with his colleagues, as he explained later to his successor Cornewall Lewis, was to 'keep his own Counsel & let the cabinet as a whole not know his plans till his mind was made up in the main, & the time close at hand'.[4] Cardwell alone, at the Board of Trade and not in the Cabinet, was in Gladstone's confidence, very helpful and fertile in suggesting expedients. Even so, Gladstone had much ado in cabinets on April 11 and 12 to quell carpers and critics. Wood, Herbert, Graham and Lansdowne were disturbed by the boldness and riskiness of many of Gladstone's projects; anxious especially about Gladstone's plans to integrate Ireland into the British tax structure. Aberdeen also worried about this. Palmerston, characteristically, betrayed breezy insensitivity and bad taste by commenting that it might seem a very good plan, but Disraeli's was a very good plan too, and yet had been beaten. In the end the various objections cancelled each other out and Gladstone won general if somewhat apprehensive Cabinet

1 M.W. Wright, *Treasury Control of the Civil Service, 1854–1874* (1969), xviii.
2 D, iv, 510.   3 PMP, iii, 144.   4 D, v, 34.

acceptance for his budget. The 'corner stone' of his whole financial plan was the renewal of the income tax, previously renewed three times since Peel reintroduced it in 1842, but within a scheme whereby it would be progressively reduced by stages until it would expire on April 5, 1860. To cover his costs Gladstone proposed to lower the income limit from £150 to £100 and apply it to Ireland. £100 in his view was the 'equatorial line of British incomes', whereby the whole of the 'educated' part of the community was brought in and the 'labouring part' left outside. By thus imposing a special tax burden on the electorate Gladstone hoped to impose a sense of responsibility for the mass of the unenfranchised, a fiscal 'doctrine of trusteeship'.[1] And by making the burden one of fixed limits Gladstone combined responsibility with relief. In return, to balance his policy on the tariff side, he would offer remissions of duties on 13 articles of food and 123 other items to stimulate consumption.

On Sunday, April 17, the eve of his budget statement, Gladstone prepared himself spiritually with Holy Communion and by reading aloud in the evening the 'MS of 1841'. Afterwards he felt obliged to wrench himself away from the *Paradiso* and 'give several hours to my figures'.[2] At Holy Communion that morning at St. James's he was edified by an extraordinary spiritual visitation which he was coming to recognise as of a type concomitant with 'occasions of very sharp pressure or trial'. Some inspiring words of Scripture, usually from the 'great storehouse' of the Psalms, would 'come home' to him, 'as if borne on angel's wings'. He would soon identify them as a series: the first occasion was in Norwich Cathedral in 1837, at the time of his first great and frustrated affair of the heart; the second was the 'harrowing' Oxford contest of 1847; and the third the morrow of the Gorham judgment. On this fraught occasion it was from Psalm 86, verse 16: 'O turn thee then unto me, & have mercy upon me: give thy strength unto thy servant, and help the son of thine handmaid.'[3]

On the 18th, after driving and walking with Catherine, Gladstone spoke for nearly five hours, to immense acclaim. Stanley reported: 'It was said that for three nights before this display he was unable to sleep from excitement, but the success was worth the suffering.'[4] Again, as in December, it was the symbolism and evangelistic rhetoric which mattered more than the technical issues. Gladstone clothed his measures in a voluminous wrapping of morality. He deliberately set out to establish his budget as being in its scope and sweep a phenomenon quite transcending the existing budgetary tradition. It was to be the touchstone of a new politics.

1 Matthew, HJ (1979), 630.
2 D, iv, 519.
3 *Ib.*, 617–18.   4 DDCP, 106.

[7]

At the end of his life, in a fragmentary memorandum of 1896 entitled 'General Retrospect', Gladstone offered a most suggestive formulation of a theory of his political career, highly tendentious but at the same time valuable as an effort at objective estimation of himself. He argued (subject to reservations of humility) that if Providence had entrusted to him a 'striking gift', it had been shown, 'at certain political junctures', in what might be termed 'appreciation of the general situation and its result'. This was quite different, he insisted, from 'simple acceptance of public opinion, founded upon the discernment that it has risen to a certain height needful for a given work, like a tide'. Rather it was 'an insight into the facts of particular eras, and their relations one to another, which generates in the mind a conviction that the materials exist for forming a public opinion, and for directing it to a particular end'. Gladstone thought that there were four occasions or 'junctures' during his career to which he considered this formulation applicable; the first was the 'renewal of the income tax in 1853'.[1]

This general theory thus raised the possibility of credentials providentially conferred authorising political prerogatives on a grand scale. Gladstone was scrupulous not to make any positive claim specifically in such terms; he could 'by no means' be sure, 'upon a calm review'; but the practical strength of his presumption was thereby hardly affected. It offers a revealing insight into the entire absence in Gladstone's view of himself as essentially an exponent of a politics in any substantial sense stemming from popular authority. In this crucial sense the core of Gladstone's political sensibility remained consistent through his movement from Conservatism to Liberalism. In distinguishing carefully between a lower opportunism founded upon merely exploiting an existing and rising public opinion and a higher intuition of creative statesmanship which forms and directs public opinion Gladstone provided himself with a most formidable method of relating to popular politics on his own terms. As a general theory it can also serve quite particularly, if retrospectively, as the charter of legitimacy for his new vocation. It was an example of the way in which Gladstone's unconscious and discrete instincts and urges could later be shaped into a revealed coherence.

As yet Gladstone had but dim inklings of any 'general situation and its result'; and indeed the collapse of the coalition at the beginning of 1855 would leave him in a sorely disconcerted and bewildered state, full of complaint about the false turn taken by politics and the 'demoralisation of Parliament with respect to its high duties'.[2] That his sense of 'insight' into

1 GP, 44791, 51.
2 'The Declining Efficiency of Parliament', QR, xcix, September 1856, 554.

the 'facts' of 1853 and his notions of the 'materials' which existed for 'forming a public opinion' and 'directing it to a particular end' were equally dim inklings can also be reasonably assumed. Gladstone was to find fulfilment of his sense of a new mission or vocation to any substantial degree far more difficult probably than he imagined in 1853. At the bottom of his disgust with the consequences of the fall of Aberdeen's government was an outraged realisation that his hopes of forming and directing a public opinion were thwarted by what he saw as the opportunist talents for debauching public virtue of Palmerston.

Still, for the present, a brilliantly successful budget made up for a lot of dimness of inklings as to the future. The rhetorical technique consisted first in Gladstone's projecting himself as a third in a heroic series after Pitt and Peel. Pitt had created the income tax, 'this colossal engine of finance', as the key to victory in the desperate conflict with revolutionary and Napoleonic France. Then Peel 'called forth from repose this giant, who had once shielded us in war, to come and assist our industrious toils in peace'. If the first income tax produced 'enduring and memorable results', the second 'has been the instrument by which you have introduced, and by which . . . ere long you may perfect, the reform, the effective reform, of your commercial and fiscal system'. Now, 'if we rightly use the income tax' it would be the means of 'achieving a great good immediately for England, and ultimately to mankind'. The second aspect of Gladstone's technique was the rhetoric of courage, urgency, and decisiveness. The House must not 'nibble at this great public question'. 'You must be bold, you must be intelligible, you must be decisive.' 'You must not palter with it;' there must be a 'real substantial plan', not 'some paltry proposal to shirk the difficulty'. Gladstone assured the Commons that he, for his part, did not seek to 'evade the difficulties of our position'; there would be no 'narrow or flimsy expedients'. No one could suppose that the government was 'paltering' or that Gladstone was not presenting a proposal which was 'substantive and intelligent' to bring 'to completion the noble work of commercial reform which is so far advanced'.

The third, and most important, feature of Gladstone's rhetoric distinguished him from Pitt and Peel rather than stressed his links with them. Gladstone saw himself as being in a position to point towards a future golden era. His scheme to extinguish the income tax by 1860 he offered as a token or augury of good omen; an auspicious sign of the good times at hand when the noble work of commercial reform should begin to show forth its fruits of prosperity. The logic of his argument implied that the end of the income tax marked the end of an era of desperate struggles and toils. This he underlined with his plan for 'a great and beneficial remission of taxes' of two millions which fulfilled Peel's principles of unleashing productivity and stimulating consumption. The imagery of the promised land – 'Now I have the downward road before me and the plains of Italy are in my view' – Gladstone linked with the theme of reconciliation of classes and interests. He made much of his change in the legacy duty to cause it to fall on land as well as income, thus abolishing a traditional privilege and obliging real property to bear its share of national burdens at the same rate as 'intelligence and skill'. His bringing of Ireland within a uniform tax system with Britain ('the advantage of which I hardly know how to appreciate') Gladstone also presented as a token of a more auspicious era for the union.[1]

Certainly Gladstone's 'appreciation' of the situation was not so dim that he had no inklings of a public opinion likely to be responsive to such rhetoric. Later he explained his budget recipe to Algernon West: 'Get up your figures thoroughly and exhaustively, so as to have them absolutely at your fingers' ends, and then give them out as if the *whole* WORLD was interested in them.'[2] With his first budget he launched his myth as the keeper of the Victorian financial conscience. Russell reported to the Queen that Mr. Gladstone's statement was one of the most powerful financial speeches ever made in the House of Commons. 'Mr. Pitt in his days of glory might have been more imposing, but he could not have been more persuasive.' Prince Albert, trusting that Gladstone's Christian humility would not allow him to become 'dangerously elated', could not resist the gesture of sending Russell's report to the Queen for Gladstone himself to read.[3] Aberdeen was sure that as a finance minister Gladstone had placed himself 'fully on the level of Sir Robert Peel'. And Clarendon declared that it was 'the most perfect financial statement ever heard within the walls of Parlt for such it is allowed to be by friend & foe'.[4] Greville's opinion was that it had raised Gladstone 'to a great political elevation, and, what is of far greater consequence than the measure itself, has given the country assurance of a *man* equal to great political necessities, and fit to lead parties and direct governments'.[5] Karl Marx's jeering hostility was also in its way a measure of Gladstone's new public eminence. Marx combined Butler's Hudibras and Sue's Rodolphe de Gérolstein to dub 'Hudibrasiac Rodolpho Gladstone' as 'certainly a master of this sort of financial alchymics'.[6] Gladstone recorded himself as receiving 'innumerable marks of kindness: enough to make me feel ashamed'.[7] By May 5 his letters were 'to be reckoned only by the hundred: the Priv. Sec.s are quite overwhelmed & we are obliged to get large fresh aid'.[8] Disraeli prudently took the line that Gladstone had followed, though in a caricatured and exaggerated form, his own financial projects.

1 H, cxxv, 1350–1422.
2 *Kilbracken*, 147.   3 Q & G, i, 103.
4 Conacher, 70.   5 *Greville*, vi, 419.
6 S.S. Prawer, *Karl Marx and World Literature* (1976), 185.
7 D, iv, 519.   8 *Ib.*, 523.

Despite some restiveness on the part of the Irish and the landed interest, Gladstone got his proposals through early in May. By now he was in a state of exhaustion, having recourse to 'blue pills', and in his extremity even taking to riding for exercise and distraction. He noted on May 11: 'an adventure, after so long cessation.' While in London Gladstone kept up his riding for nearly a year, eventually being 'glad to get rid of a personal luxury and indulgence'.[1]

[8]

Immediately in the wake of his budget success there followed a distressing little episode. Walking through Leicester Square after the opera (Donizetti's *Lucrezia Borgia*: Grisi, Mario, Ronconi) on the night of May 10 Gladstone was accosted by a woman who asked for money. While in conversation with her in Panton Street, he was approached by one Wilson, a young unemployed Scottish commercial traveller, who announced that he recognised Gladstone, much admired his public character, but felt it necessary to expose him to the *Morning Herald* as an immoral frequenter of prostitutes, unless Gladstone promised to find him a position in Somerset House or elsewhere. Gladstone indignantly repudiated both the charge and the menace, and escorted the woman to her home in King Street, Soho, pursued by Wilson, who persisted with his threats. Gladstone then attempted, unavailingly, to shake off the vociferous and embarrassing would-be blackmailer; and, after failing to find a policeman in Regent Street, eventually came across P.C. Joy, C.187, in Sackville Street. The odd trio then went off to Vine Street Station, by which time Wilson was in tears and very contrite, protesting that his only motive was that Gladstone should be exposed 'that he might take it as a moral reproof from one so humble as I was'.[2]

Despite unavoidable and unwelcome publicity, Gladstone decided that he had no alternative but to press charges as a deterrent against future attempts at blackmail. The wretched Wilson accordingly was sent for trial and on June 17 sentenced to twelve months' hard labour. Gladstone's counsel referred to his client's 'benevolence, and particularly in reference to this unfortunate class of society', as being 'well known to all who had the honour of his society'.[3] It is likely, however, that many who had the honour of Gladstone's society were astonished at these revelations. 'Much interest was excited' at the remand and committal hearings at Marlborough Street Court on May 11 and 13, when Gladstone appeared to make a deposition, the Marquis of Stafford and Mr. William

1 D, v, 42.   2 *Times*, May 12, 1853, 5.   3 *Ib.*, June 16, 1853, 7.

Scholefield, Liberal M.P. for Birmingham, being attentively present. Greville remarked on May 15 that the incident 'created for the moment great surprise, curiosity, and interest, but has almost entirely passed away already, not having been taken up politically, and there being a general disposition to believe his story and to give him credit for having had no improper motive or purpose. Nevertheless it is a very strange affair, and has not yet been satisfactorily explained.'[1] Gladstone became the butt of many a sly witticism, such as Clarendon's comment to the Duchess of Manchester on 'our Jesuit', with his 'benevolent nocturnal rambles'.[2] Gladstone confessed to his diary that: 'These talkings of mine are certainly not within the rules of worldly prudence: I am not sure that Christian prudence sanctions them for such a one as me; but my aim & intention did not warrant the charge wh. doubtless has been sent to teach me wisdom & which I therefore welcome.'[3] Neither variety of prudence persuaded Gladstone against resuming the good work; which he did, rather more actively than usual, in June. At the same time he took steps to intercede on Wilson's behalf. He pointed out to the police authorities that Wilson was 'not a common rogue but has apparently a reckless fanaticism about him that partakes almost of madness'; and pointed out further that, after all, there was 'a *primâ facie* case against me'. He asked the police to 'simplify & expedite the matter as much as possible'; and in August, through the good offices of Palmerston, the Home Secretary, arranged for Wilson's early release.[4]

Probably even more embarrassing in its way was a letter which appeared in *The Times* on May 13 from 'J.S.' of the Temple. J.S. gave an account of an incident in May 1852 concerning two young women being annoyed by an elderly man at the top of the Haymarket. The altercation attracted the attention of a gentleman passing by who rescued the young ladies, gave one of them money, put them into a cab and sent them home. Further, J.S., in his professional capacity, had reason to know that the same gentleman made enquiries the following day, and since then had been a 'kind and disinterested' friend to the unfortunate girls. This incident, J.S. informed the readers of *The Times*, reflected the 'highest honour upon Mr. Gladstone' – for such, it transpired, was the identity of the benevolent gentleman, an identity discovered by J.S. by 'mere chance'. J.S. defined his object in writing his letter as, *à propos* of the current proceedings, 'to show how Mr. Gladstone acted in an analogous case with which I am acquainted, and to suggest, as a fair inference from that, that his motives were equally pure and honourable in the case now reported'.[5] Messrs Palmer's, *The Times*'s indexers, chose to suggest a slightly cynical colouring to the affair by indexing the incident: 'Glad-

1 *Greville*, vi, 422.   2 A.L. Kennedy (ed.), *My Dear Duchess* (1956), 90.
3 D, iv, 525.   4 GP, 44528, 142, 153–54, 178.   5 *Times*, May 13, 1853, 8.

stone (Rt. Hon. W.E.) and the two Girls in the Haymarket a Disinterested Case.'[1] Greville commented that it was 'creditable in these days of political rancour and bitterness that no malignant attempt has been made to vilify him by his opponents or by the hostile part of the press'.[2]

[9]

Imperturbably, Gladstone compounded the personal luxury and indulgence of a stable with a bout of art collecting. May 31 found him gazing 'with much pleasure at my Murillo: though I have some misgiving about *my* laying out so much money on a picture'.[3] Was he tempted to add to this 'Virgin and Child' (now at Hawarden) the Giorgione 'Adoration of the Virgin' which he viewed at Christie's on June 23? He assuaged his aesthetic lusts by turning to porcelain, in which by the beginning of 1854 he was 'dabbling' heavily. The session continued busy enough. There was the problem of Sir Charles Barry's new Palace of Westminster to be dealt with. A supplemental vote would be necessary. There were the arrears in Barry's own claims to remuneration; on the other hand there was Barry's financial fecklessness ('I deeply regret to find the state of embarrassment into which the accounts and claims for the new Houses of Parliament have come ...').[4] There was a good deal of tidying up of budgetary loose ends. £17 millions of Exchequer Bills coming due involved much ado with the City. The Colonial Church and India Bills required attention. There was, reported Gladstone to Graham, 'a storm in the department of Woods' where its officers 'launch denunciations at one another of ruin to Dean Forest especially'. What did Graham know of the person at the centre of this storm, one Kennedy, Commissioner of Woods and Forests since 1850?[5] What Graham apparently did not know was that Kennedy was a friend and retainer of Russell's; and that accordingly Gladstone would be well-advised to take that into account. Such was the deceptively calm origin of a tempest which would almost blow the coalition apart. On May 30 Gladstone's work 'touched 17 hours very nearly'; and on June 3 he lamented 'this whirl which carries me off my balance'. Designs for the new Australian coinage caused problems with the Queen: Prince Albert conveyed her complaint that they 'deprived H.M. of part of her intellect by making her forehead excessively flat and retreating'. And the Prince himself had projects to be attended to: what about housing the learned societies in the vicinity of Hyde Park Corner

1 Index to *The Times*, April-June 1853, 21.
2 *Greville, ib.*   3 D, iv, 531.
4 G to Barry, May 10, 1853. GP, 44528, 137.   5 *Ib.*, 146.

and moving the National Gallery to Kensington?[1] Gladstone derived what spiritual and mental refreshment he could from the Tractarian fiction of Miss Charlotte Yonge's *Heir of Redclyffe*. Far in the background was the faintly nagging anxiety aroused by the shadow of impending conflict in the Near East: the Russian quarrel with the Turks was dragging in Britain and France, who sent their fleets to the Dardanelles to bolster the Turks. The Russians in turn, on July 2, crossed the Pruth and occupied the principalities of Moldavia and Wallachia, offering to withdraw if the British and French fleets did likewise. The social aspect was likewise intense. Being at Downing Street put the Gladstones in a better position for grand entertaining: they gave a dinner of twenty-eight covers in honour of the Queen's birthday on May 24. They attended at the Palace a dinner in honour of the blind King of Hanover, who had been so edified by the sight of George IV's funeral ('There is such a depth of touching expression in his countenance as is rarely to be witnessed').[2] Dining with Molesworth, the Radical representative in the cabinet, struck Gladstone as 'the height of luxury'.[3] At the Greenwich fish dinner the chairman Palmerston 'kept up the ball admirably well'. Afterwards Gladstone attended at Lady Palmerston's reception from which he slipped away to see the beautiful Elizabeth Collins: 'Late. Pretty well knocked up.'[4]

In such a pretty well knocked up state Gladstone repaired with his family to recuperate in the western Highlands. There he did a little unconvincing deerstalking in August. September was rather a ducal month: first with the Sutherlands at Dunrobin (spoiled by erysipelas – Gladstone had more 'bed illness' than since scarlet fever as a child); later at Drumlanrig with the Buccleuchs. The stay with the Sutherlands had two important consequences. The one, immediate, was that Gladstone was out of reach when Aberdeen wanted to consult him on the question of making way for Russell, in the spirit of the understanding of December 1852. There would have been no doubt as to Gladstone's advice on such an issue; but in any case Aberdeen felt that the pressures of the Eastern crisis made his continuation in the lead desirable. The other was that it established a rapport of special significance for Gladstone with the Duchess, Harriet (*née* Howard of Castle Howard), a formidable, intelligent and pious woman with whose mind Gladstone could join in serious matters of religion and politics in a manner impossible with Catherine.

After a brief pause at Hawarden serious affairs recommenced at the beginning of October with cabinets in London and a signal speech at Manchester on October 12 for the inauguration of the Peel monument. This was Gladstone's first major encounter with that public whose opinion his appreciation of the general situation and his insight into the

1 Q & G, i, 105–07.   2 D, iv, 538.
3 *Ib.*, 542.   4 *Ib.*, 549.

facts of the era would fit him to form and direct. Manchester for its part certainly received Gladstone very much in a spirit appropriate to his new and greatly enhanced public stature. He was the 'eminent statesman' whose 'comprehensive and consistent financial scheme', with its 'admirable commercial measures', had marked him out as deserving well of the interests which Manchester saw itself as representing. Avowing himself Peel's 'pupil and his follower', Gladstone for his part paid tribute to the capital of Free Trade's 'advanced intelligence' and to the 'prominent part' it played in influencing the fortunes and destinies of the country; and to the exhibition it offered of the elevation through industry and art of all classes, not only of the 'educated classes', but the whole feeling of the community. This certainly was the aspect of Manchester which most impressed itself on Gladstone. The audience at the Peel dedication he noted was 'of *men* almost exclusively, & working men. There I spoke, to the cracking of my voice.'[1] At the foundation-laying of a new school the following day, Gladstone, with a novel *frisson* of sensibility, 'had again to speak to an assembly of the *people*'. Something of a sense of thrill at adventuring into strange new reaches of political experience had been evident earlier at the first of such exotic occasions, the coal whippers' meeting at Shadwell. But this was something on an immensely bigger and more exciting scale. Gladstone was starting to enrich the texture of his new vocation with an ingredient of the virtuous masses.

It was provoking indeed that Gladstone could not indulge himself to the hilt at Manchester with issues appropriate to the moral qualities of intelligence and elevation which its people so eminently manifested; financial questions, abolition of the paper duties as a further, and vital, measure of exempting great manufactures from costs and contributing to the wider education of the public through a cheaper press, defence of the Aberdeen ministry. Instead, circumstances obliged him to divert valuable time and energy to the unrewarding Eastern question. The Turks, emboldened by British and French encouragement, had declared war against Russia on October 4. The British fleet had passed through the Dardanelles and was now riding at Constantinople itself. Gladstone was only too well aware of the pressures of the anti-Russian party in the Cabinet, led by Palmerston, to have the fleet pass out through the Bosphorus into the Black Sea and thus confront the Russians with an unambiguous menace. Aberdeen stubbornly resisted this bellicosity, but was in danger of being overborne by the current of opinion. The newly-enthroned Napoleon III in France was ready to inaugurate the Second Empire with a glorious war against the greatest pillar of the system of 1815. Nicholas himself felt Russia under threat, and stiffened his responses accordingly. The British 'national' public was spoiling for

1 *Ib.*, 562.

war against Russia in defence of the liberties of Europe. They saw the gallant Turks as resisters of the grim Muscovite despotism which had enslaved the Poles and delivered the Hungarians into servitude. This public looked increasingly to Palmerston to represent its will and press for its measures. At Manchester Gladstone ranged himself ostentatiously beside Aberdeen. He warned against the 'glare of glory', and denounced war as the enemy of freedom and of the 'real moral and social advancement of man'. He extolled Aberdeen's policy of 'peace and negotiation', lamenting that unfortunately it was devoid of glamour and romantic excitement. Like that old philhellene 'Athenian' Aberdeen, Gladstone could not take the Turks seriously as defenders of the liberties of Europe. He saw the Ottoman Empire as 'full of anomaly, full of misery and full of difficulty'.[1]

Back in London Gladstone coped with Tom's vexing tiresomeness, which had pursued him incessantly throughout the year. Gladstone's attempts to mollify his resentful eldest brother by demonstrating that his apparent neglect was caused by inescapable pressures of public business failed to convince Tom.[2] In November Gladstone sent Catherine 'more of the *Tom* correspondence. Either he or I, an impartial person would say, must be mad: perhaps both – yet I have really tried to write for the best, & feel that I am not angry but sorry for one who with good intentions & notions of duty causes much trouble to other people but yet more to himself.'[3] That was perhaps not the best moment for Prince Albert to launch a little jest by putting it to Gladstone that the solution to the problem of a new barracks would be for the Ordnance Department to take over Burlington House. Gladstone's grave reply, replete with conclusive reasons, forced the discomfited Prince to reveal himself as talking 'merely in joke'.[4] That was never a safe thing to do with Gladstone without making very clear preliminary signals.

In the meantime Gladstone took refuge from the baronet of Fasque and from the gloom of impending war by immersing himself in the Civil Service reform question. He did not allow even Elizabeth Collins to be much of a distraction now (though on occasion he still had to adjure himself to 'remember Hooker on the torch'). As a member of the Council of King's College, the Anglican foundation in London, he could not avoid being involved in the scandalous case of the prosecution of his old Oxford friend F. D. Maurice for heresy. (This made him call guiltily to mind his own behaviour in the earlier case of Hampden.) Gladstone had in the previous year collided at Oxford with another noted specimen of the liberal Anglican school in the form of the Rev. Benjamin Jowett. Gladstone found one of his University sermons 'very remarkable, but

1 *Times*, October 12, 1853, 5; 13 October, 7.   2 Magnus, 62–63.
3 G to CG, November 19, 1853. GGP, 28/4.   4 Q & G, i, 107–108.

unsettling'.[1] Jowett would soon also (in 1855) be denounced as a heretic; but in the meantime Gladstone found his unsettling qualities very serviceable. Jowett was one of the leaders of the reform party at Oxford. Gladstone, impressed by the commissioners' report, was converting himself to the notion that Oxford could not avoid a large measure of reform and would best be reformed by its friends. The Oxford reformers were now looking to him as their best hope. Jowett aimed to change Oxford from an aristocratic finishing school and an Anglican seminary into a serious secular institution which would train undergraduates for positions of responsible leadership in government, politics and the empire. His immediate objective was to get the provision of candidates for a reformed Civil Service into the hands of a reformed Oxford. His initial tactical manoeuvre in this campaign was to get himself on the committee studying the analogous question of Indian Civil Service reform which was preparing recommendations for Wood's new India Bill, itself in turn necessitated by the expiry of the East India Company's charter. Wood's policy was a radical recasting of Indian government, while retaining the principle of dual control between company and government. Trevelyan was very much involved with this question, and Jowett struck up a good working relationship with him as two reformers sharing very similar aims. Trevelyan's brother-in-law, Macaulay, another old India hand, gave invaluable and weighty support. And via Trevelyan on the Indian aspect of Civil Service reform Jowett came into the same collaborative relationship with Gladstone's man, Northcote.

Thus Jowett, the embodiment of the intimately complex inter-connectedness of Oxford, India and the Treasury, returned repeatedly upon Gladstone at this time. He wrote to Gladstone in July 1853: 'I cannot conceive a greater boon which could be conferred on the University than a share in the Indian appointments.' He exploited a shamelessly wheedling approach: 'You love Oxford too well not to do what you can for it.'[2] Gladstone loved Oxford for reasons quite alien from Jowett's liberal secularity. He wanted to save Oxford for the Church; and he had a deep sentimental attachment to its aristocratic tone. But there was scope for a working compromise. 'Whether wisely or not,' Gladstone told Jowett, 'I love Oxford well: and I know no subject which has a larger place in my heart than that of the improvement of her institutions, the adjustment of the great questions now in agitation respecting her, and her restoration to repose, and as connected with it the independence, which is essential to the effective pursuit of her exalted calling.'[3] The logic of Jowett's argument about the grand role to be played by the universities as

1 D, iv, 390.
2 R.J. Moore, 'The Abolition of Patronage in the Indian Civil Service', HJ (1964), 250–51.
3 G to Jowett, December 16, 1853. GP, 44529, 16–17.

exponents of the morality of merit was compelling. Getting Oxford's (and Cambridge's) hands on the Indian Civil Service meant destroying the monopoly of the Company's college at Haileybury; which was accordingly done. The unreformed Home Civil Service proved a much tougher nut to crack.

The instructions with which Gladstone charged Northcote in April urged him not to be 'intensive and exhaustive' but rather 'reflective' upon the detailed departmental reports already completed from which 'conclusions of general validity' might be drawn.[1] The report which Northcote and Trevelyan presented to Gladstone on November 28 recommended that it was desirable that the best brains of the country be attracted to the Civil Service; and that this would be possible only if recruitment by patronage were replaced by a system embodying the principles of competition and merit; and if the work of the service be adjusted accordingly by demarcating strictly between a higher, directive sphere of administration and a lower mechanical sphere of copying and petty routine executive functions; and if promotion within the service were determined on merit as against seniority. Gladstone was convinced that this was a worthwhile cause to press on the Cabinet. He accepted readily the wider implication of the Northcote-Trevelyan recommendations: that there was a definable 'public interest' which now, rightly, took precedence of the traditional notion that government existed to serve the Crown and was in turn sustained by the Crown's influence. He was not thinking in terms of recruiting to the service from 'out of doors'; from, say, the 'advanced intelligence' and 'the *people*' he had recently saluted at Manchester. In much the same spirit Gladstone was conspicuously unforthcoming with encouragement or support for Russell's project for a new Reform Bill.[2] His doctrine of the 'fiscal trusteeship' of the income tax of 1853 was indeed incompatible with a wider franchise. He admitted to the suspicious Shaftesbury that Reform was now no longer a 'mere abstract question';[3] nonetheless, for all that it was formally on the official political agenda, he could not see the point of trying, like Russell, to weld a new wider franchise on to the old unreformed apparatus of administration. That incompatibility would simply lead to popular demands for further organic reform. But he did suppose that government would best serve the Crown by a reciprocal application of principles of advanced intelligence to the structure and modes of its organs. As Gladstone put it to Graham: 'This is *my* contribution to parliamentary reform.'[4] If indeed what Gladstone had saluted at Manchester represented in some sense or

1 Wright, *Treasury Control*, xiii.
2 Conacher, 297.
3 G to Shaftesbury, November 16, 1853. GP, 44529, 3. Ashley became 7th Earl of Shaftesbury in 1851.
4 Morley, i, 511.

some degree the public opinion it would be his vocation to form and direct, then it followed necessarily that he, as a man of government, should give the lead in putting its machinery on to a footing from which it would be able to respond appropriately to such requirements as Gladstone's appreciation of the situation or insight into the facts might cause him to formulate. Gladstone's views on Civil Service reform were very much an expression of the *'étatisme'* which has been identified as an important and growing ingredient of his politics in this period.[1]

Both the eventual shape and detail of the Northcote-Trevelyan report owed much to Gladstone's intervention. On December 3 he told Trevelyan that he had read his 'able paper on the Organization of the permanent Civil Service', that he looked upon it as a document of 'great importance'; and that he was 'most anxious that it should be in such a form as, if it does not at once secure the execution of the design shall give it a good start to advance it some way on its road to a state of vital activity'. But on some points he wanted it 'fortified and modified'. He was a critic, Gladstone assured Trevelyan, because he felt 'so thoroughly and heartily associated with your feelings & purposes in the matter. I am keenly anxious to strike a real blow at Parliamentary Patronage.' Bold in principle, the report was timid in application. Everything must be done to prevent its failing 'through the reciprocal jealousy of Departments'; which could degenerate into a 'selfish squabble, strongly flavoured by hypocrisy'. Gladstone identified the 'weakest point' of the proposals as they stood as connecting itself 'with this remark: it will I am afraid be viewed as a device for the aggrandisement of the functionaries of the Treasury at the expense, it may be said by the plunder of other Departments'. The report withheld any plan of dealing with patronage of the Treasury in Customs and Inland Revenue, by introducing 'effective competition'; but it was 'here that the most appointments are made & on by far the largest scale'. It was quite correct to envisage piecemeal applications; but it was vital to 'get the principle sanctioned in its full breadth: & particularly let it be applied to the Treasury with unsparing rigour'. A 'large & bold design', Gladstone urged, was 'more practicable, as well as more just, than any one of narrower limits'.

> Dealing equally with the cherished privilege of patronage wherever you can make it amenable to your reforming process, you will plant the scheme on firm & solid ground, will get rid of a multitude of objections which would disguise the main issue, & will place the issue clearly in the public view, thus commencing, if you do not at once carry through, a conflict which can have but one ending & that a good one.

Furthermore, Gladstone took exception to the recommendation that

1 Matthew, D, v, xxxii-iii.

clerkships in the higher offices should be disposed of by selection among the successful candidates and that their selection should 'rest with the First Lord of the Treasury, who would give due weight to the recommendations of his colleagues & also *of his Parliamentary* supporters'. Having 'slain Patronage in principle by your admirable opening statement & your first recommendations you revive it by these words' and give it a ground from which it could 'wriggle itself once more into possession of all the space from which it had been ejected'. 'Pray let this disappear.' Gladstone could not accept power being given to the Treasury as Northcote and Trevelyan proposed on grounds of tactical caution; characteristically, his style was one of aggressive frontal assault: assert a 'great & salutary principle', one calculated 'above all to be made palpable to the public mind'.[1] The receptivity of the 'public mind' was indeed now Gladstone's most intense political concern. When Trevelyan proposed that the revised report be published and widely distributed for purposes of propaganda Gladstone responded positively: while in general averse to the 'gratuitous distribution of documents and works prepared at the public expense', the 'novelty of the subject opened by the Report on the Civil Service and the great importance of enabling the most intelligent portion of the middle and lower class to form a judgment upon it' justified his approval.[2]

Had Gladstone foreseen the length of the conflict before him to secure acceptance of the recommendations he might have been more tolerant of Northcote's and Trevelyan's placatory tactic. In enlisting the support of his colleagues Gladstone found most of the Peelites amenable. Graham, however, was inclined to resistance. He could not conceive of any system but the existing one of patronage which would guarantee the filling of appointments by candidates in whom ministers of the Crown could repose confidence and trust. It was, he insisted, 'a Qualification to be a Gentleman: and no other attainment can compensate for the want of this inestimable merit'.[3] He remained sceptical at Gladstone's counter-arguments, but declared himself open to persuasion. Russell was much more obstinate. He refused to admit that the Indian reforms were a relevant precedent. Imbued with the most Whiggish proneness to aristocratic cliqueishness and exclusivity, Russell interpreted the Northcote-Trevelyan proposals as implicitly but deliberately anti-aristocratical and anti-monarchical. He considered the criticisms of the patronage system as grossly exaggerated; and in any case the best brains could always be hired from outside the Service when needed. He denounced the proposed reforms as an attempt 'to substitute talent & cramming for character',[4] a kind of administrative Jacobinism, whereby

1 G to Trevelyan, December 3, 1853. GP, 44529, 11–12.
2 G to Trevelyan, March 1, 1854. *Ib.*, 60.
3 Conacher, 319.   4 *Ib.*, 321:

clever and industrious persons of low extraction could form a social and political cancer within the machinery of state. Gladstone countered copiously with reassuring arguments that the tendency of the reforms would 'strengthen and multiply the ties between the higher classes and the possession of administrative power'. As a member for Oxford University he looked forward 'eagerly' to their operation. He assured Russell that he had 'a strong impression that the aristocracy of this country are even superior in natural gifts, on the average, to the mass; but it is plain that with their acquired advantages, their *insensible education*, irrespective of book-learning, they have an immense superiority'. He asked Russell to remember that 'at the Revolution we passed over from Prerogative to Patronage, and that since the Revolution we have also passed from bribery to influence'. Gladstone could not think that this process was to 'end here'; and 'after all we have seen of the good sense and good feeling of the community', he cherished the hope, perhaps too sanguine though it might be, that the day was now near at hand, or actually come, when 'we may safely give yet one more new and striking sign of rational confidence in the intelligence & character of the people'.[1] Despite having his 'self-sufficiency' thus 'punctured',[2] Russell remained unmoved by this appeal to 'advanced intelligence', denounced the scheme again as 'harshly republican', and reaffirmed his opposition.

Russell's negative was endorsed by his Whig colleagues (except Granville); and thus by the beginning of 1854 the question was in stalemate. The Queen, too, had 'considerable misgiving', which Gladstone attempted to allay by pointing out that 'previous industry and self-denial which proficiency evinces, are rarely separated from general habits of virtue'.[3] Gladstone hoped to help things forward by taking the initiative with a scheme for Oxford reform – which issue, after all, Russell himself had been responsible for forcing in 1850. This was the obvious tactic to outflank the Whig leader, and Gladstone forwarded to him a 'rough draft' of an Oxford Bill in December 1853. By now Gladstone was working under increasing pressures of urgency. There was the 'Wine Duty agitation', which was 'active, and may be formidable'; there were cruel pressures on indigent Church schools by Education Department directives that tiled floors be replaced by boards; and was Customs 'under any and what amount of *engagement* to admit the packages of the Orleans family free of duty'? There was the decimal coinage question to be kept in view. But over-shadowing all was the deteriorating situation in the Near East. On November 30 the Russians destroyed the Turkish Black Sea fleet at Sinope; and demands that the British fleet at Constantinople should pass through the Bosphorus into the Black Sea mounted to an excited

2 Ib., 322.
2 J. M. Prest, 'Gladstone and Russell', *Trans. Roy. Hist. Soc.* (1966), 47.
3 Q & G, i, 111–12.

crescendo. The Cabinet began to crack under the strain. Palmerston let it be known that he advocated this patriotically belligerent course; and indeed, paradoxically, his position as Home Secretary allowed him more freedom to assert himself than he would have had at the Foreign Office. When on December 16 Palmerston resigned in protest at Russell's insistence on bringing forward a new Reform Bill, there was a widespread and quite accurate understanding 'out of doors' that he was protesting also at what he considered to be the appeasing pusillanimity of the Prime Minister. Palmerston's popularity with the 'national' public was now such that Aberdeen had to take him back to keep the Cabinet intact on terms which crucially weakened the influence of the peace party. Gladstone's own anxiety for the continuation of the coalition was such that he confessed to Aberdeen that he 'had wishes that Palmerston was back again on account of the Eastern question'[1]. It was also true that Gladstone largely shared Palmerston's distaste for Reform. Certainly Gladstone did not feel himself in a position to stand forth boldly as an advocate of peace in conformity with his Manchester doctrine of October 1853. His failure to 'muster courage' at this juncture and brave public obloquy was later a matter of great regret to some of his most fervent supporters, embarrassed at the painful spectacle of his 'bolting in the middle of the war'.[2] Such were the pressures and anxieties that Gladstone kept his Christmas in London for the first time since the epochal year of 1842. (He was nevertheless able to assure the Bishop of Moray and Inverness on Christmas Day: 'I think frequently of the subject of lay organization in the Scottish Episcopal Communion.')[3]

[10]

The new year indeed opened inauspiciously: on January 3, 1854 the British and French fleets entered the Black Sea. Imminent war threatened to blight Gladstone's plans and projects. It was some compensation that on January 7 Catherine gave birth to a 'dear little boy', christened Herbert John. The birth was difficult. Catherine was now in her forties and her labours were encouraged by the beating of a drum. Herbert, their fourth son, proved to be the youngest of the Gladstone brood. Perhaps it was a mood of paternal indulgence which led Gladstone to concede to the Chief Baron of the Exchequer that 'candles supplied for the personal use of the Judges on the Bench ... ought to be of wax'; and likewise agreed that 'black sealing wax should be furnished for them in case of family

1 G & P, 44.
2 Smith, *My Memory of Gladstone*, 21–22.   3 GP, 44529, 19.

mourning'.[1] The ending of Catherine's childbearing period left Gladstone in a vulnerable state on the 'sad & perplexing subject' of his rescue mission. He had kept this work up fairly regularly when in London. He lay awake on the night of January 20 musing on the rather mortifying calculation that he had conversed with something like eighty or ninety of these 'unhappy beings', but could claim positively only one case of successful rescue. 'Yet this were much more than enough for all the labour & the time, had it been purely spent in my part. But the case is far otherwise: & tho' probably in none of these instances have I not spoken good words, yet so bewildered have I been that they constitute the chief burden of my soul.'[2]

It was another burden on Gladstone's soul that he failed early in 1854 to break out of the stalemate on Civil Service reform. At a cabinet on January 26 his scheme ran into stiff opposition from Russell, Lansdowne, Clarendon, Wood, and Lord Chancellor Cranworth. Trevelyan's rather unscrupulous attempts to manipulate the press and especially his part in orchestrating an agitation in *The Times* were undoubtedly counter-productive. Propaganda for the reforms was too much directed at indiscriminate and exaggerated denigration of the Service; which was much resented by the majority of its officers. It soon became clear that opposition was too strong to permit any further progress in 1854. Few people shared Gladstone's *étatist* predispositions; and many, like Russell, who were in favour of reform in a general way, were not favourable to reforms which seemed likely to create a bureaucratic state within the state. Little more could be attempted before the Aberdeen coalition itself collapsed at the beginning of 1855. Nor did it help that in May 1854 Gladstone, as a result of the enquiries he had set in train the previous year,[3] dismissed from a commissionership of Woods and Forests T. F. Kennedy, who happened to be a connection and protégé of Russell. Gladstone resolutely declined Russell's repeated requests that Kennedy be reinstated. For Russell the matter was partly a duty to stand loyally by an old friend in the very spirit of patronage which he was defending against Gladstone's meritocratic reform project; but increasingly it took on the character of an obsession to assert his seniority and prestige. Sensitive to a morbid degree from the beginning of the coalition at his 'humiliation' and 'degradation' at having to step down from the first place in politics and accept the Peelites as an equal power, Russell's vanity turned rancid during 1854, with the Kennedy case a focus of mounting rage and frustration. Gladstone's inflexibility was perhaps justifiable on the merits of the case; but he should have taken into consideration also, for the benefit of the government whose fall he would lament so bitterly,

1 G to Sir F. Pollock, January 16, 1854. GP, 44529, 20.
2 D, iv, 586.   3 See above, 275.

the expediency of humouring the peppery Whig chief. Later he confessed to Aberdeen about Russell: 'Had I been aware of his personal interest in Mr. Kennedy, I should have communicated with him before taking any step of a decisive nature.'[1] By the end of 1854 Gladstone was appalled at the extent to which a small matter provoked by him should have become, in a crazily absurd way, a serious threat to the stability of the coalition.

Meanwhile, Gladstone leavened the preparation of his budget with Art. He purchased for the nation from Herr Kruger of Minden for £2,500 fifty-two pictures of the 'Westphalian School' and twenty of 'other German and Netherlands Schools'; but he did not feel at all sure, as he informed Aberdeen, that Canova's 'Magdalene' was 'worth £1,500 to the nation'; nor did he concur with Russell's view that Hayter's picture of the reformed House of Commons was worth four or five thousand pounds. On the other hand, he was prepared to purchase Madame Gherardini's collection of models.

Gladstone announced his financial plans for 1854 on March 6, a few days before the formal declaration of war on Russia. His mood was appropriately subdued. He did not disguise the bitterness of his regret at losing the opportunity for a further million or more of tax remissions; nor did he disguise his regret at the all-but declared war itself. At a time when patriotic uplift might have been thought in order, Gladstone chose instead to characterise the expenses of war as a 'moral check' which it had pleased the Almighty to impose upon 'ambition and lust of conquest'; and to warn against the 'pomp and circumstance' and 'glory and excitement' about war which invests it with charm and blinds men to its evils and miseries. Gladstone urged strongly a policy of paying for the war by increased direct taxation rather than having recourse to loans and indirect taxes. This he advocated partly as a species of 'moral check' and partly on the strength of his interpretation of Pitt's war finance. Borrowing was 'a course not required by our necessities, and therefore unworthy of our character'. The 'necessity of meeting from year to year' the expenditure entailed by the war would be 'a salutary and wholesome check'. By thus measuring the cost of any benefit calculated to be gained war would be to waged by 'rational and intelligent beings', attending not only to the 'necessity of the war' but to the 'first and earliest prospects of concluding an honourable peace'.[2] To his Radical brother Robertson ('my brother is a supporter of the Government and something more: a little of what the Americans call a barn-burner'),[3] Gladstone observed that war had 'hitherto been to us Englishmen but a remote and abstract idea: and when we say we are going to War, or as now we must say at war, we do

1 G to Aberdeen, November 7, 1854. GP, 44529, 171–72.
2 H, cxxxi, 357–89.   3 GP, 44529, 72.

not know what we mean. It will dawn upon us by degrees, and in forms for the most part eminently disagreeable.'[1]

These 'first and early prospects' of peace were certainly Gladstone's measure of the financial necessities of the war; and their consequences for him were certainly 'eminently disagreeable'. He increased the income tax for six months from 7d to 10½d. He asked for a sum of about £50 per head of the forces earmarked for the expedition to the east; and estimated for a deficit of £2.8 million. Essentially he saw himself as directing a holding operation: to keep the general position of 1853 as intact as the exigencies of war would allow. He was reluctant to accede to French proposals of a substantial 'advance of money' to the Turks. He recalled the frightful lengths to which the policy of subsidy had been carried in the last war; and insisted that Turkey was at least as able to borrow for herself on terms 'as good as those upon which even the Government of Austria could now borrow'.[2]

Thus Gladstone made himself a hostage to fortune; and events decreed not only that there would be no honourable and early peace, but that the war would be waged in a manner which made it a byword for incompetence and imbecility. Gladstone, moreover, was in dispute over financial policy with the Bank of England, as represented in the Commons particularly by Thomas Hankey, a former governor. Disraeli launched an effective criticism on March 22; and in Stanley's opinion Gladstone's reply 'failed of its purpose'. This was 'Disraeli's first victory over his rival in finance'.[3] Gladstone had no doubt that 'misapprehension about the Government and the Bank' was 'owing to the joint efforts and effusions of Mr. Disraeli and Mr. Hankey'. 'The truth is,' he assured Robertson with more than a touch of paranoia, 'that it is common to periods of this kind to be disturbed by panic and we now have for the first time a man calling himself a party leader and not unwilling to gain notoriety by inflaming apprehensions mischievous only to the Country.'[4] Gladstone would remain in office only for a further ten months. During that time he clung obstinately but ineffectually to his initial premises. What is so noticeable about Gladstone at this time, particularly in contrast to his successor at the Exchequer, Sir George Cornewall Lewis, is a certain helpless inflexibility, a lack of resourcefulness and consequently, ultimately, 'evasions and sophistries'.[5] Partly this was because he committed himself to a monetary doctrine derived from the famous 1828 Select Committee of the Commons on Public Income and Expenditure and the influence of the economist Sir Henry Parnell, enshrined in Peel's Bank

1 G to Robertson G, March 29, 1854. *Ib.*, 72–73.
2 G to Clarendon, March 18, 1854. *Ib.*, 67.
3 DDCP, 123.
4 G to Robertson G, March 29, 1854. GP, *Ib.*
5 O. Anderson, *A Liberal State at War* (1967), 195.

Charter Act of 1844, and fixated on the 'burden' of the national debt; partly it was because his own obsession with his new vocation in turn led him to invest in this already excessively moralistic financial policy an overwhelming and unbalancing element of his own intense moralism. This obsessiveness accounts for the extraordinary way in which he exposed himself to criticism from Treasury and City experts by shuffling and quite unconvincing assertions that his borrowings to finance the war were not really borrowing at all. This sorry process he commenced in April 1854 with an issue of £6 million of Exchequer Bonds ostensibly redeemable in phases over the next six years but in fact never redeemed and eventually added to the funded debt. This fiasco seriously compromised Gladstone's financial reputation. His attempted manipulation of Exchequer Bills also provoked charges of 'surreptitious abandonment of the policy of taxes, not loans' from such very acute critics as Lord Monteagle, the former Thomas Spring-Rice and a distinguished former Chancellor.[1] It was as well, in fact, for Gladstone's reputation that the Aberdeen coalition fell at the beginning of 1855, for by then the discrepancy between his doctrine and his policy was of embarrassing proportions: He was contemplating a loan of £12 million and a large increase in indirect taxation; responsibility for which, in the event, he was quite happy to pin on to Cornewall Lewis. It was only the way in which from 1860 he contrived to restore a credible financial moralism which allowed his admirers to look back and retrospectively include his first period at the Exchequer, on the strength of the *éclat* of 1852–53, as a signal triumph.

In such circumstances of largely self-induced disaster it was no wonder that Gladstone groaned about a 'tumult of business wh. follows & whirls me day & night, so that I cannot attain to recollection much less compunction'.[2] On March 19 he noted: 'I have been more overcome & undone by this day than by any day's *labour* for a long time, and I cannot describe the end of it otherwise than as being stunned by God's mercy.'[3] He braced himself to confront the consequences of a failure of tenders for bonds on May 2 in a mood of defiant self-pity: 'I shall have rough weather: but this tries what a man is made of. I am sure a little trial is needed: & probably a little is as much as I am good for.'[4] Greville observed on April 2 the 'discredit' into which Gladstone had fallen by his 'rash, obstinate, injudicious' behaviour and mismanagement: in 1853 'marked out as a future Prime Minister'; now with his prestige in tatters. The failure of Gladstone's Exchequer Bill scheme Greville judged 'very injurious'.[5]

1 O. Anderson, 'Loans versus Taxes: British Financial Policy in the Crimean War', *Economic History Review*, xvi (1963–4), 315.
2 D, iv, 611.   3 *Ib.*, 603.
4 *Ib.*, 615.   5 *Greville*, vii, 29, 35.

Gladstone's explanations about Exchequer Bills to Monteagle (Chairman of the Board of Audit) did not convince;[1] and the relationship between Exchequer and Audit remained cool for the rest of Gladstone's term of office. In his clashes with the authorities of the Bank of England he went so far as to disclaim 'affected and sarcastic politeness' and even to declare that the 'old fashion' of 'English pugilism' by which combatants shook hands before they fought was an unaffordable expenditure of valuable time.[2] His immediate object was to put an end to time-honoured conventions whereby the Bank held for its own benefit at certain times monies due to the government, thus obliging the Exchequer to borrow to tide itself over the intervals: conventions lucrative to the Bank but in Gladstone's opinion (for which in due course he would gain legal sanction) detrimental to the public interest. His larger purpose was to subordinate the Bank decisively to the authority of a responsible 'Ministry of Finance' – an *étatist* and French style of designation Gladstone was now prone to employ. On the day before his supplementary budget of May 8 'in the agony of my work' of 'labour and turmoil', he was visited by one of those angelically borne presentiments of Scripture which he marked as moments of high revelation amid his intercourse with the Almighty. And indeed Greville considered that his defence of his policy was 'honourable and creditable' and did much to restore his stock, especially in view of the 'imprudence' of Disraeli's attack.[3] But the real damage had been done. On top of all this the Gladstones lost their cook ('I saw Mrs. Higginson this morning about dinner which led to her money matters and that again to her departure when we both rather nearly if not quite cried').[4]

Solaces and mitigations were few. One was that Gladstone managed to persuade W. K. Hamilton, an old friend of Eton days, to accept the bishopric of Salisbury. Hamilton had been hovering on the point of following Manning over to Rome, and Gladstone was able to hail this success as 'a new & auspicious day for the Church of England!'[5] Another consolation was the passage of the Oxford University Bill, which Gladstone drew up and piloted with the loving devotion he applied in every relationship with Oxford. He defended the 'clerical element' against charges of being the 'bane and pest' of the university, but he was obliged to accept the ending of religious tests for members below the status of masters of arts. 'The governing and teaching power shall remain entire and intact with the Established Church,' he reassured the Provost of Oriel; 'but Dissenters shall have all that does not interfere with this appropriation of the governing and teaching power.'[6] The bill went on to

1 G to Monteagle, March 29, 1854. GP, 44529, 72.
2 Morley, i, 519.   3 *Greville*, vii, 37.
4 G to CG, May 23, 1854. GGP, 28/5.
5 D, iv, 602.   6 GP, 44529, 190.

a smooth course through the Lords, despite the university's Chancellor, Derby, in July. Much in the same spirit of offering sensible concessions Gladstone took the opportunity in the 1854 session to put into practice his doctrine of the Church's advantage in giving 'gold for freedom' by proposing a compromise solution to the perennial church rates question. The freedom he aimed at was reserving church vestries to Anglicans. He did not succeed; but he signalled his willingness to deal with moderate Dissent. There were less contentious matters. Prince Albert raised the question of a Duccio at Christie's for the National Gallery; but, though it was decided not to bid, it was a pleasure to speak at the Royal Academy dinner on the theme of providing public money for the encouragement of the arts and to give practical earnest of benevolence by arranging to purchase and convert Burlington House and thus provide a new home for the Royal Academy and other learned societies, leaving room for convenient concentration of government offices in Somerset House. Poor Sir Charles Barry remained unextricated from his financial embarrassments at the new Palace of Westminster. Gladstone sympathised but remained sternly the 'Cerberus of the public purse'. He kept an eye all the beadier on G. G. Scott's restoration projects for Westminster Abbey. There was also the question of the new Law Courts to consider; Gladstone inclined on grounds of both convenience and economy for the Lincoln's Inn Fields site as against the Strand. He took pains to furnish Robertson at Liverpool with a useful supply of magistracies (recommending Robertson to Palmerston as a 'strong Radical' with 'good will to the Government, though we lag sadly behind him').[1] It was a blessing to see Selwyn back on a visit from New Zealand in May; and no doubt Lady Glynne's death at Hagley that month could without undue callousness be classified in a category of mixed blessings. (One of the blessings was a moiety of Lady Glynne's estate worth £16,500.17s.2d.)[2] He kept Italy in view. From Panizzi he had 'bitter accounts of Poerio and Settembrini from their several dungeons'. He asked Clarendon (who by now had succeeded the restless Russell at the Foreign Office): 'Is it possible to do anything for them?' In default of this, he wanted Clarendon to get the Neapolitan Ambassador, Carini, up to the Foreign Office and do a 'good and Christian work' and 'baste him across the shoulders with your best cane'.[3] To Lord Holland Gladstone avowed that 'were not the cases of Naples and Rome in their different ways so intertwined with other and different questions I confess it would in my mind be difficult to assign bounds for the measures they would justify and require'.[4] He even had

1 G to Palmerston, May 30, 1854. GP, 44529, 102.
2 GGP, 94/13. Secret Account Book, 7.
3 G to Clarendon, April 18 and 19, 1854. GP, 44529, 84.
4 G to Holland, April 18, 1854. *Ib.*,

time to read Disraeli's *Life of Lord George Bentinck* and note it as 'a remarkable & interesting work'.[1]

But such solaces and mitigations were of no avail against the shifting avalanche of troubles which threatened to engulf the government. Of those troubles Lord John Russell was not least. After having caused immense dislocation at the beginning of 1853 in leaving the Foreign Office, he now, in June 1854, caused even more difficulty by insisting on taking the Lord Presidency, against all precedents. Gladstone, heavily embroiled in the Kennedy affair, had no sympathy whatever for Russell's sense of resentment at having been eclipsed. He thought Russell's behaviour 'bad & discreditable'; that the changes were 'more worthy . . . of a set of clowns at Astley's or mountebanks on a village stage than of an English Cabinet'; and ascribed a poisonous influence to Lady John's 'depths' of 'restlessness & folly' in bringing her husband 'both to a pitch of wilfulness & to an abyss of vacillation & infirmity of purpose, which are in themselves a chapter in the history of human nature'.[2] By July Gladstone himself was in a state of physical collapse, forbidden by his doctor to deal with business (though on the matter of the Turkish loan he wrote to Clarendon: 'I have made a compact with my Doctor that I am to write to you this letter by way of getting the subject off my mind').[3]

Much worse, however, were the strains telling on the government in consequence of general public frustration about the conduct of the Russian war. Having withdrawn from the Principalities, the Russians had removed the greatest original pretext for war. The British expeditionary force under Lord Raglan, sitting uselessly and dysenteritically in Bulgaria, began to look ridiculous. To bring it back, without having struck a decisive blow, would reduce the whole affair to ignominious farce. The 'treachery' of the Austrians and the Prussians in not joining eagerly in a crusade to liberate Poland (and thus conveniently bear the brunt of the war) came as a shock of disappointment to the 'national' public. The government began to search maps for ways of getting at the Russians. The arsenal at Sebastopol in the Crimea looked like a possible target for a swift raiding and reducing operation. From April the Cabinet pondered this way out of the impasse. Naval operations in the Baltic were equally unimpressive and ineffectual. The general sense of anti-climax led the more excited patriots to detect Russophile conspiracies on the part of Prince Albert and Aberdeen. The Prime Minister was indeed vulnerable to these dissatisfactions. He had no heart for the war. Palmerston, sitting strategically in the wings in the Home Office, could wait for the national call for strong leadership to prosecute the kind of war originally envisaged. Russell, terrified of being trumped by Palmerston after having

1 D, iv, 611.   2 Conacher, 407–8.
3 G to Clarendon, July 4, 1854. GP, 44529, 14.

been eclipsed by Aberdeen, grew increasingly restless, demanding to get control of war policy and insisting that part of the deal in December 1852 to form the coalition had been that he would take over from Aberdeen after a decent interval. Mainly at Russell's instigation Newcastle's responsibility for War and Colonies was divided, and in an evil hour Newcastle decided to stay with the War Department. The Whig-Peelite fault line widened ominously. Disraeli divined this line of weakness accurately in a notable speech in March 1854, when he drew an invidious contrast between the 'two systems of policy' contending for direction of Britain's response to the Eastern question. There was 'that school of opinions, which I call British opinions', advocated by Palmerston and Russell, believing in the vitality of Turkey, and in Turkey's future as an independent and progressive country, forming a powerful and sufficient barrier against Russian expansion. Against this was the 'other school, which I call the school of Russian politics', believing that Turkey was exhausted, and that nothing could be done to prevent anarchy, but by 'gradually enfranchising the Christian population', and which 'contemplates the possibility of Russia occupying the Bosphorus'. Aberdeen, during his 'long and consistent career', had pursued this policy; in 1829, in 1844, when he 'entered into a virtual agreement' with the Emperor Nicholas for 'ultimate partition and intermediate interference'; and as soon as Aberdeen became first minister in 1852 Nicholas renewed his efforts.[1]

Thus, even more precisely than Gladstone's Manchester speech of October 1853, Disraeli in March 1854 prefigured his Eastern policy of the 1870s, when he set out to emulate 'national' Palmerstonism as against the 'cosmopolitan' feebleness of Aberdeen's heir, Gladstone. But, for his immediate purpose, Disraeli's attack was even more precisely *à propos*. His lead was followed in July in debates which damaged the government and wounded Aberdeen both by the extent to which Palmerston emerged as the available alternative war leader and by what he considered a lack of support from his Peelite friends. Russell alone made a fist of defending the government's policy: but being defended by Russell had its own peculiar dangers. On July 24 Aberdeen, whose woundedness disturbed Graham, asked Gladstone in a note sent by his son Arthur Gordon specifically to come to his aid: 'If my father is personally attacked tonight, he is very desirous that *you* should speak in his defence.' Gladstone, oppressed at having a few days earlier to ask for a special vote of credit of £3 millions for additional war expenditure, felt quite unequal to the task: he protested that he was 'commonly supposed to be tarred with the same stick'.[2] On the 25th Gladstone found Aberdeen 'deeply wounded';[3] but still felt too inhibited to intervene, and preferred to suppose that a rattling

1 H, cxxxii, 298.   2 Conacher, 418.   3 D, iv, 636.

speech from Herbert 'put all right'. He supposed wrongly, and got a stinger from Gordon, who regretted Gladstone's paralysis, 'because I know how restless my father feels about it believing as he does that a defence from you *coming from the heart as it would do*, would go much further to set him right with the public than a few conventional proprieties from Lord John'. Gladstone could only respond feebly and inaccurately that Aberdeen's reputation 'remains unscathed'.[1]

[11]

Prodded by parliament, public, and a thunderous campaign in *The Times*, ministers set seriously to finding a way of striking at the Russians. Since virtually all the army Britain could scrape together was already in Turkey with the French forces, the Baltic was ruled out. A grand campaign to strike at Russia through the Principalities was forbidden by the Austrians. The Caucasus was too remote. Sebastopol, already marked as a feasible target, practically imposed itself for want of anything better. It was alleged to be a vital naval base; but in any case it had to be reduced in order to justify all the fuss and expense. The final decision to go for Sebastopol was taken at a Cabinet dinner given by Russell at Pembroke Lodge in Richmond Park. Argyll gave Gladstone a lift back in his carriage in the 'sweet and calm air of a glorious summer night'. Argyll was scathing on the absence of any realistic purpose in the proceedings. 'Discussion on the objects of the war, without guidance from something like authority, will be taken up by the different parties in a Popular Assembly each bidding against the other in clap-trap sayings.' There were already demands for the liberation of Poland and Finland. Clarendon was keen to drag in 'Italy' as a good cause for the next peace congress, rather like the slave trade at Vienna in 1814–15. Aberdeen was incapable of asserting himself as such an 'authority'. By default Palmerston was allowed to press himself forward. Gladstone made no bid to interpose himself in the spirit of 1853. Argyll made a special point of stressing that Gladstone admitted 'no misgivings' about the decision to go for Sebastopol. 'It was not in the habit of his mind to go back upon decisions once reached. On the contrary, he was always disposed to repel doubts and hesitations, even those which he had felt before. An assured and even passionate advocacy generally took the place of any former hesitations.'[2] As in January 1854, at the time of Palmerston's resignation, Gladstone's overriding concern was to keep the coalition in being as a powerful and successful government. In the circumstances of war his vocation

1 Conacher, *ib.*　　2 Argyll, i, 477.

depended more on the government than the government depended on his vocation. That he was demoralised by the failures of his financial policy in 1854 is also very probable.

For Gladstone it was an especially welcome relief to escape from such painful embarrassments and distasteful problems for a weekend with his new friends the Sutherlands at Cliveden, where he sculled on the Thames – 'the first time for many many years.' At Eton on the Sunday he heard a 'noble sermon' from Bishop Selwyn ('but one to make me deeply ashamed'). That evening Argyll edified the company with readings from Tennyson's *In Memoriam*, which must have stirred many bitter-sweet memories of Eton days with Hallam.[1] Week-ending at Cliveden would become one of Gladstone's most frequent and important modes of social relaxation. Back in London there was the distressing case of one of his private secretaries, Frank Lawley, yet another of Catherine's cousinhood, younger son of Lord Wenlock, Fellow of All Souls, and Peelite M.P. for Beverley, who had been speculating with the funds. According to Stanley, Gladstone and Newcastle 'suffered greatly in public estimation' by attempting to smuggle Lawley out to South Australia as governor 'while under suspicion of violating official confidence for stock jobbing purposes'.[2] Then to Ramsgate and Broadstairs in mid-August for relaxation, with much bathing with the boys. There was a passing scare with an illness of Willy, whom Gladstone was coaching for confirmation. There was an interlude at Osborne at the end of August, with enjoyable conversations with Prince Albert on 'art, metropolis improvements, & finance' (the question of the National Gallery was a particular concern). Then back to Kent, with pleasant excursions to Walmer, Betteshanger, Canterbury, and Sandwich. Gladstone finished *Jane Eyre*, which he judged 'a very remarkable but jarring book'.[3] Even more jarring was Robert Wilberforce's book which caused Gladstone 'very great pain' as the work of 'an overborne and bewildered man',[4] teetering on the brink of submission to Rome. There was no end of leaks in the national coffers to be plugged. Was it true, he asked Sir John Young, the Irish Secretary, that certain of the Queen's Colleges were 'mere establishments of public alms', where students paid only a trifle of their costs and were subsidised by the public bounty? The case of the 'very weak college of Galway' was especially in his mind; if so, 'the case is ugly'. Perhaps, if Cork were any better, there might be an amalgamation ('I imagine Belfast from common fame to be a thriving plant').[5] There were only brief passages in London until the new session commenced in mid-December, one of which was to sit to Mr. Munro for a bust, 'of which I am rather ashamed, but the act is

1 D, iv, 637.   2 DDCP, 126; D, iv, 638.   3 D, iv, 648.
4 G to CG, October 17, 1854. GGP, 28/5. D, iv, 654.
5 G to Young, November 17, 1854. GP, 44529, 180.

not spontaneous'. By the time the sculpture was exhibited at the Royal Academy in 1855 Gladstone was out of office.

The latest chance to end the war by diplomacy faded with the collapse of the Vienna negotiations at the beginning of September. Palmerston, as delighted at diplomatic failure as Aberdeen was despondent, led the pressure for military success. Sebastopol became an urgent objective. Raglan accepted without enthusiasm his orders to capture and reduce it. The season was already late. Newcastle despairingly encouraged him: 'God grant that success may reward you and justify us!'[1] At Hawarden on October 11 Gladstone's 'reading time' was 'absorbed in the wonderful details of the Battle of Alma & its sequel'. Unfortunately one of its sequels was not the one intended: the swift capture of Sebastopol. With the Russians in a state of confusion an improvised dash of less than twenty miles would almost certainly have brought off the *coup*. But Raglan allowed himself to be dissuaded by the dying French commander, Saint-Arnaud, and the golden moment passed, and with it the chance of success that would have rewarded Raglan and justified the government. The lost opportunity was not redeemed by the famous action at Balaklava late in October and by victory at Inkerman in November. The prospect of being bogged down in a siege through the Crimean winter confronted the ill-equipped and scantily-provisioned army and the dismayed government.

Meanwhile, after battling unsuccessfully to dissuade Robert Wilberforce from following his brother Henry into the Roman Church, Gladstone prepared to return from Hawarden to a series of pre-session cabinets which commenced in mid-November and which could hardly fail to be profoundly depressing. He was already sufficiently depressed by guilty introspection as to Catherine's suffering from his 'selfishness'. He wrote on arriving in London:

> You have kindly & generously foregone many things *before* as well as during the days of pressure for money which, according to the usages of society, others would have expected & would have had . . . It is vindicating our own true liberty when we can shake off ourselves some of the artificial wants which modern luxury & self-indulgence have so sadly multiplied in our moderate rank & station of life. I have not believe me been wanting in the feeling of honour that was due to you: but I have said little upon it – from a variety of causes, some of them perhaps sound and reasonable, but I fear not all so: I am afraid the selfishness which is the basis of my character, & the habit of my mind when unchecked by reflection, has been one or even the principal one: & that it makes me take as matter of course what really demanded more

1 Conacher, 454.

of special acknowledgement & praise. I have the more reason to lament this, as it naturally led you to misinterpret my real feelings & I *am* sorry for it. But in truth this is only one among a multitude of daily occasions in which I find myself coming short of my clear & positive duty and failing in *justice* to 'my neighbour' – failures which I persuade myself are in some degree owing to an absorbed preoccupied & overtaxed mind, & which cause me to regard with nothing less than positive horror such an idea as that of ending my life in the tumultuous sphere in which my lot is now cast. I have said all this not because I thought you wanted it but for my own sake rather. I can not forgive you for there [is] nothing to forgive. I am hurried but hope *you* may understand what I have said & supply its defects.[1]

Russell by now was in a frantic state, partly because of well-founded doubts about his colleagues' competence to wage war, partly because of an overweening and quite unjustified confidence in his own capacity to succeed where Aberdeen was failing. His initial manoeuvre was to attempt to bully Aberdeen into replacing Newcastle at the War Office with Palmerston. 'J.R. again!' was Gladstone's eloquent comment.[2] Gladstone's Peelite loyalties blinded him to the strength of Russell's case that extraordinary measures needed to be implemented if the government were to survive. Russell no doubt was completely intolerable as a cabinet colleague; but what he was arguing for – a new drive and energy – was what was needed; and, when the crash came, it was Russell rather than Aberdeen's friends whom the Commons, rightly, preferred to believe. Gladstone chose to direct his exasperation at Lady John as if she were the only motivating force behind Russell's antics. 'We have a little woman to deal with who is of necessity as inevitable as the gates of a certain place: and it is perfectly vain for Lord A. to make concessions to her.'[3] Gladstone had his own exasperating problems: by November it was clear that he could no longer realistically hold to his original plan not to increase indirect taxation; and he gloomily set about framing a scheme for a house tax. 'Contentious questions between the Bank and the Government respectively' were as sharply contested as ever, with depressingly constant 'tourneys' also with Monteagle at the Board of Audit.[4]

By December, having failed to bully Aberdeen, Russell was ready to bolt. At a fraught cabinet on December 4 he announced his intention to resign on the issue of the conduct of the war. He was convinced that Newcastle must be dislodged in Palmerston's favour as a signal to the public of resolution and determination. He made clear also his conviction that he regarded Aberdeen's hebetude 'as the source of evil';[5] and his

1 G to CG, November 11, 1854. GGP, 28/5.
2 D, iv, 662.　　　3 Conacher, 494.
4 G to Hubbard, March 1, 1855. GP, 44530, 33.　　　5 PMP, iii, 150.

tactic, equally clearly, was to terrorise the Cabinet into displacing Aberdeen and yielding the premiership to himself. At an even more fraught cabinet dinner on the 6th he persisted in his intention, but offered to remain on until the Christmas recess. The government thus met parliament with Russell's 'menace' hanging over its head. His dispute with Gladstone over the Kennedy case was now at a new pitch of fraughtness. Gladstone recorded 'a strange & again a childish scene' at a cabinet on December 9.[1] 'Some little heat', he reported to Catherine; J.R. 'rather had to back out'.[2] To Aberdeen on December 17 he 'vented' his 'overflowing disgust at the conduct of Ld J. & the degradation of the Cabinet'.[3] Gladstone's contribution to the defence of the government was to quote Napoleon: 'he who has made war without many errors has not made war long'; which observation, he added, applied also to the 'political portion of the great game of war'. He appealed for credit in the name of Alma and Inkerman: 'You have fought two battles with splendid success . . . you may hope for still greater successes.'[4] Though ministers weathered the storm before the Christmas recess, Aberdeen could no longer disguise from himself the extent to which his personal lack of popularity weakened his government. His formerly faithful ally, Delane of *The Times*, passed over increasingly to a harsh and critical tone, diverting his strictures from the quartermaster's department to the high command in the Crimea. The next logical step would be to turn against the War Office itself. Gladstone himself felt the sting of *The Times*'s strictures. He protested to Delane that 'after so much valuable support' to the government in 'giving effect to their views of financial policy under critical circumstances' it was a shock to find an article asserting 'either directly, or by clear implication' that the 'state of the Exchequer' was 'a cause of the early assembling of Parliament'; and that the measures of war had 'hitherto been governed by a regard to expense'. There was 'no foundation whatever', Gladstone insisted, for such suppositions.[5] To his consternation Gladstone found himself under attack as having '"starved" the Crimean War'; an issue about which he was still acutely sensitive in 1859.[6]

By December 23 Newcastle had started to get seriously rattled by dire reports of the general collapse of the system for provisioning and equipping the army in the Crimea. Raglan, always excessively unforthcoming with information, relapsed into a kind of stoic paralysis, overwhelmed by the dimensions of the administrative breakdown. While his colleagues retreated for their Christmases, Newcastle was left in Pall

1 D, iv, 666.   2 G to CG, December 9, 1854, 28/5.
3 D, iv, 667–8.   4 H, cxxxvi, 233, 237.
5 G to Delane, November 28, 1854. GP, 44529, 182–83.
6 G to Griswell, June 24, 1859. GP, 44530, 38.

Mall desperately struggling to restore the situation. Military drafts for the Crimea could no longer be filled, and it was decided to hire mercenaries. Gladstone had much ado explaining to the indignant Robertson the necessity of 'recourse to foreign soldiers'.[1] For his own part, Gladstone assured the Master of Pembroke that the charge that the problems of the army were due to financial economy was 'foolish' and 'cruelly unjust to the people of England'.[2] In such circumstances he was tremendously relieved to get back to Hawarden, the more so as Willy was to receive his first communion. He assuaged his pent-up feelings by arranging his new bookshelves and books. He noted on Christmas day: 'As for me I was troubled during the morning about my feud in the Cabinet: brute passions were in my mind with the thought of the newborn Christ . . . but at the Altar the Son of God came to me and bid them be still.'[3] He told Aberdeen on New Year's Day that he had reached his *'ultima Thule* in concession' on the Kennedy affair.[4] But the dispute took for Gladstone a much nastier turn a few days later when a move was announced for a Select Committee of the Commons to look into it. Gladstone was outraged, his executive hackles instantly on the rise. 'We must look,' he instructed one of his Treasury subordinates, 'to the principle of aggression on the Executive power involved in the appointment of this Committee.' What were the precedents for investigations of dismissals of civil servants by their official and responsible superiors?[5]

The 'little piddling war with Johnny' continued when cabinets resumed on January 9, 1855. Russell hung on to office in order to out-bluff Aberdeen. Gladstone was anxious to force a 'rupture with Lord John, be the consequences what they may'.[6] Aberdeen thought, rightly, that his judgment was warped by the Kennedy feud. But soon Gladstone's awareness of the weight of the avalanche moving against the government began, belatedly, to restore some perspective to his outlook. When he dined with the Trevelyans on January 16 Macaulay recorded that 'nothing could be more lamentable than his account of affairs in the Crimea'.[7] Newcastle came to the conclusion on January 22, the eve of the new session, that he must sacrifice himself for the sake of the government. When parliament met on the 23rd, Roebuck, the Radical Member for Sheffield, gave notice of a motion for a committee of inquiry into the conduct of the war.

This was the signal for Russell to remove himself as expeditiously as possible from the target area. He resigned on the ground that he could not conscientiously oppose Roebuck's motion. This called the coalition into

1 G to Robertson G, December 30, 1854. *Ib.*, 5.
2 G to Jeune, February 14, 1855. *Ib.*, 25.   3 D, iv, 669.
4 G to Aberdeen, January 1, 1855. *Ib.*, 5.
5 G to Wilson, January 4, 1855. *Ib.*, 7.
6 Conacher, 532.   7 Trevelyan, *Macaulay*, 309.

question. Gladstone later indulged in speculative hindsight as to the coalition possibly becoming a 'real & final amalgamation'; but 'the mortar still being wet, Lord John Russell's powder magazine blew the whole fabric into the air'.[1] He insisted that, apart from the 'uneasiness' created by Russell, 'there never was a more complete success than that of the late Cabinet in its internal relations generally', and that the 'prevailing harmony' was much as in the case of Peel's ministry. 'On NO single occasion did it ever happen that in any difference of opinion it could be traced to who was Whig or who was not Whig.'[2] This was unconvincing special pleading; a papering-over of a fault-line of a sufficiently defined nature. Aberdeen and the Peelites were for staying on; the Whigs, other than Palmerston, for following Russell's example. Newcastle, upstaged by both Roebuck and Russell, offered himself as a ritual sacrifice to appease public anger. Palmerston agreed to replace him, with the Leadership of the Commons; but such manoeuvres were by now hopelessly overtaken by events. Gladstone glowed with Peelite resentment against the Whigs and Russell in particular; and Roebuck's move for an inquiry he saw as a larger but not more outrageous version of 'aggression on the Executive power' which already threatened him on the Kennedy case. He was indignant at Whig moves to drop Newcastle altogether rather than reallocating him; and, when Clarendon floated the notion that Russell could return if Newcastle went, Gladstone denounced it as 'quite out of the question: and the idea fell stillborn'. His animus against Russell was such that he insisted that there should be no announcement in terms that the Cabinet resigned because Lord John had resigned: 'We resigned as a body because some of us thought it necessary to resign on account of his resignation, and the rest of the Cabinet could not remain without this portion of their colleagues.' The Queen, almost as furious against Russell as was Gladstone, urged reconsideration; and to Gladstone's relief the Whigs agreed to stay on 'instead of flying from Roebuck's motion'. The Cabinet would remain in being and place itself manfully at the mercy of the House of Commons.[3]

Russell's exculpatory speech on January 26, Gladstone had to confess, 'carried the House with him as Herbert observed while he was speaking'. Gladstone conceded that it was 'tempered with some grains of policy' as well as 'a contemplation of another possible premiership'. Palmerston's reply was 'wretched'. Wood groaned: 'And this is to be our leader!' When Palmerston sat down Gladstone could hardly restrain himself from asking, 'Can anything more be said?' On top of everything else, Gladstone found himself having to be polite to Lady John in the ladies'

1 D, v, 210.
2 G to Milnes, February 12, 1855. GP, 44530, 23.
3 PMP, iii, 153–155.

gallery, but made his sentiments plain enough by telling her that Lord John's speech had been 'very kind but that I did not agree in his mode of viewing or putting the facts'.[1] Gladstone had his chance in the debate on the 29th to make this point publicly. He defended Newcastle and Raglan and vindicated the government's policy. He reserved his particular virulence for the proposed committee of inquiry, condemning it as an illegitimate invasion by parliament of the executive sphere, likely to be subversive of the effectiveness of the army in the field and offensive to the French. Were the motion to be carried, his 'last words as a member of the cabinet of Lord Aberdeen' must be 'words of solemn and earnest protest against a proceeding which has no foundation either in the constitution or in the practice of preceding parliaments, which is useless and mischievous for the purpose which it appears to contemplate, and which . . . is full of danger to the power, dignity, and usefulness of the Commons of England'.[2] What Gladstone really meant was that he regarded the committee as 'placing in the hands of a small number of Members of Parliament duties which appertain essentially to the executive government', and that no government submitting to such a proceeding 'ever can or ever ought to enjoy the respect of Parliament'.[3] Stanley noted that, though Gladstone delivered a 'very powerful, ingenious harangue', it was 'but coldly received'.[4] Gladstone spoke as an *étatist*, a defender of executive privilege; but he spoke also as a man to all appearances blatantly defending his own interests and his own reputation; and the Commons of England sufficiently answered him on both counts by carrying Roebuck's motion by 304 to 148.

[12]

Aberdeen's Cabinet met for the last time on January 30 and exchanged 'friendly adieus'. As Aberdeen proceeded to Windsor under doleful winter skies Gladstone recorded 'a day of personal lightheartedness: but the problem for the nation is no small one'.[5] The Queen sent for Derby; who proposed that Palmerston, Gladstone and Herbert should join him. Palmerston, as emissary, approached Gladstone in a rather languid way. Gladstone put up a handy Peelite obstacle by demanding whether Graham was to be included. He also insisted on retaining the Exchequer, which, as Stanley remarked, 'Disraeli could not in honour or consistency surrender'.[6] Palmerston in fact was merely manoeuvring Derby out of the way to make his own path clear. In any case, as Derby soon came to

1 D, v, 210.   2 H, cxxxvi, 1180, 1205–6.   3 PMP, iii, 180.
4 DDCP, 129.   5 D, v, 9.   6 DDCP, 131.

realise, by now Gladstone's distaste for the Conservative party was as nothing to the Conservative party's distaste for Gladstone. Derby estimated that had he included Gladstone in a government he would have lost 50 or 60 votes, 'such is the intensity of feeling among the best of my supporters against him'. Gladstone's refusal saved Derby from 'imminent risk of a great disaster'.[1] Gladstone meanwhile had the pleasure of assuring Palmerston that if *he*, Palmerston, were to form a government it 'could not have any reasonable prospect of stable parliamentary support'. Gladstone's wish was very much father to that thought; for he still hoped that a blocking of all alternative avenues would lead to Aberdeen's being recalled. Perhaps it was with a premonition that Palmerston was now to be the great enemy that Gladstone on February 1 offered his hand to Disraeli 'which was very kindly accepted'. Despite Herbert's arguments for joining a Derby government as the best prospect for making peace, Gladstone insisted that he would not move without Aberdeen's approval, nor would he separate from Graham, and if the Peelites joined they must join 'in force'. In any case Palmerston declined Derby's proposal and that was the end of any chance of a Derby ministry. Herbert and Gladstone thereupon set off for dinner at Grillion's, 'where we had a small but merry party, Herbert even beyond himself amusing'.[2]

Gladstone's official inclinations were for a Derby-Peelite combination or a homogeneous Whig ministry under Lansdowne. But when Lansdowne on February 2 was in a position when much might have been made of him Gladstone let the chance slip. Lansdowne asked Gladstone whether he would serve under him as Chancellor of the Exchequer; if Gladstone declined Lansdowne indicated that there would be little point in his persisting in his effort to fulfil the Queen's request to form a ministry. Gladstone 'declined at once and positively'. The coalition under Lord Aberdeen, he told Lansdowne, had worked to his 'entire satisfaction', but he was 'indisposed to partake in it under any other form'. Having thus committed himself so far to gain Gladstone, Lansdowne was 'naturally vexed, but he did not enter into particulars and remained carefully reticent'.[3] He might have done well to relax his reticence as to Gladstone's complacent delusions that Palmerston had no chance of a majority. Gladstone later confessed that his motives were not easy to analyse. The best he could offer was the rationale that, while perfectly satisfied to be in a 'Peelite government which had Whigs or Radicals in it, I was not ready to be in a Whig government which had Peelites in it'.[4] Which indeed was an eloquent commentary on the Peelites' view of their

1 J.R. Jones, 'The Conservatives and Gladstone in 1855', EHR, lxxvii (1962), 95–98. DDCP, 132–33.
2 PMP, iii, 156–7.   3 *Ib.*, i, 131.   4 *Ib.*, 249.

role in the coalition. Gladstone called on Aberdeen to get his blessing to join a Derby ministry if necessary. Russell was announced at half-past two and 'sat till three – his hat shaking in his hand'. The Queen was reduced to the extremity of asking him to explore the possibilities, and he asked Gladstone to stay on with him. Gladstone responded that the old coalition under Aberdeen would be better than any new one; the Peelite position under Russell would be 'false'. Charitably, Gladstone 'did not enter on the question whether particular objections applied to him'. Upon the whole, not surprisingly, Russell's tone was 'low and doubtful'; and he departed '*re infecta*'.[1]

Nevertheless, despite much talk of a Lansdowne cabinet, the prospect began to take shape of Palmerston as first minister. A dismaying notion began to seep into Gladstone's mind that he was witnessing the ultimate and degrading logical consequences of Peel's destruction of the old party system. Russell's negative capacities for damage thus let loose were bad enough. But what of Palmerston's positive powers for evil? Gladstone conferred anxiously with Graham on February 4. Herbert joined them with the news that Palmerston now had the Queen's commission. Gladstone was convinced still that Palmerston could have no parliamentary majority; that he would cause alarm abroad; that he was 'not fit for the duties of the office of Prime Minister'; and Aberdeen had not been condemned and excluded, and might, others having failed, go on. It was Herbert's duty to try to instil some sense into Gladstone's head. Aberdeen was entirely discredited and out of the question. Palmerston had a very good chance of a majority. If the Peelites refused to join him they would look 'too nice'. Herbert in any case was willing to go in. Gladstone remained fertile with obstinate delusions. Aberdeen was the 'fittest man to be minister', while 'Lord Palmerston is in no way equal to the duties which fall upon a Prime Minister'. If the vote of the 29th did condemn and exclude Aberdeen, it did so because he stood for peace, which Gladstone stood for also. A Palmerston government with Derby and Russell aloof would be but a new coalition liable to all the frailties of the old. Confidence abroad would be seriously shaken. And, as to financial prospects, 'maintaining such a financial policy as I think requisite' would be a very doubtful business.[2] It was this obstinacy which blinded Gladstone to the Lansdowne alternative. It would not be long before he rued this as the greatest blunder of his career. In 1896 he described his refusal of Lansdowne's proposal on February 2 as 'one of the most important as well as least pardonable errors of my political life'.[3] But it is unlikely that Gladstone's adhesion to Lansdowne could have stemmed the tide running for Palmerston. The lesson learned slowly and painfully by Gladstone over the next four years was that Palmerston was

1 *Ib.*, iii, 161–63.   2 *Ib.*, 167–8.   3 *Ib.*, i, 131.

the one principal political figure who commanded anything like wide public confidence.

Palmerston saw Gladstone on the night of the 4th ('a rather sad Sunday!').[1] He broke the news that there was 'no other government in view'. Lansdowne had promised to join. He wanted Gladstone to stay on. Gladstone went to Aberdeen again to get his blessing, at 11.30 p.m. Aberdeen urged Gladstone to swallow his objections and bow to the power of public opinion. Gladstone retired morosely to bed at 3 a.m., oppressed by the thought of the 'irksome and painful' task ahead of having to brace himself to go with Palmerston. On February 5, however, the Peelites conferred and, mainly at Gladstone's instigation and despite Aberdeen's promptings, sent Palmerston their refusal. They baulked at going in while Aberdeen insisted on staying out. However, a meeting of the Peelites outside the cabinet condemned this course. Aberdeen finally undertook to extract from Palmerston a statement about foreign policy which would enable him to declare his confidence in the new ministry. Gladstone proclaimed himself 'ready to make the sacrifice of personal feeling', ready to see Aberdeen expelled by 'a censure equally applicable to myself, and yet to remain in my office', ready to 'overlook not merely the inferior fitness but the real and manifest unfitness of Palmerston for that office', ready to enter on a venture with him without any reasonable prospect of parliamentary support 'upon the one sole and all-embracing ground that the prosecution of the war with vigour and the prosecution of it to and for peace was now the question of the day to which every other must give way'.[2] He flinched before disapproving Peelite colleagues – notably the stricken Newcastle. Granville was 'sorry beyond expression: he almost looked displeased which for him is much'. (But Granville himself came in anyway as Lord President.) 'The truth is', Gladstone concluded, 'the world is drunk about a Palmerston government: and if we humour it in its drunkenness it will rightly refuse to admit the excuse when restored to soberness it condemns what we have done.' One 'most noble victim' had been struck down', and we were 'set to feast over the remains'. 'The thing is bad and the mode worse.' It was something to manage to persuade Graham to join. Gladstone was determined that the 'moral union and association' with Aberdeen must continue and be publicly known to continue. After dealing distractedly with domestic exigencies – 'a great event with us': a new butler – he swallowed his nasty pill on February 6 and sourly accepted Palmerston's invitation; and set this off with a pathetic scene of final parting from Aberdeen, the noble victim sacrificed for his 'wisdom and virtue'.[3]

Palmerston's ministry was the old coalition less Aberdeen, Newcastle and Russell, who was shunted off to the Vienna Conference of the powers

1 D, v, 14.   2 PMP, iii, 173–4.   3 *Ib.*

(where he botched his part in the negotiations memorably). Urged on by Panizzi, Gladstone did not neglect the opportunity to plead with Russell that if 'Italian questions' arose 'your humanity as well as your love of freedom' would be exerted on behalf of the unhappy prisoners in Naples.[1] Otherwise, in a thoroughly sulky humour, he took care to find fault with everything. On the first day in the Commons, on February 7, he did not think 'appearances over favourable'.[2] He characterised Palmerston's first cabinet on the 8th as 'acephalous'; which naturally did not 'relieve the gloom' of his impressions. There was feeble talk of striking a deal whereby the Commons were to give up their Roebuck committee while ministers in their turn would undertake an investigation under the authority of the Crown. Should Raglan be recalled? Palmerston 'tossed among us' this notion, 'without any clear broad or strong views of his own, as if for what chance might bring'.[3] How very different from the masterful ways of Sir Robert!

At a further cabinet on February 17 Palmerston had to report glumly that the Commons were clearly set on having their inquiry. The backbenchers were naturally determined to maintain their unwonted advantage over the arrogant Treasury bench. Gladstone, its most arrogant occupant, 'went so far as to say that if the inquiry into the state of the army were allowed by this government it neither could nor ought to enjoy a week's credit or authority in the House of Commons and intimated that I could not see any way to this concession under any circumstance'.[4] The simple lesson of the vote of January 29 had not penetrated Gladstone's consciousness, so frenzied were his feelings. Much of the earlier instability and sense of displacement had recurred. The Queen and the Prince sensibly urged submission. At a cabinet on the 20th there was a majority decision, equally sensible, that a determined 'House of Commons could not be opposed and to resign after a fortnight in office would reduce ministers to a laughing stock. Gladstone's frenzy conversely intensified. Behind and inside it was much more than his constitutional objections to unwarrantable invasion of executive prerogatives, his objections as to relations with France, as to the duty to support those in command in the field, as to the discipline and obedience of the army, as to the 'onesided' partiality of such an inquiry. There was a welling bitterness about the treatment of Aberdeen. Above all there was an awareness that his financial programme of 1854, as subsuming the crucial landmark budget of 1853, was now bankrupt. To carry on would mean confessing failure. Doing that in 1845 had been painful enough. A second confession would be unbearable. There was a special and personal appropriateness in the urgency of Gladstone's

1 G to Russell, February 14, 1855, GP, 44530, 26.
2 PMP, iii, 175.   3 *Ib.*,176–7.   4 *Ib.*, 179.

pressing upon Granville the necessity of appointing a national 'day of Humiliation'.[1]

Argyll recorded that the cabinet of February 20 was his only experience of witnessing Gladstone directing at him 'for a moment some considerable irritation'.[2] The implication of Gladstone's position was that the executive should call the bluff of the Commons by threatening, in effect, to strike. His point was valid that parliament would not inflict Roebuck's committee on a government in which it had confidence. But that did not help the fact that it was not the fault of parliament if there was not a government in which it could easily repose confidence. Gladstone was speaking the constitutional language of a most severely old-fashioned type, as if still in a political world when governments made Houses of Commons, and not the other way around. Along with Herbert and Graham, and despite entreaties from Prince Albert, Gladstone resigned on February 21.[3] He was with difficulty dissuaded by his two Peelite colleagues from proposing a counter-motion of resolutions preserving the integrity of executive government from illegitimate usurpation. They pointed out, crushingly, that smallness of support would expose the cause to ridicule. Gladstone's explanatory speech on the 23rd dwelt pathetically on the fate of the 'trusted', 'admired', 'eulogized' colleague of Sir Robert Peel, Lord Aberdeen, 'a man who has been much misunderstood', 'dismissed by a blow darkly aimed'. He denied passionately that he was a 'deserter'; the government, in submitting to an invasion by the legislature, had made a 'fatal choice'.[4] Yet the awkward fact remained that Gladstone was receding from his earlier position that the great issue of the war and the peace took precedence of 'every other' question. The clue to this blatantly unresolved contradiction is almost certainly Gladstone's despair over financial policy and the collapse of his vocation. His sense of proportion, never very secure at the best of times, evaporated in the intense heat of his fanatical insistence that the political crisis had been subsumed and thereby somehow cancelled by the constitutional monstrosity of the Roebuck committee. 'My belief is that by our resignations we have dealt the best blow in our power ... at the most dangerous measure of the present day.'[5] 'However tainted we may be, I aver with confidence that we have resigned our offices in resistance to the most revolutionary proceeding of this our day.'[6] Gladstone would

1 G to Granville, February 12, 1855. GP, 44530, 23.
2 Argyll, i, 537.
3 Robertson Gladstone to G, May 12, 1855: 'It does not appear, admitting you had some cause, you were fully justified in going out of office ... Administrative Reform will become the order of the day, or it will end in a general clearance of the aristocratic class, *unless they* qualify themselves elsewhere than at the Universities.' GP, 56445.
4 H, cxxxvi, 1823–1841.
5 G to W. James, February 23, 1855. GP, 44530, 30.
6 G to C. Marriot, February 27, 1855. *Ib.*, 32.

find that his 'taint' – especially the accusation that he had 'starved' the war – was not so easily washed away.

Cardwell displayed a touching Peelite loyalty by declining Palmerston's offer of promotion from the Board of Trade. On the 25th Gladstone handed over at the Treasury to Cornewall Lewis, assuring him of all aid and support: 'He might command me precisely as if instead of resigning I had only removed to another department.'[1] On the 28th Gladstone handed back his seals of office at the Palace, discoursing on the demoralised state of politics, and on the consoling fact that the Throne had for a long time been gaining in stability. As for the Palmerston government, it was also no doubt in some sense a consolation to be able to assure Prince Albert, with some asperity, that it would 'not last a twelvemonth'.[2]

1 PMP, iii, 189.   2 *Ib.*, 190–92.

CHAPTER VI

'WHAT CONNECTIONS CAN BE FORMED WITH PUBLIC APPROVAL': 1855—1859

[1]

During the next six weeks Gladstone nursed his bile by occupying himself largely with his splenetic and unpublishable 'Party as it was and as it is'. The fifty densely-wrought manuscript sheets of this 'sketch' of political events from 1835 to 1855 elaborated the sombre assurance with which he had taken his leave of the Queen and Prince Albert: that the Court would find 'little peace or comfort' until 'Parliament should have returned to its old organisation in two political parties: that at present we were in a false position, and that both sides of the House were demoralised'.[1]

In this piece Gladstone compounded a fundamental misreading of the future by concocting a wilfully misread interpretation of the past. Politics in fact were about to enter into a decade of comparative stability which would, at its end, be celebrated by Walter Bagehot in his *The English Constitution* as a golden era of repose, threatened by the onset of turmoils and strifes, fomented by Gladstone himself more than anyone else. There was a sense, indeed, in which Gladstone, within even a few years, would have accepted some validity in a view such as Bagehot's: for stability in the sense of a stable parliamentary base for government was but one half of the case. Gladstone's painfully and reluctantly gained and yet more painfully and reluctantly postponed vocational mission required the restoration of what he saw as the essential greatness of Peel's ministry: a government enabled by a stable parliamentary base to be dynamic, innovative, wielding mighty powers to mighty effect. Gladstone's deepest complaint about the prospect he viewed in 1855 was not so much about instability in itself, but rather the extent to which, in the hands of Palmerston and his cronies, instability would be concomitant with negation and sterility in domestic policy, and, in all probability, with yet more recklessness and bluster in foreign affairs. His reading of Palmerston's ministry was that it would be weak and incompetent. As to army reform he informed Dr. Jeune of Pembroke: 'Lord Palmerston has wonderful favour and acceptance', but Gladstone could not see 'a

1 PMP, iii, 190.

Government with such strength as may be necessary to deal with that question'.[1] By the same token, such a government could not cope with war. 'Politically the future is quite dark,' he told Northcote: 'but in one way or other Parliament must get back to its old *binary* organization and probably some question of peace and war will impart the initiatory movement.'[2]

There was, accordingly, a very strong element discernible in Gladstone at this moment of a peculiarly Peelite resentment at disinheritance. To the *étatist* predispositions of 1853 was now joined the executive arrogance of 1855. As Peel's kind of government was the finest possible kind of government to be had in the circumstances of England in the mid-nineteenth century, so the peculiar guardians of Peel's faith were the finest possible executors of the obligations and duties which its capacities imposed upon government. A system of politics which militated against the Peelites was thus *ipso facto* morally reprobate; for a Peelite was, Gladstone confidently asserted, so much superior in quality, so 'much above *par* as a member of Parliament'[3], 'not a dandy or a coxcomb among them'.[4] Resentment at disinheritance and Peelite arrogance required Gladstone in 1855 to invent the fiction that in the decade prior to 1845 the 'normal state' of 'party connection' had been in 'full and brilliant blossom'. In those years, formed in the 'great Epoch of the Reform Bill', 'great works' had been achieved by both the Melbourne government and by 'that grand political combination' of which Peel was the 'centre and mainstay'. 'Since then we have had properly speaking no parties; that is none in the best sense of the term; none compact and organised after the ancient manner.' The fictional character of Gladstone's notions is perhaps best conveyed by his insistence that 'the session of 1845 closed like the calmest of summer sunsets without a whisper in the air or a spot upon the sky'.[5]

Tendentiousness of such breathtaking quality was perhaps the only effective means of sustaining Gladstone's purpose in not allowing that Peel's party had been in its way as 'bedevilled by faction' as Russell's was. Gladstone's explanation of the 'downward course' of politics thus had to be couched in melodramatically unconvincing personal terms. 'On the horizon a cloud, though no bigger than a man's hand', emerged. 'Mr. Benjamin Disraeli came out from the ranks, in 1842', restless with 'political disappointment'. (So much for the unspotted sky of 1845.) Then there was Lord Stanley's strange and inexplicable and sudden change of attitude over repealing the Corn Law. Above all, of course, the giant

1 G to Jeune, February 14, 1855. GP, 44530, 25.
2 G to Northcote, March 5, 1855. *Ib.*, 36.
3 GP, 44745, 209.   4 Vincent, xxi.
5 GP, *ib.*, 173, 177–8, 182.

figure of Peel, showing 'too much of the front of Pride', pulling down the Temple of 'strict party order and organization' like another Samson Agonistes. Peel's role indeed was 'perhaps even a determining influence over the present positions of leading men, and the actual forms and relations of party'. The 'spirit of wrath' presiding over the debates of 1846 was exacerbated by the 'lofty name and the political reputation of Lord Stanley, the hard conscientious obstinacy of Lord George Bentinck, the subtle self-seeking which History will probably impute to Mr. Disraeli, and on the part of Sir Robert Peel something like the proud indifference of a wounded spirit to spend labour in soothing passion and conciliating support.' On top of that, Peel's conduct from 1846 to 1850 'was a mistake'. If he did not 'deceive' the House with his 'systematic support' for Russell, he 'misled' it. Peel was blameable in Gladstone's eyes for not fighting to recover the soul of the Conservative party. More: his 'great and massive figure' stood in the way of the obvious alternative course. Why did he not advise his followers to join the 'Whig or rather Liberal' party? Why did he leave his particular friends and followers as 'superfluous baggage of the world', 'very inconvenient and even dangerous personages'? This slightly absurd catalogue of complaint, invoking Peel to account for the consequences of Gladstone's own fanaticism as the self-appointed watchdog and keeper of the purity of the Peelite faith, mounts to a crescendo of pathos: 'Why did he leave them hanging between earth and heaven, between wind and water?' 'Did he mean them to be eternally divorced from their old friends and eternally prohibited from making new? Did he contemplate the dying out of a party connection altogether and the substitution of philosophical for Parliamentary Government?'[1]

Was Gladstone seriously blaming Peel for his predicament? Or merely conferring upon his own sense of inadequacy and frustration and inability to move decisively in either direction a spurious dignity it could not otherwise have claimed?

The great characteristic of the obliteration of the old dividing lines of party, according to Gladstone, was a 'singular state of things', in which 'political differences no longer lie between parties but within parties. The most Conservative Liberal and the most Liberal Conservative not only are near one another; but probably the one of these two persons (and each of them represents a class) who retains the Conservative designation is for any practical purpose, though his traditions and associations are the other way, the more liberal of the two.' The Peelites, Gladstone pointed out, were 'more with strong or advanced Liberals on Public Economy and Colonial Policy than with Whigs. There was some cause for gratification in that the parties now stood much nearer; yet Gladstone much regretted the passing of a party system 'highly salutary in its general character both

1 *Ib.*, 188, 184, 190, 217, 194.

moral and political' by means of a discipline which ennobled public life by mutual confidence and obligation and guarded against the temptation to seek the applause of opponents. Gladstone looked apprehensively to the future: 'To resist popular pressure there must be some firmness of texture in the resisting body'; and this is the 'tissue of political party', depending upon 'reciprocal sympathies, upon the confidence of man in man, and above all of parties in leaders'. Now, one party in the House of Commons is 'too weak for its work, and the other has its strength so ill-adapted that it is neutralised by inward disorder'. The Russell government, 'half-smitten with feebleness from the beginning', had become the type of the new dispensation; with the egregious Palmerston as its 'great illustration'.[1]

It took long for Gladstone's bile to subside. (He eventually published a comparatively polite version of his effusion in the *Quarterly* for October 1856 as 'The Declining Efficiency of Parliament'.) Nor did an incident of family distress help: a first cousin, W.T. Goalen, confidential employee of a railway company, was imprisoned for embezzlement. Gladstone made himself the medium of two petitions to Home Secretaries (Grey in 1855 and Lewis in 1859) for commutation of sentence.[2] Meanwhile his detestation of the 'great illustration', the great profiteer from disaster, grew no less. 'I greatly felt being turned out of office,' he later explained to Bishop Wilberforce, 'I saw great things to do. I longed to do them. I am losing the best years of my life out of my natural service . . .'[3] Argyll, visiting Gladstone at Hawarden in 1855, was disturbed at evidences of frustration and violent impulses under uncertain control. 'I saw how unsafe was his judgment'; which Argyll connected with his observation that Gladstone was 'too destructive' in the management of woodlands 'partly due to his eagerness in the personal handling of the axe'.[4] At Cliveden Gladstone grumbled that nowhere had Palmerston 'that peculiar guiding influence' which his experience of Peel had taught him 'to associate with the idea of premiership', and which was 'not wholly lacking in Lord Aberdeen'.[5] 'Puss' Granville, with that instinct for soothing tact which would make him Gladstone's favourite confidant, confided: 'I think you are well out of it.' Granville added the even more grateful assurance that he had 'always anticipated that Palmerston would die with a great fame *unless* he came to lead the House of Commons or to be a Prime Minister'.[6] Sustained by such comforting delusions, Gladstone grimly confronted the thankless life of exile. 'I have been deeply interested in the business of my office,' he told Brougham; 'but now that we are out I rather feel myself in the way except as to finance and I

1 *Ib.*, 199, 200, 215, 188.   2 GP, 44530, 32, 101.
3 *Wilberforce*, ii, 349.   4 Argyll, ii, 2.
5 PMP, iii, 192.   6 *Ib.*, 193.

propose to keep myself as little in politics at present as I can well contrive.'[1]

It was not in fact likely that Gladstone could so contrive to restrain himself. Nor, though 'well out of it', was Gladstone silent in the House. He had some renown to keep polished; and some credit to restore. He gave notice on March 19 of his determination 'completely to set free the press', whether cheap or dear, from the taxation which inhibited 'the handling of public events and news of all kinds, and to apply to this subject those principles of free commerce which have been extended with such efficacy to the general mercantile transactions of the country'.[2] He assisted the passage of the Newspaper Duties Bill in association with Cobden and Milner Gibson, two representatives of the pressure group for Promoting the Repeal of the Taxes on Knowledge, and two Radical enemies of *The Times*. The old flat rate stamp duty had given *The Times* an advantage over its rivals; now the new system of postage rates by weight helped smaller papers, and became the charter of a new Radical and provincial press. For many years to come Gladstone would suffer the weight of *The Times*'s displeasure. Moreover, the newspaper issue put into more prominence the concomitant question of repealing the paper duties, which had been on Gladstone's agenda since 1853. He was accordingly alert also on the issue of possible backsliding on tariffs: 'the grand and main object of Parliament' had been 'to destroy protective duties'.[3] He was severely critical of the Customs Duties Bill for letting in the 'thin end of the wedge of protection'; and he was hostile to further additions to the wine duty ('already the scandal of our tariff') when tea, coffee, and sugar were better able to bear necessary burdens. He was still singing his old song about the evils of a loan policy. The 'funding system' was a 'misfortune and a curse to mankind', mortgaging industry and encouraging resort to war.[4] He was stout also in defending executive government from the criticisms of the Administrative Reform movement, an aggressively bourgeois pressure group dedicated to the proposition that the war could not be brought to a satisfactory conclusion unless policy and its implementation were wrested from the grasp of an incompetent aristocracy. Gladstone eloquently repelled attempts to pin the blame for administrative deficiencies on the aristocratic class, recruited as it was 'from among the very best of the people', whose record was written 'in the most glorious pages of the history of the country'. He was all in favour of merit, as his advocacy for Civil Service reform amply testified; and he could also testify that the Aberdeen Cabinet, than which 'no Cabinet could have been more aristocratically composed', conceived and matured the plan to surrender patronage in Civil Service recruiting;

1 G to Brougham, March 2, 1855. GP, 44530, 34.
2 H, cxxxvii, 794.   3 *Ib.*, 1898.   4 *Ib.*, 1801–03.

and Gladstone offered his testimony as bearing more weight in that he was the only one of the fifteen noblemen and gentlemen who composed it who would not fairly be said to belong to the aristocracy. Considering the obstacles put in his way when Gladstone pressed his case for reform, this was more than a little disingenuous. But doubtless Gladstone was on firmer ground when he insisted that the essential problem of the Civil Service lay not with the aristocracy but in the inferior quality of its lower and middle ranks.[1]

Defence of the Divine Law obliged Gladstone to offer vehement resistance to the Marriage Law Amendment Bill, which would, among other things, have permitted marriage to a deceased wife's sister. Gladstone, fearing the opening of a 'floodgate which no earthly power can shut', took pains to correct widespread misapprehensions in the Commons as to the true interpretation of the 18th verse of the 18th chapter of the Book of Leviticus.[2] It was appropriate that a degree of polite contact should have been re-established with Hope. Gladstone dined with Lady Hope in March to meet 'Jim' ('Not as in other days!').[3] More memories of the old vocation crowded in on him when a little later he occupied himself in arranging his correspondence files. 'In selecting Manning's through the long years of our intercourse I again go through that sad experience.'[4] The years since 1851 – the 'saddest year' – had seen much of Gladstone's religious turmoil subside. Moreover, the apparatus of the 'Engagement', which was so important in sustaining him in the fraught and delicate process of abandoning his State and Church programme while yet staying in politics, now ceased to figure in his life. Gladstone was now a hardened political specimen. When he needed resource from political distress he turned to religion in the guise of classical studies.[5]

[2]

Displaced once more, destabilised and restless, Gladstone found relief in these years in venting himself also in the higher journalism. He was, of course, no stranger to dealings with the major periodicals. Since 1843 some fourteen items could be credited to him. But he seems to have felt the need now for a medium through which he could express his sense of the political process in a manner less inhibited than parliamentary convention (or, for that matter, parliamentary recesses) allowed to a resigned minister and privy councillor. Under the cover of anonymity he

1 *Ib.*, cxxxviii, 2099–2106, 139, 728.   2 *Ib.*, 270–71.
3 D, v, 36.   4 *Ib.*, 57.   5 Matthew, D, v, lviii-ix.

could give his feelings of frustration and outrage something nearer their true value. In the Rev. Whitwell Elwin, Rector of Booton since 1849 and Lockhart's successor as editor of the *Quarterly Review* since 1853, he found a ready and willing collaborator. The 'Party as it was' piece was a false step; but it set the general tone and manner accurately enough. Gladstone's anonymity soon proved to be merely formal. Aberdeen warned him that it would be well to proceed 'with the prospect of discovery, for the secret cannot be perfectly kept'. Aberdeen illustrated his warning with the testimony of a local Aberdeenshire squire, who offered no better authority for his confident statements as to Gladstone's authorship than that 'everybody said so'. And, if squires in remote Aberdeenshire were in on the secret, it was prudent to assume that effectually it was no secret at all.[1] Gladstone inaugurated this new phase of aggressive journalism with an article on 'Sardinia and Rome' in the *Quarterly* for June 1855, an account of the resistance being offered by the Vatican to legislation designed to reduce the temporal powers of the Roman Church in the Piedmontese State. It was characteristic that Gladstone should revert to an Italian theme by way of a fulmination against popery. (He enjoyed 'three hours in close conversation with Montalembert whom I was so happy as to have for a fellow traveller' in the train from Oxford, where the French Catholic luminary had received the degree of D.C.L.) Of more moment, in view of the crucial part the Italian question would play in influencing the course of his political development towards the resolution of 1859, was Gladstone's avowal that the 'doom of the Pope's temporal power is in all appearance sealed' and that in its example of 'tempered liberty', avoiding either absolutism or anarchy, the Turin government offered a model to Italy and thus made Piedmont's position and policy 'pregnant ... with important results'.[2]

There was, still, the war. The only aspect of it at all tending to mitigate Gladstone's distress was Piedmont's intervention on the side of France and Britain. The issue of the military convention with the Kingdom of Sardinia in March 1855 produced from Gladstone another important statement as to Piedmont's special claims to sympathy and respect as a country that, 'amidst difficulties almost unprecedented, has succeeded in establishing for herself the blessings of a free government'.[3] His old anti-Romanism, now excited anew by such manifestations of the Vatican's post-revolutionary ultramontane reaction as the Austrian concordat and the promulgation of the dogma of the Immaculate Conception of the Virgin, merged with the implications he had unwittingly set in train at Naples. Ever since the Neapolitan affair Gladstone had been marked by the *Risorgimentisti* as a promising object of attention and cultivation.

1 Aberdeen to G, December 11, 1856. GP, 43701, 343.
2 QR, xcvii, 41–70.   3 H, cxxxvii, 1086.

Antonio Panizzi at the British Museum and Giacomo Lacaita, now professor of Italian at Queen's College, London, were their invaluable links. The Farini translation added immensely to Gladstone's attractiveness from that point of view. Massimo d'Azeglio engaged him in earnest discussions in 1853.[1] Gladstone gave a breakfast party in 1854 in honour of Daniel Manin, the hero of revolutionary Venice (though he found Manin disconcertingly 'wild').[2] Cavour made a point of meeting Gladstone on his visit to London in December 1855 (Gladstone reporting to Catherine that 'Cavour is not distinguished looking but his ability comes out in his conversation').[3] He paid tribute to the memory of Vincenzo Gioberti, the Piedmontese philosopher and statesman (died 1852), whose 'literary and public life was one long gallant strenuous effort to reestablish, in the country of his birth ... the long banished harmony between religion and civilization: between divine truth in the Christian dogma subject to the conditions under which he held it, and the movement of human thought'. To Gladstone the 'whole question seems to be whether the Court of Rome can be saved in spite of itself? There is not the smallest hope of spontaneous wisdom or prudence from that quarter.'[4]

One advantage of being out of office was that Gladstone was much freer to revive the argument he had first adumbrated at Manchester in 1853 in opposition to the war policy associated with Palmerston. Now he developed this into a formidable critique. Russell had left the Vienna conference of March 1855 ready to press upon the government the Austrian proposals for a negotiated end to the war on the basis of equality and 'counterpoise' between the two sides. But his courage failed him when it came to the point; and he went along with Palmerston's determination to capture Sebastopol and hobble Russia permanently by neutralising the Black Sea. Argyll's view was that Gladstone's 'ingenious mind invented for itself the fable that our policy was completely changed when we did not accept the Austrian terms, and that it was now perfectly consistent in him to oppose and condemn the war into which he had helped to plunge us, and in particular the great military enterprise which was the most significant indication of its aims, and which he was one of the loudest to applaud'.[5] These strictures were justified. Gladstone had sold his soul to the Palmerstonian war aim of capturing Sebastopol as the price of keeping the coalition afloat. Now he was purchasing his soul back at what Argyll considered a rather cheap rate.

In the big debate on the prosecution of the war in May 1855 Gladstone insisted that the true and legitimate objects of the war had been substantially attained. Russia's overweening notions of her prerogatives

1 D, iv, 53.   2 *Ib.*, 630.
3 Bassett, 112.   4 GP, 44746, 62.   5 Argyll, ii, 30.

had been sharply repudiated by Europe and now the Russians were displaying 'a different language and a different spirit'. The great need now was to come quickly to reasonable terms and abandon all ideas of imposing a punitive and humiliating peace on the Russians – particularly if the real origin of the trouble, the 'internal state or institutions of Turkey', were ignored. Gladstone 'despaired' of any contrivances to hobble Russian power permanently being forced upon Russia; 'the more I feel the extreme indignity which, if so forced, it inflicts upon her; and there is no policy, I think, which is so false and dangerous as to inflict upon Russia indignity without taking away strength.' The proposed stipulation that Russian warships should be banned from the Black Sea Gladstone denounced as an 'imperfect remedy for the past, imperfect justice as between the parties, and an imperfect security or guarantee for the future'.[1] No power of the first order could be permanently coerced; it was quite futile to attempt to bind Russia down; there was no further point in obsessively persevering in the siege of Sebastopol, the capture of which would mean nothing and achieve nothing.[2]

These were golden words of wisdom; but the effect was spoiled by a note of dogmatic zealotry, especially in a tendency to uncritical Russophilism which alienated potential support. 'Gladstone, as usual, overdid his part', noted Argyll: this he would continue to do for the next several years. Argyll remarked that Gladstone 'could always argue in private life with perfect temper'; but 'upon any question on which he was keenly interested, and on which his mind was irrevocably made up, he could not even entertain an opposing thought. Under such circumstances, his mind was essentially fanatical . . .'[3] Stanley also noted of Gladstone's part in the debate 'especially' that he 'injured the peace party in general opinion'.[4] Very much in this spirit Gladstone rounded off his critique in the 1855 session with a ferocious attack on the projected Turkish loan, denouncing it as a subsidy in disguise to prop up the 'corrupt agents of a weak and uncertain Government'. Palmerston certainly had cause for annoyance at Gladstone's tenacious hostility; and some cause for concern at what appeared to be the making of a 'Gladstone–Dizzy coalition'. In the spirit of their handshake of February 1st, Gladstone and Disraeli gave every appearance of having concluded a 'Treaty of Alliance' or a 'compact upon the Peace Principle'.[5] But Derby vetoed Disraeli's scheme; and Gladstone's counter-productive rage made his pursuit of Palmerston as vain as his pursuit of the Turks.

He pursued also the question of the Neapolitan prisoners he had raised with Clarendon in April of 1854. Gladstone's words on that occasion as to

1 H, cxxxviii, 1055, 1046, 1057–60.   2 *Ib.*, 1810–25.
3 Argyll, i, 561.   4 DDCP, 134.
5 J. R. Vincent, 'The Parliamentary Dimension of the Crimean War', *Trans. Roy. Hist. Soc.* (1981), 44, 47.

the difficulty of assigning bounds to the measures justified and required by the case took on a curious and conspiratorial immediacy in the summer of 1855. Panizzi was party to a plot to liberate six of the prisoners on the island of San Stefano by force. For this daring purpose he appealed to friends for money to charter a steamship. He consulted Gladstone; who coolly set about abetting this 'flagrant violation of the canons of conduct between civilized states'[1] by advising the Principal Librarian of the British Museum to apply to Palmerston and Clarendon for a grant from the Secret Service Fund. He provided also £100 of his own money (for decency's sake given under the cover of Catherine's name) and promised £200 more from friends. Palmerston and Clarendon were also perfectly willing to connive (Hudson and Temple among the diplomatists in Italy were already heavily implicated); and only the bad luck of the *Isle of Thanet's* shipwreck in October 1855 prevented Panizzi from launching his desperate enterprise. The remaining fund was entrusted to Gladstone for the relief of dependants of the prisoners.[2]

Naturally during these months Gladstone awaited impatiently signs of the imminent and much-desired collapse of Palmerston's ministry. He assured Catherine on July 13 that the 'prevailing idea' was that the government 'cannot escape from their frightful and unexampled position', and that the 'most probable issue will be Derby's advent to power.'[3] Perhaps sanguineness as to that happy outcome helped to inspire Gladstone to order some new waistcoats which he hoped and indeed expected would command Catherine's 'approval nay admiration'.

Frustration in politics helped to drive Gladstone towards a major countervailing diversion. At Hawarden he noted on August 6, 1855: 'Began the Iliad: with serious intentions of working out something on old Homer if I can.'[4] His intentions were to expand the thesis he had urged against Lachmann in 1847 that the Homeric epics were indeed by Homer and not stitched together out of fragmentary lays, and that their author composed them at no great distance in time and place from the events described. But added to that he now had a much larger and deeper purpose. Gladstone had convinced himself that Homer's stature as by far the greatest poet in the pre-Christian world pointed to his being the medium of a divine legation. God's revelation as vouchsafed to the Jews had been transmitted by them in what Gladstone considered a narrow and inadequate manner: theologically correct, but lacking in wisdom and guidance about human nature and human society. As a politician with a vocation to order human affairs in conformity with God's purposes, Gladstone assiduously studied the Old Testament seeking divine inspiration as to his directions and his duties. Increasingly he had become

1 G. B. Henderson, 'Lord Palmerston and the Secret Service Fund', EHR, liii (1938), 485–87.
2 E. Miller, *The Prince of Librarians* (1967), chap. 13.   3 Bassett, 110.   4 D, v, 68.

dissatisfied with the Hebrew Scriptures as a statesman's manual; at the same time he came to see Homer as the provider of the kind of hints, illuminations, and insights about man, society and politics he was looking for. The logic was impeccable: if Gladstone was convinced of the validity of his vocation, and if in reading Homer he felt himself inspired by revelations bearing directly on the purposes and directions of his vocation, it followed that those revelations in some manner must have been provided as an essential item of God's providential economy.

Imbued with this somewhat crack-brained religio-politico-literary enthusiasm, Gladstone set off with the family for a vacation at Penmaenmawr between Conway and Bangor on the North Wales coast. It was a convenient spot to reach from Hawarden, combining the charms both of sea and mountain.[1] He did not allow the attractions and activities of the resort and the sublimities of Snowdonia to distract him long from Homer. After setting his 'little goods to rights' he recommenced work immediately on arrival on September 3. At the parish church he attended services in Welsh and was distressed at 'some irreverence of kinds wh. wd. not occur in England'; and he concluded that the language did not make 'favourable impressions'.[2] This experience doubtless contributed to his refusal in 1856 to accept the opinion beginning to form widely in Wales that a command of Welsh ought to be an essential qualification for appointment to a Welsh bishopric (it would be an 'error to recognise a knowledge of the Welsh tongue as dispensing with any of the still more essential qualifications for the Episcopal office')[3]. The war was inescapable. Dr. Thomas Short, his former tutor at Christ Church, Bishop of St. Asaph and old friend of Keble and Pusey, Gladstone found '*warlike* to a degree and in a manner which carries the mark of belonging to a general distemper'.[4] The Gladstones departed on September 27, Gladstone accusing himself of having 'lived too happily for one who thinks as I do about the course of events and the responsibilities of needless war'.[5] Penmaenmawr suited Gladstone very well; and this was to be the first of many happy stays in the resort. On the way back to Hawarden Gladstone 'sat up late' at Bodelwyddan 'reading the detailed accounts from Sebastopol: wh. were for England grievous'.[6] The Homer project, meanwhile, had taken root.

Clearly Gladstone missed the life and work of office. That was a gap even Homer could not fill. His case now, moreover, was quite different from what it had been in his earlier stretches away from the Treasury bench. Resignation over Maynooth had been his individual, free deci-

---

1 K.G. Robbins, 'Palmerston, Bright and Gladstone in North Wales', *Transactions of the Caernarvonshire Historical Society*' xli (1980).

2 D, v, 76. 3 *Ib.*, 165; *Liverpool Evening Mail*, October 18, 1856, 2.
4 D, v, 73. 5 *Ib.*, 77. 6 *Ib.*, 77.

sion; and during the period of both the Russell and Derby governments between 1846 and 1852 he had been a member of a group deliberately giving countenance to ministers. Now, for the first time, he was unwillingly out of office at a period of critical importance, with time and opportunities wasting, with the political lead in the hands of a man he despised, oppressed by a sense of resentment and disinheritance. Gladstone expressed his frustration partly in complaints against himself: 'In my increasing difficulties with respect of doing what I dislike I trace the greater weakness of the brain *relatively* to its work than ten years back.'[1] After returning to Hawarden from the North Wales excursion: 'I find feebleness & timidity for duty, & a disposition to Epicurean self-indulgence is growing upon me, . . . the time for trying to brace myself somewhat has arrived.'[2] Certainly the long Hawarden retreats offered many tempting epicurean moments. Gladstone 'luxuriated in Burke' in November, and likewise in December in Macaulay's new third volume, which he judged 'quite equal to England's expectation'.[3] Gladstone occupied himself much in arranging his books at Hawarden ('here about 6000'),. which he could now trust were 'in tolerable order'. Back in London in January 1856 he immediately 'went to work at 9 p.m. on my books & worked till 2 a.m.'[4] A few days later he was book-buying at Quaritch's. This kind of innocent labour had a soothingly therapeutic effect. Perhaps this therapy was helpful on the occasion at Lady Waldegrave's when Gladstone's charming hostess 'stood up' to him on the issue of General Lord Lucan's censure and recall from the Crimea and, as one observer noted, 'he did not half like the want of reverence with which she treated him'.[5]

[3]

Gladstone braced himself for the sterner tasks of the new parliamentary session by speaking 'fully on Parlty. Churchmatters' with the Rev. Mr. Keble ('how few are like him!')[6]. Sessional business helped Gladstone to recover his poise. He intervened vigorously on the issue of unwarrantable borrowing powers of government. He had the satisfaction of offering sardonic comment on the anti-climax of the much-vaunted report of the parliamentary commission on the conduct of the war. But his major preoccupation was to prepare the way for a return to office when Palmerston had been got rid of and politics restored to a proper footing. In February 1856 Gladstone drew up an outline of a comprehensive financial

1 *Ib.*, 66.   2 *Ib.*, 83.   3 *Ib.*, 85, 92.
4 *Ib.*, 97–8.   5 O. W. Hewett, *Strawberry Fair* (1956), 120.   6 D, v, 99.

policy. He listed twenty-one projects: an initial group of three, including the strengthening of the Audit department, aimed to bring financial policy under stricter accountability and 'controul of the Finance Department'; the next three bore on the problems of managing the national debt, including a stricter subordination of the role of the Bank of England as the agent of the state and limitations of the powers of the 'Minister of Finance' to manipulate redemption policy; a seventh proposal envisaged making 'provision for efficient departmental aid & counsel to the Minister of Finance & for the compilation & continuance of proper Financial Records'; the eighth raised the question of the authority of the British government over the management of Indian finance; the ninth considered extending the issues of government stocks; a block of four schemes concerned reduction or abolition of duties, especially on paper and wine; two proposals related to the plan to extinguish the income tax by 1860 and consequent adjustments; and the final six projects raised questions about banking and currency.[1] Gladstone's guiding notions in this 'unique example of mid-Victorian political planning',[2] were 'to complete the construction of a real department of Finance' and to 'bring all really public accounts under the control of the Treasury'.[3]

With this programme, the ultimate completion of which in his future term as Chancellor has been aptly cited as a 'remarkable, perhaps unique, achievement in Victorian politics',[4] Gladstone signalled the revitalising of his second vocation. He was picking up the threads of the aborted mission of 1853 and forming them into the sinews of a grand strategy for a financial policy big enough and bold enough to remoralise politics by the sheer weight of its gravitational pull. It was a highly characteristic expression of his amalgam of Peelism, *étatisme*, and aggression. Most of the aggression was directed at the Bank of England, which Gladstone never forgave for obstructing him in 1854. In that year he had instructed two of his officers at the Treasury to examine the relations between the Bank and the State.[5] That report (by Spearman and Anderson) was now prepared; it would be put in the hands of the governors of the Bank in 1857; it would be one of Gladstone's major policy documents should he return to the Exchequer. He determined also to 'make further provision for the custody & management of monies in the hands of the public: & for security of depositors in Savings Banks & the like.'[6] This was the germ of his later project for popular savings banks operating by means of the Post Office network. In this way he calculated that he could strike a blow not only for small depositors but also at the Bank: for ready access by government to such a mass of deposits would help to spare the Treasury having to go begging in Threadneedle Street. In a letter to Aberdeen of

1 *Ib.*, 104–06.   2 Matthew, *ib.*, 104 n. 18.   3 *Ib.*, 107.
4 Matthew, *ib.*, xxix.   5 GP, 44531, 53.   6 D, v, 107.

March 13 he elaborated his strategy. The war was coming to an end. A time for new departures was at hand. Care must be taken not to be caught unawares by the new circumstances of the 'great civil juncture' of the peace. It would be necessary to reduce 'vast establishments' and to satisfy 'corresponding claims'. These were questions demanding a 'determined and vigorous policy'. The expenditure of the state other than fixed charges and the servicing of the debt had trebled within a period of three years, from twenty to more than sixty millions. 'The duties connected with our establishments & our finances are in my opinion the primary and urgent duties to be performed upon a return from war to peace.' Moreover, the disorganisation of political parties over the previous decade was a 'capital evil' which 'discredits government, retards legislation, diminishes the respect necessary for the efficiency of Parliament, and is thus unfavourable, by a sure though circuitous process, to the stability of our institutions'. This 'chronic evil of executive weakness' could not be overcome by the mere willingness of political men to form a government 'with a policy to seek'. Any such willingness would be more than counteracted by 'less of compactness among their followers, more of feeble and half-hearted support'. Gladstone's conclusion was that no strong government was possible 'unless it be in a marked manner founded upon a policy'. Thus the needs of public affairs and the peculiar state of parties and parliament 'lead up to the same point'.

Yet a strong government with a programme of strong measures was in itself no longer enough. There was a new and powerful element in public life: public opinion. This public opinion had been 'irritated and wounded'; and the public mind would 'not be at rest, unless under the consciousness that those who are to govern recognise the nature and magnitude of the work they will have to perform'. The present moment, he assured Aberdeen, was 'one that calls for measures'. Political men will be estimated 'chiefly with reference to measures'. For himself, Gladstone was 'inclined to resolve to enter no government, actual or possible, without an adequate assurance, that it will take its stand upon such a policy as I have generally indicated'. It would be better 'to decline taking any part in public affairs upon such an occasion as the next turn of the wheel is likely to present', and 'to wait for an opportunity when arrangements more advantageous to the nation could be made', rather than 'to enter a weak government in the rather presumptuous hope of making it by personal adhesion one degree less weak'. The presumption was rather that Gladstone must stipulate for the Exchequer. The key now was 'doings and practical intentions of the minister, and upon a corresponding conviction wrought by them upon the public mind'.[1]

For Gladstone, formulating the financial programme of February 1856

1 PMP, iii, 195–98.

and its associated political strategy of March were crucially important steps in his feeling his way towards a more mature relationship between his sense of vocation and his sense of 'insight' into the means whereby that vocation could be realised in politics by masterful invocation and manipulation of the 'public mind'. The immediate problem was to get a government not only strong in itself but one in which Gladstone could take command of finance and which could elicit a sufficient response from public opinion. There was thus the problem of getting Lewis out of the Exchequer and of keeping Disraeli out. These criteria would dominate and ultimately resolve Gladstone's calculations in the next few years as to the kind of ministry it would be best for him to join.

Certainly the Peelites were clear, upon further discussion of the available permutations, 'adding names', that neither Palmerston nor Russell would be satisfactory 'as ministers with reference to the administrative work to be done'. They could just conceive the possibility of returning to office with control of all the spending and financial departments or with full confidence in the holders of them, 'even with Palmerston as head'; though it would be better still if both Palmerston and Russell could 'disappear', with perhaps Clarendon being allowed to come to the top as a sop to Whig feeling. Graham carefully passed this on to Charles 'Punch' Greville, clerk to the Privy Council and notorious political gossip, for discreet circulation, with the additional rider that Palmerston was really 'out of the question' and Russell 'a case for the House of Lords'.[1]

Naturally Derby and his friends were also given the benefit of this splendidly self-deluding Peelite thinking. Gladstone, engaged to consult with his Oxford University colleague Heathcote about various impending questions, turned the occasion to advantage by reading to him the letter to Aberdeen of March 13 and by suggesting Heathcote's 'conveying to Lord Derby's friends our idea of the dangers impending and to be avoided'. Heathcote duly mediated with Derby. The latter, sensibly cautious, confined himself to enquiring about the intentions of the Peelites as to acting together and pointing out that he could not summarily discard his own people to make room for them *en bloc*. A little later, on April 19, Derby enquired through Heathcote whether the Peelites, if unwilling to take office with him, might nevertheless grant him the same friendly countenance he himself and Graham had given to Peel in 1835, which later grew into a political identification. Gladstone was ready to concede that this case was 'a possible one', and indeed he could 'even conceive circumstances in which it might be the best of the alternatives before us'.[2] With the detested Palmerston in power Gladstone was peculiarly prone to lean in this direction: a revived version of

1 *Ib.*, 199–200.　　2 *Ib.*, 206–7.

his insistence in 1852 that a junction with the Whigs and Liberals was the Peelites' 'least natural position'. It was noted, especially by alarmed Liberals who nursed hopes of luring Gladstone into Liberalism, that he was often to be seen at the Carlton Club, where he was (unlike the Duke of Newcastle) 'very civilly received'.[1] For the rest, Gladstone could only wait grimly and hope. He consoled himself by reflecting that 'Justice might for some reasons have properly been represented dumb no less than blind: dumb, though strong'.

> For most of her great operations are those which she achieves in silence. She has a natural hold on man. Noisy passion shakes & strains but cannot destroy it. Such influences exhaust themselves: but she labours night and day in calm and as Time flows on she first mitigates & at last redresses what is wrong.[2]

It was particularly provoking that shortly afterwards the Queen conferred the Garter on Palmerston.

[4]

Meanwhile Gladstone kept up a steady level of sessional activity. He pressed keenly on the question of reducing public expenditure (he was unhappy with the salary account for the National Gallery being as high as £3,000) and he was hostile to more 'paid officers of the Crown' being generated by the government's Education Bill. He dealt with Russell's resolutions pressing for a policy to put education 'within the reach of every child' in a manner which a later Liberal admirer wonderingly described as 'almost incredibly reactionary'.[3] Gladstone extolled local control, voluntary exertion, and 'the moral influences operative upon character, the human love, that are obtained through the medium of the voluntary principle carried out by men whose main motive is one of Christian philanthropy'. He declared himself a firm opponent both of rate support for schools and of compulsion; and condemned Russell's resolutions as being 'adverse to the national character', substituting what was 'mechanical, technical, and formal for that which is free, open, elastic and expansive'.[4] All these elements were vividly on display when Gladstone laid on May 8, 1856 the foundation stone of a Church school providing free education for the children of costermongers and poor inhabitants of Golden Lane and Whitecross Street in the parish of St. Thomas, Charterhouse. He plugged away at the Civil Service reform

1 Hewett, *Strawberry Fair*, 120.   2 GP, 44746, 5. (March 12, 1856).
3 Prest, *Russell*, 378; Reid, 388.   4 H, cxli, 1422.

issue, dismissing as 'idle, pusillanimous, womanish' all fears about the Civil Service being made so strong in skill and knowledge as to threaten the 'free action and institutions of the country'.[1] He repeated with emphasis his critique of the peace treaty: that the great benefit of the war had been the 'moral demonstration on the part of Europe' impressing itself upon the mind of Russia; that what was so 'remarkable' was the 'purity in the origin of the war' as an expression of the moral community of the concert, and that such issues as the security of the Indian empire had not been a powerful motive. The scheme to neutralize the Black Sea was a 'series of pitfalls'. The real problem, untouched by the treaty, was the condition of the Christians in Turkey, with immense danger of 'future complications'. Moreover, Gladstone was particularly anxious to insist that the ninth article of the Treaty of Paris did not mean a renunciation of the right to intervene in the internal affairs of the Ottoman Empire. He complained especially of the government's 'niggardliness' over the appeal for freedom and independence of the Danubian principalities of Moldavia and Wallachia – an issue he was beginning to build up as a personal cause.[2] To reinforce this critique Gladstone let fly in *The Gentleman's Magazine* in July 1856 another very heavy and destructive barrage on 'The War and the Peace', excoriating the Turks and their apologists and excusing Russian absolutism as being of a type with India rather than with any relevance to western Europe.

This strong emphasis on foreign affairs distinguished even Gladstone's intervention in the budget debate, where he left Lewis alone and took the opportunity yet again to extol the Piedmontese and to stress his sense of the utmost importance of maintaining abroad a conviction of 'our sense of the duty' of lending the Piedmontese 'every support that the moral influence of England can give'. This led to a rare and brief gleam of courtesy to Palmerston as a fellow admirer of Piedmont's role of exhibiting a 'right example to Italy' and of the certain reward of all her efforts and endurances that would eventually come from that example 'and the consequences flowing from it'.[3] (Cavour shrewdly improved the shining hour by making a point of ostentatiously requesting a copy of Gladstone's 1853 budget speech. Corti, the Piedmontese minister, assured Gladstone that Cavour would 'not fail to appreciate this new proof of your goodness'; and added for good measure the gratuitous information that 'the outbreak at Massa was a ridiculous affair got up by the Mazzinians and, I firmly believe, countenanced by the Austrian Authorities in order to compromise our government'.)[4] Gladstone thus signalled a kind of reciprocal response to Palmerston's signals to him at the time of the Neapolitan pamphlet. It was but a passing moment; but a

1 H, clvi, 945–46.   2 *Ib.*, cxlii, 94–98; D, v; 152.   3 H, cxlvi, 142, 175.
4 GP, 44386, ff. 95, 97–98. (Corti wrote 1852 but it is clear he meant 1853.)

kind of a germ of an important conjunction in the making. Despite provoking Palmerston's 'extraordinary asperity' with 'an innocent little speech enough' criticising the government's handling of the dispute with the United States over the Foreign Enlistment Act, Gladstone found himself after dining at Grillion's Club at the Queen's concert, 'where Lord Palmerston had some conv. with me in great good humour' – 'a most merry conversation', as he described it to Catherine.[1] Perhaps Palmerston would not have been so merry had he known of Gladstone's impending *Quarterly Review* article on 'The Declining Efficiency of Parliament', by which he meant mainly the rising intolerableness of Palmerston.

Gladstone took his leave of the 1856 session in a flurry of ecclesiastical cares. There was the sad question of pensions for Scottish bishops, and indeed the sadness of the neglect of the Scottish Episcopalian Church generally. There were problems about the retirements of the Bishops of London and Durham (Gladstone found himself obliged to intervene pertinaciously on fifteen occasions; 'we have been utterly smashed on the second reading of the Bishops' Bill ... it is another proof of the disorganized condition of the House').[2] There was the vexing question of the salary of Bishop Selwyn of New Zealand. There was time for social distraction: a breakfast at Stafford House with the Duchess of Sutherland and royalties (the Prince of Prussia, the later German Emperor William I, made an 'agreeable impression').[3] A good deal of the bile in Gladstone's system was released in the *Quarterly* article, dilating on the 'decay of zeal and abeyance of political duty' in parliament, a politer version of the 'Party as it was' piece; but still sufficiently abusive of Palmerston. The defects of the Prime Minister, it was clear to Gladstone, 'must inevitably prevent his ever taking rank among the great ministers of England'. Compared with the 'immense energies of Peel' Palmerston's conceptions were 'vague, flat, bald, and shallow, in an unprecedented degree'. Aberdeen had said in 1854 that any government in these days must be both conservative and liberal; it was the peculiar distinction of Palmerston's system to represent and exacerbate the vices of the respective parties – Liberal restlessness and Conservative inertness. Perhaps recalling that fraught moment in the Carlton Club at the end of 1852 when he was threatened with being tossed over into the Reform, Gladstone (so often and long a resident in Carlton Gardens or Carlton House Terrace) pointed a political parable: 'He who turns from Pall Mall towards the Park between the Reform and the Carlton Clubs will perceive that each of those stately fabrics is mirrored in the windows of the other.'[4] Unquestionably Gladstone was beginning to see himself as in some significant measure the embodiment of Peel's immense and benevolent potency as against

1 D, v, 146; Bassett, 113.   2 G to CG, July 23, 1856. GGP, 28/5.
3 D, v, 143.   4 QR, September 1856, 558, 562, 564.

Palmerston's negativism and shallowness. Would it be reserved for him to replace Palmerstonism with a system of politics which would fruitfully release the virtuous energies of the great component parties – the constructive and progressive reforms of Liberalism tempered and solidified by the intelligent caution and traditional wisdom of Conservatism? It was not for Gladstone in these years leading to the ministry of 1859 ever a question simply of choosing between entities which could be vapidly labelled either 'Liberalism' or 'Conservatism'. It was always a question rather of calculating the combination likely to induce the best possible opportunities in terms of the criteria set out in February and March 1856.

The domestic dimension, at any rate, was serene. Gladstone immensely enjoyed taking his two elder boys riding and to the theatre. Moving back to Carlton House Terrace – no. 11 this time – was a 'stiff day's work', but well worth it for the improved facilities. He filled Goulburn's place as a Trustee of the British Museum (Panizzi had written in January 1856: 'Now, between us, you ought to be his successor in the Trust');[1] a responsibility he greatly relished. Gladstone was much in attendance at Christie's sales in 1856; and at the Academy exhibition he joined in the pious hue and cry against Holman Hunt's 'awful' 'Scapegoat'.[2] Hawarden that summer and autumn especially was fulfilling its promise. There was hope from new coal borings ('I have settled & signed on I hope all the material points for the Coal Lease this morning').[3] 'The new walk called mine gives a road to Church a very little longer & opens the park delightfully.' In September he 'worked on the walk, aided by the boys'.[4] The Thomas Gladstones came, together with Helen, in July, in a warm atmosphere of family reunion ('this visit has been good in many ways: we are much pleased with our nieces').[5] Helen indeed was growing rather fat ('Aunt J.,' as Gladstone reported to Catherine, 'says that she is far beyond the dimensions of Elizabeth whom we have heretofore considered the *ne plus ultra* (see if you can make that out) of circumference').[6] Willy and Stephy were doing gratifyingly well at Eton. Gladstone immersed himself congenially in forestry and in purchasing a 'fine young horse' for £58. Above all he observed with satisfaction the climb back to prosperity of the estate. The coal leases looked well; and walks to the new coal pits were now a feature of Hawarden social life. At the end of the year there was a 'long *sederunt*' and a 'review of the general state of Stephen's affairs'. The 'deadly struggle' had been 'carried on with as much success as on the whole we could have hoped'. On December 4 he noted proudly: 'we burned a fire with the Hawarden coal a 2f.6. seam

1 Foot, 'Gladstone and Panizzi', *Br. Library Journal* (1979), 52. 2 D, v, 131.
3 G to CG, March 28, 1856. GGP, 28/5. 4 D, v, 145, 158.
5 *Ib.*, 149–50. 6 G to CG, January 24, 58. GGP, 28/6.

found'. On December 24: 'Without the coal we can get on, & mend, but only at a snail's pace. All rapid movement depends on it.'[1] On Boxing Day Gladstone assessed the value of his personal goods and estate at upwards of £187,000. After all expenses and burdens were deducted £2,000 per annum was available for the maintenance and growth of Willy's inheritance. On his forty-seventh birthday Gladstone allowed that 'blessings have abounded even more than usual: & a long unbroken country sojourn has been a great spiritual mercy'.[2]

A special feature of spiritual mercy at this time was yet another family excursion in North and Mid-Wales. Gladstone was 'delighted with the Inn and the place' at Bala and found opportunities to display his new sylvicultural expertise in admiring old churchyard yews at Llangwn. There was reading of the harrowing account by the Italian patriot Felice Orsini of his incarceration in the Austrian fortress at Mantua. There was bathing at Aberdovey and admiration for the 'extraordinary beauty' of Lyffant glen. Aberystwyth, however, was rather a let-down: a 'violent attack of diarrhoea' obliging recourse to sal volatile was topped off by an altercation with the landlady of the Bellevue about the bill. The route back via Devil's Bridge and Llanidloes to Powis Castle ('exceedingly beautiful') gave Gladstone the pleasure of long 'Crimean & Army' conversations with Colonel Herbert, M.P. for Ludlow, of receiving the hospitality of Sir Watkin Williams Wynn, and of encountering '3 excellent clergymen' at Oteley Park, Ellesmere. The Gladstones regained Hawarden on September 18 and Gladstone launched himself back into Homer, for which purpose he was now deep in Max Muller's *Essay on Comparative Mythology*. He published a chip from his workshop in the *Quarterly* in January 1857, 'Homer and his Successors in Epic Poetry', in which he demonstrated Homer's superiority to the 'courtierlike' Virgil and the 'extravagant' Tasso.

In the intervals of Homeric work, always rather grudged – he was impatient when 'an explosion among the men-servants, & enquiries connected with it' interrupted his scholarly routine[3] – Gladstone ruminated on the sorry case of Maurice, now ejected from his chair at King's, London, for heresy; and was prompted to write apologetically to that veteran victim of Puseyite and Evangelical rancour, Bishop Hampden of Hereford, expressing 'regret' for his part in the campaign against Hampden's appointment to the Regius chair of Divinity and explaining 'that which ... brought back to my mind the injustice of which I had incautiously been guilty in 1836 was my being called upon as a member of the Council of King's College in London to concur in a measure similar in principle with respect to Mr. Maurice'.[4] He was now working also on a

1 D, v, 180.   2 *Ib.*, 182.
3 *Ib.*, 158.   4 GP, 44386, 215 (draft).

'projected political article' for the *Quarterly*: a 'very difficult task: not what to say, but how to say it'.[1] Elwin, the *Quarterly* editor, was ambitious to provide good offices to reconcile Gladstone with Derby. To Aberdeen and Elwin Gladstone despatched 'anxious letters which occupied most of my day in thought & writing' on the expediency of a 'conference on the state of public affairs',[2] 'with a view to ascertain whether there would be any chance of . . . an understanding as to the course to be pursued during the coming session, which might not only lead to greater harmony . . . but possibly tend hereafter to the reunion of the now discordant Conservative elements'.[3] Graham was quite sure that Gladstone would seat himself at the opening of the new session on the opposition bench. Aberdeen thought he was 'too hasty' in imagining this; but 'thought it probable this step would not long be delayed'; although it was clear that 'much prudence and circumspection would be required' on Gladstone's part before he arrived at such a decision. 'As you agreed to join Palmerston, after I had left the Government', Aberdeen reminded Gladstone, 'I think it will never do now to attempt his overthrow, without more specific or assignable cause.' Strong apprehension of a 'mischievous policy' or 'general disapprobation and mistrust' would not be sufficient. To this advice Aberdeen felt the need to add some candidly pointed admonition:

> Your position in the House of Commons is very peculiar. With an admitted superiority of character and of intellectual power above any other member, I fear that you do not really possess the sympathy of the House at large, while you have incurred the strong dislike of a considerable portion of Lord Derby's followers. Your recent conduct has not been fully understood; but it has been very unpopular and any new course which is not perfectly intelligible, and clearly justified by the necessity of the case will only add to this unpopularity.[4]

Perhaps this gave Gladstone pause; but his excited eagerness as to Derby is evident in his calculation on December 20 that the 19th was 'the *first* day when in course of post anything cd. have come from Ld D.'[5] Bishop Wilberforce of Oxford, visiting Hawarden in November, noted how '*very* strong against Palmerston' Gladstone was, and how 'manifestly' he leaned 'to a Conservative alliance'.[6] Greville recorded current rumours that Gladstone was to become leader of the opposition in the Commons *vice* Disraeli, which he judged 'wild and improbable'; but he heard from George Byng and Sir William Jolliffe (the Conservative whip) that 'necessities have modified their extreme repugnance to Gladstone, and that they may now be willing to accept him as Leader (eventually)'.[7] The

1 D, v, 179. 2 *Ib.*, 176. 3 PMP, iii, 210.
4 Aberdeen to G, December 5, 1856. GP, 43071, 332–34.
5 PMP, iii, 179. 6 *Wilberforce*, ii, 335–6. 7 *Greville*, vii, 251–52.

new article, dashed off between December 15 and 20, certainly testified, as an exercise in Palmerstonophobic spleen, to Gladstone's readiness. Unfortunately Elwin, in his first communications to Derby in December, did not make it clear that he was writing with Gladstone's knowledge and sanction; and accordingly it was not until late January 1857 that Derby realised that Gladstone had been waiting to hear from him. In the midst of this misunderstanding Gladstone reported despondently to Aberdeen that the 'great Derby case has for the present at least ended in smoke'.[1]

Despite this provoking hitch, Gladstone found much to be thankful for in his Christmas and New Year self-adjurations. Into politics he felt himself 'drawn deeper every year'. In the 'growing anxieties & struggles of the Church' he had 'no less share than heretofore'. 'Literature' had of late 'acquired a new & powerful hold' on him. 'The fortunes of my wife's family' 'have had with all their dry detail all the most exciting & arduous interest of romance for me during nine years and more'. And 'seven children growing up around us' were each the 'object of deeper thoughts & feelings & of higher hopes'.[2]

[5]

'The difficult task' of writing about political prospects and without compromising a possible Conservative reunion Gladstone solved mainly by unsparing condemnation of the record of 'the present Liberal Administration', spiced with an extra virulence in his abuse of Palmerston. 'Prospects Political and Financial' in effect rebuked the Prime Minister for failing to rise to the occasion as defined by Gladstone's earlier article on 'The Declining Efficiency of Parliament'. Set against Palmerston's legislative sterility, his 'marked fecundity in the noble art of parliamentary evasion', his lack of political courage, his carelessness of domestic interests, his 'brawling' foreign policy, his 'deliberate extravagance', his 'daring abrogation of the rules heretofore observed by all Governments', his offensive impiety about questions of marriage and divorce and the abolition of ecclesiastical courts, Gladstone offered a model of an alternative government. This would take as its primary duty a policy of real retrenchment and economy. Gladstone laid heavy stress on the sacredness of the policy of 1853: that 'covenant' must be kept; and he cited 'Lord Aberdeen and his political friends' as its guardians and guarantors. The alternative model would exhibit the 'art of governing well – prudently, honourably, energetically', making 'full use' of 'great resources and materials', 'labouring to extend the spirit of union for great

1 GP, 43071, 353.   2 D, v, 183.

public objects', and by 'frank and practical acknowledgement' that while 'heady innovation' must be resisted, reforms were needed by the country to 'husband its resources', 'lighten its labours', and 'improve its laws'.[1]

As an exercise in providing an encouraging atmosphere for negotiations with Derby the *Quarterly* article left something to be desired. The Peelite emphasis on heroic energy was not in accord with the dispositions of the bulk of Derby's followers; and would tend to make them all the more aware of the utility of Palmerston's hobbling of the Liberal party. Derby himself could not have been much encouraged by Gladstone's emphasis on the Peelites as a *bloc*. Still, Gladstone set out resolutely on a pre-sessional political tour. From Westwood, near Droitwich, the seat of Sir John Pakington, Derby's Colonial and War Secretary in the 1852 Conservative Cabinet, he proceeded to Wilton where he had a 'long sitting' with Sidney Herbert and Aberdeen 'about our position: tried at a letter to Lord D.'[2] Derby, by now belatedly aware of what was afoot, declared that he would be glad to confer with Gladstone at St. James's Square as soon as Gladstone reached London. Gladstone paused at his brother John Neilson's place at Bowden Park, Chippenham (John's 'head not strong'), and visited Lacock Abbey and Bowood. Then at Oxford he inspected Butterfield's startling new chapel at Balliol and engaged in 'Homeric talks with all persons whom I find fit to victimise'. He reported to Catherine that as far as he could see the Oxford people were in 'good humour' and he did not '*hear* any evil reports' about himself.[3] He arrived in Carlton House Terrace on January 31 to find domestic chaos 'deeper & more hopeless than usual in a new (but most promising) house' and rather discomposed by 'a great gumboil & some neuralgia'.

He was sufficiently composed by February 3, however, to maul the government in the debate on the Address for its irresponsibly extravagant domestic policy and a foreign policy in a 'state of perpetual disquietude by one broil after another', as witness the latest quarrel with China provoked by the authorities in Hong Kong.[4] This set the scene for Gladstone's call on Derby on February 4. They conferred for three hours. Gladstone declared himself anxious to end the Peelite isolation, denouncing himself as a 'public nuisance'. He informed Derby that he 'deliberately disapproved of the government of Lord Palmerston and was prepared and desirous to aid in any proper measure which might lead to its displacement'. So strong were his objections that he was 'content to act thus without inquiring who was to follow', for he was convinced 'that anyone who might follow would govern with less prejudice to the public interests'. To Derby this was merely a form of evasion. He wanted Gladstone to commit himself to joining a Conservative ministry, regard-

1 QR, January 1857, 246–284.   2 D, v, 189.
3 Bassett, 114.   4 H, cxliv, 139–45.

less of Graham and Herbert. Instead of this, he found himself being assured by Gladstone that his opinions of Lord Palmerston's government were 'very much in harmony with those of Lord Aberdeen, Sir J. Graham, and Herbert'. Well versed in Peelite protestations (rather like Manning and Hope formerly on the theme of Gladstone's political duty to the Church) Derby responded cautiously by pointing out that it was 'material' for him, in the event of being commissioned by the Queen, 'to consider beforehand on what strength he could rely', and by reminding Gladstone of the feelings of his party. He 'adverted to the offers he had made in 1851 and 1855. The fact of an overture made and not accepted had led to much bitterness or anger towards us among a portion of his adherents'. This 'irritation' among some Conservatives, Derby furthermore pointed out, 'was kept up by its being observed that a small body of men, of eminence . . . kept together and acted in concert apart from either great party', necessarily giving rise to unsettling expectations and disappointments. There was, added Derby, an impression among the much greater section of Conservatives who sincerely desired the reunion of the party that, while Graham and Herbert leaned towards the Liberals, Gladstone was much more likely to incline towards the Conservatives.[1]

It does not appear that Derby managed to extract an unambiguous response from Gladstone. Undoubtedly Gladstone was eager to escape from Peelite anomalousness; but he was not prepared to pay the price of declaring a willingness to break with his brethren. Though both Aberdeen and Graham were beginning to fade into the shadows of elder statesmanship the link with Herbert remained particularly close and intense. Every move by Derby to emphasise Gladstone's isolated position in the group was countered by a move by Gladstone, still very much in his original manner as a kind of Peelite whip, to assert its continued unity and cohesion. Aberdeen's warnings about his unpopularity among the bulk of the Derbyites made Gladstone studious in these weeks to devote himself 'to financial points currently exciting deep prejudice among the squires'.[2] But at the same time he made sure that negotiations about a joint attitude to the budget were conducted as between two parties. Disraeli was strong for reducing the direct income tax; Gladstone insisted rather on reductions of indirect tea and sugar duties. There was the awkward question as to whether Disraeli or Gladstone should take the lead in moving the agreed resolution. His Peelite colleagues urged Gladstone to insist on taking the motion into his own hands as the standard-bearer of the principles of 1853; but Gladstone explained that 'from motives which I could neither describe nor conquer I was quite unable to undertake to enter into any squabble or competition with him for the possession of a post of prominence'. Disraeli tended to obtrude

1 PMP, iii, 213–14.   2 Vincent, DDCP, 147.

awkwardly into Peelite calculations. 'We had much conversation on political prospects': Graham wished to see Gladstone lead the Commons under Lord John as Prime Minister in the Lords; but admitted that 'the same thing would do under Lord Derby but for Disraeli who could not be thrown away like a sucked orange'.[1]

After all these bold manoeuvres for Derby's benefit it was rather humiliating that over the proposal to extend the country franchise on February 19 the Peelite group should have split. Gladstone and Herbert voted with the government and the Conservatives to stop the bill and Graham and Cardwell followed Russell and the bulk of the 'unofficial Liberal' minority: 'a bad night for Peelism'.[2] Gladstone did his best to repair the damage with a fierce attack on Lewis's budget the following day. But the fierceness of this attack went far beyond the necessities of the case as between Peelites and Derbyites. It was an assault so brutal as to recall Argyll's observations at Hawarden in 1855 as to how 'unsafe' Gladstone's judgment was, and how his 'destructiveness' was expressed in an 'eagerness in a personal handling of the axe'. Argyll now judged Gladstone's performance over Lewis's budget 'very overstrained, and unfair in argument in the highest degree. Lewis himself, one of the most passionless and amiable of men, spoke of it as so personally bitter that he was quite amazed.'[3] To the equally astonished Stanley the occasion remained a vivid memory ever after: he would measure evidences of Gladstone's 'excessive irritability' and bitterness 'rarely equalled in Parliament' against it as a kind of standard gauge.[4] He observed Gladstone's manner of speaking with 'that peculiar vehemence, like that of a man under personal provocation, which has marked his displays during this session'.[5] Greville likewise observed Gladstone 'so inflamed by spite and ill-humour that all prudence and discretion forsook him; he appears ready to say and do anything and to act with everybody if he can only contribute to upset the Government, though it is not easy to discover the cause of the bitterness, or what schemes of future conduct he has devised for himself'.[6]

Greville's reading of Gladstone quite lacked – very understandably and indeed necessarily – any awareness of the turmoil within Gladstone stemming from his frustration at his thwarted vocation. Given such awareness, the cause and the 'schemes of future conduct' are as plain as day. Gladstone's assault on Disraeli in December 1852 had contained much of the same brutality and much of the same purpose. Other than its frustration and aggression, the salient feature of this speech was Gladstone's intense concern to maintain and enhance the buoyancy of his credit of 1853. It was of the essence that he should be in an unchallengeably

1 PMP, iii, 216. 2 D, v, 200. 3 Argyll, ii, 72–73.
4 DDCP, 216. 5 *Ib.*, 149–50. 6 *Greville*, vii, 273.

strong position to claim the Exchequer when the opportunity arrived to take office in a strong ministry 'in a marked manner founded upon a policy', as he had stipulated to Aberdeen in March 1856. This was the indispensable condition of his resuming and fulfilling his new vocation as (in fact if not necessarily in form) the practitioner of the 'doings and practical intentions of the minister' with respect to the 'measures' called for by the times and as the demiurge and focus of the 'corresponding conviction wrought by them in the public mind'. For this grand purpose Gladstone had to project himself anew as the custodian and tutelary genius of the tradition of Peel. His mode was to assert the principles of 1853 as the sacred repository of financial truth and virtue, the touchstone on which all subsequent policies had to be tested. Lewis's alloys he found decidedly base. Lewis took, in Bagehot's opinion, a 'stricter and simpler view of finance' than Gladstone; and Lewis also gave 'especial satisfaction to the City', which Gladstone conspicuously had not done. But Lewis's worst crime was to break the 'fundamental law of the currency', Peel's Bank Act.[1] Thus, for Gladstone, the government's financial proposals were 'in every point contradictory' to the criteria established in 1853. 'Everything for which we have been labouring during the last fifteen years', the 'principles of finance which were introduced amid difficulties and struggles' had been 'thrown overboard, condemned, repudiated' by a fecklessly immoral budget which neglected to repair deficiencies, failed to balance revenue and expenditure, which ignored the need to simplify and consolidate financial laws or to reform the tariff (and which, specifically, left untouched the wine duty which thus remained the greatest impediment to an enlarged commercial intercourse with France). This indictment Gladstone carefully larded with allusions calculated to burnish his personal myth: 'I remember periods – for instance 1842 . . . '; 'the rule by which I had to abide in 1853 . . . '; 'well do I recollect the day when Sir Robert Peel . . . '[2]

In the same spirit of resuscitating the spirit of 1853 Gladstone converted his 'Memorandum of Finance' of February 1856 into official printed form as a twenty-eight page *Memorandum on Financial Control* of April 1857. To assure 'a more simple and effectual check upon the issue and appropriation of the public money' and a 'correct application of the moneys granted for the public service', Gladstone envisaged a Finance Committee of the Commons to inspect and 'revise' Treasury accounts. To complete the oversight of parliament, Gladstone proposed that the government should be required to lay accounts, and the reports upon them, before the Commons and move on a future day *'that they be received'*. He proposed also that the checks exercised by the Audit Board over the government's

1 Bagehot, *Biographical Studies*, 241–42.
2 H, cxliv, 985–87, 999, 1,000, 1,015.

financial proceedings should also be 'exhibited' to the Commons and the public at the close of every quarter; and within a brief period after the close of every financial year they were to be subjected to the scrutiny of the Finance Committee of the House and submitted finally to the sanction of the House itself.[1] This document represented Gladstone's anticipations of an early end to Palmerston's ministry and his own imminent return to office.

Almost immediately on top of the budget another chance of striking at Palmerston presented itself in the form of the outcry against the gunboat diplomacy practised by the government against China. The Chinese authorities in Canton had arrested on a charge of piracy the *lorcha* registered in Hong Kong as *Arrow* and flying the British flag. For Palmerston it was another case of *Civis Romanus sum*, combined with his old complaint of 1840 that the Chinese refused to treat other powers as equal parties in legal or international disputes. On the latter ground Palmerston had in fact good cause to defend the actions of Bowring, the Governor of Hong Kong; but he was overconfident as to his ability to repeat his triumph over the Don Pacifico affair in the Commons. Still, his position was not to all appearances dangerous; and Cobden, who led the attack, despairingly predicted that yet again Palmerston would escape his deserved retribution. It is possible that Gladstone's immensely eloquent and passionate intervention on the fourth and last night of the debate, on March 3, condemning Palmerston's 'defence of the indefensible' and appealing to the House for a 'message of mercy and peace', may have turned the few crucial votes.[2] One of Gladstone's audience declared: 'Nobody denies that his speech was the finest delivered in the memory of man in the House of Commons.'[3] To his surprise Palmerston was beaten by 263 to 247, with Disraeli, Russell, and Roebuck among the majority alongside Gladstone and Cobden.

The discomfited Prime Minister denounced the majority as a mere 'combination' out for political advantage. He was echoed by *Punch*, which interpreted the vote as 'For hauling down the British Flag, apologizing to the Chinese, and putting DERBY, DIZZY and GLADSTONE in office.'[4] Whatever may have been the justice of such an accusation against Disraeli, Gladstone, as he soon made clear, was innocent. But he was, also, exultant in a measure far beyond anything Disraeli was capable of or could indeed have desired. The Commons had wiped the stain of dishonour of 1850 from its escutcheon. It had righted the wrong done to China in 1840. Above all, it had administered a stinging rebuff to the

1 St. Deiniol's Library, Hawarden: G *Speeches and Writings*, iii, 1.
2 H, *ib.*, 1841, 1794, 1808.
3 D. Hurd, *The Arrow War* (1967), 66, 70.
4 *Punch*, March 14, 1857, 101.

'great illustration' of the demoralised politics of the times. No wonder Gladstone went home that night 'being excited which is rare with me'.[1] Palmerston had contrived to stay on twice the twelvemonth Gladstone had disgustedly allotted to him in February 1855; the excitement of seeing him go at last was correspondingly the more intense. Gladstone's reading of the event was bound to be within the context of his moral critique as set forth in *Quarterly* articles on·'The Declining Efficiency of Parliament' in September 1856 and 'Prospects Political and Financial' in January 1857 and in the unpublished 'Party as it was and as it is' of April 1855 and a second unpublished piece he began in March 1857 on the 'situation' in anticipation of Palmerston's repudiation by the electorate.[2] Once the war itself had ended Palmerston confronted Gladstone as the great, conspicuous obstacle to the attainment of a regenerated politics which would be the vehicle of his redemptive vocation. Getting rid of Palmerston was the first necessary step in the beginnings of regeneration. 'Times are changed, & men!'[3]

Events thus moved much more swiftly than either Derby or Gladstone could have envisaged in early February. On March 5 Palmerston announced that the Commons would be dissolved, not without a sharp altercation with Gladstone, who, with Cobden, demanded in vain a statement that the government would reverse its China policy. Gladstone conferred again with Derby that day and, in view of the impending elections, discussed the expediency of not 'knocking our heads against one another at every election as we did in 1852'. Gladstone evaded anything like a treaty of co-operation with the Conservatives, offering Derby nothing more specific than engaging to exert himself to his uttermost against the Palmerstonian member for Flintshire, Mostyn.[4] In fact Gladstone was already pushing the hapless Sir Stephen Glynne into the lists as champion of righteousness and justice against the supporter of a government 'guided by a man without conviction of duty: by a man who systematically panders to whatever is questionable or bad in the public mind: who lives simply on the dissension of those who disapprove of his policy'. To encourage his reluctant brother-in-law Gladstone urged that being a member of parliament in these days did not impose the same strain as under the 'close and constant fighting' of former times, and that 'increased facilities of locomotion' added greatly to their freedom 'as you may well judge from my having pitched at Hawarden during the month of June in two successive years'.[5]

Not even the pressures of an imminent general election could coagulate the Derbyite and Peelite Conservatives. Gladstone saw himself as having every motive for keeping his options open. Presumably he could, if

1 D, v, 202.   2 GP, 44747, 53–81.
3 D, v, 203.   4 PMP, iii, 220–21.   5 Bassett, 114–5.

necessary, join a Derby cabinet without preliminary binding commitment; therefore why make one? If the electorate were to return a new House of Commons which would consummate the process begun in the old House of emancipating politics from the degenerate Palmerstonian thraldom, a prospect would be opened of a wholesale and wholesome recasting of old combinations into new and much superior forms. In the light of such a splendid and alluring vision Derbyite Conservatism did not look all that impressive to Gladstone. Derby himself made it clear that on the question of retrenching expenditure he expected difficulties with some of his people 'who were greatly afraid of military reductions'. Nor was either Derby or Gladstone unaware of the important residue among Conservatives of abiding resentment and dislike of Gladstone, especially on grounds of his alleged crypto-Romanism. (A revealing outburst of this feeling broke through the surface on February 27 in the person of Bentinck, M.P. for West Norfolk, who denounced Gladstone and his friends for 'anti-Protestantism' and identification with 'democratic measures'.[1])

On Gladstone's side the problem about the Derbyite Conservatives was deeper: no less, indeed, than a whole dimension of the necessary prerequisites as outlined in 1856 to Aberdeen for re-accrediting his vocation. He put it to Derby thus: 'It seemed to me it was high time for them to consider whether they would or would not endeavour to attract towards themselves such a strength of public opinion as would really put them in a condition to undertake the government of the country: without which they could not be a real opposition according to the spirit of our parliamentary system.'[2] This point about 'strength of public opinion' was in truth the lodestone which guided Gladstone through doubts and waverings to his eventual, and supremely ironic, junction with Palmerston in 1859. In the intervening months two general elections obliged Gladstone to bow, with infinite distaste, to three ineluctable facts which would exert sovereign authority over his ultimate decisions. The first was that any notion of a new and higher and readily available politics deriving from a moral repudiation of Palmerstonism by the constituencies was a rank delusion. That would be the work of decades rather than years. The second, as demonstrated by the election of 1857, was that to the extent that there was a responsive public opinion it responded more readily to Palmerston than to anyone else. The third, as confirmed by the election of 1859, was that the Derbyite Conservatives had, accordingly, revealed themselves as having failed in two successive general elections to attract towards themselves such a strength of public opinion as would really put them in a position to undertake the government of the country.

Thus a fundamental duality of criteria imposed by Gladstone upon

1 H, cxliv, 1791.   2 PMP, iii, 221 (March 6, 1857).

himself worked its logical way through a painful series of eliminations. His point of departure was established in 1853 and defined in 1856. Strong government and strong measures, as represented by the 1853 budget, wrought in the public mind, as represented by Manchester, a corresponding conviction. Gladstone cited 1853 as the first case of his awareness of his providential gift of 'insight' enabling him to articulate the two criteria and to form the materials of public opinion and direct its energies towards ends formulated by himself. In early March 1857 Gladstone still looked at politics and political prospects in the mood of confidence or even arrogance of one imbued with a prerogative of mission, equipped with the appropriate policy and poised to renew the articulation of the two by forming and guiding a new public opinion made available for his purposes by the elimination of Palmerston. He felt he could treat with Derby from a position of strength. If all went according to plan the Derbyites would be no more than a marginal element. The fragility of his link with Derby is illustrated by his declining Elwin's invitation to review Guizot's article on Peel for the *Quarterly*: 'It leads one over tender ground, & naturally prompts a distribution of praise and blame in accounting for our present political evils. At the present moment looking upon *dishonour* as the great characteristic of Lord Palmerston's govt. I would not willingly run the *risk* of wounding Ld Derby or any friend of his.'[1]

Wounding Lord Palmerston, on the other hand, was a duty as well as a pleasure. The fanatical obsessiveness of Gladstone's animosity against Palmerston in these years made him a bore to his friends as well as to the public.[2] Nothing better exemplifies this obsessiveness than the indictment Gladstone began composing, mainly on Carlton Club notepaper, in March 1857 by way of a projected contribution to the election campaign. Apparently Gladstone envisaged another letter addressed to Lord Aberdeen with Palmerston as the target instead of 'King Bomba'. The same obligation of duty which had prompted him in 1851, Gladstone declared, called him once again to appeal to Aberdeen's name as 'better adapted than any other to represent in their natural conjunction the claims of humanity and the interests of public law and order'.[3] Essentially it was another (equally unpublishable) version of 'Party as it was and as it is', with abuse of the Tories and Disraeli replaced by added vitriol directed against Palmerston as the real creator of the war with Russia, as the reducer of British elections to plebiscites suitable for a Bonapartist despotism, as a common bully governed by a fundamental 'frivolity' and 'levity', as one in whom the 'foundation & staple of the character is defective and wholly without that relation to truth and nature and

1 D, v, 207 (March 27, 1857).
2 Argyll, ii, 51–52.   3 GP, 44747, 76.

genuine earnestness which is the boast & ornament of England'.[1] Of more moment as a revealing glimpse of the drift of Gladstone's attitudes about party was his analysis of Palmerston's role in distorting and frustrating the energies of Liberalism: 'He brings up the friends of peace in thick array to defend every quarrel which his "blustering foreign policy" has raised. He rallies the friends of Hume behind profligate public expenditure; rallies progressives behind a barren legislative programme.' Above all, the new members of parliament to be returned in the elections must not support the present ministry 'because they are called a Liberal Administration in doing acts of which all parties but especially a party which glories in the name of Liberal ought to be ashamed'.[2] Gladstone took pleasure in seeing Palmerston off at the close of the session with a barrage of pertinacious hostility on the Navy estimates.

Unchallenged at Oxford, Gladstone campaigned hard for Stephen in Flintshire as well as assisting further afield in Chester and Liverpool. His excitement was noted. Argyll observed a 'campaign of oratory, all over the country, for the purpose of influencing its decision'. He told Aberdeen: 'Gladstone has been making a speech in every town – every village – every cottage – everywhere he had room to stand, and at Liverpool it was an avowed canvass for Derby.'[3] The early confidence faltered by late March: 'Up to this time we are sanguine: but the evidences are still indefinite.'[4] The evidences soon became very definite and exceedingly grievous. A surge of support for Palmerston in the country unseated Cobden at Huddersfield and Bright and Gibson at Manchester; and Gladstone at Mold had bitter cause to lament 'the thrusting of the Election into Passion week'. By April 7 sombre reality asserted itself: 'soon the signs of a defeat which became smashing & woeful as the day advanced' returned Sir Stephen (standing as a 'Liberal Conservative') to his private station. The sturdy voters of Flintshire, not uninfluenced by the Palmerstonian sentiments of the Marquess of Westminster (Gladstone counted this as wanton betrayal), faithfully reflected the national mood. The Glynnes and the Gladstones 'digested as well as we could the defeat of yesterday which cut us deeply rather as a scandal & offence of the county than as a personal or family disappointment'.[5] Scandal and offence were compounded by John Neilson's being dismissed by the voters of Devizes. Palmerston improved his parliamentary position handsomely to the tune of the best part of fifty seats, leaving the Derbyite and Peelite Conservatives in a marked and humiliating minority.

The effect on Gladstone was shattering. The deliciously promising fruit of the China vote turned nauseatingly sour. As early as March 31, when the horrid shape of things to come was sufficiently outlined, Gladstone

1 *Ib.*, 63–69, 57, 77.   2 *Ib.*, 55, 62.
3 Argyll, ii, 75.   4 D, v, 209.   5 *Ib.*, 213.

addressed 'dismal ruminations' to Aberdeen, consisting mainly of an outline of the hopeless position of 'Peelism'. His fear was 'not only lest it should be extinguished, but lest it should have gone out, as is said, with a stench'. A 'creditable exit' seemed 'peculiarly needful' in the new parliament. But whither? Every argument of honour and consistency pointed to reunion with the Derbyites. Not only did protection not now stand in the way; on every great question of the hour, foreign policy, expenditure, taxation, the Peelites were 'in general agreement with Lord Derby & the bulk of his party'. What could be worse for the characters of the Peelites than 'to have it said that, having professed to quarrel with our party on a particular question in 1846, we not only consummated the rupture just when the Conservative party had made it a main object to defend our principles & measures in finance, & the principles of Foreign policy which are peculiarly yours'? Would not such conduct 'bear the marks both of duplicity & of an undying hatred'? Would not any other course expose the Peelites to the charge of having been 'all along covert party men, only of a new party, & likewise without the courage to say so'? What sort of light would such duplicity 'reflect upon the character of Sir Robert Peel & upon his never recalled declarations that the course he took upon the Corn Law in 1846 was not a breach of his obligations rightly understood to those who had raised him to power'?

So much for positive motives for Conservative reunion. The argument was equally cogent against union with Liberalism. The circumstances which had made the coalition of 1852 possible no longer obtained. On all the great questions of the hour the bulk of the Liberal party, 'in consequence of taking Lord Palmerston for its leader', had 'placed itself in almost continual, at least in very frequent, antagonism with us'. How could men who acted thus in 1852 possibly justify incorporating themselves with the Liberal party in 1857? There was, indeed, the possible alternative of Lord John Russell, unreconciled with Palmerston ever since the fiasco of his Vienna negotiations in the summer of 1855 and, even in eclipse, potentially formidable if only because of his dangerous itch for parliamentary reform and educational meddling. How could the Peelites become parties 'to such tampering with our institutions'? If it were a question of moving closer to Liberalism by means of an alliance with Russell and his friends, how could the Peelites, on any great subject of public policy – foreign, retrenchment, taxation, reform, education, church, 'Ecclesiastical questions in Ireland', law – be 'naturally guided to, and justified in, party union with Liberalism at this time'? Graham, Cardwell, and now Herbert, were drifting in this direction. Gladstone deplored this as unwarrantable pre-emption of events; and could not bring himself to believe that Graham 'in his heart' was persuaded that parliamentary reform was the present want of the country. 'Our whole safety, for ultimate vindication,' Gladstone insisted, could be found only 'in our following with perfect good faith the guidance which events afford'. For his own part Gladstone could not but feel that if they were to separate (not by any act of his) he could not find ground in the new House 'for the sole of my foot to rest upon'; which was perhaps a surprising conclusion to a compelling argument, on the face of it, for a return to the bosom of Conservatism. Instead, Gladstone's conclusions were reminiscent of the pathos of the years of the disintegration of his first vocation: 'I do not look to spending in political life the last of my strength: I only await the day when the evidence of facts shall convince me that I have no reasonable expectation of doing good there, & certainly both the fact & the manner of the severance that is now hanging over us are the most significant indications that have yet been afforded me towards a proof, which I dare say the next few years will carry to demonstration.'[1]

The crucial point here, behind the camouflage of pathos, is in fact Gladstone's neglect ultimately to pitch himself over the brink to which his casuistical finesse had carried him. There was, embedded in the verbiage, one small remark which weighed heavier than all the rest. It was the only item of his analysis which told against Derby: 'Lord Derby is much weaker than he was in 1852.' Within the terms of Gladstone's new dual criterion for determining the optimum shape of future politics, that was a decisive verdict. Combined with the equally brief but pregnant remark that Russell constituted an alternative recourse, it was a damning verdict. And Aberdeen responded with perfect tact by taking the cue to draw the moral from Gladstone's tale – a moral Gladstone was both unable and unwilling to draw for himself: 'It is clear that we must accustom outselves to the conviction that there is no such thing as a distinctive Peelite part in existence'; Aberdeen indeed considered 'the amalgamation of Peel's friends with the liberal party to have practically taken place'; and he believed too that 'in this age of progress the liberal party must ultimately govern the country'; and he only hoped that 'their supremacy may be established without mischief or confusion'. In all this, Aberdeen pointed out, Gladstone would be 'free to act as your conscience may dictate; and there can be no doubt that until the moment for decision shall arrive, your true place is by the side of Graham and Herbert, both from political affinity & from private friendship'. Such a decision would require 'very mature reflection & an impartial estimate of the future'. Constituted as the present parliament was, 'and situated as political parties actually are', Aberdeen believed that 'the future, & indeed the early future, is big with great events; but that you will do well to preserve your present position until you find yourself in the face of a real emergency'.[2] Aberdeen's expressions of the 'warmest interest' in Gladstone's 'personal success &

1 *Ib.*, 210–11.   2 Aberdeen to G, April 3, 1857. GP, 43071, 364.

reputation' told him what he wanted to hear. Following with 'perfect good faith' the 'guidance which events afford' was an elastic formula which would enable Gladstone to place himself at the disposal of an event of his own choosing. Just as Gladstone spent the years between Maynooth and Gorham evading the 'proof' which those years carried to a quite convincing 'demonstration' of the bankruptcy of his State-Church programme, so now he settled down to evading the logic of his professions that there was no way out of the Peelite dead-end, compatible with honour and consistency, other than reunion with Derbyite Conservatism.

[6]

Graham's apprehensions at the prospect of 'open defection' by Gladstone to the Conservative benches on the opposition side of the House on the opening of the new parliament were needless.[1] When the parliament opened on April 30, 1857 Gladstone duly resumed his seat, along with Graham and Herbert, on the government side, below the gangway; the traditional place of men, as he explained with scrupulous gratuitousness to Herbert, 'who, having been out of office, may be either practically connected with, or wholly dissociated from the existing Government'.[2] His distress about the results of the election was exacerbated by the embarrassment of Catherine's connection James Stuart Wortley's putting himself forward as a candidate for the Speakership: 'For I am quite certain that it would be a violation of public duty in its first principles either to propose or support one just recovered from such a terrible illness attended with such peculiar features.'[3] The extent to which Palmerston's comprehensive rout of his enemies had knocked the stuffing out of Gladstone is best gauged by the fact that he did not open his mouth in the Commons until June 19, and then only for insignificant interventions. Stanley noted that 'Gladstone, either from ill-health, pique, or prudence, stays away'.[4] Pique undoubtedly predominated. The intensity of Gladstone's frustrations was marked by recourse to the scourge on May 29. Not until July 20 was he back in anything like his pre-election form, spurred by the impious secularity of the Divorce and Matrimonial Causes Bill.

To some extent Gladstone compounded for his unwonted parliamentary silence by another of his series of expostulations in the *Quarterly*. The new piece, 'The New Parliament and Its Work', was substantially the

1 Parker, *Graham*, ii, 308–9.   2 D, v, 218.
3 G to CG, March 27, 1857. GGP, 28/5.   4 DDCP, 151.

abortive letter to Aberdeen adjusted to the painful reversal of electoral expectations. The prevalent note was a sullen petulance. Not only was it an age of sophisters, economists, and calculators; but now 'another step in the downward series' had been taken. An 'age of charlatanism, of time-serving, and of something very nearly resembling imposture' appeared to have arrived. The Commons, 'shorn of many intellectual ornaments and of much moral strength', reflected a new dominance of local motives and interests in the boroughs; a new dominance of the 'retail mind' in place of the 'old order of gentlemen'. The government was entirely bereft of any sense of mission. 'As we had once a Barebones Parliament, so now we are to have a Palmerston Parliament', thanks to an incomprehensible election 'of great and general insincerity' which ignored the real problems of the country to pay homage to an unworthy minister whose turpitude stained every aspect of public life, not excluding a disgraceful episcopal policy of promoting Low Churchmen who could not even claim rank as mediocrities. The Conservatives knew all this: 'yet with a shrug or a sigh, they fold their arms, and provisionally accept Lord Palmerston as for the moment a necessity'. Peelism, that repository of political virtue, that peculiar guardian of the models of financial policy of 1842, 1845, and 1853, was now unhappily extinct. 'Some few, like Mr. Gladstone and Mr. Sidney Herbert, have apparently avoided any profession of allegiance to a party, but it seems likely that henceforth they will only be known as individuals, and as representing some particular shade of the one party or the other.'[1]

Through all this diatribe two positive notes only gleamed. The first was that Palmerston in 1857 had at his behest no real 'homogeneous band'. The 'ground is mined beneath his feet'. He presided over a 'mass of motley materials'. And there was still Lord John Russell to be contended with as a likely agent of instability in a 'miscellaneous and confused' parliament. The other was that Palmerston might yet perform one service: he 'may yet die the martyr of the Constitution'. He might, true to his 'domestic no-policy', refuse to countenance a 'democratic measure of reform'. In such a case Gladstone trusted that, 'irrespective of general confidence', Palmerston would 'receive from the independent portions of the House a warm support, stinted neither by the recollection of what they have disapproved, nor by any unworthy jealousy of his perpetuating his power'. Gladstone then sketched some features of a non-democratic Reform measure that would, presumably, gain his warm and unstinted support: it would preserve the distinct character of county representation founded upon 'beneficial interests' and property as against mere occupancy as in boroughs; it would preserve close boroughs as indispensable nurseries of statesmanship.[2]

1 QR, April 1857, 541, 566, 552, 543–45, 561, 573.   2 *Ib.*, 561, 583.

Recuperation from the numbing shock of the elections was aided by election to The Club, the famous convivial dining club founded by Dr. Johnson. Gladstone dined for the first time on April 21. On the 22nd he made a 'purchase of fine china wh. ought to be the last'; which also no doubt speeded convalescence, together with much therapeutic arranging of pieces in their cases. He busied himself hanging his precious Murillo in Carlton House Terrace, and lighting the Wilson. Entertaining the Royal Academy was a gratifying but arduous distraction. Gladstone fretted about how the house would look for an occasion 'which seems almost too audacious for us'. The best of the porcelain, he told Catherine, ought to be brought into more conspicuousness; 'both this & the pictures ought now to be put into really good order'. Gladstone had 'more confidence in the pictures I have myself bought than in the china into which fancy & a peculiar antiquarian knowledge of its own go so far to determine value'.[1] There was the opening of the new Reading Room at the British Museum to be attended; and Mr. Madot's painting of 'Slender wooing Anne Page' was purchased at the Academy exhibition. He dined with the Herberts and Graham 'as if Peelism were not dead'. He sat to Marochetti for a bust at Catherine's desire 'but I confess with a bad conscience'. The exigencies of the sculptor's art caused Gladstone to remove the 'quasi-beard' he had been cultivating. It was indeed an iconographic period: Gladstone had sat in 1855 for one of the exponents of the new photographic art, Mr. Maynall of Regent Street; and in 1859 he sat twice to the rising artist George Frederick Watts, whose 1857 portrait of Tennyson caused a stir. He kept up his Italian interests. He saw much of Panizzi, who possibly apprised him of Delane's undertaking to place the weight of *The Times* behind the Piedmontese cause in Italy. One of Gladstone's last pronouncements before the dissolution was to berate the Neapolitan government *à propos* of the arrest of the Piedmontese vessel *Cagliari* with some English aboard. Now, at the end of May, he met Felice Orsini, exponent of Mazzinian propaganda and refugee from Austrian dungeons, whose account of his sufferings Gladstone had recently been reading amid the beauty of West Wales. Orsini's fate and the fate of Palmerston's government would shortly be strangely entangled.

Rescue work continued in a rather desultory and not very satisfying manner. Gladstone complained of his 'half-heartedness' on May 29 and administered the discipline by way of retribution. That Willy was admitted to Christ Church at the beginning of June was a signal comfort. (That he had to pay £6–£8 to the servants on leaving Eton was a signal discomfort: unknown in Gladstone's own time.) Gladstone deeply enjoyed the occasion, redolent of so many happy or poignant memories.

1 G to CG, March 23, 1857. GGP, 28/6.

He did the usual pleasant Oxford rounds[1] and then proceeded to Cliveden for fireworks and thence to Salisbury where Bishop Hamilton confirmed Agnes. It was also highly gratifying that Willy, with three friends, should be chosen to accompany the Prince of Wales for an educational excursion that summer to Königswinter on the Rhine and then to Switzerland. It made one feel, he told Catherine, 'what I suspected, viz that the Prince of Wales has not been educated up to his position'; being 'kept in childhood beyond his term' had made him 'wanton'; but the fault lay with his teachers. 'I rejoice that Willy's whole soul loathes the tuft-hunting.'[2] There was a refreshing break in early July at Glenalmond to examine for prizes and meet the new warden, Hannah (*vice* Charles Wordsworth, now Bishop of St. Andrews), who made a good impression, mainly, it appears, by catering to Gladstone's insatiable appetite for 'long Homeric conversations'. He lectured the college on 'Christian and Classical Education' (in the train back he got from a Newcastle man in return a 'good Lecture on the Iron Trade').[3]

As the wounds healed Gladstone gradually picked up the threads of parliamentary life. The divorce question provoked a good deal of activity as well as another *Quarterly* article condemning the tendency of the times as 'restless, violent, feeble' when dealing with matters other than those 'mechanical and external'. He lamented the 'general decay of the spirit of traditionary discipline' as evidenced by the proposal to transfer matrimonial causes from ecclesiastical to secular courts and to allow petitions for divorce by husbands (for wife's adultery) and by wives (for husband's incestuous adultery, rape, bigamy, bestiality, or adultery coupled with cruelty); as well as by profane attempts to overturn the Table of Prohibited Degrees.[4] The Lords were making a 'deplorable business' of the Divorce Bill, he complained to Catherine, 'but what can you expect when the Bp of Exeter and De Tabley support the Bill, and when George [Lyttelton] had no opinion of it?' To Catherine again he confided that parliamentary affairs were 'very black'. The 'poor Church gets deeper and deeper into the mire'. The fear grew upon Gladstone 'from year to year that when I finally leave Parliament I shall not leave the great question of Church and State better but perhaps even worse than I found it'.[5] Certainly he resisted the bill tenaciously, making seventy-three interventions, fighting clause by clause, between July 24 and August 17.[6] His big speech on July 31 on the second reading dwelt on the horrors of bringing divorce to the doors of all classes. Stanley described the harangue as 'learned and

1 D, v, 228. The *Diary* reference to attending New College chapel at 4 a.m. is a slip of G's pen – alas! – for p.m.
2 G to CG, August 4, 1857. GGP, 28/5.   3 D, v, 236.
4 QR, July 1857, 'The Bill for Divorce', 523.   5 Bassett, 115, 116.
6 This performance was used against him by Parnell's followers in the early 1880s when Gladstone tried to cut down parliamentary obstruction.

impassioned'; but it 'lost a great part of its effect when Sir G. Grey published the fact of a similar Bill having been brought in by Lord Aberdeen's cabinet', thus revealing that Gladstone's 'religious scruples dated from less than three years back'.[1] Gladstone never forgave Palmerston's forcing through the Divorce Act by his 'merciless' use of his parliamentary strength when he had 'nothing to contend against but decency and reason'.[2]

Considering the conspicuous part played by Gladstone in assisting Lincoln to get his divorce this vehemence was, to say the least of it, unwise as well as unbalanced. The obvious public riposte was delivered by counsel for the plaintiff in a case of *crim. con.* citing Gladstone as a precedent. In *The Times* judicial report on August 12 it was recounted that 'the Journals of the House of Lords bore testimony to the fact that a right hon. gentleman, who was once a Minister of the Crown, had tracked the wife of a noble duke, who afterwards obtained a divorce, all through Italy, and appeared as a witness to prove her adultery'. Counsel pleaded that his client (an upholsterer of Charlotte Street, Fitzroy Square, whose wife was indulging in a liaison with a man who answered his advertisement for capital to expand his business) should not be blamed for employing the same method of surveillance.[3] It was knockabout courtroom comedy; and, as a clownish burlesque, all the more embarrassing. Acting on advice from Graham and Heathcote, Gladstone denied these 'untruths': his purpose had been 'alike friendly and in the interests of both parties'. But his vulnerability as to the collecting of evidence was not convincingly disposed of.[4] This embarrassing incident did nothing to ease Gladstone's despondency. 'Partly the Divorce Bill,' he told Catherine, 'and partly the grief with which I view the state of the House of Commons, its relations to the Govt. and (what I think) the constant loss of character and sacrifice of public interests give me a touch of mingled excitement and depression which will make me feel it an immense relief when this turmoil is over and I get back to Hawarden and the children.'[5]

In such a mood of 'mingled excitement and depression' Gladstone resumed his old campaign against 'great expenditure'. 'Step by step, inch by inch', without formal or sufficient discussion, the country was being drawn into a project for new War and Foreign Offices, 'one of the most astounding and incredible schemes that, in a financial point of view, has ever been presented to a civilized country'.[6] He harried the bureaucrats over their superannuation, shocked by the proposal that the 'proper remuneration to be given to public servants' should be taken from the

1 DDCP, 152. See Grey's statement H, cxlvii, 858–59. The bill to set up a Court of Divorce was abandoned for parliamentary reasons in July 1854.
2 Q R, *ib.*, 529, 530.
3 *Times*, August 12, 1857, 11.   4 H, cxlvii, 1691–3.
5 Bassett, 116–7.   6 H, *ib.*, 364–5 (July 24, 1857).

hands of the Commons and handed to arbitrators: 'There is infection in diseases of this kind.'[1] He was scathing about a vote of £40,000 for an industrial museum in Scotland; the increasing general scale of the miscellaneous estimates was a scandal; and Gladstone did not fail to point to the nefarious link between great expenditure and the deplorable 'spirit of our foreign policy'. And on that theme he had the pleasure of harrying Palmerston over the Suez Canal project which he vindicated against Foreign Office jealousy and extolled as a 'great stroke for the benefit of mankind'. Gladstone also opened the question of Danubian principalities, rejoicing that the elections rigged by the Turks and the Austrians with the connivance of the British government to keep them separated and thus to obstruct the forming of a Romanian national state had been quashed at the instance of the Emperor Napoleon.[2]

Family tragedy interrupted Gladstone's parliamentary convalescence. Mary Lyttelton, in defiance of her doctor's advice, had become pregnant for the twelfth time. The birth of the child in February was fraught with severe complications. While Gladstone wrestled with the Divorce Bill, Catherine was at Hagley watching over her fading sister. A telegram summoned Gladstone on August 16; he could not resist diving back immediately to London and the iniquitous Divorce Bill; but he was back up again when Mary died, serenely, on the 18th.[3] George Lyttelton was prostrate. 'He fully accepts the will of God & to see his behaviour is most edifying.'[4] Gladstone set about framing a scheme to collaborate with Lyttelton in a selection of translations to distract his grief. After the funeral the Gladstones were back in Hawarden on the 28th, where Gladstone solaced himself with Homer leavened with Döllinger and a long course of Walter Scott. There were the new coal bore holes to be admired. But the obsessions were no less obsessive: 'We had a Palmerston Conversation till $\frac{1}{2}$ p.12.'[5] Homer, on the whole, predominated. When the Dowager Lady Lyttelton and her party called at Hawarden in October they found themselves obliged to participate in 'Homeric conv.'. Gladstone published in the *Oxford Essays* of 1857 'The Place of Homer in Classical Education and in Historical Inquiry' which was to form the Prolegomena of the first volume for his forthcoming *Studies on Homer*. By this time Gladstone was well enough advanced with the book to 'begin

1 *Ib.*, 660.   2 *Ib.*, 1667–70 (August 14, 1857).
3 The heavy distractions both of the Divorce Bill and of Mary's death allowed little time for Gladstone to notice the great and sanguinary event known as the 'Indian Mutiny'. He caught up on Indian papers and documents on July 27 and read the latest account of the events on August 12. But his only comment appears to have been made on the occasion of his speech at the annual meeting of the Society for the aid of Foreign Missions, when he drew attention to the 'lesson of humility' taught by the horrific occurrences. (Reid, 395). Certainly this theme of humility would be at the bottom of his attitude in the following year to the reshaping of the British government of India.
4 D, v, 246–7.   5 *Ib.*, 252.

Contents: but a good deal of licking down & filing & some rewriting remain'. He enjoyed his task so much that he felt the necessity to reassure himself that he was 'quite sound in conscience as to the work on Homer which now occupies so much of my mind & time'.[1] When he finished the *Homer* manuscript on February 10, 1858 he wished he 'felt as hopeful about the execution as the design. If it were even tolerably done, it would be a good service to religion as well as to literature: and I mistrustfully offer it up to God.' The only untoward incidents to disturb the placid Hawarden routine were the bizarre setting on fire of the church on October 29 (providing a good restoration job for George Gilbert Scott) and the scandalising discovery in November that 'one of the servants in the house is an unbeliever': 'Eli, the reading youth'.[2]

[7]

Placid times ended abruptly in the new year, when on January 14, 1858 an attempt was made by a group of Italian exiles to assassinate Napoleon III by means of bombs. Among the perpetrators was Gladstone's acquaintance Felice Orsini. The operation was planned in the vicinity of Leicester Square; and the bombs (as the French authorities soon discovered) were manufactured in Birmingham. The French government, under pressure from an anglophobe public mood, made stiff representations about Britain's giving irresponsible latitude to dangerous refugees. Orsini was tried in France in February and executed on March 13. The affair embarrassed Gladstone, one of Orsini's most illustrious patrons. (No doubt it was gratifying, meanwhile, to have tribute paid to him by a more respectable representative of the Italian cause in Farini's *La Diplomazia e la questione Italiana. . . . lettera al Signor G. Gladstone.*) Palmerston took Count Walewski's point about giving asylum to assassins to the extent of agreeing that it would be appropriate to convert conspiracy to murder from a misdemeanour to a felony. As with his careless recognition of Louis Napoleon's *coup d'état* in 1851, Palmerston's careless complaisance towards Walewski in 1858 cost him dear. The patriotic claptrap of the 'national' public which normally sustained him now turned against him as a truckler to French insolence; Palmerston was weakly allowing the law of England to be altered at the dictates of a foreign absolutism. Since his great success in 1857 he had also grown arrogant, and alienated many of his supporters with injudicious appointments. As Palmerston faltered, Gladstone instinctively pounced. In the competition in humbug which ensued Gladstone's contribution was not least. He solemnly

1 *Ib.*, 270.   2 *Ib.*, 262.

defended freedom against repressive measures which would be 'a blow and a discouragement to that sacred cause in every country in the world'. With unctuous pathos he spoke of grave times for liberty. 'We live in the nineteenth century. We talk of progress. We believe that we are advancing but . . . there is . . . a downward and backward movement.'[1] All Palmerston's enemies rejoiced at having him at a disadvantage on his own ground. Ministers were astonishingly beaten on February 19 by 215 to 234. The only really promising sign before the division, Gladstone recounted, 'was that Palmerston was actually rabid'.[2] Gladstone was ecstatic. 'It almost revived the China night.'[3] Some eighty disgruntled Liberals turned against their chief. Palmerston tendered his resignation to the Queen on February 20. On the 21st Gladstone wrote to Catherine from the Oxford and Cambridge Club that it was a 'most bewildered and uncertain house but at last they were screwed up to it. Last year we struck one vote for humanity – this year for honour: God be praised.' So elated was Gladstone that he felt it greatly amiss that Catherine was not with him to share the happiness of the event: 'Last year you were here. This year you are not, and this is what I do not like. In hours of great joy as well as great sorrow it is very sad to be away from you. I thought of bolting by the 6 a.m. train four hours hence – but the crisis is important and I dare not.' Gladstone's excitement at the fall of the 'great fustian Ministry' was almost disturbing in its intensity. Later, in another *Quarterly* piece, he gloated on the shortness of the interval for Palmerston between the 'summit of the Capitoline Hill and the precipice of the Tarpeian Rock'. 'England has cause to be glad that she is quit of him as her guide.' He also allowed his wishes to father his thoughts to a highly incautious degree. Palmerston could not 'under any ordinary circumstances, whatever be his longings, resume the station he had lost'.[4]

Marking his sense of the high solemnity of the occasion by taking Holy Communion at no less a church than Westminster Abbey on the evening of Sunday, February 21, Gladstone went directly 'from the sacred feast' to Lord Aberdeen's. There a message from Derby caught up with him, offering him an unspecified place in a Conservative cabinet. Herbert was sent for and Gladstone drafted a negative reply. Graham also arrived and heard it. With 'slight modifications' it went. 'The case though grave was not doubtful.' Gladstone went off into the night with Herbert; and they parted 'with the fervent wish that in public life we might never part'.[5]

The argument of March 13, 1856 applied decisively. It was important that Palmerston had gone out; but it was not necessarily important that the 'next turn of the wheel' had put Derby in. And, apart from anything

1 H, cxlviii, 1819–20.   2 Bassett, 120.   3 D, v, 279.
4 QR, 'The Past and Present Administrations' (October 1858), 543–4, 546.
5 D, v, 279.

else, Gladstone's plans presupposed an unchallenged claim to the Exchequer; and his disinclination to compete with Disraeli remained as strong as ever: 'we could not', as he said in April 1856, 'bargain Disraeli out of the saddle'.[1] Yet the very coolness and briskness of Gladstone's response marked a stage in his emancipation from some of the 'main practical principles' by which his political understanding had been anchored. The further movement of such 'processes' of detachment would remain 'exceeding slow'; but the general trend was 'not doubtful'. The process of Gladstone's shedding his purely Conservative identity in the late 1850s bears many analogies with the manner of his dismantling his State and Church programme in the late 1840s, not least in his profound unwillingness to admit to himself or anyone else that the process itself was under way. Very much in the same manner of constantly reassuring himself by reassuring Manning and Hope that his commitment to his original vocation remained intact, in these years Gladstone made his preparations for reimplementing his second vocation within a context of excessively prim meticulousness as to formalities, of a rigid punctiliousness as to not allowing any ostensible anticipation of events, and of an intense reluctance especially to renounce his Peelite loyalties. The more he felt the political ground shifting beneath him the more he invoked old images of stability. He was never more studiously a Conservative than at the time of his coming to the conclusion that Conservatism could not be an adequate vehicle for his renewed vocation.

As with the disintegration of Gladstone's first vocation, the subterranean pressures beneath the reintegration of his second vocation occasionally broke through to the surface. He had already cited (if only as a paradox) public economy and colonial policy as two issues on which the Peelites were more with the 'strong or advanced Liberals'. This was generally true also of foreign policy issues such as the Greek case in 1850 or China or the Russian war. The implications of Gladstone's attitude to the Italian question were by no means as clearly 'Liberal' in the 1850s as they came to seem later. His Italophilism derived from anti-Romanism more than from anything else. In the same way, his incipient Austrophobia owed more to the concordat of 1855 than to resentment at Schwarzenberg in 1851. The point of his Neapolitan indictment, that absolutism and Romanism forced Italians to be Liberals because they were not allowed to be Conservatives, remained as valid for him as ever. His recent defence of Piedmont against the Vatican repeated the essential features of this indictment. Certainly nothing broke through to the surface in the 1850s which exposed the subterranean shifts as revealingly and compromisingly as his 1847 'march of mind' outburst on the Jewish disabilities issue.

1 PMP, iii, 206.

On February 22 Palmerston announced his resignation in the Commons. Gladstone noted: 'Palmerston died with propriety, Disraeli with bad tact anticipated his leadership.'[1] But even Disraeli's tactlessness could not dampen Gladstone's elation. As he had earlier assured Derby, he was so eager to be rid of Palmerston that he would welcome any replacement. Now, in the *Quarterly*, he rejoiced in emancipation from Palmerston's thraldom. What a relief that 'new actors are upon the stage'! The intensity of his relief can perhaps best be judged by the persistence of the humbug that was the means of its attainment. It was not too much to say, insisted Gladstone, that 'Europe at large applauded the vote by which Lord Palmerston fell from the giddy summit of power'. It was felt that 'a great stroke had been struck, and that in an evil day, for freedom, for justice, and for national honour and independence'. Naturally Gladstone was full of happy analogies with the 'vote for humanity' of 1857. 'The conspirators of the far-famed China vote of March 1857, Mr. Disraeli, Mr. Roebuck, and the friends of Sir Robert Peel, once more rubbed shoulders together. The Parthian drank of Arar, and the Germans of the Tigris . . . but they were now, as Lord Derby observed, conspirators no longer – they were patriots.'[2] It was exhilarating to find oneself in a role as unaccustomed as it seemed auspicious. The 'extraordinary asperity' of Gladstone's 'extreme antipathy' to Palmerston in this 'bitter though able review' caused more head-shaking.[3]

In high glee Gladstone celebrated what he trusted was the definitive end of Palmerston with attendances at Christie's sale room and with shopping for 'further extensions' to his porcelain cabinets. He could now boast that 'our China has grown almost into a collection'. Early in March he made his last sitting for the Marochetti bust ('a product of extraordinary power: I would it were another subject')[4]. Excitement had made it difficult to get down to the 'wretched' article on the fall of the government he prepared for the *Quarterly*, from which he so long 'flinched' and 'pottered'. Gladstone in truth became rather manic about restoring pictures and refurbishing frames. 'Shall we hang the large Severn in the dining room over the side-board? Another is Richmond's suggestion. He is *enthusiastic* about the large Murillo. It must be cleaned.' It must also be lowered; and Richmond advised a red ground on the wall to give it effect. Gladstone also had an 'experienced and accomplished' dealer in to look at the porcelain, which at last had been arranged 'in something like a proper way'.[5] To crown all, the Homer book came out at the end of March. 'My book came from Parker's in a fit state for sale: I was

1 D, v, 280.   2 QR, April 1858, 571–2.   3 *Greville*, vii, 363.
4 D, v, 280, 282, 283, 288, 289. The bust was destroyed in the Mansion House during the London blitz of 1940.
5 G to CG, March 31, 1858. *Ib.*

weak enough to spend two hours in reading it.' Even Catherine read it ('I take in your reading "Homer": it shows what love can do').[1] The confident fortitude of mind Gladstone derived from his conviction of vocation and mission is nowhere better illustrated than in his fond indulgence for this work in the face of the criticisms of the scholarly world.

Studies on Homer and the Homeric World, in three stout volumes, was received with general eyebrow-raising. Gladstone's argument for unity of authorship and the proximity of the author to the epic story was in itself acceptable enough; but Gladstone was distinctly out of his depth in most of the more abstruse reaches of the technicalities. It was his insistence that the Homeric religion contained elements of divine truth and that those elements must have proceeded from divine revelation and that they therefore reflect the 'authority of a providential order' and amount to a species of 'supplementary revelation' that startled his readers.[2] Jowett dismissed it as 'mere nonsense'. Mark Pattison, another of the Oxford reformers, compared *Studies on Homer* to Bishop Warburton's *Divine Legation of Moses*, one of the grand oddities of misdirected eighteenth-century erudition. Twentieth-century classical scholarship inclines to see Gladstone's 'marked eccentricity' as 'recalling the oddest aberrations of seventeenth-century enthusiasts', or as being 'strangely reminiscent of the doctrines of the British Israelites'.[3] 'But while the Jewish records exhibit to us,' Gladstone affirmed, 'the link between man and the other world in the earliest times, the poems of Homer show us the being, of whom God was pleased to be thus mindful, in the free unsuspecting play of his actual nature.' The Jewish dispensation shows a state of things 'essentially special and exceptional'; in Homer 'we see our kind set to work out for itself, under the lights which common life and experience supplied, the deep problem of his destiny'. Homer's religion, Gladstone insisted, was 'a true Theology corrupted'; it had not its basis in nature-worship; it 'could not have sprung from invention only'. Section X of volume ii, 'The office of the Homeric Poems in relation to that of the early Books of Holy Scripture', caused most of the eyebrow-raising: the uniqueness of the Homeric Poems put them 'in a certain relation to the Scriptures, that no other work of man can be compared to them'. Thus: 'if we are right in the belief that we are not to look for the early development of humanity in the pages of Jewish and patriarchal history, but rather to believe that it was given to another people, and the office of recording it to the father, not only of poetry, but of letters, does it seem difficult to read in this arrangement the purpose of the Most High, and herewith the wisdom of that purpose?'[4] Gladstone noted a review in *The*

1 G to CG, September 1, 1858. GGP 18/6.
2 H. Lloyd Jones, 'Gladstone on Homer', *Times Literary Supplement*, January 3, 1975, 17.
3 *Ib.*, 25. Tollemache, 12.   4 *Studies on Homer*, i, 7; ii, 9–13, 522.

National Review in July 'which ought to humble me'.[1] That review, by the Oxford scholar and historian Edward Freeman, warrants attention both for its quality and its representativeness. He accused Gladstone of meddling with ethnology 'without the needful training' and of treating mythology 'from a wholly false point of view'. He drew attention to Gladstone's 'strange fondness for bringing in references to Scripture, and a strange mixture of timidity and daring in his way of dealing with them'. We are not allowed to pay literary homage to Hebrew warriors and statesmen; but we are invoked 'with a daring which many would call irreverent', to see the shadow of the Trinity in Zeus, Poseidon, and Aidoneus. Gladstone's doctrine at bottom, concluded Freeman, was 'simply unintelligible'. Why could not he accept Hebrew writings for what they are – history, politics, poetry, as well as theology?[2] Gladstone, however, remained imperturbably unhumbled.

In the spirit of indulgence to the new actors upon the stage Gladstone offered a very friendly response to Disraeli's budgetary proposals in April, expressing hopes that the policy of extinguishing the income tax would be adhered to and that the overall scale of expenditure would be reduced to something like £53 or £54 millions as against the scandalous existing level of £63.6 millions. Likewise on Church Rates Abolition he was all sweetness and light and co-operation with ministers, urging an end to all reasonable Dissenting grievances but pleading for delay to mitigate the immediate severing of the Church from its traditional mode of local financing. He was less satisfied with ministers' proposals for recasting the government of India in the aftermath of the Mutiny, offering sombre thoughts as to the doubtful 'efficacy of our Parliamentary institutions in defending the interests and the institutions of the people of India' and in maintaining 'our respect, our care and tenderness towards the feelings and prejudices of those over whom we happen to be placed'. He was particularly apprehensive at the dangers of unconstitutional exercise of power by the executive through the medium of the Indian finances and the Indian Army; and objected to the wide powers of the proposed new office of Secretary of State as inimical to Treasury control over the spending of money, citing the instance of the division of responsibilities between the Secretary at War and the Secretary of State for War in support.[3] Gladstone's general indulgence to the Conservative government in the 1858 session worried those Liberals who looked to him as the greatest potential recruit to their cause. John Bright, who increasingly saw in Gladstone the means of breaking out of the bounds of politics set by Palmerston and Derby, grew anxious. Gladstone's alleged

1 D, v, 309.
2 Republished by Freeman in *Historical Essays*, 2 series (1873), 67–68, 72, 92.
3 H, cxlix, 1683–4, 2195–98 (April 26 and May 3, 1858).

'backsliding towards the Tories' panicked Lady Waldegrave and her friends into inviting the Gladstones to Strawberry Hill at Twickenham for a course of Liberal stiffening.[1]

[8]

Unquestionably Gladstone's *chef d'oeuvre* of the 1858 session was his great speech on May 4 to his motion urging the Commons and the government to uphold the cause of the Romanians against the Turks and the Austrians. The implications of this occasion ultimately, if indirectly, made a decisive contribution to the stiffening of Gladstone's liberalism. He had been following the question closely ever since he began corresponding with Bratiano in 1856; and he conferred with the Romanian statesmen on April 27. He had made a point of stressing its importance in his latest *Quarterly* article. Now, with Palmerston out of the way, an opportunity presented itself for striking a blow combining the humanity of the China case in 1857 with the honour of the refugees' case in February 1858. The Foreign Office and Bulwer's embassy in Constantinople (pushing aside the dissentient Stratford Canning) colluded with the Turks and the Austrians to stifle the Romanian state at birth. Gladstone had already rejoiced that France, together with Russia, had secured the quashing of the elections rigged to produce a vote against the union of Moldavia and Wallachia. The question was now poised. A conference would soon meet in Paris. It was vital to give support to the French. Gladstone trusted that the new Conservative ministry which had no motives for adherence to Palmerston's Crimean policy could be persuaded to take a new line, in concert especially with the French, to patronise Romanian unity and independence as one of the few positive achievements in an otherwise largely barren war.

The 1858 Romanian speech is a document of crucial significance for the development of Gladstone's outlook on foreign affairs. It provided, in a considered form, the positive dimension of his negative critiques of what by now was becoming identifiable as the 'Crimean' aspect of Palmerstonism, as offered in his Manchester speech of 1853 and his speeches against the continuance of the war in 1855 and on the spuriousness of the peace in 1856. There were times when his frustrated excitement on this issue broke out of the restraints of what was judicious, prudent and, above all, politic; and this was especially the case with the 'War and Peace' article in the *Gentleman's Magazine* of July 1856. In this, in the intervals of abusing the Turks and Islam, Gladstone painted

1 Morley, i, 579; Hewett, *Strawberry Fair*, 137.

glowing vision of 'we or our children' seeing 'the noble spectacle of a Greek Christian empire with Constantinople as its capital', a 'wholesome check upon Russia in the interests of Europe, a strong bulwark against Papal aggressions on behalf of Christendom'. The substance of the piece, however, was to the effect that Russia was a largely innocent victim of events: she had been sucked into Turkish affairs by the criminal debility of the Ottoman empire. 'The position of Russia in the East is of necessity commanding; and her destinies there, unless sedulously spoiled by herself, must be magnificent. She is the natural head of Eastern Christendom.' This was incautious enough; but to top it off with a lyrical evocation of the magnificence of Nicholas I (the impact of 1844 remained very immediate), his 'towering form', the 'lightning of his eye', 'his imperial, his almost superhuman presence', the grandeur of his role as the 'immovable stay and pillar of continental Europe' during the 'disastrous disclosure and miserable retrogression' of 1848,[1] compromised Gladstone's credit as a guide on Eastern affairs very seriously. It is clear that many of Gladstone's friends and admirers such as Argyll were embarrassed by this foolishly extravagant Russophilism much as they were bored by Gladstone's obsessive vindictiveness against Palmerston.[2]

This general loss of credit undoubtedly undermined Gladstone's plea for the Romanians in 1858. Ironically, though he rehearsed all his former prejudices, his speech was a model of restraint and good sense. He argued that there was no chance of the British or the French people being always ready in the future to pay £50 or £100 millions to prop up the Turks; and that therefore the logical, sensible, rational, as well as humane, liberal and generous course was to promote emancipation of Christian subject peoples under the anyway rotting Ottoman yoke. If Russian aggression was the principal fear then 'surely the best resistance to be offered to Russia is by the strength and freedom of those countries that will have to resist her. You want to place a living barrier between her and Turkey. There is no barrier, then, like the breasts of free men.'[3] Russophile extravagance was replaced by shrewd contrasts between Russia and Austria, to Austrian disadvantage. This strong new Austrophobic emphasis was an important shift, with obvious implications for the Italian question (it was not convenient for Austria 'to have freedom in conjunction with prosperity close by her threshold; but that is her fault, not mine').[4]

That Palmerston would oppose Gladstone's Romanian initiative was to be expected: the Crimean War had been fought to maintain the integrity and independence of the Ottoman empire; it would be absurd to set about undermining that independence and integrity in the peace. The crucial

1 *Gentleman's Magazine*, July 1856, 141–155.   2 Argyll, ii, 160.
3 H, xl, 59.   4 *Ib.*, 58.

disappointment for Gladstone was that Disraeli, speaking authoritatively for Malmesbury at the Foreign Office, echoed Palmerston's argument and placed the Conservative government firmly on the side of the Crimean policy. Gladstone accordingly lost by 292 to 114, noting grimly: 'and with it goes another broken promise to a people.'[1] He had no disposition whatever to blame himself in any degree for compromising his own case; but he now had a considerable disposition to feel a grievance against the Conservative government. This was an immediate consequence of great importance for two reasons: first, it was yet another jolt which helped to shift Gladstone's political understanding further from its old anchorage; second, it confronted him for the first time with the realisation that on a major field of foreign policy there was nothing to choose between Palmerston and Derby. In a longer perspective, the Romanian case of 1858 fixed both Gladstone and Disraeli more firmly in their respective postures of 1853 and 1854. Romania thus points forward with curious precision to the dénouement of this developing antagonism in the 1870s. Gladstone's golden phrase of 1858, 'breasts of free men', became a *leitmotiv* of the opposition in 1876–78 to Disraeli's Palmerstonian policy. And it was also a matter of curious precision that in 1858 Gladstone should have found a supporter for his motion (if not for his emotion) in the young Lord Robert Cecil (who earned himself a pained rebuke from Disraeli), who was also, as Marquess of Salisbury, to play a singularly consistent role in the 1870s.

[9]

Gladstone's broodings over Romania were soon interrupted by a cabinet crisis. Ellenborough, President of the Board of Control for India, resigned in May 1858 after a dispute with Canning, the Governor General, over the settlement of the Oude, annexed in 1856. Palmerston perpetrated, according to Gladstone, a 'gigantic blunder' in attacking the government on Canning's behalf; an attack which recoiled upon himself and strengthened Derby.[2] Gladstone's generally sympathetic attitude on Indian policy encouraged Derby to make another effort to entice his 'only half-regained Eurydice'. On May 22, with Spencer Walpole as emissary, he offered Gladstone a choice of the Board of Control of the Colonial Office. He sweetened the enticement with the understanding that if Gladstone accepted it might be a means towards a more extended union with the Peelites thereafter. To facilitate the transaction, it was made clear that Disraeli was willing to surrender the Leadership of the Commons to Graham.

1 D, v, 295.   2 QR, October 1858, 545.

For Gladstone nothing had happened to make him feel that the criteria of March 1856 as applied to February 1858 were to any extent being fulfilled by events. A great matter like the reshaping of India was naturally tempting; and it was indeed 'handsome' on Disraeli's part to waive his claims. And, while 'no broad and palpable differences of opinion upon public questions of principle' separated him from the Conservative government, the same applied to the Liberals, excepting Lord Palmerston's 'temper and views of public conduct'. Nay, it was hard to show broad differences of public principle between the government and the opposition. It was true that Gladstone differed from the government on issues of Indian legislation and upon the Romanian question: yet he differed at least as much on these matters with the government's opponents. 'I said however,' as Gladstone reported to Aberdeen and Graham, 'that in my view the proposal . . . could not be entertained.' Much as he felt the 'personal misfortune and public inconvenience' of being 'thrown out of party connection', it still remained the case that 'a man at the bottom of the well must not try to get out, however disagreeable his position, until a rope or a ladder is put down to him'. His 'clear opinion' was that by joining the government he would 'shock the public sentiment' and would 'make no essential, no important change in their position'. No individual could effect the reconstruction of a party or 'that process, call it what we may, which would place the government in such a condition as materially to enlarge and strengthen its hold upon public opinion, and change in its favour the present distribution of political strength throughout the country'. To underline his disappointment over the Romanian case, Gladstone added pointedly the lament that the government was falling into 'the groove of Lord Palmerston's eastern policy', relying on the ineffectual support of Austria and alienating France and thereby impelling her towards Russia.[1]

This sting in the tail illustrates tellingly the alienating effect of Disraeli's support for Palmerston on Romania. But the substance of Gladstone's refusal was still encapsulated in the point he put to Derby on March 5, 1857: that it was 'high time' for the Conservatives to 'attract to themselves such a strength of public opinion as would really put them in a condition to undertake the government of the country'. It is clear from Gladstone's response to Walpole that he did not think that the Conservatives had succeeded in doing this; it is also clear that Gladstone felt himself in some sense responsible to a 'public sentiment' which would be 'shocked' by his joining the Conservatives; which is to say that, to the extent that a public opinion of dimensions appropriate to the occasion existed, it was a Liberal public opinion; and moreover that Gladstone felt himself obliged to defer to its will, at least to the extent of not deliberately or directly affronting it.

1 PMP, iii, 222–24.

Finally, it is clear that Gladstone assumed that the rescuing hand which would lower the rope or the ladder to him at the bottom of the political well would be the strong hand of that public opinion which would materially enlarge and strengthen the political force in the country of the party chosen to fulfil its purposes – purposes, that is to say, already chosen for it by Gladstone. And those chosen purposes required that Gladstone should resume control of the levers of finance. It was indeed 'handsome' of Disraeli to renounce the leadership of the House; but it was not enough. Again, the logic was impeccable.

From his two Peelite mentors Gladstone got contradictory advice. Graham, the most Liberal-leaning of the Peelites, advised Gladstone to go with Derby. His motive was the passing of opportunities. 'Time is wearing fast away. You have attained the utmost vigor of your understanding and of your powers. Present opportunities are not to be neglected in the vain expectation of better, which *may* arise, but which may also never come. Without some risk no great advantage is ever gained.' Graham could not possibly assist by accepting Disraeli's offer; it was too late. Graham saw himself, along with Aberdeen, as henceforth a political bystander rather than a participant. There was no further point in clinging to a Peelite position: 'The little band is broken up.' Newcastle stood aloof, awaiting his opportunities; Herbert and Cardwell would go with the Liberals. 'The result is, that you stand alone.' Gladstone could join Derby with 'perfect honor'. His natural affinities in that direction were strong; the India Board at this decisive juncture was a worthy task; his 'honest liberal tendencies' would 'soon leaven the whole lump'. As for the Leadership of the House, Gladstone could not make Disraeli's abdication a 'condition *precedent*'. 'But side by side you would soon virtually supersede him.' Disraeli would relinquish as soon as he could without disgrace; 'pre-eminence would be yours, let the official arrangements be what they may'. A dissolution could not be far distant. Derby would either continue as head of the government or retire at the head of a most powerful party. In any case Derby in the Lords and Gladstone in the Commons acting in concert for Conservatism 'cannot be dreary'. Parliamentary reform must soon become a prominent question; and Gladstone was more likely to agree on this subject with Lord Derby than with Lord John Russell. Graham would rejoice to see Gladstone's 'honest virtue' and 'great abilities' actively engaged in great affairs and not wasted in fruitless controversy, even at the cost of some official but no personal break in their relationship. Graham recommended Gladstone to seek the opinion of Lord Aberdeen, which 'ought to have great weight with you. . . . He regards you with warm affection, and would wish to leave you on the right road to present honor and to future fame.'[1]

1 *Ib.*, 225–227.

Aberdeen's opinion is recorded with a laconic and decisive authority: 'Like myself decidedly of opinion that it is impossible for me, acting alone, to join Lord Derby's administration under the present circumstances; nor does either of us foresee any circumstances in which that step would be possible or would promise public advantage.'[1] Graham's advice comprehended every point except the one at the centre. Aberdeen had already put his finger accurately on it with his simple doctrine that in 'this age of progress' Liberalism must command politics. Gladstone was not prepared merely to be the leaven of the lump. Nor did he see the matter in terms of the 'risk' of missing his chance of jumping at the turning of the wheel of political fortune. On the contrary, he could feel confidently passive. It was not a question of fortune but of great new forces. He was at the bottom of the well waiting for the public opinion his insight told him was forming to lower the rope or the ladder. His discomfort in the meanwhile was acute; but there was no serious alternative to patient waiting.

All this made Disraeli's intrusion in aid of Derby at once so decidedly handsome and so peculiarly infelicitous. The Peelites had laid it down in negotiations with Heathcote in April 1856 that the Leadership of the Commons was a matter of 'most vital consequence', and that while Gladstone looked upon it himself with 'doubt and dread', Disraeli's holding it would be one of the '*data*' of the case 'which might be seriously affected by it'.[2] 'I think it of such paramount importance to the public interest,' Disraeli accordingly wrote to Gladstone on May 25 (with a dramatic absence of the conventional preliminaries), 'that you should assume at this time a commanding position in the administration of affairs that I feel it a solemn duty to lay before you some facts that you may not decide under a misapprehension.' Keenly aware of the widely held view that 'our mutual relations have caused the great difficulty in accomplishing a result which I have always anxiously desired', Disraeli begged Gladstone to 'listen without prejudice' to a brief narrative of the various offers he had made to give up the Leadership of the Commons to Palmerston or Graham in order to make the way clear for Gladstone. Did not Gladstone think the time had come when he 'might deign to be magnanimous'? Disraeli appealed to the precedent of Canning's sacrifice of his feelings for the benefit of the Tory party in joining with Castlereagh. 'I may be removed from the scene or I may wish to be removed from the scene.' There was, as Disraeli with exquisite ineptness reminded Gladstone, 'a Power, greater than ourselves, that disposes of all this'.[3]

This last note, from Disraeli, was jarringly false; but not so jarring as Gladstone's unworthily nonchalant response: all the more so in that Gladstone was perfectly justified in the main point of his explanation,

1 *Ib.*, 227.　　2 *Ib.*, 206.　　3 Blake, *Disraeli* 383–84.

that the problem of their mutual relations was not the 'main difficulty' in the way. The difficulties, he assured Disraeli, were 'broader than you may have supposed'. It was a question not only of connections which make harmonious and effective cabinet co-operation possible; it was a question also of 'what connections can be formed with public approval'.[1]

In any assessment in 1858 of Gladstone's political difficulties on the grounds of personal relations, Palmerston now far outweighed Disraeli. Perhaps no vendetta in modern politics up to that point had ever been more pertinaciously waged than that waged by Gladstone against Palmerston. In this respect Palmerston eclipsed Disraeli, who in the earlier 1850s had been shaping so promisingly as the prime antagonist Gladstone seemed to be in need of. In refusing Derby and Disraeli, Gladstone well knew that he risked having eventually to accept Palmerston as the unavoidable price he would have to pay in order to be hauled out of the well. That kind of risk, as against the risk defined by Graham, he was willing to take. In any case, Gladstone was in the process of convincing himself that Palmerston, already seventy-four and not a little discredited, was a spent force. Nor, again, is there reason to suppose that Gladstone did not accept the entire accuracy of Graham's prognostication of the likely shape of any future political partnership between himself and Disraeli. In the final analysis, for all its failure to rise to the level of the occasion set by Disraeli's generosity, Gladstone's refusal derived from higher and better motives than personal dislike. In his eyes Disraeli's merit lay in making a rather painful decision marginally less painful.

In a last bid, Derby, choosing to regard Gladstone's reply to him as a 'réponse argumentative' rather than a 'refus catégorique', concocted a desperate plan to have Gladstone 'take India under the shield and cover of Lord Ab. joining the Cabinet . . . without office'.[2] Aberdeen's refusal to lend any countenance to this bizarre expedient doomed it to quick extinction.

[10]

As if to bear testimony to his disinterested cordiality to the Conservative administration Gladstone launched out on yet another parliamentary assault on Palmerston, this time on the theme 'whether we are to protest against the use of the political influence of this country for the purpose of preventing the making of the canal across the Isthmus of Suez'. He pilloried the 'vicious system' of which Palmerston when in office was the 'main author', the system of arbitrary and gratuitous interference to

1 M & B, i, 1559.   2 *Ib.*, 1561.

thwart a project 'beneficial to mankind' on grounds worse than 'null and valueless,' because they 'place England at issue with the world, and commit us to a contest in which we must necessarily fail'. Not even Austria had supported Palmerston and his friends in their 'blatantly political', 'most unwise' and 'ungenerous' intrigues. Let the canal stand or fall as a commercial enterprise. Gladstone declared himself 'unwilling to set up the Indian empire of Great Britain in opposition to the general interest of mankind, or the general sentiment of Europe'.[1] Disraeli, thus challenged as on the case of Romania to distance the Conservative government from Palmerstonism, responded on this occasion with a judicious evasiveness which fended Gladstone off while not provoking him into a greater sense of grievance.

At Lady Jersey's reception on June 19 Gladstone did indeed vent 'some dissatisfaction with the Govt.'[2]. But he chose not to cause difficulties for what he later described as 'the regular, the undisputed, let us add the generally successful administration of public affairs by a Government which is, or is supposed to be, politically opposed to the large majority of the House of Commons'. Gladstone's primary motive for thus under-lining the point that Derby's minority government existed with 'pretty general approval, with nearly universal acquiescence', was in fact to explain this 'singular anomaly, this curious twist in constitutional history', as a consequence of the final collapse of Palmerston's political credit. Gladstone refuted indignantly shallow efforts to account for Derby's survival on grounds of Conservative 'plagiarism' of Liberalism, of purchasing office by 'sacrifices offered to the genius of radicalism represented in the person of Mr. John Bright' on such matters as church rates. Gladstone inclined rather to be severe on that 'knot of politicians commonly called the Manchester School'. No: the essence of the explanation, insisted Gladstone, was that too many of Palmerston's betrayed followers 'have written this sentence upon the tablets of their heart: "*Come what may, Lord Palmerston shall not again be minister*"'. It was a proscription, continued Gladstone, not only of a person, but of a 'system of misgovernment at home and abroad'. Palmerston clearly was finished: 'That sun has set, and has set, if we read the signs of the times aright, not to rise again.'[3]

There is no reason to suppose that Gladstone was not perfectly serious in this rather frantic exercise in wishful thinking. Obviously it helped to bolster his confidence that he had done the right thing in refusing Derby and Disraeli. The thought of risking Palmerston as the alternative must have been, even to one as generally self-assured as Gladstone, unnerving. But more probably it was that very self-assurance which lay behind the wish which fathered the thought. Gladstone was playing a bold

1 H, cl, 1385–92.   2 D, v, 306.   3 QR, October 1858, 515–41.

game for high stakes. He saw himself as the destined heir of a post-Palmerstonian dispensation. He never lacked ambition. One of the staples of Peelite talk was Gladstone's leading the Commons (for all his protestations of 'doubt and dread') with a conveniently recessive prime minister in the Lords. There is no reason in any case to suppose that Gladstone did not see himself now as an eminently eligible first minister. It was often enough predicted. He was nearly fifty: older than Peel was in 1834; only a little younger than Peel was in 1841. He now had his own 'system' fully prepared and unchallengeably accredited (to his own satisfaction) by both human reason and divine mandate. He had good reason to feel justified in rejecting the Conservatives as lacking indispensable 'bottom' in the country. Nor was it unreasonable to calculate that Palmerston might well be out of the way. Frustration exacerbated his impatience. Out of these came his misreading of the signs of the times.

Meanwhile there were distractions enough. A distressing heresy-hunt to root out 'ritualism' among the Scottish episcopalians pursued Bishop Forbes of Brechin, an old friend of Fasque days. Worse, two tutors at Glenalmond were dismissed (one of them, William Bright, eventually found refuge in the regius chair of Ecclesiastical History at Oxford and a canonry at Christ Church). Rescue work continued its regular London routine, with the added spice once more of searching in vain for Elizabeth Collins, and of searching at Somerset House also in vain for a wedding certificate that might have established her saved condition. Gladstone went twice to see *Lear* at the Princess Theatre ('Kean's is a very considerable performance'). At a concert at the Palace he 'renewed acquaintance with the K. of Belgians & the heir apparent'. He entertained the late King Louis Philippe's son, the Duc d'Aumale, and party, at breakfast. The session was not in itself particularly taxing; but doubtless Gladstone relished his usual long summer retreats at Hawarden no less. The Hawarden routine now included 'ordinarily a family song or dance after dinner'. There he diverted himself in 'reviewing some part of my old verses: here & there amending'. On the whole he found them better than he had supposed. 'But that fountain has stopped. I grieve to add that they exhibit my present moral and spiritual state in a very humbling light.' After purging himself with a bout of timber-cutting Gladstone returned briefly to London to catch up on reviews of his *Studies on Homer*, to read Tennyson, and to work on a draft of his new article excoriating Palmerston. *The Times*'s eight-column review of *Homer* (which found 'not a little amusement occasioned by the futility of his reasoning, and the insignificance of his results') he thought 'exceedingly clever'.[1] A sardonic reader of this review, perhaps better found as a classical scholar than Gladstone, Karl Marx, drew Friedrich Engels's attention: 'Hast du in der

1 D, v, 304, 320, 315, 318. *Times*, August 12, 1858, 7.

Times die kritik über Gladstones Buch über Homer gesehen? Es ist manches Amusante dadrinnen (in der Kritik). Ein Werk wie das von G. ist übrigens characteristisch für die Unfähigkeit der Engländer, in Philologie etwas zu machen.'[1]

The new excoriation of Palmerston, published in the October *Quarterly* on 'The Past and Present Administration', notable for its tribute to the merits of Derby's government, is even more noteworthy as the fullest, most considered, and most effective indictment made by Gladstone against the 'Crimean' policy. On the origins of the war: 'The symptom was seen in the aggressive tendencies of Russia: the disease lay in the condition of Turkey.' The Treaty of Paris, mistaking the symptom for the disease, was doomed to futility. In Turkey the 'governing body is dead, while the body of the governed is alive'. Palmerston, on the subject of Turkey, exhibited the 'strongest alternatives between levity and fanaticism' in his absurd misconception that Turkey would become a progressive country if only the Russians could be fended off; and 'his fanaticism has unfortunately become the policy of England'. (Gladstone cited Clarendon in point, but carefully ignored the guilt of Malmesbury, the villain of the Romanian case, beyond hoping that the Foreign Secretary and the government of Lord Derby would soon 'throw off the last rags of the Clarendon livery'.) The true problem was the 'organic maladjustment' inside Turkey, especially the European part of Turkey, which diplomacy 'can no more counteract, than Mrs. Partington and her broom could dispose of the incoming Atlantic'. Gladstone characterised Palmerston's most grotesque diplomatic chimera as the 'great frock-coat-and-trousers question', the introduction of Turkey into the European community. It was an equally grotesque error to suppose that Turkey '*governs* her provinces at all'; in reality the Ottoman Empire was simply a 'great savage incursion of brute force', 'like a deluge of blood rained from the windows of heaven'. Mere 'military possession, and taxation by virtue of military possession, were the climax, according to Turkish intellect, of the architectonic science of politics'. The Turk's folly was to pretend to govern; his wisdom was to make terms with the higher intelligence of the peoples under his iron heel and leave them to organise things. And now, after centuries of this bleak hopelessness, came the 'diplomatic chimera of Lord Palmerston', with his pathetic and fanatic faith in Hatt-i-humayans, magniloquent but empty Turkish schemes of reform. 'It would be impossible adequately to describe within the space at our command the dangers of the Ottoman Empire.' Russian ambition was the least of them.

1 *Times Literary Supplement*, January 3, 1975, 16: 'Have you seen the review of Gladstone's book on Homer in *The Times*? There is much that is amusing (in the review). A work like this by G. is extremely typical of the incompetence of the English to achieve anything in classical scholarship.'

Turkey was radically corrupt, unwieldy, its finances embarrassed, its administration exhausted, its classes divided, at its heart a mass of seething Islamic fanaticism. Gladstone looked forward eagerly to the speedy downfall of this mouldering structure of oppression; and could already detect signs, in Belgrade, Montenegro, Crete, the Lebanon, Smyrna, Jeddah, that Turkey was beginning the process of convulsive volcanic disintegration.[1]

In its extraordinary accuracy of prevision, not less than the perspicuity of its (admittedly somewhat over-heated) understanding, this piece was a landmark, taking bearings and setting out directions for a fundamental revision of and constructive alternative to the Eastern policy being pursued by both the Palmerston and Derby governments. Gladstone was clear that the day 'must surely come' when the Derby government would renounce a policy so repugnant to decency and humanity. And it is also clear that, quite apart from thus putting the Conservatives on probation with the implied stipulation that they would have to improve on their Romanian performance, Gladstone was defining the shape of an Eastern policy appropriate to a post-Palmerstonian politics which would find its accredited formative exponent in himself.

[11]

Having despatched this envenomed barb against Palmerston, Gladstone set off from Hawarden in early September for a tour *en famille* of the Scottish Highlands by way of Graham's seat at Netherby in Cumberland. Graham showed him the 'heads of two Reform Bills' prepared by Russell. 'He made little comment,' reported Graham to Russell, 'but thought it would be unwise prematurely to fix details. He was less hostile to Reform than I expected, and he expressed an opinion that no Government could now stand which blinked the question.'[2] In fact, as Gladstone was to reveal in the debates on the government's Reform Bill in the 1859 session, the issue rather bored him. It did not as yet fit in very immediately with his notions of an energized public opinion. His awareness of vocation and mission required no mandate from any form of popular authority. He regarded the fuss and bother of parliamentary reform as a controversial but unsubstantial diversion of energy, likely to be a hindrance rather than a help towards achieving the programme he had mapped out. The logic of Gladstone's sense of his political role meant that the only kind of parliamentary reform ever likely to attract him as representing some

1 QR, October 1858, pp.554–5, 556–58, 560.
2 Parker, *Graham*, ii, 360.

degree of popular endorsement of his mandate would have to be much
more extensive than the kind of tinkering, 'homoeopathic' doses being
proposed in the 1850s; and Gladstone felt no great need of any
endorsement founded directly on the parliamentary franchise greater
than that Peel had been able to summon in the 1840s and he himself had
invoked in 1853.

From Netherby the Gladstones repaired again by way of Drumlanrig to
the Sutherlands at Dunrobin, where Gladstone did some entirely
unconvincing deerstalking (his shooting was so bad he took it as 'a new
sign of something impaired in my sight').[1] 'For once' Gladstone dis-
obeyed his doctor's instructions to nurse a sprained ankle ('I could only
douche it in a burn') to revisit the 'scenes of 1820' in Dingwall. Thence to
Aberdeen's seat at Haddo. Gladstone observed Aberdeen now distinctly
aged, if still spry (the 'old man in good health'). They discussed Reform,
Gladstone reporting his inability, or perhaps his unwillingness, to
understand Graham's position. At Haddo a curious letter caught up with
Gladstone at the beginning of October: an invitation from Edward
Bulwer-Lytton, the new Colonial Secretary, to go to the Ionian Islands
Protectorate as a special commissioner to investigate the situation there
and advise the government as to the best remedies for its problems. The
origin of his odd notion was a proposal (quite preposterous) by Robert
Phillimore that Gladstone should be sent as a commissioner to negotiate
various disputes with the Neapolitan government. The idea was taken up
by Lord Carnarvon, the Colonial Under-Secretary, transferred to the less
unsuitable case of the Ionian Islands, and pressed upon Bulwer-Lytton.
The scheme had obvious attractions from the government's point of view.
The protectorate was a difficult problem; and advice from a political
heavyweight of cabinet status could relieve ministers of the embarrassment of choice. And of course it might prove to be the first step in
Gladstone's return to Conservatism, all the more sure for being tangential
and indirect.

Somewhat nonplussed, Gladstone proceeded to the highlight of the
tour, a return to Fasque, on October 6. Sir Thomas and Louisa were all
graciousness; the old soreness was now healed. 'Much is changed, some
very well, all in the spirit of love for the place: yet I miss some marks of my
Father, our foundation stone.'[2] There were solemn attendances at the
chapel ('a very sacred place to me & mine'); he wrote a 'long letter to Willy
on his going to Oxford'; and there were conversations with Tom 'resp.
Helen & the Residuary Estate accounts'. The late Miss Emily Brontë's
Wuthering Heights was receiving his best attention. After seeing Willy off
to Oxford, Gladstone completed the family atmosphere of his tour by
calling at Robertson's in Liverpool. While at Liverpool on October 16 he

1 D, v, 324.   2 *Ib.*, 329.

'commenced Ionian I. papers' and pressed hard to finish them by the 18th. The essence of the problem was that the protectorate over the Islands, conferred upon Britain by the Treaty of Vienna in 1815, had been administered as a colonial despotism tempered very ineffectually by a few constitutional devices. Unrest and repression in 1849 led to a revised constitution which served only to expose the contradictions more openly. Sentiment in the Islands was strong for union with Greece. Sir John Young, the High Commissioner since 1855, failed to reconcile the Ionians to a continuation of the protectorate; and in June 1857, at the end of his tether, recommended to the government either handing over all the islands to Greece or annexing the northern group of Corfu and Paxo as a crown colony and leaving the southern group – Leukadia, Cephalonia, Ithaca, and Zante – to join Greece. Gladstone's immediate response was to '*conceive* that the ultimate incorporation of the islands, except Corfu . . . and Paxo, with Greece might be desirable, & I can even suppose the same of an early resort to that measure'.[1] But he had as yet not decided definitely whether to accept Lytton's invitation.

Back in London, on October 19, Gladstone mulled over the pros and cons. He talked with Lytton at the Colonial Office. 'We have had a long confabulation,' he told Catherine; '& he is going to make the needful enquiries of Young . . . Nothing in the nature of a new bar has presented itself . . . I could easily have had Young recalled but hope to avoid that.'[2] It was a delicate matter: Young was an Eton and Oxford contemporary, a privy councillor, and had been Chief Secretary for Ireland in Aberdeen's administration (hence the government's need for a very senior emissary). Against acceptance were considerations of domestic inconvenience, of being away from the political centre at a possibly crucial juncture, of exposing himself to mockery by being so great a man stooping to so petty a chore (the population involved was barely 250,000). Success would gain Gladstone no credit; failure might well do serious damage to his reputation. It would be easy to ridicule his mission as an expedition into Homeric topography. People were still shaking their heads over *Studies on Homer*. Was it prudent to commit an even more indiscreet act of eccentricity?

These items contra were formidable; but for Gladstone they were outweighed in the end by those pro. His peculiar self-sufficiency compounded of innocence and assurance made him impervious to fears of ridicule or mockery. Undoubtedly the Homeric aspect was attractive. A chance to travel always lured him. He had not been to Greece or within convenient proximity to Greece. Doing a service for Derby's government at a safely non-committal distance would be both a harmless substitute for serious commitment and a practical way of striking back

1 *Ib.*, 329.   2 G to CG, October 19, 1858. GGP, 18/6.

at Palmerston. More telling was the chance to strike a blow for Britain's international reputation by repairing the damage done by the 'atrocities' committed in the repressive measures of 1849. Schwarzenberg had made much of these proceedings in his dealings with Aberdeen over Naples in 1851; and this still rankled with Gladstone. He rehearsed his grievance (quite false) in his latest *Quarterly* article that Schwarzenberg 'did not stir' to respond to the appeal.[1] That the matter itself was of small scale did not deter him. His superb self-confidence very readily made of it a *magnum in parvo*: 'It may seem strange,' he later recorded, 'but so it is that my time & thoughts are as closely occupied and absorbed in the affairs of these little Islands as they have been at almost any period in Parliamentary business . . . The complexity of the case is inversely (so to speak) as the extent of the sphere.'[2] Above all, Gladstone was frustrated, impatient, and restless. An opportunity to escape, if only briefly, from the sterile parliamentary scene would have immense attractions. Graham had recommended joining with Derby to provide 'active official duties' as a way to emancipate himself from 'fruitless controversy'.[3] Taking on the Ionian job would be the next best available thing. It is evident, moreover, that Gladstone still hankered after his old ambition to govern men rather than packages and currencies. The tone of his later reports and comments testify to an overweening assurance in himself as a ruler of men. Had he not been Secretary of State for the Colonies? And had he not recently been offered the immense commission to reshape the government of India? And was he not equipped with very clear principles about the correct relationship between metropolitan governments and their dependencies?

At Hawarden once more, Gladstone discussed with Catherine the 'domestic bearings' of the invitation. Why not continue the spirit of the Highland tour and go *en famille*? 'As I reflected more,' he noted on October 26, 'I become more disinclined to refuse.' Both Catherine and Agnes (now sixteen) were willing to accompany him. On October 27: 'Made up my mind to go, if there be no personal obstacle *ex parte*.' He set to work on the *Odyssey* and 'made out the topographical extracts'. He telegraphed his acceptance to Lytton on the 30th; in London he persuaded Lacaita to go with the party (the Islands had for centuries been subject to the Venetian Republic). He wrote to Aberdeen: 'My Lilliputian die is cast and I am going . . . I hope you will not disapprove of this proceeding . . . Only be assured of one thing: it is but the consequence of having become entangled unawares in such circumstances as left me no right to secede.' This was humbug; it continued: 'My circumspection, perhaps wretched in quality, has in mere amount been enormous: and I am deliberately persuaded that if I had not said a syllable to Lytton I ought

1 QR, October 1858, 540.   2 D, v, 359.   3 PMP, iii, 225, 227.

on the whole to go for the limited purpose now worked out for me.'[1] Aberdeen told John Bright that he wondered Bulwer-Lytton had not asked Gladstone 'to black his boots for him, and advised him strongly not to go, as did other friends of his. But his Homeric fancies prevailed, and he went – must be damaged by it.'[2] Arthur Gordon (as a mollifying compliment to his father Aberdeen) would be secretary. At Windsor on November 5 he kissed hands as High Commissioner Extraordinary and then examined more Ionian Islands material at the Colonial Office.[3] It would be a kind of counter-Naples: a mission of mercy and reconciliation, not of wrath.

[12]

By November 8 the party (less Lacaita, who was to follow on a little later) reached Brussels ('Agnes & I were sick with all the servants'). An invitation to dine with King Leopold was the occasion of an ominous *faux pas*. Arthur Gordon, unable to choose quite the right waistcoat, kept Gladstone waiting in the King's carriage for fifteen or more minutes, fretting and then fuming. Eventually Gordon sauntered down, unapologetic, and was equally unapologetic when they were received by the waiting King and his other guests. Gordon – the incident still rankled in 1894 – 'never tried to shield Mr.G.'[4] Gordon never really reinstated himself in Gladstone's estimation after this atrocity to the Belgian protocol; and it was only the circumstance that Aberdeen had confided his son to Gladstone's tutelage that kept their relationship intact.

Somewhat ruffled, the party departed for Brunswick via Cologne (Gladstone again viewed the cathedral 'wh. now as ever rather disappoints me'), much enjoying the antiquities of north Germany for the first time. From Magdeburg they reached Berlin, where Gladstone visited the porcelain manufactory '& was désillusionné at the various objects in the London market'. Berlin he thought was 'chiefly seen in externals of which there are a great mass tho' not with first rate interest'. He considered the standard of the Schauspielhaus decidedly not first rate. Dresden, where Lacaita joined them, offered a 'most rich treat' in the great picture gallery and many opportunities of delving in and purchasing fine old china. Gladstone was mortified to find that invariably his official status 'do what we will, causes an increase of expence'.[5] At Prague

1 G to Aberdeen, October 30, 1858. GP, 43071, 393.
2 *Diaries of John Bright*, 235.
3 D, v, 332–36.
4 J.B.Conacher, *Victorian Studies*, ii, 155; D, v, 336.
5 D, v, 337–38.

he 'debated Inscription on the Radetzky monument with A.Gordon'[1] and followed George Eliot's recent footsteps in visiting the 'singularly dismal but curious synagogue & Friedhof of the Jews' in the Josefstadt quarter.

They reached Vienna on November 18, and put up at the Erzherzog Karl Hotel in the Kärtnerstrasse (Gladstone already commenting on the *Schlämperei*: 'train late, as seems common'). There was much to be done with the cathedral, the galleries, old Vienna porcelain, traversing 'the mazy town in all possible directions' (though the opera did not detain him more than twenty minutes). But what promised to be a most enjoyable touristic interlude was compromised by a second, and much more important, incident of ill-omen. From London came news that the confidential dispatch sent by Young in 1857 recommending the annexation of Corfu and Paxo as one of the alternative courses of policy had been spirited out of the Colonial Office and published in one of the morning papers. This was an enormous embarrassment for Gladstone, prospectively in the Ionian Islands themselves, where the notion of partition was anathema, and immediately in Vienna, where to the Austrian government, with no motive for hugging Gladstone to its bosom at the best of times, ceding any or all of the islands to Greece was anathema. It was lucky in a way that Gladstone was on the spot to dispel as much as he could of the unfortunate impression. There was much to-ing and fro-ing with the ambassador, Lord Augustus Loftus, and the Austrian Foreign Minister, Count Buol-Schauenstein (Schwarzenberg's messenger to Aberdeen in July 1851) whom Gladstone tried to reassure by emphasising that he had no title to arrange either 'total or partial annexation of the Islands to Greece'.[2]

After paying his formal respects to the ancient Prince Metternich (who had been Austrian Chancellor and Foreign Minister when Gladstone was born) and calling on the great Interior Minister, Baron Bruck, and leaving the Ballhausplatz as pacified as he could, Gladstone went on to Trieste 'by what is I suppose the most beautiful and wonderful railway in the world. Its especial glories are the Semmering pass & the ascent of the Saave.' At Trieste they were soothed by the 'admirable Austrian Band near our windows till almost 12' (the 'Inn good but very dear'). There H.M.S. *Terrible* awaited them; and the party embarked for Corfu, calling at Pola (Gladstone bravely 'rose & managed dinner'). He was gratified by a view of Gargano, the great spur of Italy, and thrilled on the morning of November 24 with a prospect of the 'grand Acroceraunian range' on the eastern shore of the Adriatic. The first sight of Corfu prompted a disputed point of Homeric scholarship *à propos* of a line in the *Odyssey*: 'Homer

---

1 Field-Marshal Count Radetzky had died in January 1858. For the monument, see
  F. Hubmann, *The Habsburg Empire* (1972), 173.
2 D, v, 340.

probably meant a *mirage* wh. is common.'[1] They 'sailed on tracking the land with glasses all the way & reached Corfu between 11 & 12. Landed with military honours and other forms at one.' As High Commissioner, Gladstone rated a seventeen-gun salute; but his unfamiliarity with the etiquette of inspecting a guard of honour caused some awkwardness.[2]

After initial presentations and compliments Gladstone closeted himself with 'my old friend' Young ('He is good and judges justly but without force of character: Lady Y. not wise'); and occupied himself congenially turning his proposed address to the Ionian Senate into Italian. No party or interest on the island looked on Gladstone with any cordiality. The Italianized aristocracy distrusted him as an proponent of annexation to Britain; the Greek populace distrusted him as an opponent of cession to Greece; the British establishment distrusted him as pro-Greek. Gladstone went on his way imperturbably. In performing the social rounds he enjoyed especially conversations with the Greek Orthodox archbishop and priests. He shared with the Anglican High Church generally a disposition to cultivate relationships with Orthodoxy as having a common interest in resisting Romish aggression. He admired their monasteries and was particularly gratified to be shown the mortal remains of St. Theodora and St. Spiridion. Gladstone's tendency towards ostentatious reverence for the Orthodox cloth caused some anxiety. Lytton enquired gravely whether Gladstone had actually, as reported, kissed the hand of a bishop, since questions might be asked in parliament. Gladstone unashamedly confessed the deed.[3] Certainly questions were asked in the public prints of the more embattled Protestant sects. 'Is there any foundation for the incredible story that Mr. Gladstone while Her Majesty's High Commissioner to the Ionian Islands publicly knelt and kissed the hand of a Greek bishop?'[4] There was much canvassing of 'proof' that Gladstone had 'partaken of Mass'; and there was a more casual but widespread resentment that he had been 'obsequious to the half-barbarous priests of Corfu'.[5] Arthur Gordon himself deplored Gladstone's proneness to 'kissing the pudgy hands of every bishop he could get hold of.'[6]

On the secular side Gladstone 'got through a quadrille' with 'huge difficulty' and otherwise indulged himself in an orgy of following what he fondly believed were Homer's tracks; though it was puzzling that his topographical observations did not invariably accord with those of the Homeric text.[7] He visited Leukadia, Odysseus's Ithaca, Cephalonia, (where he was beset with a demonstration for union with Greece), Zante,

1 *Ib.*, 341.   2 A. Ponsonby, *Henry Ponsonby* (1942), 309.
3 Morley, i, 609.   4 GP, 44763, 162.
5 St.Deiniol's Library, Gladstone Pamphlets, xx, 23; Hudson, *Munby*, 294.
6 J.K.Chapman, *The Career of Arthur Hamilton Gordon, First Lord Stanmore* (1964), 12.
7 Morley, i, 603.

whence 'a noble view down to the S. mountains of Peloponnesus' called him across to Greece. There he set foot on December 18, after marvelling at the grand scenery while sailing up the Gulf of Corinth. He marched across the Isthmus, 'exulting in the views, & unconscious of brigands'. On the Aegean side H.M.S. *Scourge* was waiting to carry the party to Piraeus, the port of Athens. After embarking Gladstone had an opportunity to turn his earlier shooting mishap to advantage: 'My maimed hand being shown, persuaded a poor seaman to have a crushed finger amputated: & all went well' (though Gladstone was appalled at the badness of the wine administered to stiffen the man's resolve). On reaching Athens the exigencies of protocol required due respects being paid to the Bavarian King Otto and his Oldenburg consort ('he utters with some difficulty'). The Greek government, still smarting from the chastisement at the Anglo-French occupation of Piraeus in 1857, and at a loss to fathom Gladstone's motives and intentions, warily cultivated him; to the extent of rather impeding his main purpose of seeing the sights. The snow-covered Acropolis was almost intoxicating: 'The view – the ruins – & the sculptures, taken together are almost too much for one day.' There were books to be purchased as well as a curious carving from Mount Athos. After luxuriating in the prospects of Acrocorinth, Gladstone was back in Corfu by Christmas Eve. On Christmas Day he 'had three hours with Sir J. Young on *the* question of his return home'.[1] For Gladstone had decided to pack Young off and take over as High Commissioner himself. He had a plausible case in that Young's position was compromised by the unauthorised publication of his despatch of June 1857; and he came quickly to the conclusion that Young lacked the necessary force of character. It was Young's misfortune at that moment to stand in the way between Gladstone and the tempting immediacy of executive power. Gladstone's ruthlessness was a measure of his frustration since February 1855; and he was prone to the dangerous presumption that his own strength of character and his experience in dealing with refractory tariffs and delinquent budgets fitted him to succeed in the Ionian Islands where Young had failed. His tour at the Colonial Office was long enough to feed his appetite to rule men but short enough to shield him from any likely unhappy consequences of it.

The result was that Gladstone lived in a world of fantasy, 'immersed'; as he put it himself, 'in a work of justice and mercy'. Just as he saw in the Ionian microcosm a task worthy of macrocosmic devotion, so it is possible to deduce much at large about Gladstone immersed in this small episode. His 'work', as he saw it, was to put a decisive stop to all ideas in the Islands of union with Greece. His observations in Athens satisfied him that union there was viewed with 'mixed feelings'; which no doubt was

1 D, v, 348–351.

true enough. But what official Athens thought bore but a marginal relevance to popular opinion either in Greece or in the Islands. (King Otto's deference to the susceptibilities of conservative Europe on the issue played a large part in his deposition in 1862.) Gladstone's 'vast despatch'[1] to Lytton of December 28 recommended concessions to 'popular principles of government' by promoting the powers of the legislature against those of the executive (and especially the police) on the grounds that the Ionians were not absolutely disqualified from 'discharging the duties political freedom must entail'. No doubt there would be initial difficulties; but with 'kindly treatment' under favourable circumstances the 'influence of England working through the medium of their free will' might be 'almost unbounded'. Expression of a desire for union with Greece, since it was due neither to aversion to England nor to foreign intrigue, should not be treated as a crime, provided it be legal in form, respectful in terms, and not associated with any tendency to public disorder. It was indeed a sentiment universal in the Islands, but tempered by the realization that the British government would not permit it and that 'Eastern Europe has not yet reached the state in which alone such a reunion ought to be an object of immediate or practical desire'. There were both enthusiasts for union and exploiters of enthusiasm. It was an error to 'suppose that the cry for union with Greece means only what it seems to mean'. All dissatisfactions found vent in it. Decided improvements in government 'would of themselves greatly diminish the available forces of enthusiasm of the unionists'. Her Majesty's government should 'undeceive the country by an explicit declaration coming direct from the highest authority to the regularly elected organ of the Ionian people' that union was not permissible; and Gladstone would not despair of 'seeing a practical stop put to the serious mischiefs of the present agitation', and the Assembly thus brought to its senses setting about its modest tasks of attending to the business of the protectorate. Ionians of 'station and intelligence', like their opposite numbers in Greece, were well aware of the necessity of subordinating the dream of *enosis* to the 'dictates of other and larger interests', particularly as connected with the 'present state of Eastern Europe'. It would be an act of 'criminal folly on the part of England were she to give the slightest encouragement to so crude a project'. The Ionian question was a 'small question', a 'narrow part of a very great question, one no less, in all likelihood, than the reconstruction of all political society in South-Eastern Europe'. If it were allowable of the Greek family, the 'best and safest means both of meeting that day when it comes, and of accelerating its tranquil arrival', would be to have trained 'some, at least, of the severed portions of that race in the peaceable and steady exercise of local liberty'.

1 Matthew, *ib.*, 358n.

Should the present Assembly, 'seduced into a temper of political fanaticism', refuse to accept these recommendations, it should be dissolved and the Ionian electors given the opportunity of 'repairing the errors of its temporary Representatives'. In any case, the British government would cease to be responsible in the eyes of Europe for any political and administrative evils.[1]

From a man who had very recently advocated a very large dose of reconstruction of the political society of South-Eastern Europe in the form of a Romanian national state, and who had not hesitated to publish (if incognito) a vision of a restored Greek empire once more in possession of Constantinople, the restraint of these recommendations was indeed remarkable. True, this restraint was largely induced by the contradictions of Gladstone's situation as somewhat of a philhellene with an initial penchant for Young's partition proposal, who had nonetheless to work within limits set by the public law of Europe: which knew not philhellenism and cared not for partition. Perhaps the most remarkable feature in the recommendations, from the point of view of eliciting some indications towards a fuller understanding of Gladstone's mind, is the extent to which he ingenuously imported into South-Eastern Europe his own peculiarly Peelite assumptions as to the crucial role of Ionians 'of station and intelligence' and of a deferential Ionian electorate's reinforcing their position. No doubt this bizarre degree of misapprehension was not the least of the reasons why Lytton and the government received Gladstone's recommendations so gratefully. Gladstone told ministers what they wanted to hear: that *enosis* was no great problem; that the difficulties could be met by a judiciously liberal concession of colonial self-government; and that Gladstone himself was the man to handle the job. Lytton telegraphed on January 11, 1859: 'The Queen accepts. Your Commission is made out.' Not everyone was grateful. There was much indignation at the hard treatment of Young. *The Times* dilated on 'one of those acts of eccentricity which tend so grievously to tarnish a brilliant reputation'; and confessed that 'after all the experience we have had, we have no right to be astonished at anything Mr. Gladstone may do'.[2] To those who knew Gladstone particularly well the absurd side of his taking over suggested itself alarmingly. Herbert exploded: 'I cannot say how much I am annoyed about Gladstone . . . What an infernal position he has placed himself in! He really is not safe to go about out of Lord Aberdeen's room.'[3] Graham fretted that Gladstone had ruined his career. Aberdeen, a connoisseur of Gladstone's *métier* for getting things somewhat out of proportion, was able to reassure him: '*Ah! But he is terrible on the rebound.*'[4]

1 *Ib.*, 354–58.   2 *Times*, January 13, 1859, 8.
3 Lord Stanmore, *Sidney Herbert* (1906), ii, 167.   4 Morley, i, 613.

For a while, Gladstone himself fretted about his chances of a rebound. He told Aberdeen that he did not care 'for the misconstructions of the act of taking the office; but there is no doubt that I have run some risk as to time'. As to Young's dismissal he insisted that as he had thought fit to attempt to change the mode of government of the protectorate 'now at the eleventh hour & under circumstances of extreme disadvantage, I could not shrink from undertaking the principal part of the burden'.[1] He was dismayed to discover that by assuming the High Commissionership he automatically vacated his seat for Oxford University. 'A very great blow,' he telegraphed to Lytton.[2] Nor would it be possible to be re-elected while he remained in his new office. The thought of what might be afoot in Oxford while his back was turned gave him painful anxiety. Already steps were being taken to appoint a new commissioner to rescue him from his predicament. Sir Henry Storks, a military man with experience in Mauritius, was hastily shipped out. Meanwhile, Gladstone just as hastily resigned his office on 1 February to facilitate a prompt and uncomplicated re-election for parliament. It was thus, absurdly, as a High Commissioner who had resigned and reverted to his commissionership extraordinary, and who as it happened was not as yet aware whether or not his successor had been appointed, that Gladstone, with highly doubtful legitimacy, addressed the Ionian Senate on February 5. The point was that it hardly mattered whether his legitimacy was doubtful or otherwise. The Ionian Assembly had no intention of taking his promises of a 'prompt adjustment' to their constitution seriously. Instead, the Assembly devoted itself to drawing up a petition in which it made clear the 'disposition' of the Ionian people for *enosis* with Greece. Gladstone was reduced to semantic censorship to keep the text decently respectful. He took solace in a course of rescue work among the Corfiote *hetaerae*.

By now relations with Arthur Gordon were once more strained. Gladstone complained on January 22 that Gordon had 'not done his work & that his heart was not in it'.[3] Poor Gordon was in fact distracted by having fallen in love with Agnes; but possibly he suffered also from a shrewd awareness of the futility of Gladstone's hectic proceedings. At his father's insistence, Gordon ignored Mrs Gladstone's demands that he resign; and his response to Gladstone's instructions not to waste the public's money by reading letters from Lord Aberdeen in working hours was 'rude'. Gordon viewed the Ionian affair as 'a political drama alternately tragical and comical, not unmixed with occasional scenes of the broadest farce, but always picturesque'.[4] Something of the general character of slightly farcical irrelevance of the whole affair is suggested in the luridly exotic circumstances of Gladstone's escapade in Albania at the

1 G to Aberdeen, January 31, 1859. GP, 43071, 397.   2 Magnus, 137.
3 D, v, 364.   4 Chapman, *Stanmore*, 12–13.

beginning of February, where, the guest of an ancient chieftainess at Philiates, he and his party ate a Turkish repast in 'rude abundance' and Gladstone smoked his 'first & last Chibouk'. He much enjoyed the Asiatic picturesqueness and positively relished the barbaric splendour, despite all the distressing evidences of 'indolence, decay, stagnation'. Indeed, Gordon noted with perhaps a certain degree of the keener perception which is refined by malice, that Gladstone was very much in his element when calling on Lacaita to recite Italian poetry in the manner of a pasha summoning his bard – though perhaps the manner of a Homeric hero. summoning Homer might have been the more apt image. After the ladies of the party were led off to the harem for the night, Gladstone and his male entourage were packed tightly on the floor under quilts of Brusa silk and gold, tucked in by gorgeously attired Albanians. Gladstone, in high fettle, quipped whether or no they were in contravention of the provisions of Lord Shaftesbury's recent Lodging House Act.[1]

Whatever Lacaita's merits as a bard in Albania, his skills as a gleaner of depressingly accurate information in Corfu were not to be gainsaid. It was he who finally made it clear to Gladstone that the Ionian Assembly would not be swayed from its purpose of union: his 'ingatherings of rumour are all bad'. Earlier, Gladstone was annoyed at Storks's appointment, feeling that his authority would be compromised; by February 16, when Storks arrived, it was indeed as if on a rescue mission. The Ionian Assembly rejected all Gladstone's proposals and pointedly, by remaining in session, omitted to bid him farewell at his departure on February 19. Gladstone nevertheless left as imperturbably convinced of the value of his mission of 'labouring for truth and justice' as when he arrived. He was no more successful in persuading the Ionians to renounce *enosis* than he would have been in persuading Australians that they would have to accept the continuance and expansion of the system of penal transportation. His three massive and elaborate reports, printed for the use of the Cabinet, faded into obscurity. It was felt that, in the circumstances of the Italian war, it would be inexpedient to lay documents before parliament which bore on the question of the rights of subject peoples within the jurisdiction of the public law of Europe.

[13]

After a rough passage, including sea-sickness 'at the lowest depths' ('with the utmost effort could I get through my prayers'), the party arrived again at Pola; and reached Venice by February 23. Gladstone,

1 Morley, i, 608.

delighted to renew memories of 1832, admired the Austrian military music, found the Venice opera 'good but ballet ad nauseam, chiefly mere muscle'. There was tension in the air: 'Caffè Restaurant, sunshine, music, all the right incidents & no wrong ones'; but all under the shadow of impending war as Piedmont, with France behind her, challenged Austria. The Gladstones dined as guests of the viceroy, the Archduke Ferdinand Maximilian and the Archduchess Charlotte – Gladstone found the young archduke, brother of the Emperor Francis Joseph, 'kind, intelligent, ingenuous & earnest'[1] – the future, tragic Emperor and Empress of Mexico. Ominous military mobilisation and concentration dominated the scene: at Vicenza, Gladstone noted Austrian cavalry and artillery about to march; more cavalry on the road with a van and·pickets, some with drawn swords. At Verona whitecoat regiments passed in review; at Milan pickets were in the streets: 'as I write,' Gladstone noted that night, 'I hear the tread of horses patrolling the streets. Dark omens!'[2]

Milan, however, was otherwise all sightseeing, antiquities, and porcelain-hunting. Turin was much more serious. The Piedmontese politicians could hardly fail to mark the passage of so distinguished a friend of their country; and it was natural that they should make every discreet effort to convert him into a partisan of their cause. They took care that Gladstone should be met at the railway station by the sympathetic British minister, Sir James Hudson; and Gladstone then spent an hour alone with Count Cavour, who was 'confidential down to a certain date', which is, presumably, to say down to his meeting with the Emperor Napoleon at Plombières in July 1858 when it was agreed in principle that Austrian power should be driven out of Italy. After seeing Farini and other notabilities Gladstone indulged himself in what was now plainly a neurotic porcelain addiction: 'More transactions in China: I have now done my work for the year in this line: or nearly.' He then dined with Cavour '$5\frac{1}{2}$–$8\frac{1}{2}$'.

As the Gladstones diligenced, sledged, and entrained their way home across the Alps and France ('Still on & on: Agnes as well as C. an excellent traveller') he noted: 'Much rumination.'[3] No doubt what he had learned from Cavour was much to be ruminated upon. Cavour was embarking on a frightening gamble: French intervention depending on Austria's being goaded into a false step. Gladstone marked this portentousness by getting in two church services in Paris on Sunday and, even more, by refraining from porcelain purchasing. He reached Carlton House Terrace on the morning of March 8; and plunged back into his metropolitan routine. That day he saw Herbert, Graham, and Cardwell as well as Lytton. He took his oath in the Commons, and even did some rescue

1 D, v, 372. The archduchess was a daughter of King Leopold of the Belgians.
2 *Ib.*, 373.   3 *Ib.*, 377.

work. On the 9th he voted (unavailingly) for the government's 'very feeble Ch. Rate Bill'. On the 10th he had Panizzi and Lacaita to dinner and read Mr. Mill's new treatise *On Liberty*. (It was gratifying to be able to recommend Lacaita for a knighthood of St. Michael and St. George for his services in the Ionian Islands; but this caused trouble with Arthur Gordon, who demanded 'the little cross of the C.M.G. . . . I rather encouraged it than otherwise as being a good thing for the order'.)[1] Panizzi was running the Neapolitan Exiles Committee: Poerio and Settembrini escaped from the ship bearing them to exile in America, landed at Queenstown and were now in the Committee's care. Gladstone attended a meeting of the committee on the 15th. Soon he was reading Farini's letter to Lord John Russell on the Italian crisis. On April 4th he held a dinner in Poerio's honour with fifteen guests and an evening party later. On April 9 he met the young disciple of Döllinger and rising intellectual leader in England of liberal Roman Catholicism, Sir John Acton, who had indeed recently been in Italy with Döllinger and who was especially attractive to Gladstone because of his resistance to the Vatican's ultramontanism. On April 11 he lunched at Stafford House where the Sutherlands gave a reception for the Neapolitans.

The Italian theme was indeed in the ascendant. The only other question which claimed a serious share of Gladstone's attention was Disraeli's Reform Bill. This was an unconvincing affair, the lowest common denominator of Derby's willingness to offer and Palmerston's willingness to accept. Disraeli attempted later to disguise its essentially homoeopathic character by implausible claims that it would have increased the enfranchised constituency by 'absolutely a larger addition' than the 1832 Act.[2] But to the public its reputation was damaged by John Bright's sneer at 'fancy franchises'. Gladstone recorded himself as 'sorely puzzled' by the question on March 21; and read both Mill and Bagehot unavailingly for enlightenment. In the Commons on March 29 Gladstone defended Disraeli's Bill against a hostile amendment by Russell advocating a greater extension of the borough franchise. But Gladstone confessed himself only a little more enthusiastic for the bill than for the amendment. He could see in the question 'no substantial difference of opinion traceable to differences in this House between political parties'. He agreed with Bright that parliament should proceed to settle Reform 'in a spirit of trust towards the people, and for several years past we have been getting all the proceedings of legislation more and more upon that sound and satisfactory basis'. He agreed with Russell that the 'lowering of the suffrage in the boroughs was the main purpose of having a Reform bill,

1 G to CG, April 9, 1859. GGP, 28/6. July 20, 1859 (*ib*): 'Arthur Gordon has written to Lacaita in the 3rd person!' G himself declined the grand cross of the order.
2 H, cliv, 131.

and that unless we are to have that lowering of the suffrage, it would be better that we should not waste our time on this subject'. But he told Russell that, if he could see in Russell's resolution 'the prospect of a powerful Government, and a combination of men ready to carry through a measure of reform not immoderate in its form', he would support it. But Russell, like Disraeli, was not strong enough to command a strong bill. Given a choice of weak, unsatisfactory schemes, Gladstone would choose the government's as the more likely to put an end to the unwholesome agitation in the country.

The criteria determining Gladstone's judgment on Reform were clearly still those set out in March 1856. It was not sufficiently an issue dividing parties; and it was not an issue proposed by a strong government as a means of fulfilling ends purposed by a strong government. Gladstone's consequent lack of interest and candid advocacy of the expediency of a speedy settlement so that parliament could get on to 'the many other demands on our time' shocked the more earnest and committed reformers. In later years, when he had a reputation as a reformer to cherish, Gladstone was embarrassed and querulous at revelations of this insensibility. He remonstrated peevishly in 1893 when Arthur Gordon tactlessly exposed in his life of his father Aberdeen the extent to which Gladstone was 'reluctant to engage in any fresh measure of Parliamentary Reform'. 'You had accepted honestly,' Gordon firmly reminded Gladstone, 'but it was thought rather coldly, the Reform measure of the Aberdeen Government, and when that proposal was withdrawn by Lord John it was supposed that you reverted to your position of 1852.' Gordon had no difficulty in overwhelming Gladstone's objections with evidence that with both Aberdeen and Herbert the 'impression current' in 1857 was that Gladstone was 'an opponent of Parliamentary Reform'; Herbert testifying that, while he was not 'enamoured' of Reform, he yet wanted more than Gladstone, who wanted 'none at all'. Gordon cited Aberdeen as advising Gladstone that the 'proper opportunity' for his joining Derby would be the production by Palmerston's government of a Reform Bill; and to this he added testimony to the same effect from Graham.[1] The only aspect of the 1859 bill which evoked any enthusiasm from Gladstone was the glory of small nomination boroughs as nurseries of statesmanship (he cited Pelham, Chatham, Fox, Pitt, Canning, and Peel); and the only passage of eloquence and feeling was his jeering at Palmerston's evasiveness over Reform – saved from it in 1855 by war, in 1856 by peace, in 1857 by the dissolution of parliament, and in 1858 by the dissolution of his government.[2] The fact was that Gladstone had been as fully the beneficiary of these circumstances as had Palmerston.

1 Gordon to G, February 19, 1893. GP, 44322, 140.
2 H, *ib.*, 153, 1049, 1051, 1053, 1066, 1067.

Support of this calibre was not likely to save the bill: Russell and Bright defeated Disraeli and Gladstone on the seventh night of the debate on March 31 by 330 to 291. Derby and Disraeli, sustained by the Queen's resentment at what she regarded as Russell's mischievousness, announced on April 4 that they had advised Her Majesty that the government should not resign and that the Commons should be dissolved. (Gladstone 'worked most of the day upon my China, which is now really a collection'.) He joined in the 'universal dissatisfaction' (apart from the Radicals) at the government's decision to dissolve rather than resign after only two years had passed since the last elections. Gladstone himself, as in 1857, was not incommoded by a contest for Oxford; and had time to devote himself to an article for the *Quarterly* on the war in Italy. He signalled the restoration of the ascendancy of the Italian question by making his last appearance in the session on April 18 a sharp rebuke to Disraeli for characterising Austria's policy as one of 'dignified concilia-tion' as against the 'embarrassing, perplexing, and ambiguous' conduct of the Piedmontese government. Gladstone contended that, without accepting the extreme thesis that the only satisfactory solution would be the expulsion of Austria from Italy and a great alteration of the Treaties of 1815, nevertheless Palmerston was to be supported in championing Piedmont's right to a place in any conference of the powers and should not be obliged to disarm.[1] A particular animus against Austria had become a distinctive feature of Gladstone's foreign outlook, especially since his speech on the Danubian principalities of May 1858, which inaugurated his tactic of extolling Russia by way of denigrating Austria. What was new and important in his outlook as shaped by events in 1859 was the extent to which his earlier obsession with Turkey and the Eastern question evaporated, leaving Austria (with the papacy as a subsidiary adjunct) exposed in invidious singularity to his disapproval.

When Phillimore remarked after meeting Gladstone in May 1859 that 'Foreign politics seemed to have the chief place in his mind',[2] it is necessary to qualify this observation in the light of that evaporation of his concern with the Eastern question; and to be aware that, in a situation where for Gladstone the pressing immanence of making fundamental choices was of the essence, the logic of his having nothing to choose between Derby and Palmerston on the Eastern question was working itself out by pointing to an alternative area where choice was to be had. The contrast in this respect between 1858 and 1859 is highly instructive. Gladstone's thinking in 1858 was dominated overwhelmingly by a conviction of the disastrousness of the pro-Turkish Crimean policy. Compared with this, his complaints in other quarters were relatively mild; and indeed hostility to Rome was the guiding theme. France was

1 H, cliii, 1882–3.   2 Morley, i, 624.

culpable for pursuing a clerical policy and for propping up the papal throne. Austria was culpable for abandoning in 1855 its 'single pledge to freedom' in the Josephine code and by abandoning in the new 'ill-omened' concordat (which had 'not yet attained to one-half of the notoriety it deserves and must acquire') that 'fabric which the wisdom, probity and energy' of the Emperor Francis Joseph's ancestors con-structed 'against Romish aggression'. Likewise, Naples weakly relin-quished its traditional ecclesiastical independence; leaving the Piedmon-tese alone in vindicating their religious liberties against 'Romish ambition and intrigue'.[1]

By April 1859 Gladstone both shifted and narrowed his focus crucially. It was not only that Italy now monopolised his attention; he now insisted that the 'true state of the question' was not 'as between Austria and France, but as between Austria and Italy'. This was taking his cue from Cavour. To French connivance at Cavour's goading the Austrians, Gladstone now added his own connivance. He withdrew France from the range of his censure and argued that, whereas hitherto Italy had been obscured by France, now Italy had emerged into its rightful place at the forefront of the question. But much the most important consideration bearing upon Gladstone's shifting of his focus at this time was his awareness that, whereas he had failed to raise any significant degree of public response by his strictures against Palmerston and the Crimean policy, a public opinion was now distinctly in being; and that opinion was decisively 'Italian'. Hitherto Gladstone judged English feeling to be anti-Italian: they 'believe, as they are taught, that Austria stands wholly on the defensive'. Gladstone protested to Hudson in Turin that he mistrusted every '*nostrum* for Italy except that of local freedom'; yet that was enough to have him 'booked even in high quarters as an *ultra* Italian'.[2] 'Within the last few weeks,' Gladstone noted, '... there has certainly been a change in the tone of English opinion.' Certainly Austria, even at her best, could 'never attract much of enthusiasm in England'. But now, by demanding the right to reduce Piedmont to the status of a compliant satellite, Austria has exposed herself to the British public as the villain of the affair. That public was coming to awareness that there was not a 'yard of Italian soil' upon which Austria had not 'trodden with her iron heel'; and that the 'thirst for national independence in Italy is inseparably associated with the hope of relief from political servitude and from heavy practical grievance'. As for the Pope, 'let him have dignity, let him have security, let him have wealth ... but let us not dream of free institutions under a papal monarch'. And as to the sacredness of the public law of Europe as laid down by the treaties of 1815: if Austria had

1 QR, October 1858, 550-51.
2 D. Beales, *England and Italy, 1859–1860* (1961), 53.

used her position in Lombardy-Venetia to dominate Italy 'her own title to Lombardy-Venetia is thereby reciprocally and greatly impaired'. Did Austrian interests in any case require her to hold Lombardy-Venetia? Would not a modified form of suzerainty in the manner of Servia and the Principalities to the Ottoman Porte serve as a model? Whatever befalls, a 'new combination among the Italian States at large' must replace the existing dispensation.[1] Elwin nervously reported to Gladstone the scandal caused to *Quarterly* readers by this revolutionary effusion.

The tirade against the Crimean policy of October 1858 proved, in fact, to be Gladstone's last exercise in that *genre* until public opinion forced him back upon it in 1876. This is, in its way, the most revealing measure of how crucially decisive was the role of public opinion in guiding Gladstone towards his goal in 1859. At last, for Gladstone, a 'public mind' was responding to events with a 'corresponding conviction', and in a manner (quite unlike 1857) conformable with the movement of his own mind. It was not a public opinion of formidable dimensions; and no doubt its most substantial feature was Gladstone's need of it; and certainly it was not an important factor in the general election; but it could be seen as a token of a better age. Compared with this fundamental datum, the manner in which men and ministries were to be reassembled after the elections was in itself relatively of much less importance so long as that reassembling reciprocated public opinion by providing the materials of a strong government with strong measures. Circumstances decreed, in effect, that the *desiderata* defined by Gladstone in March 1856 were to be attained back to front: but by 1859 Gladstone was in no position to quibble. Given that he discerned the kind of responsiveness in the public mind for which he had since 1853 been looking in vain, and given that Derby and Disraeli, far from mending their ways as revealed in the Romanian case, were aggravating their fault by their Austrophile inclinations, it followed that Gladstone was moving, willy-nilly, closer to Palmerston. That could not, alas, be helped. Unlike the Reform question or the Eastern question, the Italian question possessed for Gladstone the supreme utility of tending to make the divisions between parties more distinct. Financial policy remained for Gladstone the lodestar of politics; but no public was as yet formed to be directed by his insights on it. Much of his later insistence on the crucial role for him in 1859 of the 'overwhelming interest and weight of the Italian question' bore therefore the character and 'flavour of self-justification'.[2] As in 1857, Palmerston in 1859 was the nearest thing to a minister whose 'doings and intentions' 'wrought a corresponding conviction upon the public mind'. Much as Gladstone might deplore the painful irony of this circumstance, he could not evade its logic. Residual

1 QR, April 1859, 'The War in Italy', pp.530–61.
2 Beales, *England and Italy*, 87–91.

notions of wriggling out of it were much weakened when, in an election speech in his constituency at Tiverton at the end of April, Palmerston, with inspired opportunism, abandoned his bland prepared text and launched into an open avowal that he hoped that the coming war would end with the Germans being driven out of Italy. Aberdeen, who of all his contemporaries knew Gladstone best, remarked to Graham that Palmerston's 'brilliant stroke' at Tiverton had 'secured Gladstone, who is ready to act with him, or under him, notwithstanding the three articles of the Quarterly and the thousand imprecations of late years'.[1]

With things thus tending to come together in a generally desirable coherence, despite obvious reservations about Palmerston, Gladstone could afford to take a rather loftily detached view of the elections. He was the object of careful scrutiny by the Liberal chiefs. He reported to Catherine on April 9: 'Of all the birds in the air Sir J. Acton (the son) called on me this morning (before going to Ireland to stand) to ask a lot of questions about politics. This I conclude was a fishing visit prompted by senior persons.'[2] It was widely assumed that the Conservatives would make up much of the ground they had rather fortuitously lost in 1857. But there was no evidence that they might break out of the national minority to which the events of 1846 had condemned them. By now Gladstone had no desire that they should. He responded with a markedly cool objectivity to the news of initial Conservative gains. He visited the Carlton on April 30, 'wh. was excited & more pleased than the facts quite seem to justify'. Derby and Disraeli in the result duly failed to break out of their electoral impasse. They improved their position to something just over 300 seats, which made it worth their while to make another series of judicious offers to enable them to carry on. One agreeable feature was that John Neilson regained the Devizes seat he had lost in 1857. Disraeli, fertile as ever with expedients, made the usual unavailing overtures to Palmerston. The Liberal and Peelite majority in the Commons was by no means united. The situation was reminiscent of the beginnings of the Abredeen coalition at the end of 1852. It might be as difficult to form a new coalition as it had been to form the old. Russell was inclined to insist on the first place or none at all, and Sidney Herbert had some ado arguing him out of it.

As soon as the elections were over Gladstone repaired to Oxford with Catherine and Stephy, who was to be confirmed by Bishop Wilberforce. It was pleasant to lunch in Willy's rooms in Peckwater (and three days later to congratulate him on his junior studentship at Christ Church). It was pleasant also to be inducted, together with Heathcote, as one of the first

1 Parker, *Graham*, ii, 388.
2 G to CG, April 9, 1859, 28/6. Acton was standing for Carlow. Granville was his step-father.

honorary fellows of All Souls. From Oxford he went on to Chevening, where he relaxed in conversation with Argyll ('who is free from all gall & guile') whom he heard strongly criticising Derby's Austrophile Italian policy. As to the general shape of future politics, Gladstone was thinking of a much broader coalition, 'an engrafting of Palmerston upon Lord Derby, dethroning Disraeli from the leadership of the House of Commons, arranging for a moderate Reform bill, placing the foreign office in other hands, but not in Disraeli's'.[1] Graham indeed told Russell that this project was the most probable solution of existing difficulties. Possibly this reflected a Peelite desire to keep Palmerston out of the first place. Palmerston himself knew that the key to the problem lay in his coming to an understanding with Russell. There was to be a meeting of the Liberal party. Prodded by Herbert, Russell made the initial overture to Palmerston on May 18. On the 20th Palmerston drove down to see Russell when it was agreed that Derby would be turned out by a vote of no-confidence, that there would be a broad new ministry committed to a Reform Bill satisfactory to Lord John. The question of who should lead was to be left with constitutional propriety to the discretion of the Queen.

Naturally Gladstone, with vivid memories of the collapse of the Aberdeen coalition and its sad aftermath, was, as Phillimore recorded on June 1, 'much harassed and distressed at his position relative to the government and opposition'.[2] He remained firm against anticipating events; and would therefore not desert Derby. But the prospect of being once more in close political proximity to both Russell and Palmerston was now alarmingly near. Herbert sent him a copy of his letter to Russell of May 17 urging Russell to join in a general anti-Derby front. This letter, together with Herbert's covering note confessing 'very gloomy' anticipations for the future, caused Gladstone 'some reflection'.[3] Perhaps his harassed and distressed state was exacerbated by the tensions of a new bout of rescue work which led to an application of the discipline on May 25 (now a rare recourse: the last occasion had been in May 1857). He saw Palmerston on May 28 and made it clear that he would continue consistently to support Derby's government against a motion of no-confidence (though he would vote against Derby on any motion as to the merits of the dissolution of parliament). The one point apart from the dissolution he had specifically against Derby was that he distrusted Malmesbury's handling of foreign affairs at so critical a time. Then, after another taste of Lady Waldegrave's eager entertainment at Strawberry Hill, a 'formidable and highly political' dinner party at Lord Carlisle's, talks with Graham, Cardwell, Stratford de Redcliffe, Argyll, Palmerston and Herbert, Gladstone went off to the Sutherlands at Cliveden early in June where Argyll 'read Tennyson aloud to us: very high strains indeed'.

1 Morley, i, 623.   2 *Ib.*, 624.   3 D, v, 394.

On June 4, at Magenta, the first great battle took place between the Franco-Piedmontese and Austrian armies: which led to an Austrian retirement and the yielding of Milan. On Sunday, June 5 Gladstone conversed with Argyll 'on public affairs & my own position'; and consented to entertain the Cliveden party in the evening by singing, at the cost of some qualms as to the decency of thus straining the sabbath, 'but it seemed too small to fight'.[1]

On June 6, on the eve of the new session, the Liberal party gathered in Willis's Rooms. Herbert attended as a token of the goodwill of the former Peelite group. Palmerston and Russell announced their reconciliation and their reciprocal willingness to serve under the other. Bright and Herbert made encouraging utterances. The calculations were that there was now a certain majority to beat Derby and Disraeli. The motion of no-confidence was moved on June 7 by the rising young Whig M.P. for North Lancashire, Spencer Cavendish, Marquess of Hartington and heir to the great dukedom of Devonshire. Gladstone held firm to his consistent intention to uphold the government, despite the menaces of Mrs. Sidney Herbert ('who threatened me').[2] Through the several nights of debate all the eminences of the House gave forth – Disraeli, Palmerston, Russell, Bright, Graham, Milner Gibson, Herbert, Lewis, Pakington, Roebuck – except Gladstone; who registered his silent vote for Derby and Disraeli in the division on June 10. The government failed narrowly to hold its own, by 310 to 323.

The Queen, confronted with the dire prospect of Palmerston and Russell, tried to dodge by pleading her unwillingness to make an invidious choice between two so equally eminent claimants, and nominated Granville as an acceptably innocuous compromise. Palmerston, though offended, was willing to go through the motions of accepting Granville's offer of the Leadership of the Commons, knowing well that Russell, while content to be second in the government, would not be third, especially to a political stripling; and was confident that the Queen, forced to 'encounter the difficulty of making a choice', would not choose 'selfish, peevish Johnny'.[3] Gladstone 'learned Granville's proceedings' on June 11, no doubt with mixed feelings. Granville never indeed got so far as consulting Gladstone; and abandoned his futile proceedings as soon as he decently could. Palmerston was called in; and on the 13th Gladstone received his summons to attend. To stiffen his resolve, now ultimately confronted with the swallowing of a pill larger and nastier than that of 1855, Gladstone twice had recourse to Herbert's doses of moral reinforcement. 'Went to Ld P. by his desire at night: & accepted my old office.'[4]

1 *Ib.*, 398.   2 *Ib.*, 399.
3 Prest, *Russell*, 384.   4 D, v, 400.

CHAPTER VII

'THE HORIZON ENLARGES, THE SKY SHIFTS, AROUND ME': 1859–1862

[1]

Accepting his 'old office' was indeed for Gladstone very much of the essence of the matter. He told Herbert next day that 'he would not have joined the Government otherwise'.[1] Lady Clarendon was indignant that Gladstone should have 'insisted': 'Why he who voted in the last division with the Derby ministry should not only be asked to join this one, *but be allowed to choose his office*, I cannot conceive, or rather, I *can* conceive, for I know that it is for his power of speaking. They want his tongue and they dread it in opposition. And so, tho' G. Lewis had accepted the office . . . he has been requested to make way for Gladstone, which accordingly he has done and accepts the Home Office instead.'[2] More assuredly than ever, Gladstone saw the fulfilment of the Peelite tradition of financial policy as the crux of social stability and class reconciliation. Palmerston hoped to resume with the Chancellor who had served him well at the Exchequer when Gladstone deserted him in 1855. Cornewall Lewis had taken over a difficult task and acquitted himself creditably. He rescued the war finance from Gladstone's narrow moralistic dogmatism and nursed the revenue capably up to the change of government and Disraeli's take-over in 1858. Lewis's genius was empirical; but Gladstone's complaints and criticisms between 1855 and 1858 owed more to bad temper and frustration than to merits and principles. His ostentatious indulgence to Disraeli in 1858–59 only underlined this factiousness of humour. Palmerston certainly owed Lewis much gratitude and Gladstone none. Perhaps it was a certain sense of guilt which led Gladstone in 1861 to an oblique apology by way of confessing that 'in 1857 the temper of the public mind had undergone a change which I failed to discern: and I attacked the Government and the Chancellor . . . for doing what the country desired though I did not'.[3] Yet unquestionably Gladstone's ability in 1859 to oblige Palmerston to shunt Lewis aside into the Home Office derived from a relationship with the 'country' cultivated since 1853 with which Lewis could not compete. The extent to which Gladstone was

1 Stanmore, *Herbert*, ii, 200.   2 H. Maxwell, *Clarendon* (1913), ii, 186.   3 G & P, 196.

able in 1859 to impose demarcation terms upon Palmerston is not clear. It emerged during a dispute in 1861 that Palmerston had disclaimed any ambitions to behave like Peel and be the real as well as the nominal First Lord of the Treasury. In asking Gladstone 'to take Charge of the Exchequer I clearly understood that the Management of the Finances of the Country subject always to the Concurrence of the Cabinet should be left to you'.[1] A formula somewhat in these terms was probably agreed with Gladstone in 1859.

It was thus an appointment distasteful to Palmerston and painful to Lewis. And – despite Argyll's being 'most movingly kind'[2] – to many who had observed Gladstone's ferocious impugning of Palmerston since 1855 there was something indecent about it. 'Lord Aberdeen,' Gladstone himself noted wryly, 'holds me the most extravagant and abandoned of English politicians.'[3] Bright, with whom Gladstone's celebration of rotten boroughs and refusal to vote against Derby rankled hard, pronounced Gladstone's acceptance of office under Palmerston as – even in one so 'eccentric' – 'wholly unjustifiable'.[4] Gladstone's niece Lucy Lyttelton noted the 'uproar in the midst of which we are all simmering' raised by Uncle William's taking office under Palmerston, 'view his well known antipathy to the Premier.'[5] Gladstone was sensitive on this score. He spoke later (to Acton, in 1864) of 'differences and collisions' but 'no resentments'.[6] This was easy for Gladstone to say: he had been on the giving, not the receiving, end. For Palmerston, a proud and combative man, the offer to Gladstone in 1859 was a matter entirely of expediency untinged by any element of forgiveness. Shaftesbury, his stepson-in-law and confidant, recorded that Palmerston feared Gladstone's 'character, his views, and his temperament, greatly. He rarely spoke severely of any one. Bright and Gladstone were the only two of whom he used strong language.' Shaftesbury recounted that when Derby dissolved the parliament in 1859 Palmerston urged him to 'do all that lay in my power to secure Gladstone's seat for the University' as tending usefully to act as a brake on his restless movement.[7]

There was no problem for Shaftesbury in Oxford in the uncontested election of May 1859; but Gladstone himself soon became indignantly aware that there were many among his university constituents who shared Aberdeen's or (for very different reasons) Bright's view of the dubiousness or unjustifiability of his proceedings. They put up the Marquess of Chandos[8] to challenge Gladstone when he presented

1 *Ib.*, 176.   2 D, v, 400.
3 Stanmore, 197.   4 K. G. Robbins, *John Bright* (1979), 151.
5 *The Diary of Lady Frederick Cavendish*, i, 192–3.
6 Morley, i, 628.   7 E. Hodder, *Shaftesbury* (1887), iii, 187–88.
8 Richard Temple-Nugent-Brydges-Chandos-Grenville, b. 1823, M.P. for Buckingham 1846–57; succeeded as 3rd Duke of Buckingham 1861.

himself for re-election on acceptance of office. 'I confess,' Gladstone wrote acidly to the Warden of All Souls, 'I should have felt some confidence in that under these circumstances an adverse judgment as to the effect of my position on my principles would have been reserved until it had been in some degree founded upon overt acts.'[1] After two easy passages in 1857 and earlier in 1859 Gladstone was intensely annoyed at being subjected once more to the kind of anxiety Perceval had caused him at the end of 1852. 'I am sore about the Oxford Election,' he noted on June 20, 'but I try to keep myself in order: it discourages & demoralises me, while, such are the riddles of *my* "human nature" it also quickens mere devotional sensibility. O that I had wings.'[2] He was later to declare that, although in retrospect he did not regret his parliamentary connection with Oxford, he felt he had been 'cheated into it' by his 'ignorance'. Had he been able to anticipate all the 'controversies that were to arise' and the effect this would have on his position, 'I never should have ventured to charge myself with the responsibilities of member for the University'.[3] As it happened, Gladstone still commanded sufficient credit in the university to get him through on July 1 by a margin of 191 votes out of 1,900, rather better than the 173 margin of 1847 or that of 149 in January 1853. Still, the indignity of being subjected to scrutiny left Gladstone from now on very restless about his Oxford seat. The salient points that came home to him were that neither Inglis nor Heathcote had ever been contested; that indeed his bid for the second seat in 1847 was the first occasion of a contest for the university since the 1832 Reform; and that, while he had held the seat without challenge on three occasions (1857, February 1859 – the Ionian imbroglio – and May 1859), this contest was his fourth, and correspondingly tiresome in a constituency supposedly above the vulgar rough-and-tumble of common politics. (There had been only two contests for Cambridge University since 1832.) Gladstone was sensitive on this score: he later referred to his seat's having 'often been the subject of contest', but was careful to insist that he had always had a majority among both resident and non-resident electors.[4] He was prone also to stress his readiness to retire from the university representation and to allow the 'interests and aims' of the electors of Oxford to be stated by 'someone whose opinions were more congenial to their own'.[5] 'Under these circumstances I naturally ask myself a question... How far am I responsible for this state of things and for having been, much against my will, the occasion of such frequent & serious disturbance to the University?' He could foresee no change in his own attitude, no 'abatement'; 'for

1 G. to F. K. Leighton, June 22, 1859. GP, 44530, 36.
2 D, v, 402.
3 G to Granville Vernon, July 28, 1865. GP, 44535, 96.
4 H, clxiv, 832, 837 (12 July 1861).
5 H, clxi, 1017 (February 27, 1861).

no one can yet venture safely to predict what form political combinations in this country are ultimately to assume.' And, as for his opponents, there was no likelihood that having fought four times, they 'will not be loath to fight it a fifth or a sixth'.[1] He thanked the Master of Balliol for his labours and apologised for having been 'the occasion, so many times over, of their imposition'.[2] That he was becoming restless not only about his dignity but about the inconveniences of being hobbled in his political movement was a point that would bear in upon him slowly but surely.

In the meantime Gladstone was much with Palmerston at Cambridge House in Piccadilly 'for political arrangements' ('B. of Trade propose Cobden'). Palmerston indeed made a strong bid to secure Cobden for his Cabinet. But Cobden was possessed of an 'unspoken sense of a loss of personal dignity and self-respect that would follow official subordination to a Minister of whom he had thought and spoken so ill as he had thought and spoken of Lord Palmerston'; and he was clear that, given his recorded opinions of Palmerston's public conduct, in which opinions he had experienced no change, he would ruin himself in his own eyes if he were to follow the 'monstrous' course of accepting Palmerston's offer unless Palmerston were to make a declaration of a change of view.[3] Milner Gibson was eventually slotted in to the Board of Trade. Russell insisted on the Foreign Office (much to the chagrin of Clarendon, who excluded himself in dudgeon); Herbert went to the War Office; Newcastle to the Colonial Office; Wood went back to the India Office; Somerset to the Admiralty; Grey to the Duchy of Lancaster; Granville and Argyll sustained the new Lord Chancellor, Campbell, in the Lords. There were hopes at Hawarden and Hagley that George Lyttelton might get something (he badly needed the money). 'Do not let *anything* ooze out,' Gladstone warned Catherine, 'of what I said rather prematurely about a place for G. – it is too remote & shadowy – the chances are very small that anything might be in my power.'[4] Nothing in the end could be done for Lyttelton. Gladstone filled in the intervals of administration-making with sittings to Mr. Watts ('very agreeable'), who was to complete two portraits that year.[5] At Stafford House on June 17 he heard Tennyson read his 'Guinevere' ('A memorable time'). On the 18th he was sworn in and received his seals at Windsor. Already he was deep in reading the Cabinet's Italian papers which would lead by the end of June to a memorandum. On June 24 the confused and bloody collision at Solferino reinforced the Austrians' disposition to entrench themselves in their Quadrilateral. Would Napoleon III, his confidence equally shaken, have

1 G to Rawlinson, July 5, 1859. GP, 44530, 45.
2 G to Scott, July 6, 1859. *Ib.*, 46.
3 Morley, *Cobden*, 699; 693.
4 G to CG, April 22, 1859. GGP, 28/6.
5 One in the National Portrait Gallery; the other at Hawarden.

the stomach to assault the formidable group of fortresses?

While the great events in north Italy thus relapsed into an uneasy lull, Gladstone found Tennyson suddenly highly intriguing; and made the first step in a pursuit to consummate a marriage of true minds which was to last, with decreasing reciprocality on the Laureate's part, until Tennyson's death in 1892. This new phase of their hitherto rather distant relationship commenced, with an accurate inauspiciousness, with Tennyson's declining an invitation to breakfast, though declaring himself gratified that 'My dear Mr. Gladstone' was not disappointed with 'Guinevere'. 'I used occasionally,' he recalled by way of apology, 'to breakfast with Mr. Rogers & Mr. Hallam, but they were men of so great an age that it would have been irreverent to refuse their invitations.'[1] It was perhaps strange that after nearly thirty years since Arthur's death his two most conspicuous admirers should not have been on terms. Did their claims to the affection of Mr. Hallam's charming son still cause an awkwardness? It may well have been so. But, if so, Gladstone set out with assiduity to make up for lost time and missed chances. And, as Gladstone marked his new sense of intellectual community with Tennyson, he received from John Stuart Mill a copy of the newly published *On Liberty*. In acknowledging a 'sense of the instruction to be derived from your writings', now 'doubly strong' (he had already read it), Gladstone invited Mill to fill the breakfast slot left vacant by Tennyson (with the added inducement that the social lion was to be the Orleanist pretender the Comte de Paris).[2]

[2]

It was one thing for Gladstone to get his 'old office' back; it was quite another to get back the old sense of rapport and homogeneity and stability which had sustained and inspired him in the good days of the Peel and Aberdeen administrations. Serious, or disagreeable, politics were not long in obtruding themselves. 'My office indeed is at this time not a pleasant one: for on every side the prospect of it is dark with increased charges and increased burdens, while the distance is worse than the fore-ground.'[3] The first whiff of the long quinquennium of conflict between Gladstone and his chief came before the end of June with a brush over the issue of the Suez Canal. But Italy offered for the present welcome occasions of co-operation. Gladstone declared himself a man

1 Tennyson to G, June 21, 1859. GP, 44391, 370.
2 G to Mill, July 5, 1859. GP, 44530, 44.
3 G to Storks, July 25, 1859. *Ib.*, 53.

beyond most others of peace, yet 'still my heart bounds with hope when I think of what Italy has long suffered and of the prospect opened for her deliverance'.[1] He made clear to Russell his confidence that he would be summoned from Flintshire 'even on *short* notice in case of a Cabinet on Italian matters'.[2] Gladstone assured Massari (one of Cavour's lieutenants) that 'among the very first and foremost motives which have guided me in returning to office . . . perhaps I should go further and say the very first of them all, has been a consideration of the great Italian question in its present state, and of the important though I hope pacific part which England may have to play in bringing it a happy settlement'.[3]

The 'present state' of the great Italian question was indeed the Emperor Napoleon's lack of stomach for taking on the Quadrilateral and his consequent readiness to come to terms with the Emperor Francis Joseph. They met at Villafranca on July 11 and agreed that, apart from Austria's ceding most of Lombardy to France for retrocession to Piedmont, the Pope and the other princes formerly under Austria's aegis would be restored to their sovereignties, and the Pope would become the head of an Italian confederation of which Austria's Venetian territories would be part. It seemed that Piedmontese aspirations to become the nucleus of a Kingdom of North Italy from the Tyrrhenian to the Adriatic seas had received a decisive check. Gladstone's cabinet memorandum of June 30, apart from the issue of papal sovereignty, was not entirely remote from the spirit of Villafranca. He agreed with Palmerston in seeing no prejudice to British interests in the formation of a Kingdom of North Italy but he was anxious at Piedmontese temptations to 'domineer' and be a bad neighbour to Austria in the future. Doubtless she would want some annexations but her ambitions must be kept within bounds. There were evidences of resistance to Piedmontese 'sheer ambition' in Tuscany. The two great desiderata were first, the 'cessation of direct dominion of Austria in Italy', and second an 'essential change' in the temporal prerogatives of the papacy. It was necessary to get Austrian consent to any lasting settlement; so perhaps Lombardy-Venetia could best be given to the sovereignty of that Archduke Ferdinand Maximilian who had impressed Gladstone so favourably at Venice? As for the Pope, he must be handled by Europe and not left to deal alone with his former subjects, which would lead to a Mazzinian republic and thus the discrediting of the 'cause of temperate freedom'. The Pope should be given guarantees as to dignity, independence, security, wealth; but his sovereignty must be reduced to a 'suzerainty'. Britain should play a 'European' role in strengthening the hand of the Emperor Napoleon in coming to a

1 G to Damaschino, July 8, 1859. *Ib.*, 46.
2 G to Russell, August 18, 1859. *Ib.*, 62.
3 Beales, *England and Italy*, 87.

co-operative policy with Austria to secure these ends.[1] This was a formula for about as conservative an Italophilism as could be in July 1859.

However fascinating, the Italian question could not delay the press of mundane problems which crowded in upon the new Chancellor of the Exchequer. Gladstone would be plagued for years by the matter of the newly established Galway packet and postal contract, presently in the hands of the Atlantic Steam Navigation Company and losing the government nearly a million pounds annually. This arrangement was being challenged by the older-established British shipping lines, who set up a collecting depot at Queenstown; a scheme backed for its economy and efficiency by Rowland Hill at the Post Office. The Galway contract was a vested Irish interest and Gladstone prudently moved for a Commons select committee to investigate. He found it necessary to defend the Civil Service Commission from critics who were not aware that the 'present position of the system is only in a stage of transition'. There were questions about the National Gallery: should it be moved from Trafalgar Square to the Burlington House site? And should a National Portrait Gallery be deducted from it? Gladstone had grave doubts – mainly financial – on both scores. There were problems about housing the Royal Academy in Burlington House; and the question was still unresolved as to whether to purchase that painting by Hayter of the first reformed House of Commons in which the young Gladstone brothers cut handsome if obscure figures. There was the vexed question of Mr. Scott's designs for the new Foreign Office; and the passionate battle between the partisans of the Gothic and Italian styles. Gladstone's predilection for the renaissance solution owed much to his sense of a 'very important difference' in the costs between the rival styles.[2] There was also the distasteful necessity on July 13 of voting unsuccessfully with the bulk of the Conservatives in a 'wretched division' against the latest attempt to solve the church rate problem.[3] There was also the question of Reform, which Russell had stipulated as the price of his collaboration with Palmerston. Gladstone guardedly explained to Brougham that the question contained 'all the elements of a false position.' On the one hand the 'good sense and practical turn' of the English people suggested confidence in a 'tolerable solution'; but, on the other, 'what ministries it will scatter on its road may be very uncertain'. It seemed to Gladstone that a settlement would be 'more safe than a postponement'. Security for the 'good use of the present franchise' lay, he thought, 'not so much in the competency of the voter as in his willingness to defer to others more competent & in his respect for the established order'. Of 'this security

1 Beales, 96.
2 H, cliv, 800–05; 1067–68; clv, 892, 899–901, 918–20.
3 D, v, 409. The issue was régarded by Ministers as an 'open' one.

much may be hoped for upon a lower & broader basis; and that in defining what that basis should be it might be well to rule cases of doubt in favour of rather than against Extension'.[1] These were bold words. But Gladstone remained indisposed to action. Apart from caution as to the possible scattering of ministries, Reform still lay outside the centre of his sense of vocational mission, essentially irrelevant to his larger and immediate purposes. By October Gladstone apologised that the government had 'made no progress whatever' on the question; and that, for himself, 'sordid considerations compounded of alarm at the state and prospects of our expenditure' made him 'inapt to embrace any constitutional question'.[2]

Above and beyond such matters was the need to get up a provisional budget by July 18. A deficit of five millions had to be coped with. There were no obstacles: at a cabinet on the 16th 'two hours took my budget through, *pur et simple*'. Gladstone's principal expedient was a sharp hoist in the income tax from 5d to 9d. In his statement on the 18th he stressed in careful, measured and unpolemical language the necessity for 'increased efforts' to meet the 'unusually enlarged' expenditure caused by the augmentation of the armed services estimates by more than £5 million. A lucky bonus in the form of £2 million falling to the revenue by the ending of Long Annuities must not be allowed to be 'dragged unnoticed into the general vortex of expenditure'.[3] After this stop-gap Gladstone had leisure on the 19th to meditate on 'the future of our finance'. There was the vital question of reaccrediting his vocation. There were the principles and projects of 1856 to be set into beneficent motion. As he saw it, Gladstone was confronted with the circumstances that his heroically Peelite stroke of 1853 in renewing the income tax for the strictly limited purpose of emancipating finance finally from the sway of error and restrictiveness had been allowed to fail by default. Exigencies of war and Whiggish empiricism and fecklessness had degraded the income tax into yet another mere perennial device to service an illegitimate inflation of the gross expenditure of the State by 22½ per cent compared with 1853. 'I am indeed exceedingly fond of my office, but the lavish temper (as I admit) of the times makes my duty one perpetual and wearying battle which I should not like to sustain for more than a certain time.'[4] In hot and mocking dispute with Disraeli, Gladstone insisted on 1853 as the crucial bench mark of financial 'principles of high policy': 'I demur . . . entirely to the doctrine of the right hon. Gentleman that this growth in the civil expenditure is a thing natural, normal, and proportioned to the state of

1 G to Brougham, August 23, 1859. GP. 44530, 64.
2 G to Brougham, October 11, 1859. *Ib.*, 41–2.
3 H, cliv, 1389–1407.
4 G to J. D. Acland, September 9, 1859. GP, 44530, 73.

the country'.[1] He remarked to Catherine on 'nice and close fighting' and on Disraeli's concocting 'a popular motion to trip me up.' In the new circumstances of 1859 it was necessary for Gladstone to readjust his resentments and his targets. Palmerston was now (publicly at any rate) out of range. The indulgence of 1858–59 to Disraeli would thus be withdrawn. 'I am afraid that the truce between us is over and that we shall have to pitch in as before.'[2]

As to meditations on the 'future of our finance', Gladstone disclosed himself to his brother Robertson at the beginning of August. He defended his augmentation of the income tax 'regardless of charges of inconsistency', because it was 'necessary for the public service on its present enormous scale'. 'But let me own to you fairly that I am not converted in my general views of the tax itself. I view it as a grand instrument for war, and for special occasions, and for fixed reforms. But I shall rejoice to see the day when it may be dispensed with as an ordinary instrument of finance.' Economy was the 'first and great article' of his financial creed. 'The controversy between direct and indirect taxation holds a minor though important place.' Gladstone insisted that he had not 'the smallest doubt we should at this moment have had a smaller expenditure if financial reformers' – of whom Robertson was a prominent specimen – 'had not directed . . . their chief attention not to the question of how much of expenditure and taxes shall we have, but to the question how it should be raised.' There was no 'leverage' in existence which could 'displace either direct or indirect taxation from the system of a country which in one way or another raises nearer ninety than eighty millions a year'. Hume was, Gladstone pointed out, 'all for direct taxation: but he bestowed his chief care upon expenditure. I sorely feel his loss'.[3] Against the generally sound argument that if you had only direct taxes you would have economical government was the undeniable fact that it was the income tax which had been the principal source of extravagance since the ending of the twenty-five years of 'good spirit' which obtained before the Russian war. And memories of the war sentiment of that time made Gladstone sceptical of Liberalism. 'The Liberal side of the House is certainly at this time the more pacific and economical: but the manufacturing and mercantile classes have had much to do with promoting wars and likewise annexations or assumptions of territorial power and responsibility which are in some respects as dangerous and bad.'[4] Indeed, Gladstone could well envisage the Conservatives seizing the initiative on economy. 'It is pretty evident,' he noted on September 9, 'from Mr. Disraeli's advice

1 H, clv, 183–87.
2 Bassett, 125.
3 G to Robertson G, August 2, 1859. GP, *Ib.*, 57.
4 G to Robertson G, August 18, 1859. *Ib.*, 63.

about arrangements with France that he is laying himself out, quite properly I think, for a run in the sense of economy.'[1]

Once the immediately critical exigencies of finance had been dealt with Gladstone recurred to what was becoming a new obsession: he read Tennyson's newly-published 'Idylls' on July 14; noting in the very midst of his budget preparations: 'Tennyson: who has grasped me with a strong hand.' An urge to acquit himself with a comprehensive statement including the earlier 'In Memoriam', 'Maud' and 'The Princess' asserted itself irresistibly. He wrote to Elwin of the *Quarterly* on August 16: 'Will you let me try my hand on a review of Tennyson. . . I have never felt fanatical about him; but his late work has laid hold of me with a power that I have not felt, I ought to say not suffered, for many years.'[2] From the evidence of his article in the October *Quarterly* Gladstone seems to have been gripped by a sense of a dual vocation, an intersection of Tennyson the seasoned Liberal Laureate and himself as the new Liberal statesman in alliance as prophet and practitioner of a better age. Perhaps this dream of Literature and Politics in moral harmony was all the more attractive to Gladstone confronted with the depressing reality of Palmerston. A cabinet on August 6 he described glumly (and in Greek) as 'only a place for conversation'; and he was loftily sardonic on Palmerston's sanguine view that 'it looks well'. There were the distractions of preparing to install himself at Downing Street – he kept up Carlton House Terrace for the family – and in dispatching the brood in various vacation directions – the two elder boys to a tour in Wales and the 'tinies' to Hawarden. There was a Council at Osborne and conversation with Prince Albert and thereby an opportunity to meet Helen, who had settled in 1858 at St. Helen's Priory nearby. She came over to Osborne to see her brother and 'was asked in by Gen. Grey had luncheon with us all and renewed her acquaintance with Newcastle & Elgin'.[3] 'Much conv. in evg. She promised to write to Tom' – presumably about the Residuary Estate Account. (Newcastle's private affairs were not less of an anxiety: 'Phillimore hears of the deranged state of Newcastle's family. I think his temper has suffered perceptibly.')[4] Then to Cliveden and driving and boating with the Laboucheres. 'Read Tennyson, Tennyson, Tennyson.'[5]

The old avocations were not entirely displaced. The theatre remained close to Gladstone's heart. He presided at a dinner given by fellow-Etonians to Charles Kean, whom he praised for raising the moral tone of the stage and whose famous production of *The Corsican Brothers* he would enjoy later in the season. Theatre-land of course was always convenient for expeditions of rescue in the West End. Gladstone first met Maria

1 G to Lord Granville Somerset, September 9, 1859. *Ib.*, 74.
2 D, V, 410.   3 G to CG, August 14, 1859. GGP, 28/6.
4 G to CG, July 15, 1859. *Ib.*   5 D, v, 415–16.

Summerhayes at the end of July, 'full in the highest degree both of interest and of beauty'. He was 'long' with her on August 4 and soon he was proposing that she sit to Dyce for a portrait commissioned by him. (She now appears with fetching demureness in the Aberdeen Art Gallery as 'Lady with the coronet of Jasmine'.)[1] He saw her to say farewell on leaving for Hawarden, and wrote to her immediately after arriving. He warned himself on September 1: 'My thoughts of S require to be limited & purged.' On September 16 he read Tennyson's 'Princess' with her ('much & variously moved').[2]

The 'heat is sweltering', complained Gladstone from his seat in the Commons on July 18. 'Tomorrow we are to have the question discussed upon the expediency of returning to November Sessions and getting rid of July and August . . . I have a charming letter from old Stephy . . . He says the boys at Eton generally think Austria ought to get out of Italy altogether.'[3] 'Foreign policy is at present the chief subject of my hopeful interest,' he told Acland.[4] Gladstone had the satisfaction of making his farewell to the session by an *'oretta* on Italian affairs: my best off-hand speech, or least bad'. He was caustic on Disraeli's complaints about the government's partisanship. Gladstone's retort (as Kettle to Pot) was that it had been the Derby-Disraeli government which was partisan – for Austria. Lord Palmerston's government was, Gladstone artlessly insisted, 'neutral' – and in the manner of Canning in 1823 as the model and as having 'vindicated the character of England'.[5] At the traditional Greenwich fish dinner for ministers, as Gladstone reported to Catherine, 'Argyll & I talked Tennyson like mad all the dinner.' Gladstone also felt himself in a Tennysonian mood of guilt in relation to Catherine: 'Your closing words dearest C. cannot be bad for you or for any one but they send me "grovelling" like Guinevere when Arthur comes.'[6] The Cabinet parted for the vacation on August 17 and Gladstone returned to Hawarden to find the church 'admirably rebuilt & restored'; but with the recent death of Henry Glynne's daughter Nora casting a shadow ('God had made him for calm & placid life in the affections and the repose of home').[7] Catherine was also much troubled by distressing menopausal recurrences: 'C. on her back: with certain appearances, long disused.' The doctors were reassuring about an 'effort to regain equilibrium at a stage of transition'. There was an enlivening interlude for a special Cabinet in London at the end of August. Palmerston and Russell had fallen foul of the Queen over Italy. She objected to Lord John's cavalier attitude to the

1 *Ib.*, 413–15. *Victorian Studies*, xix, (1975) 93. GP, 44392, 111. The portrait is also reproduced in the *Diaries*, v.
2 D, v, 418–24.   3 G to CG, July 18, 1859. GGP, 28/6.
4 G to J. D. Acland, September 9, 1859. GP, 44530, 73.
5 H, clv, 1139–55.   6 G to CG, August 11, 1859. GGP, 28/6.
7 G to CG, July 18, 1859. *Ib.*

rights of legitimate sovereigns; and 'kicked'. Lord John, 'in a *state*', ran to Palmerston; who thereupon wrote to the Queen in a manner 'too *brusque* to address to her as a Sovereign & as a woman'. Gladstone described the behaviour of his two senior colleagues to Argyll as 'hasty, inconsiderate, & eminently *juvenile*'.[1] 'Meantime here in the heart of London & at the head quarters of politics,' Gladstone told Catherine from 11 Downing Street, 'I have the prospect of a most quiet Sunday sitting by the single window in the drawing room that opens, in very good & cool air . . . The drawing room is wonderfully perked up by the pictures & prints now hung & looks quite human.'[2]

Back at Hawarden once more Gladstone found China, Italy and Tennyson competing for his attention as he prepared for another Penmaenmawr vacation early in September. The case with China was that the Peking government was refusing to ratify the provisions of the Treaty of Tientsin imposed upon them by Britain, France, Russia and the United States in June 1858. The purpose of the treaty was to bring China, however unwillingly, out of her isolation of assumed superiority and into the comity of nations by establishing diplomatic relations, opening ports, and making agreements on tariffs and trade. Gladstone could not object to this in principle. Especially he could not object to the provision permitting work by Christian missions. Besides, having swallowed the camel of Palmerston he would not strain at the gnat of a coercive China policy, even when Palmerston paraded drastic projects of an 'attack and occupation of Pekin' or a blockade of the Chinese coast. Instead, Gladstone spoke of his 'extreme grief' at the 'sadness' of the repulse of the British assault on the Taku forts.[3] His guiding notion was to extend his advocacy of Anglo-French concert from Italy to the Yang-tse, with an 'adequate' force to be sent to secure ratification of the treaty and 'just and necessary' satisfaction.[4] When challenged by the Duchess of Sutherland as to whether the Chinese war was 'just' Gladstone prevaricated:

> I condemn the policy out of which its occasion sprang: of the particular facts of 1857 I think now, as I thought then: I feel the burden and the misery for is not too strong a word, of being obliged to take decisions in a moment upon statements which may be biased & must be incomplete. . . . All I can say in *answer* to your question is that I do not think the Govt have since they heard of the disaster at the Teiko taken any unjust resolution. But I do not feel myself now in such possession of all the facts of the case as to be able to pronounce upon it conclusively.[5]

1 D, v, 420–21.   2 G to CG, August 28, 1859. *Ib.*
3 G & P, 111–12.   4 D, v, 425.
5 G to Duchess of Sutherland, December 12, 1860. GP, 44531, 91.

The Italian case was that all the assumptions of June and July – and not least the Villafranca agreements – were being swiftly overtaken by events. Parma, Modena, Tuscany and the Romagna were now moving towards union with Piedmont. Gladstone tended to move along with them. He could not 'but continue to hope' more than he feared, he told Palmerston, 'for the Italians of the four associated districts'.[1] On the one hand, as he told Clarendon, 'annexation to Sardinia may have to be waived, on the other their Sovereigns will I hope & believe continue deposed as I am afraid they too richly deserve & some other arrangement will be made. Matters seem to look in this direction.' Still, it had always seemed to Gladstone that 'there were two sides to the question of Sardinian aggrandisement. There is surely an equilibrium of Italy as well as of Europe.' But the notion that 'some other arrangement' might preserve that equilibrium against the Piedmontese was hardly a tenable position by now. And as for the Pope: 'To say . . . that the question of the Papal States is not Italian but Catholic, is simply to establish a war of life and death between human nature and religion, with human nature in the right.'[2] Indeed Gladstone's tendencies to flow with the Piedmontese tide were too much for Elwin of the *Quarterly*, who declined Gladstone's proposal to expose the iniquities of the Modenese government.

At Penmaenmawr Gladstone corrected the proofs of his Tennyson article and found his sea-dips 'a very *powerful* agent'. There was an interlude at Liverpool to see Robertson about plans for a new post office and to look for the site of a new church at Seaforth. On the way back he paused for three crucial days at Hawarden. It had been arranged that Cobden would call. 'Robertson is coming to Hawarden on Monday! cannot resist the attraction of Cobden,' Gladstone told Catherine. 'We shall indeed be a "happy family" there.'[3] 'I came last night,' he reported on the 11th, 'and found the Dean and the Hopes. When Lady Mildred [Hope] was gone both gentlemen went to sleep: I am afraid it was when I was asking Stephen a question or two about the coal pit . . . Cobden comes tomorrow forenoon Robertson not till the afternoon . . . Stephen has sentenced us to dine at half past four!'[4] On September 12 Cobden arrived, and there was 'further conv. with Mr. Cobden on Tariffs & relations with France. We are closely & warmly agreed.'[5] 'Cobden came early', he informed Catherine; 'nothing could go better than the luncheon but I am afraid the dinner will be rather sorny[6] with local Clergy. I have had a walk & a long talk with Cobden who I think pleases & is pleased.'[7] This was the germ of the Treaty of Commerce to dismantle protective

1 G & P, *ib.*
2 G to Clarendon, November 26, 1859. Bodleian MS, Clar. Dep. C523.
3 G to CG, September 10, 1859. GGP, 28/6.
4 G to CG, September 11, 1859. *Ib.*   5 D, v, 424.
6 'Obtruded upon'.   7 C to CG, September 12, 1859. GGP, 28/6.

barriers between France and Britain which Gladstone incorporated into his 1860 budget. All he told Palmerston at the time was that Cobden was 'very anxious for a reduction of wine duties with a view to improved relations with France. He is going to Paris.'[1] Cobden had been primed for the project during the summer by the Saint-Simonian free trader Michel Chevalier and by Bright. Their notion was a grand stroke of international commercial concord which would proclaim an example to the world and rescue Anglo-French relations from the dangerous strains and tensions attaching to the French aggression against Austria and rumoured French expansionist ambitions. The method would have to be by diplomatic treaty: there was no chance of getting a reciprocal free trade scheme through the protectionist French chambers or past the protectionist Minister of Finance, Magne. But on the other hand the Emperor Napoleon was prone to sympathise with Saint-Simonian notions (the Suez Canal was another); and, if he could be persuaded, he possessed the necessary constitutional powers. For Cobden it was an opportunity to pull off something grand outside the government he had proudly declined to join. There would be objections from purists that free trade was incompatible with commercial treaties; but this would be no serious impediment. For Gladstone it was the kind of big stroke which marched well with his predisposition for heroic and large-scale acts of beneficent executive power: nothing could more dramatically exemplify his 1856 doctrine that the key to future politics would be the 'doings and practical intentions of the minister, and a corresponding conviction wrought by them upon the public mind'. Here was a providential opportunity to do something bold by means of the leeway allowed by the falling in of the £2 millions of annuity payments. And that an international dimension of peace should be added to two domestic dimensions of economic morality made the scheme much more than twice as attractive.

Having secured Gladstone's undertakings of full support and co-operation, Cobden sounded Palmerston and Russell in London. There was little in the way of cheer or encouragement from them, but no obstacles or objections either; so Cobden went hopefully on his way to Paris. Gladstone meanwhile resumed his Penmaenmawr sojourn, interspersed with occasional cabinets in London and bachelor eating at the University Club (his partiality for club fare such as 'my beloved mutton chops' had long been one of his little jokes with Catherine[2]) and expeditions with Miss Summerhayes. With her on September 17 there was 'a scene of rebuke not to be easily forgotten' – though who was rebuking whom is not entirely clear.[3] After dining at Herbert's on the 19th he met her at eleven and brought her to Downing Street for an hour 'espy. to see the pictures'. He assured himself that 'all is there on the way, if

1 G & P, *ib.*   2 Bassett, 118.   3 D, v, 425.

there be no illusion, to order & good: the case is no common one: may God grant that all go right. To me this is no trivial matter, for evil or for good.'[1]

There were two weeks more back with the family at Penmaenmawr (bathing in the rain brought on a nasty 'tight chest') and then Hawarden, where Gladstone viewed the prospect of the trial for heresy of Bishop Forbes, friend of both Pusey and Döllinger, 'with pain and even more than pain, with shame'. There was a critical cabinet on September 24 on the French negotiations (Gladstone was proud of his expertise as a railway traveller: 'I was in Downing Street this morning at ¼ past eleven, and I slept full half the way & made myself rather a killing bed').[2] It was a solace also that the Tennyson article came out in the new *Quarterly*. This marked Gladstone's first major excursion into contemporary English letters; though his main purpose was to enrol Tennyson in the ranks of progressive politics. His rebukes to Tennyson for behaviour unbecoming to this role, such as the warlike conclusion to 'Maud' or aggressive attitudes to the French or for patches of hysteria or morbidity, were all the more stern and strict; and stung Tennyson accordingly. He defined Tennyson's 'business' in terms which he would employ increasingly to define his own.

> Mr. Tennyson is too intimately and essentially the poet of the nineteenth century to separate himself from its leading characteristics, the progress of physical science, and a vast commercial, mechanical, and industrial development. Whatever he may say or do in an occasional fit, he cannot long either cross or lose its sympathies; for while he elevates, as well as adorns it, he is flesh of its flesh and bone of its bone. We fondly believe it is his business to do much towards the solution of that problem, so fearful from its magnitude, how to harmonise this new draught of external power and activity with the old and more mellow wine of faith, self-devotion, loyalty, reverence, and discipline.[3]

For Gladstone the Arthurian romance in the 'Idylls' had 'every recommendation' for this purpose: 'It is national: it is Christian. It is also human in the largest and deepest sense. . .' Tennyson's poetry had raised 'the character and the hopes of the age and the country which produced it.' On the way back to London on October 14 Gladstone was 'getting Guinevere by heart' as a kind of testimony of his own sense of a vocation to raise the character and hopes of his age and his country.

That would depend much, in the immediate perspective, on Cobden's proceedings in France. Gladstone conferred with Chevalier. 'All this is

1 *Ib.*, 427.
2 G to CG, September 24, 1859. GGP, 28/6.   3 *Gleanings*, ii, 145.

merely mapping out the way which it would be possible to tread,' he
reported to Cobden. 'You know my views & desires but the time has not
yet come when they could be laid before the Govt. at large (though I am
glad to find that you have communicated with Ld P & Ld JR) and therefore
of course I have no authority whatever to commit them.'[1] While he waited
on the fortunes of Cobden's negotiations Gladstone had more than
enough to occupy him. He discussed the Reform question with Lewis
('my great wish is to promote what will in a liberal spirit get it to a
settlement but a departmental instinct leads me towards preferring
ceteris paribus a rating franchise').[2] There was Summerhayes, 'for whom
I wish to exert myself'. There was a trip to Holyhead to witness the trials
of Brunel's 12,000-ton *Great Eastern* and to attend a public dinner on board
('the ship of an overpowering vastness'; and he was gratified that Lord
Chandos was 'marked in his attentions'). Back in London, he missed
Summerhayes after a play at the Haymarket ('Rem in T [rafalgar] Square
from 11½ to one'). One of his rescue techniques now was to distribute
copies of Henry Gladwyn Jebb's *Out of the Depths* (1859), a romance of a
prostitute rescued by an aristocratic priest. Gladstone discussed this
congenial theme with Catherine along with the 'State of the departed' '&
kindred subjects'.[3] At Hawarden briefly he worked on translations in
German and English as part of his literary schemes with Lyttelton ('an
agreeable way for a C. of E. to pass his time'). There were charades at the
Rectory; and a 'letter from Ld Abn handwriting much aged & broken'.[4] At
the Rectory Gladstone met Henry Glynne's new intended. 'From what I
saw, he reported to Catherine, 'I quite join in the favourable judgment
on Miss Lowder.' He could also report that the brickworks at Oak Farm
was 'in substance let which is good.' And at length Catherine visited
Cliveden. 'Your account of the place and of its mistress are *very*
interesting and I am very glad you have at last made out the visit. It
seemed almost unnatural that you should not have been there and I am
sorry on every ground, for my own muddle therein, not to have
accompanied you to it.'[5] Then to Cambridge for an honorary doctorate,
along with Bishop Wilberforce of Oxford and Sir George Grey. He found
the audience in the Senate House 'crowded & very warm' and detected
that the 'spirit of the young men was excellent especy. as indicated in
whatever touched religion'. He took advantage of the occasion to discuss
with Wilberforce the Bishop of Brechin's dire problems with his synod;
and, the guest of the Vice-Chancellor, Latimer Neville, Master of
Magdalene, read Lady Charlotte Guest's edition of Welsh legends,

1 G to Cobden, October 20, 1859. GP, 44530, 97.
2 G to Lewis, October 17, 1859. *Ib.*, 95.
3 D, v, 442.
4 G to CG, October 8, 1859. GGP, 28/6.
5 G to CG, 4, 5, October 7, 1859. *Ib.*

Mabinogion. After another round of Cambridge socializing and sight-seeing the Gladstones repaired to Audley End, the seat of Neville's brother Lord Braybrooke, where Catherine had spent much time with cousins in her girlhood. There he wrestled to 'bring into order' the porcelain collection; which sparked off another bout of purchasing when he returned to London ('Went into the City: & hunted China in Holborn etc.'). There were always official dinners: at Guy's Hospital he was 'much pleased' with the Duke of Cambridge's 'frankness & evident *application* of mind.' At the Guildhall he 'thanked in a roar i.e. roared my thanks for the H. of C.'

Cabinets started seriously again in November. Gladstone was not sanguine about prospects. 'But as to Cabinets I do not know that I shall be able to put in anything satisfactory', he reported on October 20. 'We are plagued and vexed with foolish proposals which however there is ample good sense to put down but I dare not take the responsibility for myself, of voluntarily remaining away while uneasy questions are afloat.' One of them was the 'wretched Morocco question', about which Russell was fussing. 'The little man gets less & less *solid* as he grows older'; in Peel's time such an issue would not have detained the Cabinet in town.[1] There was a new scheme for cabinet committees to screen legislative proposals. True to his earlier indifference to the Reform issue, Gladstone tried to 'beg off the Committee of the Cabinet on Reform: but without success.' There was much ado humouring Palmerston on such trivia as telegraphic communication with Balmoral and Prince Albert's request for money for research on 'Magnetical observations' (Palmerston was always stout in favour of the claims of science: Gladstone secured the vote on June 12, 1862; by which time the Prince was no longer in a position to be gratified). There were details about the Prince of Wales's visit to Canada. It was gratifying to see Aberdeen and observe him improved in health and appearance: '& what is to us an inexpressible relief he is less painfully downcast and despondent about Italian affairs.'[2] At Windsor Gladstone walked with the Dean (Gerald Wellesley) and the Queen's new chaplain Charles Kingsley ('whom I much like'). He was delighted with the 'freshness' of Princess Alice at dinner and after a long conversation with the Prince the Queen said, 'You must prepare a large Budget.'[3] That Gladstone had every intention of doing. By now things were taking shape in Cobden's negotiations with the French.

Cobden had started conferring with Chevalier and Rouher, the Minister of Commerce, on October 25. He had an audience with the Emperor at Saint-Cloud on the 27th. Then he saw Fould, a former Finance

1 G to CG, 20, October 21, 1859. *Ib.*
2 G to Clarendon, November 26, 1859. Bodleian MS, Clar. Dep. C523.
3 D, v, 438 (November 14, 1859).

Minister. Gladstone and Chevalier were by now corresponding, mainly about the problems of overcoming suspicion and resistance in both countries. Cobden, back in London on November 3, saw Gladstone: 'really almost the only Cabinet Minister of five years' standing,' he told Bright, 'who is not afraid to let his heart guide his head a little at times.'[1] Certainly neither Palmerston nor Russell was any more encouraging than they had been earlier. But Cobden was indefatigably back in Paris on November 17 with much negotiation with Rouher and Fould. 'Cobden exerts himself usefully in Paris,' Gladstone told Catherine: 'don't say a word of this.'[2] He saw the Emperor again at the Tuileries on December 21, when he 'explained to him that Mr. Gladstone . . . was anxious to prepare his Budget for the ensuing session of Parliament, and that it would be a convenience to him to be informed as soon as possible whether the French Government had decided to agree to a commercial treaty, as in that case he would make arrangements accordingly; that he did not wish to be in possession of the details, but merely to know whether the principle of the treaty was determined upon'. The Emperor returned assurances as to the principle of reciprocal free trade; it was a matter of settling questions of detail.[3]

The ground was now laid. From now on the negotiations would be taken on to the plane of formal diplomacy. Gladstone prodded Russell (he recommended Jourdan's pamphlet *Guerre à l'Anglais* as a 'remarkable indication') and was fertile with copious drafts of official instructions for the negotiators. Doubtless also he extolled the project when dining with the Palmerstons on November 17 (noting perhaps a little hopefully that 'she at length seems *aging*'). Russell's persistence in pressing on with the Reform Bill was an annoying distraction; but Gladstone managed to get deep into budgetary details in conferences with the Financial Secretary of the Treasury, Laing. Sweeping the remaining protective duties from the British tariff would leave large holes in the revenue which would have to be filled. Licences on public houses, eating and coffee houses? A hop duty? New stamp duties? Gladstone was sure that this was the moment to begin clearing away the greatest remaining restrictive item among the customs and excise duties, the paper duty, and thus redeem the implied pledge he had given in Manchester in October 1853 and the pledge he had given to himself in the 'Memorandum on Finance' in February 1856. Immediate abolition would leave a very large hole in the revenue indeed, and would require some nimble manoeuvring in the new estimates.

All this led on November 25 to Gladstone's making his first major aggressive initiative against the spending departments; which resulted in an exchange of preliminary ranging shots on the issue of the naval

1 Morley, *Cobden*, 717.
2 G to CG, December 6, 1859. GGP, 28/6.			3 Morley, *ib.*, 720–21.

construction programme provoked by the recent design in France of the first iron-built and shot-proof warship, the *Gloire*. Two iron-plated ships had already been commenced under the late government. Somerset proposed the construction of a new and smaller and less expensive type of iron-plated ship. Gladstone assured Palmerston that he 'entirely and cordially' concurred in Somerset's plan as the 'most formidable and efficient which is in our power to employ'; but he asked Palmerston to consider in return with Somerset 'whether it is really wise to continue the present outlay on so great a scale for the building of those maritime castles which we call line of battle ships and which seem to be constructed on the principle precisely opposite to all land fortifications, and to aim at presenting as large a surface as possible to the destroying fire of an enemy'. Gladstone hastened to reassure Palmerston that he was not speaking '*now*' with 'any view to the reduction of our outlay on building as a whole though I may think something desirable in that sense: but rather to the transfer from an apparently inferior to a probably superior mode of applying our resources'. Palmerston, convinced of the need to keep defence expenditure up to the mark required by the tense European situation, responded unpropitiously. 'Command of the Ocean', he informed Gladstone on November 29, depended on the strongest fleet of line of battleships.[1] Already Gladstone was exclaiming dolefully: 'a divided Govt.!'

At a cabinet on November 30 Gladstone found himself 'very *lonely* on the question of Military Estimates'. A few days later there was 'stiff work' on the estimates; 'I gained some points & lost more. We are in excess, & in fever.' The 'fever' of widespread public apprehension of a French invasion expressed itself in the form of a volunteer movement and pressure for a policy of defensive fortifications along the south coast. Palmerston and other members of his government were ready enough to give a lead to this sentiment rather than merely respond to it. 'Old woman as I am,' Gladstone confessed, 'my fears still run in the line that our charges and accusations against the French, may ultimately become the groundwork of the very mischief we apprehend.'[2] Herbert joined with Palmerston in a determination to secure the vital points of southern England from vulnerability to invasion. He put up proposals which Palmerston was anxious to get adopted. He wanted a cabinet on December 16 to decide that all great naval arsenals and other important ports should be secured at the cost of something between £10 and £11 millions. Palmerston made his determination quite clear: it was not a question of whether, but of how. Extra taxation or a loan? 'We have had Suez Canal but not definitively. All present were more or less in the right

1 G & P, 113–14.
2 G to Brougham, November 8, 1859. GP, 44530, 107.

sense except Lord P. – We were not ripe however for decision and nothing fresh seems to be known. Herbert's military plans are the grand trouble. I am going to dine early with him however.'[1] The only other response Gladstone had to hand was to forward 'encouraging' letters from Cobden.

On this menacing note the political year closed. At a time of crucial consequence, when Gladstone particularly needed as much remissive capacity in the revenue as he could get, he was being burdened with large extra demands which, moreover, had the effect of contradicting the dimension of 'peace' which was at the foundations of the great commercial treaty operation. He retreated with Argyll to Trentham with the Sutherlands for repose: Harriet, Duchess of Sutherland (a granddaughter of the legendary Georgiana, Duchess of Devonshire) was becoming a kind of Egeria for Gladstone, wise, soothing, knowledgeable (in 1859 she assumed again the office of Mistress of the Robes to the Queen). It is not likely, however, that Gladstone was soothed there by reading the much talked-of book by Charles Darwin, *On the Origin of Species by Natural Selection*, which offered evolutionary explanations of natural phenomena incompatible with orthodox Christian interpretations of Holy Writ. With Argyll he went on up to Edinburgh for a session of the University Court, which pre-elected him as Rector. Scotland was an oppressive reminder of Forbes's trial for heresy, due to commence in February. At Hawarden he worked on translations of sapphics from Bishop Heber as part of his literary project with Lyttelton: 'And so I bid to verse composition in a dead language a probable lifelong farewell.' Talks with the Hawarden agent revealed that Stephen Glynne's affairs were 'still somewhat an anxious & critical matter to consider'. There was more criticism than anxiety in discussions with Lord Richard Cavendish of the shortcomings of Arthur Gordon, who was due for the New Year. And Gladstone was confronted with that fact familiar to fathers of finding that his son had surpassed him in stature: at a family measuring in stockings or slippers Gladstone was found to be 5 feet 10¾ inches; while Willy made 5 feet 11 inches.

But the ending of 1859 confronted Gladstone above all with the fact that he had passed his fiftieth year. 'Behold me then arrived at the close of half a century in this wayward world! Half a century! What do those little words enfold! Grace & glory, sin & shame, fears, joys, pains, emotions, labours, efforts; what a marvel is this life, what a miracle the construction of it for our discipline?' He felt more than ever cause to 'hang down the head'; yet cause too to be thankful: 'this morning' – December 29 – 'came into my room my wife and seven children.' Again the disturbingly powerful sense of resentment at the onset of age came over Gladstone:

1 G to CG, December 16, 1859. GCP, 28/6.

'Yet there is in me a resistance to the passage of Time as if I could lay hands on it & stop it: as if youth were yet in me & life & youth were one.'[1]

[4]

To start the New Year of 1860 on the right foot and to relieve his feelings on the services and fortifications issues Gladstone launched an attack on the education estimates. (There had very nearly been a wrong foot. Gladstone recounted on January 5: 'At Richmond I was obstructed in getting into the train & had to jump into a 2nd class carriage when it was moving rather fast, helped by a porter, a thing I should not have done at my time of life if there had been a moment to reflect.')[2] Government provision of *per capita* grants to schools claiming them on the basis of complying with the requirements as to teaching and inspection as laid down by the Education Department's Code now amounted to nearly a fifth of the entire civil expenditure of the state. Gladstone was sure that there were opportunities for economy. For example, 'State endowment' of pupil teachers aged thirteen 'at such an age among the peasantry is like a pure gift – I think no great inconvenience would attend its limitation or withdrawal'. On expenditure on education generally he warned that the 'gigantic system on which we are proceeding is one that after a time unless *early* subjected to a gradual contraction, must end by exploding'.[3] Gladstone was fortunate that on this question he was pushing with rather than against the grain of official opinion. Even Russell admitted that the growing cost of the grant system would have to be slackened. The commission on elementary education chaired by the Duke of Newcastle would present its findings in 1861, which did not tell in the direction of liberal expansiveness. And in Robert Lowe, the new Vice-President of the Privy Council and head of the Education Department, Gladstone had a willing collaborator in the quest for substantial reductions in expenditure. They had had earlier dealings in the areas of university and Civil Service reform; and Lowe's faith in the efficacy of examinations recommended him warmly to Gladstone's favour. Lowe's zeal both for economy and examinations was the key to the controversial Revised Code of 1861 whereby government grants were tied strictly to a retrospective principle of 'payment by results'.

It was also an alleviation of strained feelings for Gladstone to recur to the 'very first' motive which had guided him into his problematical relationship with Palmerston. As one linked notoriously with Palmerston

1 D, v, 449–50.
2 G to CG, January 5, 1860. GGP, 28/6.   3 D, v, 451–2.

and Russell as the 'Italian party' in the Cabinet Gladstone made a point of registering his sense of the movement of events in that quarter. On January 3, 1860 he sat up till 2 a.m. composing a long letter for Russell's benefit '& had an almost sleepless night for it'. His objections of June 1859 to the 'domineering' tendencies of Piedmont were now eclipsed by fears that Austria might try to intervene to restore the validity of the Villafranca agreement as formalised by the Treaty of Zurich in November. Gladstone was anxious that Britain should back France to deter any such intervention. He argued that since Britain and France could never unite 'for any European purpose which is radically unjust' it followed that they represented the spirit of Europe's moral community; and their role was to supervise the free choice of the peoples of Tuscany, Parma, Modena, the Romagna (and perhaps also other parts of the papal dominions such as Umbria and the Marches). Gladstone covered himself technically by treating Piedmont along with Austria as an external power which should not be permitted to impose itself by force upon the peoples of central Italy. On the other hand, if Piedmont were to accept the justice of the Anglo-French European mission, her alliance would be welcome. Gladstone's other main point was that public opinion in England had moved 'rapidly and steadily in favour of the Italians', and 'when the Englishman has taken his side he loves measures of decision'. The government would have public support if by allying with France 'we take the measures most likely to give effect' to ensuring Austria's exclusion and 'we ought cheerfully to stake in so noble a cause the existence of an administration'.[1]

At Pembroke Lodge Gladstone 'passed the evening with Lord John & his family. Lord John & I had much conv. on Italy'. Palmerston meanwhile proposed 'common and united action with France & Sardinia'. Gladstone agreed 'in every particular' except that he would not reckon 'in the improbable event of a war, upon confining our share of it within narrow bounds'. It certainly testified to the strength of Gladstone's Italophilism that he contemplated even so improbable a contingency of war with such nonchalance. His combativeness doubtless owed much to his readiness to show a bold front to threatening fulminations from Rome, which he thought constituted 'something of a challenge to all governments as such'.[2] Clarendon, much more shrewdly suspicious of France, was indignant at the 'present intention of Pam., J. R., and Gladstone' to 'cram this policy down the throats of their twelve colleagues'.[3]

The great fact of the Italian situation as Gladstone wrote his glowing Francophile and Italophile sentiments was that the Piedmontese were

1 Beales, *England and Italy*, 118–19; K. Bourne, *The Foreign Policy of Victorian England, 1830–1902* (1970), 347–59.
2 Bourne, 354; D, v, 453–4.   3 Beales, 124.

managing with French connivance their union with the duchies and Romagna at the price of purchasing the Emperor Napoleon's acquiescence by agreeing to cede Savoy and Nice to France. Given, however, Gladstone's strong predisposition (reinforced powerfully by the commercial treaty question) to make the rosiest interpretation of French motives, he was in no position to react very convincingly against the consummation of Franco-Piedmontese connivance in March 1860 when Turin got its votes for union and Louis Napoleon got Savoy and Nice. And though as far as ever from any idea of either the practicality or desirability of Italian unity, Gladstone was in an equally weak position to object when in May 1860 Cavour in turn was to connive with Garibaldi's expedition to Sicily at the expense of the French as well as the Neapolitan governments.

For the time being, however, Gladstone could immerse himself devotedly in preparations for the commercial treaty as an appropriate and exemplary parallel policy to his ideal of an Anglo-French mission on behalf of Europe to supervise the unfettered freedom of the central Italians to decide their own destiny. There was a curious mixture of *étatist* executive predispositions and perhaps memories of the overpowering potency of the *Great Eastern* in Gladstone's remark to Brougham at this time about Napoleon III: 'For my own part at this moment, and on the given conditions of the case, I really desire no more than to live in the same boat with him, a stoker or sub-stoker on his engine.'[1] There were only occasional excursions to ply his rescue trade (there was an 'unsuccessful hunt in Seymour Street' on January 8 after dining at Admiralty House and talking about Italy; later: 'Again I was baffled: but will not desist.') The cabinet committee on parliamentary reform and the imbroglio over the architecture of the new Foreign Office obtruded awkwardly; but Gladstone pressed on indefatigably with his treaty instructions, his correspondence with Cobden, and his study of the Wine Duties Report, which he attended to with the particular concern of one who had long felt the wine duties to be the great 'scandal' of the tariff. Gladstone's strategy was to embody the treaty in his budget rather than, as Pitt did in 1786 and 1787, keep them separate. (He called on Lord Stanhope's historical expertise as to Pitt's mode of operation.)[2] Gladstone was very willing to pay the price of volume of work in return for the advantages of bigness and drama. On January 16 he expounded the treaty

---

1 G to Brougham, January 18, 1860. GP, 44530, 146. This was an indiscreet thing to say to so malicious a gossip as Brougham. And sure enough there was an odd echo of this odd remark in a letter from Argyll on February 3, 1860: 'There is a story going about town which has been repeated to me – "that Gladstone now expresses unbounded confidence in the Emperor, even to acting stoker in his train" – a weak invention of the enemy, but showing the direction of the attack. . .' (Argyll, ii, 154).
2 G to Stanhope, January 17, 1860. GP, 44530, 144.

to the sceptical Graham: 'the operation for which I have been living. I have seen in it not merely the increase of influence for a peaceful solution of the Italian question, not merely the extension almost to consummation of the Tariff Reforms begun in 1842, but also the means of allaying the passions that menace danger, and of stemming the fears which in my opinion have done us so much discredit.'[1] He reported to Cobden on January 19 that the 'prejudice or opinion against proceeding in the form of Treaty is strong' – both Graham and Grey, for example, were opposed; but Cobden must not suppose that Gladstone was therefore 'desponding or indifferent'. It was unfortunate that Bright could not fill Cobden's place in England – he raised too many hackles. 'But give us a Treaty,' Gladstone assured Cobden, 'carrying *bona fides* on its face (I do not doubt its being in the heart) and I have no fear of its fate.'[2]

At a cabinet on the 21st Gladstone saw the treaty through safely. It was signed at Paris on January 23. Gladstone dined that evening at Palmerston's. 'My mind is relieved,' he noted on the 25th: 'I have now a standing ground & weapons in my hand.' That Gladstone felt the need of ground and weapons is evident from Bright's report of a conversation at Downing Street that day: 'He is miserable at the reckless expenditure got up by the tax-eating and War party. His language is very strong, for he feels it deeply.' Speaking of the treaty, Gladstone said 'he was more obliged to Cobden than he could express in words – he had done it all – and that no other man could have done it. He considers it a grand success, and its results could hardly be too much thought of, etc.' Bright urged Gladstone to be staunch on the repeal of the paper duties, a cause which the Radicals regarded as logically completing the 'freeing' of the press by the abolition of the stamp duty on newspapers in 1855. Graham happened to come in while Bright was there, and while a sceptic about the treaty was equally 'strong for repeal of the Paper Duty'. Gladstone responded by inviting his two visitors to dine.[3] In other quarters there was lively speculation about Gladstone's intentions as to the paper question. His old enemy Monteagle assured Clarendon that though Gladstone was 'audacious enough for many things', he would bet Clarendon 'any money' that Gladstone 'had not dared to think of *that*'.[4]

The 'tax-eating and War party' were certainly hard at work. Gladstone 'read & wrote on the Fortifications' on January 22, especially the report calling for a further £11 millions for dockyard works. At a cabinet on January 28 he 'opened the remissions of taxes: with good effect.' But on the 31st it was 'very stiff. I carried my remissions but the Depts. carried their great Estimates.' Gladstone audaciously pressed through his plan to abolish the paper duty against strong resistance from Palmerston and the

1 D, v, 457.   2 *Ib.*, 458.
3 Bright, *Diaries*, 244.   4 Maxwell, *Clarendon*, ii, 208.

'stationary' party on financial matters. Palmerston opposed almost all remissions, the better to finance armaments; others preferred to reduce the income tax along the lines of the 1853 plan. On February 2 Gladstone worked late '& found with great vexation' a new demand for £500,000 'upsetting all'.

To add to the vexation Henry Glynne, a widower now for a decade, was being obstinate about his 'new attachment', Miss Lowder. Gladstone had revised his earlier good impression. Now he thought the lady 'not quite what we could wish', and a 'great care' to Catherine 'because of her nieces'. Opinion at Carlton House Terrace soon hardened sharply. On February 5 Gladstone 'saw Wortley and Phillimore: resp. this great mistake of Henry's'. Catherine on February 7 'had more comfort and support respecting Henry's error'. Meanwhile, on the eve of his epochal budget statement, Gladstone succumbed to congested lungs and a croaking throat. His statement had to be postponed from February 6 to 10. It was a testimony both to the drama of the occasion and to Gladstone's political reputation that *The Times* should remark that no other question was being asked but 'How is Mr. Gladstone's throat?' *The Times* also harked back to England's awaiting in suspense Peel's arrival back in London in 1834 as the only comparable moment. Now, 'the most conspicuous disciple of that great statesman has his moment of concentrated attention'; but in any event 'it seemed just a little ridiculous that all Europe should hold its breath because an English gentleman cannot make an oration in his best manner'. For all that *The Times* was firmly of the view that free trade and commercial treaties were contradictions in terms, it was, like the country and the world, all agog to hear the 'great secret of the impending Budget', the fate of 'that bitter ninepence' of the 1859 income tax and, not least, what the French Emperor had 'given to Mr. Gladstone to put in his bag'.[1]

The imposed delay Gladstone turned to account by writing from his sick-bed to Palmerston on February 7 on the theme of 'the most serious differences amongst us with respect to a loan for Fortifications, and this being the case I had thought it clearly for the interest of all that we should reserve that question until we had got through the French treaty, the Budget, and the chief Estimates'. He was allowing for a sum out of which the first year's interest on such a loan could be sustained; but he regarded the notion of carrying it further at present as a 'betrayal of my public duty'. He reminded Palmerston further that only in a 'full belief that the subject of fortifications was postponed did I become a party to the Military & Naval Estimates as they now stand'. Palmerston, soothing and pacifying, let the fortifications issue rest for the present and arranged for a cabinet at Gladstone's house.[2] Probably Gladstone's illness was, as

1 *Times*, February 6, 1860.   2 G & P, 123–4.

Greville thought, 'unlucky' in that it allowed time for critics of the treaty to gather strength.[1] Outside the shielding embrace of the budget the treaty stood naked and exposed: the interests that would be damaged by French competition were immediate and vocal; its benefits were as yet abstract and prospective. 'Clarendon shook his head.' The great banker Overstone pronounced adversely. *The Times* thundered against it. Certainly Gladstone did not delay any longer than absolutely necessary. His doctor, according to Greville, advised that Gladstone should have taken two months' rest instead of two days.

On February 10 Gladstone was able to speak '5–9 without great exhaustion: aided by a great stock of egg & wine'; 'the most arduous operation I had ever had in Parliament.' He conducted the operation on what was by now a familiar pattern: 1853 the model and benchmark; the means and ends as defined by the catalogue of February and the doctrine of March 1856. He explained his thinking later to Palmerston.

> I found in 1860 that all the reforming legislation which had achieved such vast results, had been suspended for seven years. We were then raising by duties doomed in 1853 from twelve to thirteen millions. . . . Had the expenditure of 1853 been resumed, there would notwithstanding the Russian War have been in my opinion room for all these three things 1. abolition of Income Tax by or near 1860, 2. remission of increases on Tea and Sugar within the same time, 3. the prosecution of the commercial reforms.[2]

This argument of what might have been was necessarily partial and prejudiced. Its more important function was to reinforce the mythology launched in 1852. In place of Disraeli the angel of the hosts of enchanters and magicians there was now a septennate of failure and regression to be grappled with. The rhetoric, though more gravely and magisterially produced, was of the same theatricalised politics and the same morality play of finance.

The theme of failure and regression since 1852 Gladstone founded on the text that between 1842 and 1853 there was a 12 per cent increase in national wealth (measured by the criterion of the income tax) coincident with an increase of $8\frac{3}{4}$ per cent in government expenditure. Between 1853 and 1859 wealth increased by $16\frac{1}{2}$ per cent, expenditure by 58 per cent. His moral was that parliament had let slip its control of the public purse strings. 'I may at once venture to state frankly that I am not satisfied with the state of the public expenditure, and the rapid rate of its growth. I trust, therefore, that we mean in a great degree to retrace our steps.' Gladstone further pointed to the 'one great and conspicuous head of increase – that on the Military and Naval Estimates'. On the other theme of positive

1 *Greville*, vii, 458.   2 G & P, 195.

uplift the commercial treaty provided virtually limitless scope for rhetoric on the theme of 'new departures', a 'determined and vigorous policy', of strong government 'in a marked manner, founded upon a policy', 'boldly and readily' carrying the reform of commercial legislation to its completion. Gladstone paid tribute to the Emperor Napoleon for his benign solicitude and to Cobden for his 'great and memorable service', 'decorated neither by rank nor title'. As the key to the knitting 'together in amity these two great nations' there would be 'a sweep, clean, entire, and absolute, of manufactured goods from the face of the British tariff'.

One of Gladstone's particular satisfactions was in proposing a drastic reduction of the wine duty, insisting that it was quite wrong to hold that the English had no taste for light French wines and that the preference for port, sherry and highly brandied wine was fixed and immutable. He cited in point the case of the injured sailor on H.M.S. *Scourge*, obliged to have recourse to an abominable quality of wine because of the effects of the duty. Equally gratifying to Gladstone was his proposal to abolish the duty on paper as an impediment to manufacture and as inhibiting the circulation of knowledge and information. In thus going out of his way to stress the link between paper duty abolition and the former newspaper stamp duty and the extent to which his proposal was calculated to encourage 'cheap literature' Gladstone was rather recklessly over-confident. To go further, and to celebrate the growth of a provincial Liberal and Radical press consequent on the abolition of the stamp duty as a phenomenon 'highly creditable to the conductors of what is called the cheap press,' was to issue, in effect, a challenge to the Palmerstonian majority as much as to the Conservative minority of the Commons. Gladstone let himself appear here to be speaking in accents more suitable to John Bright. The offence thus caused was compounded by the circumstance that Gladstone had to replace the losses to the revenue from reduced or abolished duties in the tariff or the excise by raising the income tax by 1d to 10d. He even went so far as to point to the advantages of a round shilling of income tax as a means of dispensing with the remaining war duties on tea and sugar. And his peroration was a return to his original challenge to the 'one great and conspicuous head of increase' in expenditure: those who were anxious about national defence should realise that measures calculated to 'strike away the shackles from the arm of industry, which give new incentive and new reward to toil', which give the people 'increased confidence in their rulers, that which makes them feel and know that they are treated with justice' – such measures are in themselves 'no small, no feeble, and no transitory part of national defence'.[1]

On the following day Gladstone retreated to Labouchere's place at

1 H, clvi, 812–72.

Stoke to recuperate amid a 'kind welcome & pleasant party'. All immediate indications suggested that he had carried it off, with something of a repetition of his success in 1853. Palmerston put the best face he could on it and hoped Gladstone was 'none the worse for that Triumph on Friday for which the Government is much the better' (though he was worried on the question of game licences). Bright was ecstatic: 'How infinitely he excels the ordinary race of statesmen!' Greville recorded that Gladstone *consensu omnium* achieved one of the greatest triumphs that the House of Commons ever witnessed. Everybody I have heard from admits that it was a magnificent display, not to be surpassed in ability and execution, and that it carried the House of Commons completely with him'. Gladstone himself noted on February 17 that his 'correspondence is now counted in hundreds of letters daily'.[1]

It remained a question how long Gladstone could sustain this momentum of success to get through his consequent piecemeal legislation. He managed the initial stages in late February. Greville again recorded on February 22 that 'everybody agrees that nothing could be more brilliant and complete than Gladstone's triumph'. On February 24 Gladstone 'greatly rejoiced' in the division putting through both his tariff and financial proposals in principle; and again Greville noted 'another triumph'. Gladstone made 'a splendid speech, and obtained a majority of 116, which puts an end to the contest. He is now *the* great man of the day'.[2] Gladstone dealt with the besieging hordes of protesting deputations with deft assurance. When a temperance group remonstrated against making French wines available to the masses 'the Alliance deputation could do little but quote formulae and testimonials; all the sophistication, subtlety, imagination and success lay with Gladstone'.[3]

Greville's assumption, however, as to an end being put to the contest was premature. The commercial treaty was vulnerable; and after the initial impact of oratorial prowess faded the budget itself began to suffer by association. To criticisms that it should have been a 'smaller' budget, Gladstone later asserted that 'if it had been a smaller boat it would not have lived in such a sea. . . I admit that political motives greatly concurred to recommend the Budget. . . It was a Budget of peace, and peace wanted it'.[4] There were the rather esoteric criticisms by the new editor of *The Economist*, Walter Bagehot, who pronounced Gladstone more 'adhesive' to projects than to principles and detected an 'entire inconsistency in abstract principle between the Budget of 1853 and the Budget of 1860'.[5]

1 G & P, 126; Bright, 248; *Greville*, viii, 296.
2 *Greville*, vii, 460.
3 B. Harrison, *Drink and the Victorians*, (1971) 248.
4 G & P, 196.   5 *Biographical Studies*, 104–05.

More telling was burgeoning resentment over the 'democratic' implications of the paper duty proposal. Gladstone spoke with 'weapons in his
hand'; he had deliberately made of his budget a combative and challenging proposition; it was not wonderful that his challenge should be taken
up. Palmerston made no secret of his hostility. Clarendon, a suspicious
observer on the outside, deduced the darkest prognostications about
Gladstone: a man with 'a fervent imagination, which furnishes facts and
arguments in support of them'; an 'audacious innovator, because he has
an insatiable desire for popularity'; in his notions of government 'a far
more sincere Republican than Bright, for his ungratified personal vanity
makes him wish to subvert the institutions and the classes that stand in
the way of his ambition'; Gladstone and Bright 'converging from different
points to the same end'.[1]

This was the voice of sourness and misapprehension. But it was a
misapprehension which stemmed from a distinct, if narrow and distorted, shrewdness of perception. Gladstone's reputation for being able
to convince himself of the utter righteousness of whatever opinion he was
urging at any given time was by now widespread. Acton, writing in the
liberal Catholic *Rambler* later in 1860, commented that 'Mr. Gladstone is
equally remarkable for the highest moral integrity and rectitude and for
the utmost intellectual duplicity. . . His excessive earnestness of conviction is the great secret of the persuasiveness of his eloquence; but that
earnestness is founded on an incredible power of persuading himself. . .
He cannot see the flaw in his own case, though in an adversary's nothing
escapes him'.[2] Part of the intensity of Gladstone's early religious
struggles to form his first vocation passed by political transference in the
later 1840s and the beginning of the 1850s into a condition something akin
to a secular equivalent of spiritual pride. Already this had expressed itself
virulently in the crisis of 1855 in executive arrogance. There was to be a
serious crisis in the 1860 session in Gladstone's relationship with the
House of Commons. A disposition to hector and drive provoked
resentment and resistance. Greville noted that Gladstone was 'said to
have become subject to much excitement, and more bitter in the House of
Commons than was his wont. The severe working of his brain and the
wonderful success he has attained may account for this, and having had
his way and triumphed over all opposition in the Cabinet, it is not strange
that he should brook none anywhere else.'[3]

After a break at Brighton early in March ('Much walking & sea: also
visited the China shops') Gladstone returned refreshed to help defeat the
Duke of Cambridge's efforts to retain purchase of army commissions

1 *Greville*, vii, 459, 462.
2 D. Woodruff, *Essays on Church and State by Lord Acton* (1952), 451.
3 *Greville*, vii, 462.

above the·rank of major and to see the commercial treaty through the Commons on March 9: 'a most prosperous ending to a great transaction in wh. I heartily thank God for having given me a share.' Gladstone had particular reason to rejoice at that moment. The French announced their intention to annex Savoy and Nice and touched off a francophobic spasm in British public opinion, with a boost (encouraged by rousing verse from Tennyson) to the movement to form a Volunteer Rifle Corps. Gladstone's protestations as to the budget's having 'political motives' and its being a 'budget of peace' took on an extra significance. His own view as to the merits of the French act was that there was justification in the case of Savoy but not of Nice; but in any event he emphasised that British interests were not involved 'and there was not the shadow of a case of honour'.[1] He argued that the Savoy-Nice issue made all the more reason to 'unite cordially with France in a great act of policy'. And he could not but 'cherish the cheerful and sanguine expectation' that the treaty 'will, of itself, do something to make the year 1860 one memorable – memorable because fruitful of blessings – in the annals of Europe and of mankind'.[2] Ever after Gladstone insisted that free trade in 1860 came to 'involve also through the French treaty the question of peace and war: for such was the irritation of men and parties in that year . . . that the choice lay between closer bonds of amity through the treaty, and the tension of relations almost certain to result in rupture'.[3] This interpretation of the treaty of commerce as the 'only sedation', the one 'counter-irritant to counter-act war passion',[4] exaggerated its role. It is most unlikely that it made the difference between peace and war; but Savoy and Nice certainly compromised drastically Gladstone's chances of fending off further demands for armaments and fortifications.

As so often happened with Gladstone, solemn public transactions proceeded majestically against a background of domestic scuffling. Poor Henry Glynne's efforts to break out of his Hawarden estate corral continued with feeble persistence. The feebleness came from Henry ('always gentle he is more tender in manner than ever,' as Gladstone remarked[5]); the persistence came from the object of his 'great mistake' and 'error'. Miss Lowder was showing fight, necessitating a conclave on February 14 'on the unsatisfactory marriage'; and a letter was 'concocted' for Sir Stephen to sign. There were more consultations with lawyers and family in March, Gladstone 'much offended with the L. Letters'. By March 18 there was progress, and talk of a 'delay of H.G.'s marriage'. Gladstone did indeed observe that Henry looked 'much pulled & worn' at Lady Wenlock's in London. To make up for all this Agnes was presented at a Drawing Room, 'fair & simple as the snowdrops that she carried'.

1 PMP, i, 85.   2 H, clvii, 310, 326.
3 PMP, 74.   4 Beales, 139.   5 D, v, 420.

Gladstone also assuaged himself much by haunting Messrs. Christie's auction rooms. He thought it appropriate to resign from the Carlton Club.

The *éclat* of the budget started to fade by the end of March. There were disturbing evidences of a mounting reaction against paper duties repeal which Palmerston did nothing to discountenance. Horsman, the Liberal M.P. for Stroud, who specialised in being a candid friend to the government, denounced Gladstone's repeal bill on March 12 as pregnant with dangerous implications and as exposing the 'new career' upon which Gladstone had embarked of 'agitating class interests' and of abandoning Peel's principles.[1] Palmerston's schemes for defence spending matched the francophobe public mood. He represented a widespread public view that this was not the time to dispense with lucrative indirect sources of revenue. He put it to Gladstone on March 29 that it would be a good idea to postpone the repeal of the duties both as excise and customs 'till after Easter'. Palmerston was solicitous also to encourage Gladstone to find £150,000 much pressed for by Herbert, reinforcing his urgings with dark prognostications on the menacing state of European affairs. (Gladstone's line on that aspect of things was to accuse Russell of using 'most questionable language' in warning the French.[2]) Palmerston returned to the attack, pointing out that it would be quite easy to find Herbert's £150,000 if repeal of the paper duties were put off till next year.[3] Gladstone conferred with Herbert on April 2 '& we fought long on his proposal to augment forces'. This dispute between the Treasury and the War Office lasted through the summer. Clarendon (who claimed that Aberdeen had assured him that Gladstone and Herbert 'would never go on together') eagerly detected a 'state of antagonism' between the two Peelites, and persuaded himself that Herbert would retire before the end of the session.[4] Gladstone later recorded how saddened he was by Herbert's falling 'under the influence of the prevailing French panic'. 'He warned me that I was in danger of overlooking a great danger, that of invasion from France. I on my part dubbed him "the captain-general of alarmists".'[5]

In cabinet on April 3 Gladstone 'rather stiffly resisted augmentation of the Estimates (Army) & objected even to increase of force not involving charge: Ld P. at length suggested an expedient to avoid it'. He escaped to Brighton, when on doctor's orders Lenten disciplines were relaxed. Thus recruited, Gladstone counter-attacked with a cabinet paper threatening a 13d or 14d income tax if military retrenchment, especially on expeditions, colonies, and fortifications, were not achieved. Leaving his colleagues to chew on that, Gladstone departed for Edinburgh to deliver his inaugural address as Lord Rector of the university. He advised the Scottish

1 H, clvii, 420–21.   2 D, v, 476.
3 G & P, 131–32.   4 *Greville, ib.*   5 PMP, i, 80.

academic youth that above and beyond professional knowledge and intellectual training the work of a university was to inculcate a 'temper and aim' to subordinate all else to the 'conscience and the will of God,' with virtue and the moral law as guides.[1] Back in Downing Street, with virtue and the moral law as guides, Gladstone stuck firmly to his intention to repeal the paper duties. To Palmerston he appealed on April 20: 'How could we recede when we have got the equivalent in the shape of the full Income Tax? Would not this seem to stand in the light of a fraud upon Parliament?' Palmerston obstinately would not see it in that light; and repeated his litany of China operations, European dangers, and the likely deficit in the coming year.[2]

Worse was to come. On April 24 Gladstone had to digest the incredible fact that Palmerston wanted the paper duties repeal postponed until the next budget, with arguments that in the present state of world affairs no 'sane man' would throw away part of our 'permanent revenue'.[3] Gladstone turned for therapeutic soothing to arranging his porcelain collection ('wh will be a work of *time*'). He indulged himself in a breakfast mainly for artists – 'saw Mr. Holman Hunt for the first time' – which was very *à propos* for some of his official concerns at the time, such as ventilation of the National Gallery and the controversy over the Foreign Office designs (a pamphlet entitled *Shall Gothic Architecture be denied fair play*? was an item of his current reading). Gladstone got his first dispiriting taste of the turn of the tide against him when he spoke on the Representation of the People Bill on May 3 to an 'adverse & difficult House'. He did not help his case by incautiously claiming 'some credit for sincerity in my desire to see this question disposed of'. Given his record of indifference bordering on contempt for the issue, Gladstone should not have been surprised to be greeted with '*Ironical cheers*';[4] but then, being Gladstone, he was. Then, at a cabinet on the 5th, Gladstone had to endure listening to Palmerston speaking '3/4 hour agt Paper Duties Bill! I had to reply.' Gladstone managed to carry his point in cabinet: the bill for repeal would go forward. As if these problems of finance were not enough Gladstone found himself grappling with both Palmerston and Russell on foreign affairs. 'More wild schemes of foreign alliance are afloat! Our old men (2) are unhappily our youngest.'[5] When Gladstone spoke in the Commons on May 8 on his Paper Duty Repeal Bill he again found himself speaking to 'a very adverse House'. The bill only scraped through by 219 to 210, and went on up to the Lords already morally defeated.

Gladstone's mood at that juncture would not have been lightened by

1 *Gleanings*, vii, 'Inaugural Address on the Work of Universities', April 16, 1860.
2 G & P, 132–33.
3 PMP, iii, 230.   4 H, clviii, 628.   5 D, v, 485.

reading Frederick Temple's essay on 'The education of the world' in *Essays and Reviews*, the newly published and soon-to-become notorious collection of liberal Anglican critiques of orthodox religious authority. After a ball at Downing Street ('Workman & confusion in the House') and more porcelain arranging Gladstone escaped to a Cliveden weekend, now his favourite resort near London (and where he was often unaccompanied by Catherine). The spring and summer of 1860 was to be an intense season of Clivedens. When he wrote later that 'friendships with women' had formed 'no small part' of his life, and that 'in every principal case' they were women older than himself, to be prized for their 'great glory', 'their gift of judging character', it was Harriet Sutherland whom he had mainly in mind.[1] Catherine responded to this relationship with what has been aptly termed a 'pragmatic detachment'.[2] She was aware of her incapacity to meet her husband's intellectual demands; she was not prepared to compromise an attachment which served to the advantage of his career. At Cliveden Gladstone stood up for the 'men of 1661, who drove out the Presbyterians at the Savoy conference'; and heard a 'pale Curate' preach 'well & like a man near the unseen world' at Hedsor Church. The principal event of the stay, however, was that his Egeria, the Duchess, took the opportunity to give Gladstone 'excellent advice in a manner delicate beyond all conception' about 'sensitiveness in the H. of C.'[3] Gladstone was later to make much of the 'redeeming qualities' inculcated by political life considered as a profession, and especially to insist that there was no 'finer school of temper than the House of Commons'.[4] The lessons of that school he was finding difficult to learn in 1860.

Looking back from 1897 Gladstone designated the sessions of 1860 and 1861 as 'the most trying part of my whole political life', his 'nadir in public estimation'. He identified three 'causes at work' which 'entirely altered by their joint operation' the formerly favourable 'complexion of the scene'. First, Palmerston's determination to go ahead with the fortifications project, although blocked by Gladstone for the early part of the session, 'hung over as a difficulty ready to become very serious when associated with other difficulties'. Secondly, Russell, 'most unhappily', insisted, despite the claims of the budget measures, on pressing on with his Reform Bill, which many on the government side, led by Palmerston himself, 'scarcely loved' any better than the Conservative opposition. The opposition were therefore able to play on a 'widespread though largely latent sentiment' in the House to obstruct the measure. When Russell demanded right of way for Reform as against the budget Gladstone records himself as pleading, 'Lord John, I will go down on my knees to

1 *Ib.*, lxiii–iv.   2 Marlow, *Mr. and Mrs. Gladstone*, 78.
3 D, v, 487.   4 PMP, i, 138–39.

you, to intreat you not to press that request.' Russell's insistence delayed the paper duties repeal measure, thus allowing time for its enemies to gain strength and confidence. Its derisory majority exposed Gladstone's vulnerability. His weakness attracted aggression. As he recalled with bitterness undimmed by four decades, 'around the carcass the vultures now gathered in overwhelming force'.[1] Greville noted with astonishment the extent of the reversal of fortune. With a little better management by the Conservatives the narrow majority for repeal might have been put in a minority; all of which was 'now encouraging the House of Lords . . . to throw out the Resolution when it comes before them'.[2]

And indeed Gladstone noted on May 15 that the 'meditated aggression of the Lords presses more & more upon my mind'. Constitutional convention reserved to the Commons the control of supply; but while it was clearly understood that the Lords might not amend financial measures there remained the question as to whether they might return such bills *in toto* to the Commons. There were no modern precedents for such an action. Gladstone's sense of outrage led him to talk in terms of the 'pending *coup d'Etat*'. It also made him, conspicuously, a Radical hero. He told his 'barn-burning' brother Robertson: 'This is a most serious matter, 100 times as much so as would have been the mere rejection of the Bill in the House of Commons.' He would have to consider carefully 'what I should endeavour to urge upon my colleagues'.[3] A meeting of Whig peers on the 17th did little to stiffen optimism. Gladstone loyally muted his apprehensions by attending the Queen's Birthday Drawing Room on the 18th 'in robe' and gave a Birthday dinner (from which he slipped away for a rescue expedition). At another of his dinners the following day Lady Waldegrave told him 'her mind about myself'; which was that there was much Whig dissatisfaction with his playing the Radical game. He anxiously consulted Granville about Derby's crucial speech on May 20 advising their lordships that the needs of the revenue were paramount and that the paper duties could not be sacrificed. Were Palmerston and Derby in collusion? Palmerston certainly told the Queen that he 'felt bound in Duty' to say that the Lords would 'perform a good public Service' if they threw out the bill.[4] (Gladstone could find time nevertheless to talk 'sombrely with Bp Wilberforce' – no doubt about the scandalous *Essays and Reviews*.) The blow fell on May 21 when the Lords rejected the repeal bill 193–104. Lady Palmerston was observed to applaud triumphantly in the Ladies' Gallery. The Queen told Uncle Leopold that it was a *'very good thing'*.[5] On the 22nd a 'rather stiff' cabinet failed to accede to demands by Gladstone, backed by Russell and Gibson,

1 *Ib.*, 86.   2 *Greville*, vii, 476.
3 G to Robertson G, May 15, 1860. GP, 44531, 4.
4 J. Ridley, *Lord Palmerston* (1970), 497.   5 LQV, iii, 401.

for something decisive by way of visiting the displeasure of the Commons upon the Lords. Palmerston reported to the Queen that it was decided that precedents would be searched for as a device for keeping the government's options open while at the same time doing something to 'in some degree satisfy those who think some step necessary'.[1] Gladstone, very probably, was not much mollified by Palmerston's consolatory remark that he could well understand Gladstone's disappointment at the defeat of his bill because he was himself very disappointed by the failure of his horse to win the Derby.[2]

On May 26 Gladstone took refuge at Cliveden once more and mused over the 'hairbreath scapes of which so many occur in these strange times & with our strangely constructed Cabinet' and on the 'great question now depending between the Lords and the English nation'. Palmerston had been thwarted in this nefarious attempt to do nothing and to allow the Lords to get away with establishing a 'reviewing power' over the 'most vital function' of the House of Commons and thus set up a 'divided responsibility' for fixing the revenue. Behind Gladstone, Russell and Gibson in their demand for 'decided action' were Argyll, Newcastle and Villiers, sure that there was 'some step necessary'. Palmerston, supported by Campbell, Wood, Granville and 'in substance' Lewis, 'gave in & adopted with but middling grace the proposition to set out with enquiries: & with the intention to make as little of the matter as he could'. But a 'dignified declaration' by Russell on May 25 put everything right. Gladstone could hope that in this grave matter at least we have turned the corner'.[3] A Radical campaign against the House of Lords demanded that the bill be sent up a second time, backed by adequate menaces. But, by 'careful steering' on Gladstone's part and he presumed also on Palmerston's, 'all occasion of scandal was avoided.'[4] A series of resolutions would be put to the Commons asserting and defending their prerogatives. 'It was one of those difficult passages of life,' explained Gladstone to Bright, 'in which any conclusion offers only a choice of doubts hazards & embarrassments.' He could not wonder that Bright advocated a frontal assault; but pointed out that 'Mr. Cobden sent me opposite opinion'. But nothing could in Gladstone's eyes 'attenuate the magnitude of the event. Notwithstanding the Treaty, notwithstanding the progress towards freedom & peace in Italy, it has left, for us, a great black mark on the year 1860; & both the H. of C. and its members are smaller than they were.'[5] As in the case of the Bank of England in 1854, the failure of the Lords to fall in with Gladstone's plans called in upon themselves his unforgiving and unrelenting enmity. Gladstone diversified his campaign by presenting the Cabinet on 24 May with a

1 *Ib.*, 401–02.　　2 Ridley, *ib.*　　3 PMP, iii, 228–29.
4 *Ib.*, i, 87.　　5 G to Bright, August 17, 1860. GP, 44531, 38.

memorandum objecting to fortifications and fortification loans in which he stressed the 'dangers to liberty' and to the constitution that would be offered by five or six 'great fortresses' in 'the hands of the Executive'.[1] Palmerston considered this 'absurd & nonsensical'.[2]

Cliveden that visit was all the more delightful, with drives to Windsor Forest and Virginia Water through hours of 'wonderfully fine & varied woodland scenery.' On May 30 Gladstone went on the Thames ('My threefingered hand soon blisters'). That evening he amused himself by drawing up a character of the Cabinet. 'We are not Mr. Burke's famous Mosaic' – the wonderfully contrived Chatham Cabinet of 1766 – 'but we are a mosaic in solution that is to say a Kaleidoscope when as the instrument turns the three separate pieces readjust themselves & all comes out in perfectly novel combinations.' There were the 'Italians', the 'combative' exponents of foreign policy, the 'alarmed, or most martial', in defence expenditure, the 'onward' party in finance, the 'liberal' side on reform, the proponents of a 'large measure' of redistribution of parliamentary constituencies, the group 'strong for remedy' on the paper duties question; and to each of these groups was an opposed counterpart. Gladstone put himself in the 'Italian' combination (his one link with Palmerston), the 'other way' on defence expenditure, among the 'onward' men on finance (with Lewis 'first and foremost' among the 'stationary men'), with the 'strong for remedy' men on the paper duties, and (a matter of significance) among the 'liberal men' on franchise reform. 'It is easy to judge', noted Gladstone, 'what an odd shifting of parts takes place in our discussions.' But the oddness of the kaleidoscopic permutations was not random. It was equally significant that his analysis should positively correlate Gladstone with the advanced Liberal Milner Gibson alone on all important issues, with Argyll the next nearest. Herbert was on the other side on Italy, foreign policy, defence expenditure, finance, reform, and paper duties. He linked with Gladstone only on the relatively uncontroversial issue of Church affairs (patronage was not a cabinet matter and hence not an occasion of 'struggle.').[3] Here was evidence, quiet but insidious, of the ending of the Peelite connection and – conceivably – the beginning of another kind of connection.

[6]

A cabinet on June 2 – a distasteful interlude from Cliveden – revealed that whatever grounds there were for hoping that the corner had been turned on the paper duties question did not apply to fortifications. Palmerston's

1 GP, 44749, 142–157.   2 D, v, 490.   3 PMP, iii, 233–36.

views on the absurdity and nonsensicality of Gladstone's objections led to Gladstone's noting, 'My resignation *all but* settled.'[1] After dining at the Palace and conversing with the King of the Belgians and Prince Albert Gladstone returned to Cliveden – 'what courtesy, warmth, & grace.' There, Argyll, a fellow guest, showed his 'mediating' letter to Palmerston suggesting a reduced programme of fortifications to be financed on an annual basis by taxation or loan as expedient. With these good offices easing the way Gladstone conferred on June 6 '12¼ – 1½' with Palmerston. 'Nothing could be more kind and frank than his manner,' reported Gladstone to Argyll. 'The *matter* was first to warn me of the evils and hazards attending, for me, the operation of resigning, secondly to express his own strong sense of the obligation to persevere.' Palmerston explained that in his life he had always had two great objects before him: to suppress the slave trade and to put England in a state of defence. For the latter object Gladstone understood him 'distinctly to adhere' to the whole fortification plan, its immediate commencement, and to its financing by one form or another of borrowing. 'Little doubt,' concluded Gladstone, 'can remain of the nature of the question which I have to decide: nor can I see such a question in any light but one.' Had he realised that Palmerston 'entertained this purpose' when he formed his government Gladstone would not have joined, but would have helped as well as he could from another bench its Italian purposes. 'Still I am far indeed from regretting to have joined it, which is quite another matter.'[2]

This characteristic distinction was rather reminiscent of Gladstone's nimbly drawing back from the brink of his wholly convincing argument in March 1857 that there was no alternative but Conservative reunion. Perhaps he saw the point of Palmerston's formulation of evils and hazards: 'If he resigned nobody would believe that a man of his ability & experience & Statesmanlike Position left the Govt. because he would not have the country defended;' they would say, however unjustly, that Gladstone was 'afraid of the financial consequences of his Budget, & running away from them'; and 'moreover that out of office he would be thrown into Companionship with Bright which would be Ruin to him as a Public Man'.[3] But it was Gladstone's analysis of the kaleidoscopic character of the Cabinet which gave him decisive pause. 'It is the nature of one disease sometimes to drive out another: and such may be the case with our complications.' One could never be certain whether the fortifications complication or the reform complication or the Lords complication or the Chinese complication or the new taxes complication 'will come uppermost'. 'Any one of them might kill a Government: but the whole may perchance cure it.'[4]

1 D, v, 494.   2 *Ib.*, 495.
3 *Ib* n.   4 *Ib.*

This was indeed at best a somewhat desperate mode of optimism and Gladstone's mood remained correspondingly grim. His tactic, in effect, was to play a waiting game and hope for the coming of better times. Palmerston, after all, was getting on for eighty and could not last much longer. In 1859 Gladstone had committed his chances of fulfilling his vocation to one side of the new great political divide. There could be no going back to the other side. Even were Radicalism strong enough to promise a viable alternative Gladstone was by no means disposed to embrace it. Bright's tributes to his 'fine conscientiousness' on the paper duties and the commercial treaty[1] caused Gladstone something of the same uneasiness as did the Liberals and the Leaguers eagerly claiming him for their own when he was disowned by the Duke at Newark in 1846. Bernal Osborne later shrewdly defined Gladstone's position as 'content to remain in office and mark time, and wait until the occasion for action arrives'.[2]

Even so, this general rule would constantly be subject to exceptions at times of particularly heavy political squall. Gladstone's grimness of mood made him urge the duty of the government's resigning when on June 9 Russell announced to the Cabinet that he was dropping his Reform Bill. Gladstone's comment was a sardonic, 'Marvellous!' Palmerston's collusive role in opposition to franchise reform was to Gladstone only too painfully similar to his collusive opposition to paper duties repeal. Gladstone's new-found enthusiasm for reform was an accidental by-product of the paper duties crisis. Palmerston recorded that 'Gladstone urged that we ought all to resign as we had come in on Reform. . . . Gladstone's motive evidently was, to cover under a general Resignation his own failure as to Budget, & to escape from being a Party to a Fortification Loan.'[3] Despite taking to riding again and attending at Christie's and Phillip's' rooms Gladstone was described by Clarendon to Lewis as '*rabid*' about fortifications.[4] Cobden later made embarrassing allegations that Gladstone deliberately absented himself 'in a marked manner' from the House during debates on this issue to manifest his dispproval. Gladstone insisted that his absences were due 'in the main to accident', and repudiated the notion that he would do anything so futile or so culpable as to evade or diminish his ministerial reponsibility.[5] It is a measure of the tension of Gladstone's personal relations with Palmerston at this time that an application to the Prime Minister to be permitted to offer suggestions as to Church preferment had to be made through Herbert.[6] After attending a review of 20,000 Volunteers in Hyde Park ('a very noble spectacle') Gladstone retreated again to Cliveden where were,

1 Robbins, *Bright*, 151.   2 H, clix, 2096.
3 D, v, 496.   4 Maxwell, *Clarendon*, ii, 215.
5 H, clxviii, 176.   6 G & P, 137.

congenially, Bishop Wilberforce and Argyll: Argyll talked of 'our strange position';[1] and the Bishop preached 'a noble sermon'.

A new and disturbing feature of the 'strange position' was Palmerston's evident intention to let the House of Lords issue slide into oblivion. A cabinet on June 30 Gladstone described as 'Ugly!' On July 2 Gladstone was alone in his refusal to accept a composite series of resolutions of protest which did not embody an undertaking to proceed on legislative and not merely declaratory terms. Palmerston reported to the Queen that when all the other members had left the room 'Mr. Gladstone requested Viscount Palmerston to submit to your Majesty that he could no longer continue to carry on the business of his Department'. Palmerston protested that he 'really could not undertake the communication which Mr. Gladstone wished to be submitted to your Majesty' and 'earnestly entreated' Gladstone 'to reconsider the matter'. Palmerston promised to hold up the resolutions to give Gladstone 'more time to think and more room to turn round in'. Gibson had no intention of resigning; nor Argyll. Palmerston's view was that 'Mr. Gladstone, having failed to become master of the Cabinet by a threat of resignation, will in the end yield to the almost unanimous decision of his colleagues'.[2] The Queen reported to Uncle Leopold that Mr. Gladstone was 'terribly excited'.[3] Gladstone was not too excited to exercise some more nimble brinkmanship by asserting, notwithstanding the Cabinet's decision, his 'personal liberty' to 'concur in any proposal' that might come along to vindicate the rights of the Commons by action once Palmerston's resolutions were 'disposed of'.[4] On July 5, his opportunity came to 'break the ice' with a virulent assault on the 'gigantic innovation' and 'great encroachment' of the Lords, the 'most gigantic and the most dangerous that has been attempted in our times'; reserving for himself above and beyond the government's proposals 'entire freedom to adopt any mode which may have the slightest hope of success for vindicating by action the rights of this House'.[5]

The government's proposals were in no danger of being eclipsed by Gladstone's offer to flout the principle of ministerial responsibility as the means of acting as the Commons's vindicating conscience. Gladstone succeeded in making himself appear something of a Don Quixote, with Bright cast as his Sancho Panza. Palmerston enjoyed composing his report to the Queen, giving full ironic value to the Radical Digby Seymour's praise for Gladstone, who, 'he said, if he lost his place in the Cabinet in consequence of that speech would be rewarded by a Throne in the affections of the Nation'.[6] With Gladstone's position of weakness thus

1 Argyll, ii, 164.   2 LQV, iii, 403.
3 *Ib.*, 404.   4 G & P, 139–40.
5 H, clix, 1430–31.   6 LQV, iii, 404.

exposed, Palmerston could go ahead to settle arrangements for the Fortifications Bill. 'Impossible to say whether Gladstone will go or stay;'[1] but in the event Gladstone stayed. He was pleased at least with Palmerston's agreement not to include a religious enumeration in the new census to avoid exacerbating relations between Church and Dissent as the 1851 census had done. With the decline of the Dissenting campaign on the church rates question after its peak in 1859 Gladstone felt that the Church could afford to relax somewhat in a position of strength. He relaxed by viewing Holman Hunt's 'wonderful picture' of 'The Finding of the Saviour in the Temple' exhibited in the German Gallery, Bond Street. He made more enquiries after Miss Summerhayes. He coped with the Queen's objections to the designs for the new coinage (the 'portrait is so *frightful* that the Queen cannot sanction it').[2] He also 'worked on finance: to be ready with my plan'. On July 16 he composed his 'last shot in the locker', thirty-eight points on the folly of the fortifications scheme. It was embarrassing that in the Ways and Means Committee of the Commons on that day Gladstone had to make an apologetic statement about his need for £2,336,000 and an increase on the duties of ardent spirits. This was damagingly open to the interpretation (put by Bernal Osborne) that at the time of proposing the paper duties repeal Gladstone was 'totally ignorant how the finances of the country stood'. And it enabled Palmerston to exploit an opportunity to point to Gladstone as the source of the government's revenue problems.[3]

By now Gladstone was in retreat. On July 20 on the Savings Bank Monies Bill he suffered his '*first* defeat on a measure of finance in the H. of C. This ought to be very good for me: & I earnestly wish to make it so.'He left the cabinet on July 21 early to avoid the fortifications issue ('that the discussion might be free' was his formulation) and attended Sir Joseph Paxton's fête at the Crystal Palace at Sydenham; and Argyll 'fought my battle in my absence'. Palmerston was adamant as to substance. Gladstone remained firm (at Sydenham) as to its unacceptability; and even indulged in the notion that were he to resign 'one or two more might have done the same. The Cabinet with its small majority was not in a condition to stand a surgical operation such as an amputation of this kind.'[4] Gladstone was spared the responsibility of performing such drastic surgery. Argyll and Herbert sought him out amid the groves of Sydenham; and 'seemed', as Gladstone reported to Graham, 'to bring good news'. Gladstone professed to find that 'concessions have been made beyond my expectation, at the last moment & under great pressure'.[5] The indications are that Argyll and Herbert put a face on the transactions (the concession had to do with the annual basis of the

1 D, v, 503n.   2 Q & G, i, 117–19.
3 H, clix, 1963–80, 2093, 2097.   4 PMP, i, 87.   5 D, v, 506.

financing) which enabled Gladstone so to interpret them; and he was able to go off to Cliveden to walk and boat as a minister possessed both of office and integrity. Palmerston's interpretation was less flattering: 'He evidently has throughout been playing a game of Brag & trying to bully the Cabinet & finding he has failed he has given in.'[1]

In any event Palmerston had already made contingency plans to survive a 'surgical operation'. Derby and Disraeli conveyed an undertaking that 'if Mr. Gladstone were to propose a democratic Budget making a great transfer of burthens from indirect to direct Taxation, and if, the Cabinet refusing its concurrence, Mr. Gladstone were to retire, the Conservative Party would give the Government substantial support'; and that 'no step would in such case be taken to produce a change of Government'.[2] (This pledge, to which the Queen was privy, would be renewed in 1861.) The Exchequer would have been offered to Lewis, and the Queen, as Clarendon assured Lewis, would have accepted Gladstone's resignation 'with satisfaction'.[3] She was indeed wholly with Palmerston on defence expenditure. Lewis had the pleasure of responding to Clarendon that Gladstone had backed down on fortifications because the Cabinet took 'the measure of his foot'.[4] Palmerston assured the Queen that any future obstruction from Gladstone would follow the same pattern: 'ineffectual opposition and ultimate acquiescence.'[5]

There were still plenty of squabbles and testy exchanges between Gladstone and Palmerston; but after the cabinet of July 25 which settled the 'distinct basis' of the fortifications scheme their antagonism faded with the approaching of the end of the session. They were of one mind in thinking that 'we should act upon Captain Fowke's plan for the National Gallery': that is, to replace the Wilkins building with one by the designer of the Albert Hall.[6] Gladstone was also able to assure Palmerston that £5,000 for the Belvedere Murillo was 'dear at this price', despite Eastlake's recommendation.[7] Gladstone relaxed with visits to the sculptor Matthew Noble's studio in Bruton Street; to an exhibition of Bussoli's drawings of the Italian war in company with the Duchess of Sutherland and Argyll; to Theed's studio to see the statue of George IV designed for parliament; to view Mr. Herbert's 'noble cartoon' for the peers' robing room. In the Commons on August 6 for the equalisation of French and British excises Gladstone found 'a favourable House', and a 'most kind & indeed notable reception afterwards'. Being back on terms with the Commons was a gratifying conclusion to a most trying session. It was no less gratifying that in the Lords Derby had overreached himself of late. 'This time the

1 *Ib.*   2 LQV, iii, 429.
3 Maxwell, *Clarendon*, ii, 220.   4 *Ib.*
5 B. Connell, *Regina v Palmerston*, (1962) 321.
6 G to Laing, April 11, 1860. GP, 44530, 188.
7 G to Palmerston, July 19, 1860. GP, 44531, 31.

Lords have got the worst of it,' Gladstone was able to point out to Bright. 'Derby was betrayed by Monteagle into a premature & coarse effort to improve upon his great triumph of the Paper Duties. But it will not do and though very loath they are to recede.' It was well that they should receive a check; 'well especially for them: and for them it would have been best had they been checked at once.'[1] Then to Phillimore's 'pleasant retreat' near Henley, 'so adorned by the cheerful & contented spirit of the inhabitants'. After croquet on August 13 Catherine departed for Hawarden by way of Hagley. Gladstone returned to London to clear up the miscellaneous business of the session and to put in some rescue operations and work on 'my chaos of books a little'. After having incautiously charged himself with coping with his private secretary's work 'at this *dead* time' and finding himself unexpectedly inundated, he reached Hawarden thankfully on August 27.

[7]

No sooner had Gladstone settled in at Hawarden than came news of a 'new vagary' of Henry Glynne's: a Miss Rose this time, formerly governess to his motherless daughters. Added to which was the consideration that Stephen's prospects at the pit and bore hole diggings were 'still in the main tantalising & uncertain'. The 'long struggle' was still to be protracted, with Oak Farm a 'sad wreck'. But it was encouraging that 'much is afloat' at both Hawarden and Oak Farm.[2] Resort to Penmaenmawr yet again at the beginning of September, in Mr. Harrison's 'new & most excellently prepared house.' Thither came news of Henry Glynne's engagement to Miss Rose: 'startling & precipitate, & by no means what one would wish: yet it may come in lieu of worse.' Presumably anything was preferable to Miss Lowder. But the old machinery nevertheless was set in motion again. 'Conv. on Henry's matter & on his letter to Miss Rose. We now hope they are not *engaged*. Letter to Miss R. framed on consultation.'[3] Meanwhile, in the intervals of the usual strenuous course of bathing, walking, and sightseeing, there was Aristotle's *Politics* to be construed with Willy, Tacitus, Tosti on the Council of Constance, and Madame de Sévigné: 'but I begin to think this group with my business is a little hard for pure holiday: so I may let in some lighter material.' This meant Walter Scott in copious doses and some tales from *Blackwood's*. 'Began, audacious work! a paraphrastic translation of the Politics.' He drove with Willy and Stephy to Bangor and

1 G to Bright, August 17, 1860. GP, 44351, 38.
2 D, v, 521.   3 *Ib.*, 514–18.

saw 'inside & out, the wonderful Britannia Bridge'. Then, via the 'excellent' Victoria Inn at Llanrwst, return to Hawarden at the end of September, with some invigorating woodcutting.

There were autumnal interludes in London for such things as King's College Council and pre-sessional cabinets. Bishop Selwyn was copious with painful news from New Zealand of that 'arbitrament by force' which the English were 'far too prone to resort to'.[1] To Newcastle Gladstone was eloquent on the 'hopeless & incurable faults of our plan of attempting to manage such controversies whether on paper or in the field from the other end of the globe. I think the doom of that system is written even if its hour be not yet come.'[2] He dutifully kept up with the latest fiction (Wilkie Collins's *Woman in White* struck him as 'far better than Adam Bede though I do not know if it rises quite as high'.)[3] He kept his vendetta against the Bank turning over. 1854 was still a sore memory ('I am anxious,' he informed the Governor, 'to examine more minutely than I have yet had the opportunity of doing some facts connected with the operation of *fear*, in periods of pressure in the money market, on the Bank reserve'). He had his Treasury sleuths hunting up the records of the management of the National Debt; and he was determined to turn the findings of the Spearman-Anderson report he had instigated in 1854 to account.[4] He contemplated depriving the Bank of a large part of the fees it charged for managing the Debt; and abolishing entirely the 'House Money' it took for dealing with South Sea annuities.[5] He made a point of attending at St. George's in the East where services had been disrupted by anti-ritualists. 'Among the congregation was no less distinguished a person than the Chancellor of the Exchequer, who occupied a seat in the churchwardens pew.' Malcontents were present; and also the 'portly figure of Police-inspector Allison' in plain clothes. Gladstone 'did not leave the edifice until order was being restored'.[6] There were sartorial reports to Catherine ('I have bought the most killing dressing-gown you ever saw, at least on my back').[7] He regretted the necessity of refusing a plea for a loan by the Chartist Ernest Jones, whose imprisonment for sedition from 1848 to 1850 had been cited by Prince Schwarzenberg. There was a slight flurry on Italian affairs: Lord John warned the Piedmontese in a Note on August 31 not to invade Umbria and the Marches. Panizzi promptly conferred with Somerset and Gladstone (as d'Azeglio reported to Cavour) and both talked in a sense 'most favourable for our affairs and spoke with great

1 G to Selwyn, September 20, 1860. GP, 44531, 48.
2 G to Newcastle, January 30, 1861. *Ib.*, 113.
3 Bassett, 131.
4 G to Dobree, October 3 and 17, 1860. GP, 44531, 53, 62.
5 See J. Giuseppe, *The Bank of England* (1966), 117.
6 *Times*, October 15, 1860, 12.
7 G to CG, October 18, 1860. GGP, 28/6.

energy against Lord John's Note which they stigmatized as "Holy Alliance Style"'. Gladstone, it appears, was 'even more expansive'.[1] Indeed Gladstone was reconciling himself with little difficulty to the Piedmontisation of Italy which he had hitherto consistently deprecated. He was dazzled by the drama of Garibaldi's delivery of both Sicily and Naples to Victor Emmanuel. There were worrying aspects: 'Still the name of Mazzini is to me of very ill savour & I am grieved to hear that he is or is likely to be on the ground. If Garibaldi does not ship him off it will be a bad sign.'[2] He sought to improve the shining hour with a letter to Lacaita on December 1: 'We are going I hope to see a kingdom of Italy, and if it can but be solidly formed, it will indeed be a blessed sight. Now there is a question, which may be overlooked. . .': the utter necessity of Italy's avoiding the 'vicious commercial laws' of the 'protective system', by which its unity would be impaired.[3]

There was a further spell at Hawarden before the pre-sessional cabinets recommenced on November 13. Gladstone entertained visiting Lytteltons with tours of his library in the 'Temple of Peace' and of the ever-fascinating mines and colliery railway. At Chester on November 5 he attended rather unwillingly a grand review of Volunteers in the Roodee meadow: 'I had an uncomfortable speech to make: for I had to set up the Volunteers & yet cry down the alarms.' On the way back to London Gladstone stayed with his Oxford colleague Heathcote at Hursley, near Winchester (Keble was the Vicar), where he aired his restlessness about the university seat. 'Wrote at night, tentatively, an address resigning my poor seat at Oxford!' He gave as his motive his desire not to be the cause of another disputed election.[4] He did not in fact send the letter; but in drafting it Gladstone marked a distinct moment in the movement of his understanding and a distinct shift in the operation of detaching himself from one of the main practical principles by which his undertanding had been anchored.

In London Gladstone was much taken by Dion Boucicault's 'very national & also most touching' drama *Colleen Bawn* (which he saw twice again). He had time to absorb himself in the 'vast scheme' involving 'large public outlay' for new Law Courts (£800 for 'some *plans!*'). His major contribution was to argue passionately with Lewis against the proposed site in the Strand, and press for Lincoln's Inn Fields. He thought the Fields really wasted as they were: far too large for the surrounding buildings. They offered a 'magnificent opportunity of making what hardly exists in London, a *visible* public building, as well as of converting the gardens now a desert into a real lung of London by opening the space

1 Beales, 155–56.
2 G to Brougham, September 26, 1860. GP, 44531, 51.
3 GP, 44233, 155–62.   4 D, v, 531.

to the public as a little park'.[1] By now, in the quiet political season, he thought it safe to take up the opening as to Church patronage negotiated earlier with Palmerston on his behalf by Herbert. On November 16 he broached the question with the Prime Minister: hitherto having 'shrunk from recommending to your notice any particular person among my constituents as qualified to be advanced to a Bishopric', Gladstone felt the claims of the Rev. Mr. Claughton, Vicar of Kidderminster, to the vacant see of Worcester to be such as to justify his intervening.[2] Gladstone's attempting to get a foot in the patronage door represented a High Church interest concerned at the degree of influence over ecclesiastical appointments notoriously exercised by Palmerston's Low Church stepson-in-law, Shaftesbury. Gladstone 'made it a rule', as he had explained in the case of an initiative in 1854 on behalf of Jowett, 'not to offer recommendations re Church preferment to Lord Aberdeen'.[3] Now he felt that Church appointments were so dire in quality and character as to compel an attempt to offer a countervailing pressure. Palmerston, who treated God as a benign but remote foreign Great Power, responded regretfully that he felt bound to look for a Cambridge man (he was himself a son of St. John the Evangelist) as five of his seven appointments so far had been Oxonians. He did not want to revert to the old practice of alternating between Oxford and Cambridge for the episcopal bench, but he was unwilling to expose himself to the imputation of paying Cambridge back for having dispossessed him of his seat for that university in 1831. (Henry Philpott, Master of St. Catharine's, was duly preferred.)

Henry Glynne was still a distracting domestic problem. 'Much conv. on Henry & the Rose affair' took place in November. 'R. Phillimore on the Rose affair, growing daily more painful.' November 27: 'We dined with the Phillimores and discussed largely the Rose affair. I wrote a draft for C. to Miss Rose, wh. she sent: renouncing further intervention. This course her position even more than her peace requires.'[4] Miss Rose was showing even more fight than Miss Lowder; and the prospect of a scandalous breach of promise action began to take shape. Otherwise, there was a heavy social calendar ('The Aumales dined. I sat by the Duchess: rather hard on her I think'). It was a blessing that the embarrassing Chinese affair was now out of the way ('We are indeed bound all, I not least of all, to be thankful for the close of the Chinese War').[5] On December 21 an event registered with special poignancy the thinning of old landmarks: *"To Ld Aberdeen's funeral: no common occasion.'* This was the biggest personal break with the political past since Peel's death more than ten

1 G to Cowper, November 9 and 16, 1860; to Lewis, November 23, 1860. GP, 44531, 72, 76, 79.
2 G & P, 153–55.   3 G to Trevelyan, October 26, 1854. GP, 44529, 161.
4 D, v, 533–35.   5 G to Comin, December 27, 1860. GP, 44531, 99.

years earlier. Like the drafting of the letter about the Oxford seat in the previous month Aberdeen's death marked a point of disjunction. It must have aggravated the feelings recorded a few days later by Gladstone at Hawarden on completing his fifty-second year: 'I cannot believe it. I feel within me the rebellious unspoken word, I will not be old. The horizon enlarges, the sky shifts, around me. It is an age of shocks: a discipline so strong, so manifold, so rapid & whirling, that only when it is at an end, can I hope to comprehend it.'[1]

[8]

The New Year was marked by a computation of property and goods: £77,000 worth of land at Hawarden and nearby, £35,000 at Seaforth, £19,800 in London; £26,500 of money lent; £105,500 of stocks and bonds (including £20,000 of Sardinian Bonds); £8,500 of unproductive personal effects (plate, books, pictures, marbles, porcelain, etc.); less charges and differences between market and par and monies held for the House of Charity; leaving a residue of £214,550.[2] It was marked also by a missive of entreaty and encouragement from John Bright. Amid a long list of complaints about the government's policy on expenditure, the American Civil War, China, Europe, Reform, and the Anglo-French armaments race, he put it to Gladstone that the 'men whose minds are full of the traditions of the last century – your *Chief* & your *Foreign Minister*', would 'still cling to the past', and 'seek to model the present upon it'. But a 'new policy & a wiser, & a higher morality,' Bright asserted, were 'sighed for by the best of our people, & there is a prevalent feeling that *you* are destined to guide that wiser policy, & to teach that higher morality.' After informing Gladstone that Cobden had last been seen eating strawberries in Algiers, Bright resumed that he hoped that Gladstone might 'have the courage, & the success which often waits on courage', to 'set free our friends the Paper makers' and 'restore the position & the powers of the House of Commons in matters of taxation'. Bright was 'quite sure that the Towns, & our great populations, will regard the Govt. with increased favour if they see them having some regard to the pressure of taxes upon them'.[3]

In his cautiously circumspect reply Gladstone dwelt on the advantages of Bright's idea of talks to reduce Anglo-French naval rivalry.[4] He did indeed apply to Lord Clarence Paget at the Admiralty for particulars of what he gathered was a scheme promoted by the ambassador in Paris,

1 *Ib.*, 541.   2 GGP, 94/11 'Rough Book A', 83.
3 Bright to G, January 1, 1861. GP, 44112, 24.
4 Robbins, *Bright*, 152–53.

Cowley, to restrict naval establishments.[1] Did this demureness conceal a reluctance to engage himself squarely and candidly with questions which bore all too obviously on enlarging horizons and shifting skies? In invoking the role of guide and teacher Bright defined with tolerable accuracy Gladstone's own sense of the purposes of his political vocation. That accuracy did not make the definition the more commendable to Gladstone. It touched too directly on sensitive personal and political nerve-ends. Bright's theme of 'Towns, & our great populations' was all too disturbingly consequential for Gladstone not only in the hitherto rather distanced sense of what Manchester in 1853 represented for him, but also now in the very immediate and painful context of his contemplating the giving up of his Oxford University seat. It would not be long, indeed, before deputations from towns and great populations waited on him with urgent requisitions that he represent them. He had recently declared himself as witnessing with 'the most lively satisfaction the rapidly multiplying proofs that the great commercial classes of this country appreciate the great and signal service, which Mr. Cobden has rendered to them and to the nation in connection with the Treaty of Commerce between England and France'.[2] Gladstone certainly intended to get satisfaction on the paper duties issue and the House of Lords: but after the travails of 1860 he was aware of the limitations merely of 'courage'. Circumstances forced on Gladstone a Fabian strategy of holding on and waiting. And, in any calculations of weight and effectiveness applied to the political process in 1861, Palmerston and Russell and the 'traditions of the last century' still decisively outmatched John Bright and towns and great populations. Nor was it at all clear to Gladstone that he would prefer the advantage to be the other way about. (It was not long since that Gladstone had been doodling in his diary yet one more of those genealogical celebrations of his wife's and his children's impressive aristocratic and political connections.)[3] Bright shared much of Clarendon's misapprehension as to the nature and direction of Gladstone's developing relationship to towns and great populations.

But, quite apart from calculations, Gladstone faced once more the same perplexity as came upon him after he comprehended that the 'work was gone' of his first vocation. 'This whirl which carries me off balance' was the forming of his new vocation in the early 1850s. Now the 'shocks' caused by subterranean shifts and pressures were again impinging upon his consciousness in a confusing and incomprehensible manner. To an alarmed consciousness of rapid and whirling movement Gladstone

1 G to Paget, January 16, 1861. GP, 44531, 107.
2 G to Mitchell, December 4, 1860. *Ib.*, 87.
3 D, v, 520 (September 21, 1860).

instinctively opposed stasis, not least in a determination to resist the physical process of growing old, but more profoundly in a recurrence of his pattern of agonised reluctance to let go of old principles and links of stability and safe anchorages. Gladstone's clinging to his Oxford seat in the early 1860s and eventually forcing the university to disown him was very much in the same spirit of his clinging in the 1840s to a doctrine which he proclaimed still to be the purpose of his public career but which at the same time 'one might perhaps wish extinct'.

Thus Gladstone's instinct would be to evade rather than embrace the more ambitious and unspecific purport of Bright's appeal. There would be quite enough on hand for the time being with the paper duties and the Lords. It was specifically with such things in mind, however, that J.A. Froude, younger brother of the late Hurrell, put the case to Gladstone that he should take steps to mobilise support in the popular press, for which repeal of the paper duty would be the logical sequel to repeal of the stamp tax in 1855. Here precisely was a point integrally connected with towns and great populations. The management of *Fraser's Magazine* had lately fallen into his hands, he informed Gladstone; and he wished to 'place it at the disposal of the only statesman in whom since Sir Robert Peel's death I have full confidence'.[1] 'The whole subject of working through the press for the support of the measures of the financial department is very new to me,' replied Gladstone. 'I have commonly been too much absorbed in the business of the offices I have held to consider as much as I might of the modes in which my proceedings . . . would be commended favourably to public notice.' He would, he assured Froude, however, 'bear the subject in mind'.[2] He certainly felt he had cause for complaint against *The Times*. He wrote privately to that paper indignant remonstrance soon after taking office.[3] And it was not long before he was in touch with Thornton Hunt of the *Daily Telegraph*. In any case there were more immediate distractions: the Rose affair was as tiresome as ever; and a 'rather formidable missive of Miss R's' set Gladstone to work on yet another draft for Sir Stephen's signature. As against this annoyance the 'ray of hope' for Stephen's coal interests brightened promisingly; and Gladstone was able to declare on 'dearest C's birthday' that he had 'never seen her better or stronger'. At the very un-John-Bright occasion of the Hawarden Estate rent dinner on January 8 Gladstone was able to indulge his penchant for the feudal graces by discoursing 'some $\frac{1}{2}$ hour to a very friendly & well-contented audience'.

The way back to Downing Street was eased by a stop at Hagley, where problems of translating Homer were the question of the hour. Gladstone,

1 Froude to G, February 6, [1861]. GP, 44395, 146.
2 G to Froude, February 16, 1861. GP, 44351, 120.
3 G to Griswell, June 24, 1859. *Ib.*, 44530, 38.

à propos of Matthew Arnold's recent pronouncement, declared that 'when asked to believe that Homer can . . . be rendered into English hexameters, I stop short'[1] (he did not stop short, however, before the year was out, of himself embarking on a 'trochaic translation'). Preparation for cabinets involved the Navy estimates and the chances of persuading Napoleon III to agree to a limitation of naval construction rivalry. Gladstone began to mobilise outside support in aid of his coming budgetary struggles. He asked Graham to join in a 'round robin' of independent members urging reductions in naval and military expenditure to put pressure on the Cabinet. Graham declined on constitutional grounds: the 'battle of economy' must be fought in the Cabinet without outside interference.[2] 'This week is the crisis of the year for the grand heads of charge,' Gladstone wrote on January 22 '– & probably for my keeping my ground in the Govt. But I must hang on – port is close at hand.'[3] He saw Herbert on the 24th, now more frightened about expenditure '& not so panic-stricken about France: so that we may come together'.[4] On January 25 Palmerston, for his part, renewed his treaty with Derby to neutralise any threats of resignation from Gladstone.[5] Gladstone hoped that his opponents might 'relax' after the next cabinet. 'I have had two hard days of hard fighting. By dint of, what after all might be called the threat of resignation, I have got the Navy Estimates a little down, and I am now in the battle about the army . . . My battle here must very soon end. I hope for the sake of my colleagues & for my own that I shall not be fighting it again this time twelvemonth.' On the 28th, with the military estimates in prospect: 'I have some idea of going to see a Pantomime tonight.'[6] But a cabinet on January 30 to settle the Army estimates passed off without resistance from the Chancellor of the Exchequer ('As they now stand I reluctantly but quietly consented').

Prince Albert thoughtfully forwarded an article in the *Revue des Deux Mondes* on French finances in case Gladstone had not already perused it; and for nearly a month a deceptive lull lay over the financial front. Gladstone responded copiously to the Prince's gesture, with melancholy reflections on imperial finance both in France and in Austria ('After this long letter, I fear your Royal Highness will never again send me an article on French finance'); and took the occasion to return the courtesy with a copy of *Translations* by Lyttelton and himself, newly published.[7] There was business to be done with the Prince on questions of the Civil List and marriage settlements for the royal children. Gladstone also had the gratifying task of introducing his legislative plans to set up Post Office

1 G to Arnold, February 11, 1861. GP, 44351, 118. 'Pray remember my breakfasts.'
2 Parker, *Graham*, ii, 410.
3 G to CG, January 22, 1861. GGP, 28/6.
4 G to CG, January 24, 1861. *Ib.*   5 LQV, iii, 429.
6 G to CG, January 26, 28, 1861. GGP, 28/6.   7 Q & G, i, 121.

Savings Banks to improve facilities for deposits of small savings. He was free to keep abreast of Miss Rose's increasingly vexatious correspondence and of Bishop Wilberforce's outburst in the *Quarterly* against *Essays and Reviews*, which transformed a minor doctrinal scandal into a major ecclesiastical crisis. It was embarrassing that his former Christ Church tutor, Biscoe, applied for inappropriate jobs with painful persistence. He visited the 'subterranean railway' – the beginning of the Metropolitan underground line – 'a work of the utmost interest', in which he was a shareholder. At the Geographical Club he heard M. Du Chaillu and Mr. Owen on the discovery of the gorilla 'with the utmost interest'. He got his way with the Bank on the matter of its fees for the Debt and the South Sea annuities; and the cowed directors conceded as well on February 7 his demand that the quarterly dividend 'shuttings' should be shortened for the convenience of the public. On February also Gladstone received a deputation from the West Riding and declined their invitation to become a representative of industrial Yorkshire. He attended at the death of Russell's Reform Bill in cabinet on the 9th without emotion, as Palmerston used a discouraging report by the Liberal Chief Whip, Brand, to rid himself finally of a distasteful encumbrance.

It was not until the end of February that matters reverted to their normal state of contentiousness. Gladstone's temper was not improved by his having to intervene against the latest proposal to solve the perennial church rates question. His sense of commitment to defend the interests of the Church made it impossible for him to 'act in any other sense consistently with personal honour as the representative of the University of Oxford'; and he was studious to stipulate that, were his opinions to undergo a change, he would feel it proper to give the Oxford electors 'an opportunity of having their interests and claims stated in this House by some one whose opinions were more congenial to their own'. His line was that it was not a question of exemption for Dissenters but rather encouragement for those ready to contribute; the old link between payment of the rate and a seat in church was still the law but not seriously applicable either in populous town parishes or small rural parishes; the answer was to abolish rates where they were impracticable and form voluntary church vestries.[1] He took care to make sure that Keble was not 'erroneously informed' as to his position; but he confessed himself 'very uneasy at the incessant war & strife on these things.'[2] For his pains he was abused by Bright for having the same old 'misty notion' of eighteen years before: 'there is an influence in that ancient and eminent University which busies itself with the learning of the past, but sees little of the present, and shuts its eyes resolutely to the future.'[3] In such a mood

1 H, clxi, 1017–25.
2 G to Keble, February 27, 1861. GP, 44531, 122.   3 H, *ib.*, 1028.

Gladstone was startled by a sudden proposal for an extra £3 million on the Navy estimates. Gladstone composed a 'Counter Memorandum' on 'Lord P.s wild proposal, which much disturbed me'. He entered an 'objection, amounting at one point nearly to complaint', against the programme of matching French construction of iron or shot-proof ships, alleging lack of evidence as to the reality of danger and the impolicy of creating 'great alarm' and provoking the French. Gladstone added that it would be 'uncandid' to conceal his opinion that he 'ought to be supplied with further means of considering such evidence, than . . . one or two manuscript papers'. Nor could he 'undertake to dispose of this question between Monday and Wednesday afternoons'.[1] He was relieved that the 'absurd proposal of yesterday seems to have little chance: & I breathe again'.[2] He withheld a letter drafted in general terms to Palmerston of the 'unseemliness' of his renewing during the present session 'a series of struggles such as were those of last year upon the Fortifications, the Paper Duty, and the question of Taxing Bills'. The 'most natural sequel to what I have said would be at once to place my resignation in your hands'. But 'one strong public motive' disinclined Gladstone from any such step: his desire to render his account 'of the measures of last year', which could be done only by way of the forthcoming budget.[3] Palmerston, strong in the knowledge of Derby's countenance, remained, in any event, quite unapologetic, especially on the point of French susceptibilities.

'My life is a life from hand to mouth,' Gladstone complained; 'I have always too much to do, & always a great deal undone.'[4] Still, there was much riding in the Park early in March with daughters and visits to Christie's. About Oxford he continued in a state of great addlement. One side of him inclined towards continuing the work of 1854. 'I have no business to be an Oxford Reformer,' he told Thorold Rogers, 'more than my butler has to amend my manners.' Yet the notion intrigued him that fellowships must not be a 'mere prize', however honourably won; might they not 'be *more* than now connected with the discharge of duties'? And should not study in the vacation be 'promoted instead of discouraged' to end the 'irrational system of dispeopling Oxford for half the year'?[5] In that spirit Gladstone assisted in efforts to resolve the problem of Jowett's stipend as Regius Professor of Greek, blocked by the votes of both High and Low orthodoxy; and it was gratifying also to urge successfully the claims of the sympathetic Churchman Montagu Burrows to the Chichele chair of Modern History. The other side was studious to assure Keble that 'I have on all occasions voted against the abolition of Church-rates', despite the fact that his colleagues had 'given in', 'not for approving of

1 G & P, 157–58.·   2 D, vi, 13.   3 G & P, 161–62.
4 G to Brougham, March 15, 1861. GP, 44531, 129.
5 G to Rogers, January 22, 1861. GP, 44531, 111.

abolition so much as in despair of a settlement', and thus had made the question as far as the government was concerned 'an open one'. Gladstone promised to keep the issue 'carefully in view'.[1] Italy, again, offered itself pertinently as a cause of happy convergence. Gladstone observed with surprise and delight the extent of unanimity in the Commons on this question. 'There is the [Pope's] Brass Band: there are a few people who have lingering sympathies with despotism. But subject to small exceptions the Conservative and the Liberal sides really seemed to feel alike.'[2] The *fait accompli* of Piedmontisation was about to be consummated by the formal proclamation of the Kingdom of Italy; and Gladstone took the opportunity both to praise Russell for having pursued a 'national policy', 'stamped with approval throughout the body of the people of England', and to apologise for his tardy conversion to unification. 'Now let me say one word as to the yearning of the Italians for political unity. I am ashamed to say that for a long time I . . . withheld my assent and approval of those yearnings.' Gladstone's excuse was that it was 'Austria that has made Italian unity'.[3] To his tributes to France (despite Savoy) and Cavour, Gladstone added the highly Palmerstonian point that he wished Austria well north of the Alps where she would be a mainstay of the peace and order of Europe; which was not presumably the central theme of his conversation with the Hungarian revolutionary leader of 1848–49 Louis Kossuth ('a man of mark & wonderful eloquence'), to see whom he interrupted a retreat in Brighton. The sea air and 'sublime' breakers that season Gladstone found exceptionally invigorating ('found myself at night another man,' he noted on March 17); which braced him to confront yet another requisition to stand for a northern seat (this time the newly-created third division of South Lancashire). Despite Gladstone's published refusal *The Times* persisted with reports that it was 'well understood' that Gladstone could be persuaded to 'consent to stand'.[4]

   Doubtless also Gladstone was glad of Brighton's bracing ozone tonic when on March 20 he met Manning again for the first time since April 1851. The initiative was Manning's; and for Gladstone it was a 'great event': 'all was smooth: but *quantum mutatus*! Under external smoothness and conscientious kindness, there lay a chill indescribable.' Gladstone hoped on his side that it did not affect Manning so. 'He sat where Kossuth sat on Friday: how different!'[5] Part of Manning's motive appears to have been to arrange an exchange of their correspondence. Gladstone recalled many years later: 'Ah, that correspondence!' Manning proposed, 'and I

1 G to Keble, March 24, 1860. GP, 44530, 179.
2 G to Brougham, March 15, 1861. GP, 44531, 129–30.
3 H, clxi, 1565–79.
4 *Times*, March 20, 1861, 5; March 28, 10; April 2, 1861, 4.
5 D, vi, 18.

like a donkey accepted, an exchange of letters'. To Gladstone it was giving back gold in return for bronze. Later he learned 'with extreme vexation' that Manning had destroyed his Anglican letters;[1] for Gladstone always held that Manning's Anglicanism showed no declension in power or brilliance before the catastrophe of 1851. Gladstone felt that he had unwittingly been manoeuvred into collaborating in Manning's deliberate obliteration of his Anglican traces. At the same time Gladstone was doing his best to expose his Ionian traces. He tried to persuade Newcastle that it would be to the public's benefit if his report was published, as his information and insights were 'just as material to any discussion now as they were to my abortive proposals.' 'The ignorance that prevails in this country is gross.' It was believed that 'the Islands possess the full essentials for what is termed Parliamentary government'; and it was 'idle to shelter under misconceptions'.[2] Newcastle, however, preferred to cleave to the custom that reports of negotiations which have failed are not normally produced. Which was, as things turned out, very fortunate for Gladstone.

[9]

By now Palmerston was as insistent as ever as to Herbert's requirements on fortifications and Somerset's problems in casing ships with iron plates and in constructing new iron ships to match the French programme. Gladstone responded eloquently on the difficulties of the revenue. There would be a deficiency in the excise of a further £250,000 for the 1860–61 accounts; and in general he had 'never known a time when it would be so essential to proceed with great caution and full possession of the best *data*'.[3] He foresaw another dreary round of budget conflicts ahead. Fortified by porcelain arranging and reading Macaulay, Gladstone went off to Wilton for Easter. After seeing the chapter house at Salisbury with 'great delight' he rode with Herbert on Easter Monday to the local 'meet'. Gladstone spoke to the ailing Herbert 'of his health, & of my hope that for different reasons we should be both "out" soon'.[4] Was this a recurrence of

1 PMP, i, 156. Gladstone in 1894 put the proposal to exchange at the time of Manning's secession; but March 1861 seems more likely to have been the occasion. See below, 450. Gladstone was misinformed by Manning's biographer Purcell about the alleged destruction of the letters. They were discovered during the Second World War at the House of the Oblates of St. Charles in Bayswater. See Butler, 70n.
2 G. to Newcastle, March 23, 1861. GP, 44531, 133.
3 G & P, 163.
4 D, vi, 20–21. Herbert suffered from diabetes and probably also renal disease, baffling to his doctors. 'Apparently he was living on brandy'. F.B. Smith, *Florence Nightingale* (1982), 112n.

Gladstone's familiar protestations of earlier difficult times? Or did restlessness about Oxford or trepidation about towns and great populations add an extra twist? Certainly the tribulations of the early phase of budget planning in April gave good reason for wishing to be 'out'. 'Saw Lord Palmerston & explained to him my plans: wh did not meet his views. A laborious & anxious day.'[1] With a balance of £1½ million in hand Gladstone wanted to revive his paper duties repeal; at which Palmerston balked. Perhaps he would have balked even more decisively had he known of an unwonted spark of new interest which led Gladstone that day to extend his condolences to Edward Baines, the Radical M.P. and Leeds journalist, at the 'unhappy' failure of his bill to extend the borough franchise.[2] After all, Reform was no longer an obstacle;· and, with the Lords to confront, it might become an ally. Gladstone signalled another manoeuvre to turn the flank of his opponents by moving in the Commons on April 9 for a Select Committee of Public Accounts to examine audited accounts of public expenditure after they had gone through regular processes at the hands of executive government. In effect, it would be a formal parliamentary mode of criticising the expenditure of the previous year.

As his budget day approached new demands for £1,250,000 from the Admiralty, War, and India departments pressed in upon Gladstone ('hardly possible to conduct public business under these modes of proceeding'). At a cabinet on April 11: 'Explained my case 1–3. Chaos!' 'Very stiff indeed', as he described it to 'Own C.'. 'More than doubtful whether I shall get through: doubtful whether we shall go to D.St. next week.'[3] On the 12th: 'Very stiff. We "broke up" in one sense, & all but in another.' In the furious 'tug of war' Gladstone wanted to remit over a million of taxation, mainly in abolishing the paper duties, reserving a third of his balance as surplus. 'Lord P. tried to show a necessity for more expenditure on iron ships. The Duke of S. stated the case fairly, & this attempt broke down.'[4] Only Milner Gibson supported the paper duties proposal. Some preferred a reduction of the tea duty. Most were strong for reduction of income tax. Gladstone decided to plant his paper duties abolition on the coat tails of a penny off the income tax; and confront the Lords with the option of accepting or rejecting them in tandem. This tactic worked. On the following day Gladstone managed to get his plan 'as now framed' accepted, 'Ld P. yielding gracefully' and Stanley of Alderley 'almost the only kicker'; then back to Downing Street and 'worked late'. (By this time long days were a rarity to be specially noted: 'A day of over 14 h. work. Thank God for the strength.')[5] In his relief and elation

1 *Ib.*, 22.   2 *Ib.*, 23.
3 G to CG, April 11, 1861. GGP, 28/6.
4 PMP. iii, 236–37.   5 D, vi, 114 (April 10, 1862).

Gladstone reverted to Glynnese in his report to Catherine: 'I am *thruff*. It is all right. Almost unánimous.'[1] Reducing the income tax by 1d to 9d as well as repealing the paper duties would leave an estimated surplus of less than £400,000. Palmerston, as he made clear in a letter on April 14, 'acquiesced reluctantly', still convinced that his government's financial arrangements should have been 'framed upon a Principle different from that on which your Proposal has been founded'. A larger surplus was needed to cope with the contingencies of the unsettled state of Europe. Nor (with a renewed compact with the Conservatives in his pocket) did he flinch from warning Gladstone candidly that were the Commons to jib as they had done in the 1860 session, the Chancellor of the Exchequer would have to fight his own battle: 'I think it right to say beforehand that, as far as I am concerned, I do not intend to make the Fate of my administration depend upon the Decision which Parliament may come to on your Proposal.'[2]

With such cheer and encouragement from his chief's bold twist to the constitutional conventions (something of a tit for tat for Gladstone's rather similar performance over the resolutions on the Lords in the 1860 session) Gladstone delivered his financial statement on April 15. 'The figures rather made my head ache. It was the discharge of a long pent up excitement.' Gladstone celebrated the commercial treaty and the definitive end of the protective tariff. He lamented the highest taxation and expenditure (£72 million) other than in time of war. He cited, as ever, 1853 as the model from which the 'lesson to be derived' was the duty of cutting back expenditure by ten millions or so and so dispensing with the income tax. He covered his renewed proposal to repeal the paper duties by denying any personal partiality for direct as against indirect taxation; but he pointed proudly to the last twenty years as a 'memorable epoch' for remissions of indirect taxation, a great and beneficial pruning operation to restore the vigour of the stock. Then home after nine: 'Read Stanhope's Pitt. Rode alone.'

With painful memories of how Russell's Reform Bill had impeded him in the 1860 session, Gladstone was determined to push ahead without delay. This provoked more complaints from Palmerston: the Commons allow themselves to be led but not driven; it would be best to have an adjournment to enable members 'to go to distant Homes or to run over to Paris', otherwise they will turn sulky or sullen. 'You must be aware that your Budget is not much liked in the House except by the comparatively small Band of Radicals below the gangway, who are thought to be your Inspirers in Financial Matters.'[3] At the Lord Mayor's dinner on April 17 Gladstone returned thanks on behalf of the House of Commons; and, inured though he was to the Prime Minister's public tone of apology for or

1 Bassett, 135.   2 G & P, 166–67.   3 *Ib.*, 169–70.

hostility to the official financial measures of his own government, thought 'Ld P..s notice of the Budget in his speech was remarkable'. Gladstone felt himself dangerously exposed. Catherine wrote to Graham begging him to come to her husband's aid. 'He does not know I am telling you this. . . Even a few words thrown in by you would refresh William's spirit, and it would come with great weight from you.' This appeal to the venerated memory of Peel' moved Graham to intervene in the budget debate with his last considerable speech in the Commons, upholding Gladstone on the paper duties and Lords issues.[1]

The thing to do, however, was to take a long view of Palmerston's refractoriness. Lucy Lyttelton remarked on April 30: 'Uncle W. in rollicking spirits over his Budget';[2] and Gladstone diverted himself with Mill's *Considerations on Representative Government* and Du Chaillu's book on the gorilla[3] and with moving his establishment into 11 Downing Street (there had been much reconstruction and redecoration in the meantime). And a congenial 'Phil-Italian' dinner at Monckton Milnes's was an occasion for the friends of Italy to celebrate the birth of the new state. Gladstone's mode of reconciling himself to his dispensation was to argue that 'as disunited Italy has been a great source of danger to Europe, so united Italy . . . will be a stable element in the European system: and that the Italian power will both help to keep France in order, and will be more conservative of the general peace . . . than any of the great Powers now existing on the continent'.[4] And Manning's three lectures extolling *The Temporal Sovereignty of the Popes* could only reinforce Gladstone's disposition to accommodate himself to the existence of an Italian state which looked forward ultimately to displacing the Pope and establishing its capital in Rome. The lectures he thought 'mournful indeed to peruse!'[5] (later: 'Manning's Lectures Eheu!'). Doubtless it was consoling that Manning was being in some manner paid back for his faithlessness to Anglicanism by being on the losing side in Italy.

That Gladstone's tendency was to be strong on the stronger side is indeed distinctly marked in his outlook on foreign affairs since 1859. The evaporation of his former intense criticism of the Crimean policy was eloquently manifested in his silence in 1860 on the various scandals of Turkish repression in the Balkans, and especially in the atrocious

1 Parker, *Graham*, ii, 412.   2 *Diary of Lady Frederick Cavendish*, i, 115.
3 'When Du Chaillu's book come out, & the world was mad about monkeys, several were sceptical as to the Gorillas – but Gladstone said that was the only part of his book of which he felt confident, as he had sate in the House of Commons with a Gorilla for several years – G. P. Bentinck (M.P. for Norfolk). G. P. Bentinck was upwards of 6 feet 2 i. at least, with bandy legs, & the most inhuman face ever encountered. It was really a caricature of a Gorilla. Fred. Lygon, who was the best-looking fellow in the House, said, that he thought Gladstone, as usual, was unfair & that Bentinck was rather "the missing link".' (Swartz, *Disraeli's Reminiscences*, 87.)
4 G to Russell, March 17, 1861. D, vi, 19.   5 D, vi, 28.

massacres of Maronite Christians in Syria and the Lebanon: precisely the onset of that process of 'convulsive volcanic disintegration' of the Ottoman empire which he had accurately predicted. Prince Gorchakov, the Russian Chancellor, drew Europe's attention to these sour fruits of the Crimean war in his famous Circular to the Powers in 1860 in terms very reminiscent of Gladstone's strictures between 1855 and 1858; but now Gladstone was a consenting party to his government's policy of rebutting Gorchakov's critique as a revival of Russian ambitions and aggressions against Turkey. Already Irish Catholic defenders of the Papacy and Austria were baiting Gladstone for inconsistency as between his championing the cause of Italy and his reluctance to apply that same principle in, say, the case of the Greeks, with special reference to the Ionian question. Gladstone muddied the waters with much irrelevant flourishing of 'a name which must stand among the most illustrious' in the establishment of the Greek state – 'I mean the name of Mr. Canning'; but the substance of his argument was an unrelieved conformity to what had by now become a Palmerstonian 'Crimean' orthodoxy, that the independence and integrity of the Ottoman Empire was a capital interest both of Britain and of Europe. Gladstone insisted that 'it would be nothing less than a crime against the safety of Europe . . . as connected with the state and course of the great Eastern question, if England were . . to surrender the protectorate of the Ionian Islands for the purpose of uniting them to Free Greece'. The delicate bearings of such a move on the 'Greek provinces of Turkey' had to be well considered; disturbances would be fostered in Thessaly, Albania, and Crete. The 'closedness and urgency' of 'high political considerations' ruled out simple solutions.

> Men may differ as to the practicability of maintaining the Ottoman dominion in Europe; they may differ as to whether it is desirable to maintain it; but all will agree that whatever is done upon this question shall be done above-board upon principle, and with forethought; that we should not by any piecemeal measures bring into operation unawares any source of disturbance which might tend to perplex and break up a great European question, and might have a most detrimental influence upon the future not only of Corfu and Turkey, but of the entire East, and of all Europe, as connected with the great problem of the East.[1]

In effect Gladstone was resolving his dilemma by a curious conflation of his stress on the importance of an 'Italian' public opinion with the unarguable fact that the 'Crimean' policy was no less endorsed by public approval. The one case was to be celebrated; the other to be accepted as a fact of political life. His consistent line on Italy was to assert that

1 H, clxiv, 1682–89 (May 7, 1861).

Palmerston and Russell were above all exponents of 'a national and British policy'.[1] It was now expedient to transfer that doctrine eastwards.

Doubtless, as with the Chinese issue, Gladstone felt that he had enough on his hands without looking for trouble in foreign policy. By this time another aspect of foreign affairs impinged upon him. Gladstone responded to it quite gratuitously in a spirit highly conformable with the prejudices of Palmerston and the gentlemen of England. At breakfast on May 2 Sir John Acton was 'most satisfactory' on the American Civil War: which is to say, he deplored the obstinacy of President Lincoln in persisting with his hopeless project of restoring the Union by force.[2] For all that he detested the principle of slavery, as he assured the Duchess of Sutherland, Gladstone considered the war to be 'without cause' and hence foolish and wicked. It was not a war for freedom in any case. The northerners would think the same about the blacks as the southerners 'if it could happen that a tropical climate could take the place of the climate they now have, and that the same economical reasons should recommend Slavery in the North as now sustain it in the South, those ideas, legitimately worked out, would re-establish it in the North itself, despite the opposition of a philanthropic minority'.[3] Gladstone continued staunch in this view despite hobnobbing with one of Lincoln's greatest admirers, John Bright (he noted: 'walked home with Mr. Bright' in the early hours after a sitting; and Bright commiserated on May 8: 'I see Mr. Disraeli was very rude last night').

In any case the American Civil War was as yet a peripheral concern. Gladstone's immediate attention was directed at seeing his paper duties repeal through. And there was more trouble with the Irish over the Galway packet contract. Gladstone rallied to Hill's defence ('I should regard the displacement of Sir Rowland Hill as the greatest misfortune that can befall the Post Office').[4] And indeed, the passage of his Post Office Savings Banks Bill would be for Gladstone one of the great features of the 1861 session: not least because of the gratifying increased liquidity it placed at the Treasury's disposal. After purchasing pictures at Christie's ('Madame du Barry consulting Cagliostro on her future fate' by Biard, 61 guineas) and discoursing at the Royal Academy dinner (where the president, Sir Charles Eastlake, 'made me return thanks for authorpoliticians') he departed on May 18 for a Whitsun recess at his now familiar haven at Cliveden, 'leaving C. which seems but selfish'. There he found only the recently widowed Duchess Harriet and Argyll. There was 'much

1 H, clxiv, 1235.
2 'I delivered a brief . . . abstract of my American article, to the astonishment and admiration of . . . especially the ignorant Gladstone.' J. L. Atholz *et al.* (eds.), *Correspondence of Lord Acton and Richard Simpson*, ii (1973), 146.
3 G to Dss of Sutherland, May 29, 1861. GP, 44531, 167.
4 G to Stanley of Alderley, May 18, 1861. *ib.*, 159.

conversation', enlivened by excursions to Dropmore and Burnham Beeches, and a Whit Tuesday visit by boat to Eton, where he saw Stephy. He decided to prolong the visit, though not without a conscience-twinged apology to Catherine: 'This seems rather selfish.'[1] Then an emergency called Gladstone back up to Flintshire. Mostyn, whose election had caused such dishonour to the county and grief to the Glynnes and Gladstones in 1857, had died; and the prospect thus opened of Stephen Glynne's recovering his rightful status of knight of the shire. But to the consternation of Hawarden, the Grosvenors of Eaton shouldered their way to the nomination. The Westminster influence was held to have been decisive against Stephen in 1857; now the Marquess put his weight behind his brother, Lord Richard. Hawarden swallowed the affront, and Gladstone conveyed the capitulation that 'Sir Stephen's agent who is also mine will vote for Ld Rich. Grosvenor'.[2] He soothed his family hurt by the feudal pleasure of reporting to Catherine from Hawarden that 'my tenants go with Lord Richard'. He desired his agent to make 'my sentiment known to my tenants. I shall be obliged by your kindly taking the trouble to acquaint them that I sincerely desire Lord Richard Grosvenor's success.'[3] He also put Catherine to work: 'I want you *to write, & send me by return,* a note to John Bellis, labourer, Bannel, saying you are glad to hear he intends to vote for Lord R. & encouraging him to do so.'[4] The only awkwardness was yet another 'vagary' from the Reverend Henry: he threatened to vote Conservative, and Gladstone had much ado arranging to pair with him to avoid the public scandal of a Glynne being seen to vote against Grosvenor.[5] 'It is beautiful here,' Gladstone reported to Catherine; 'perhaps I shall stay and instead of coming just send my resignation.'[6]

That temptation was prompted by more than fair weather at Hawarden; a crucial test awaited Gladstone in London. The division on the paper duties repeal was due on May 30. Stanley records sitting at dinner on May 29 next to Catherine, who 'could think and speak of nothing but her husband and the division of tomorrow: she seemed astonished at any of his measures being opposed, and almost intimated that she looked on such opposition as personal to him'.[7] Repeal went through the Commons by the narrow but in the circumstances sufficient majority of 296 to 281. 'One of the greatest nights on the whole of my recollection.' (Palmerston concluded for the government 'briefly and grudgingly'.) There were moves in the Lords to repeat the controversial rejection of 1860; but Derby, though clear that the Customs and Inland Revenue Bill was

1 G to CG, May 20, 1861. GGP, 28/6.
2 G to Brand, May 10, 1861. GP, 44531.155.
3 G to Burnett, May 21, 1861. *Ib.*, 162. He instructed Burnett further (*ib.*, 167) to check the poll books to find out which voters changed or did not vote compared with 1857.
4 G to CG, May 24, 1861. GGP, 28/6   5 D, vi, 35.
6 G to CG, May 25, 1861. GGP, 28/6   7 DDCP, 171.

objectionable in substance as well in form, advised their lordships as to the inexpediency of further resistance. 'This has been a week of great excitement', Gladstone told the Duchess of Sutherland; '& I have in me I fear still a considerable stock of indignation that has to be blown off like steam: but great thankfulness & satisfaction preponderate and indeed absorb more & more everything else.' He allowed that he could 'almost hope the financial controversies of my life, I mean the great ones, are at an end'.[1] The bill went through on June 7 without a division. 'Today's debate in the Lords,' Gladstone recorded, 'was a great event for me.' It was a great event also for the new press which had been given its franchise in 1855. What Gladstone lost in the countenance of *The Times* was more than made up by his becoming the hero of the *Daily Telegraph* and its provincial fellows. Thornton Hunt of the *Telegraph* assured Gladstone: 'in all directions, I find the strongest sense of the debt due to you for what you did in the paper duties affair. Men are fully alive to the value of those services in *all* their aspects, and know [sic] one knows better than yourself what that means. There is a desire to *avoid causing you embarrassment* by any premature and obtrusive mode of expressing that feeling, but you will learn it some day.'[2]

The next stage in the 'vagaries' of Henry Glynne's ever-thwarted quest for matrimony was a threat (from Miss Rose presumably; or possibly Miss Lowder) of a breach of promise case. Phillimore ('altogether greatly horrified') advised that a financial settlement was 'decidedly preferable to going into court'.[3] This embarrassment came indirectly into public notice when the *Cork Constitution*, reflecting Irish opinion offended at the proposal to cancel the faltering Atlantic Company's Galway packet contract for mail to America, published an allegation that Gladstone had paid £5,000 to avoid a summons as a co-respondent in a divorce case. Gladstone explained on June 3 to his solicitor: 'In the present case it happens that some circumstances have happened to a relative of mine which recently caused me to be the medium of transmitting to a lady through a London Bank a sum of money: it is possible that this may have grown without any intentional falsehood into the fiction we now have to deal with.' The idea of 'legal punishment or redress', he added, was 'not to be entertained'.[4] The *canard* in fact rebounded against Gladstone's enemies. 'I am not sure,' he wrote to Robertson, 'that I ever witnessed such a burst of emotion in the H of C as at the announcement of the numbers ... after the foul Galway job had been imported into the contest.'[5] In a 'subsequent utterance' in the *Cork Constitution* the

1 G to Dss of Sutherland, June 1, 1861. GP, 44531, 168.
2 Hunt to G, August 2, 1861. GP, 44397, 3.
3 G to CG, January 19, 1861. GGP, 28/6.
4 D, vi, lxvii, 37.   5 G to Robertson G, June 1, 1861. GP, 44531, 169.

allegation was contradicted; which ended the matter with a minimum of fuss.

After giving evidence to the Colonial Military Expeditions Committee of the Commons to the effect that colonies should pay for their own defence. ('To the horror of C.O. & the Mother Country') and breakfasting with Herbert, whose ill-health impelled resignation ('sad but less sad than the present state'), Gladstone retreated to Betteshanger Park, near Sandwich in Kent, 'that nest of peace & virtue', seat of Walter James. There with Catherine and his host (a prominent Churchman and former Conservative M.P. for Hull) Gladstone debated 'Oxford v S. Lancashire in its Ch. & religious bearings as well as in others'.[1] His candidacy had been put forward without his consent for the new South Lancashire seat, due to be filled in August. He depended on Robertson to manage the affair for him. He made it clear that there would be 'nothing disparaging to Oxford in my quitting it to meet a strong and general wish in my native county'. But was there a strong and general wish? And would it be necessary to hire a secretary to handle the constituency work? The 'rather difficult and delicate business of the South Lancashire movement' weighed heavily; at a time moreover when 'we have not yet passed over the critical period of the Session'.[2] Should he allow it to go ahead, to test the ground? But would it be well in the event of a contest to risk failure? 'The time is now approaching,' Gladstone told Robertson, 'when it will have to be determined in Lancashire whether to make any offer to me or not.' What was Robertson's judgment as to likely poll support?[3] There was the tempting possibility also of the impending vacancy of the City of London seat on Russell's elevation to the House of Lords. This teasing problem continued to exercise him at Cliveden, 'this hospitable house', helped by 'much air, rest, & boat', and Stephy's coming over from Eton.

So far the 1861 session, apart from the budget itself, had been, by 1860 standards, unstrained. Through June and most of July Gladstone sailed on unruffled waters. He had the pleasure of helping to examine John Stuart Mill when the saint of rationalism gave evidence before the Income Tax Committee of the House (in favour of differential as opposed to graduated rates). Lady Waldegrave informed him in her stimulating way 'first that all, then that most, of my Colleagues in the Cabinet predicted that I should lead the Bright party'.[4] At dinner at John Neilson's he met his niece's bridegroom (Richard Lowry-Corry, 4th Earl of Belmore, of Castle Coole, Enniskillen); 'but was summoned away.' There was the 'intolerable nuisance' of correcting the proofs of his Financial Statement. He rode with Agnes; and on June 22 was 'much shocked at Herbert's

1 D, vi, 39.
2 G to Robertson G, March 20, 25, 30, 1861. GP, 44531, 132, 135, 137.
3 G to Robertson G, June 1, 1861. GP, 44531, 169.   4 D, vi, 41.

face'. To Herbert he wrote on the 29th that he was 'a good deal embarrassed about the prospect of a proposal for South Lancashire'. And indeed on July 18 a South Lancashire deputation took an hour and half to present a requisition of 7,788 electors that Gladstone stand for the seat. But already Gladstone on July 12 had a 'long & anxious' conclave with Roundell Palmer (the Solicitor-General), the Rector of Exeter College and the Provost of Queen's College (William Thomson), George Rawlinson of Exeter, and Edward Palmer of Balliol; and afterwards it was settled with Brand the Chief Whip that he 'ought not to stir'. He also saw Baron Rothschild and declined the London seat. Gladstone announced his refusal of the Lancashire requisition on July 19 in guarded terms: he could not leave Oxford despite contests unusual in that constituency; and besides, 'the Parliament is yet young'.[1]

Otherwise there was an intensive social round, much of it in the company of the Dowager Duchess Harriet (at the Royal Academy show: 'Her quickness is *marvellous*'). Gladstone dined with 'The Club' and gave a dinner for the Fine Arts Club; which he left after 12.45: 'Went off to a distant quarter to see "Mrs. Dale"' – alias Summerhayes – 'Altogether she is no common specimen of womanhood.'[2] There was much ado with the British Museum, especially Panizzi's scheme for moving the natural history collections to South Kensington. Palmerston urged that more money be spent on the promotion and encouragement of science, which he insisted was as fully deserving as the arts. The State, he pointed out to Gladstone, spent freely on 'Pictures and Medieval Curiosities', 'Frescoes, Statues, and Galleries'; yet the knowledge which science imparted 'and the Truth which it establishes redound quite as much to the Honour and Fame of a Nation as the Triumphs of art, and are often attended with Results of more practical usefulness'.[3] Was the Prime Minister – perhaps even with Darwin mischievously in mind, for the collision between Huxley and Bishop Wilberforce at the meeting of the British Association at Oxford the previous year still reverberated – being deliberately provocative? Certainly Gladstone later that year referred to himself as a 'Charlatan' in speaking for the promotion of science[4]; but he did, however, at this time take the trouble to explain to the Commons about the 'very useful invention recently made', known as methylated spirits, 'which involved the solution of a most difficult problem – how to invent a spirit which should be available for purposes of manufacture, and which could not be used as drink'.[5]

These halcyon days ended abruptly with squalls on July 19. 'What a day: my poor brain whirled.' Palmerston exploded in irascible complaint about a Treasury minute. After consulting Graham, Gladstone

1 *Times*, July 22, 1861, 12.   2 D, vi, 47.
3 G & P, 172.   4 D, vi, 65.   5 H, clxiv, 1173.

responded 'with much regret' to the 'indictment', pointing out that the Cabinet had consented to the minute months ago. Nor could Gladstone omit to add that Palmerston's language appeared to him 'of equivocal construction, and suggests the idea that you may have meant by its tone to signify that you thought the time was come when the official connection between us ought to cease'. If so, he left the matter entirely at Palmerston's discretion: the state of the finances would allow resignation at the end of the session 'without any public inconvenience'. In his agitation Gladstone lost his grip on his grammar: 'If you have no intention of this kind, please to consider the last sentence as never have been written.' He would not attend the next cabinet unless there was a positive response. Palmerston assured him 'with great Truth' that 'Termination of our official Connection' would be a 'real misfortune to myself, to the Government and to the public Service'; upon which Gladstone signified his intention to attend the cabinet.[1]

Worse than this personally bruising but publicly insubstantial collision was another communication from Palmerston on July 19, returning to the attack on the question of the French menace. At massive length, replete with ideas and projects for iron-plated and iron ships and £2 million of terminable annuities to finance them, Palmerston demanded a million more to 'take immediate and active Measures to keep pace with the French': 'no Time is to be lost.' Cherbourg was clearly being prepared as a launching base for invasion. On the matter of the immediate extra million Gladstone rather breathlessly protested that in the 'midst of a day of close and incessant pressure I should thus, while still holding the office of Chancellor of the Exchequer, be deprived of all power of examining and considering proposals which I deem to be in some points open not only to grave, but as at present advised I must add insurmountable objection'. Palmerston imperturbably brushed Gladstone aside with another enormous letter full of intricate naval technicalities on the disturbing implications of the relative naval strengths of France and Britain.[2] Gladstone protested; but did not fight. Having got his way on paper duties repeal and forced a climb-down by the Lords he had every motive of discretion not to push his luck any further in cabinet. There was a determined and conspicuously unfriendly cabinet majority set on getting its way over defence expenditure and not at all likely to tolerate another performance from Gladstone on the lines of 1860. Cornwall Lewis had now replaced Herbert at the War Office; he was both formidable and grimly unforgiving not merely at having been supplanted in 1859 but mostly from having to suffer Gladstone's airs of patronising superiority (when Lewis died in 1863 Gladstone commented that he was 'pained to think of my differences with him at one time on finance: however he took

1 G & P, 174–81.   2 *Ib.*, 172–87.

benefit by them rather than otherwise').[1] Gladstone candidly confessed
to Palmerston his motives for surrender: it might have been said that
'having set my face against an excess of Expenditure, I ought to have
considered that a holy war, and not to have receded'. However, though
he placed public economy 'somewhat higher, as a matter of duty, than
many might do', Gladstone did not think it would have been right, it
would indeed have been 'foolish and presumptuous', to have gone
beyond 'these two things, first making an effort to the utmost of my
power, at the critical moment', and secondly 'on being defeated to watch
for opportunities thereafter'. Gladstone did not, after all, as he insisted,
'recommend or desire sweeping and sudden reductions'.[2]

Still, whatever glosses might be put upon it, receding from a holy war
was a dispiriting manoeuvre. 'The political storm has blown over,' he told
Catherine, ' – but I do not think it seems an evening for riding to Holly
House nor can I honestly say that a party there would be a relaxation for
my very weary bones & wearier nerves and brain.'[3] Gladstone had to
swallow the distasteful fact that the charges for the armed services would
remain at an average of nearly 40 per cent of government expenditure for
the period 1861–1865. Nor was the Public Accounts Committee of the
Commons he set up in 1861 of any help. As with his project of a 'round
robin' at the beginning of the session and his speeches in Lancashire in
1862, it was part of a campaign to drum up extra-cabinet support. But the
Committee lacked the technical expertise to challenge the War Office and
the Admiralty convincingly; and all disputes ultimately had to be settled
in cabinet. More importantly, Gladstone was too intent on preserving his
executive prerogatives intact to give the Committee any prospective
voice in policy or expenditure. He restricted its terms of reference to
considering taxation retrospectively. He wanted no new Roebuck Committees. The price of effective parliamentary support would be to cede a
voice in expenditure policy as well as taxation in itself: that price
Gladstone was unwilling to pay.

On July 25 Gladstone recorded: 'St. James: our marriage day'; 'It was
not as it should be!' Morale was not stiffened by an unpleasant 'tirade'
from the hand of Lord Robert Cecil in the new *Quarterly*, accusing
Gladstone of playing Bright's game and of helping to destroy the limited
parliamentary franchise and the House of Lords, the only barriers
holding off the 'uncurbed dominion of the multitude'. (Gallingly close to
the bone was Cecil's gibe: 'What object Mr. Gladstone may be *consciously*
pursuing we do not, of course, venture to decide. No psychologist that
ever existed could solve such a problem.')[4] Perhaps watching 'that

1 D, vi, 195.   2 G & P, 195.
3 G to CG, July 20, 1861. GGP, 28/6.
4 QR, cx, July 1861, 'Democracy on its Trial', 285–286.

prodigy Blondin' walk at dizzy heights along ropes set up at the Crystal Palace gave Gladstone some compensating inspiration. There was dismaying news from Oxford of moves to make it possible for non-resident electors (among whom it was to be assumed that Gladstone would only have minority support) to register their votes without the necessity of travelling to Oxford. Gladstone confessed to Heathcote that he remained 'still in the maze as to the reasons which have induced you and the Committee to establish this extraordinary scheme of proxies in lieu of voting papers'.[1] But the mood of defeat was more appropriately matched by the spectacle of the mortally stricken Herbert's sinking to his grave. At the end of July Gladstone watched from Mary Stanley's house in Grosvenor Crescent Herbert's return from a fruitless quest for health abroad to Belgrave Square. 'Alas it was a sore sight.' On August 1: 'Sad & sadder accounts came from Wilton.' Herbert (a year younger than Gladstone) died on August 2. Gladstone reported from Wilton to Graham, himself too ill to attend the funeral, of what he had gleaned of the 'closing scene' ('such not only as we could have desired, but as angels might delight to look upon').[2] The funeral, 'alike sad & soothing', marked along with Aberdeen's passing at the end of 1860 a crucial snapping of Peelite drag anchors. It also marked the removal of a man widely held to be the most likely successor to Palmerston as Liberal leader. Stanley recorded on July 14 Granville's having hinted to Derby that 'an arrangement to that effect had been made!'[3]

[11]

After an audience at Osborne on August 5 when the Queen spoke 'with much interest about Herbert' Gladstone drove over to the Priory to see Helen. There he found Cardinal Wiseman and Dr. Vaughan, in whose interesting conversational company he returned to London. 'I travelled in a coupee with Card. Wiseman & his Chaplain!' he told Catherine. 'Card. W. is a man of great ability but his appearance is repulsive, almost loathsome – yet he has mind, eloquence, & imagination. Helen was perfectly lucid & natural.'[4] Herbert's passing exposed Gladstone to the attentions of the formidable and tenacious Miss Florence Nightingale, who had tried to manipulate Herbert for her projects of war office reform and now hoped to exploit Gladstone's old Peelite friendship for the same purpose. With 'a consummate piece of Gladstonian filigreed evasion',

1 G to Heathcote, July 10, 1861. GP, 44531, 183.
2 Parker, *Graham*, ii, 415.   3 DDCP, 174.
4 G to CG, August 7, 1861. GGP, 28/6.

'cautious, cold, complimentary, yet eloquent' he gingerly fended her off ('I see at once that the matter is too high for me to handle . . . I am in truth ignorant of military administration. . .').[1] As against this species of problem female 'Mrs. Dale' remained both a comfort and a distraction 'in whom my interest does not flag'.[2] As his farewell to the London season he visited Cremorne Gardens, the notorious Chelsea haunt of pleasure, where he admired the acrobat Léotard and 'afterwards explored the gardens & saw the manners: a very mixed company. Various M.P.s and Diplomatists'. From Cliveden he sent a bulletin to Catherine: 'I am scandalously strong and well. This is the Duchess's birthday.'[3] Before departing for Hawarden he took the opportunity of the vacancy in the see of Gloucester and Bristol to recommend Claughton again to Palmerston's remembrance. At Hawarden he found 'all well in this happy home'; and had time to give thought to moving the nation's collection of Turner's pictures to the projected new National Gallery. If this were not done, he advised Palmerston, 'we shall have a new source of broil.'[4] Then the Gladstones set off for a month at well-beloved Penmaenmawr.

The usual diversions of the resort that season were enlivened by 'table-turning'; at which Gladstone recorded that the 'table turned again at night, about 2 f. or 2f. 2 in diameter'. This occult occurrence 'for the first time rent my views'.[5] Perhaps an unoccult occurrence of more moment was an excursion to Liverpool to vote in the election to fill the new third seat for South Lancashire. The Liberal candidate was defeated 8,898 to 9,714; 'the losing side', as Gladstone had particular cause to remark, 'in a very significant election'.[6] Back in Penmaenmawr he ruminated on this significance through his many 'luxurious' bathes, his tours with Dean Liddell of Christ Church to Llandudno and Orme'sHead, his paraphrastic translation of Aristotle, his coaching Willy for the coming examinations, his 'gay days' with the Grosvenors and Lord Clarence Paget's party to Penrhyn Castle and his readings of *Framley Parsonage* and 'that singular & for the masses dangerous book Jack Sheppard' (Ainsworth's novel of a work-house boy who turned to highway robbery). He got bad news from Palmerston about Gloucester and Bristol: it was to go to Thomson, Provost of Queen's; though to soften the blow Palmerston graciously invited Gladstone to be the channel of communication to Thomson. (Poor Claughton had to wait for Rochester in 1867.) This event provoked an exchange of uneasy banter between the two statesmen from their respective seaside resorts. 'I hope,' Gladstone wrote to Palmerston, 'you are enjoying the sea breezes at Walmer: perhaps amusing yourself with

1 Smith, *Florence Nightingale*, 105. By 1869, Miss Nightingale condemned Gladstone as 'the most unsanitary brute that ever was.' (*Ib.*, 106).
2 D, vi, 51.   3 G to CG, August 21, 1861. GGP, 28/6.
4 G & P, 188.   5 D, vi, 59, 60.   6 *Ib.*, 55.

the inquiry how the old Britons should have prevented Caesar from landing there or hard by as I believe he did.' Palmerston's retort was that there 'would be no harm in its being shewn that the Chancellor of the Exchequer is not the *most* hard hearted of Men'.[1]

Penmaenmawr for 1861 ended with the twenty-seventh bathe and a visit to Llanllechydd Church in the Afon valley 'where the Welsh singing was noble & warming in the highest degree'; and a Welsh concert in the Hall was 'a real treat'. Back at Hawarden on September 17 Lacaita paid a 'Bibliographical visit to the Temple of Peace; and some good things were discovered'. Some bad things were also discovered: Arthur Gordon, due to leave for the governorship of New Brunswick, turned up and 'to our great surprise, made known to C. his desire to marry Agnes. I am sorry: for I do not think it will, and I doubt whether it ought.' Agnes, fortunately, was eager to co-operate in sparing her father the prospect of Gordon as his son-in-law.[2] Gladstone was happier when Dean Liddell joined the party and he could indulge himself in hazarding 'some suggestions' for the Greek-English lexicon and in anxious consultation on *Essays and Reviews*, Professor Jowett, the Athanasian Creed, '& the like subjects'. He also, very practically, took the opportunity to get the Dean to take 'dear Stephy's name' for Christ Church for October 1862. He slipped once more across to Liverpool to inaugurate the Hall of Science at St. George's Hall (this was his charlatan's performance on the promotion of science). After inspecting Robertson's 'farming operations' Gladstone saw a 'Mr. Holt, from New Orleans'. Back at Hawarden he consulted Phillimore on the question increasingly occupying his mind of the government's offering its good offices to the parties in the American Civil War.[3] The Battle of Bull Run in July 1861 seemed to indicate beyond reasonable doubt that the Confederacy could not be coerced back into the Union.

There was an interlude in London of cabinets, sittings for Watts, coping with Palmerston's demands that something be done to quell 'Declamation' in the Commons on the delicate topic of that 'sort of Alms Houses', royal 'grace and favour' residences, and examining with Professor Richard Owen the grossly overcrowded natural history departments at the British Museum. Gladstone found Palmerston looking 'extremely well', in 'excellent spirits', pressing the Gladstones 'very kindly' for a Broadlands visit. 'Altogether he is in the highest form.' However, Broadlands did not seem likely, as it looked as if the Prime Minister would be moving up to London 'bag & baggage for a little season in Novr'.[4] Gladstone used Stafford House largely as his domestic base (Catherine remained at Hawarden and Rhyl). On returning to Hawarden news of

1 G & P, 190, 192.   2 D, vi, 64.
3 *Ib.*, 65.   4 G to CG, October 17, 19, 1861. GGP, 28/6.

Graham's death at Netherby on October 25 dealt 'a most heavy blow'. On the 26th Gladstone was 'busy in reading many of Manning's old letters: an evening among the Tombs!' (Presumably this was by way of fulfilling the undertaking to exchange correspondence.) The way back to London for serious preparations for the new session was rather ducally magnificent. First Chatsworth (where Bishop Wilberforce was of the party) where Gladstone admired the 'noble Tropical conservatory' and enjoyed a 'sense of general magnificence' exceeding all particulars. The party walked over to admire Haddon Hall. From Chatsworth Gladstone was gratified to accept, though 'not without an emotion of pain', the Prince Consort's invitation to fill Graham's place as an Elder Brother of Trinity House. It was appropriate in such a setting that Gladstone should have been pursued by Palmerston's vigilance to defend landed incomes from 'capricious assertions' by insolent taxation commissioners. On the way to Blenheim Gladstone paused at Oxford, interspersed with London cabinets, to lunch in Willy's rooms, to attend the opening of the Radcliffe Camera as part of the Bodleian ('spoke *nolens volens*'), to inspect Scott's new chapel at Exeter, and to speak at the Sheldonian in favour of the Woodard Schools project to provide cheap and wholesome Anglican education for the middle classes. After being 'most kindly received' by the Marlboroughs at Blenheim ('noble park', 'vast treasures', 'majestic place') to Windsor, where the Castle was buzzing with the news of the arrest by the United States authorities of the Confederate agents Mason and Slidell on the British ship *Trent*. 'The Queen & Prince spoke much of the American news: & in the Anti-Northern sense.'[1]

On November 29 the Cabinet considered the question; and deputed Gladstone to report back to Windsor their decision that 'reparation for the seizure of Messrs. Mason and Slidell ought to be asked from the Government of the United States and that Lord Russell is to prepare a dispatch, on which the Cabinet will deliberate to-morrow, for submission to Your Majesty'.[2] Gladstone returned to Windsor later that afternoon '& reported to Q. & Prince' the further information that Russell had seen Adams, the American minister, who was 'without information and without instructions on the subject'. Gladstone shuttled back to London for the cabinet on the 30th which 'softened & abridged' Russell's draft. Later this draft was further softened at Windsor by Prince Albert, who by now appeared to be mysteriously ailing. Gladstone occupied himself with porcelain-purchasing, British Museum affairs and the question of a public memorial to Herbert before finally returning to Hawarden early in December. There he took a strong line against Canadian requests for financial aid ('she has plenty of wealth and plenty of intelligence; is she to right herself, as she may with ease, by honesty and thrift, or is she to put

1 D, vi, 76.   2 Q & G, i, 123.

her hand into the purse of England?'). On December 13 the Gladstones became 'seriously alarmed' at the news about Prince Albert, who indeed died that night; and his emending of the Cabinet's emending of Russell's original draft dispatch was his last official act. At Hawarden on the 15th the 'sad news came in the middle of the day. God help the Queen!' It was sad particularly for Gladstone since 1861 had been a time of ripening rapport in his intercourse with the Prince. On December 23 he attended the 'very solemn scene' of the funeral in St. George's Chapel at Windsor. He returned to Hawarden for Christmas, when the children 'made their morning song as usual', and joined the 'great musical Supping Festival at the Rectory' on Boxing Day. He found working on his 'Trochaic Version of Homer' 'fascinating, though not easy & difficult to leave. It threatens to become a dissipation & probably the tie must be snapped.' His birthday self-adjuration recorded that the 'strongest, though not the worst, of all in me is a rebellion (I know not what else to call it) against growing old'.[1]

[12]

1862 opened with Pope's *Rape of the Lock*: 'a wonderful work of fancy'. An even more wonderful work of fancy, thought Gladstone, was the Report of the Secretary of the Treasury of the United States. 'Fitter for a swindler than a Minister,' he told Russell; and surely meant to drive the Americans 'by financial terror into abandonment of the war'. His expenditure for the year June 1861–62 was to be £109 million; his *revenue in hand is seven millions!!*' This kind of consideration bore heavily on Gladstone's general appreciation of the situation in the war between the Union and the Confederacy. After celebrating Catherine's birthday ('How much might I say of her as a hero-woman') Gladstone went to Edinburgh for the University Court. He attended the Symposium Academicum which put him greatly in awe of Scottish professorial conviviality ('Speaking & songs. The free unbending of eminent & laborious men on a rare occasion is full of interest').[2] He exhibited something of his own brand of laboriousness by working on his Homer translation 'even in the Crewe waiting room at midnight'.[3] Otherwise these pre-sessional days saw Gladstone frequenting Cliveden, where there was debate on America and Tennyson's dedication of the forthcoming *Idylls* to 'Albert the Good': 'noble lines which in one point I ventured to remark upon'. As a former Mistress of the Robes Duchess Harriet (recently widowed herself) was an expert on the royal family: she 'read & told me much of the deepest

1 D, vi, 86.　　2 *Ib.*, 89.　　3 *Ib.*, 88.

interest about the Queen'. He drove with the Duchess to Frogmore '& discussed the Mausoleum' being planned by the Queen for the late Prince. Indeed the problem of public expenditure for monuments and memorials to the Prince was becoming a vexing question. Palmerston held that 'mourning Expenses' ought to be defrayed from the Civil List; and was not at all inclined to co-operate with the Queen's desire that Wolsey's chapel should be redecorated as a mark of Windsor's grief. Meanwhile Gladstone's trochaic dissipations with Homer continued unabated ('threatens to become a snare'). He was reduced to 'inhibiting' himself by restricting indulgence except after dinner ('This will pretty well starve it').[1] Even so, he got in '2 hours, or 3, of Homeric translation' after dining with the Phillimores on January 23.

Serious matters intruded on January 30 with a 'heavy blow in the announcement of increased Military Estimates' from Cornewall Lewis, which gave Gladstone 'a disturbed evening'. The item was for an extra £1,080,000. Gladstone worked on the 'formidable subject of the Estimates & made known to the Cabinet my difficulties'. He sent to Palmerston a general sketch of prospects for 1862–63: the long and short of which was near a million deficit. On February 1 he tried a little financial terrorism on his own account and threatened the Cabinet with an increase in the income tax. 'It went well: the tenth penny proved to be a strong physic.' £750,000 of reductions were ordered. The estimates and the Queen's Speech were settled on February 3. Gladstone felt himself at last in a position to initiate a modest counter-attack. 'Wrote Mem. on possible Reductions &c. to dispense with Income Tax. The whole question I think is can we be satisfied (I think we ought & will) with 21 millions for Army & Navy instead of 27?'[2] But what emerged most tellingly in the 1862 session was the priority given by Gladstone to executive control of prospective financial policy. Lord Robert Montagu proposed to move on March 11 for a 'Committee of the House to revise the Annual Estimates'. Gladstone reacted unpropitiously: 'The House would be slow to admit the principle of delegating to the Committee its annual duty of Inquiry, in Committee of Supply, into the proposed expenditure of the Government.' Such a committee 'might in time arrogate to itself the functions of the Executive Government and relieve it of the proper responsibility'. As to a committee to revise accounts of past expenditure, that point 'has been conceded already; the Committee of Accounts appointed in the past session was exactly in the spirit of Lord R. Montagu's proposed resolution. He is just a year too late in his suggestion.' And as to the question of extending and changing the duties and powers of the Board of Audit with a view to making it responsible to parliament alone, Gladstone's tone of severe executive *hauteur* was not less decisive than in February 1855: 'It can

1 *Ib.*, 92.   2 *Ib.*, 97.

scarcely be seriously intended by Lord Robt. Montagu that such executive functions, which can only be properly exercised by a Department fully cognisant of facts and Official precedents, should be transferred to a Committee of the House of Commons.'[1]

A sad tribulation broke in upon Gladstone at this time when his brother John Neilson's wife died after a sudden illness. At Bowden for the funeral on February 19 Gladstone observed John bearing his grief 'wh was piercing, as a man & as a Christian should'. John indeed never recovered from the shock. At Bowden were all four brothers and Helen; 'I think not assembled since my Father's death,' as William noted. He observed to John that it was the anniversary of dear Anne's death.

Death was the prevailing theme. Gladstone arrived at Cliveden again on March 16 to be coached by Duchess Harriet 'resp my coming visit to Windsor which troubles my spirit'. In trepidation at having to confront the widowed Queen he sought also the advice of the Duke of Argyll. 'I am ill fitted for these things: they want a better naturel.' On the evening of the 19th he sat in the small room in the Castle where the Prince used to sit 'feeling an uneasiness very different from any feeling with which I had ever before anticipated her approach'. When she entered 'with her usual simple dignity' Gladstone bowed and fell on his knee to kiss her hand. 'She took mine, held it for two or three moments and pressed it. She told me much by that slight action.' Their talk of public affairs was largely artificial and desultory. Gladstone spoke of social distress in Lancashire consequent on the cotton famine caused by the American war and stressed the 'admirable patience and comprehension' with which it was borne. The Queen spoke of her affliction 'as the heir of our common flesh and blood', dilating on the Prince's 'remarkable combination of gifts, naming his personal beauty among them'. (Gladstone did not record her saying anything in the way which struck Derby as 'odd' of imputing a kind of inertia or remissness on the part of the Prince in facing serious illness – 'Some people rally much better from illness than others: it is all pluck.')[2] She impressed Gladstone with the 'firm texture and elasticity of her mind, and her marked dignity and strength of character'. He invoked God's wise purpose which 'as cannot be doubted has appointed you to an eminence in the greatness of your affliction as remarkable as in your station and your previous happiness'. The Queen 'either said, or assented to when said, that this great affliction was sent to her for good'. Gladstone later was oppressed with a sense of *esprit d'escalier*: 'I might have gone a little further in the language of hope and was afterwards sorry that I did not.' He was gratified and relieved to be assured by Lady Augusta Bruce that the audience was 'agreeable' to the Queen. Gerald

1 GP, 44594, 123–24 (draft not in G's hand).
2 DDCP, 188.

Wellesley, the Dean of Windsor, confided that 'of all her ministers she seemed to me to think that you had most entered into her sorrows'.[1]

[13]

The Cabinet considered Gladstone's budget proposals on March 29. 'All smooth there.' The revenue was suffering from diminished consuming power during the previous quarter, but the deficit was caused 'entirely by supplemental estimates'. As Gladstone went off to join Catherine with the Laboucheres at Stoke he was buoyed up by a sense that the pressures were easing. In the Commons on the 31st he could note happily that 'Fortifications got their first blow'. The French panic had subsided. He delivered his financial statement on April 3 'to a most kindly House'. He caused a *sensation* – 'a general buzz I have heard around me' – by not budgeting for a surplus. He kept the income tax at 9d and offered no remissions. He explained the cause of the depressed revenue 'in the single word "America"'. He counted his first achievement as 'Minister of Finance' as having halted the growth of public expenditure; and pointed to what might otherwise have been done had not the demands of war in China and New Zealand over the past three years swallowed some £8.6 millions. This was Gladstone's most low-key budget since 1854; there were no celebrations of 1853.[2] After the alarms and excursions of 1860 and 1861 something of an equilibrium had been attained in cabinet. The Conservative opposition had in January (through Malmesbury) renewed the compact of the two previous years with Palmerston to sustain the ministry in the event of serious conflict with Gladstone; but there was no hint of any likelihood in 1862 of its being invoked. Rather, the Conservatives were starting to shift towards the advantages of pressing for a general reduction of expenditure. And for his part Gladstone ostentatiously went out of his way on April 11 in the debate in which he 'Spoke for Italy' to offer a glowing tribute to Palmerston's role as tutelary genius of a redeemed Italy: 'I do not hesitate to say that I believe a special part of the duty – I may say the mission – of the Administration of which my noble Friend is at the head, is to be the true expositor of the sense of the people of England on a question so vitally important'; through evil report and good report Palmerston 'sustained and supported the cause of Italy'; and there would not be a chapter of his life upon which Englishmen would dwell with greater satisfaction.[3]

Gladstone's sense at this time of a chapter in his own life upon which future Englishmen would dwell with most satisfaction was of getting an

1 PMP, iii, 238–44.   2 H, clxvi, 460–91.   3 *Ib.*, 933–50.

expenditure of £70 millions down to something near £60 millions; and he proceeded to Lancashire later in April to recommend this notion strongly at Stockport and Manchester, in a spirit of resuming the 'holy war' from which he had receded in 1861. Together with severe animadversions on unworthy panic and fantasies of invasion, Gladstone asked for a penitent public opinion to respond to the moral imperative of public economy. Ever since experiencing his first *frisson* at talking to the *'people'* in 1853 Gladstone held Manchester in a certain special esteem. Now it represented not only 'advanced intelligence' but the centre of 'distress and crisis' and the 'pressure of the cotton-famine'. Of his reception Gladstone noted that the 'kindness was extreme throughout: the visit very interesting & touching'. His address on April 23 at the Free Trade Hall, 'crowded with a very cordial auditory' of the Association of Lancashire and Cheshire Mechanics' Institutes, was distinguished not for political polemic but for evidences of an important new stage in his view of the development of a popular dimension of 'advanced intelligence'. In his audience with the Queen in the previous month Gladstone laid stress on his sense of the degree of the 'real political and social progress' of 'the people' as being measured not only in 'admirable patience and comprehension' but also in the 'greatly increased disposition they evinced, as compared even with the last period of pressure in 1857, to make use in their enforced leisure of the means of mental improvement'.[1] The Free Trade Hall audience precisely represented, for Gladstone, that popular, self-improving constituency. Already his attitude to franchise extension evinced a distinct shift away from his bored view of it as an irrelevance in 1859 and his hostile view of it as an obstruction in 1860. Bishop Wilberforce was struck in conversation at Cliveden on March 18 by the extent to which Gladstone was now 'strong for' an increase of the franchise.[2] Unquestionably his traumatic experience of Palmerston's collusion with Derby over the paper duties crisis in 1860 had given the movement of his mind a decisive impulse. Rather in the sense in which Gladstone saw Austria as the maker of Italian unity, the House of Lords made Gladstone a 'democrat'.

But the nature of his 'democracy' would always remain highly idiosyncratic. There would be no fundamental change in his assumption that 'advanced intelligence' as popularly developed by 'patience', 'comprehension', and 'mental improvement' would be a matter of improved capacity to respond adequately and thus deferentially to initiatives deriving from 'insight' and credentials issued from on high. Thus when Gladstone informed the Mechanics of Lancashire and Cheshire that the nineteenth century was the 'age of humane and liberal laws, the age of extended franchises, the age of warmer loyalty and more firmly estab-

1 PMP, iii, 238. 2 *Wilberforce*, iii, 46.

lished order, the age of free trade, the age of steam and railways', it was entirely and logically in accordance with his predispositions towards the prerogatives of authority and discipline to stress, as far as 'mental improvement' was concerned, that 'so it is likewise ... the age of examinations'.[1]

The theme of 'warmer loyalty' Gladstone thought fit to attach, rather blatantly, to the Prince Consort's death. Perhaps, he suggested to the throng of mechanics, amid the 'pressure of the Cotton-famine',

> in the wise counsels of Providence it was decreed that the crushing sorrow which came down as sudden as the hurricane, scarcely yet four months ago, upon the august head of our Sovereign, should serve, among other uses, that of teaching and helping her subjects to bear up under the sense of affliction and desolation... In many a humble cottage, darkened by the calamity of the past winter, the mourning inhabitants may have checked their own impatience by reflecting that, in the ancient Palace of our kings, a Woman's heart lay bleeding...[2]

Possibly this appeal touched the mechanics; certainly it struck the right note with the Queen, who wished 'from the depth of a heart which bleeds *more & more* to tell Mr. Gladstone that his Speech touched & gratified her much'; for Gladstone so *'well described* the *love* that bounds and binds the poor, broken-hearted Queen to that adored & perfect Being who was & is her *All* – but without whom *life* is *utter darkness'*.[3] But already, in the background of these sentiments, lurked an issue which was increasingly to cast a shadow on Gladstone's relations with the Queen: his emphasis on the theme of 'bearing up' was not welcome. Her 'faithful Servants and kind friends must *not deceive* themselves by *thinking* that her *efforts* will carry her on'; 'the gt amount of work & responsibility wh weighs alone upon her is *telling very* VISIBLY upon her health & strength; she gets much weaker – her health worse & her nerves terribly shattered.'[4] Gladstone was unwise to respond with further variations on the theme that as the people had taken heart from the Queen, so the Queen must take heart from the people. 'Yet they cannot shut out hope concerning a sorrow which is full of humility and self-mistrust, and which itself does not shut out, but seems to quicken, the sense of duty and draws from the tender recollection of the past and from faith in the unseen fresh devotion to its performance.'[5] The idea of drawing 'fresh devotion' out of emotional devastation was a commonplace of Gladstone's spiritual equipment; he was a bad psychologist in supposing he could apply it usefully in the case of the Queen. There was no personal response; an acknowledgement, kindly enough but brief, from Princess Alice.

1 *Gleanings,* i, 1, 2, 20.   2 *Ib.,* 2.
3 Q & G, i, 123.   4 *Ib.*   5 *Ib.,* 125.

Unaware that he had started off on a potentially dangerous tack with the Widow of Windsor, Gladstone soon became only too clearly aware that the Prime Minister's susceptibilities were as touchy and volatile as ever. Cobden's pamphlet on *The Three Panics* (of 1848, 1853 and 1862) was the sensation of the hour (Gladstone read it at Hawarden on his return from Manchester). Gladstone's speeches looked suspiciously like a part of a concerted agitation. Palmerston rebuked Gladstone for seeming 'to make it a Reproach to the Nation at large that it has forced, as you say it has, on the Parliament and the Government the high amount of Expenditure which we have at present to provide for'. Now it seemed to Palmerston 'to be rather Proof of the Superior Sagacity of the Nation, than a subject for Reproach'. Both Gladstone and Cobden were wrong to speak of panic; it was rather a matter of the country having awakened from its lethargy. The government, parliament, and the nation had 'acted in harmonious Concert'. Proof: 160,000 volunteers. Have they and parliament and the nation been wrong, 'and have Bright and Cobden and yourself been right?' They had taken the 'juster view', for the French 'hate us as a nation from the Bottom of their Hearts, and would make any sacrifice to inflict a deep Humiliation upon England'. They could not forget or forgive Aboukir, Trafalgar, the Peninsula, Waterloo, and St. Helena. Palmerston regretted that Gladstone should 'invite an agitation' to force the government of which he was a member to 'retrace those steps taken' for the 'faithful Performance of which it is responsible to the Crown and to the Nation'. Gladstone should remember that a cabinet of fourteen or fifteen men must involve the yielding of opinions to the 'Decision of the Body' (the implication that Gladstone had already got a good bit of his own way was sufficiently clear). 'Pray forgive these Remarks,' concluded Palmerston, 'and take them in the friendly spirit in which they are given.'[1]

Palmerston's point was taken up in the Commons by Disraeli and Northcote, who asserted that Gladstone's summoning up the genius of the people was a very serious impeachment of the prerogatives of the Commons. Gladstone, fresh from walking 'in the woods & among the flowers' of Hawarden ('O ubi campos!'), took everything in his stride. He was busy with his usual press of avocations: there was the Mansion House Dinner at which he thanked for the Commons, the Curates Aid meeting at which he moved a resolution, the Hop Deputation, preparations for the new Great Exhibition (opened magnificently on May 1: Gladstone chairman of the pottery jury), the Royal Academy private view, above all dinner with Palgrave and Woolner 'to meet Tennyson. Heard his Enoch Arden & much else. Parted at 1½. O noctes.'[2] Gladstone's response to Palmerston was unapologetic. It was one thing, he pointed out, to accept loyally decisions already made; it was quite another matter

1 G & P, 205–09.   2 D, vi, 118.

to concern oneself with the 'state of public feeling and opinion' in relation to the question 'of what the Estimates and public charges are to be'. Gladstone's doctrine was that if a minister of finance conceived that 'public opinion requires in matters bearing upon his department, to be either stimulated or restrained', it was his 'right and duty' to 'improve as far as he can by any arguments couched in moderate and becoming language' the 'state of opinion and feeling which may at the time prevail among the public'. Further, his 'duty thus to raise the warning voice is much enhanced, if in the department of Finance . . . he sees in the actual state of things, a real public danger or a serious mischief'. 'In all good humour', Gladstone preferred 'not being classed with Mr. Bright or even Mr. Cobden', first because he did not 'know their opinions with any precision', and secondly because as far as he did know or could guess them, 'they seem to contemplate fundamental changes in taxation which I disapprove in principle, and believe also to be unattainable in practice: and reductions of establishment and expenditure for which I am not prepared to be responsible'. Gladstone's opinion remained that 'by the firm hand of a united Government our expenditure might be and ought to be gradually reduced by some millions'. He remained unrepentantly convinced that in the last few years the English people had displayed 'less than their usual high degree of political intelligence and self-possession'. He expressed himself glad as well as sorry that he held opinions 'widely apart' from Palmerston's as to the 'spirit and intentions' of the French.[1]

Well satisfied with this version of himself in the role of guide and teacher, Gladstone went driving on May 1 with Duchess Harriet, 'and read her the letters of the week. She was pleased.' He joined the Duchess the following day at Cliveden, where she had arranged that Tennyson would be the other guest. That night Tennyson read from *Pericles*. There were more readings from and conversation with the Laureate over that memorable weekend. Gladstone's conclusion on 'this most interesting visit' was that 'I really feel I have got nearer to this great simple man'. Tennyson, who possibly was disconcerted to find himself so exposed to Gladstone's attentions in such an underpopulated house party, had a somewhat different angle on it. He found Gladstone 'a very agreeable, and intellectual and most gentlemanly man. I read the "Fisherman"[2] with which he seemed to be greatly struck.' The difficulty was that Gladstone would go on about Homer and translating Homer and otherwise tread heavily on ground Tennyson regarded as his own. ('Very pleasant and very interesting he was, even when he discoursed on Homer, where most people think him a little hobby-horsical: let him be. His hobby-horse is of the intellect and with grace.')[3]

1 G & P, 210–214.   2 *Enoch Arden*.   3 Tollemache, 16.

Back at Carlton House Terrace ('Found C. awaiting me') Gladstone grappled again with Palmerston, who retorted that while Gladstone disclaimed 'political community with Bright and Cobden, and justly', he could not 'but be aware that owing to various incidental Circumstances many People at Home and abroad connect you unjustly with them, and this False Impression is certainly not advantageous'. Palmerston reinforced this sally on May 25 by forwarding to Gladstone a copy of a flysheet: 'You may not have seen how your Name is taken in vain by People with whom I conceive you do not sympathise.' The sheet called on taxpayers to read Mr. Cobden's new pamphlet on *The Three Panics* and to cease to suffer themselves to be 'Humbugged by PALMER-STONIANISM'; it further pointed out that the Chancellor of the Exchequer had appealed for them to help him in his struggle against the same evil; and drew the moral: 'REFORM THE HOUSE OF COMMONS, and do it thoroughly this time.'[1] Gladstone responded in a conciliatory tone, but insisted that 'from the distance of prospective reductions neither honour nor (almost) decency would allow me to recede'.[2]

In these circumstances it was a matter of some embarrassment to Gladstone (and doubtless of mixed feelings for Palmerston) when on May 9 three members of the 'economico-radical party', Baxter, Forster, and Stansfeld, appealed to Gladstone for support in moving a resolution for reducing expenditure. In the House on May 8 Gladstone defended his Manchester speeches against Northcote's criticisms, repeating in substance his doctrine as laid down in his letter to Palmerston of May 2.[3] ('My work was a very nervous one, before & during: between two fires.')[4] But now, truly between two fires and confronted by an economico-radical invitation to repeat his performance over the paper duties resolutions in 1860, Gladstone backed away hurriedly, and declined to look at their draft, as he assured Palmerston. However, he felt that, in the event of a debate, he would have to say something about finance; and indeed was inclined to propose resolutions to be adopted by the Cabinet. It was a welcome sign of the times, from Gladstone's point of view, that the Conservative opposition were now wavering on expenditure. In his letter to Palmerston which had given Duchess Harriet so much pleasure Gladstone had prophesied a time when the two main parties in the Commons would be competing for possession of the policy of retrenchment; and he was 'not without fear that the liberal party shall be the hindmost'. The Conservatives were coming to the same conclusion; and their general feeling, reported by Stanley, was for 'reduced estimates, but against any vote that might seem to censure ministers for the largeness of theirs'. It 'would not be decent to use the votes of the economico-radical

1 G & P, 214–16, 221. 2 *Ib.*, 216.
3 H, clxvi, 1386–90. 4 2, vi, 121.

party as a means of defeating Lord Palmerston in a party division'.[1] The rather clumsy tactic was eventually determined upon of putting an amendment to Palmerston's amendment to Stansfeld's resolution; in the same sense as Stansfeld, but so as to avoid voting with him.

Meanwhile, Gladstone persisted with his own notion of a resolution. After all, he was a Chancellor of the Exchequer without a surplus, an occasion of '*sensation*' and '*buzz*' all about him when he delivered his budget. 'In my opinion it justifies the H. of Commons in asking the Government formally, what it thinks of the Expenditure, and whether it considers that, apart from exigencies it may and ought to undergo some reduction.' Nor was Gladstone prepared to evade any resolution in this sense by means of a procedural device.[2] Presumably Gladstone regarded Palmerston's proposal to kill two birds thriftily with one stone by naming the projected new National Gallery on the Burlington House site after Prince Albert (and sticking his statue on the front), thus solving the conundrum of an Albert Memorial, as an inadequate response to the solemnity of the expenditure question. When on May 19 Gladstone lost his Museum Bill to remove the natural history departments to South Kensington he asked: 'Economy *up*: for the day?' So the wrangle went on. On May 29: 'A troubled morning, on a letter from Ld Palmerston', who wanted to accept Horsman's amendment that existing defence expenditure was necessary. Palmerston found 'decidedly objectionable' Gladstone's proposal to include the loan raised for the fortification works in his projected comparative statement as to expenditure. Gladstone was no less stiff: 'great mistakes' had been committed in the 'costly conversion' of wooden ships of the line ('I objected to this at the time'); it was not acceptable to 'affirm now that this was right'. Then Holy Communion at St. James's: 'From that peace to an animated Cabinet which ended thoroughly well thank God.'[3]

All this was alleviated only by an 'expedition with a party, luncheon & speech included, thro' the Metropolitan Railway: most interesting', on 24 May (he took care to have photographs of the event distributed to all his companions; 'I hope the time may be near when the Piccadilly and Kensington may be taken in hand')[4] and a retreat once more on the 31st to Cliveden ('a larger party than usual'). Then on June 3 the great debate on reducing expenditure. Spencer Walpole was to move the Conservative resolution. Palmerston announced that he would treat the division as a vote of confidence. Disraeli eagerly launched his assault; but Walpole, intimidated (or angling for Palmerston's favour and the Speakership), withdrew, leaving Disraeli at a loss. Stansfeld's motion was swamped in a 'scene as notable & a rout as complete' as any Gladstone could remember.

1 DDCP, 185.   2 G & P, 223–25.
3 D, vi, 125.   4 GP, 44533, 9.

Gladstone 'sat on velvet all the time.' True, Stansfeld's motion sank without trace; but it had caused the Conservatives, and therefore the Commons as a whole, to go into convulsions. By June 23 Gladstone could discern that 'the tide has turned' on the fortifications issue. 'Lord Palmerston is now the "strong swimmer in his agony".'[1]

[14]

As the session wound down there was time for an interlude at Bowden Park to cheer the pining John Neilson. 'We invaded him in force', all but Willy (deep in Classical Moderations examinations at Oxford) and Stephy. It was 'both touching & edifying to see John with his children round him, all so good & all in their dark garb, in his own seemly House of Prayer'. On June 7 Gladstone heard of Willy's '*second* class'. 'The news was chill; but it is easy to see it may be good.' When Willy, hapless subject of so much intensive coaching at Penmaenmawr, came over rather mopingly on the 10th Gladstone advised him 'strongly to go on' to the Honours Schools to read Law and History. Then, as John mourned unconsolably, came news of the death of Charles Canning, and yet another Peelite funeral ('What warning is in his death: what comfort in his noble memory'). More Peelite memories were raised when on June 25 Gladstone took Graham's place as an Elder Brother of Trinity House, along with the Duke of Argyll ('& as such took the Declaration not to injure the Established Church!'). 'Ld Palmerston played his part well: otherwise it was highly penal.' Quite different was the occasion when the foundation stone was laid (by Catherine) for the chapel at the House of Charity ('with deep interest for C.G.: & spoke at the meeting'). The trustees of the St. Barnabas House abandoned the old former workhouse in Rose Street and moved round the corner to more commodious and elegant eighteenth-century quarters at No. 1 Greek Street, Soho Square, recently vacated by the Metropolitan Board of Works. The new chapel, designed by Joseph Clarke in the early French Gothic manner, lay on the Rose Street frontage of the former stables of the Greek Street establishment.[2] Exalted by this gratifying occasion, Gladstone was spurred to a flurry of rescue expeditions (Summerhayes seems now to have been dormant). At Palmerston's most pressing instance ('sternly cast aside any other Engagement you may have for Saturday') the Gladstones gave 'a pompous little dinner' at Carlton House Terrace for the Khedive of

1 D, vi, 130 (the line is from Byron, *Don Juan*, Canto ii st. 53).
2 The House of St. Barnabas-in-Soho at 1 Greek Street and its chapel still continue the redemptive work of their founders. The former Rose Street is now Manette Street. See above, 172.

Egypt ('& was I think well dispatched').[1] Gladstone loyally attended Palmerston at Oxford on July 2 when a D.C.L. was conferred upon the Prime Minister, who was 'extremely well received'. Gladstone made a point of inspecting the new Burne-Jones windows in the cathedral.

Five days later Gladstone forwarded to Palmerston a memorandum advising that the time was coming for intervention by Europe to mediate in the American Civil War. Gladstone reflected a growing public sentiment. The strategic advantage of the Confederacy over the Union seemed decisive: the Union had to win the war; the Confederacy merely had to avoid being defeated. Nothing since Bull Run a year before gave any convincing evidence of either the capacity or the will of the North to overwhelm the South. Even John Bright for a time despairingly admitted to Cobden that the Union would have to submit to conceding some form of recognition to the Confederacy.[2] Much of the Union's natural support in Britain remained mute or lukewarm so long as Lincoln resisted the drastic recourse of emancipating the Negro slaves. Hostility in Europe to the 'democratic' North and Lincoln and to the potentially disturbing power of the Union joined conveniently with humanitarian sentiment. Lincoln's stubbornness in the face of an unresolvable stalemate seemed a kind of bloodthirsty obstinacy. Gladstone partook, more or less, of all these prejudices. Phillimore's son later asserted that a Burkean doctrine of the right of secession weighed in Gladstone's outlook; an early version indeed of 'home rule'.[3] To them in any case Gladstone added two particular considerations: he was appalled at what he regarded as the irresponsible recklessness of the Union's financial policy; and, even more, he was becoming extremely anxious about the building up of a possibly explosive situation in Lancashire. There were manifestations of unrest and protest among unemployed cotton operatives in Manchester in June and again in September 1862; the rigorous attitude of the Poor Law Guardians in Stockport and Preston gave rise to resentment and publicity. It was one of the many ironies of Gladstone's curious involvement in the American question that his initial propelling impulse derived mainly from special knowledge of and humanitarian concern with those centres of 'advanced intelligence' whose 'patience and comprehension' under painful burdens and deprivations he celebrated as one of the most hopeful signs of the age.

On July 18 Gladstone pressed Palmerston not to commit himself against a policy of mediation. In a parliamentary statement Palmerston accordingly reserved the government's freedom of action. 'I have had a pretty satisfactory conversation about military Expenditure,' he told Catherine, 'and Lord P. has come exactly to my wish about some early

1 D, vi, 131; *Diary of Lady Frederick Cavendish*, i, 140.
2 G. M. Trevelyan, *Life of John Bright*, (1913) 302.   3 Reid, 436–37.

representation of a friendly kind to America if we can get France & Russia to join.'[1] In between lunching with Tennyson ('who was as usual most interesting' – and who returned Gladstone's trochaic translation of the first book of the *Iliad*) and an expedition to Cremorne Gardens (where he gave a copy of *Out of the Depths* to 'a person'), Gladstone dined on July 30 at Lord Campbell's '& had a most interesting conversation with Mr. Hotze a Southern in office'.[2] Henry Hotze was a Confederate agent charged with funding journalistic propaganda and sympathy for the Southern cause. His talk with Gladstone was about the fixing of the most suitable border between the North and the South when Lincoln and the Union came to their senses. Gladstone sent a memorandum of this discussion to Palmerston very much in the sense that it would be (as indeed it would have been) expert and valuable information for a government contemplating mediation to have at its disposal. There was a cabinet debate on August 2 on whether 'to move or not to move' on the question of mediation. Gladstone, it happened, left the cabinet early, with 'rather a bad conscience', as he apologised to Argyll. But he was restless with London by that time. As a consequence of 'economico-radical' machinations on the Tyne, a triumphal reception was being arranged for him as a bigger and better version of Manchester in April. (He accepted on August 2 the Mayor of Newcastle's formal invitation to a public dinner, suggesting October 7 as the most convenient date.) More immediately, affairs at Hawarden called him: there was much to be done with the Estate Trust Accounts and the pits. Even so, Gladstone signalled to Argyll his considered opinion on the American case that it was 'vain, and wholly unsustained by precedent, to say nothing shall be done till both parties are desirous of it'; but that, however, 'we ought to avoid sole action', and join with the 'weight of impartial Europe'.[3]

Hawarden was shaping promisingly: well worth cutting a cabinet for. After an inspection at Mancot on August 8 Gladstone had the 'great pleasure of reporting to Stephen & afterwards to C. the satisfactory advance & the excellent prospects opened by the boring prospects there. They promise to put an end to all anxiety respecting the debts of his Estate & the future position of the family, if only tolerable prudence continues to be observed. A happy end I trust in God to a struggle of fifteen years duration, from the crash of 1847.'[4] Besides devoting himself to a copious commentary on Stafford Northcote's recent book on financial policy Gladstone displayed a healthy interest in South Lancashire political prospects. To the government Whip, Henry Brand, he wrote on August 9 enclosing a letter 'respecting the S. Lancashire registration', and telling

1 G to CG, July 29, 1862. GGP, 29/1.
2 D, vi, 138.
3 GP, 44532, 179.   4 D, vi, 141.

Brand that if he received 'any information relating to the subject I shall trust to your being kind enough to let me know'.[1]

The Gladstones (together with John Neilson) repaired to Penmawn-mawr in mid-August, and Gladstone 'bathed forthwith'. 'The Hall', their new quarters, 'is excellent for accommodation but too much shut in, & not the *pure* Penmaenmawr air for *purists* in the matter such as we are.' This was their fifth season in the little north Welsh resort since the first visit in 1855; and now they assumed the airs of veterans. The place was rather like a synod. Thomson, the new Bishop of Gloucester, the Dean of Bangor, the Bishop of St. Asaph, the Dean of Westminster were in evidence. The Dowager Duchess of Sutherland arrived. Amid picnics, bathing, dizzy walks ('such a poor head') Gladstone read in the *Globe* of the death of the Archbishop of Canterbury; and immediately wrote to Palmerston. Perhaps he was encouraged by the success of his application earlier that month on behalf of Phillimore's claims as Queen's Advocate; but in any case, as he pointed out to Palmerston, he represented 'a constituency which is in a position different from that of every other except one only, with respect to its deep, and immediate as well as deep, concern': which was a prelude to pushing hard for Longley, the then Archbishop of York.[2] Longley was indeed translated to Canterbury; which left York vacant. Wilberforce of Oxford was passionate to get it, and pressed Gladstone for his support. Wilberforce happened to be staying with Disraeli at Hughenden at the critical time; and his host 'never knew a man more agitated.'[3] Gladstone duly wrote to Palmerston urging Wilberforce's claim eloquently, though with reservations as to his abrasiveness ('those who think he meddles too much in London would gladly see him removed from it to a spot where he would no longer be within an hour of the Metropolis').[4] Possibly this was the occasion when Palmerston remarked to Shaftesbury, 'Well, Gladstone has never behaved to me as a colleague, in such a way as to demand from me any consideration.'[5] To Wilberforce's intense chagrin and humiliation, Thomson, his former subordinate and Bishop of Gloucester for barely a year, was preferred. Wilberforce hoped that Gladstone would insist; and even Disraeli supposed that had Gladstone threatened to resign as over the paper duties issue 'he must have gained his point'.

Possibly Gladstone did not think the point worth gaining at such a cost. His mind was on Lancashire, America, and the Tyne. As to America, the 'whole of the present proceedings', he told Argyll, were an 'exaggeration and caricature of such follies as we of the old World have unhappily from time to time committed'. Nor was the 'exhibition morally very creditable'.

1 GP, 44532, 185.   2 G & P, 231–32.
3 Swartz, *Disraeli's Reminiscences*, 111.
4 G & P, 238.   5 Hodder, *Shaftesbury*, iii, 187.

There was an 'astounding contrast between the extravagance with which they inflame and stretch the doctrines of allegiance in their own case, and the democratic principles of their government'. This contrast, moreover, became 'much uglier when we take into view the manner in which they have treated all other revolters except their own, where there has been the slightest chance of their achieving success'. There were, conceded Gladstone, difficulties about mediation; problems about taking the first step; 'but I cannot subscribe to the opinion of those who think that Europe is to stand silent without limit of time and witness these horrors and absurdities.'[1] Back at Hawarden from Penmaenmawr he set to examining the park 'with a view to the little plan for employing Lancashire men' over the winter; and later took a house party out 'marking out ground for walks &c' to be made by the unemployed. (He provided work for six men at twelve shillings per week.) In the Castle Catherine took in ten factory girls to be trained for service. Catherine was much involved also in plans to set up a soup kitchen in Blackburn, where there were riots after the sentencing of poachers: 'one fears the example may spread,' as Lucy Lyttelton noted.[2] It was a busy Hawarden autumn. Gladstone presided at the Agricultural Show dinner at Mold. It was a particular pleasure to receive Professor Richard Owen and talk about the British Museum. He found Owen 'delightful': a scientist and a Christian who could talk about Greek mythology '& on other subjects' – which perhaps included Owen's sharp hostility to Darwin (whose *Origin of Species* he had attacked in 1860 in the *Edinburgh Review*). They sampled the geology of the district, Gladstone showed off his 'choice trees', and Owen in return lectured on the nocturnal Madagascan 'Aye Aye'. Soon the Tyne tour had to be prepared for. Two Tyneside Liberal M.P.s, Thomas Headlam of Newcastle and William Hutt of Gateshead, were the prime movers of the scheme to devise a 'triumphant visit to the Tyne' as a tribute to Gladstone for his services to the cause of economy, peace, and social progress during the 'grave financial difficulties', as Gladstone later described it, 'which in 1860 and 1861 went near to breaking me down'. The 'blue sky' which came over him in 1862 was the sign for a grand celebratory demonstration.[3] It seemed to Palmerston and Russell by now (September 24) that the time was fast approaching when joint mediation with France and Russia might be proposed to the Americans. Palmerston noted that Gladstone was to have 'some great Dinner given you in the early part of next Month'; and he hoped that Gladstone would not tell the country to agitate against expenditure. 'Those topics suit best Cobden & Bright and their Followers.'[4] Gladstone dutifully looked away from expenditure

1 G to Argyll, August 29, 1862. GP, 44533, 14.
2 *Diary of Lady Frederick Cavendish*, i, 148–49.
3 PMP, i, 132–33.   4 G & P, 232–33.

towards America as one of the keynotes of his forthcoming speech.

Certainly Gladstone was ready enough to humour the Prime Minister. Indeed as he told Palmerston he was about to write asking advice about what he might most usefully say. Gladstone in fact eagerly sought to make use of his opportunity to put himself prominently forward in his 'guide and teacher' role. He was glad to learn that Palmerston and Russell were thinking of mediation to procure a 'cessation of the deadly struggle in America'. It was clear that the 'progress of the Confederate Arms' was such that if it continued for even a short time the Confederacy might fairly be authorised 'with something like justice to ask of us prompt recognition'. It was desirable not to be brought to that step without first having offered our good offices and 'made a friendly effort to induce the North to recede'. A second material point was that the population of Lancashire had borne their sufferings with a fortitude and patience 'exceeding all example, and almost all belief'. But if such resignation should even once give way to excitement, 'our position in the face of America, and our influence for good might be seriously affected'; and it might appear that we were interfering in our own interests rather than in the 'general interests of humanity and peace'. French policy in Mexico was an awkward problem (they were installing as emperor that Archduke Ferdinand Maximilian, balked of his Lombardo-Venetian kingdom); hence the necessity of having Russia as a party to establish the requisite 'moral authority'. Gladstone promised to give satisfaction at the Newcastle dinner, which, he explained deprecatingly, arose out of the French treaty, was harmless, and approved by Henry Brand.[1] Thus Lancashire, the Tyne, and America all tended to push Gladstone in a direction which was, incidentally, a bonus as far as relations with Palmerston were concerned, but which in any event represented crucially for him a compelling conjunction of humanity and peace on both sides of the Atlantic. 'The case of Lancashire is deplorable,' he wrote to Arthur Gordon; 'but even this is a trifle in the eye of humanity compared with the wholesale slaughter that is going on, and its thoroughly purposeless character, since it has long been (I think) clear enough that Secession is virtually an established fact, & that Jeff. Davis & his comrades have made a nation.'[2]

After seeing Stephy off to Oxford with admonitions about the care of money Gladstone departed with Catherine on October 4 for the tour. At Hutt's seat at Gilside near Gateshead on October 7 he 'Reflected further in what I should say about Lancashire & America: for both these subjects are critical.' Lincoln's Emancipation Decree had been published in *The Times* the previous day; which proclaimed freedom for all slaves in states which

1 *Ib.*, 233–36.
2 G to Gordon, September 22, 1862. GP, 44533, 25.

should not have returned to the Union by January 1. *The Times* considered that this form of blatant inducement was 'more contemptible than it is wicked'.[1] Gladstone was in perfect accord with that sentiment. It was seemingly an act of hopelessness and recklessness, quite devoid of anything in the way of moral grandeur: by offering such a bribe Lincoln in effect was making slavery the cement of the Union. In any case Gladstone was immune to what he called 'negrophilist' enthusiasm. After admiring Newcastle ('Grey St. I think our best modern street') he went at six 'to a crowded & enthusiastic dinner of nearly 500. I was obliged to make a long oration which was admirably borne.'

Gladstone said many things of rather startling import. His remarks on the French treaty and free trade were innocuous enough; but his handling of the Lancashire cotton famine exposed a degree of moral and emotional sensitivity and involvement which his purist economist admirers later deprecated as 'excessive and impolitic indignation'.[2] Gladstone spoke *à propos* of the administration of the Poor Law in Lancashire that it should be remembered that 'the right of these people is to a sufficiency of food for the purpose of sustaining not life only, but health'. Relief committees and private charities were all very well; but 'remember that that is the sacred right of the people – a lien constituted by law upon the property which is liable for the purpose of supporting them'; and Gladstone further hoped that any relief given would be entirely devoid of any hint of reproach or circumstances of humiliation 'on account of misfortunes, of which they are as innocent as children, but which they have borne like heroes'. This invocation of the duties of property had something of the accent of the old Toryism about it; and when Gladstone then got on to the delinquencies of certain mill-owners he spoke very much as a county magnate who had lately presided at the Mold agricultural dinner and who delighted in playing the benign feudal lord at Hawarden. He stigmatised men in the manufacturing class who in the name of the rights of property and mere profit and loss were so 'insensible to the solemn and sacred claims of their noble work-people' as to sell off their cotton stocks and shut down their works. Gladstone pointed to the public indignation and charges of 'moral guilt' that would be directed against 'some great landowner' who exploited the rights of property in the same manner. After this outburst Gladstone turned to the American question as an anti-climactic official matter of routine. He could not advocate mediation, for the Cabinet had not yet formally decided upon it. But he could usefully teach and guide public opinion by pointing out authoritatively the capital and signal fact which made mediation both logical and desirable. For the Americans he pleaded a neutral temper and an avoidance of any exultation at the patently obvious and inescapable fact that their Union was dismembered

1 *Times*, October 7, 1862, 8.   2 Reid, 435.

beyond all hope of repair. As he could not mention mediation, so he could not mention diplomatic recognition of the Confederacy. But, in terms of the doctrine he had asserted to Palmerston on May 2, here was a public opinion which needed to be stimulated in the right direction on a prospective issue. 'We may have our own opinions about slavery' – Gladstone's was that the Negroes would be better off dealing with their own masters than dealing with the Federal Government of the United States – 'we may be for or against the South; but there is no doubt that Jefferson Davis and other leaders of the South have made an army; they are making, it appears, a navy; and they have made what is more than either, they have made a nation (*Loud cheers*.)'[1]

Having dropped such an authoritative hint Gladstone would not have been surprised at manifestations of response. It happened that G.J. Holyoake, the secularist campaigner and a journalist at this time with the *Newcastle Chronicle*, was deputising for the reporter for the Electric Telegraph Company, and condensed Gladstone's remark: 'There could be no doubt that Jefferson Davis had made a nation of the South. (The announcement caused great sensation.)'[2] This he later described as 'too strong'. There was, rather, 'a general movement as of unexpectedness, and "surprise" would have been a more appropriate word; but it did not come to me at the moment, and there was no time to wait for it, and the "sensational" sentence was all over London before the speech was ended'. Holyoake noted that when Gladstone returned to the theme 'with qualifications' at Middlesbrough the following day the press took no notice of them. 'The "sensation" appended to the sentence had set political commentators on fire.'[3] Gladstone caused a 'sensation' at Newcastle because he seemed to be manipulating or preparing opinion for mediation or even recognition, not because he was implicitly pro-Southern. Opinion in Lancashire was predominantly pro-Southern;[4] and it was not less likely to be so in Tyneside. Offence was taken in pro-Northern circles. Bright concluded that Gladstone's mind was too unstable for him to lead a party or a nation successfully. 'He was born of a great slave-holding family,' was his verdict to Cobden, '& I suppose the taint is ineradicable.'[5] Gladstone himself later listed his words as a 'palpable error which was of a very grave description; and which illustrates vividly that incapacity of viewing subjects all round, in their extraneous as well as their internal properties and thereby of knowing when to be silent and when to speak'.[6] But at the time Gladstone was under no such burden of apprehension. He explained to Russell that

1 *Times*, October 9, 1862, 7.   2 *Ib.*, October 8, 1862, 7.
3 Holyoake, *Bygones Worth Remembering*, i, 292–93.
4 N. Longmate, *The Hungry Mills. The Story of the Lancashire Cotton Famine, 1861–5* (1978) ch. 19. M. Ellison, *Support for Secession. Lancashire and the American Civil War* (1972).
5 Robbins, *Bright*, 164.   6 PMP, i, 132 (1896).

'according to some of the newspapers, some words which I have used at Newcastle respecting America have a wider sense than I intended'.[1] Russell, for his part, though a little concerned at Gladstone's incautious latitude in using the word 'nation',[2] eagerly looked forward to leading a mediation, to being a 'second Canning' – all the more so, perhaps, because. of his embarrassment at having been responsible for not detaining ship no. 290 at Birkenhead dockyards from slipping away in July 1862 and transmuting itself into the devastating Confederate commerce raider, *Alabama*. *The Times* commented that 'Mr. Gladstone has . . . only made a statement considerably within the truth. . . . The greater the truth, the greater the libel.'[3] Palmerston waited for one more decisive battle as the signal to proceed with the French and the Russians. It was Gladstone's misfortune to be caught publicly out on a limb when that battle – Antietam, September 17, 1862 – proved eventually to be the beginning of the end of the Confederacy's fortunes.

That fact was by no means obvious even in October 1862. Gladstone's interpretation of Antietam was that it would act as a wholesome check on the tendencies of the over-confident Confederates to become 'intoxicated by success' and produce obstacles to peace. He reported to Hudson in Florence that even J.L. Motley, 'one of the most fanatical of the Northern party is now opening his eyes'.[4] Cobden himself countenanced the notion of mediation.[5] Lee would still be victorious at Fredericksburg and Chancellorsville. The irony that the doctrine of his role as public guide and teacher which he had used as a weapon against Palmerston would rebound against him was unsuspected by Gladstone as he proceeded to play his part in the great Tyneside theatre of politics, with Joseph Cowen, prospective M.P. for Newcastle, as impresario. To the Tynesiders Lancashire was remote and America in the dimmest distance. The man they had chosen to be their hero was at hand. After an address at Gateshead on October 8 the party 'embarked in the midst of a most striking scene which was prolonged & brightened as we went down the river at the head of the fleet of some 25 steamers amidst the roar of guns & with the banks lined or dotted above & below with great multitudes of people'. Holyoake recalled thousands of miners coming up from the pits of Durham and Northumberland, fired by promises that they 'would see a sight in England, which they might not soon see again – a Chancellor of the Exchequer who was known to have a conscience'. 'Great numbers' succeeded in shaking hands with Gladstone as he embarked on the *Harry Clasper* (named after a famous Tyne oarsman). Men swam before the vessel for considerable distances; twenty-two miles of river bank were

1 G to Russell, October 17, 1862. GP, 44292, 82.
2 Russell to G, October 20, 1862. *Ib.*, 84.   3 *Times*, October 9, 1862, 8.
4 G to Hudson, September 27, 1862. GP, 44533, 27.   5 DDCP, 191.

lined with people, women holding up their children to give them a glimpse of the great man. 'The expedition ended at six, & I had as many speeches as hours. Such a pomp I probably shall never again witness: circumstances have brought upon me what I do not in any way deserve.' Gladstone admired the 'daring and comprehensive' works transforming the Tyne: the Tyne docks, Wellington Quay, Wallsend, Jarrow, South and North Shields and Tynemouth. They went back to dine at Gilside; 'C. went through everything in a wonderful manner.' Catherine indeed was enchanted. She would ever after insist that this was the first occasion on which William was accorded anything like the recognition he deserved.

From Newcastle and Sunderland on October 9 the party progressed to Middlesbrough and then to Darlington, Mr. Henry Pease, M.P. for South Durham, travelling in attendance. 'Middlesbrough was as warm or if possible even warmer.' More steamboat processions and an 'incessant flood' of information. 'The labour however is too much: giddiness came over me for a moment while I spoke at Sunderland, and I had to take hold of the table.' Gladstone was 'most happy to lie down for 15 minutes at Mr. Vaughan's in Middlesbrough'. He and Catherine retired with Lord and Lady Zetland to their house at Upleatham near Guisborough (Zetland was Lord-Lieutenant of the Yorkshire North Riding). Exhausted, Gladstone recorded that it was 'vain to think of reading writing or much reflecting on such a day'. 'I ought to be thankful: still more ought I to be ashamed.'[1]

1 D, vi, 153.

CHAPTER VIII

'SOME BETTER GLEAMS OF LIGHT' 1862–1865

[1]

By October 15 the Gladstones were back at Hawarden. There was indeed 'much reflecting' to be done as to both Lancashire and Tyneside. Gladstone was studious to assure George Holyoake that 'the manifestations of feeling at Newcastle and elsewhere were as much beyond my anticipation as my desert'.[1] Nor was Gladstone in the least inclined to retractive caution about the disunited States. At York on October 11 he evoked Canning's name and authority with a variation on Canning's famous boast of 1826: 'We may say that we turn to a country of the Old World to redress and compensate the calamities and failure of the New. (Cheers).'[2] He wrote from his railway carriage to his old friend Tupper that he did not think he had 'much claim' to the reception he had experienced in the North; 'I have come into a harvest for the moment of public favour but others tilled the land and sowed the seed.' As for the Civil War in America: 'I have found in addressing various audiences in different parts of the country that the only difficulty is to carry their assent to what may be (I think justly) said in apology for the conduct of the North.'[3]

America was the question most immediately on his mind. Although he reassured Russell that his Newcastle declaration had not been taken to signify intention on the part of the government to act, Gladstone's own disposition in the direction of mediation was stronger than ever. 'On coming to town I found Lewis had circulated a Memorandum on the American question, *against* Lord R. and yesterday I wrote one in answer which absorbed my spare time.'[4] Against his old financial rival Gladstone extolled the beneficent power of the 'vast weight of authority and force' which would be exerted by a combination with France and Russia. He argued that one of the noblest distinctions of the nineteenth century had

1 G to Holyoake, October 20, 1862. GP., 44533, 36.
2 *Times*, October 13, 1862, 4.
3 G to Tupper, October 14, 1862. GP, 44533, 31.
4 G to CG, October 24, 1862. GGP, 29/1.

been a 'gradual and sensible growth of what might be rudely called an international opinion' analogous to public opinion. It was the 'moral force' of that international opinion which had destroyed the Treaty of Zurich of 1859; now it could be mobilised to bring the Washington régime to its senses as it had brought the Vienna régime. Further delay would make loss 'more probable than gain'. Public peace might well be compromised by the distress in Lancashire; as the people of England were being 'rapidly drawn into Southern sympathies' the more difficult would it be for the British government to appear to maintain a 'friendly and impartial aspect in any proceeding'. And as to the question of slavery: any mediation from which the South would ostensibly, 'though perhaps not really', be the greater gainer should involve 'every moral influence with a view to the mitigation, or, if possible, the removal, of slavery'; and the later mediation was left, and the more the South saw the result in terms of its 'own daring and tenacity', the less easy would this be to achieve.[1] In society Gladstone 'made no secret' of his views as to the need for separation between North and South. Stanley recorded his holding forth at a dinner at the Cowpers': 'He thought Virginia must be divided, and probably Tennessee likewise.'[2]

To remonstrators he turned a blandly unapologetic front. Duchess Harriet, indignant at Gladstone's sentiments on the 'purposelessness' of the war, was informed that 'if Mr. Lincoln's lawless proclamation[s] continue for much longer & the war with them, I am afraid that destruction, which may be but for the moment ... must become permanent and final'.[3] Many Dissenters were offended. To Newman Hall, his link with Dissent, Gladstone insisted that 'negro emancipation cannot be effected, in any sense favourable to black or white, by the bloody hand of war, especially of civil war'; and he lamented deeply 'the act of those who, not swept along like the Northern Americans by a natural & scarcely avoidable excitement, undertake from an impartial position to favour in the interests of the negro the prolongation of this dreadful conflict'.[4]

Fortunately for himself, Gladstone did not carry the Cabinet against Lewis's (and Argyll's) shrewdness and Palmerston's caution. Instead, as he confessed ruefully to Catherine as she went about her 'blessed work' among the distressed Lancashire cotton operatives, he was going to the Haymarket Theatre to 'see Ld Dundreary!!!', the comic character in the rage of the season, Tom Taylor's *Our American Cousin* ('quite admirable', 'laughed to split myself').[5] So captivated was he by Dundreary that

1 G & P, 239–47.   2 DDCP, 192.
3 G to Dss of Sutherland, November 17, 1862. GP, 44533, 45.
4 G to Newman Hall, February 2, 1863. *Ib.*, 87.
5 Bassett, 141.

Gladstone went off to the Strand Theatre to see its imitation version ('very clever').

Still, Lancashire was much, and increasingly, with Gladstone. Already 432,000 people, more than one in five of the population, were in receipt of relief; Cobden called for a national subscription of a million pounds. There was the delicate matter of handling Mrs. Tennyson's scheme, as forwarded by the Laureate, to mitigate the cotton famine. Gladstone regretfully pronounced it not feasible; and took the occasion to apologise to Tennyson that he had had no time lately to progress with his Homer translation.[1] The question of the feasibility of various modes of alleviation exercised the Cabinet. Gladstone resolutely resisted pressures for direct government intervention. 'A public grant in my opinion is not to be thought of. Indeed I can hardly conceive the time when more than a loan could be asked from the State on behalf of the vast property of Lancashire.' The government had already agreed to authorise poor law unions in 'Manufacturing Districts' to borrow from the Exchequer loans to the extent of £200 million.[2] He reassured the Dean of Christ Church that the Cabinet had concluded that 'without doubt' the 'means forthcoming for relief will be ample during the present winter without any resort to that worst of all forms of aid which we are agreed should only be called in when other & better sources are exhausted'. More than half a million had been raised so far from voluntary subscriptions, and the influx was increasing and, Gladstone believed, would increase. The poor law guardians began, 'in some places at least', on 'a most niggardly scale', which had justly shocked the country; but 'this is now amended, or is mending fast'. Already the authorities at Blackburn were planning a scale of 13s. 6d. per week for each family; and 'when we consider that this is much above the average income of the peasantry of the three kingdoms is it not plain that we should *think twice* before taxing that peasantry to raise it higher?'[3]

There was other business to attend to. There were approaches to be made to Mr. John Murray, the publisher ('my sister Miss Helen Gladstone ... has some thoughts of getting up a Child's Book on the Sayings & Doings of a rather wonderful Parrot in her possession').[4] Helen indeed was 'as kind & pleasant as anything you could conceive – in great indignation with her co-religionists – inquiring so curiously about Stephy, & whether he had made up his mind to be a clergyman'.[5] There were rescue cases to be placed with milliners. A beady eye needed to be kept on the Clarendon Commission on public schools. To Lyttelton, one of its

1 G to Tennyson, November 4, 1862. GP, 44533, 42–43.
2 G to Moffatt, November 24, 1862. *Ib.* 52.
3 G to Dean of Ch.Ch., November 21, 1862. *Ib.*, 49–50.
4 G to Murray, November 18, 1862. *Ib.*, 49.
5 G to CG, October 25, 1862. GGP, 29/1.

members, Gladstone confided that he was 'jealous of the absolute imposition either of mathematics or of French'. He put mathematics 'somewhere about the point where semi-ultramontanes put the Temporal Power: I do not believe them to be part of the indispensable discipline of a highly educated mind'. Lyttelton's view was merely 'the Cambridge view'. And as for French: it was more necessary for 'the *"man of the world"* than for the "educated man"'.[1] Generally Gladstone felt himself in fine fettle. He had been 'very gay', he informed Catherine, 'with little dinners, very little ones from two & three upwards: think of 4 in all with Panizzi – 3 Stafford House'.[2] He was less gay on finishing Delarive's *Life of Cavour* ('What a deathbed: what a void')[3]. There were indeed worrying features about the new Italy. It was 'woeful that a structure of moral and political corruption should operate and form from such a vantage ground'; even so, he assured Lacaita that his confidence in the Italian people and their political leaders 'increases from day to day'.[4] His confidence also increased about his own political prospects for the next session. He believed that members of the government were 'at last possessed with the belief that some retrenchment is wanted and that I shall get in the Great Estimates with far less trouble or even by spontaneous acknowledgement far more than in the former years it has cost a life and death struggle to obtain'.[5] 'Better times now!' he exulted after a cabinet committee on the Army estimates.[6]

There was also the question, again, of the Ionian Islands, and, linked with it, of the throne of Greece. Having deposed the Wittelsbach King Otto, the Greeks were casting about for a replacement, and interested powers were pressing forward suitable candidates. Palmerston and Russell, anxious to detach Greece from Russian tutelage, were ready to offer the Ionian Islands as a bribe. The Greeks, for their part, were ready to humour the British: the Queen's second son, the Duke of Edinburgh, could have had the Athenian throne; and Lord Stanley and even Gladstone himself were mentioned (Gladstone forwarded to Hawarden a copy of the *Daily News* with a letter recommending him insisting that he could ask only 'a bit more of Dundreary and beg a week to laugh over it before answering anything seriously'. Catherine reported that little Herbert was quite taken with the idea: she would be a queen and he a prince).[7] Gladstone noted on December 8: 'Resolution to surrender the Ionian Protectorate!' He wrote to Catherine from the cabinet: 'The discussion is going on and everybody but old Bethell[8] in favour!!!'[9] The profusion of exclamation marks betrayed Gladstone's embarrassment.

1 G to Lyttelton, October 20, 1862. GP, 44533, 25.
2 G to CG, November 26, 1862. GGP, 29/1.
3 D, vi, 163.   4 G to Lacaita, December 6, 1862. GP, 44533, 61.
5 Bassett, 142.   6 D, vi, 16r4.   7 Bassett, 141–42.
8 Lord Chancellor Westbury.   9 Bassett, 142.

What he should have recommended in 1859 consistently with his anti-'Crimean' policy of 1858 was now happening in spite of him. Talk of him for the throne only sharpened the sense of embarrassment. He was in the false position of enjoying a spurious reputation for political philhellenism stemming from misconceptions about his Homerology and from the fortunate non-publication of his report as High Commissioner in 1859. Gladstone played no part in the initiative of 1862. Cornewall Lewis was careful to stress to Stanley that 'it was the doing of Lords Russell and Palmerston'.[1] Gladstone indeed supported the proposal warmly (there were sensible economies to be made); but he had to admit to Panizzi: 'I am very glad that the plan of cession of the Ionian Islands has been started . . . But I have no particle of the credit . . . I never heard of its having been decided to propose it until the Cabinet was gathering to consider it . . . '[2] All that Morley could say, very lamely, was 'as Lord Palmerston changed, so did Mr. Gladstone change'.[3] Palmerston and Russell went so far, indeed, as to urge the Turks (unavailingly) to improve the shining hour by piling upon the Ossa of British bribery the Pelion of Thessaly and Epirus; a circumstance which Gladstone would in due course exploit for all it was worth – or, rather, for much more than it was worth. But for the present, as the Greeks obliged by electing the highly acceptable Prince George of Denmark (brother of the affianced Princess of Wales to be), Gladstone could only modestly deprecate his mythological reputation, enhanced by the camouflage of the warm glow of Homeric scholarship, as the original author of the cession.[4]

[2]

At Windsor Gladstone attended for audiences with the Queen and the Prince of Wales about the Prince's settlement on his impending marriage. 'Here I am,' he wrote to Catherine, 'with six candles blazing!' He was amazed at her supposing he would have 'pluck to ask the Prince of Wales! or the Queen!!! about photographs promised or not promised'.[5] The pleasurable edge of returning to Hawarden on December 11 was somewhat blunted by news of Willy's third class in the Law and History Schools. ('Both his virtues & his faculties excellent: it would be very wrong to complain if his energy is not quite on the same scale.')[6] The *Iliad*

1 DDCP, 193.
2 G to Panizzi, January 11, 1863. GP, 44533, 77.   3 Morley, i, 620.
4 For an example of the development of this mythology: Algernon West later described how Gladstone went to the Ionian Islands 'to inquire into their grievances; the result of his mission was the cession of the islands to Greece' (*Recollections*, i, 255).
5 Bassett, 143.   6 D, vi, 167.

translations were as absorbing as ever; and Gladstone felt himself 'positively chained down' by Thiers' *Histoire du Consulat et de L'Empire*. This was his excuse for dilatory correspondence, as he told Argyll; whom he was also glad to tell that President Lincoln's latest pronouncement on negro emancipation was better in tone. 'It gives more of body and form to the idea of relieving the poor blacks: and morally it tends in some degree to set quietly aside the mischievous Proclamation of September and to become a kind of substitute for the same.'[1] Lee's victory at Fredericksburg seemed in any case to make Lincoln's improved moral tone redundant: 'Surely this will end the madness.'[2] As Gladstone remarked to the Speaker of the Commons, 'The Americans, poor things, had evidently a large stock of insanity on hand, & have spent it like gentlemen, but it must be nearly run out.'[3]

More significant than Gladstone's misreading of the American situation was the reading by which he chose to interpret Lancashire and the Tyne. At the Saturday Evening Assembly of Working Men at Chester on December 27 Gladstone offered the first fruits of his reflecting on his recent experiences in the North. This took the form of a full-scale and mature mythology of the virtue of the Lancashire cotton operatives confronting the cotton famine, with particular reference to the display of qualities worthy of conferment of the parliamentary franchise:

> No murmuring against the dispensations of God; no complaining against man; no envious comparison of their case with the case of their employers; no discontent with the Government or with the Laws; a universal and unbroken reverence for public order; under a homely or even rough exterior, a true delicacy, a true loftiness of sentiment; an unwillingness to be burdensome, a willingness to suffer patiently, a willingness to turn to account in a more frequent and more crowded resort to divine worship, and to make an enforced leisure profitable, by going back to the discipline of boyhood, and gaining once more the first elements of forgotten knowledge: all these things present a noble picture, instructive to us all . . . A picture intended for us all to look upon, and to learn from; for if cotton has done this for the men of Lancashire, cotton is but the instrument in the hand of God, and He can find some other instrument with which to do it for us, when He sees that we need the lesson and can profit by it.[4]

This 'noble picture' was a retouched and heightened version of that development of the popular dimension of 'advanced intelligence' Glad-

---

1 G to Argyll, December 19, 1862. GP 44533, 64–66.   2 D, vi, 169.
3 G to Denison, January 6, 1863. GP 44533, 75.
4 *An Address delivered at the Saturday Evening Assembly of the Working Men of Chester, December 27, 1862*, 9.

stone had saluted in April 1862 in the form of the Association of Lancashire and Cheshire Mechanics' Institutes. It was a picture which – like any great, characteristic Victorian work of art – bore an obliquely distanced relation to the realities of life. Popular life in cotton-famine Lancashire was far from being characterised by such paragons of virtue as Gladstone depicted. The point was that Gladstone made of Lancashire a stage setting for a morality drama of his own devising. He was the impresario of a curious kind of political theatre as the counterpart to his own kind of personal political theatre first made dramatically manifest in the budget issues of 1852–53. The mythology was not as yet quite in its fully matured form. Gladstone would first have to confess the fault of his own pro-Southern sympathies (largely shared by the Lancashire operatives) before he could, in 1866, add to the tale of their virtue the crowning myth that they 'knew that the source of their distress lay in the war yet they never uttered or entertained the wish that any effort should be made to put an end to it, as they held it to be a war for justice and for freedom'.[1] If providential purpose guided and sustained the role of guide and teacher, it implied equally the eventual reciprocation of the guided and the taught. For Gladstone the hand of God now touched on the franchise question.

Divine accreditation was but the logical consummation of the unfolding providential purposes and consequences which for Gladstone had always been at the heart of the commercial and financial reform programmes of his new vocation. Peel's budgets, free trade, his own great series of budgets now almost at their point of fulfilment, had, as he saw it, nurtured and emancipated a new generation, appreciative of the beneficence of its immediate political heritage, correspondingly responsive to the claims of that heritage for loyalty and deference. Gladstone could see himself on the verge of presiding over a grand synthesis of cause and effect. On December 31 he gave thanks for the 'ending well of what has been so good a year'. 'We sat, & heard the bells chime in 1863: may its course be blessed to us all.'

The new year indeed started promisingly: 'Made my *first* sketch of a budget for 1863–4. The figures, as far as I can judge, look very well.' He calculated a revenue of £71 millions, charges of £67 millions. He could envisage balanced remissions of direct income tax and indirect tax and sugar duties and still retain a surplus of half a million.[2] As he looked out on the wintry Hawarden park land, Gladstone wrote to Palmerston 'outlines which I see before me dimly moving in the mist'. Gladstone discerned the shape of an income tax reduced to 7d, which would not only be an important remission 'but a considerable political measure' as well. So would be getting the sugar duty back 'to the *peace* point.' To do this, of course, a 'firm hand' would need to be applied to the estimates,

1 Longmate, *Hungry Mills*, 244.   2 D, vi, 171.

civil and Irish as well as those of the services.[1] On January 2, with refreshing intervals of reading Carlyle's *Oliver Cromwell's Letters and Speeches* (1846), Gladstone found himself 'greatly pleased with the look of the figures – so much so that it rather interfered with my sleep!'[2]

Other shapes were discernible moving portentously in the January mists. The Chester speech had been noted by interested parties. Not the least of them was George Wilson, Manchester cotton magnate, one of Gladstone's requisitioners for the South Lancashire seat in July 1861, soon (1864) to be President of the National Reform Union and in 1865 one of Gladstone's principal sponsors in South Lancashire. Writing with 'great frankness', Gladstone explained to Wilson that the purpose of his reference 'on two occasions in conjunction with the Lancashire Distress to the question of the franchise' had been 'not in any manner to force forward the question, but to endeavour to impress the idea' that it was 'a grave and serious one', and that 'it must at some time be entertained', that it was 'desirable to dispose of it', and that the 'labouring classes' were 'worthy of a more generous treatment than was accorded to them in the House of Commons on the introduction of the Bill of 1860'. Gladstone owned that it was his opinion 'that the public mind in general' wanted 'a good deal of this preliminary manipulation' before any further parliamentary effort was made. His chief 'object of anxiety as to any effort about the franchise' was 'not that it should be early but that it should be creditable and successful: that it should not be such as those which have preceded'. But he freely added that provided it could realise the conditions he had described, then the earlier it was, the better, 'for the honour of all parties & for the public good'. Lord Russell, Gladstone carefully emphasised, would be his leader in that 'desire & intention'.[3]

This view of his role as a manipulator of the public mind was a highly characteristic aspect of Gladstone's sense of himself as accredited political guide and teacher. His financial vocation as defined in the 1850s was now substantially fulfilled; a new vocation was taking shape. Horizons were still enlarging and skies as shifting as ever. Meanwhile, as the subterranean pressures made their way, Gladstone coped with the surface phenomena. He celebrated the end of the Hawarden retreat by reciting his latest *Iliad* translations to Catherine. He softened the return to London by recourse to Drury Lane, where he 'laughed immoderately' once more at Lord Dundreary. Reading Kinglake's *Invasion of the Crimea*, however, was no laughing matter: not at all agreeable or just to the Aberdeen government ('I am afraid that Newcastle blabbed on what took place and this blabbing was much tinged with egoism').[4] There were more frowns at worrying news from Bowden Park, where the pining John Neilson

1 G & P, 248–50.   2 Bassett, 143.   3 G to Wilson, January 5, 1863. GP, 44533, 75.
4 Bassett, 144. Acton, March 5, 1863: 'A long and charming talk with Gladstone today. We have materials for demolishing Kinglake.' Altholz, *Correspondence*, iii (1975), 91.

seemed to be sinking. The family gathered early in February; John died on the 6th. This was the first death of a sibling since Anne's in 1829. The shock had a unifying effect. Robertson in particular was 'all kindness'. There was much concern with property arrangements, with John's only son, John Evelyn ('Jack'),[1] the cause of much avuncular concern. Another tie had snapped, as Gladstone broodingly noted in the railway carriage on his way back to London.

Even amid the funereal gloom of Bowden Gladstone found Palmerston in pursuit. There was the problem of the Prince of Wales's marriage settlement: Palmerston was willing for £110,000, but Gladstone insisted that when he saw the Queen at Windsor she was 'quite content' with the round £100,000.[2] Soon Gladstone was initiating members of the Commons to the 'mysteries of a trade very difficult to understand', tobacco. It was highly expedient to reduce duties to increase competition, diminish the scandalous smuggling (especially of 'Cavendish or Negro Head'), and to benefit the revenue.[3] At the first Clivedens of the season Gladstone defended unabashedly his anti-Lincoln views on the American war. He busied himself at the Treasury with the worrying (and expensive) problem of venereal disease in the armed services. He was an unabashedly *étatist* advocate of compulsory registration and examination of prostitutes in garrison, arsenal and dockyard towns and of subjecting soldiers and sailors to stoppage of pay to meet the expenses of their treatment for disease. He was in no doubt that the government ought 'in the most circumspect manner to make an effort for effectual repression'.[4] In this way Gladstone was one of the authors of the Contagious Diseases Act, smuggled through in the most circumspect manner in the 1864 session, but soon after to become notorious as the target of one of the most indefatigable and vociferous agitations of public moral purity in the later Victorian era.

Innocently unaware of all this trouble in store, Gladstone administered a rap on the knuckles to Lord Clarence Paget at the Admiralty ('Supplemental Estimates are in general most objectionable and make it impossible for the C of E to perform his duty to the H of C and to uphold any real Parliamentary control over expenditure').[5] The budget figures were still looking as good at the beginning of March as they had done at the opening of the year. On March 4 Gladstone spoke and voted for the Abolition of Declaration Bill, condemning those aspects of the Test and Corporation Act offensive to Dissenters. This was a straw in the wind. The wedding of the Prince of Wales to Princess Alexandra of Denmark at

1 1855–1945; 4th baronet 1926. In 1945 the baronetcy passed to William's line.
2 G & P, 251–52.
3 H, clxix, 330–32.   4 D, vi, 183.
5 G to Paget, February 18, 1863. GP, 44533, 90.

St. George's Chapel, Windsor, on March 10 was the 'most gorgeous sight' Gladstone had ever witnessed, '& one of the most touching'. He ventured out that night in the Strand to admire the illuminations, finding the crush at Temple Bar 'dangerous to life: not made for one of my age'. He nevertheless took the opportunity intrepidly to put in some rescue work. He was happy to assure the Bishop of Argyll that in his view a Scottish consecration 'ought to be no bar to the appointment such as that of the see of St. Asaph'.[1] Then there was a slight scuffle with Palmerston over plans for the Albert Memorial. The Prime Minister was inclined to 'give way to the Queen's feelings' and find more money. Gladstone was adamant in defence of the public purse. At Cliveden indeed on March 23 in a debate on Scott's design Gladstone found himself 'pretty nearly alone on the hard side'. Palmerston permitted himself a 'joking allusion' to the Chancellor of the Exchequer in his report to the Queen which Gladstone, sensitive to the Queen's getting any whiff of cabinet disunion and equally sensitive to any undeserved royal disfavour, took somewhat amiss.[2]

Vigilance was necessary also to defend the budget. Critics of the malt tax and the income tax had to be fended off. Gladstone was planning an audacious scheme to tax charitable bequests which involved several conclaves of revenue officers at the Treasury. It was gratifying to acknowledge the tribute of Henry Fawcett's *Manual of Political Economy*: 'Although we in England consider ourselves to have settled so many of the practical questions belonging to that science, there will always be ample reason for its active presentation.'[3] He was solicitous to cosset his pet Public Accounts Committee, eagerly appearing before them to give every satisfaction as to the regularity of the vote of credit for the China expedition in 1860, and to defend the Treasury officers working 'a most difficult system'.[4] Gladstone's effective representation of the executive in fact tended to stultify the original purpose of his brainchild. The House was growing cynical. It would not be long before Sir Henry Willoughby, one of the Committee's members, announced that he 'thought the House should know its powers and its usefulness were extremely limited'.[5] Gladstone proceeded unperturbed. On April 4 he could write to Panizzi: 'The sea of politics is smooth;' and to Argyll: 'I think an easy and short Cabinet will settle what remains of the Budget.'[6] Later that day Gladstone went for a ride in the Park. At the west end of Rotten Row he was thrown, 'which might have been most serious', but cost him only a 'few cuts &

1 G to Bp of Argyll, February 13n, 1863. *Ib.*, 89.
2 G & P, 253–58.
3 G to Fawcett, March 28, 1863. GP, 44533, 108–09.
4 G to Baring, February 14, 1863. *Ib.*, 89.
5 H, clxxvii, 455.
6 GP, *ib.*, 112.

bruises'.[1] Otherwise, there was much ado arranging with Christie's for a sale of surplus porcelain on May 5 ('serious business of *riddling* my Collection of China for the Sale'), there were British Museum trustees' meetings to be kept up (Disraeli was elected on Palmerston's motion[2]), there was the deplorable affair of 'painful disclosures' about bad language picked up by Herbert and Harry at their preparatory school in Hunstanton, Norfolk. Another Cliveden in mid-April was the occasion of an excursion to Windsor, and a 'satisfactory' ecclesiastical conversation with the neologist Professor Stanley.

On returning from Cliveden news came of Cornewall Lewis's death. He was but three years older than Gladstone; and, as with Herbert, Lewis's removal deprived Gladstone's enemies and critics of a formidable candidate to challenge for the succession to Palmerston and Russell. It was known that Palmerston himself looked to Lewis as his political heir; and Delane of *The Times* and his friends had also seen in Lewis the leader of a future anti-Radical coalition to head Gladstone off. Certainly Lewis had always been a thorn in Gladstone's side at the Exchequer; which made it all the more appropriate that at a cabinet on April 15 the budget should have been quietly settled 'as proposed.' The immediate consequence for Gladstone of Lewis's demise was in fact having to cope with Miss Florence Nightingale's determination to get her protégé de Grey (now Ripon) into the vacant War Office. Gladstone thought a secretary of state for a great spending department in the Lords would be a difficulty; but Miss Nightingale got her way.[3]

Also on April 15 Gladstone distinguished himself in debate on what he called Sir Morton Peto's 'not wise' Burials Bill: not wise because defeated 221 to 96. Gladstone had been a member of the select committee appointed in the 1862 session to examine the question of Dissenting grievances against the existing law, which permitted the burial of Dissenters in consecrated ground only if baptised (this was a particular grievance of the Baptist denomination) and by the forms of the Established Church. Gladstone enlarged on the theme of 'Christian unity and harmony', with touching allusion to 'John Bunyan in Bedford Gaol'; and was sure that the present law gave Dissenters 'some title to come before this House and ask for an alteration to the law' on the basis of 'principles of civil and religious freedom on which, for a series of years, our

1 'Kodak', an equestrian expert, recalled in 1858: 'Gladstone, theologian, politician and Editor of Homer, bestrides his celebrated white mare in Nottinghamshire, scurries along by the side of the ex-War Minister, the Duke of Newcastle.' *Notes and Queries*, 10 Series (1908), ix, 234.
2 Possibly this was the occasion of Disraeli's musing in 1863 on the position of the 'Hebrew Race in universal history' and of his notion of establishing a prize for the best essay on the question, the judges to be Professor Stanley, Gladstone, and himself (Swartz, *Disraeli's Reminiscences*, 103–04).
3 G to Nightingale, April 15, 1863. *Ib.*, 116.

legislation has been based'.[1] This marked yet another distinct movement on Gladstone's part away from strict establishmentarianism. He gained Dissenting applause; but he drew upon his head witheringly churchly rebukes from Disraeli and Lord Robert Cecil. More to the point, Gladstone attracted the hostile attentions of the M.P. for Leominster, Gathorne Hardy. Resentment against Gladstone among Oxford voters burst out yet again in a campaign to contest his re-election, with Hardy as their new champion. Gladstone professed himself to Phillimore 'frankly ... at a loss to understand the grounds which have prompted these adverse feelings'; and until they were pointed out, he was driven to believe they arose 'out of the temper which now prevails among the "friends of the Church"'. Nor could Gladstone give any pledge as to the 'mode & time of declaring any opinions' he might entertain beyond acting in the manner in which he had acted for twenty years.[2] He compounded his offence a little later in the session by his attitude to the question of Anglican subscription for taking all degrees other than the baccalaureat. Not the least of his offences, no doubt, was to extol the 'Cambridge compromise', whereby only theological degrees and membership of the Senate were thus subscribed for. 'I do not see,' Gladstone told Bishop Wilberforce on May 11, 'how the present rule of Subscription at Oxford can be maintained in argument.'[3] (No doubt it was a relief to be able to reassure the Vice-Chancellor that his new proposals about club licences for liquor would be no impediment to the traditional amenities of the common room.)[4]

[3]

While the 'friends of the Church' simmered in Oxford, Gladstone delivered on April 16 his seventh budget. He reduced income tax from 9d to 7d (thus making up for the missing year of 1862, and getting the rate down to Peel's original level of 1842), and reduced both tea and sugar duties (he waved at the House two pennyworth packets of tea, one at 1s 5d duty and the other – noticeably larger – at the proposed shilling duty). Convinced that his 1853 project of abolishing the income tax remained impracticable for the present because it was the most convenient and indispensable item of direct taxation, Gladstone introduced graduation to ease the burden of payers in the £100–£200 bracket, thus making the tax more palatable. He proposed to tax charitable bequests. He conserved a

1 H, clxx, 150–53.
2 G to Phillimore, April 20, 1863. GP, 44533, 118.
3 GP, 44533, 126–27.   4 *Ib.*, 120–21.

modest surplus of £531,000. Apart from the one item of the income tax Gladstone regarded himself as having substantially completed the programme of 1856. If he had not reduced government expenditure as decisively as he could have wished, he had checked its growth and brought it under control. With the 1863 budget he in effect presented, as he put it to the House, 'an Account for the last four years'.[1] 'It wound up I hope a chapter in finance & in my life. Thanks to God.'[2] He registered this sense by publishing later in 1863 *The Financial Statements of 1853, 1860–63* as a kind of testament of his stewardship.

Thus the budget of 1863 marked for Gladstone the end of his second vocation. What next? He noted on 17 April a 'feeling of deep unworthiness, inability to answer my vocation, & the desire of rest'. Desire for rest was understandable. The Exchequer in itself was burden enough; for Gladstone Palmerston had been an even bigger burden. The sense of inability to answer his vocation was equally understandable. As yet Gladstone had but dim and unformed notions; a general awareness that great things were to be done when the inert mass of public opinion would be animated by the manipulatory power of his insight. Such dim and unformed notions were in fact already present in his financial statement itself. Clearly their calls and demands would be oppressively formidable. Gladstone thus in effect outlined the foundations of a third vocation. The two elements were Lancashire and Ireland: he defined these as the two main areas of pressure in 1862–63. His Lancashire doctrine and its wider implications was by now a well-developed theme: the people of Lancashire displaying signally that 'power of endurance, that self-command, that cheerful, manly resignation, that true magnanimity in humble life' which gave such solemn pause for thought. The case of Ireland was different, but not less thought-provoking. Already in September 1862 Gladstone had discerned that 'among other objects in the distance, Ireland is again slowly growing into a political difficulty'.[3] Distress in Ireland was more generally diffused and not so dramatically conspicuous – indeed, one feature of the session was the resentment of Irish members that Lancashire was hogging the distress limelight.[4] Because of crop failures the value of agricultural produce in Ireland had declined over three years by nearly a half; and nearly as much as the established annual valuation of the country (£13.4 million): a state, declared Gladstone, 'not less remarkable than painful'.[5]

Leaving these portentous hints hanging in the air Gladstone went off to Windsor to be warned by the Queen not to overwork and to converse with the Prince and Princess of Wales ('All was pleasant, even delight-

1 H, clxx, 391.   2 D, vi, 195n.
3 G to Gordon, September 22, 1862. GP, 44533, 25.
4 DDCP, 196.   5 H, clxx, 205–207.

ful'). After riding in the Park for the first time after his fall and making some investments in the Royal Academy exhibition, he returned to the fray in the Commons on May 4 and failed decisively to put through his budget proposal to tax charitable bequests. His argument, impeccable as to logic and fact, was that nineteen-twentieths of 'charities' were death-bed bequests which cost their donors nothing; and that in any case the great majority of charitable foundations were more or less grossly mismanaged and inefficient. His proposal allowed charitable provision made in the donor's lifetime to be untouched by taxation. Gladstone had every right to feel strongly on this matter. Between 1831 and 1860 he had given out of income to purposes of 'Charity and Religion' a total of £18,577. Between 1861 and 1870 he would add a further £12,427 to that total.[1] His sensible and salutary scheme provoked a great outcry of muddled sentiment and protests from threatened vested interests about 'robbing the poor'. Gladstone had tried to mollify the outraged Shaftesbury that there would be 'no obstinacy in pressing our proposal about Charities if we find that it would be pressed upon an adverse or even a reluctant House'; but he felt the case must be put.[2] In the event, he felt that 'we could not fairly ask our friends to divide, & withdrew the Clauses'.[3] Defiantly, Gladstone tacked the speech on to his published collection of *Financial Statements* later in the year.

This failure at the beginning of May was compounded by embarrassment at the end. Gladstone found himself on May 29, in Palmerston's absence, prodded by Brand into defending the government's 'Crimean' policy of sustaining the Turks, lately engaged, among many similar atrocious instances, in bombarding the city of Belgrade and in inciting the Druses of Mount Lebanon to persist in the massacre of Maronite Christians. 'Spoke of the Turkish question: reluctantly.'[4] Gladstone in fact had been lucky so far to avoid this distasteful duty. The only occasion of his being flushed out into the open on the question of the evaporation of his 'Romanian' programme of 1858 was the affair of the Ionian Islands debate on May 7, 1861; and that had been Irish Roman Catholic

---

1 Gladstone's own account of his 'Expenditure on Charity and Religion' in 1897 was as follows:

	£	
1831–43	4,250	
1844–50	5,345	Adding the endowment of
1851–60	8,982	St. Deiniol's Library at
1861–70	12,427	Hawarden (£30,000) and
1871–80	10,830	small change, the grand
1881–85	10,297	total amounted to
1886–90	18,407	£114,136.5s.9d. (GGP,
1891–94	9,392	Secret Account Book,
1895–97	4,219	94/13, 167).

2 G to Shaftesbury, May 2, 1863. GP, 44533, 123.
3 D, vi, 199.   4 *Ib.*, 204.

mischief-making. But now there was Irish mischief-making of a more serious cast. W. H. Gregory, M.P. for Galway County, primed by experts in Near Eastern affairs such as the Rev. William Denton, exposed to the House a formidable dossier of Turkish iniquities committed under the aegis of British patronage. He exposed incidentally but to devastating effect the imbecilities of the campaign by the British embassy in Constantinople to counteract the Gorchakov circular of 1860. Cobden joined in the hunt, asserting the role of the Commons as 'the orators of the human race'. Palmerston (through Brand) turned the screw on Gladstone. Fortunately, it was a small House which listened to Gladstone urging the virtues of 'discretion'. 'It is our duty,' he declared, 'in compliance with the faith of treaties, to be loyal to the Turkish Government.' We must adhere to European 'purposes and interests'; Turkey must not be made the subject of foreign intrigue and foreign aggression. No doubt the French intervention in the Lebanon and Syria to rescue the Maronites had been provoked by gross outrages and was justifiable; yet 'it required to be watched with the utmost vigilance, and not altogether without some degree of suspicion'. After all, there existed a belief that the principles upon which the Crimean War had been fought were sound principles (Gladstone at least had the grace to use a form of words which avoided explicitly including himself among such believers). In any case, there had been much exaggeration as to Turkish atrocities; it was all very well to draw 'highly coloured pictures.' 'But we have got the fact of the existence of the Ottoman Empire to deal with.' Were we prepared for a 'total reversal of British policy'? (Indeed, it was to take Gladstone another thirteen years to be pushed to that point by an outraged public opinion.) Upon a firm basis of 'official obligations of good faith' an even hand must be kept between Christian and Muslim peoples, encouraging improvement by sympathetic influence and 'friendly remonstrances', leaving a 'fair and open stage' and avoiding all 'presumptuous predictions.' 'Let us firmly adhere', he perorated, 'to the ancient policy of this country', aware that it was a 'matter of profound European concern' to take care that the destruction of the Ottoman Empire 'be not made the means of introducing more serious evils and dangers more menacing than any which may attend its continuance'.[1]

It was a competent lawyer's brief, much like those for Peel defending the Corn Law in the early 1840s. Cobden reported to Chevalier that 'Gladstone was obliged to speak in reply to me, but he did it with evident reluctance'.[2] Palmerston did not feel he had cause for complaint; but Henry Bulwer, the ambassador at Constantinople, felt he did. Gregory's accusations of bad faith about Bulwer's Circular to the British Consuls in the Ottoman Empire had not been contradicted. Gladstone explained

1 H, clxxi, 140–47.   2 Morley, *Cobden*, 868.

that he had not been anxious to speak because he could not speak about Turkey and its prospects '*up* to the rather sanguine tone of Palmerston'; and because he thought that anyone speaking outside his own department 'should be careful to avoid speaking . . . at a lower pitch, so to say, than has been given by the pitch-pipe of the department itself & the debate remained in charge of Mr. Layard only'.[1]

[4]

All this was disagreeable enough to one imbued with the notion of a vocation to guide the wiser policy and to teach the higher morality. And there was the constant pressure of delicate and fraught issues. Should the form of the subscription required by the clergy to the Thirty-Nine Articles and the Prayer Book be relaxed? 'It is sometimes said,' Gladstone responded, 'that I am too apt to draw distinctions.' The distinction he drew in this case was that, while the system of clerical subscription was not incapable of improvement, parliament was on the other hand not the place in which to originate it.[2] Even more fraught was the issue of the condition of Ireland: though here Gladstone had himself practically incited (or 'manipulated') initiatives in his budget speech. The problem of the Irish establishment, like a Trojan horse full of armed men, stood waiting outside the gates of the Church; there were Irish members willing to take up Gladstone's hints and pull it in. To Colonel Dunne Gladstone declared on June 12: 'If the hon. and gallant Gentleman asks me whether, admitting the distress of Ireland, I have myself anything to offer in the way of a boon, I must be very guarded in my answer.' His discussion of fiscal aspects only made more eloquent the great undiscussed question hanging in the air. Nevertheless, the implication of his conclusion was unfiscal and plain: 'We must look to the influence of good laws, liberal legislation, and thorough and hearty equality in our endeavour to apply the principles of justice and freedom to all three countries . . . '[3]

Opinion in cabinet on the Irish Church Establishment was well reflected in the remarks made by Lewis to Stanley back in July 1862: it was the real difficulty of the day; while it remained there was no hope of conciliating the Irish Catholics; yet the difficulty of dealing with it was so great as to prohibit action.[4] Roundell Palmer testified later that Gladstone told him in 1863 that he had 'made up his mind on the subject, and that he should not be able to keep himself from giving public expression to his feelings. How far or near that might be practicable, he could not foresee;

1 G to Bulwer, July 4, 1863. GP, 44533, 145. A. H. Layard (1817–94), famed as the excavator of Nineveh, was parliamentary Under Secretary at the Foreign Office.
2 H, clxxi, 625.   3 H, clxxi, 835.   4 DDCP, 190.

but, under the circumstances, he wanted his friends connected with the University of Oxford to consider whether or not they would desire for that reason a change in the representation of the University.' Gladstone testified for himself: 'I did not give my nights and days to the question . . . yet the question continually flitted, as it were, before me.'[1] It certainly flitted like a ghostlike presence through the debate of June 12, 1863.

Why had Gladstone come by 1863 to 'make up his mind' about the Church of Ireland? Considering that the question had lain on him in 1846 'like a nightmare' and that ever since Maynooth he felt himself open to the imputation of being bound, 'so far as consistency binds, to strip the Irish Church', it was hardly before time. By the 1860s it was ever more a fixed feature of his ecclesiastical thinking that, as he had put it in 1845, it was in the 'highest interest of the Church to give gold for freedom'.[2] In the intervening years his fears had lessened as to the 'process' which separated the 'work of the State from the work of the Christian faith'. As a 'consenting party, in a certain sense, and relatively to certain purposes, to that process of separation', Gladstone was now by the 1860s capable of taking views about the English establishment much more relaxed than those he agonisedly took in the 1840s. He no longer confused the failure of his own State and Church programme with the failure either of the State or of the Church. But the logic which allowed him to relax about the English establishment (and indeed to consort with Dissenters) by no means applied in the case of Ireland. On the other hand, nor did that logic positively and inescapably enjoin upon him the duty of Irish dis-establishment.

The case of the Church of Ireland was that by giving gold it would gain not only freedom for itself but would emancipate the vast majority of the Irish population, Catholic and Dissenting Protestant, from subjection (even if by now highly attenuated) to an alien or unwelcome establishment of religion. But that, again, was hardly a new revelation. Nor was it a revelation that 'Ireland forces upon us' great social along with great religious questions; or that the question of the Irish Church could not be separated from the 'general question of Ireland'. These, again, were Gladstone's own phrases of the 1840s. What was new and important for Gladstone in 1863 was that he needed body and work for his forming vocation. The logic which pressed itself upon him with an irresistible cogency now was that, if what he could make of Lancashire and the Tyne as representing body in terms of numbers and releasable energy was available, what would be the most appropriate work upon which to set those numbers and energies? What would a guide to a wiser policy and a teacher of a higher morality properly offer as the great national task of the time?

1 *A Chapter of Autobiography* (1868), 40.
2 On September 8, 1863 G pressed the President of Maynooth to join his breakfast parties when in London in the season (GP, 44533, 164).

The eventual 'proposal of religious equality for Ireland in 1868' Gladstone was later to cite as the second of the four occasions of his life when, conceivably, his 'appreciation of the general situation and its result,' his 'insight into the facts of particular eras, and their relations one to another', generated a 'conviction' that the 'materials' existed for 'forming a public opinion, and for directing it to a particular end.'[1] From Gladstone's own point of view he was subject to imperatives of quite categorical authority. The pattern of things seemed to have about it attributes quite reasonably interpretable as being of providential dispensation. The great works symbolised by 1842, 1846, 1853 and 1860 had borne their fruits; those fruits, manifested on the Mersey and the Tyne, constituted a mighty new social and political energy; how could it be otherwise than that he was somehow appointed to form and direct such 'materials' to a particular end? Lewis himself, a statesman of polar difference, had sufficiently defined that end: the Irish Church was the 'great difficulty of the day'. What possible alternative of comparable stature was there? For Gladstone the statesmanly test was to demonstrate that the difficulty was not so great as to prohibit action.

That demonstration would be determined both by capacities and chances. Everything, in fact, looked promising. As for capacities, Gladstone, now in his early fifties, stood in the optimum phase of mature physical and mental vigour. As for chances, Palmerston, the great obstacle, could not hold out much longer. Russell, hopelessly adrift at the Foreign Office, could only live politically for one object; and that, a second Reform Bill, coincided precisely with Gladstone's own grand prospective necessity. Herbert and Lewis, the other possible obstacles, were both out of the way. No one now took Newcastle seriously except himself. Gladstone was poised advantageously to enter upon an inheritance of a brilliance unprecedented in the nineteenth century.

[5]

All these grand and high prospective considerations did not immunise Gladstone from the slings and arrows, or even banana skins, of outrageously commonplace political fortune. He was still prone to gross mishandling of the Commons. Such was the case on June 15 with the affairs of the scheme to purchase the South Kensington exhibition buildings and site. Gladstone was over-eager because of his zeal to transfer to South Kensington the scientific collections of the British

1 GP, 44791, 51. 'General Retrospect', (1897). See above, p.270. The first occasion was 'The renewal of the Income Tax in 1853'.

Museum. He was zealously fighting a battle also for the Queen, who did not scruple to canvass members personally with what was felt to be 'an indecent eagerness' for her Albert Memorial projects.[1] The Queen had made herself unpopular because of her insistence on remaining in widowed seclusion. Gladstone incautiously allowed himself to be the target of a double resentment. Having cast himself so often as a paladin of economy his urgings for purchase were received with 'laughter and derisive cheers'. His 'dictatorial manner and want of tact' were again as evident as in 1860. There was even talk of persuading Roundell Palmer to give up the law and take over the leadership of the Whigs left vacant by Herbert and Lewis. Disraeli had the pleasure of coming to Gladstone's rescue. He reported to General Grey, the Queen's secretary: 'Gladstone made much too clever a speech – sarcastic instead of conciliating – and sent them all to dinner in a bad humour', amid a 'din quite demoniac', and a 'regular panic' among the front benches. 'I sent to Gladstone not to divide – but he insisted.' Something indeed was saved from the wreckage: Gladstone got the land if not the buildings. Palmerston had the gratification of reporting to the Queen that no doubt Mr. Gladstone, through his 'extreme eagerness', was 'unfortunate in the conception and in the execution of his speech'.[2]

There was the affair also of backtracking on the American question. Lee's victory at Chancellorsville at the beginning of May led to a bid at the end of June by Roebuck in the Commons to secure recognition for the Confederacy and mediation to end the war. Napoleon III (already deep in Mexican schemes) was ready; but Palmerston was even more markedly cautious than in January. As in the case of the Ionian Islands, as Palmerston changed, so did Gladstone. He noted a new 'strong counter-current of feeling' in Britain against the South's 'strict adherence to slavery'; and intervention would only stimulate a patriotic reaction in the North and risk 'making worse that which is already sufficiently horrible'. 'Doubt', he declared, 'ought to be ruled on the side of safety.'[3] And safety was the keynote of his response to the other problematic foreign questions. Rather as in the Turkish affair, Gladstone was pushed into defending the government's policy of not intervening against the Russian suppression of the latest Polish uprising. In this case at least he had the opportunity of going with rather than against the grain of his instincts. The friends of the Poles held language 'of a sanguine and therefore speculative nature'; the Emperor of Russia 'has some claims too on our sympathy'; and as to charges that the government had threatened the Russians and then left the Poles in the lurch Gladstone could wheel out his trusty precedent of the illustrious Mr. Canning's policy to the French

1 DDCP, 198–99.
2 LQV, 2 ser., i, 96–98.   3 H, clxxi, 1801–12.

invasion of Spain in 1823.[1] The affair of the quarrel between the Danes and the Germans over the 'Danish Duchies' of Schleswig and Holstein worried Gladstone (though not, as it happened, because of Palmerston's highly incautious announcement on July 23 that, should Denmark find herself at war with the powers of the Germanic Confederation, Denmark would not stand alone. Gladstone later fretted that Palmerston spoke 'entirely on his own motion, and without the authority or knowledge of his Cabinet'; but at the time, like most others, he failed to notice the event)[2].

Nearer to home but not less dangerous in its way was the issue at the end of the session of abolishing Church subscription for higher degrees at Oxford. Given the umbrage which had been taken at Gladstone's attitude on the burials question in April, and the apprehension already gathering about his views on the Irish Church, this question took on an extra significance. Gladstone's statement on July 24, 1863 that he confessed that he did not know upon what principle the present state of subscription at Oxford could be justified and recommending the Cambridge system of permitting non-Anglicans any non-theological degree and allowing them to found halls and hostels was another nail in his Oxford coffin.[3] The ministerial fish dinner at Greenwich the following day came as a welcome change, enlivened by conversations with Brand on 'prospects of the party' and with Palmerston 'on our pronunciation of the ancient languages!' But Gladstone was 'hurt by the tone of some papers about me today, in their review of the Session'.[4] He consoled himself with what promised to be a rare rescue success. A beautiful young woman 'at the very top of the tree', as he described her to Catherine, with an open carriage and pair daily in the Park, was now disposed to a nunnery, but in any case was prepared to become an inmate of the Clewer refuge, provided only that her King Charles spaniel be cared for. Gladstone was happy to give all necessary assurances on this stipulation; and the dog soon became a notable feature of the Hawarden ménage.[5]

The 1863 session had proven unexpectedly taxing (Gladstone remarked on July 5: 'Walk with C. – now rare'). Probably therefore he did not receive with unalloyed joy Palmerston's notice on August 12 that part of the recess would have to be spent as minister-in-waiting: 'I know the Queen would like you to take your Turn, as you have not done Suit & Service at Balmoral.'[6] Nor was it with unmixed feelings that he directed on August 25 that £50,000 be provided for the Albert Memorial.[7] There were, moreover, vexing problems with artists in state employ getting up to the nefarious tricks of their trade at the public's expense; in this case,

1 H, clxxii, 1095–1102.   2 PMP, i, 89–90.   3 H, *ib.*, 1383–87.
4 D, vi, 217.   5 Bassett, 145–46; D, vi, 216–17.
6 G & P, 264.   7 G to Phipps, August 25, 1863. GP, 44533, 160.

the completion of the Nelson monument in Trafalgar Square. 'Does Sir E. Landseer mean to give us four designs of Lions or only one?' 'You may think it strange,' he wrote to the Commissioner of Works and Buildings, 'that I should suggest the idea of anything so flat and poor as the repetition of the same design on the four pedestals or bases. And I should have thought so too, had I not learned that Baron Marochetti had repeated the same Angel!! on the four tablets of the monument at Scutari for which I am told he received above £17,000.'[1] Gladstone was to note sardonically that on the question of the gun metal for the Albert Memorial Mr. Scott treated the Prime Minister's injunctions 'as so much waste paper, or waste vapour'.[2] He got on better with the sculptor Thomas Woolner. There were sittings at Hawarden in the intervals between London and Penmaenmawr for a clay bust, from which two marble copies were to be made.[3]

Back at Hawarden there was much ado with plans for a branch railway line to the Dee (the Wrexham, Mold and Connah's Quay Railway); and a new reaping machine to be viewed 'at work in a glorious field of wheat'. Stephen's affairs were 'at present grave tho' not menacing'; and Gladstone with indefatigable optimism set about once more 'trying Lord Dudley for the O.F.'[4] The now habitual resort to Penmaenmawr was inaugurated with a great walk from Llangollen to Pentre Foelas – 'rather too much for my stiffening limbs. My day of long stretches is I think gone by.'[5] There were still hill walks with the boys (he much missed Harry and Herbert when they departed for school). The reading programme was as formidable as usual: David Hartley's *Observations on Man* (1749), Pausanias, Boswell's *Johnson*, Bartlett's *Life of Butler*, and much on the case of the heretical Bishop Colenso of Natal and Charles II's Act of Uniformity as applied to Oxford. The question of the *Alabama* caused anxiety: Gladstone reported to Argyll that, with Palmerston now much more sensitive to the susceptibilities of the Union government, 'a *most private* order' had been given not to seize the ironclads in the Birkenhead building yards but to forbid their quitting the Mersey.[6] The question of those Confederate rams '(for such I suppose they really are)' Gladstone found 'most difficult and perplexing'. Should parliament be recalled? The age was 'anti-doctrinaire, & abhors abstract principles beyond all bounds of reason'.[7] This did not divert him from problems of minting florins and half-crowns (the latter were wearing out and there would be a danger of a

1 G to W. F. Cowper, August 25, 1863. *Ib.*, 159.
2 G & P, 260–61.
3 One at Hawarden; the other, presented by Gladstone's election committee, in the Ashmolean Museum, Oxford.
4 D, vi, 219–23.   5 *Ib.*, 223.
6 G to Argyll, September 8, 1863. GP, 44533, 163.
7 G to Argyll, September 13, 1863. *Ib.*, 165.

dearth of sixpences when the former began to grow numerous). Lord and Lady Enfield were there; and the Bishop of London and Mrs. Tait (there were questions of clergy discipline). Willy, already admitted to Lincoln's Inn, prepared for his All Souls fellowship examination; Helen for confirmation. Gladstone was glad to be able to rejoice along with Argyll about Jefferson Davis's recent proclamation on the slavery issue: 'a great & glad event. I am perhaps not so wide of you as [you] think.' Although Gladstone still remained convinced that it was 'highly criminal to attempt the extirpation of mere slavery as such by war', should however it please God in his wisdom 'so to overrule the passions of men as to make this war conduce to the abolition of so pernicious a system', Gladstone was most cordially ready to sympathise with Argyll's feelings of joy, '& shall likewise be prepared to give you much credit as a prophet'.[1]

Penmaenmawr was changing. 'The place grows and is getting gradually spoiled,' Gladstone told Argyll. 'But it will for some time yet not lose its illusions.' One of the nuisances of the 1863 season was Bishop Colenso himself, campaigning against his condemnation for heresy, and 'desirous to preach in a tent here'. Fortunately, the deposed prelate ('evidently a foolish man') was dissuaded.[2] Argyll's invitation to Inverary was highly tempting: but 'I fear I must not listen to the siren voice that invites me'. 'If we could but make this part of the year indefinitely long! and the Parliamentary part indefinitely short.' It had in fact been the coolest of all Penmaenmawr Septembers, as Gladstone reported to Robertson. Nevertheless, there were twenty-one bathes before Gladstone departed for Balmoral on the 24th.

Passing through Liverpool Gladstone found 'loyal Robertson' waiting in the rain and willing to provide a sustaining luncheon. With this and by providing himself with a new stock of gloves and a 'superlative' wide-awake hat, Gladstone braced himself for Balmoral. On arrival he reported to Catherine that the area had 'got a polish', though it vexingly lacked the boon of an Episcopalian church, thus obliging Gladstone to drive to Ballater for communion and to arrange morning and evening services in his own room. 'Suit and Service' was enlivened by the drama of the Queen's being overset while driving in her 'sociable' at night. When Gladstone 'lectured her a little' for imprudence she insisted that 'all her habits were founded on the Prince's wishes and directions and she could not alter them'. He was warmed by the 'beautifully domestic' atmosphere but explained to Catherine that he felt too constrained, too much on 'one's good behaviour', which had the effect of 'throwing the mind too much inwards', to be a faithful reporter of conversation. Accordingly, he made a special effort to oblige: there was much talk about

1 *Ib.*
2 *Ib.*

the Queen's Prussian grandchildren – little Prince Willy[1] 'called them all '*stumpfnase*, pugnosed'; about the beauties of Lord Palmerston's hand-writing, about '*Mr. Disraeli's* style in his letters to the Queen', the children's plays at Windsor, Shakespeare, Scott, the German language in England, Guizot's translation of the Prince's speeches. He gave Catherine a touching picture of the three Prussian grandchildren playing with his 'rusty old stick'. Gladstone was also able to commend himself as a courtier by summoning up enough German to produce a translation from Schiller's *Wallenstein* very close to the Queen's bereaved heart and by lending her a copy of *The Female Jesuit, or a Spy in the Family* (Lady Augusta Bruce reported that Her Majesty 'could hardly put it down and had been much occupied by it').[2] The Queen was 'all as one could wish', though much distracted by the Schleswig-Holstein problem and very prone to Albert's pro-Prussian views. Gladstone himself was more distracted by the problem of the Confederate rams, about which he thought Russell was being 'very incautious'. 'I would write and tell him so,' he told Catherine, 'but that as I made an incautious speech about America myself last year I do not feel entitled to take so much upon me . . .'[3] His new readiness to give Argyll credit as a prophet was the first step towards ultimate recognition of the Newcastle declaration as a major error of judgment.

The affairs of Trinity College, Glenalmond, and university matters at Edinburgh were taken in on the run down for a cabinet on October 13 (he dashed off from dining with the Edinburgh physicians for the London train, 'changing in the carriage'). 'Here I am again,' he wrote from his office to Catherine, 'at the old desk in the old room, where I have bent many a time over my work with an anxious brow.' Gladstone conveyed to the Cabinet the Queen's views on the Danish Duchies question. He was soon back up at Hawarden for Helen's confirmation by the Bishop of Oxford. There was 'much conversation with the Bp on what might follow Ld Palmerston. He will have me hold for the first place: I say no.'[4] Gladstone would be loyal to 'the little man'. Back at Hawarden again after a family gathering at Hagley the Gladstones were confronted with a 'strange & sad account resp. Lord Palmerston', which, 'if it is not met, must produce fruits'. O'Kane, an Irish journalist, cited Palmerston as co-respondent in a divorce action, claiming damages of £20,000. (Though somewhat flattered at the age of eighty, Palmerston was not amused at the society joke: 'She may be Kane, but is he Abel?') Catherine was avid

1 Friedrich Wilhelm Victor Albrecht, 1859–1941; as William II King of Prussia and German Emperor 1888–1918. The other children were Princess Victoria Charlotte (b.1860) and Prince Albrecht Wilhelm Heinrich (b.1862).
2 C. Pearl, *The Girl with the Swansdown Seat* (1956), 212–13.
3 Bassett, 146–52; D, vi, 227–29; G & P, 267.
4 D, vi, 232.

for gossip: 'I will report to you the first or any other whispers that I may hear about the P. affair,' Gladstone assured her on November 10; although all he could offer was a feeble anecdote about Clarendon's blundering tactlessness with Lady Palmerston. There was the excruciating problem of a possible invitation by the Palmerstons to Broadlands. At a party at the Granvilles' Lady Palmerston complained at the Gladstones' not having stayed there; but Gladstone was insistent that any such invitation must be avoided in 'present circumstances'.[1] Palmerston himself he reported 'seriously hit, not exactly in health, but in spirit, force, and tone. The dart sticks.'[2]

An excursion to Burslem on October 26 to lay the foundation stone of the Wedgwood Memorial Institute gave Gladstone an opportunity to discourse on the general laws of industrial production, the benign self-regulation of trade, the science of political economy, and the just limits, as enshrined in the Factory Acts, of that science. 'The very same age, which has seen the State strike off the fetters of industry has also seen it interpose, with a judicious boldness, for the protection of labour.'[3] This was another straw in the wind of his developing enthusiasm for a measure of working-class franchise. Back at Hawarden there was little joy on the domestic front when Willy returned from Oxford without an All Souls fellowship. 'What next?' Willy seemed strangely reluctant to be pushed into a parliamentary seat. On November 5 Gladstone could exclaim: 'A domestic evening: how rare!' Gladstone had time to write to Charles Sumner, the American statesman and abolitionist, on the theme that he disapproved of war to end slavery but would be glad if slavery ended as the consequence of war. 'I could go further & say it will please me much if by the war the union shall be re-established. But it would be a shabby way of currying favour with you to state a proposition which though in its terms strictly true contemplates a contingency which as it seems to me is wholly unattainable.'[4]

There was the next session to be thought about. Gladstone told Catherine on November 20 that the resolutions of the Commons on economy in 1862 'exercised an influence which is now much weakened'; but he would take all his measures 'to go as far as I can in pressing for a reduction'. He wrote accordingly that day to Palmerston that a probable surplus of two millions would 'create a great *expectation* of reduction in taxes'. Palmerston responded unpropitiously. The surplus proved that the estimates had been framed 'on the safe side, which is a great Merit'; it would be pleasant to reduce, but 'the present Aspect of things in

1 G to CG, November 10, 13, 19, 1863. GGP, 29/1.
2 Bassett, 157. O'Kane could not prove his marriage, and his action failed.
3 *Wedgwood. An Address* (1863), 11–13.
4 G to Sumner, November 5, 1863. GP, 44533, 187.

America in Europe in Asia is very discouraging as to the Prudence of making any material Reduction'. As ever, he was scathing about 'Clap Trap' economies.[1] Writing to Catherine in cabinet, Gladstone found the European aspect indeed rather worrying: 'This Danish business is a very nice one in itself & with the Queen. She is rather wild & Lord R. does not show much tact in managing her.'[2] After a therapeutic china-hunting expedition with Catherine (and getting down to reading Motley's *Rise of the United Netherlands* and Froude on Queen Elizabeth) Gladstone found the cabinet on the estimates on December 1 disappointing: 'The Estimates postponed: the sky not being clear. I mean the Cabinet sky.'[3]

Nor was the Oxford sky very clear. George Wilson made overtures from Manchester about South Lancashire. Gladstone wrote to Robertson: 'My position at Oxford must I fear be regarded as very doubtful. But if Mr. Wilson thinks it necessary to proceed *now* to a definite arrangement, I think it would be well that . . . he should correspond with Mr. Brand who could keep me informed.'[4] By thus distancing himself, Gladstone could show clean hands to Oxford. Wilson and Robertson found Gladstone a difficult prospect: the more doubtful Oxford became, the more reluctant was Gladstone to make a clean and convenient break. A passage at Windsor found Gladstone sitting by the late Prince's favourite child, the Crown Princess of Prussia ('She is very remarkable') and dining *en famille* with the Queen. He took an opportunity to visit the Frogmore mausoleum. Back at Hawarden the Castle was buzzing with the question: will Lucy Lyttelton become engaged to Hartington's younger brother, Frederick Cavendish? ('*Some* result is expected.') Gladstone, meanwhile, was much harassed with Church appointments '(I think these Church preferments will be the death of me').[5] To the Dean of Windsor: 'I doubt if Dean Elliot would do. He has I am told married a divorced wife, of course in the teeth of ecclesiastical law.' And it was most distressing that two of his friends at Oxford, Bradley and Church, were being made the 'objects of a secret and slanderous proscription' in their quest for professional advancement.[6] Still, Gladstone could count his blessings in his end-of-year birthday reflections. 'No mercy of God to me is more wondrous than the absence of sorrow or anxiety about my children.' There were as ever the perils of 'lurking unextracted sin'. Had he adequately fulfilled his vocations? 'My life has not been inactive. But of what kind has been its activity? . . . It seems to have been & to be a series of efforts to be and do

1 Bassett, 168; G & P, 269–71.
2 G to CG, November 23, 1863. GGP, 29/1.
3 D, vi, 240.
4 G to Robertson G, December 1, 1863. GP, 44534, 5.
5 G to Wortley, December 11, 1863. *Ib.*, 11.
6 G to Wellesley, December 11, 1863. *Ib.* Gilbert Elliot was Dean of Bristol.

what is beyond my natural force.' Nevertheless: 'In other quarters some better gleams of light.'[1]

[6]

The new year of 1864 opened with prospects for the estimates much less rosy than they had seemed a year before. Gladstone consoled himself by setting to work on January 4 on his latest Post Office Savings Banks project. He had in view a scheme for cheap life assurances for the working classes. He diverted himself with the opening of the new village reading room at Buckley, which he used as the occasion for a discourse on free trade and savings banks and improving the lot of working men by providing them with new mental resources. But his most eloquent passage was on the defence of public houses as ministering to the 'wants of mankind'. The use of stimulants by whole communities was not to be 'altogether dispensed with', always provided there was a 'moderate and rational and Christianlike use of such things'.[2] This marked one of the earliest moments of Gladstone's long conflict with the rising forces of the anti-alcohol movement. Otherwise, there were further adjustments about America: he wrote to John Stuart Mill about neutrality in a manner which that leading advocate of the Union found 'on the whole very satisfactory'.[3] There would be further adjustments that spring consequent on the French exploitation of the opportunity to install the Archduke Ferdinand Maximilian as Emperor of Mexico: 'one of the greatest political blunders ever perpetrated,' Gladstone told Disraeli; 'certainly, the greatest political blunder of his time.'[4] There was a gratifying communication about foreign membership of the *Institut de France* conveyed by Guizot, which prompted from Gladstone (for Guizot, too, was eminently a survivor) *tristes* sentiments: 'How busy death has been . . . with those together with whom I have trodden the thorny road of politics!'[5] But always the mundane task recalled Gladstone to his duty: 'I cannot say,' he informed the Commissioner of Works and Buildings on January 26, 'that I am well satisfied with Sir E. Landseer's tone in this business of the lions . . . '[6]

The 1864 session opened under the shadow of the Danish annexation of Schleswig and the punitive invasion of the duchies by Austria and Prussia. Palmerston's bluff had been called. Russell was eager to honour

1 D, vi, 245.   2 *Times*, January 7, 1864.   3 D, vi, 248n.
4 Swartz, *Disraeli's Reminiscences*, 121.
5 G to Guizot, January 21, 1864. GP, 44534, 31.
6 G to W. F. Cowper, January 26, 1864. *Ib.*, 32. Laura Thistlethwayte (*née* Bell), is supposed to have helped Landseer in the carving.

the commitment to the Danes; Palmerston held back, hoping to prod the French into co-operation. In the debate on the Address in Reply on February 4 Gladstone denied accusations of a 'divided cabinet', defended the government's impartial policy on the German-Danish dispute and insisted that he and Milner Gibson were absolutely content to be 'represented to the country and the House of Commons by the able and luminous speech of my noble Friend at the head of the Government'.[1] Gladstone was even less convincing in response to demands for reduced expenditure. He found himself haplessly regurgitating the old arguments of Disraeli and Palmerston that the 'increased wealth of the country made it necessary that increased expenditure should be incurred'.[2] He was much happier on the same day introducing the first reading of his Government Annuities Bill offering Post Office facilities for small and cheap life assurances to encourage 'frugal habits among the industrious classes'. Gladstone explained to Newman Hall the purposes of his 'labour for our friends of the labouring class in another shape': 'I have introduced a Bill which aims at giving them increased facilities for making provision for old age and death of Deferred Annuities & by small Life Assurances. It has involved me in a smart contest, and obliged me to give much attention to a subject lying somewhat beyond my ordinary province. I don't intend to fail through want of effort.'[3] His allusion to a 'smart contest' referred to the M.P. for Dudley, H.B. Sheridan, who set himself up as defender of the life assurance interests. Gladstone set about this culprit in much the same punitive spirit he had directed against the Bank; and distinguished himself during March in a series of bruising clashes with Sheridan, some of which excited the House to uproar. On March 18 Gladstone was reduced to expressing his 'sincere regret' at imputations he had made.[4] 'I have had a narrow escape from a vote of censure,' he reported to Robertson, 'for denouncing a corrupt & fraudulent society. But I have done a public duty: & am at ease.'[5] Stanley commented that 'Gladstone has more than ever established his character for honest imprudence'.[5]

It was not as if business was lacking to keep Gladstone out of mischief. 'What about Cobden's pension?' he asked Russell; was it not time 'either to move, or virtually to abandon the idea of moving'? But Russell declared his despair of persuading Palmerston to agree to pensioning Cobden.[7]

1 H, clxxiii, 131–36.   2 *Ib.* 476–77.
3 G to Newman Hall, February 29, 1864. GP, 44534, 47.
4 H, clxxiv, 191–211, 305.
5 G to Robertson G, March 19, 1864. GP, 44534, 55. Sheridan was M.P. for Dudley 1857–1886, when he was defeated as a Gladstonian Liberal.
6 DDCP, 212.
7 G to Russell, February 5, 1864. GP, 44534, 38; Russell to G February 29, 1864, GP, 44292, 132.

There was an Osborne audience ('Every time she improves upon me by her simple & noble qualities')[1] and much entertaining (it was a triumph to entice Tennyson). Some of the business was sufficiently unpleasant. Lucy Lyttelton thought that her Uncle W. looked 'terribly fagged' after having been 'badgered in the House in re his excellent Government Annuities speech' (and 'Atie P[uss]' looked just as bad, 'more overwhelmed with hard work than ever', in her innumerable charities, 'and her season and societytums', and being 'deep in politics', and being 'everything to Uncle W – all at once').[2] Buxton's resolution on February 9 condemning the bombardment of Kagashima in 1863 confronted Gladstone with another, and worse, Don Pacifico episode. Fortunately he was not required in this instance to perjure himself in the name of collective cabinet responsibility. But unhappy memories of that competent lawyer's brief on behalf of the Turks in May 1863 were possibly raised when Gladstone put it to Russell that the latest information on Turkish finances disclosed 'a state of things somewhat ominous' with regard to future payments of the guaranteed loan.[3]

Much more ominous was the news on February 8 of the judgment by the Judicial Committee of the Privy Council on the *Essays and Reviews* case. The shock here was that Tait, the Bishop of London, voted with the lay judges against the two archbishops and cleared the defendants of the charges of heresy; thus, by abolishing Eternity of Punishment and dismissing Hell with costs, depriving orthodox members of the Church of England of their last hope of everlasting damnation.[4] What hope was there now of making the heretic Colenso's deprivation stick in the courts? Gladstone launched himself into a campaign in collaboration with Bishop Wilberforce to increase the episcopal element in the Judicial Committee for the purposes of ecclesiastical appeal.[5] Even Gladstone's countryhouse weekends took on a distinctly theological tone. At Polesden Lacey he devoted himself much to the Colenso case and the problem of 'Eternity of punishment', one of the weaker points in the Church's defences. At Cliveden he conversed with Argyll on 'Future Punishment' ('We had a delightful evening').[6] 'I am sorry to say,' he wrote to Keble, 'the more I have thought of it the worse it seems . . . in matters of faith what is called judicial construction will be found to mean liberty of simple contradiction to solemn engagements . . . ' A question of an isolated point of religion involved through a chain of reasoning the 'whole fabric of Christian belief'.[7]

Throughout all these distractions Gladstone kept the crucial Reform

1 D, vi, 256.   2 *Diary of Lady Frederick Cavendish*, i, 205.
3 G to Russell, February 22, 1864. GP, *ib.*, 45.   4 See above, 217.
5 On this theme see M. D. Stephens, 'Gladstone and the Composition of the Final Court in Ecclesiastical Causes, 1850–1873', HJ, 1966.
6 D, vi, 266–67.   7 G to Keble, March 31, 1864. GP, 44534, 61.

issue steadily in view. It was very likely, indeed, that he might well find an occasion during the session to make a deliberate declaration. It was known that Edward Baines, M.P. for Leeds, was planning to introduce a bill to lower the borough franchise from the existing £10 rateable qualification to £6. Gladstone kept Robertson abreast: 'I am not however one of those who think there is much present danger of a monopoly of political power in the hands of the most numerous class & I confess I wish their share of it were *sensibly* enlarged.' Apart from that it was sad to see 'both the Federals & Confederates in America 'more confident than ever'; but Gladstone was pleased to report that nothing had occurred to 'damp my hopes of avoiding any share in those unhappy quarrels on the Continent'.[1] The Austrians and the Prussians, having cleared the Danes out of Schleswig early in February, now commenced an invasion of Denmark proper. Palmerston and Russell were doing their best to get Britain involved on the Danish side. 'Those two dreadful old men,' as the Queen described them on February 25 to Uncle Leopold,[2] were hopelessly out of their depth in dealing with Bismarck. Britain was in fact poised on the brink of a collapse of credit as a European great power. The evident tussles between the war and peace factions in cabinet attracted opposition censure. Gladstone, put up on February 22 to answer Disraeli's well-found accusations of incompetence, resorted to evasive manoeuvres, using sarcasm as a substitute for argument. He described the encounter as 'a little "scene"'.[3] He characterised Britain's European role feebly as that of a 'friendly bystander'.[4] This phrase was justly seized upon by Robert Cecil: was this a declaration that Britain had abdicated as a great power? This kind of pressure stirred Palmerston and Russell to greater efforts. At a cabinet on February 24 Gladstone led the protest of the peace faction against communications, without cabinet sanction, with Russia and France proposing naval demonstrations in the Baltic; and succeeded in getting the Cabinet to decline sending a British squadron to Copenhagen.[5]

As Britain's European credit crumbled Gladstone worked on his forthcoming budget. He was under pressure from the barley interests to make remissions on the malt tax. Disraeli was indeed 'haunted' by a fear that Gladstone might put himself at the head of a movement to abolish the tax altogether and thus threaten Conservatism's ascendancy in the agricultural constituencies.[6] Possibly Gladstone was tempted; but repeal would leave £6 millions to find somewhere else. He was inclined rather to propitiate property more generally with remissions on the fire insurance duty. In any case Oxford soon obtruded in the form of the old question of

1 G to Robertson G., February 20, 1864. GP, *ib.*, 44.
2 LQV, 2 series, i, 168.   3 D, vi, 258.
4 H, clxxiii, 869–71.   5 D, vi, 258.   6 DDCP, 210.

the Tests Abolition Bill. Gladstone, in damaging conflict with his university colleague Heathcote, urged a compromise formula, deploring the attitude of 'indiscriminate resistance to almost every measure aiming at relaxation or relief'. His advocacy of what was known as the 'Cambridge compromise' did not, however, spare him denunciation from one of the Cambridge University members, Selwyn,[1] larded with bitter references to the Burials Bill and the Endowed Schools Bill, to the effect that 'on every occasion when they had taken a single step in the path of concession it had not led to the settlement of the question, but had been treated as a stepping stone to further aggression'.[2] This was very much the view of Gladstone's Oxford critics, who would not have been reassured, for example, by Gladstone's conferring on March 23 with Newman Hall, notoriously one of the chiefs of Dissenting agitation. Gladstone formulated on March 6 a private definition that he would jealously conserve 'national or public endowments for religion' or even *'exclusive temporal privileges and possessions of ecclesiastical establishments and other communions except* in cases where they fail to answer in some reasonable degree to the wants & wishes of society at large'. This applied equally to Ireland or Oxford. It was on the theological side that Gladstone was more prone to stiffness and resistance: he opposed 'all attempts at remodelling the Christian faith'; but viewed 'rather with hope than with apprehension' the 'free action of the religious life within the measure of the laws in the various sections of the Christian world', as 'affording the best promise, under the conditions of the time in which we live, for maintaining in its vigour the Christianity of the country'.[3] It was no wonder that many Dissenters deludedly saw Gladstone as more than half way on a progress from *The State in its Relations with the Church* of 1838 to eventual acceptance of the ideal of 'a free church in a free state'.

March 1864 generally was a difficult month. There was the awkward case of James Stansfeld, Member for Halifax and a Lord of the Admiralty, ingenuous patron of Mazzini, implicated unwittingly in yet another assassination plot against Napoleon III. Gladstone's defence was that the French *Procureur-général* was taking a severely *ex parte* line in duty; and, in any case, when it came to one man's word against another's, was not Mr. Stansfeld an English gentleman?[4] On the occasion of the cession of the Ionian Islands Gladstone confined himself decently to a cool state- ment in which he emphasised that it was no great injury to the Greeks if the Austrians, as the price of their acquiescence, insisted on the demo- lition of the fortresses.[5] By now Clarendon had returned to the Cabinet;

1 A brother of the Bishop of New Zealand: C. J. Selwyn, later Solicitor-General and a Lord Justice of Appeal.
2 H, clxxiv, 127, 132–35, 141. 3 D, vi, 261–62.
4 H, *ib.*, 278–82. 5 *Ib.*, 377–80.

and if Gladstone had lost one good enemy in Cornewall Lewis, he gained an even better one in the new Chancellor of the Duchy of Lancaster. It was a relief to get away to the Rothschild mansion at Mentmore ('a sumptuous residence') and enjoy some 'excellent preaching' on Palm Sunday. At Cliveden at the beginning of April he worked on the budget and read Kingsley's latest retort in his polemic with Newman (*What then Does Dr. Newman Mean?*). Perhaps he recalled his regrets to Kingsley in 1860 that 'a Chancellor of the Exchequer must report himself wholly without means or hope of lifting *the* most deserving clergyman out of gloom into light'.[1] He went back to town with Sir John Acton ('whom the more I see the more I like').

On April 7 Gladstone delivered his financial statement. 'The plan seemed to be well received. Nothing more than these occasions makes me feel and know myself to be *so* poor a creature.' It was well received because, with a surplus of £2,352,000 in hand, Gladstone could reduce income tax by a further 1d to 6d, reduce the fire insurance duty, and on the direct side, reduce the sugar duty again. Thus, as he happily put it, the surplus grew 'fine by degrees and beautifully less'. He decided against remission of the malt duty; but 'property' was well enough pleased. Gladstone still had grave doubts lest the income tax 'creep unawares into perpetuity', for in his view its cornucopic effect was incompatible with 'reasonable public thrift'. But as against this he could point to a distinct abatement of expenditure as compared with 1859. He invoked 1842: the 'commencement of the great work of Parliament with respect to commercial legislation'; and particularly Gladstone stressed the 'essential and vital connection between the growth of the industry of the country and the legislative process pursued within the last quarter of a century'. This was indeed at the core of his new sense of vocation. So also was his celebration of the 'astonishing development of modern commerce', of locomotion, the electric telegraph, cheap postage, the progress of machinery; and the concomitant decrease in pauperism and in the burden of the public debt.[2]

[7]

Soon after the budget followed the Garibaldi episode. The Hero of the Risorgimento had arrived early in April to pay a visit of gratitude to the

1 G to Kingsley, September 28, 1860. GP, 44531, 51.
2 H, clxxiv, 537–93. *Diary of Lady Frederick Cavendish*, April 8, 1864: 'Uncle W., speaking of certain plays moving one to tears, said that there was something that made him feel ready to cry in his Budget! – viz. the description he gave of the gigantic power and prosperity of England' (i, 207).

British people. Ministers were more than somewhat nervous. The governments of France, Austria, and Russia looked upon Garibaldi as little better than a criminal; and the Italian government regarded him with mixed feelings at best. Radical elements in Britain prepared to receive him both as the genius of European Revolution and as a mighty stimulus to the 'movement' in Britain itself. There were plans for a grand provincial progress over four to six weeks. Garibaldi's managers had provisionally accepted something over thirty engagements. Gladstone, as a fully accredited member of the 'Italian party', offered his services to Palmerston: 'I do not know what persons in office are to do with him: but you will lead, & we shall follow suit.'[1] Palmerston's strategy was to keep Garibaldi tightly confined to London, to hobble him closely with a press of 'respectable' admirers, and to get rid of him as quickly as might be. One of his most important devices to these ends was Gladstone.

Given Gladstone's predispositions there was nothing surprising or untoward in such a spoiling role. In the first place, he would have no particular affection for a campaign of democratic incitement conducted by one who was Europe's most notorious anti-clerical and revolutionary freemason, even if that animus was directed against the Roman Church. More important, as one who saw his vocation as former and director of public opinion, as teacher, guide, and, in his own special term, manipulator, Gladstone had no motive for encouraging rival performers in the field; performers, moreover, who were likely to get both the directions and the distances wrong. After the initial mass demonstrations on Garibaldi's arrival the Sutherlands deftly enveloped Garibaldi in their hospitable embrace, aided and abetted by other grandees such as the Shaftesburys. Gladstone went to Chiswick on April 12 to inspect the phenomenon: 'We were quite satisfied with him.' He had the tact to do Gladstone's part for Italy 'much more than justice'. The following evening there was a dinner and evening party at Stafford House – 'a magnificent festival'. In the immense crush on the staircase Garibaldi caught sight of Gladstone and insisted on shaking his hand, with a cry of 'Precursore!'[2] Disconcerted admirers noted that the General 'spits abundantly'; but he established his social ascendancy by being the only man ever to smoke a cigar in the Dowager Duchess of Sutherland's boudoir in Stafford House. At that same occasion Gladstone had a 'long talk' with John Bright about Ireland and the Irish Church. Bright recorded him as thinking 'when the Liberal party is restored to life, that question would come up for settlement, and he should regard it as one of the great purposes of the party, although it would necessarily separate him from the University of Oxford.'[3] Gladstone went 'by desperate push', to see

1 G & P, 279.
2 MRDF. Under that same staircase Lucy Lyttelton and Frederick Cavendish were deciding at that moment to get married.   3 Trevelyan, *Bright*, 331.

Garibaldi welcomed at the Opera. He could even indulge in a touch of his own sentimental populism: 'It was good, but not like the *people*.' It was the 'people' precisely who were being edged out. Through Panizzi Gladstone dropped a 'heavy hint' to Garibaldi that it was high time for the sake both of health and public calm that the tour should end.[1] At Stafford House on April 17, following a dinner party the previous evening at the Palmerstons', Garibaldi in a conversation with Gladstone 'agreed to give up the provincial tour'.[2] Gladstone himself received the now disonsolate General at Carlton House Terrace on the 20th. There was a crowd outside the door, 'all in the best humour'; the hall and the stair were full before dinner, with redoubtable Aunt Johanna Robertson in her eighty-ninth year 'stationed in the front'. A 'hostile deputation invaded us at ten: but we ejected them'. 'My nerves would not let me – old hack as I am – sleep till after five.' Gladstone wrote to Clarendon on April 23:

> I am to see Garibaldi at Cliveden this evening & it is possible that some occasion may offer there for obtaining from him a further declaration. But since I received your note the following circumstance has occurred. Clarence Paget has been to me, & reports that Mrs Schwabe, a well known and zealous but anti Mazzinian Liberal in Italian matters, who is also a friend of Garibaldi's, has acquainted him that Garibaldi himself has made known to her that according to his own painful impression the English Government do consider the prolongation of his stay in England very embarrassing and are very anxious that he should go.
>
> What a pity, if this is so, that this simple & heroic man could not speak his mind plainly to me but wrapped himself in the depths of diplomatic reserve, instead of acting like Lord Aberdeen who used to say 'I have a habit of believing people'.[3]

At the farewell Cliveden party for Garibaldi Gladstone attempted to explore the spiritual void; but the 'utmost' he could extract from the General was the view that it would be 'sad if the Italian people should lose its faith'.[4] Garibaldi abruptly departed from England shortly afterwards.

Indeed Palmerston had led and Gladstone followed suit to the extent of being deputed by his colleagues as the right man to put personal pressure on the General. Ostensibly politics was not mentioned. As Gladstone insisted rather unctuously, 'there was nothing political in the conversation ... not one syllable about the desire of the Government that the General should leave escaped my lips'.[5] Palmerston contrived that his medical henchman, Dr. Ferguson,[6] should write an opinion that

1 Foot, 'Gladstone and Panizzi', *Br. Lib. Journ.*, v, 52.   2 D, vi, 268–69.
3 G to Clarendon, 23 April 1864. Bodleian MS Clar. Dep. c.523.
4 D, vi, 270–71.   5 *Ib.*, 269.
6 Identified as 'probably' Dr. Robert Ferguson (1799–1865), physician extraordinary and accoucheur to the Queen 1857. DDCP, 372 n.25.

Garibaldi's health would not stand the strain of an exhausting provincial tour (an opinion publicly refuted by Garibaldi's personal physician). In view of the hostile criticism of the government's procedures engendered by the affair, and in particular for his own part in it, Gladstone later made a statement in the Commons in which he outlined his 'share in the proceedings'. He was told by the Duke of Sutherland that the Duke and other friends of the General were beginning to 'entertain considerable doubts in regard to the state of his health' through his 'protracted labours' and his 'meditated excursion to the provinces'. Dr. Ferguson at their request examined the General. Gladstone was then called to Stafford House to consider what advice to tender. Dr. Ferguson was explicit that the General's strength would not be equal to the exhaustion of such a tour. The conclusion was accordingly arrived at that 'our duty was to advise the General to contract very greatly the circle of his provisional excursions'. Gladstone was requested personally to advise the General not only that his health would not stand the strain but that in any case his reputation would lose in 'real dignity' from so many receptions being frequently repeated. The General replied that to avoid the invidiousness of curtailment he would prefer to abandon the projected tour altogether.[1]

Despite Gladstone's statement a widespread opinion persisted that, as Stanley put it, 'the pretext of health cannot be seriously put forward'.[2] Gladstone persisted equally with his own version of the innocence, as he put it to Manning, of 'persons in authority'. 'But I believe they acted wisely in dealing with it as they dealt.' Once the General was safely away, Gladstone could afford to defend him from Manning's charges of Mazzinianism and revolutionary conspiracy. 'As to his attenuated belief, I view it with the deepest sorrow & concern: I need not repeat an opinion, always painful to pronounce, as to the principal causes to which it is referable, or as to the chief seat of responsibility for it.'[3]

[8]

Throughout the exotic interlude of the Garibaldi affair routine business continued. Gladstone got the second reading of his Life Annuities and Life Assurances Bill through unchallenged on April 11. He confided to J. D. Acland: 'In one word I am sanguine as to politics: less sanguine as to faith, and I hope wrongly, because the latter subject must in the end look back into the former.'[4] The *Essays and Reviews* judgment hung like a dark

1 H, clxxiv, 1423–25 (April 21, 1864). 　　2 DDCP, 214.
3 G to Manning, July 2, 1864. GP, 44534, 97.
4 G to Acland, April 12, 1864. *Ib.*, 66.

cloud. It would be 'futile' on his part, wrote Gladstone to Keble, to try to be a prime mover in any plan relating to the replacement or reform of the Judicial Committee. That must originate among the bishops.[1] This time, prodded by Wilberforce of Oxford, there was some movement among the right reverend brethren: the Archbishop of Canterbury earned himself an Address of Thanks. Things were rather fraught at the renegade Bishop of London's reception on May 4; but Tait 'spoke kindly & proposed a conversation'.[2] Gladstone felt ruefully bound to confess that though Manning had 'made himself in many respects less a man than the caricature of a man, and the $\phi\theta o\rho\grave{a}$[3] of a powerful intelligence', he was nearer the truth about the state of the 'principle of belief among us' than many more reasonable people.[4]

As against these rather lowering ruminations, it was a signal matter of family rejoicing that Lucy Lyttelton and Frederick Cavendish announced their engagement on April 21 ('We all cried laughed congratulated & what not'). Gladstone cleaved his way among multifarious concerns. Was the portrait of Archbishop Laud acquired by the National Portrait Gallery for £75 really by Van Dyke? There was the more congenial duty of visiting the Royal Academy Exhibition, dining with the Academy and speaking 'chiefly respecting Mr. Dyce', the recently deceased High Church artist.[5] He made known to the Commons his conservative views as to the Public Schools Commission he had already conveyed privately to Lyttelton: he would have no truck with modern languages; Greek and Latin were the essential stuff of a gentleman's education. ('In many countries there are no educated men but authors and students. But it is the proud distinction of England to have a large body of highly educated gentlemen.')[6] He was put to shifts to fend off the direct tax advocates who were pressing for a select committee. Gladstone warned them that they were proposing a task which would 'infallibly break their backs'. 'I do not deny that the direct tax is the perfect tax'; but the revenue was far too complex a system to be susceptible to simple perfection.[7]

A flurry about the Schleswig-Holstein problem made the beginning of May 1864 uncomfortable. Russell's suggestion that a British squadron should warn the Austrians off the Baltic startled Gladstone: 'Such a proposal from Lord R! only Ld P. supported, & that but half.' Even so, Palmerston saw fit in a conversation with Apponyi, the Austrian ambassador, to convey the threat. Gladstone judged the 'Dangers renewed' at a cabinet on May 2. He was inclined to the solution of partition: northern Schleswig to go to Denmark, and the rest of the two

1 G to Keble, April 13, 1864. *Ib.*, 67.
2 D, vi, 273.   3 Corruption.
4 G to Lyttelton, May 17, 1864. GP, 44534, 80.
5 D, vi, 272.   6 H, clxxv, 129.   7 *Ib.*, 275–77.

duchies to form a new separate entity within the German Confederation. 'In one way or another, we shall have to come at the opinion of both Duchies in this matter; & I do not think that under any circs. we can be parties to overruling it by force.' The people of the Duchies were 'not part of the Danish nation; & were not conquered & acquired by the Danes, as Ireland was by England'.[1] Despite the resistance of the 'War "party" as it might be called Ld P. Ld R. S[tanley] of A[lderley] & the Chancellor', a draft by Russell to Vienna was cancelled. The Queen, alerted by her agent in the Cabinet, Granville, intervened decisively. Palmerston's bellicose statement to Apponyi was explained away as purely private. 'All went well.'[2] Resignation by Palmerston and Russell was in fact 'a distinct possibility' in early May 1864.[3]

All this took place behind the scenes. Russell's efforts to help the Danes by proposing arbitration were wrecked by Danish obstinacy; which did not deter Russell as spokesman of a blusteringly pro-Danish British public opinion from offering them further incitement by virtually repeating Palmerston's undertakings of the previous July of British intervention in the last resort. The sorry dénouement of Danish fecklessness and British windbaggery would not occur until later in June. In the meantime the lively immediate feature of the session proved to be Baines's £6 Borough Franchise Bill, introduced on May 11. With this bill Baines was casting a fly across the political waters with the hope very much in mind that Gladstone might rise to the bait. Gladstone, after all, had been semaphoring signals rather freely in recent months. Quite apart from public pronouncements there were the letters to such as George Wilson of Manchester and to Robertson Gladstone of Liverpool (Robertson especially was still closely in touch). The import of these letters ('much frankness', *'sensibly* enlarged') had circulated widely among the 'forward' or radical elements of Liberalism in the great centres. And if Gladstone sought occasions of 'preliminary manipulation' here was a splendid opportunity. On May 10, almost as if to prime him on the theme of the responsible virtue of the artisan class, a deputation from the Amalgamated Society of Engineers waited on Gladstone with a request that he modify the regulations so as to allow trade unions to deposit their funds in the State's Post Office banks.

The House of Commons was thus 'prepared for some momentous utterance' from Gladstone when Baines's bill came up on that Wednesday morning. 'Rumours had been rife' that Gladstone would speak; the House was 'fully prepared for a startling declaration'; and, although it was only at the very beginning of a morning sitting, 'a considerable

1 D, vi, 273.　　2 *Ib.*, 274.
3 W. E. Mosse, 'Queen Victoria and her Ministers in the Schleswig-Holstein Crisis, 1863–1864.' EHR (1963), 277.

audience was already collected to hear him'.[1] Palmerston was appropriately apprehensive. He wrote to Gladstone that morning: 'I hope that in what you may say about Baines's Bill you will not commit yourself and the Government as to any particular amount of Borough Franchise.' The £6 franchise, Palmerston warned, had 'gone to the Bottom'; 'and *if* at any future Time our Government should have to bring in a Reform Bill which the present State of public opinion does not appear to favor', it was 'of great Importance' that ministers should not be 'pledged'. There was a danger of the working classes, under the control of trade unions and 'directing Agitators', swamping the classes above them.[2] Palmerston prudently decided that his absence from the debate would be expedient.

Immediately after the bill and the Opposition amendment were briefly proposed and seconded Gladstone rose. His first point was that the Liberal side of the House was not at all unanimous on the question, and it was agreed by all Liberals that it would at present not be advisable or justifiable for the government to submit such a measure to parliament. Why then would he not vote against Mr. Baines's bill? Because the parliamentary history on Reform since 1851 had been 'a most unsatisfactory chapter'. Gladstone was convinced that the 'discussion of the question in the House of Commons must, through that gentle process by which Parliamentary debates act on the public mind', gradually help to bring home the conviction that it was for the interests of the country 'that this matter should be entertained; and that it ought, if we are wise, to be brought to an early settlement'. A favourable state of the public mind was necessary; 'but the public mind is guided, and opinion modified, by the debate of Parliament.' If he deeply deplored the state of opinion in the Opposition, he was 'far from being satisfied with the state of opinion on this side of the House'. Was there really no choice between excluding forty-nine out of every fifty working men on the one hand 'and on the other a "domestic revolution"'? We were told that the working men do not agitate; but was it desirable that we should wait until they did agitate? If there was to be any class feeling it would be because of 'resentment at exclusion, and a sense of injustice'. This would be to lose the great advantage of the 'altered temper' of the times compared with sixty years ago. Now the old antagonisms had faded; there was a prevalence of social trust. Had he not only yesterday received a deputation of trade unionists eager to invest their funds in the Post Office bank? A 'very small but very significant indication, among thousands of others'. The labouring classes no longer agitated, insisted Gladstone, because they spent their time improving their minds and ensuring the marvellous success of the co-operative movement. He cited the example of Lancashire: 'self-command, self-control, respect for order, patience under suffering,

1 QR, July 1864, 259.   2 G & P, 279–80.

confidence in the law, regard for superiors.' Surely these were the criteria for the franchise?

Thus far, Gladstone had exhibited his 'manipulatory' theme and shown cause why. Then he suddenly shifted the fulcrum of his argument and challenged his opponents to show cause why not. His implication was that presumption was for if there was no proof against. Hence the slipping out of Gladstone's notorious utterance: 'And I venture to say that every man who is not presumably incapacitated by some consideration of personal unfitness or of political danger is morally entitled to come within the pale of the Constitution.' As he explained afterwards in the 'Advertisement' to his authorised version of the speech, it was not 'a deliberate and studied announcement'. It was 'drawn forth on the moment by a course of argument from the opponents of the measure', who appeared to assume that the present limitations of the franchise required no defence and were 'good and normal'.[1] Something radically new seemed to have been injected into what had so far been a routine restatement of several of Gladstone's previous public utterances. The 'advanced' Liberals 'shouted with delight'; 'a murmur of consternation ran through the rest of the House.' Gladstone saw 'how acute was the impression he produced, and made a floundering attempt to retrace his steps'.

> Of course, in giving utterance to such a proposition, I do not recede from the protest I have previously made against sudden, or violent, or excessive, or intoxicating change; but I apply it with confidence to this effect, that fitness for the franchise, when it is shown to exist – as I say it is shown to exist in the case of a select portion of the working class – is not repelled on sufficient grounds from the portals of the Constitution by the allegation that things are well as they are.

By thus repeating at the end of his reassurance the principle of moral right as against utility Gladstone added fuel to the flames rather than dampening them. 'He did not succeed in reassuring his astounded hearers. The rapturous cheers of his Radical allies accompanied him to the end of his speech.'[2] But it was precisely the very manipulatory character of Gladstone's sense of his relationship with the franchise question which allowed him to make so apparently radical a departure.

That peroration returned to the well-worn theme of 'binding and blending and knitting of hearts together'. It had been given to them of that generation 'to witness, advancing as it were under our very eyes from day to day, the most blessed of social processes': the 'process which

1 *Speech of the Chancellor of the Exchequer on the Bill for the Extension of the Suffrage in Towns, May 11, 1864*, 3–4.
2 QR, *ib.*, 260.

unites together not the interests only but the feelings of all the several classes of the community'. Hearts should be bound together 'by a reasonable extension, at fitting times, and among select portions of the people, of every benefit and every privilege that can be justly conferred upon them'.[1]

That night, puzzled, Gladstone recorded: 'Some sensation. It appears to me that it was due less to me than to the change in the hearers & in the public mind from the professions at least if not the principles of 1859.'[2] This was in one way wilful self-delusion. Gladstone's celebration of close boroughs in 1859 had disgusted Bright. His last statement on Reform in the Commons in 1860 blandly demanding credit for his sincerity had been received, justly, with ironical cheers.[3] In fact there had been a crucial shift in Gladstone's own attitude to the question, set originally in motion more by the paper duties crisis in 1861 than by anything else; but even at that point still a matter of tentative opportunism and contingent convenience. Behind Gladstone's spurious claims to virtuous consistency was the simple but sovereign (and unacknowledgeable) circumstance that, whereas to the vocation formed by the 1853 budget and the programme of 1856 franchise reform was at best an irrelevance and likely to be even a damaging distraction and diversion, to the vocation shaping itself after 1863 franchise reform was indispensably of the very essence. Gladstone's consistency lay in his role, one way or another, as manipulator. His honest puzzlement derived from a lack of imaginative capacity to appreciate that a wide gap existed necessarily between his interior understanding and the understanding of the unadept world.

Clearly, it would be as well to get back promptly and soothingly to Palmerston. 'Others will give you a better account of the impression left by what I said than myself. But as to the intention and the words, while I am warmly in favour of an extension of the Borough Franchise, I hope I did not commit the Government to *any*thing: nor myself to a particular form of franchise.' Gladstone redefined himself disarmingly as being in favour of 'a sensible and considerable, but not excessive enlargement'; meaning such an enlargement 'as we *contended* would have been produced by our proposal in 1860'.[4]

But this propitiation did not get around the real difficulty. The phrase that struck home was the one about moral entitlement. Undoubtedly it conveyed more than Gladstone intended it to convey. As the *Quarterly Review* diagnosed shrewdly, with Gladstone there was often an 'unlucky contradiction between his meaning and his words', owing to a 'style of reasoning peculiar to himself' and baffling to the English, for they do not understand logical gymnastics; and 'when a great performer makes a

1 H, clxxv, 312–27.   2 D, vi, 275.
3 See above, 414.   4 G & P, 280.

jump, they cannot be brought to comprehend that it is only the beginning of a summersault which, when completed will leave him standing very much as he was before'. A passion for 'sweeping general principles' had steadily adhered to Gladstone, observed the *Quarterly*, through his whole varied mental history. 'Widely as his intellectual position differs now from that which he occupied when he wrote his essay on the "Relations of the State and the Church", this habit of thought retains as strong a hold over him as ever.' Gladstone was not comfortable unless he could base his proposed action 'upon the foundation of some simple, large, grand first principle, which, applied to the existing condition of the world, would turn society upside down'. But this result would be in no way Gladstone's intention. His actual objects were moderate enough. 'Accordingly he proceeds to cut down his great first principle by limitation after limitation until, for practical purposes, the merest shred of it is left behind.'[1]

This assessment, perceptively recalling Gladstone's 'schoolman' and 'Butlerian' predispositions, spoke perhaps more truly than it knew by invoking his first vocation of 1838. The filiation of descent back from the Borough Franchise declaration to *The State in its Relations with the Church* by way of the Peelite years of the 1840s and the intermediate vocation of the 1850s was indeed the inner logic of Gladstone's career. Beside the fact that for Gladstone the grand programme was working out according to plan the *Quarterly*'s strictures on his 'unphilosophical' mode of laying down rules which were swallowed up by their own exceptions were trivial. Still, its conclusion was correct that if Gladstone was 'generally supposed to have taken up the battle-cry for manhood suffrage, he has only himself to thank for it'.

People other than Gladstone himself naturally measured the velocity of impact in terms of the stark contrast between Gladstone the reformer of 1859–60 and Gladstone the reformer of 1864. That night, Stanley, at the Cosmopolitan Club, reported that Gladstone was the 'general subject of conversation'. There was agreement that 'he had broken with the old Whigs and placed himself at the head of the movement party'. It was felt on all hands that he was the 'inevitable leader: and at the same time (apart from this last move) that the *hauteur* of his manners, his want of skill in dealing with men, and . . . his pedantic stiffness in adhering to his own opinions as rigidly in small matters as in great, will make him most unpopular in that capacity'. He was, Stanley concluded, 'universally respected, admired, and, except by Bright and a few of that school, disliked'.[2]

Neither respect nor admiration, however, featured in Palmerston's unpropitiated response. 'You lay down broadly the Doctrine of Universal Suffrage which I can never accept.' Palmerston entirely denied that 'every

1 QR, July 1864, 261–62.   2 DDCP, 215–16.

sane and not disqualified man has a moral right to vote'. The franchise was a privilege to be earned. Gladstone's speech was not such as might have been expected from the Treasury Bench. 'Your speech may win Lancashire for you, though that is doubtful but I fear it will tend to lose England for you.' He regretted also Gladstone's exhorting the trade union deputation to agitate.[1] Gladstone protested next day (May 13) that his words were 'neither strange nor new nor extreme'. As with his Oxford critics, he tended more and more to be 'at a loss to conceive' why he gave offence. 'I have no desire to force the question forward.' But 'such influence as argument and statement without profession of political intentions can exercise upon the public mind' he 'heartily' desired 'to see exercised in favour of an extension of the franchise', that the question might if possible 'be disposed of for another generation to come, while it remains manageable and before it runs the risk of becoming formidable'.[2]

This doctrine of pre-emption, like Gladstone's distinction between 'force' and the consequences of the manipulatory influence of argument and statement, combined, to his critics and enemies, veiled menace with casuistry. Brand, the whip, was 'startled'.[3] Stanley dined on the 12th with the Clarendons. 'Among other things Lord C. said of Gladstone that a physician in attendance on him had declared that he would die insane.' (Stanley believed this was Dr. Ferguson, the same who had been so obliging in the Garibaldi affair.[4]) And Stanley reflected that it was true that 'an excessive irritability' had appeared in Gladstone on 'various occasions, and especially in the spring of 1857'.[5] Among Gladstone's colleagues Charles Wood equally disapproved, though agreeing with Stanley that the language was 'so vague as to pledge him to nothing'. Wood thought it indicated 'no settled conviction, but is only one of Gladstone's odd inexplicable freaks: would not be surprised if he were to make another speech in the opposite sense next week'. He thought that after Palmerston, Gladstone was 'inevitable, but most dangerous'.[6]

Press comment did nothing to minimise the significance of the event. Delane's *Times* thought that Gladstone's making such a declaration was 'a thing so strange and so startling that we can scarcely yet realise the full importance of the event'. By shifting the burden of proof as to fitness for the franchise he had possessed himself 'at once of a formula which leaves the one side nothing more to fear, and the other nothing more to desire'.[7] The *Daily Telegraph* seized the opportunity to exploit the occasion to the

1 G & P, 281–82.   2 *Ib.*, 282–83.

3 W. E. Williams, *Rise of Gladstone to the Leadership of the Liberal Party, 1859–1868* (1934), 101.

4 Certainly Gladstone had known Ferguson (who was a lecturer at King's College, London) since April 28, 1845. (D, iii, 450).

5 DDCP, 216.   6 *Ib.*, 217.   7 May 13, 1864.

hilt: 'Sincerely and in the name of England, we thank Mr. Gladstone for the courageous manifesto which he pronounced on Wednesday.' It had 'echoed already through the land like the clarion of a leader who trusts his cause, his followers, and himself, and who sounds a general advance'. A dozen 'veracious, manly, and outspoken words' had put the 'Conservative reaction' into limbo; the great Liberal party was once more a living power; Gladstone had unfurled again the labarum of the crusade of progress. By this 'bold and wise step Mr. Gladstone had advanced to the very front of the great Liberal party'.[1] Sentiments of the same character of caricature and hyperbole came also from the *Morning Star*, which pointed out that 'Chartism itself did not assert more than the title to the franchise' than did Mr. Gladstone: an 'event of the largest promise'.[2] Palmerston had to rebuke the editor of the *Observer* for his favourable leaders;[3] and the Queen wrote to Palmerston 'deeply grieved at this strange and independent act of Mr. Gladstone's'. He should not have made such an 'imprudent declaration' as a member of the government.[4]

Under this barrage of rather equally misconceived praise and blame Gladstone retreated to Brighton: 'I lay on the shingle & enjoyed the sea' (though he found the water 'over-warm' for bathing).[5] 'Many thanks for all you say respecting my speech on the Franchise Bill', he wrote to Robertson. 'I have been astounded to find it the cause & occasion of such a row.' After all, his exceptions could be used to exclude almost everybody. 'I shall be very glad indeed, if what I said has any tendency to bring about a sounder state of opinion & a more consistent conduct – in any case I believe I have spoken truth.' For the rest of the session Gladstone had 'some hope of being more quiet'.[6] To this end he decided to publish a corrected version of his speech with an explanatory preface. Palmerston advised against a preface on the ground that it would have the effect of seeming 'more formal and deliberate'.[7] Palmerston mobilised Brand in support: it would give the speech 'too much importance'. A single footnote to clarify the one sentence upon which the 'whole fabric of exaggeration has been built' would be sufficient.[8] Gladstone insisted. It would get rid of the 'accretion' of unwarranted assumptions. 'My speech has been talked into importance.'[9] His 'Advertisement' argued that 'objection has been taken, and even alarm expressed', under a misconception. One of his grounds for exclusion from the franchise would certainly be any 'disturbance of the equilibrium of the constituent body, or through virtual monopoly of power in a single class'. Further, he 'spoke without reference to the present'; it was not the time to 'attempt

1 May 13, 1864.   2 May 12, 1864.
3 Ridley, *Palmerston*, 564–65.   4 LQV, 2 series, i, 189–90.
5 D, vi, 276.   6 G to Robertson G, May 17, 1864. GP, 44534, 79–80.
7 G & P, 185.   8 Williams, *Rise of Gladstone*, 101.   9 G & P, 287.

the solution of problems of real intricacy, which belong wholly to the future, and which are little likely to become practical except for another generation'. His great fear was that unwittingly he had raised false hopes and would cause 'disappointment'.[1] Gladstone's attempt to talk it out of importance was wholly futile. 'You may be amused,' he told the Provost of Oriel, 'at seeing that the bubble of my "democratic" speech has burst.'[2] There was little disposition in Oxford to see any such thing, let alone be amused at it. The *Quarterly* accurately characterised the 'celebrated Preface' as giving the impression of wanting to 'draw back a little' but of not knowing exactly how to do it.[3] In the midst of it all Gladstone loyally on May 24 put on a Birthday dinner for twenty-eight persons '& full dress evg party afterwards'. On the 28th: 'At Ld Dudley's & Mr. Disraeli's, on the roofs, for the Review: the spectacle was very grand, the natural features aiding wonderfully.'[4]

[9]

For the rest of the 1864 session Gladstone did indeed attempt to realise his 'hope of being quiet'. On June 3, he wrote a minute for Russell's benefit 'on transport of Circassians'.[5] These were Muslims preferring emigration from the Caucasus rather than rule by the Russians. The scheme was to plant them among the Christians in Turkey (they were to form the bulk of the 'bashi-bazouks' of such notoriety in 1876). To the British 'Crimean' public they were gallant victims of Russian aggression;[6] to critics of that policy they were (as they proved indeed to be) a potential source of difficulty for Christian-Muslim relations in the Balkans. Gladstone's interest in the matter is evidence of a subterranean persistence of the attitudes of 1855–58. His immediate concern was financial. Turkish financial irregularities Gladstone unremittingly frowned upon in these years ('Of course,' he told the Deputy Governor of the Bank, 'you will not allow M. Musurus to go to sleep').[7] Now the Turkish ambassador was instructed to 'take up ships in England for transport of Circassians'; a transport which led to the Secretary of the Embassy at Constantinople reporting to Russell of the 'Horrible affair' of ship loads of Circassians being sent to Cyprus. There was much ado sending stocks of biscuits for

1 *Speech of the Chancellor of the Exchequer on the Bill for the Extension of the Suffrage in Towns, May 11, 1864,* 3–4.
2 G to Provost of Oriel, June 1, 1864. GP, *ib.,* 86.   3 QR, July 1864, 260.
4 D, vi, 278. Disraeli lived at 1 Grosvenor Gate, Lord Dudley in Park Lane, overlooking Hyde Park.
5 D, vi, 280.   6 E.g., QR, July 1864: 'The Circassian Exodus'.
7 GP, 44531, 102. Musurus Bey was the Turkish ambassador.

their relief.[1] There were on Gladstone's part other examples at this time of the same interest. When in August 1865 Lyons was about to go off as Bulwer's successor as ambassador at Constantinople, Gladstone forwarded to him a letter from the Rev. William Denton, who 'enters keenly' into questions respecting Servia and Montenegro; and who was criticising a consul of whom Mr. Layard thought highly (Denton had earlier been a thorn in Bulwer's side in 1863). Denton, explained Gladstone to Lyons, 'takes a side in them, but the other side you are sure to hear amply'.[2] These were trifles; but with a certain prophetic significance.

Another occasion of sadly prophetic significance was the marriage of Lucy Lyttelton to Frederick Cavendish in the Abbey on June 7. The Gladstones afterwards gave a reception for two to three hundred guests at Carlton House Terrace. Cavendish, Granville's private secretary and soon (1865) to become Liberal M.P. for Yorkshire West Riding, became also Gladstone's family favourite (his mother was a sister of Dowager Duchess Harriet of Sutherland; whose mother in turn was a daughter of the 5th Duke of Devonshire, Frederick Cavendish's great-grandfather: thus the cousinhood impinged upon Gladstone from several directions). Less agreeable things also impinged upon Gladstone. He complained to Somerset: 'I find with dismay that the Mersey Ironclads are to be bought by means of a Supplementary Estimate.'[3] Having earlier fended off the direct tax lobby, he now defended the income tax from its critics. Until an equally serviceable replacement could be found it could not be safely dispensed with.[4] He had an opportunity on the National Education (Ireland) Bill to expound his now standard Irish theme: 'My desire would certainly be in dealing with such a question . . . to apply the same principle of equity and consideration to the feelings of our fellow-subjects in Ireland as in England.'[5]

Otherwise, there was the current literary debate to be kept up with. He read with 'much interest & pleasure', as he assured Matthew Arnold, 'your remarkable work on Middle-Class Education', *A French Eton*.[6] His Thursday breakfast parties at ten after Easter continued unabated as a feature of sessional social life. One of the guests, Stanley, recorded the lineaments of one such party in June 1864. He noted Gladstone's 'evident mortification' at the sinking of the *Alabama* off Cherbourg, and his astonishment at the eagerness of the 'negrophilists' to sacrifice three white lives in order to set free one black man, even after it was shown that there was no disposition among the negroes to rise in their own cause. 'He could have understood the American feeling of dislike to the

1 PRO, FO/78/1804, 162; PRO/30/22, 93. Stuart to Russell, October 26, 1864.
2 G to Lyons, August 14, 1865. GP, 44535, 109.
3 G to Somerset, June 11, 1864. GP, 44534, 90.
4 H, clxxv, 1750.		5 H, clxxvi, 224.
6 G to Arnold, June 20, 1864. GP, 44534, 93.

breaking up of the Union, but not the fanaticism of English sympathis-
ers.' He extolled Garibaldi (a by-product of his current feud with
Manning over Italy and the Pope), and denounced the amalgamation of
the Secretaryship-at-War with the War Office as lessening the control of
the Exchequer and parliament. ('Mrs. G. as usual with her, begged of all
the party for a charity which she is promoting: a silly habit, which brings
her into ridicule. I gave my share: some evaded her request, but that is an
awkward thing to do to a lady in her own house.')[1]

There was also, as it happened, yet another scuffle with Palmerston
over Gladstone's reception of an address by the working men of York
thanking him for his 'defence of the working classes'. Palmerston jibbed
on the ground of ministerial responsibility, quite in his old style.
Gladstone noted grimly: 'A letter of Ld Palmerston's at night caused me
displeasure.'[2] He protested himself at a loss to understand, also very
much in his old style, how Lord Palmerston could so misinterpret his
entirely legitimate pointing to the necessity of future retrenchment; nor,
after having 'gone to great lengths . . . to meet your views', could he give
any 'pledge of indefinitely prolonged acquiescence in the present scale of
expenditure'.[3] This brisk exchange of shots gave promise of skirmishes or
better to come; but all such exercises in routine modes of internecine
hostilities were soon engulfed in the catastrophe of the government's
foreign policy.

On the question of British responsibilities in the German-Danish
conflict over Schleswig-Holstein, Gladstone tended to be on the 'quiet'
side. It would not be correct to say that he was an advocate of 'peace' in
any consistent intellectually or morally principled manner, such as was
the case in this instance with Cobden and Bright. As in 1860 with Austria,
Gladstone was quite prepared in 1864 to conceive the possibility or
necessity of British intervention or even belligerency. His position,
perfectly consistent within its own terms, was that neither the possibility
nor the necessity presented themselves. The situation by June was that
the Danes, in desperate straits, were calling on Britain to honour the
undertakings made on their own behalfs earlier by Palmerston and
latterly by Russell. A cabinet on June 11 Gladstone found 'very stiff'; 'but
all went well': that is, the 'war' party was held at bay. Gladstone had a
chance on June 16 to redeem his character somewhat with the Queen.
What he had to tell her was music to her germanophile ears: that among
her confidential advisers there was an indisposition to aid the Danes;
adding indeed that some held that 'in no circumstances' material aid
should be given; and indeed Gladstone said he inclined to that view
himself, for the responsibility of this country alone going to war would be
too serious and too heavy, unpledged as we were by any binding

1 DDCP, 219–20.   2 D, vi, 282.   3 G & P, 288–89.

promise. The country, Gladstone assured the Queen, had no real wish to go to war, and public excitement arose entirely from 'misapprehension of the question'.[1] There were rumours, reported Thornton Hunt of the *Telegraph*, that Russell, Clarendon, and Gladstone himself had resigned: *'any* information on the subject would be prized'.[2] Had France and Russia been willing to collaborate Gladstone almost certainly would have taken a more positive line: the Germanic powers would have felt the weight of that European moral authority which Gladstone had been eager to press upon the Federal régime in Washington. But Napoleon III stipulated too heavy a Bonapartist price for his readiness to fight a great war on the Rhine; and the Russians were not prepared to serve a Europe which had victimised them in 1856. Gladstone's reputation as an advocate of non-intervention in 1864 arose essentially out of his making a virtue of necessity.

The crucial cabinets met on June 24 and 25. The former, described by Wood as a 'long and not a conclusive Cabinet', was against war either single-handed or in conjunction with France; leaving the option open as to what Britain might do were the existence of Denmark as an independent entity or the security of Copenhagen itself put in doubt. Wood, Granville, Gladstone and Milner Gibson were for the 'decided peace line'; and Wood thought 'the peace side' was the 'heaviest'.[3] Gladstone thought it 'a grave issue well discussed'. Both parties to the conflict were condemned within a general disposition to non-interference. The decision was deferred as to whether to express total indifference. On the 25th 'we divided, & came to a tolerable, not the best conclusion': Britain would not intervene in the present dispute, but should Denmark's existence as an independent state be challenged a 'fresh decision' would be needed.[4] This was a fudge, as Gladstone's reference to 'not the best' indicated. His definition of 'best' would have been collaboration with France, or, even better, France and Russia. The government drifted into non-intervention in 1864 much as it drifted into intervention in 1854. Gladstone wrote to Catherine: 'One line after the Cabinet to say that after an interesting discussion we have come to an united & in the main a peaceful decision. So the Opposition will find no gaps in the ranks.'[5]

That Gladstone should have been so preoccupied with fending off the Opposition was a curious commentary on an epochal diplomatic scuttle. Later, Gladstone was fertile with *esprit d'escalier*: stressing his readiness to challenge Austria and Prussia had the French been willing to collaborate; which unwillingness he judged (with reason) Louis Napoleon's greatest

1 LQV, 2 series, i, 220–21.
2 Hunt to G, June 22, 1864. GP, 44403, 142.
3 LQV, *Ib.*, 228–29.   4 D, vi, 284.
5 G to CG, June 25, 1864. GGP, 29/1.

mistake, for had there been war in 1864, 'France with Great Britain on her side never would have undergone the crushing defeat which she had to encounter in 1870–1 ... That is to say the whole course of subsequent European history would in all likelihood have been changed.'[1] The extent to which Gladstone's 'decided peace line' was fortuitous rather than immanent is measured by his 'astonished' reaction to the 'strength and unanimity of the parliamentary declaration in favour of peace'. He told Enfield that 'it made a new era in our foreign policy'.[2] Ironically, Gladstone's political credit gained from the collapse of Britain's international credit. What was clearly a shattering blow to Palmerston was readily construed as the passing of an old era and a signal manifestation of Gladstone's coming into his own. In substance, Palmerston and Gladstone were not all that far apart on the Danish-German question. Palmerston stressed British interests; Gladstone a wider notion of the interests of the European community. But for both the key was persuading the French to co-operate. French unwillingness ruined Palmerston but made a hero of Gladstone as an apostle of peace. The widespread misapprehension that Gladstone shared the non-interventionism of the Manchester School stuck to him, despite irritated denials, ever after.

Derby and Disraeli decided on a motion of censure rather than of no-confidence. On balance, Derby preferred to keep Palmerston in office rather than to cope with the consequences of his fall. Palmerston appealed to Gladstone on June 28: 'We shall want a great Gun to reply to Disraeli. Would you be prepared to follow him?' It would be well, he urged later, 'not to be too hard' on the Danes. 'It is true that they were wrong in the Beginning and have been wrong in the End, but they have been most unjustly used by the Germans and the sympathies in the Majority of the House and in the Nation are Danish.'[3] Gladstone dutifully read all the recommended Blue Books; but in spite – or, perhaps, because – of this he decided on July 4 to 'throw over all my heavy armament: & fought *light*'. This method had the merit of allowing avoidance of the fatigues of grappling with the substantial issues and freeing Gladstone to make a prancing, fencing, evasive farrago in answer to Disraeli, full of clever debating points and adroit manipulation of textual intricacies, rounded off with jeers at Disraeli's willingness to wound but fearing to kill by confining himself to censure rather than no-confidence, and by another of his curiously obsessive evocations of Canning. The government's Danish policy a failure? Was Mr. Canning's Spanish policy in 1823 a failure? There was 'no more honourable chapter to be found in the whole history of our foreign policy'.[4]

1 PMP, i, 91. 2 DDCP, 222.
3 G & P, 289–90.   4 H, clxxvi, 751–74.

The motion of censure in the Commons was defeated on July 8 by 313 to 295. The government was in a minority in the Lords of 168 to 177. The 'two dreadful old men' were both thoroughly discomfited. Gladstone's fudging speech aptly reflected the discredit of the episode. Gladstone gave indications of an awareness of this. 'This debate ought to be an epoch in Foreign Policy: we have much to learn. Ld P.'s speech was unequivocally weak: in the mental & the bodily sense.'[1]

[10]

The remainder of the 1864 session passed on a muted note. What was Gladstone's opinion of the proposed demolition of Claremont House? What to do about pensions for government servants in the Ionian Islands? Should the government give guarantees to the Metropolitan Board of Works for the Thames Embankment and Metropolis Improvements? The National Gallery and National Portrait Gallery continued as rich sources of broils. On the social side there was a three-hour Sunday sitting with Manning on 'Italy, & on home matters'.[2] Gladstone dined with Woolner to meet Tennyson, who obligingly read poetry. There was much dining at Panizzi's (on one occasion 'conversation especially with M. Mérimée').[3] On July 22 an observer noted Gladstone in Pall Mall, 'walking along unnoticed and alone. He looked at me in passing, and so enabled me the better to notice his brilliant flashing eyes and the stern and somewhat cynical melancholy of his mouth. At once, I said to myself, that is by far the most powerful face I have seen today.'[4] Possibly the stern melancholy of Gladstone's visage owed something to anticipations of the morrow's cabinet: 'Two hours stiff Cabinet chiefly on Canada Defences.' (Palmerston's version: 'Gladstone insufferably tiresome and obstinate against fortifying Quebec.')[5] That day there was a Council at Osborne. The Queen, as Gladstone reported to Catherine, 'asked particularly' about Palmerston's 'health and strength, without expressing any *wish* one way or another, which seems intelligible enough'. Gladstone 'told her a fact which surprised me a few days ago when I happened to follow him up the stairs to the H. of C. – he frequently took two steps at a time – and this, too, when no one saw him'.[6]

The Prime Minister's provoking capacity for survival was all the more *à propos* in view of the still audible reverberations set off by the franchise speech of May 11. To a resolution sent by a meeting of working men at Newark in early July Gladstone replied that while he was 'not friendly to

1 D, vi, 288.   2 *Ib.*, 285.   3 *Ib.*, 293.
4 Hudson, *Munby*, 200.   5 D, vi, 291 and n.   6 Bassett, 160.

changes either sudden or violent', he could not wonder that the men of his old constituency should 'regret' the 'almost entire withdrawal (as I presume it to be), in places like Newark, from their class of the privilege of the suffrage'; and he hoped to see public opinion 'move gradually and steadily in the direction of such measures as, while neither deranging nor disturbing society, would sensibly widen the basis of our institutions, and contribute in proportion to their stability and strength'.[1] On the other hand, Gladstone was chary of public demonstrations. He told Newman Hall, who specialised in Dissenting patronage of working class movements, that 'it would not be well to give further notoriety' by receiving a deputation.[2] George Melly proposed a visit to York. Gladstone replied that he 'could hardly go to York in particular with propriety for any public occasion at present, and particularly to meet the working men, as one meeting would almost certainly lead to some political demonstration'. Though Gladstone did not 'shrink from performing such duties as occasion may suggest in the House of Commons', yet, 'out of regard for what I consider morbid nerves,' he felt he 'ought not to seek the multiplication of such opportunities' where he had 'no local or other special call'.[3]

Gladstone himself was not immune from the reverberations caused by his own speech. Enlarging horizons and shifting skies were as alarming and unsettling as ever. The Oxford side of him remained sensitive to hostile vibrations. Walking with the Tory M.P. for Lancashire, John Wilson-Patten (an Oxford voter), he declared himself 'disgusted at being classed, as he now generally is, with the ultra-liberals: says he cannot imagine what he has said or done to earn that character, declares himself a Conservative in feeling: above all is perplexed at the effect produced by his speech on reform, which he meant and believed to be moderate in tone'.[4] In other moods Gladstone's Conservative feeling was subject to modification; as when, two weeks later, in conversation with Enfield, Liberal M.P. for Middlesex, he 'thought it would not do to go to a dissolution without some proof that they really were the Liberal party (his own words)'. The two questions on which Gladstone thought 'action possible' were 'reform and the Irish Church'. He 'would not explain as to the latter – what he thought ought to be done, but talked of the establishment as a "hideous blot" and used other strong language'. Gladstone expressed 'a personal wish that the present cabinet should fall, on the ground that it had grown indolent and feeble, and wants some years of opposition to give it new life'. Enfield remarked to Stanley that this might seem 'an odd speech from a minister but it is quite in Gladstone's line'. Enfield foresaw the Whigs' forming a separate party

1 GP, 44534, 97.   2 D, vi, 291.
3 G to Melly, August 8, 1864. GP, 44534, 111.   4 DDCP, 221.

such as the Peelites after 1846.[1] These shifting moods reflected a new version of a pattern as old as Gladstone's political career: the forming of each new vocation manifested itself in painful conflict between the imperatives of the 'discipline' of an 'age of shocks' and the deep instinct to cling to links of stability and safe anchorages.

Back at Hawarden in early August 1864 Gladstone had the pleasure of examining the new rooms built on to the north-west corner of the Castle, 'especially with a view to the vast undertaking of moving my books'. For the ground-floor room in the new block was to be the definitive 'Temple of Peace'. The exterior, in a rather coarse and heavy 'Victorian' style, contrasted with the more refined Regency Gothick of Sir Stephen's father's reconstruction at the beginning of the century. The 'Temple of Peace' had two pairs of windows on the west side looking up to the ruins of the old castle on a knoll to the west of the new; near the left-hand window Gladstone would set his two small desks. The other group of windows looked out from the north or entrance front. A passage (eventually book-lined and known to the family as the 'chapel of ease') linked the Temple with the centre of the Castle; and a doorway connected Gladstone's study-library with the neighbouring old great drawing-room. (False book backs on the drawing-room side of the door included such whimsical titles as *Beehive Houses* By a member of the Archaeojollical Society, *Hailstone's Descent from Snowdon, Ascent of Cader Idris* by Anthony Strollup Esq., *Witchcraft* by a Lancashire Lady, and four volumes of *An Israelite without Guile* by Ben Disraeli, Esq.) Studying the measurements of the new room was indeed a matter of high import to one who, like Gladstone, prided himself on his craft in the science of bookcase arrangement. It would in fact take a year before the library was substantially housed in its new quarters.

Immediate prospects for the estate at Hawarden were still somewhat doubtful. The Mancot coal seams proved disappointing. Gladstone worked on the 'rudiments of a scheme' to place Stephen 'high & dry': which was that Gladstone should purchase the reversion of the estate on behalf of his and Catherine's line subject to the lives of both Stephen and Henry (and subject to Henry's matrimonial fever being finally quieted). This would be a constant concern for the next year. Another immediate concern was Lancashire. As the Oxford situation deteriorated an expedient line of retreat suggested itself ever more insistently. In London Gladstone rather tended to flinch from confronting squarely the implications of his problem. Now there was need to make a reconnaissance in force to survey prospects and test the ground. A speaking tour in October to inaugurate the serious part of the year would be sensible. Gladstone wrote to Robertson on August 9: 'I hope to write soon about "comin'

1 *Ib.*, 222–23.

hover".'[1] He came over to Court Hey on August 25 and talked with Robertson of 'divers matters'. Meanwhile there was much to talk about with Bishop Wilberforce of Oxford on the matter of the Court of Appeal; and the Bishop was subjected to Gladstonian singing evenings ('Truly I am an old bird, & begin to crack in the upper region'). After a dinner at the Rectory on August 29 Gladstone 'tried to prepare H. Glynne for the probable necessity of some measures with a view to Stephen's relief & security in the possession of the property'.

The family, reinforced by a Bowden contingent, progressed once more to Penmaenmawr. The Bishop of Oxford rather maliciously noted Gladstone's weakness on heights ('curious to see his strong mind so unbend; his head easily giddy; cannot bear even the near approach to a precipice').[2] Willy was proving more 'satisfactory': his 'disinclination to try Parliament seems to be removed'. Gladstone indulged himself again in Pausanias and in rereading *Vanity Fair* ('very remarkable & on the whole a *good* book') and by giving a 'grand dinner party' of eleven covers ('haunch of venison & champagne'). He was much taken by W. Galt's *Railway Reform,* a scheme for state purchase of the railways under the terms of Gladstone's 1844 Act. After seeing Harry off to Eton the family encampment broke up; and Gladstone set out for Scotland.

The pattern of 1863 repeated itself with another Suit and Service as Minister in Attendance at Balmoral. The Queen's proposal that the whole Gladstone family should settle in the guest cottage at Abergeldie fell through ('to C. a disappointment. I felt both ways'). On this occasion the dramatic accident was not the oversetting of the Queen's sociable but, on October 1, the rending of Gladstone's pantaloons. He recounted to Catherine on the 2nd: 'I ended writing to you at 20 min or more past 8, and dress in the costume takes rather long, and she dines at $8\frac{1}{2}$ rather punctually: in my hurry I drew up the *pants* violently when lo! they rent frightfully! and I had to write then and there a note to Prince Alfred beseeching him to make my excuses for improper dress, after which with immense hurry I got ready in time.' He observed that the Queen drank her claret 'strengthened, I should have thought spoiled, with whiskey'.[3]

There were serious concerns also at Balmoral. 'I feel much pain', he wrote to Russell, 'in looking at the Irish difficulty, slowly growing up again.'[4] The more he read of Galt's scheme for state purchase and leasing out of railways the more his *étatist* instincts recommended it to him. At Balmoral he complained of 'much mental lassitude' and a disposition not only to 'shrink from public business but from hard books. It is uphill work'.[5] It was indeed on that day of rent pantaloons, October 1, in such a shrinking frame of mind as he contemplated the immensity of shifting

1 G to Robertson G. August 9, 1864. GP, 44534, 112.   2 D, vi, 298n.
3 Bassett, 161–63.   4 Prest, 'Gladstone and Russell', *Trans. Roy. Hist. Soc.* (1966), 53.
5 D, vi, 303.

skies and enlarging horizons, that Gladstone wrote to George Wilson of Manchester, now president of the Reform Union, pleading that those interested in the extension of the franchise should be thoroughly dissuaded from 'taking any step to connect my name with it, outside the walls of Parliament; I mean in any manner requiring presentation of an address'. Already there were people seeking to damage the cause by alleging that his speech on Baines's bill was 'an attempt to create a faction in support of myself'. Proceedings involving Gladstone outside parliament could be made to bear that dangerous misconstruction.[1] Gladstone, in less of a shrinking mood by October 6, also 'fired off' at Palmerston a formidable screed on taxation and expenditure. The logic behind Gladstone's initiative was that the catastrophe of the government's foreign policy could be turned compensatingly to good account. The obvious deduction to be drawn was that, if Britain abdicated as an interventionist European Great Power, the armaments expenditure appropriate to such a role need no longer be sustained. Gladstone was already clear that the events of the summer of 1864 'ought to be an epoch in Foreign Policy'. He had no doubts as to how such an epoch would most advantageously be inaugurated. Here was an opportunity to strike a decisive blow against Services estimates and achieve a fundamental shift in the budgetary balance which even at the time of his 'testamentary' budget of 1863 he had not dreamed would be possible. After all, it was in February 1862 that Gladstone had asked himself whether £21 or £27 millions was the right charge for defence, and concluded that 'we ought & will' be satisfied with £21 millions. Gladstone thus framed his letter to the Prime Minister possessed with a special sense that much was at stake.

On the civil side, he pointed out, the upward growth of expenditure had been arrested – thanks largely to a 'salutary reform' of the education department (he had earlier written to Granville a heartfelt tribute to Lowe and the 'sincerity & efficacy of his efforts for retrenchment'[2]; with cause: the Treasury grant for education dropped from something like £800,000 to £600,000 between 1861 and 1865).[3] But on the military side Gladstone put it sternly to Palmerston: 'Can we maintain that . . . twenty-six millions and a half. . . is really necessary to maintain the peace establishments of this country in a state of efficiency?' (He added that he would soon be speaking in Lancashire. 'In anything I may have to say, I shall endeavour to observe caution.')[4] Gladstone had felt the letter to Palmerston 'lying on me like a nightmare'. It was indeed impossible politically (and personally) for Gladstone openly to tell Palmerston that he was being asked to pay for the failure of the policy by which he had made his reputation. It was a

1 M. Cowling, *1867: Disraeli, Gladstone and Revolution* (1967), 31.
2 G to Granville, April 2, 1864. GP, 44534, 62.
3 Vincent, 222.   4 G & P, 292–96.

delicate matter for Gladstone to hit the right note of deductive implication. He meant it, as he told Catherine, 'to be moderate'; 'but unless he concurs it may lead to consequences between this and February. What is really painful is to believe that he will not agree unless through apprehension.'[1]

After a detour via Fasque where he discussed Bowden arrangements with Sir Thomas ('I urged the case of little Jack') Gladstone launched himself into the Lancashire tour. The novel element as compared with 1862 was the prominent role played by Robertson Gladstone. Robertson ('if possible more kind than ever')[2] massively embodied two important new links in Gladstone's public life: Dissent and Radicalism. He functioned now as Gladstone's principal impresario in Lancashire. His seat at Court Hey became Gladstone's field headquarters. Throughout the circuit of Bolton, Farnworth Park near Bolton, Liverpool (under the auspices of Robertson and the '*élite* of the commercial aristocracy of the city') and Manchester, Gladstone developed what were now his standard themes: the benign revolution in class relations, the great role of the legislation of the past twenty-five years, the 1853 budget, the commercial treaty, the 'moral and political consequences' of paper duty repeal in its effects on the popular press, the lessons of the cotton famine, the prospect of a 'brilliant chapter' in the future. The enthusiasm of the response he elicited was rather more than he bargained for. 'Great and real enthusiasm', he noted of the Farnworth occasion; 'I was much struck with the people.' The tour 'grew to proportions', as he later described it, 'that were in one point of view at least inconveniently large'.[3] When he came to haven on October 14 with the Dowager Countess of Ellesmere at Worsley, Gladstone reflected on the ending of an 'exhausting, flattering, I hope not intoxicating circuit. God knows I have not courted them: I hope I do not rely on them: I pray I may turn them to account for good'. Gladstone thus defined sufficiently for his own purposes the essential distinction between demagogy and *étatist* manipulation. He weakened from these soundly manipulatory sentiments sufficiently to add: 'It is however impossible not to love the people from whom such manifestations come, as met me in every quarter.' He retired 'somewhat haunted by dreams of halls, & lines of people, & great assemblies'.[4]

[11]

From two points of view the Lancashire tour of October 1864 was entirely satisfactory. In the short term, it proved to be a promising preview of a

1 Bassett, 162.   2 D, vi, 306.
3 G to Baines, December 28, 1864. GP, 44534, 175.   4 D, vi, 307.

possible recourse in the event (necessarily soon) of a general election; in the longer term, Gladstone could be reassured that the impetus of his campaign to form, manipulate, and direct a public opinion was being sustained. (There was, also, an incidental bonus: at Manchester, inspecting the 'beautiful Assize Courts', he met their architect Alfred Waterhouse; with important consequences for the future Natural History Museum at South Kensington.[1]) At Hawarden again there was a brief respite before he resumed the war of attrition with the Prime Minister. The library problem was 'a critical business for the lower room is *raw*'. By October 22, 2,000 books were installed and Gladstone, having completed the monumental task of sorting his correspondence up to 1858, moved into the new Temple of Peace to contemplate frowningly Palmerston's robustly unyielding response to his query from Balmoral as to whether £26.5 millions were really necessary to maintain peace establishments on an efficient footing. Palmerston, oblivious to any implications about deducing salutary lessons from the Danish affair, insisted that facts, not abstract principles, must prevail. He warned Gladstone that he was falling into the 'Fallacy of Joseph Hume' in confusing the principles of private and public economy. With an individual, expenditure had to be adjusted to income; but with the State 'Income ought to be adapted to meet that Expenditure'. There would be no chance of reductions in defence charges at a time when 'Inventions of Science and the Progress of Improvements have much increased these Branches of Expenditure'.[2]

Gladstone inaugurated his new Temple of Peace by replying to Palmerston 'in a rather decisive tone, for I feel conscious of right & necessity'.[3] He feared indeed, he told Palmerston, that he had 'not conveyed clearly to your mind the gravity of the situation in which I stand'. He had been a party to present arrangements only on condition of the prospective reductions which he had several times publicly referred to. Gladstone could not accept £25 millions as a 'proper charge' in such a time and place 'as this latter half of the nineteenth century affords'.[4] Palmerston rejoined, grappling indefatigably on every point. Gladstone was disposed to 'propound a Theory' that 'a Chancellor of the Exchequer, who . . . cannot have the aptitude and knowledge of a War Minister, or of a First Lord of the Admiralty', was nevertheless to be entitled 'to come to an arbitrary Conclusion, as to the proper amount of our Naval and Military Establishments'; and 'to impose this Will upon the Government . . . under Pain of those consequences which his Colleagues would of course deeply regret'. The generation gap between the two statesmen yawned unbridgeably when Palmerston met Gladstone's point about 'this latter half of the nineteenth century' with a blaze of rhetoric about the

1 *Ib.*, 306.   2 G & P, 297–304.
3 D, vi, 308.   4 G & P, 305–08.

undying resentments deep in every Frenchman's heart: the Nile, Trafalgar, the Peninsula, Waterloo, St. Helena.[1]

In the midst of this polemic with Palmerston Gladstone had news of Newcastle's death ('the very last of those contemporaries who were also my political friends. How it speaks to me!')[2]. He set off for Clumber on October 26 to attend the funeral at Markham Clinton on the 27th; then on to recently purchased Worksop Manor as executor of the embarrassed estate and trustee for its problematic heirs. 'He died in the room where he had been sitting before and after dinner,' he reported to Catherine, '– where, 32 years ago, a stripling, I came over from Newark in fear and trembling to see the Duke his father where a stiff horseshoe semi circle sat round the fire in evenings – where that rigour melted away in Lady Lincoln's time. . .'[3] From Worksop Gladstone told Catherine: 'You can hardly imagine the state of Newcastle's papers.' The Queen was avid for details of the demise and the funeral, which she acknowledged with a dirge on her own case ('isolated, broken-hearted & shattered', 'now the oak is felled & the ivy is gradually dying off – *crushed* for ever').[4]

On November 9 Gladstone prepared despondently to resume his wrangle with his chief. 'I received the enclosed very unfavourable letter from Lord Palmerston,' he reported to Catherine (after what he clearly considered to be an unwarranted delay); 'I send it with draft of my reply.' 'This *sort* of controversy keeps my nerves too highly strung, and makes me sensitive, fretful, and impatient. I am not by nature brave, I am always between two fears, and I am more afraid of running away than of holding my ground.'[5] Gladstone duly disclaimed ambitions to impose his will on his colleagues; his desire, he explained, rather begging the question, was to 'avoid the renewal of struggles in the Cabinet such as might wear that unseemly habit'. He requested that their correspondence be circulated.[6] (For her part, the Queen returned the letters to her Prime Minister with a 'cordial and unqualified approval of every word said by Lord Palmerston'.)[7]

Incongruously and ironically, two days later Gladstone found himself toasting 'The Army, Navy, and Volunteers of England' in the Freemasons' Tavern on the annual festival of the St. Martin's Division of the Volunteer Corps. He contrived to extol the movement as part of a 'pacific apparatus' of defence and as a middle class phenomenon linking classes in harmony.[8] Also rather incongruous but of more moment was an occasion in which his developing link with Newman Hall began to take specific shape. To Catherine he reported on November 15: 'I am going up

1 *Ib.*, 310–14.   2 D, vi, 308.   3 Bassett, 163–64.
4 G to CG, October 29, 1864. GG, 29/1; Q & G, i, 128–29.
5 Bassett, 164.   6 G & P, 314–15.
7 LQV, 2 ser., i, 243–44.   8 *Times*, November 11, 1864.

to Mr. Newman Hall's to meet some Dissenting Ministers at tea! What odd predicaments & situations life abounds with.'[1] There he met Robert Vaughan, Baldwin Brown, R. W. Dale of Birmingham, and other luminaries of Dissent. 'They behaved extremely well to me.'[2] Indeed they would. They had high hopes of Gladstone. He seemed to be shaping promisingly on both the Oxford and the Irish disestablishment fronts, as well as on the franchise question. That Gladstone should have written on the same day to Keble on the issue of extending the English Courts of Appeal in Ecclesiastical Causes to Ireland was a measure of his sense of odd predicaments. The immediate point at issue was that Gladstone had detected a plot concocted by Palmerston and Lord Chancellor Westbury to invent new legal links between the English and Irish Church establishments; and in later years he would recount proudly how he called in that veteran enemy of the Irish establishment, Russell, to scuttle the 'ingenious scheme'.[3] The larger point was that Keble was the leading proponent among Oxford Churchmen of Gladstone's cause as Oxford's – and the Church's – parliamentary representative. It was indeed on November 30, 1864, while writing to the *Guardian* to protest against the campaign in Oxford against Gladstone's candidature, that Keble suffered a stroke which betokened his death fifteen months later.

In November Gladstone settled into his pre-sessional London life. He maintained his rescue work at a steady pace (collaborating occasionally with James Stuart-Wortley, the former Solicitor-General, who concerned himself with aiding the husbands or other male attachments of Gladstone's subjects). The theological problem of everlasting punishment, brought up by the *Essays and Reviews* case, continued to exert its fascination. He wrote to the Rev. Sir George Prevost: 'In what a hurricane of religious agitation & severance we live ... What is it to be in our children's time? But the centre is immoveable.'[4] As for severance, Gladstone kept up his polemic with Manning, with particular reference now to the encyclical *Quanta cura* recently promulgated (December 8), with its notorious appendage, the *Syllabus errorum*, anathematising every principle cherished by nineteenth-century liberalism; and also to the Pope's temporal sovereignty. He accused Manning of fighting 'in the name of religion against natural right & justice'; of subjecting peoples 'to serve the theories of ecclesiastical power'.[5] Gladstone was also having his own battles with domestic ecclesiastical power: he was harassed with disputes about his plan to build another church at Seaforth; and submitted the case indignantly to the Ecclesiastical Commissioners. As

1 GGP, 29/1.   2 D, vi, 313.
3 *Rendel*, 120. G to Keble, November 15, 1864. GP, 44534, 158.
4 G to Prevost, December 15, 1864. GP, 44534, 164.
5 G to Manning, December 26, 1864. *Ib.*, 174–75.

against these vexations, it was always a special pleasure to dine at Francis Palgrave's to meet Tennyson ('saw him after a late evening. He read us the Grandmother')[1]. Gladstone was working hard on his own poetical account on his Homer translations: 'some lines will take an hour', as he ruefully remarked of his 'Shield of Achilles'.[2] A cabinet on November 29 was chiefly on the estimates, '& as to the Navy stiff enough'. The railways question was also on his mind. So obsessed did he become that he made of it a kind of ludicrously Lilliputian version of his grand political campaigns. 'I have *promoted* the public discussion of the subject of Railways,' he informed Argyll, 'as a needful preliminary, in this case, to forming a public opinion.'[3] Again there was work to be done at Clumber with other executors and trustees and the unsatisfactory young Duke ('turned my back on Clumber . . . I wish I were without misgivings for it or what belongs to it').[4]

Before departing from Clumber on December 10 Gladstone wrote to a new acquaintance (who had been a friend of the late Duke's), a Mrs. Thistlethwayte (*née* Laura Eliza Jane Seymour, daughter of Captain R. H. Bell of Bellbrook, Co. Antrim, bailiff on the estates of the Marquess of Hertford). After a spectacular career as a Dublin belle and then as one of the more 'notorious Hetaerae' of Hyde Park, Laura Bell had married in 1852 Captain Augustus Thistlethwayte, a former military gentleman resident in Grosvenor Square.[5] The captain was of good family (his mother, Tryphena, was a daughter of Bishop Bathurst of Norwich); but of odd humour and uncertain temper. (It was his custom to fire a pistol at the ceiling to summon a servant.) His estate was only 500 acres; 'but all lay between the Edgware and Bayswater Roads.'[6] Laura's extravagance compelled him on several occasions to advertise that he would not be responsible for her debts. She was a very beautiful lady, 'the greatest beauty of the age', according to T. H. Escott, described by the artist J. R. Herbert as 'half sybil, half prophetess, with beauty enough at times to

1 Published with 'Enoch Arden' later that year. D, vi, 314.
2 *Ib.*, 320.
3 G to Argyll, 20 Dec. 1864. GP, 44534, 172.
4 *Ib.*, 318. These misgivings were well founded. The new Duke had married in 1861 in defiance of his father the bastard daughter of the banker H. T. Hope in order to get his debts paid off. The 'Beckford disease' touched his brothers and sister: Lord Arthur, spendthrift and worthless, 'enslaved by an unmentionable perversion', was charged in 1870 with transvestism and died while out on bail: Lady Susan eloped in 1859 with Lord Adolphus Vane-Tempest, a syphilitic alcoholic wastrel, who died a maniac in 1864: Lord Albert married a woman who shut herself up in a Roman Catholic convent in Kensington and escaped to live with the co-respondent in the subsequent divorce action. Lord Edward alone avoided the Beckford inheritance. (Surtees, *The Beckford Inheritance*, 131–34.)
5 The *Army Lists* of 1850 and 1851 disclose that Augustus Frederick Thistlethwayte entered the Army on December 29, 1846, joined the 26th Foot (The Cameronians) as ensign on February 9, 1849 and retired in 1850.
6 MRDF.

make one secretly offer praises and thanks to the great Maker of it'.[1] Landseer was reputedly one of her lovers.[2] An affair with Jung Bahador, the Nepalese minister, made her one of the 'sights of the town'. It was said the Opera House stood to view her departure. She seems to have undergone some kind of 'ethical' religious regeneration shortly after the time of her marriage; about which she lectured at the London Polytechnic as 'a sinner saved by the grace through faith in the hands of God'. Her appearance on the platform 'was a realization of beauty and art', her graceful hands adorned with 'large diamond rings'.[3] Although respectably married, and a well-known equestrienne in Rotten Row (where Gladstone probably met her), Mrs. Thistlethwayte's equivocal reputation, her 'past' as a notorious figure of the demi-monde, made her reminiscent in some ways of an earlier Irish beauty, Margaret Power of Knockbrit, Co. Tipperary, Countess of Blessington. She was thus not a 'case' for Gladstone in the sense that his two previous most disturbing cases – Collins and Summerhayes – had been. (He was still seeing Summerhayes – or Dale – occasionally, though without the anguish of other days.) But, perhaps all the more because of her 'saved' condition and her profession as a female evangelist, Mrs. Thistlethwayte's attractiveness was to prove even more unsettling.

At Hawarden Gladstone mingled contentedly with a large but 'choice' house party ('Both the Talbot ladies are very striking: Lady A. charming in a high degree'; they were also equal to conversations on Dante). He divided the last days of 1864 between Homer-translating ('tried doing the same bit of the Shield into Trochaics with much more difficulty'), the railway question, 'talking Italy' with Lady Feilding, and getting to know some of the younger generation such as Lionel Tollemache (later to be one of his more notable personal memoirists) and Charles Wood, later Lord Halifax and the leading Anglo-Catholic layman ('he is devoted, after the manner of 25 years or 20 years ago').[4] To Edward Baines he wrote declining an invitation to make a pre-sessional appearance in the West Riding. After the somewhat hectic circuit in Lancashire Gladstone 'felt that propriety required me at once to resolve that nothing resembling it should take place during the present recess'.[5] On December 29: 'And now for fifty-five years have I cumbered this earth, & while others my betters go, I am not removed. May the *whole* intention of my life be to be given to God during what remains of it.' On the eve of the new year what came home to Gladstone most signally was a sense that 'all the ascent seems to lie yet before me, none behind'.

While briefly in London Gladstone celebrated the launching of 1865 by

1 D, v, lxii, n.1.   2 MRDF. See above, 496 n.6.
3 C. Pearl, *The Girl with the Swansdown Seat*, 120–22.
4 D, vi, 318–20.   5 G to Baines, December 28, 1864. GP, 44534, 175.

accompanying Miss Burdett-Coutts, the banking heiress and philanthropist, to the Covent Garden pantomime. He found this much more amusing than a large house party with his Cheshire neighbours the Westminsters at Eaton a few days later ('it is always rather heavy here: the hosts seem bored with their work & anxious to end it').[1] Before departing from Hawarden for Cliveden on January 17 (with Harry in tow, bound for Eton), Gladstone thoughtfully arranged to sign a conveyance over to twenty-year-old Stephy making him a Flintshire freeholder (and therefore a useful 'faggot' voter in the forthcoming elections).[2] At Cliveden there was much talk with Duchess Harriet on the Queen's 'retirement & its effect on her influence'. He inaugurated the London sessional rescue season by dealing with 'a sort of wild case'. A cabinet on the 19th was in its way a sort of wild case too: 'about as rough as any of the roughest times.' As he complained to Catherine, he had had 'no effective or broad support' on the Navy estimates; 'platoon firing more or less in my sense from Argyll and Gibson – four or five more silent – the rest hostile.' Although there was thankfully an evident 'unwillingness to have a row', these 'batterings' Gladstone found 'sore work'; 'but I must go through.' Going through meant two more stiff memoranda on the Defence of British North America and Navy estimates reduction. Lords Palmerston and Russell 'really are our old women on these subjects'.[3]

In the intervals of batterings Gladstone haunted Tattersall's horse auctioneers fruitlessly to catch the errant Lord Albert Clinton, wrote to Mrs. Thistlethwayte, prepared Herbert for the idea of going to Eton, and saw a deputation of working men 'on opening of Museums at night – much other kindred matter'.[4] Cabinet battle was joined again on the naval estimates on January 28. 'The morning went fast but wretchedly. Seldom, thank God, have I a day to which I could apply this epithet. Last night I could have done anything to shut out the thought of the coming battle. This is very weak: but it is the effect of the constant recurrence of such things: estimates always settled at dagger's point.' In cabinet Gladstone found himself decisively out-gunned. 'I reserved my judgment.' Talks with Clarence Paget (Secretary of the Admiralty) and Hugh Childers (then a Lord of the Admiralty) offered no hope of redress; and Gladstone, defeated, 'sent my assent to Lord P.', conceding that feeling was generally against him, but allowing that concessions, inadequate but conciliatory, had been made to him; and so acquiesced 'reluctantly' in the proposed Navy estimates.[5] Gladstone retreated in some disorder to Lady Wenlock's 'hospitable house at Brighton'. 'Still tempest-tost' on the morrow, Sunday, he soothed himself with Hove churchgoing and then rejoined Catherine for an Osborne (two hours with Helen on

1 D, vi, 325.   2 Stephy would be twenty-one on April 4, 1865.
3 Bassett, 165.   4 D, vi, 329–30.   5 G & P, 320.

the way), the highlight of which was partnering the Prince of Wales at whist.

With February 1865 came problems of budgetary preparation. Palmerston set about exploiting his advantage with a long disquisition from Brocket on the merits of not reducing the income tax further. It was, he pointed out, a tax exclusively on the upper and middle classes. Reduction would have the appearance of unfairness to classes who pay only indirect taxes, and who paid, moreover, a much higher proportion of their income in taxes. Hence a reduction of the income tax to 5d would be tolerable; but 4d would look like a move to abolition. A further point urged by the Prime Minister was that the income tax had the merit of being a tax which tended to become more productive of revenue. Its cornucopic character was, indeed, precisely Gladstone's complaint against it. Gladstone was ready to concede that ultimate extinction of the tax was not possible in the present state of opinion. 'And this is a large admission,' he stressed to Palmerston, 'when it is recollected that about half of us were members of a Government, which formally submitted a plan for that purpose . . . bearing more or [less] resemblance to a promise . . . ' The 1853 budget was ever Gladstone's favourite political child. But he contested the assumption that a reduction to 4d would imply abolition. At 5d income tax would yield £6,200,000: an 'unmanageable' sum; hence reduction was essential. Gladstone still thought 'as a matter of individual feeling and honour' that parliament should get to the point of planned extinction provided for in 1853 and then determine about retention or abolition in a 'condition of freedom'.[1] Gladstone braced himself on February 3 with a congenial discussion of the railway question at the Political Economy Club.

[12]

The session of 1865 was to be the last of the 1859 parliament. The political atmosphere was heavy with the sense of the ending of an era. There was much talk of Palmerston's not meeting the new House of Commons after the elections but retiring to the Lords to assist in Gladstone's assumption of the leadership of the Commons and to mediate in likely quarrels. Stanley recorded on February 14 that of Gladstone 'the language held on his own side is, "He must lead, there is no one who can compete with him, and yet his temper and restlessness make him entirely unfit"'. *The Times* was his declared enemy. His colleagues, 'to put it in its mildest form', were 'not cordial friends'. He was decidedly unpopular with the Opposition. 'His strength lies in his extraordinary gift of speech, his

1 *Ib.*, 320–22.

great general ability, and the support of the mercantile class in the manufacturing towns.'[1]

One man's nervousness about Gladstone's 'temper and restlessness' was another man's hopeful anticipation. And such hopeful anticipation was indeed likely to be expressed by the representatives of the mercantile class in manufacturing towns. Just as the 1864 session opened in the knowledge that Edward Baines of Leeds would introduce his Borough Franchise Bill, so the 1865 session opened with the announcement that Lewis Llewelyn Dillwyn, Quaker M.P. for Swansea, would move a resolution that the Church of Ireland was in a very unsatisfactory state and that the early attention of Her Majesty's Government to its situation was desirable. As with Baines's bill, Dillwyn's resolution was framed very much with a view to the irresistible temptation it would proffer to Gladstone's temper and restlessness.

Meanwhile, as both nervousness and anticipation stewed quietly together, and as both budget and Irish Church hovered, Gladstone attended to his multifarious concerns. He had to break the news to Newman Hall that there was little prospect of an early recognition of the claims of persons other than members of the established religion to share in the government of the colleges of Oxford and Cambridge.[2] The following day, Sunday, he read the 'MS of 1847' aloud (presumably as a prophylactic) and then 'Sat alone an hour with Mrs. Thistlethwayte: to speak of the D. of Newcastle: but much also of religion, & some of herself.' Soon he was reading 'Notes on Genesis (Mrs. T.s gift)'.[3] The enormous range of Gladstone's concerns was extended on February 15 by his meeting the Archpriest Wassilieff, a leading Russian Orthodox advocate of closer links with Anglicanism. Although not a member of the Eastern Churches Association founded in 1863 (it was delicate political ground) Gladstone was familiar with its members, and approved its strategy of outflanking Roman Catholicism.[4] It was no doubt with mixed feelings that he offered Cobden the chairmanship of the Board of Audit (it was an enormous relief to be rid at last of the obnoxious Monteagle and the apostle of Free Trade was in financial straits); a function, Gladstone emphasised, to be strengthened and raised in conformity with the recommendation of the Committee of Public Accounts of 1857. More to the point, the salary was to be increased from £1,500 to £2,000.[5] As for the treaty of commerce with Austria, Gladstone inclined to agree with Russell that little was to be expected from the Austrians, but shared at the same time his reluctance to refuse. Austrian benightedness was, after all, only

1 DDCP, 228.
2. G to Newman Hall, February 4, 1865. GP, 44535, 11.   3 D, vi, 332–33.
4 On this theme see Matthew, 'Gladstone, Vaticanism and the Question of the East', in *Studies in Church History* xv, ed. D. Baker, 426.
5 G to Cobden, February 10, 1865. GP, 44535, 14.

to be expected; and the same could be said for Portugal and Denmark. But Gladstone found himself sorely provoked by the 'disgraceful behaviour of Italy!!!' over rag duties. He complained to Milner Gibson that Austria and the others 'are all bad – but the case of Italy is really too bad'.[1] (He had, after all, particularly warned Lacaita in 1860.) He was as keen as ever to do something big about the railways. He told Stanley of his plans for a commission on which Bright could serve (a kind of political house training) to examine a scheme to buy up the companies' interests and lease them out on short terms and stringent conditions. He was sure the railway companies had 'too much influence' and were an unhealthy 'power in the state', besides being wasteful and inefficient. In any event he was sure that parliamentary and Board of Trade supervision should be much more stringent. Gladstone's *étatist* zeal, even when prompted by Stanley, did not extend however to taking over the whole of the telegraphic system by the Post Office: he was ready enough in principle, but 'doubted the expediency: telegraphs . . . might be superseded and the capital invested in them be lost'.[2]

The first whiff of the Irish case came before the end of February. In a debate upon the state of Ireland, Irish members, resentful at the attention lavished on Lancashire for a degree of distress chronic in Ireland, called for measures to induce improvement and prosperity. Gladstone could not respond positively as Chancellor of the Exchequer. His doctrine of 'equality of treatment' ruled out Ireland as a fiscal special case. This was the point he had stressed also in Lancashire in laying it down that a public grant was not to be thought of, and that a loan of £200 millions guaranteed by the 'vast property' of Lancashire was as far as he would go. He extolled Lancashire as exhibiting triumphantly the 'infinite superiority' of the 'voluntary system', the machinery of which he celebrated as 'a great and important fact in itself'. The Irish case was far different. There was no vast property there upon which a triumphant voluntary principle could exhibit its infinite superiority. Yet it was impossible for Gladstone to respond otherwise. He deplored vague resolutions about relief measures (tax exemptions, public works, Shannon improvements) which raised expectations but which offered no matured mode giving effect to benevolent feelings.[3]

It was one thing, however, to fend off the Irish as a notoriously economical Chancellor of the Exchequer. It was quite another to fend off the question of the Irish Church as one who had watched it with a kind of fascinated horror since 1845. By 1865 Gladstone was absolutely clear that if the case of the Irish Church was fairly and squarely presented in the House of Commons there was no way consistent with personal integrity,

1 G to Gibson, February 25, 1865. GP., 44535, 23.
2 DDCP, 229–30.   3 H, clxxvii, 676–84.

political decency, and parliamentary honour by which he could evade it. Oxford would have to be prepared for the traumatic event. He conferred with Phillimore on March 2 'respecting Oxford seat & Irish Church'. Phillimore recorded: 'Full discussion-as to G's views on Irish Ch. & communicating with Oxf. Constituency. Resolved that G. shd. speak on Dillwyn's forthcoming motion in Parlt. & *after* that our circular should issue. At present the enemy has quite failed in his canvass. But –.'[1] On the side of setting up a line of possible retreat Gladstone was already consulting Brand who in turn was in touch with the Lancashire people. Characteristically, now that things were at a point of decision, Gladstone-felt it was his duty to take a stiff line. 'Nothing would induce me at my time of life to look that constituency in the face, except being assured that it was politically for the advantage of those with whom I am in union.' He was impatient for the 'Lancashire folks' to get down to expressing their views and intentions and settling the matter. 'Let some kind of Caucus down there dispose of the affair.'[2] After all, it was a delicate juggling operation. It would not do his prospects for the university any good if word got about that he was ardently wooing South Lancashire. The Lancashire folks were getting a dose of the *hauteur* which Gladstone's colleagues knew well.

In such a nervous atmosphere it was not surprising that, as Stanley observed, Gladstone's 'social unpopularity' appeared to be increasing. 'His colleagues detest him, and make little scruple in saying so – Wood and Clarendon more particularly. He is complained of as overbearing and dictatorial beyond what is permitted even to men of his eminence, while his eccentricities attract ridicule.' Stanley had a story of Gladstone staying at Lord Chesham's (Latimer House – Gladstone actually stayed there February 24-27) and passing Sunday evening 'in singing hymns with his wife, the Bishop of Oxford, who was present, reluctantly compelled to join but revenging himself afterwards by telling the story'. There were stories also of Gladstone's frantic porcelain purchases being secretly countermanded by Mrs. Gladstone. Malicious rumours were certainly rampant. Harriet, Lady Clanricarde (Canning's only daughter), who detested Gladstone quite as much as did any of his colleagues, assured Stanley that Gladstone had told her he believed in phrenology. 'He assured her, she says, that in his own case the external shape of his head had changed with his mental progress.'[3] Suspicion of Gladstone as a crypto-Roman Catholic was as much as ever a source of hostility. Herbert's widow's conversion was ascribed to Gladstone's influence. At a levée on March 22 Palmerston confided anxiously to Clarendon that he

1 D, vi, 338n.   2 G to Brand, February 27, 1865. GP, 44535, 25.
3 DDCP, 228, 231–32. Gladstone undoubtedly dabbled in the cult, as he did also in spiritualism.

had 'the best reason for knowing' that if Gladstone were rejected at Oxford and 'returned for a constituency like S. Lancashire', he would 'within six months profess himself a R. Catholic'. Even Clarendon, convinced as he was of Gladstone's incipient insanity, scouted this as extravagant, a product of Gladstone's excuses for Lady Herbert, his language about the Colenso case, and his ambiguity about the Irish Church.[1]

Certainly Gladstone's increasing isolation among his colleagues led to a sense of dissociation. The nearer he got to South Lancashire the more his Liverpool origins were remembered. Stanley, himself the heir of the greatest of Lancashire magnates, observed: 'Between him and the Whig party there is a fundamental difference. They are sceptical, he is dogmatic and inclined to religious enthusiasm: they are oligarchic and territorial by tradition: his connections are mercantile and popular: they are bound together by close family and social ties, he is isolated, will never consent to share power, but like Peel, if he makes any friends, will choose them only among men young enough to be his pupils.' Yet Stanley judged that these differences, 'though fatal to friendship, may give way before the necessity of political union: at least for a time'.[2] There were occasions when, even with his own connections, the kind of Gladstone sketched by Stanley could rub painfully against the kind of Whig he sketched also. When George Lyttelton presumed in April 1865 to express some misgivings his brother-in-law called him tersely to order: 'Please to recollect that we have got to govern millions of hard hands; that this must be done by force, fraud, or goodwill; that the latter has been tried and is answering; that none have profited more by this change of system since the corn law and the Six Acts, than those who complain of it.'[3] 'It is certain,' Stanley noted on March 22, 'that of late G. has been in an excited and irritable condition, for which nothing in the state of public business appears to account...'[4]

It was indeed on March 22 that Gladstone dined with the Thistle-thwaytes, remaining 'till near 12: an extraordinary but interesting scene'.[5] Catherine accompanied him on his social visits to Mrs. Thistle-thwayte's evangelical tea parties; but the deeper personal and emotional relationship Gladstone formed with the lady was an aspect of his life which he did not share with his wife.[6] Gladstone had written thrice to Mrs. Thistlethwayte earlier in the month, while working on the 'Rudi-ments of a Budget' (partly in bed 'to get quit of my sore throat'). As the editor of his journal has put it, in Mrs. Thistlethwayte Gladstone had

---

1 *Ib.*, 230.   2 *Ib.*, 230.
3 Morley, ii, 133.   4 DDCP, 230.   5 D, vi, 343.
6 See Matthew's comments, D, v, lxiv-v. Gladstone's letters to Mr. T were included by his secretaries in his letter copy books; but not those to Mrs. T. For them, see *ib.*, lxii, n.5.

found 'an ideal object of fascination: educated enough to understand something of his mind, young enough to offer beauty, religious enough to seem redeemed, but exotic enough to stand outside the ring of society women with whom he usually corresponded on religion'.[1] Thus invigorated, he mounted his chestnut on March 17 for his first canter in Rotten Row and went later to inspect the new Wales baby at Marlborough House ('really a cheering infant, & the Princess was a perfect Mother' – the future George V). Dining with the Apponyis at the Austrian Embassy on March 27 was doubtless more the sort of steadying occasion Gladstone needed to brace himself for the Irish Church debate due the following day.

Gladstone's relationship to the Irish Church question was in one important respect markedly different from that of the franchise. Most of his colleagues in the Cabinet were critical of or even hostile to the Church of Ireland as an establishment. It was not Gladstone's opinion about the Irish Church which caused nervousness; it was that he might propose to do something drastic about it soon. Stanley reported a rumour 'widely circulated' in mid-March 1865 that 'ministers intended supporting Dillwyn's motion'. Wood informed him that the rumour was unfounded: the subject had 'not even been seriously discussed'. Wood himself believed the Irish establishment 'an abomination' and believed that most public men felt the same thing; 'but an attempt to meddle with it would be madness – that he should be sorry to answer for what Gladstone might or might not say on any question (laughing) but he was not aware of any intention to support Dillwyn even indirectly. Certainly no joint action would be taken by the cabinet.'[2] Palmerston felt that a word in season would not be amiss. He wrote to Gladstone on the 27th: 'I understand that you propose to state Tomorrow on Dillwyn's Motion about the Irish Church your personal views on the Matter, as an Individual but not as a Member of the Government.' But was it possible for a 'Member of a Government speaking from the Treasury Bench to sever himself from the Body Corporate to which he belongs, as to be able to express decided opinions as an Individual, and leave himself free to act upon different opinions, or to abstain from acting upon those opinions when required to act as a Member of the Government taking Part in the Decision of the Body'?

This was a shrewd question. Probably it gave Gladstone pause; especially as Palmerston reinforced it by pointing to the possibility of a future dilemma, if Gladstone were to differ from colleagues, of either silence or acquiescence or the bringing before the public unnecessarily or prematurely differences of opinion among responsible ministers.[3] There was also, of course, Oxford to think about; and he had no particular desire

1 Matthew, *ib.*, lxiii.　　　2 DDCP, 229.　　　3 G & P, 326.

to have another 'row'. However this may be, in his approach to the question on the 28th Gladstone certainly did all he reasonably could to accommodate Palmerston's cautionary counsel. Gladstone actually saw Palmerston on the 27th; which almost certainly accounts for the fact that Gladstone delivered his statement – for all that he felt it 'a case of lifesave: I could not say less'[1] – as a member of the government. He opened by announcing that ministers were 'not able to concur' in the motion, though at the same time they were 'not prepared to deny the abstract truth' of that part of it which propounded that the Church of Ireland was in a very unsatisfactory state. Ministers could not support the whole motion unless they were willing now or soon to bring in 'some plan for the purpose of removing that unsatisfactory character'. Such a course – admitting the problem but 'declining to look the truth fully in the face' – would not be very popular. But that could not be helped: 'This, perhaps, is not so much a question for the present as for future consideration.' Gladstone then retailed all the stock arguments: the failure of the Irish Church as a Protestant mission; the advantages to the Irish Church as a missionary church of not being an anomalous establishment; the present situation hindering rather than helping its popularity; the mistake of supposing that 'the exclusive establishment of one religion is in all circumstances favourable to the progress of that religion'; the mistake of supposing that disestablishment in Ireland would harm the establishment of religion in England. All this indicated that in the present position of the Church of Ireland were 'elements which show that her difficulties cannot be surmounted by the wisdom of her rulers or by the piety and devotion of her clergy, but that they are the essential elements of a false position'. What was the remedy? The issue bristled with problems. Look at the damage the Liberal party did to itself in 1834 and 1835. This was a 'serious warning'. The 'dictates of propriety and good sense' compel ministers' not supporting the motion and not making a promise 'it would be out of our power to fulfil'.[2]

This highly circumspect declaration virtually killed the debate. Dillwyn's motion fell flat. Goschen was soon able to move and carry an adjournment. When Dillwyn a month later tried desperately to 'induce the Government to assist' him in resuscitating his motion Grey quietly buried it. As Gladstone had said, it was a question for the future rather than the present. Gladstone later testified that had anyone asked him in the first half of 1865 'How soon will it come in?' he would have replied, 'Heaven knows; perhaps it will be five years, perhaps it will be ten.' There was a further, personal consideration. By 1865, Gladstone pointed out, he had completed thirty-three years of a laborious career. He had followed most of his contemporaries to their graves. It was hard to find in the

1 D, vi, 344.   2 H, clxxviii, 421–34.

whole history of the country someone permitted to reach the fortieth year of labour in the House of Commons. Hence he did not have in 1865 a sense of a practical application to '*himself*' personally.[1] This was a fair point; though it is also material to recall that as he contemplated 1865 Gladstone expressed a sense of feeling that all the ascent seemed to lie yet before him, none behind. That Gladstone should be in two minds on the question was not wonderful. On the one hand the momentum of his career was not retarded by any impediments either of health or lack of vocational credentials. On the other hand dismantling the Irish establishment, unlike any of the practical objects of his previous vocations, had about it a negative or destructive character. The role of destroyer of an edifice hallowed by the ages went counter to all Gladstone's deepest instincts. Moreover, for the first time, Gladstone would also be putting himself in the firing line of a widespread and strongly-felt resentment. The unpopularity provoked by the paper duties issue took him unawares; and was, in any case, comparatively restricted and incurred furthermore in a positively constructive cause. The Irish Church was a quite different matter. It would be a case of deliberately grasping a virulent nettle.

But above all the crucial factor which determined Gladstone's assessment of the political equation in the 1850s remained in full sovereign authority: Gladstone had yet to be convinced that there would be a public opinion – a 'movement of the public mind' was his later phrase – correspondently responsive to the 'insight' expressed in his 'temper and restlessness'. Gladstone – to adapt the phraseology he applied, a little absurdly, to the railways issue – had '*promoted* the public discussion of the subject' as 'a needful preliminary, in this case, to forming a public opinion'. That opinion had still to be formed and manipulated. It is certainly true that Gladstone entertained no high hopes whatever of the formative powers of the elections soon to be held. He proved indeed to be as astonished at the apparent popularity of ministers as he had at the strength and unanimity of the sentiment for peace in June 1864. Gladstone was no prophet. The cast of his mind about the government was quite accurately reflected in his remarks to Enfield in July 1864: the present Cabinet should fall, on the grounds that it had grown indolent and feeble, and wanted some years of opposition to give it new life. There were, further, the grounds unspoken but more specific, that Gladstone had fulfilled his budgetary programme and the vocation expressed by it; and that therefore he had no immediate need of a government base or fulcrum. Enfield's comment, also, that such an 'odd' opinion was 'quite in Gladstone's line' was an accurate assessment of Gladstone's outlook in March 1864 and, even more pertinently, at the very height of the election campaign in July 1865.

1 *A Chapter of Autobiography*, 45.

It was thus not simply a matter of circumspection for Gladstone, whether in the long view of the difficulties of the case, or the short view of the difficulties of Oxford. It was a matter, rather, of applying something of the same kind of fundamental misreading to England which he was still stubbornly applying to America. The difficulties of Oxford were certainly too close for comfort. What was sufficiently circumspect to mollify Palmerston was by no means apt to pacify a suspicious and largely clerical constituency. As the elections approached Gladstone was approached by his old acquaintance the headmaster of Glenalmond, Hannah, who enquired on behalf of a former Oxford pupil, now a Dean in the Irish Church, as to Gladstone's view of that body. Gladstone responded with an elucidating gloss on his words about the Church of Ireland calculated to be as balm to the soreness of Oxford wounds. He stressed that the question of the Irish Church was 'remote, and apparently out of all bearing on the practical politics of the day'; hence he had no scheme or basis of a scheme in mind. He had only one clear landmark in view: that the Union should be preserved and that the Irish bishops should retain their seats in the House of Lords. He stressed, secondly, that the question was difficult, and that hence he offered no views about a mode of operation. He offered also for sympathetic consideration the 'broad distinction' to be made in politics between 'abstract' and 'practical' views. This was the reason why he had been so long silent on the question; and why probably he would be so again. But he trusted it would be understood why he was unwilling both as a minister and as a Member of Parliament for Oxford University to allow the question to be debated an indefinite number of times and remain silent.[1] Which was about as placatory an effort as was decently possible; and gave substance to Palmerston's comment earlier to Shaftesbury about the expedience of keeping Gladstone tied down by his university seat.

[13]

The 'first day with a taste of spring' in 1865 – March 30 – Gladstone devoted to a meeting of the Colonial Bishoprics Trust, of which he was treasurer. The trust decided, to Gladstone's approval, to take an opinion as to stopping Colenso's stipend as Bishop of Natal (Colenso successfully challenged this in an action in the Court of Chancery in 1866). Thence Gladstone proceeded to Marlborough House and what was to prove his last meeting with the aged King Leopold of the Belgians (the king died on December 10). Soon there was yet another contemporary to follow to his

1 *A Chapter of Autobiography*, 42–3. Hannah to G, June 8, 1865. GP, 44406, 272–74; G to Hannah, June 8, 1865. *Ib.*, 276–77.

grave. On May 3 Gladstone was 'much shocked by reading Cobden's death in the morning papers'. The funeral at West Lavington was notable for Bright's weeping at the graveside and for slyly remarking afterwards 'amid soothing words' "I doubt if he'd have liked the 6 parsons though"'. (The mourners went 'afterwards to his house which I was anxious to know'.) Russell urged that the widow be granted a pension of £1,500 a year: 'Cobden loved the Crown: Bright does not.'[1] But in his own household Gladstone could rejoice in the growth of new life. Stephy's twenty-first birthday was a particularly happy event. 'C. & I gave him a copy of her portrait. His young life is full of promise of the best kind.'[2] The boy seemed gratifyingly steady in a vocation for Holy Orders. Willy's career, however, was more problematical. Gladstone was at shifts to arrange for Willy to contest a seat at Chester in the coming elections. A rival Liberal candidate had to be elbowed out of the running. But with the editor of the *Chester Chronicle* on his side, primed with serviceable material, Gladstone prevailed. As with Gladstone's useful connections with the *Daily Telegraph*, he could doubtless reflect on the manifold fruits of paper duties repeal. It was also, with memories of the 1861 Flintshire election in mind, a gratifying assertion of Hawarden power in Grosvenor territory. Amid preparations for the budget Gladstone attended to every detail of the Chester campaign ('Wrote for Willy answer to requisition').[3]

For Easter Gladstone repaired to salubrious Brighton. He diverted himself by attending a Volunteer review. 'Saw Punch there: & a fortune teller (not on her art); also heard a sermon.'[4] From Brighton he wrote to Palmerston with a sketch of a budget he proposed to put before the Cabinet. One penny or two off the income tax? Gladstone preferred 2d, to be balanced by a tax of 4d in the pound on the value of all rateable buildings. Palmerston, afflicted with gout, could not attend the cabinet; but he made his views on the impolicy of imposing new taxes on property vigorously clear.[5] Gladstone found himself much fatigued by alternating 'between manipulating forms of Budget & discussing Chester electioneering'. This, perhaps, was hardly surprising if Willy was not allowed even to write his own answer to the Chester requisition. And, as a young Gladstone was being manipulated into the Commons, in an old Gladstone renewed ambitions stirred. Gladstone learned from Louisa in London that Tom, after an absence from the Commons since 1842, was determined to contest Kincardineshire as a Tory, on the pending retirement of the sitting Tory member, unopposed since 1832.

As budget day approached Gladstone was 'much vexed with neuralgia'; and much more vexed on budget morning, April 27, to find in his *Times* that his intentions had been 'leaked'. (Palmerston confided the

1 D, vi, 347; Russell to G, April 19, 1865. GP, 44292, 156.   2 D, vi, 346.
3 *Ib.*, 351.   4 *Ib.*, 349.   5 G & P, 330–31.

details to Delane 'two days before publication, and even before the final settlement of its provisions in cabinet'.)[1] Gladstone smoothed his ruffled feathers by calling at Christie's and putting down a bid of 58 guineas for J. Leech's 'The Sad Sea Waves'. His financial statement, the seventh in series and ninth of his time at the Exchequer, would be the last of the present parliament. He had already designated 1863 as the winding up of a great chapter of finance. He had, it was true, failed in 1864 in his last *blitzkrieg* against the military estimates. He confessed that, while the 'ordinary Civil Expenditure of the country, as a whole, has ceased to exhibit an increase', the real increase in all public expenditure *per annum* as compared with 1853 was ten millions. That was the measure of his sense of what he had failed to achieve against Palmerston. He was able to cover himself with the consideration that there had never been a period in the country's history when the expenditure had been 'more entirely in consonance with the general ideas, wishes, and feelings of the nation at large'. On the positive side, Gladstone could point to the almost disturbing buoyancy of the revenue: 1d of income tax used to mean £1 million of revenue; now it meant £1.3 million. Accordingly income tax would be reduced by 2d to 4d, its 'proper *minimum* ' to make collection economical. Tea and fire assurance duties were further reduced; and a start made on the malt duty. But the substantial feature of the 1865 budget was Gladstone's valedictory and celebratory rhetoric. It was clear, he thought, from watching the increasing prosperity of France, Belgium and Holland that they were following Britain's example. Let it be hoped that Austria would soon join. Gladstone followed a eulogy to Cobden by declaring that it was 'no small honour to the kingdoms of the Crown that, in regard to locomotion, so in regard to the freedom of trade and industry, it has been given to them to lead the vanguard and bear the banner of civilization'. It might 'be given to our acts' Gladstone suggested, quoting Arthur's hopes for his Round Table in Tennyson's *Guinevere*,

> To serve as models for the mighty world,
> And be the fair beginning of a time.

'To be the beginning of a time, richly fraught not only with economical advantages . . . but fraught more richly still with results which promote and confirm the union of class with class among ourselves, and even, as we may hope, of nation with nation throughout the wide surface of the earth.'[2]

As was not surprising, this combination of tax reductions and unction was 'indulgently received as usual'. Then off to recuperate with Duchess Harriet at Chiswick, where were Argylls and Howards. The budget leak to *The Times* still rankled; and when Gladstone returned to Downing

1 DDCP, 231.   2 H, clxxviii, 1086–1120g.

Street (there was a break for the Royal Academy Exhibition: 'This is a charming occupation: but my eyes feel the pressure of it') he, 'and others of his colleagues', made 'no disguise of their annoyance at this unusual course'.[1] Palmerston – whose 'gout' earlier in the month had in fact been much more serious, 'the beginning of the end', his physician judged[2] – took it all blandly in his stride. That was more than Gladstone could do with Mrs. Thistlethwayte's latest lecture on April 30 ('In afternoon heard Mrs. Thistlethwayte at the Polytechnic. I do not much wish to repeat it'). Nor could Gladstone easily affect nonchalance with the coming a second time round of Baines's franchise bill. After bracing himself with a Cliveden weekend and another visit to Christie's early in May he 'resolutely avoided speaking on the Baines's Bill for fear of aggravating matters'. He did vote for it, however; in a minority of 214 to 288. Enough government members joined with the Conservatives to defeat it: a preview of the Conservative-'Adullamite' alliance of 1866.[3]

The great business of establishing the Natural History collections of the British Museum at South Kensington progressed, though Gladstone fell foul of Professor Richard Owen on the question of space to be available. Gladstone regretted that there should be 'some singular misapprehension between us'; but was also able to ask Owen to 'accept my best thanks for your memoir on the Gorilla, which I shall read with great interest'.[4] In very fact Gladstone was scheming a *coup* of economy by cramming the site with a bundle of homeless or distressed museums, including the National Portrait Gallery; and Owen had every reason to be alarmed. The indispensable Captain Fowke was already working on his designs.[5] He was in 'great force' dining with the Frederick Cavendishes on May 23, Lucy enjoying the 'great treat' of 'hearing him in his swing of brilliant talk, and drawing out my Fred's energetic opinions!' (Uncle William thought Mr. Hare's electoral scheme 'somewhat of a dream'.)[6] There was another pleasant Cliveden early in June with driving ('I *fed* myself upon the cornfields all the way'), boating expeditions, writing agitatedly amid 'roaring-hot' weather to Argyll about the *Alabama* case. Gladstone was also 'astounded at the Qn's not coming back on the Pcess's Confinement. She ought never to have gone: but staying is a fresh error. What a misfortune it is to sovereigns to be so little open directly to remark in personal matters.'[7]

1 DDCP, 231.
2 *Ib.* Lucy Cavendish observed Palmerston on May 27 looking 'very old and stiff and shaky'. *Diary of Lady Frederick Cavendish*, i, 265.
3 D, vi, 353.   4 G to Owen, May 16, 1865. GP, 44535, 59.
5 On Fowke's death in December 1865 the project was taken over and completely replanned by Alfred Waterhouse.
6 *Diary of Lady Frederick Cavendish*, i, 265.
7 G to Argyll, June 6, 1865. GP *ib.*, 66–7.

Then, even more embarrassing than the Baines bill, came around yet again Tests Abolition (Oxford), that perennial nuisance. Retorting to Lord Robert Cecil was in itself satisfying enough, but it was painful to be seen to be differing from his Oxford colleague Heathcote. Gladstone appealed for his compromise of relaxing the tests and giving Dissenters 'all that we may safely give them, still maintaining intact the principle that the government of the university and of the colleges should be so lodged in the Church of England as to give ample and adequate security for the religious instruction and discipline of the University'.[1] On the other side, Gladstone found himself reduced to defending his compromise from dissatisfied Dissenters who insisted on a 'footing of equality'. Equality, he informed Newman Hall, was 'I think a principle to be applied according to times & circumstances'; and he thought an 'all or nothing' attitude in the present circumstances a great pity.[2] More congenial was the achievement of a large extension of the powers and duties of the Board of Audit – a cherished ambition ever since 1857. Gratifying also was Palmerston's complaisance in the case of the bishopric of Chester. Gladstone recommended Jacobson, Regius Professor of Divinity at Oxford. Palmerston acceded swiftly, granting Gladstone the pleasure of informing the 'Son of Jacob', though pointing out that 'by rights it is the Turn of Cambridge to furnish a Bishop'. Behind his gracious amenability was a practical motive: 'I thought that the appointment of Jacobson would be useful to you with Reference to your oncoming election and so Cambridge may well wait for the next vacancy.' Jacobson, it so happened, was chairman of Gladstone's committee at Oxford. (Gladstone elatedly returned his sense of 'great obligation' in the name of 'the children of Abraham and Isaac, and the children of all the tribes of this many-coloured world'.)[3]

As he successfully mitred one bishop, Gladstone unsuccessfully strove to unmitre another. Colenso, in the teeth of his metropolitan in Capetown and forty of the forty-one bishops of the Church of England and Ireland (Thirlwall of St. David's dissenting), found both legal and moral support to a degree with thwarted Gladstone and the other heresy-hunting Colonial Bishoprics Trustees. There was 'much conversation' with Bishop Wilberforce on Colenso on June 25 in preparation for the Convocation of Canterbury; but all to no avail. This kind of doctrinal conservatism became increasingly for Gladstone a necessary psychological counterpoise to his ecclesiastical liberalism. That liberalism, evinced at Oxford, now began to focus also on Ireland. On May 17 Gladstone voted for the Roman Catholic Oath Bill to relieve Catholics of certain impediments fastened on them at the time of emancipation in 1829; though he did not contribute to the debate. (It was in this debate that the Roman Catholic

1 H, clxxx, 221.
2 G to Hall, June 18, 1865. GP, 44535, 73.   3 G & P, 338–39.

M.P. for Co. Louth, Tristram Kennedy, used the phrase about the representatives of his co-religionists being 'muzzled'; as taken up by Derby in the Lords on June 26 the word became notorious – a kind of sessional catch-phrase.)[1] But he did intervene on June 20 in the University Education (Ireland) Bill which offered relief to conscientious obligations of Roman Catholics. Gladstone earlier (June 8) had privately concluded that 'our present position ... seems to me totally untenable'. Civil disabilities were still in 1865 attached in Ireland to religious opinions in education for medicine and law. 'How can we expect contentment among Irishmen under such circumstances, even if well bribed with Galway contracts, & the like?'[2] Gladstone was ready to entertain the notion of a Roman Catholic University in Ireland as a way of avoiding the civil disabilities problem; but government thinking leaned rather to the view that the existing non-denominational system based on the 'Queen's Colleges' founded by Peel in the 1840s should be amended to cater for Roman Catholic susceptibilities, rather on the model of London University. 'The Queen's Colleges,' as he put it, 'were wisely devised to meet a purpose; but we must admit that the colleges were made for the people of Ireland, and not the people of Ireland for the colleges.'[3] At all events Gladstone was able to rejoice in 1865 that on the Irish College and University question 'we have taken a just as well as prudent step'.[4]

As to the justice and prudence of Gladstone's ecclesiastical liberalism opinion among Oxford University voters increasingly divided. Gladstone was at pains to scotch rumours that his own loyalties were divided between Oxford and Lancashire. He carefully informed one of his most influential Oxford supporters that he had had no communication with Lancashire during the present year, and when he last did communicate, it was quite understood by them that 'the Univ. had me at her command'. Anyone, as far as he was concerned, was at liberty to say to any Oxford voter that 'as far as depends upon my own will & act', Gladstone was a candidate for Oxford and Oxford only.[5] His attitude to South Lancashire was, as he explained to Arthur Gordon, 'simply passive'. He certainly thought by July 11 that he would get in for Lancashire if they saw him failing at Oxford; 'which on the whole does not seem to be expected'.[6]

June closed with a social flourish. There was a large breakfast party on the 22nd ('The Duke of Brabant' – soon to be Leopold II of the Belgians – 'was so kind as to come'). Then on the 28th was the 'great affair' of a ball. The Prince of Wales arrived at Carlton House Terrace before eleven '& went I think at half past 2. A very lively ball.' The Prince returned the

1 H, clxxix, 473; clxxx, 789.   2 D, vi, 360–61.
3 H, clxxx, 586.   4 *Ib.*, 364.
5 G to J. T. Coleridge, June 22, 1865. GP, 44535, 75.
6 G to Gordon, July 11, 1865. *Ib.*, 84.

compliment by inviting Gladstone to be received by the Queen of the Netherlands at Marlborough House. Certain personal distresses, public and private, rather compromised the end-of-session pleasure. There was the 'sad business of Westbury': the Lord Chancellor, censured by the Commons for weakly countenancing misdemeanours among relatives, was forced to resign – 'he is very loath to die'. Old Aunt Johanna seemed to be in a critical state, causing much anxiety. There was the 'strange incredible horror' about Catherine's cousin: not further enlarged upon, but possibly to do with the efforts of James Stuart-Wortley, lately victim of a bout of insanity, to get back into the Commons by claiming Gladstone's endorsement as a candidate for Sheffield.[1] On July 7 Gladstone passed two hours with one of his rescue cases; he was observed walking in the Mall: 'A slight man of moderate height, with sprightly tremulous gait; a face of great power; hard, yet pathetic, worn with struggles & thought: the cheeks deeply lined, the mouth set & compressed, the eyes half-closed, looking inwards.'[2]

[14]

The general election was at hand. 'I trust God will look mercifully on His poor overburdened creature,' prayed Gladstone, 'as he trips and stumbles along the road of life.'[3] The road along which Gladstone had just passed was the familiar smooth one to Cliveden. He misjudged the elections both in general and particular. He did not expect any surge of public support for the government; and he did rather expect to be returned for Oxford. 'I am become for the time,' he wrote to Arthur Gordon, 'a popular character.' As far as Gladstone felt himself justified in 'appropriating or enjoying any of this popularity, it is on account of what I did, or prevented from being done, in 1859–61, when the storm whistled loud enough around me'.[4] But how popular would this make him among the university constituency? There would almost certainly be a much increased poll because of the new arrangements for postal voting for university electors. Palmerston hoped against hope that Jacobson had not been mitred in vain. As in 1859 he urged Shaftesbury to do all he could to secure Gladstone's return. '"He is a dangerous man"', said P.'; then Palmerston added, alluding to Derby's famous usage of the previous month: '"Keep him in Oxford, and he is partially muzzled; but send him elsewhere, and he will run wild."'[5] Gladstone conscientiously voted in

1 D, vi, 366.   2 Hudson, *Munby*, 226.   3 D, vi, 368.
4 G to Gordon, July 11, 1865. GP, 44535, 84.
5 Hodder, *Shaftesbury*, iii, 188.

Westminster for Grosvenor and John Stuart Mill and had the pleasure of congratulating Mill on his election 'in spite of the public-houses and the cabs'. He thanked Mill for the gift of a new edition of his great work on political economy: 'Hoping we may hereafter meet oftener, if I can get into the assembly of which you are now a member.'[1]

At Hawarden the following day there was good news of the Chester poll. Gladstone was immensely gratified to greet Willy at Chester later as the new M.P., with his mother. 'We drove to the Mayor's & supped there in great glee.' (The venture cost Gladstone more than £2,200 and nearly £1,500 more subscribed in the town.)[2] On the 13th news of the first day's poll at Oxford was bad: 'of little consequence: besides, I am callous.' Willy made a triumphant entry to Hawarden, 'drawn by the people'. Gladstone was callously detached enough on July 15 to ruminate on Stephen's affairs, '& a conversation with C. Some rather large plan seems needed.' But Sunday the 16th was sorely disturbed with telegrams and messages. 'We had to discuss Oxford & Lancashire contingencies.' 'Always in straits the Bible in Church supplies my need. Today it was in 1st Lesson I Jer. 19: "And they shall fight against thee: but they shall not prevail against thee, for I am with thee saith the Lord, to deliver thee."' He spent the morning of the 17th 'framing a plan for a great change as to Stephen's affairs'. That afternoon, it was clear that Oxford was lost. 'A dear dream is dispelled: God's will be done.' He telegraphed George Wilson in Manchester. The Oxford result came through on July 18: Heathcote, 3,236; Hardy, 1,904; Gladstone, 1,724. Gladstone had kept his core of support among the resident members of the university, but suffered much from the postal electorate. That day he wrote off to Palmerston – who by now was denouncing the 'gross folly' of the university voters in setting Gladstone loose – about Princess Mary of Cambridge's allowance on her marriage to the Duke of Teck. 'I write in extreme haste, just setting out, after my defeat at Oxford, for a short but sharp Lancashire campaign.'[3] He was on his way to Manchester before noon, examining figures in the railway carriage and writing his addresses of farewell to Oxford and greeting to Lancashire. To Oxford he declared that he left the 'incidents of the political relation' between the university and himself 'to the judgment of the future'; to 'my native county' he extolled the legislation of twenty-five years, asked for 'confirmation of that verdict' and a pronouncement 'with significance as to the direction in which you desire the wheels of State to move'. He hoped, before his words could be read, 'to be among you, in the hives of your teeming enterprise'.[4] He conferred with a Liverpool agent at Chester and reached Manchester at 2.30, settling with George

---

1 G to Mill, July 11, 1865. GP, *ib.*, 85. This endorsement caused offence among Oxford voters: Radstock to G, June 23, 1865. GP, 44406, 317–20.   2 D, vi, 380.
3 G & P, 340.   4 *Speeches and Addresses delivered at the Elections of 1865*, 38–39.

Wilson the preliminaries about his address. There was news of Sir
Thomas Gladstone's humiliating defeat at Kincardineshire ('Tom has
made what is called a mess of it').[1] Tom received his political *coup de grâce*
from a Scottish electorate just as his father had. Gladstone went on to the
Exchange, and then to the Free Trade Hall.

There Gladstone found 6,000 people and unbounded enthusiasm. It
was political theatre of the kind he relished. 'At last, my friends, I am
come amongst you. And I am come – to use an expression which has of
late become very famous, and which, if I judge the matter rightly, is not
likely soon to be forgotten – I am come among you "unmuzzled".' For
unbounded enthusiasm he returned pathos: 'I have loved the University
of Oxford with a deep and passionate love; and so I shall love it to the
end.' 'But now, by no act of mine, I am free to come among you. And,
having been thus set free . . . at the eleventh hour, a candidate without
even an Address, I make my appeal to the heart and mind of South
Lancashire.' His review of the 'beneficent and blessed' process of reform,
however, was anything but the prelude to a rousing prediction of more
and better soon to come. Rather, he stressed that he had been six years in
office and really needed a holiday; and that the political health of the
Liberal party would doubtless be improved by a short spell in opposition.
Once refreshed and back in office at some future time, the Liberal party's
policy would be based on 'those old words announced five-and-thirty
years ago', 'Peace, Retrenchment, Reform', together with a fourth
principle: the promotion of civil and religious liberty consistent with a
deep attachment to the Church. 'I am for the policy which steadily refuses
to seek either to extend that Church, or to defend it, by means of opposing
disability, or of maintaining odious distinction against our Roman
Catholic or Dissenting fellow-subjects.' As to the franchise: 'Never have I
spoken a word which, fairly interpreted, gave the smallest countenance
to the schemes . . . of any who would favour or promote the adoption of
precipitate or wholesale measures. . . ' Would that this question could be
kept outside the 'vortex of party politics'.[2]

As 'unmuzzling', this was strange 'stuff. To launch a campaign by
announcing that one wished for a spell of rest in opposition and that one's
party was in no fit condition to undertake the government was a
procedure baffling to the party activists around George Wilson and the
campaign manager, Robert Philips, former M.P. and now candidate for
Bury, in whom Gladstone had confided his electoral fate. On the strength
of that kind of appeal to the heart and mind of South Lancashire, and
considering the extreme shortness of the notice, it was a question as to
whether the electorate could be delivered. Unperturbed, Gladstone

1 D, vi, 373.
2 *Speeches and Addresses delivered at the Election of 1865*, 1, 4, 11, 14.

pressed on to Liverpool, where he dined with Robertson in the office of the family firm. His speech at Liverpool, amid the 'roar of Dale-street and of Castle-street', was not much more *à propos*. He had 'clung to the representation of the University with desperate fondness'; but he had 'striven to unite that which is represented by Oxford and that which is represented by Lancashire'. Oxford represented England's past. 'I come into South Lancashire, and I find here around me an assemblage of different phenomena. I find the development of industry; I find the growth of enterprise; I find the progress of social philanthropy; I find the prevalence of toleration; and I find an ardent desire for freedom.' But nonetheless Gladstone insisted that 'if there be a duty that more than another should be held incumbent upon the public men of England', it was 'the duty of establishing and maintaining a harmony between the past of our glorious country, and the future that is still in store for her'. In case anyone should have missed the point, Gladstone added for good measure: 'I am a member of a Liberal Government. I am in association with the Liberal party. I have never swerved from what I conceived to be those truly Conservative objects and desires with which I entered life.'[1] Gladstone later prefaced the published edition of his election speeches with the line from *King Lear*: 'He'll shape his old course in a country new.'

Thus, though unmuzzled, Gladstone hardly left any fang marks on the body politic. This was part of his general miscalculation about the elections; which in turn derived from his fundamental misreading of the pace of political movement. When he wrote tactfully to Tom on July 19 from Robertson's place at Court Hey describing himself also as a defeated candidate, he commented: 'The course of the Elections has a little surprised me. I did not expect them to be so favourable to the Government.'[2] Gladstone reported himself to George Lyttelton as 'at the present swimming in a flood of popular enthusiasm: but I do not know what the figures will in their rigour say tomorrow. However all looks well.'[3] But in truth his situation was much less well than Gladstone supposed. This might have cheered his despondent enemies. Clarendon predicted the 'inevitable political future' as Russell and Gladstone, with the latter having 'all the real power'. Stanley noted that 'dislike and fear of Gladstone are the strongest feelings in Lord C.'s mind where politics are concerned'. Even the tolerant Stanley observed that Gladstone was canvassing along with his brother Robertson, 'whose extreme violence of opinion is notorious'; and Lady Brownlow contributed items about Gladstone's having 'a sister in confinement' and Robertson's being 'on

1 *Ib.*, 17–19.
2 G to Thomas G. July 19, 1865. GP, 44535, 87.
3 G to Lyttelton, July 19, 1865. *Ib.*, 87.

some points hardly sane';[1] which prompted Stanley to recall yet again that in 1857 Gladstone's mind had been 'obviously off its balance'.[2]

When Gladstone and Robertson went in early for the poll on the 20th there were anxious moments. That evening at Hawarden Gladstone seemed set for second place (there were three seats); and the church bells were rung, people came into the park with a band, and Gladstone had to address them to the cheers of a Volunteer camp. Gladstone wrote to Philips the following day thanking him for the 'efficient & important part' he played in managing the campaign 'which promises I hope so well'.[3] But, thanking another activist for his 'great exertions', Gladstone observed that the poll 'appears to prove that the hold of the Liberal party upon the representation is by no means established';[4] and to Hornby, rather ungraciously: 'Had I known before the late Election the inferiority of the Liberal party in numbers, I should have felt myself placed in some difficulty. Probably you were not fully aware of it.'[5] Gladstone eventually scraped rather humiliatingly into third place, the only Liberal to gain a seat, with his two other Liberal running-mates sharing the bottom of the poll. On July 22 Gladstone was able to assure an audience at Newton on the declaration of the poll: 'If I came here a wounded man, you have healed my wound.' He recorded: 'It has been a time of whirling thoughts, of deep emotion, of thankfulness as far as the soil of my heart can yield it.'[6] But as he put it to Rathbone, the Liverpool magnate: 'We sailed close to the wind.'[7]

Palmerston, 'well-satisfied with G.'s moderation in S. Lancs', [8] was ready with congratulations, 'though many Friends would have preferred seeing you still for Oxford'.[9] At a cabinet on July 24 ('All in good humour') Gladstone had to digest the amazing fact that the government had gained 26 seats. At Osborne the following day, however, the Queen's humour was a trifle strained. For the first time Gladstone noticed a distancing: 'She looked extremely well and was kind: but in all her conversations with me she is evidently hemmed in, stops at a certain point, & keeps back the thought which occurs.'[10] Probably the Queen shared the thoughts which led Stanley the following day to remark that 'Gladstone's speeches are watched with extreme and increasing interest: he has become the central figure in our politics, and his importance is far more likely to increase than to diminish'.[11] Certainly what was worrying her

1 Tilney Bassett testified that he 'had seen a photograph of the enormous Robertson driving himself into Liverpool from Court Hey behind an eight-in-hand of sheep' (MRDF).
2 DDCP, 233.   3 G to Philips, July 21, 1865. GP, 44535, 87.
4 G to Wrigley, July 21, 1865. *Ib.*, 90.
5 G to Hornby, July 26, 1865. *Ib.*, 95.   6 D, vi, 372.
7 G to Rathbone, July 21, 1865. GP, *ib.*, 90.90.   8 DDCP, 233.
9 G & P, 341.   10 D, vi, 372.   11 DDCP, 233.

was what was worrying any careful, non-radical observer of the politics of recent years: on the Tyne in October 1862 Gladstone was the focus of a great popular demonstration; so was he, in much the same way, in October 1864 in Lancashire. For all Gladstone's 'moderation' in Lancashire in July 1865, his speeches were, in Stanley's word, 'effective', [1] not so much in what they actually said, but more in their emblematic character as gestures of recognition from one who saw the function of a commanding public reputation as a concern to establish and maintain a harmony between the old order and the new. What dismayed many observers was Gladstone's evidently settling into a pattern of speeches intended for a national audience; which increasingly, moreover, emphasised that status by tending to concentrate on one major theme at a time. Gladstone explained disingenuously: 'I do not in politics attend to a role wh. some have laid down for preachers, viz: that they shd deliver the whole gospel in every sermon.'[2]

From the point of view of Gladstone's commitment to his renewed vocation, such a role was essential and inescapable. In order to manipulate, one had to engage. 'God knows,' he had asserted in October 1864, 'I have not courted them.' Given his purposes and his attitudes, whether manipulatory or *étatist*, this was true, or true enough: though there was present an element which might not unfairly be defined in some such term. There was more than a touch of blandishment: the flattery which coaxes. Still, Gladstone emphatically was not a demagogue. From the point of view, however, of one not attuned in any revealing degree to the inwardness of Gladstone's politics, that fact was by no means obvious. Some, such as Clarendon, saw Gladstone bidding to pre-empt Bright from the leadership of the Radical party. Others, like the Queen, were puzzled and apprehensive. Another such was Manning. Gladstone denied his charges of 'extremism'. 'I profess myself a disciple of Butler; the greatest of all enemies to extremes. But in a cold or lukewarm period, and such is this in public affairs, every thing which moves and lives is called extreme . . . Your caution about self-control however I do accept – it is very valuable – I am sadly lacking in that great quality.'[3]

[15]

Certainly, after a close shave in Lancashire on top of a deep wound at Oxford, Gladstone needed all the self-control he could muster. Any

1 *Ib.*
2 G to Stuart-Wortley, August 31, 1865. GP, 44535, 119.
3 G to Manning, July 21, 1865. *Ib.*, 89.

lingering temptations to bitterness he tried to suppress. He assured the Provost of Oriel that, 'though with weakened hands', he remained the devoted servant of the university; and he conscientiously fulfilled his last official obligations.[1] Of Oxford he told Manning: 'My feelings towards her are those of sorrow, leavened perhaps with pride. But I am for the moment a stunned man: the more so because without a moment of repose I had to plunge into the whirlpools of South Lancashire, & swim there for my life which as you see has been given me.'[2] To Heathcote he reported that he hardly yet knew what his feelings were. 'I know a vital cord is snapped: I know nothing else, except it be that to the indictment under which I have been condemned I plead not guilty.' Gladstone had 'gloomy surmises' about the Church. 'It is a question between gold & faith: and the gold always carries it against the faith.' It was, he felt sure, 'absolutely necessary that some people should be ready to be (from their point of view) sacrificed in the endeavour to open minds and eyes, which will not read the signs of the times'.[3] This was the theme also of Gladstone's comment to Keble: 'It is difft to speak of Oxf. without seeming either cold or unmanly . . . The separation is a sharp one, but it is not difft to believe, perhaps to see, that it is for the best . . . '[4]

The sense that dismissal from Oxford was for the best in view of the need to open minds and eyes which would not read the signs of the times came out rather more aggressively and ominously when Gladstone put the point to the American Charles Sumner that 'it is plain that those who cast me out of Oxf. have committed a mistake: it is not so clear that they have done either to me or to the public an injury'.[5] The note of retribution that would fall on Oxford as wilfully being culpably of the blindness that will not see the signs of the times Gladstone related back to his theme in Liverpool that he was trying to link the past as symbolised by Oxford with the future as symbolised by Lancashire. His message to Bishop Wilberforce of Oxford was that in its wilful blindness Oxford and what it symbolised would do itself much hurt. 'I do not doubt that this to me great event is all for good . . . I am not angry, only sorry, & that deeply. For my revenge – which I do not desire but would battle if I could – all lies in that little word "future" in my address, which I wrote with a consciousness that it is deeply charged with meaning, and that that which shall come will come.'[6] Gladstone added sententiously to this already sufficiently menacing prophecy of retribution: 'There have been two great deaths or transmigrations of spirit, in my political existence.

1 G to Prov. of Oriel, July 21, 1865. *Ib.*, 89–90.
2 G to Manning, July 21, 1865. *Ib.*, 89.
3 G to Heathcote, July 21, 1865. *Ib.*, 88.
4 G to Keble, August 17, 1865. *Ib.*, 111–12.
5 G to Sumner, August 25, 1865. *Ib.*, 116.
6 G to Wilberforce, July 21, 1865. *Ib.*, 88–89.

One, very slow, the breaking of ties with my original party. The other very short & sharp, the breaking of the tie with Oxford. There will probably be a third and no more.' When Wilberforce with his intrepid insensitivity demanded to know the plain meaning of this 'oracular' utterance, Gladstone thought it would better remain in its 'proper darkness'.[1] Did he have in mind those pregnant words to Catherine in 1845 about its being the highest interest of the Church to give gold for freedom, and that he had a 'growing belief' that he would never be able to do much good for the Church in parliament 'except after having seemed first a traitor to it and being reviled as such'?[2]

More difficult than digesting unexpected dismissal from Oxford was digesting the significance of the unexpected new Liberal parliamentary strength. Clearly, Gladstone was disconcerted at being baulked of a much longed-for spell of repose and relief from the pressures of office. He had geared himself for his second vocation by just such an interlude of withdrawal. His calculations as to the pace of political movement were that the Irish Church would be an affair five, perhaps ten, years off; and that the franchise would not be 'practical except for another generation'. He was unwilling to confront the further prospect of remorselessly immediate and undelimited responsibility. To Sir Francis Crossley, Bart., the Halifax carpet magnate and M.P. for West Riding, he confided: 'I scarcely venture to look forward in politics. The large gains however at the elections do not altogether tend to mere ease. We shall know better by and by what the Liberal party in the new Parliament is made of. As far as its members go, they tend to indicate a strength, which would make it highly responsible to the country for the efficient performance of its duties.'[3] At the cabinet on the 24th he was noted as being 'quiet and subdued'.[4] As he put it to Bishop Wilberforce, though he had lost with Oxford his role as the Church's official defender, he enjoyed no corresponding sense of having gained any alternative source of credit: he saw himself now as a person 'wholly extraneous, on one great class of question. With regard to legislation & Cabinet matters, I am still an unit.'[5] When Robertson, in the course of accounting the election expenses, proposed a visit to Ormskirk, Gladstone agreed it would be a 'proper measure' but not at the present; his duty was to be quiet after having been so conspicuous and give the reporters nothing to say.[6] This new Gladstone enchanted Palmerston, who flattered himself that Reform could be fobbed off with a commission of enquiry or perhaps even remain a dead letter. Clarendon, reported Stanley, 'tries to undeceive him'.[7]

---

1 Magnus, 174.   2 See above, 183.
3 G to Crossley, July 25, 1865. GP, 44535, 94.   4 DDCP, 233.
5 G to Wilberforce, July 21, 1865. GP, 44535, 88–89.
6 G to Robertson G. August 4, 1865. *Ib.*, 102.   7 DDCP, 233.

Clarendon's instinct was the sounder. Gladstone's powers of recuperation and adaptation were, like all his powers, formidable. 'It is fearful,' he wrote on July 28, 'to think of the immense development of the deeper and more formidable problems since the time of Sir R. Peel.'[1] But by August 7 he was starting to get his old resentments back in working order again. He hoped that the new parliament would be an improvement 'in times like these, when the late almost insane desire for expenditure has not yet wholly faded away'.[2] And by August 10, thanking Edmond Beales for an 'obliging letter' from the Executive of the Reform League, he declared that their 'indulgent judgment' 'may serve as a new encouragement to the steady performance of duty during whatever may remain to me of political life'.[3] Already he was adjusting his sights on an old but for long exempted target of aggression. 'Demagogism of late yrs has fallen almost wholly into the possession of the followers of Mr. D'Israeli, for by demagogism I understand especially the dealing largely in promises wh. on the principles of the promise, are incapable of fulfilment.' For example, Gladstone had indignantly in mind the 'manner the opposition have been for the last 6 yrs the active agents in stimulating & extending expenditure: & the promoters of Economy are the only persons who are entitled to hold out any hopes of the reduction of the Malt Tax'.[4] As the principal stimulator and extender of expenditure tottered to his grave Gladstone shifted his Conservative collaborators into the prime target spot. And it would be a good reason for sticking on at the Treasury if only to keep Disraeli's hands away from the credit of repealing the malt tax.

After winding up a few last executive affairs (a conclave with Cardwell led to military operations in New Zealand being peremptorily curtailed) and talking with Prosper Mérimée at Stafford House on Hellenic studies, Gladstone was up at Hawarden before the end of July. He found Catherine 'rather suffering: overdone, & no wonder'. There was much labour in arranging bookcases and shifting books. There was a long letter to Mrs. Thistlethwayte on July 31 and also 'long conversation with Mr. Burnett on S. R. G.'s affairs & mentioned my new plan which he much liked'. Panizzi resisted enticements to come up; but was conquered by Gladstone's efforts in fourteen quatrains of doggerel Italian verse. He arrived in company with Mérimée, examined Gladstone's latest bibliographical specimens, was much taken by the *Glossary of the Glynne Language* (his unauthorised removal of it for further inspection in London threw Gladstone into a fit of comic perturbation), and talked with Gladstone 'on the franchise & my own future'.[5] Gladstone used the

1 G to G. Vernon, July 28, 1865. GP, 44535, 96.
2 G to Dunlop, August 7, 1865. *Ib.*, 104.
3 G to Beales, August 10, 1865. *Ib.*, 107.
4 G to Gurdon, July 29, 1865. *Ib.*, 98.
5 D, vi, 378.

occasion of his retrieval of the *Glossary* to enquire whether Panizzi had any news of Palmerston: 'I have found him just of late so slack in writing.'[1] On the American question he was by now deprived of his last illusions. 'On the whole the histy. of yr great war,' he told Sumner, 'impresses me with no feeling so much as this; that it is, as I now learn, hazardous in the extreme for us to pronounce upon Amern questions of the future.' The 'heroic resistance' of six millions to twenty millions and the 'courage & perseverance' to overcome it represented energies which 'surpassed our scale & measure'. He would content himself now with offering the Union 'moral support' to finish off its great task in hand.[2] By now the government found itself confronted with the American demand for arbitration and damages for the depredations of the *Alabama*. Determined to retrieve something from the wreckage of his American misconstructions, Gladstone began to envisage the possibility that a moral cause might be extractable from the principle of international arbitration. His initial move was to deflect Russell cautiously from immediate and outright rejection of the American case. He pointed out to the Foreign Secretary that 'due diligence' and 'good faith and honesty' were not the same thing; and argued strongly for keeping the option of arbitration open, for all that he inclined to believe that 'the demand for arbitration is unreasonable in a high degree, and even that we have some reason to complain of its having been made'. 'But still,' Gladstone urged, 'with these feelings, and without any disposition to say "yes" to the demand, I should have thought we were not prepared to say "no", and our proper course was to lead the Americans to bring out the whole of their pleas and arguments, that we might have them fully before us previously to coming to a decision of great delicacy and moment.'[3]

On the 'very serious question of the family estate' on August 25 'all was discussed in my absence.' Gladstone remained sensitive on the possibility of misconstruction; and there was still the delicate matter of poor Henry Glynne's feelings; but Phillimore and Lord Devon, who acted as assessors, assured him that they 'decidedly repelled every other alternative except the sale of the reversion'. Gladstone insisted when discussing the proposed arrangements with Catherine on 'the impossibility of *my* being in it'. The estate would be settled on Willy. Lady Wenlock 'warmly approved'; and Gladstone started looking into his investment portfolio to see what might be realised. As to Willy, the principal beneficiary: 'He is most satisfactory though taciturn.'[4] Willy, no doubt, felt his own sensitivities as to the Gladstone take-over.

1 Foot, 'Gladstone and Panizzi', *Br. Lib. Journ.*, v, 54.
2 G to Sumner, August 25, 1865. GP, 44535, 116.
3 G to Russell, September 2, 1865. GP, 44292, 164.
4 D, vi, 380–83.

The arrangement was that Gladstone was to pay Sir Stephen Glynne 'for the reversion of Hawarden after the lives of himself & Mr. [Henry] Glynne in round numbers £57,000: or 5% on the unpaid part of it, within the limit of the time allowed for the settlement of the whole transaction'. Gladstone was to 'begin with cancelling on that day Sir Stephen's debt to me, now standing at £14,000; which leaves me his debtor for (in round numbers) £43,000'. This would involve a deduction from Gladstone's annual income for the next and subsequent years of £2,700 p.a.; leaving his probable income for 1866 at £6,200 independent of salary.[1] Without salary, Carlton House Terrace would probably have to be given up. He estimated its sale value furnished and with stable as 'not less than £20,000'.[2] It would all be rather an upheaval. Gladstone calculated this a price well worth paying. 'So far as this divests me of a considerable part of my property in favour of my son, and also so far as it tends to give Stephen a position of complete ease, & to take off the heaviest cares of his excellent agents, this serious affair is a great pleasure & comfort to me.' For Gladstone another principal consideration was that it also promised 'to leave my mind more free for the public duties to which I daily feel myself more & more unequal'. Raising so large a sum would 'cost some time & thought but this will be mere work & not anxiety'.[3]

Once this big decision was made Gladstone could relax. He thanked Hartington for a box of game from the Duke of Devonshire's moors: 'What a pleasant interval of calm in public affairs.'[4] Duchess Harriet of Sutherland arrived at Hawarden and Gladstone read Consul Longworth's report on Bulgaria,[5] another of the small instances of the subterranean persistence of his old pre-1859 anti-Crimean line. He deprecated to Phillimore any notion of a 'memorial' statue at Oxford subscribed by his former election committee and supporters[6] (though monument there eventually was, in the form of one of Woolner's marble busts on a specially designed plinth). Then for 1865 there would be a Scottish tour as in 1858 instead of Penmaenmawr. The ducal pattern persisted: Drumlanrig, Inverary, Dunrobin. Gladstone kept in lively touch with Bishop Wilberforce about Prayer Book alterations and with Cardwell about the 'shameful proceedings in New Z.' Colonials behaved, it seemed, 'so much below the level of free men'.[7] Argyll, who disapproved strongly of Gladstone's tree-felling propensities, made sure that his guest, despite neuralgia, inspected his 'grand trees' at Inverary.

From Inverary at the beginning of October Gladstone was called back to Liverpool by the death of Robertson's wife, Mary Ellen, the Unitarian girl

1 GGP, 94/13. Secret Account Book. Mem. January 1, 1866.
2 D, vi, 405.   3 *Ib.*, 380.
4 G to Hartington, September 7, 1865. GP, 44535, 121.   5 D, vi, 384.
6 G to Phillimore, September 18, 1865. GP, 44535, 127.
7 G to Cardwell, September 28, 1865. *Ib.*, 128.

whose marriage in 1836 had provoked such an exhibition of bigoted spleen on William's part. Much as in John Neilson's case, Robertson collapsed. Gladstone arrived to a 'tempest of grief'. He stayed loyally with stricken Robertson ('I am much with him, would that I could do more to *heal* his grief')[1], consoling himself with work on his farewell address to Edinburgh University and perusing Sherlock on Future Punishment. He called again at Court Hey on October 17 on his way to Clumber to attend Newcastle's memorial service. On the 18th at Clumber he conversed 'with misgivings early in the day respecting Lord Palmerston's illness'. The news, he told Catherine, was 'bewildering'.[2] 'At 6½ a Telegram came announcing his death & made me giddy.' To Catherine: 'I think it was you who had long said, "you will see he will go off suddenly." This is an event that has made my brain spin.'

The Queen, Gladstone thought, clearly should send for Russell. 'With such consideration as I can give the matter at this moment I write to *him*.'[3] 'Your former place as her Minister,' he told Russell, 'your powers, experience, services, and renown, do not leave room for doubt that you will be sent for.' Gladstone disclaimed any pretensions to a place by 'pledge' in the new ministry; but argued that in any event 'any Government now to be formed cannot be wholly a continuation, it must be in some degree a new commencement'. 'Sore with conflicts about the public expenditure', Gladstone was 'most willing to retire'; but on the other hand, he felt bound to pursue the progressive reduction of military and naval establishments; and, on 'the general field of politics', he was quite willing to serve under Russell's banner 'in the exact capacity I now fill'.[4] This last stipulation was intended to leave Russell free to dispose the leadership of the Commons. Meanwhile Gladstone diverted himself with his Edinburgh address and sorting the Clumber papers, 'almost in despair'. October 20 Gladstone found an 'uneasy day from political anticipation. Went to see the poultry farm, and the Brood Mares & Foals Establishment'. He was oppressed by a 'sense of coming trouble': the Queen should have come·to London; she should have sent for Russell. 'I fear she has done neither.' She was, he feared, 'settling into a groove, out of which someone ought to draw her'.[5] In fact, the Queen had already (on October 15) very sensibly made arrangements with Russell that he should assume the premiership in the event of Palmerston's death. Gladstone went down to London on October 21 and saw Russell on the 23rd. Russell asked Gladstone to continue at the Exchequer and pressed on him the Leadership of the Commons. He accepted on the 24th, rather dubious as to his competency, and rightly sure that Grey was better qualified. He intervened to get Palmerston an Abbey funeral, a little annoyed that

1 D, vi, 389.   2 *Ib.*, 391; Bassett, 166.
3 Bassett, 167.   4 S. Walpole, *Lord John Russell* (1891), ii, 422.   5 Bassett, 167–68.

Russell had not stirred himself; and noted sardonically that on one day *The Times* put him up for Prime Minister and the following day knocked him down. 'There is a rumour,' he reported to Catherine, 'that it was the old story, Delane out of town.'[1] Stanley judged Gladstone's Leadership of the Commons as 'in any case inevitable'.[2] As Bagehot had put it in 1860: 'England is a country governed mainly by labour and by speech. Mr. Gladstone will work and can speak, and the result is what we see.'[3] At a cabinet on the 28th Gladstone had the 'charge of leading' fastened upon him. Palmerston's funeral the previous day was 'a solemn & touching scene'. That day, at Hughenden, Disraeli 'talked a good deal of Gladstone', Stanley recorded, 'puzzled by his persistence in High Church opinions: which he cannot think affected, for where is the motive? Yet which it is hard for him to think that a man of such talent can really hold.'[4] Other people were thinking a good deal about Gladstone also. On Sunday Gladstone found himself 'Prevented from Ch. in aft. by Mrs. Thistlethwayte, detailing to me a sad story of her affliction'. Clarendon could only hope rather despairingly: 'Gladstone's temper and want of tact are what we all know: but he has looked into himself, he has been warned by a personal friend (a woman: no man could do it)' – Dowager Duchess Harriet of Sutherland – 'and he is determined to conciliate the House if possible.'[5] Shaftesbury, shattered by the loss of his father-in-law and link with the great political world, remembered Palmerston's warning: 'Gladstone will soon have it all his own way; and, whenever he gets my place, we shall have strange doings.'[6]

---

1 Bassett, 169.   2 DDCP, 237.
3 Bagehot, *Biographical Studies*, 101.
4 DDCP, 238.   5 *Ib.*, 238–39.
6 Hodder, *Shaftesbury*, iii, 187.

Index